The Greatest Taboo

The Greatest Taboo
Homosexuality in Black Communities

Edited by Delroy Constantine-Simms

With a Foreword by
Henry Louis Gates Jr.

alyson books
los angeles | new york

MANUFACTURED IN THE UNITED STATES OF AMERICA.

THIS TRADE PAPERBACK ORIGINAL IS PUBLISHED BY ALYSON PUBLICATIONS,
P.O. BOX 4371, LOS ANGELES, CALIFORNIA 90078-4371.
DISTRIBUTION IN THE UNITED KINGDOM BY TURNAROUND PUBLISHER SERVICES LTD.,
UNIT 3, OLYMPIA TRADING ESTATE, COBURG ROAD, WOOD GREEN,
LONDON N22 6TZ ENGLAND.

FIRST EDITION: JANUARY 2001

01 02 03 04 05 a 10 9 8 7 6 5 4 3 2

ISBN 1-55583-564-3

LIBRARY OF CONGRESS CATALOGING-IN-PUBLICATION DATA
  THE GREATEST TABOO : HOMOSEXUALITY IN BLACK COMMUNITIES / EDITED BY DELROY CONSTANTINE-SIMMS ; WITH A FOREWORD BY HENRY LOUIS GATES JR.
    ISBN 1-55583-564-3
    1. AFRO-AMERICAN GAYS. 2. AFRO-AMERICANS—ATTITUDES. 3. HOMOPHOBIA—UNITED STATES. 4. AFRO-AMERICAN CHURCHES. 5. AFRO-AMERICAN ARTS. 6. HOMOSEXUALITY—AFRICA. I. CONSTANTINE-SIMMS, DELROY.
  HQ76.3.U5 G74 2001
  305.9'0664—DC21   00-045391

CREDITS
•LINDON BARRETT'S "BLACK MEN IN THE MIX" FIRST APPEARED IN *CALLALOO*, 20.1 (1997): 106-26. CHARLES H. ROWELL. REPRINTED BY PERMISSION OF THE JOHNS HOPKINS UNIVERSITY PRESS.
•CHERYL L. COLE'S "CONTAINING AIDS," FIRST APPEARED IN *QUEER THEORY/SOCIOLOGY*, EDITED BY S. SEIDMAN. CAMBRIDGE, MA: BLACKWELL, 1996.
•PHILIP BRIAN HARPER'S "ELOQUENCE AND EPITAPH" FIRST APPEARED IN *WRITING AIDS*, EDITED BY T. MURPHY AND S. POIRIER. NEW YORK: COLUMBIA UNIVERSITY PRESS, 1993: 117-139.
•BELL HOOKS'S "HOMOPHOBIA IN BLACK COMMUNITIES" FIRST APPEARED IN *TALKING BACK*, BOSTON: SOUTH END PRESS, 1989: 120-127.
•LAURA JAMISON'S "A FEISTY FEMALE RAPPER BREAKS A HIP-HOP TABOO" FIRST APPEARED IN *THE NEW YORK TIMES*, JAN. 10, 1998.
•E. PATRICK JOHNSON'S "FEELING THE SPIRIT IN THE DARK" FIRST APPEARED IN *CALLALOO*, 21.2 (1998): 399-416. CHARLES H. ROWELL. REPRINTED BY PERMISSION OF THE JOHNS HOPKINS UNIVERSITY PRESS.
•DWIGHT MCBRIDE'S "CAN THE QUEEN SPEAK?" FIRST APPEARED IN *CALLALOO*, 21.2 (1998): 363-379. CHARLES H. ROWELL. REPRINTED BY PERMISSION OF THE JOHNS HOPKINS UNIVERSITY PRESS.
•RICHARD BRUCE NUGENT'S POEM, "WHO ASKS THIS THING?" IS © 2000 BY THOMAS H. WIRTH.
•ANTHONY'S THOMAS'S "THE HOUSE THE KIDS BUILT" FIRST APPEARED IN *OUT/LOOK*, 2.1 (SUMMER 1989): 24-33
•TOURE'S "HIP HOP'S CLOSET" FIRST APPEARED IN THE *VILLAGE VOICE*, AUG. 27, 1996.
•GLORIA WEKKER'S "MATI-ISM AND BLACK LESBIANISM" FIRST APPEARED IN *THE JOURNAL OF HOMOSEXUALITY*, 24 (3/4), 1993.
•COVER PHOTOGRAPHY AND DESIGN BY PHILIP PIROLO.

Consultants

John L. Peterson
Gregory Herek
Steven Fullwood
Stanley Wei
Walter Wink
Marcel Vige
Bill Stanford Pincheon
Betti Ellerson
Kheven LaGroane
Sanford Gaylord
Bruce Morrow
Michelle Escumbise

Contents

Iconic Signifiers of the Gay Harlem Renaissance

Heterosexism and Homophobia in Popular Black Music

Homosexuality in Popular Black Literature

The Silent Mythology Surrounding AIDS and Public Icons

Acknowledgments

Deepest thanks to Stanley Wei, Henry Louis Gates, Jr., Carole Baptiste, Gail Pringle, Karen Hutchinson, The Write Thing, Angela Davis, bell hooks, Maya Angelou, Terry McMillan, the NAACP, Rupaul, the late Sylvester, *Ebony* magazine, *Essence* magazine, the late Justin Fashanu, Angela "Red" Spence, Kofi Kari-Kari, Mica Paris, Blacknet UK, *The Voice* newspaper, *The Daily Challenge, The Amsterdam News, The Gleaner, The New Nation, The Caribbean Times, The Miami Times, Gemini News Service*, Jane Wilson, *Pride* magazine, Jackee Holder, Hilary Patton, Diane Buck, Sandra Springer, Angela Brown and Scott Brassart of Alyson Publications, University of Essex, Dr. Colin Samson, Professor Ken Plummer, Yaso Hakim, Michelle Escumbise, Pablo Menfasawe-Imani, Courtier Newland, Dotun Adebayo, Steve Pope, Warren G, Vibe Magazine, *The Source* magazine, Henry Winkler, Paul Gilroy, Stuart Hall, Kobena Mercer, Hilda Shongu M'Gadza, Sylvia Shephard, the White Family, the Simms Family, the Simpson Family, Stephen Small, Michael Barnett, Lloyd Bryson, Ruth Brian, Patrick Vernon, the New Testament Church of God—Wolverhampton, the residents of Heath, Goldie, Lee Pinkerton, all my school friends at Wednesfield High School, Wulfrun College, Bilston College, Mr. Wootton, and Mr. John Avis.

In addition, my gratitude goes out to Hendon College, Enfield College, University of East London, the Sonja Haynes Black Cultural Center at UNC-Chapel Hill, Millerville State University, Cornel West, Toni Morrison, Alice Walker, *Think Doctor publication*, Angela Dodzie, Michael E. Dyson, Gerald Horne, Beverly Greene, Tracey Skelton, *The Jamaican Weekly Gleaner,* Associated Press, Reuters News Agency, New Cross Hospital–Wolverhampton, all the people of Wolverhampton, OutRage, GLAAD, Blacksene.com, Blacknet Typing Services, and all my friends in New York City. Also, thanks to all the people I have fallen out of touch with over the years, with a few exceptions, of course!

Most importantly, a very special thank-you must go to Saratha Shan and Yaso Hakim for all their kindness and support over the last two years. And last but not least, thank you, Caroline "Ayotola" Joseph for your brilliant sense of real professionalism in assisting me with this project. You delivered when it counted. I couldn't have finished this project without you and your team.

Foreword

Henry Louis Gates Jr.

All prejudices are not equal. But that doesn't mean there's no comparison between the predicaments of gays and blacks.

For some veterans of the civil rights era, it's a matter of stolen prestige. "It is a misappropriation for members of the gay leadership to identify the April 25 March on Washington with the Rev. Martin Luther King Jr.'s 1963 mobilization," one such veteran, the Reverend Dennis G. Kuby, wrote in a letter to the editor that appeared in *The New York Times* on the day of the 1993 march. Four days later, testifying before the Senate Armed Services Committee's hearings on the issues of gays in the military, Lieutenant General Calvin Waller, United States Army (retired), was more vociferous. General Waller, who, as General Norman Schwarzkopf's second-in-command, was the highest-ranking black officer in the Gulf War's theater of operations, contemptuously dismissed any linkage between the gay rights and civil rights movements. "I had no choice regarding my race when I was delivered from my mother's womb," General Waller said. "To compare my service in America's armed forces with the interrogation and avowed homosexual is personally offensive to me." This sentiment—that gays are pretenders to the throne of disadvantage that properly belongs to black Americans, that their relation to the rhetoric of civil rights is one of unearned opportunism—is surprisingly widespread. "The backlash is on the streets among blacks and black pastors who do not want to be aligned with homosexuals," the Reverend Lou Sheldon, chairman of the Traditional Values Coalition, crowed to *The New York Times* in the aftermath of the march. That the national Association for the Advancement of Colored Peopled endorsed the April 25th march made the insult all the deeper for those who disparage the gay-rights movement as the politics of imposture—Liberace in Rosa Parks drag. "Gays are not subject to water hoses or police dogs, denied access to lunch counters or prevented from voting," the Reverend Kuby asserted. On the contrary, "most gays are perceived as well-educated, socially mobile, and financially comfortable." Even some of those sympathetic to gay rights are unhappy with the models of oppression and victim-hood that they take to be enshrined in the civil rights discourse that many gay advocates have adopted. For those blacks and whites who viewed the 1993 March on Washington with skepticism, to be gay is merely an inconvenience; to be black is to inherit a legacy of hardship and inequity. For them, there's no comparison. But the reason the national conversation on the subject has reached an impasse isn't that there's simply no comparison; it's that there's no "simple" comparison.

Prejudices, of course, don't exist in the abstract; they all come with distinctive and distinguishing historical peculiarities. In short, they have content as well as form. Underplaying the differences blinds us to the signature traits of other forms of social hatred. Indeed, in judging other prejudices by the one you know best, you may fail to recognize those other prejudices as prejudices.

To take a quick and fairly obvious example, it has been observed that while antiblack racism charges its object with inferiority, anti-Semitism charges its object with iniquity. The racist believes that blacks are incapable of running anything by themselves. The anti-Semite believes (in one popular bit of folklore) that 13 rabbis rule the world.

How do gays fit into this scheme? Uneasily. Take that hard-ridden analogy between blacks and gays. Much of the ongoing debate over gay rights has fixated—and foundered—on the vexed distinction between "status" and "behavior." The paradox here can be formulat-ed as follows: Most people think of racial identity as a matter of (racial) status, but they respond to it as behavior. Most people think of sexual identity as a matter of (sexual) behavior, but they respond to it as sta-tus. Accordingly, people who fear and dislike blacks are typically pre-occupied with the threat that they think blacks' aggressive behavior poses to them. Hence they're inclined to make exceptions for the kind-ly, "civilized" blacks: That's why *The Cosby Show* could be so popular among white South Africans. By contrast, the repugnance that many people feel toward gays concerns, in the first instance, the status ascribed to them. Disapproval of a sexual practice is transmuted into the demonization of a sexual species.

In other respects too, antigay propaganda sounds less like antiblack rhetoric than like classical anti-Jewish rhetoric: Both evoke the image of the small, cliquish minority that nevertheless commands disproportionate and sinister worldly influence. More broadly, atti-tudes toward homosexuals are bound up with sexism and the attitudes toward gender that feminism, with impressive—though only partial—success, asks us to reexamine.

That doesn't mean that the race analogy is without merit or that there are no relevant points of comparison. Just as blacks have historically been represented as sexually uncontrollable beasts, ready to pounce on an unwilling victim with little provocation, a similar vision of the predatory homosexual has been insinuated, often quite subtly, into the defense of the ban on gays in the military.

But can gays really claim anything like the "victim status" inherited by black Americans? "They admit to holding positions at the highest levels of power in education, government, business, and entertainment," Martin Mawyer, president of the Christian Action Network, complains, "yet in the same breath they claim to be suffering discrimination in employment." Actually, the question itself is sand trap. First, why should oppression, however it's measured, be a prerequisite for legal protection? Surely there's a consensus that it would be wrongful and unlawful for someone to discriminate against Unitarians in housing or employment, however secure American Unitarians were as a group. Granted, no one can legislate affection or approval. But the simple fact that people enjoy legal protections from religious discrimination neither confers nor requires victimization. Why is the case of sexual orientation any different?

Second, trying to establish a pecking order of oppression is generally a waste of time: That's something we learned from a long-standing dialogue in the feminist movement. People figured out that you could speak of the subordination of women without claiming, absurdly, that every woman (Margaret Thatcher, say) was subordinate to every man. Now the single greatest predictor of people's economic success is the economic and educational level of their parents. Since gays, like women, seem to be evenly distributed among classes and races, the compounding effect of transgenerational poverty, which is the largest factor in the relative deprivation of black America, simply doesn't apply. Much of black suffering stems from historical racism; most gay suffering stems from contemporary hatred. It's also the case that marketing surveys showing that gays have a higher-than-average income and education level are generally designed to impress potential advertisers in gay publications; quite possibly, the surveys reveal the characteristics only of gays who are willing to identify themselves as such in a questionnaire. Few people would be surprised to learn that secretiveness on this matter varies inversely with education and income level.

What makes the race analogy complicated is that gays, as demographic composites, do indeed "have it better" than blacks—and yet in many ways contemporary homophobia is more virulent than contemporary racism. According to one monitoring group, one in four gay men has been physically assaulted as a result of his perceived sexual orientation; about 50% have been threatened with violence. (For lesbians, the incidence is lower but still disturbing.) A moral consensus now exists in this country that discriminating against blacks as teachers, priests, or tenants is simply wrong. (That doesn't mean it doesn't happen.) For much of the country, however, the moral legitimacy of homosexuals, as homosexuals, remains much in question. When Bill Crews, for the past nine years the mayor of the well-scrubbed hamlet of Melbourne, Iowa, returned home after the 1993 march, at which he had publicly disclosed his homosexuality for the first time, he found MELBOURNE HATES GAYS and FAGGOTS spray-painted on his house. What makes the closet so crowded is that gays are, as a rule, still socialized—usually by their nearest and dearest—into shame.

Mainstream religious figures—ranging from Catholic archbishops to orthodox rabbis—continue to enjoin us to "hate the sin": It has been a long time since anyone respectable urged us to, as it were, hate the skin. Jimmy Swaggart, on the other hand, could assure his millions of followers that the Bible says homosexuals are "worthy of death" and get away with it. Similar access to mass media is not available to those who voice equivalent attitudes toward blacks. In short, measured by their position in society, gays on the average seem privileged relative to blacks; measured by the acceptance of hostile attitudes toward them, gays are worse off than blacks. So are they as "oppressed"? The question presupposes a measuring rod that does not and cannot exist.

To complicate matters further, disapproval of homosexuality has been a characteristic of much of the black nationalist ideology that has reappeared in the aftermath of the civil rights era. "Homosexuality is a deviation from Afrocentric thought because it makes the person evaluate his own physical needs above the teachings of national consciousness," writes Dr. Molefi Kete Asante, of Temple University, who directs the black studies program there, one of the country's largest. Asante believes that "we can no longer allow our social lives to be controlled by European decadence," and argues that "the redemptive power of Afrocentricity" provides hope of a cure for those afflicted, through (the formulation has a regrettably fascist ring) "the submergence of their own wills into the collective will of our people."

In the end, the plaintive rhetoric of the Reverend Kuby and those civil rights veterans who share his sense of unease is notable for a small but significant omission: any reference to those blacks who are also gay. And in this immediate context one particular black gay man comes to mind. It's actually curious that those who feel that the example of the 1963 March on Washington has been misappropriated seem to have forgotten about him since it was he, after all, who organized that heroic march. His name, of course, was Bayard Rustin, and it's quite likely that if he had been alive he would have attended the March on Washington 30 years later.

By a poignant historical irony, it was in no small part because of his homosexuality—and the fear that it would be used to discredit the mobilization—that Rustin was prevented from being named director of the 1963 march; the title went to A. Philip Randolph, and he accepted it only on the condition that he could then deputize Rustin to do the arduous work of coordinating the mass protest. Rustin accepted the terms readily. In 1963 it was necessary to choose which of two unreasoning prejudices to resist, and Rustin chose without bitterness or recrimination. Thirty years later, people marched so his successors wouldn't have to make that costly choice.

Introduction

It was the first day of Black History Month 1994, and I was scheduled to attend a meeting at the Schomburg Center in Harlem. My family, however, had other ambitions. My forceful aunt strongly recommended that I should attend church to give thanks to the Lord for my safe arrival to America. At the back of my mind I felt like telling her I had already done my fair share of thanking the Lord when I arrived at JFK, and I'd be doing the same when I returned to London. Besides, I had my own agenda and I intended to stick to it. Religion was not on my list of things to experience. I tried every line and tact possible to avoid going to a place that I only attended at weddings, christenings, and funerals. My family, however, was not interested in my excuses, and I surrendered under serious duress. They encouraged me in true Caribbean style to "get on the bus" or face the consequences later. I felt like quoting one of those rally cries you often see in old news footage of civil rights protesters marching in the South in the early 1960s: "I am a man." But I kept quiet because I knew that for the next few weeks I would have to put up and shut up if I wanted a quiet life. Given the price of lodging in New York, I came to the conclusion that silent protest is sometimes the best option.

When our bus arrived at the church, I received the usual questions and comments: "Have you seen the queen? You have a nice accent. When are you going to cut those damn dirty dreadlocks?" I responded quietly to one woman, "When you decide to cut that tired weave you've been wearing for the last ten years!" Just to piss them off even more, I spoke in a Caribbean accent. They hated it. Too many people assume that because I'm British born and bred, I will assume the attitude and try to speak the Queen's English among Caribbeans. Just like Southerners who come to the North who suddenly forget what certain Southern terms mean. Y'all know the type of folks I be talkin' 'bout. I can't deny the British influence on my accent and mannerisms, but I don't know the British national anthem, I didn't weep for Princess Diana, and I always cheer when Britain loses at sport. (Regardless of how many Black people are playing, I just can't support them while they represent the British flag.) That's how British I am. Anyway, it was Sunday evening. Well, actually morning, but it felt like I'd been listening to the pastor preach and preach and preach nonstop for hours without as much as a piss break. Enough was enough, so I went to the toilet—that is, the toilet in the home that I was forced to leave to attend church against my will. While I was in the kitchen eating Caribbean-style rice and peas (without permission), my old university friend Michael called and told me he was in New York on vacation from his editing job in Miami. We arranged to meet outside Harlem Hospital at 4 P.M. He was damn late as usual. To say I cursed him out is an understatement. But in true Michael style he ignored me. Bastard! Once that little episode had ended, we went on our usual mission of book hunting. In all my journeys to America I had never realized it before, but New York City is awash with "Black" publications on every conceivable "Black" issue. Even the illegal street traders on 125th Street in Harlem had books we had never seen or heard of before. We were very tempted to buy, but as we had British accents we didn't think it was a good idea to flash the cash, so to speak. Don't get me wrong— not all of them are crooks. But it just so happens that as soon as people hear a Black man with dreadlocks speak with a British accent heads turn. Why, I do not know.

Eventually Michael and I found ourselves outside the Barnes and Noble bookstore in Greenwich Village, which we entered to escape the cold. We were soon approached by a smartly dressed salesman who handed me a leaflet explaining that Barnes and Nobles's contribution to Black History Month was a sale in their "Black books" section. We didn't hesitate in asking for directions. What we found was awesome, such was the wealth and variety of material; we were just hoping that MasterCard and Visa wouldn't let us down that day. But fortunately they did us justice and came through. Whilst standing in the bookstore foyer contemplating the spurious options for our journey home—taxi (which, incidentally, rarely stops for Black men) or the infamous subway—we heard a commotion and witnessed a group of African American youths giving chase to a group of mainly white gay men. The continuous chants of "Boom Bye Bye" and "Let's get them queens" revealed that the intended victims were gay, and the violent intentions of the aggressors were evident by the weapons they wielded.

Michael and I became transfixed by the activity around us, and any noble human feelings of disgust, shock, and shame seemed lost amidst our bestial instincts to see "the kill." We compounded our interest by videotaping the incident and woefully wishing that the event would become sufficiently and progressively violent to make it compelling viewing and, more importantly, to merit us a mention in the American mainstream press.

Such was our misplaced journalistic zeal, we were able to justify to ourselves the filming of the incident as something we had neither previously seen nor experienced. This was certainly not true. We understood exactly what those white gay men were facing and how they must have felt. This incident should have served as a reminder of the numerous times our friends and families had experienced similar life-threatening situations—including being harassed by racists while onlookers did nothing and while others awaited their demise. Sadly, some of our friends had been caught and seriously injured, while others had not lived to tell the tale. We should have feared the same fate for those white gay men being chased in Greenwich Village. They say white men can't run or jump, but from what I saw they certainly dealt with that myth in fine style. If they hadn't had the ability to run when their lives depended on it, the consequences could have been fatal.

After the chase ended, a sense of order was swiftly reestablished by "New York's finest." (On this occasion they didn't ram a broomstick up anyone's ass in the course of carrying out their duty.) It later emerged that the African American men giving chase and the white men being chased were part of a group of gay youths who had been involved in an earlier incident between a Black and white gay couple, which had started in one of a café frequented by gay patrons. According to eyewitness reports, it was a domestic dispute between two gay men, one Black and one white, who had both accused the other of infidelity. In the white man's anger, he had called his ex-partner a "nigger bitch," and a large-scale fight ensued.

It is noteworthy that not all the "chasers" were gay and that many of the African American men had simply joined the chase thinking it was a racially motivated incident. It was equally surprising that none of the Black gay men involved in the chase appeared concerned that some of their counterparts were shouting "Boom Bye Bye." The ultimate question is: Would these Black gay men have reacted the same way if a group of African American heterosexual men had been chasing them chanting the very slogans? I doubt it.

After a few moments of madness and a long discussion in a nearby café regarding the incident, common sense eventually prevailed, and Michael and I agreed not to pass the video on to the media or to file the report for professional or personal gain. At this point, I felt I should have stayed in church and listened to the usual brimstone-and-fire lyrics rather than experience the feelings I did. Amidst our discussion, we realized that the "great taboo" of Black homosexuality needed to be discussed in a more constructive manner beyond the usual sensationalist perspective. Given the sensitive nature of homosexuality and the reactions it provokes, we decided to first broach discussion on the issue through academic publications. This approach does not refute the impracticality of open discussion, but rather chooses to recognize the need to establish an appropriate forum to address the issues that affect the Black community as a whole. The subject of homosexuality is in itself sufficiently contentious and provocative to many heterosexuals. This notwithstanding, we agreed further that discussion is vital and must take into account the pride and the passion that any such debate necessarily invokes. Which is why we opted to publish a book as opposed to an academic or feature piece. Initially this book was supposed to be an anthology of Black perspectives that were either sympathetic to or antagonistic toward the subject of homosexuality. Interestingly enough, the only responses we received from those prepared to discuss homosexuality in the Black community were from Black gay and lesbian writers and their supporters. Those who were intolerant of the subject failed to respond, despite having been encouraged to contribute their views. We decided to continue the project based on the views and ideas of gay and lesbian journalists, academics, and basically anyone who could string together a good argument, regardless of race or sexuality.

The poor response from the "antagonists" was not from lack of trying; invitations were sent via the media, the Internet, and various academic journals. Individuals reputed for their candor and radicalism were also approached. The notable absence of such views in this anthology indicates, in our view, an unwillingness to be recognized on a wider, and possibly global platform, as being homophobic—because that is essentially what they are. Some more than others, but homophobic they all are, preferring to hide their prejudices behind irrational Afrocentric intellectualism combined with misinterpreted biblical doctrine. We hope that the quality of discussion and analysis in this collection will generate further thought and prompt serious examinations of the subject within the heterosexual and Black community as a whole.

—Delroy Constantine-Simms

Negotiating the Racial Politics of Black Sexual Identity

My Gay Problem, Your Black Problem

Earl Ofari Hutchinson, Ph.D.

The circus-like hype over the ABC/Disney show *Ellen* has passed. But the problem of homophobia hasn't. It's still deeply entrenched in many Americans. And that includes many African Americans, especially African American men. For two reasons, I still can't forget a scene I saw in a movie during the mid 1970s. One, it was the first time I had ever seen two men passionately kiss on the screen. Two, the mostly Black audience went wild, screaming, jeering, and hooting in the theater.

It took several minutes for the crowd to quiet down and for the ushers to restore order. As I left the theater I listened to the young men talk. Their contempt and disgust for these two men spilled out into the street and parking lot. They called them "faggots," "punks," and "sissies." It seemed as if they were trying to scrape off themselves the slime that the scene of these two men kissing had left on them.

A year or so later I was at a local political meeting. Afterward, while talking with a friend, a young Black man came up to us. My friend winked at me and whispered, "He's queer," and quickly walked away. I stood there alone with him, and after a moment of awkward silence we started talking. I mentioned that I was a jogger. His eyes immediately lit up, and he said he was too. He quickly suggested that maybe we could go jogging together. I didn't know anything about this man, or what he was, and I suspect my friend didn't either. But I still froze in naked panic. I thought about the young men who ridiculed the gays at the theater. At the time I thought their antics were downright silly and in poor taste. I now realized that I was no different than they.

I had the same horror of and prejudice against gays as they had. But why? Did they threaten me? Did they stir deep and violent passions in so many of us? Did I feel an even more intense dislike for a Black man who was gay? Did they threaten and challenge my fragile masculinity at the basest and most ambiguous level? They did. And this forced me to take a deep soul search into my own homophobic fears. And even though I hated what I saw and had no rational explanation for these fears, I understood why they were buried deep in me. From cradle to grave, much of America drilled into Black men the thought that they are less than men. This made many Black men believe and accept the gender propaganda that the only real men in American society were white men. In a vain attempt to recapture their denied masculinity, many Black men mirrored America's traditional fear and hatred of homosexuality. They swallowed whole the phony and perverse John Wayne definition of manhood, that real men talked and acted tough, shed no tears, and never showed their emotions. These were the prized strengths of manhood. When men broke the prescribed male code of conduct and showed their feelings, they were harangued as weaklings and their manhood was questioned.

Many Black men who bought this malarkey did not heap the same scorn on women who were lesbians. White and Black gay women did not pose the same threat as gay men. They were women, and that meant that they were fair game to be demeaned and marginalized by many men. Many Blacks, in an attempt to distance themselves from gays and avoid confronting their own biases, dismissed homosexuality as "their thing." Translated: Homosexuality was a perverse contrivance of white males and females that reflected the decadence of white America. They made no distinction between white gays and other whites. To them whites were whites were whites. Also, many Blacks listened to countless numbers of Black ministers shout and condemn to fire and brimstone any man who dared think about, yearn for, or God forbid, actually engage in the "godless" and "unnatural act" of having a sexual relationship with another man. If they had any doubts about it, they fell back on the good book. They could, as generations of Bible-toting white preachers did, flip to the oft-cited line in Leviticus that sternly calls men being with men "the abomination." While many Americans made gays their gender bogeymen, many Blacks made Black gay men their bogeymen and waged open warfare against them. Black gay men became the pariahs among pariahs, and wherever possible, every attempt was made to drum them out of Black life. Some of these efforts have been especially pathetic. Civil Rights leader Bayard Rustin, a known gay and the major mover and shaker behind the 1963 March on Washington, was all but banned by March leaders from speaking or having any visible public role at the March. A popular Black nationalist magazine of that day took frequent and giddy delight in calling Rustin "the little fairy." No Black leader publicly challenged its homophobia. In *Soul On Ice*, published in 1969, then-radical-Black Eldridge Cleaver viciously mugged James Baldwin for his homosexuality and declared homosexuality the ultimate "racial death wish." No Black leader publicly challenged Cleaver on this point, and his outrageous fad theories on sexuality were praised by an entire generation of radical wanna-bes as if they were *the* word from on high. A decade later Black gay filmmaker Marlon Riggs hoped that the hostile public attitudes of many Blacks toward gays had lessened enough to at least permit a civil discussion among them about masculinity and homophobia. In a purposely ambiguous and veiled concession to the antigay mood, Riggs stole a bit of the rhetoric of Black militants and proclaimed that "Black men loving Black men is the revolutionary act of our times." It didn't work. Riggs found that antigay bigotry was just as entrenched as ever among many Blacks. Have Black attitudes toward gays undergone much of a change today? Hardly.

Rappers such as Ice Cube still rapped "Real niggers ain't gay." Leading Afrocentrists swore that "homosexuality is a deviation from Afrocentricity." And bushels of Black ministers, with generous support from their white Christian fundamentalist brethren, still branded homosexuality "a sin before God." Some Blacks escalated their low-intensity warfare against gays to a blood-soaked rhetorical battleground.

Nation of Islam leader Louis Farrakhan made it almost part of his divine mission to attack homosexuality. Even though the Million Man March publicly welcomed gays and treated civilly the ones who participated, no one really believed that this represented a sea of change in attitude among Blacks toward gays. If some did, Farrakhan quickly dispelled that notion in a TV interview with Evans and Novack in March 1997. He made it clear that he still regarded homosexuality as an "unnatural act" and would discourage the practice whenever and wherever he could. The traditional civil rights leaders continued to denounce homophobia and urge support of gay rights. They reminded Blacks that homophobia and racism were two sides of the same coin and that many of the same white conservatives from Pat Buchanan to Jerry Falwell who relentlessly savaged gays were the same ones who relentlessly savaged civil rights.

They were right, but their argument still cut little weight with many Blacks. The one and only comprehensive survey conducted in 1995 that measured Black attitudes toward gays found that Blacks, like whites, hadn't slackened up on their hostility one bit toward gays. More damning and ominous for Blacks, they still continued to pile special scorn on Black gay men. Even the one potential bright spot in this had a taint. The survey found that there was less antigay sentiment among the more educated, less religious, and more affluent Blacks, but only if the gay male was white. They still cast Black gay men deep in the netherworld of contempt. That antigay feeling runs so deep among many African Americans that there is a virtual blackout of any discussion or activities of Black gay men. Black gays and lesbians have held a number of national Black gay conferences since 1987, yet there has been only the slightest mention of them in the Black press. The national gay and lesbian publication *BLK* might as well gather dust in the Smithsonian for all that most Blacks know about it. Black gay men continue to feel like men without a people. They carry the triple burden of being Black, male, and gay. They are rejected by many Blacks and sense that they are only barely tolerated by white gays. Many Black gay men feel trapped, tormented, and confused by this quandary. They still spend sleepless nights and endless days figuring out ways to repress, hide, and deny their sexuality from family members, friends, and society.

Black gay men worry that the hatred of other Black men toward them won't change as long as they feel that their manhood is subverted and accept America's artificial standard of what a man is, and as long as antigay attitudes remain firmly rooted in America.

This will only change when more Black leaders understand that when you scratch a homophobe underneath, you'll invariably find a racist. And it will change when more Black men realize that Black gay bashing will win no brownie points with conservatives and will certainly not make them any more sympathetic to Black causes. Former Nation of Islam national spokesman Khalid Muhammad found that out. In a widely publicized speech in 1993, he made one of the most devastating and disgusting public assaults ever on gays. Yet he is still one of the most vilified Black men in America.

The Million Man March leaders upheld the spirit of the March by including gays. This was a positive step in that it was a tacit recognition that Black gay men face many of the same problems as all Black men. But it in no way meant that the majority of Black men were willing to completely accept Black gay men as brothers and equals. In time, more Black men will come out of the closet, and more Black men will meet them, get to know them better, or in some cases discover that they have known them all along. This will force even more Black men to reexamine their own faulty definitions of manhood and confront their own homophobia. This will go far toward ridding them of their fear of

Black gays as their bogeymen. But mostly I hope that more Black men are wise enough to see that they should be the last ones in America to jettison other Blacks who may be in a position to make valuable contributions to the struggle for political and economic empowerment. It took time for me to learn all of this, but I did, because I no longer wanted my gay problem to be my Black problem.

Are You Black First or Are You Queer?

Gregory Conerly

Introduction

Are you black first or are you queer? This question embodies a central
conflict many African American lesbians, bisexuals, and gays (lesbigays) experience in dealing with two identities that are often at odds
with each other. The answer to this question varies. For example, in his
1989 documentary *Tongues Untied*, Marlon Riggs argues that the two
identities are inseparable. Others, however, see one identity as more
important than the other, and have organized their social and sexual
lives as well as their political activism around their choice. Hence,
African American lesbians and gays have responded to this conflict
between their racial/ethnic and sexual-preference identities by situating
themselves in cultures in which one identity or the other is marginalized, both identities are centered, both identities are marginalized, or
some combination of these.

The choices for African American bisexuals are more complex
because we live in a culture that sees sexual orientation as either a
gay/lesbian or straight proposition. Bisexuals generally lack institutional and other forms of communal supports specific to them.
Therefore, they are often forced to either emphasize a preference for
one gender over the other and socialize in those cultural spaces that
support their gender preference, or go back and forth between straight
and lesbian or gay communities. African American gays and lesbians
usually have the option of socializing in a community where their sexual identity is centered. Bisexuals usually do not.

Johnson (1982) has done the most extensive research on the
dynamics of the choice of primary group affiliation and the justifica-
tions for that choice. His study, like the general academic discourse on
this issue, unfortunately has focused only on gay men thus far. Using
questionnaires, Johnson sampled 60 black gay men to see whether they
saw their black or gay identity as being central to them. He called those
black gays who chose the predominantly heterosexual black culture as
their primary communal affiliation "black-identified" gays. These men

were generally less open about their sexual preference (but still felt positively about it), were uncomfortable about expressing any form of intimacy with other men in public, had greater involvement with other blacks, and preferred black lovers. They felt their black identities were more important because skin color is more visible than sexual orientation, which they could hide. Hence, they believed skin color had a greater influence on how others interacted with them.

Johnson labeled those black gays who chose the predominantly white gay culture as their primary communal affiliation "gay-identified" blacks. They were generally more open about their sexual preference, more comfortable expressing affection for other men in public, had greater involvement with whites, and preferred white lovers. Their gay identity was more important to them because they felt the gay community was more tolerant than the black community, sexual orientation affected their social lives more than race, and they felt more oppressed by their sexual preference than by their race.

While Johnson's study is useful in identifying two groups of black gays, he chose not to analyze other potential groups. For example, some black gays in his sample felt both identities were equally important, but he did not identify their characteristics. The same was true of those gay men who saw another identity, such as one based on religion or class status, as being the identity they considered most important. Johnson also did not examine whether his subjects' primary identity choice had changed over time, giving the impression that once the choice is made, it is fixed. Through an examination of his experiences, Marlon Riggs suggests in *Tongues Untied* that the primary communal affiliation for some black lesbigays changes over time. In the documentary Riggs moves among three communities at various times in his life: mostly heterosexual black spaces, mostly white gay spaces, and black gay spaces.

Other academics (Peterson, 1992; Loiacano, 1989) have also examined this issue. But like Johnson, none have analyzed the social and political implications of choosing to affiliate oneself with one culture or the other. One major consequence of having a primary communal affiliation is that conflicts have occurred between black lesbigays who have chosen to affiliate with different primary cultures, and between them and the larger black or lesbian and gay cultures within which they are marginalized. In particular, many criticize those who have chosen white lesbigay culture as their primary social world because they see them as denying their black cultural heritage (Jordan,

1990). While some heterosexual blacks see all black lesbigays as denying their blackness, because to them, homosexuality is something they associate with white culture, many black lesbigays are much more aware of the divisions among them.

In this essay I focus on power relationships among black lesbians and gays who choose different primary communities. First I examine the context for this antagonism by exploring why some black lesbigay racial/ethnic and sexual orientation identities are in conflict. Then I focus on a central theme of the debate on primary community choice, the politics of what it "really" means to be black. I conclude by looking at how African American lesbigays might move beyond the "blacker than thou" debate—or at least recast it in different terms. I examine the politics of blackness by looking at the major anthologies produced thus far that have focused, either in whole or in a substantial part, on the writings of black lesbians and gay men: Essex Hemphill's *Brother to Brother*; Barbara Smith's *Home Girls*; Joseph Beam's *In the Life*, Michael Smith's *Black Men/White Men*; Makeda Silvera's *Piece of My Heart*; Cary Alan Johnson, Colin Robinson and Terence Taylor's *Other Countries: Black Gay Voices*; B. Michael Hunter's *Sojourner: Black Gay Voices in the Age of AIDS*; Catherine E. McKinley and L. Joyce Delaney's *Afrekete: An Anthology of Black Lesbian Writing*; and Cherrie Moraga and Gloria Anzaldua's *This Bridge Called My Back*. These texts are part of a larger discourse that represents one of the more prominent ways black lesbians and gays have tried to create a distinctive culture of their own—through creative works. As Hemphill (1991) has argued, through these works they have left affirmative "evidence of being" about their lives and cultures. Unfortunately, the editors of these anthologies generally have not included African Americans with bisexual identities. Evidence of their being is, for the most part, still lacking.

I focus on anthologies because they feature a multiplicity of black gay and lesbian voices, and their editors usually claim to speak to and/or for them. Barbara Smith (1983), for example, wrote in her introduction to *Home Girls* that she saw the anthology as a space where the "girls from the neighborhood and from the block, the girls we grew up with" could be themselves. Colin Robinson notes in his introduction to *Other Countries* that the anthology "is a celebration of the importance of difference. Not only the difference [black gay men] share, but our own internal diversity as a community" (Johnson, et al. 1988). And Joseph Beam (1986) proclaims that he and the other contributors to *In the Life* speak for, among others, "the brothers whose silence has cost them their sanity," and "the 2,500 brothers who have died of AIDS" (Beam, 1986). Sometimes editors note gaps in the kinds of voices they present. Hemphill (1991), for example, states in his introduction that *Brother to Brother* does not address topics such as older gays and interracial relationships. Although these anthologies feature a multiplicity of voices, with one exception they present an overwhelmingly black-identified vision of what it means to be black and lesbian or gay. Hence, the same discourse that has been instrumental in fostering a collective African American lesbian and gay identity has itself alienated and marginalized some individuals.

RISE OF AFRICAN AMERICAN LESBIGAY DISCOURSE

This discourse began in earnest in the late 1970s for two reasons (D'Emilio, 1993). One is the politicization of sexual and gender identities brought on by the lesbigay and feminist movements. As a result, women and those with some level of a same-sex sexual preference achieved greater visibility. They also were able to provide a social context in which they could create a discourse centering on their experiences and countering dominant, oppressive discourses on these identities. Through their activism, they tried to end a variety of cultural practices that were oppressive to them and forced many to rethink what it meant to be a woman/man and lesbigay/straight—with varying degrees of success. They also created their own cultural institutions, such as music festivals, publishing companies, bars, and community service centers.

The other reason for the rise of this discourse relates to race/ethnicity and gender divisions within the movements themselves. Increasingly, an awareness grew among lesbigays of color that the larger movements were not addressing the multiple oppressions and other kinds of identity-specific experiences they faced. In fact, the movements often perpetuated these oppressions. Joseph Beam expressed this sentiment in his introduction to *In the Life*, an anthology of African American gay male fiction, poetry, and essays.

It is possible to read thoroughly two or three consecutive issues of *The Advocate*, the national biweekly gay newsmagazine, and never encounter, in words or images, black gay men. It is possible to peruse the pages of *212* magazine's special issue on Washington, D.C., and see no black faces. It is possible to leaf through any of the major gay men's porno magazines, *In Touch, Drummer, Mandate, Blueboy,* or *Honcho,* and never lay eyes on a black Adonis. And it is certainly possible to read an entire year of *Christopher Street* and think there are no black gay writers worthy of the incestuous bed of New York's gay literati. We ain't family. Very clearly, gay male means: white, middle-class, youthful, Nautilized, and probably butch; there is no room for black gay men within the confines of this gay Pentagon (Beam, 1986).

The Combahee River Collective has made similar criticisms about "the white women's movement," arguing that white feminists have made little effort to deal with their racism or develop a comprehensive knowledge of racial politics and the cultures of people of color (Smith, 1983). African American lesbigays responded to this in two major ways. One was to pressure the leaders of these movements to move beyond single identity politics and address multiple oppressions. The other was to create a discourse that focused on their experiences. And a major focus of this discourse has been the conflict between their sexual preference and racial/ethnic identities.

SOURCES OF IDENTITY CONFLICT

This conflict exists for several reasons. One is that, for the most part, cultural, social, and political institutions specifically for black lesbians and gays are rare. Major cities such as Washington D.C., Atlanta, and Chicago contain a handful of predominantly black lesbian and gay bars, churches, and social and political organizations. There is a growing black lesbian and gay press, with magazines such as *SBC* getting national distribution. But most of these efforts are short-lived or their publications come out irregularly. Institutions specifically for bisexuals are nearly nonexistent. Many African American lesbigays also experience conflict between their two identities because they perceive racism among white lesbigays and heterosexism among straight blacks. A number of black lesbians and gays have described the discrimination against and sexual stereotyping of them by white lesbigays. They have also focused on the antilesbigay remarks made by many African American political leaders and intellectuals, the verbal and physical assaults perpetrated against them by heterosexual blacks, and ostracism from family, friends, and neighbors. Since their racial/ethnic or sexual orientation identity is often marginalized in both cultures, many black lesbigays do not feel fully accepted in either.

A third reason for the conflict in identities is the lack of overlap between the mostly white lesbigay culture and the mostly heterosexual black culture. They tend to be separated culturally, politically, and, in those areas where black and lesbigay cultures have a spatial presence, geographically. Sometimes antagonism exists between the two groups. One area of tension has been white gay male involvement in gentrifying some lower-class predominantly black neighborhoods in several major cities. This has reduced the amount of low-income housing available to blacks. Some black organizations and leaders, such as the NAACP, bell hooks, Jesse Jackson, and most members of the Black Congressional Caucus have come out in favor of lesbigay rights. But there is still a long way to go, especially in regard to white lesbigays building coalitions with African American leaders on political issues that affect all blacks, not just those affecting black lesbigays. This rift between the two cultures forces many African American lesbians and gays to choose a primary affiliation with one culture or the other, or to go back and forth between both. They have also created their own spaces, usually in the context of the larger cultures within which they are marginalized. For example, many black lesbigay churches founded by the late Dr. James Tinney and others are rooted in traditional African American ways of worship (Tinney, 1986).

Social movements for equality based on race, gender, and sexuality have greatly affected the ability of black lesbigays to choose or move back and forth between communities. The resulting antidiscrimination legislation, greater social visibility, awareness of issues related to these movements, and a (slow) decline in the acceptability of prejudice and discrimination have had several effects. They have led to greater access to public accommodations, greater social and economic independence, and a growing number of businesses and organizations geared to lesbigays. Barriers remain for black lesbigays, however, when they try to negotiate their marginalized identities in community spaces. But African American lesbigays now live in a social context in which their concerns must be given consideration, even if it is token. They also have a variety of legal and political weapons at their disposal.

THE POLITICS OF BLACKNESS

There are many kinds of black-identified lesbigays and lesbigay-identified blacks. The political and social animosity between them, however, has centered on two subgroups: black-identified Afrocentrists and gay-identified interracialists. The Afrocentrists tend to have zeal for what they identify as African-influenced cultural traditions, values, and practices. Interracialists are known primarily for their sexual attraction to whites, even though other kinds of interracial relationships, such as those between blacks and other people of color, are possible. For the most part, this antagonism has been explicit only in black gay male textual discourse. Perhaps this is because, as Lloyd Jordan (1990) argues, "men are more prone to convert difference into dispute." Perhaps it also reflects the more marginalized status of black lesbian discourse. For example, in the anthologies I examined, while most of the anthologies that feature black gay male writings do so exclusively, only one of the anthologies that feature black lesbians does—the most recent one, *Afrekete*. Black lesbians are usually presented within some larger context, such as among writings by black feminists (*Home Girls*), feminists of color (*This Bridge Called My Back*), or lesbians of color (*Piece of My Heart*). In those instances in which there is a clear articulation of race/ethnicity, constructions of African American lesbian and gay identity are usually black-identified. This is particularly true of the earlier anthologies in which there is only a partial focus on black lesbians. Here, discussions of interracialists are almost nonexistent. In those instances where interracialist voices are heard, they are tokens, and the emphasis is on black self-hatred. For example, Makeda Silvera, editor of the lesbians-of-color anthology *Piece of My Heart*, published a letter from one of the contributors, Judy Nicholson. Nicholson wanted to withdraw some of the poems she had submitted for publication because "They are poems of naïveté from my paler lesbian days. They reflect a period in my life when I stayed hidden in my own writing and instead lauded the 'beauty' of my White lovers...I do not know me enough to love me, to love my blackness, and to love other Black lesbians" (Nicholson 1991, 106).

Within this discourse, it has been the interracialists who have had to defend themselves. But black-identified gays and lesbians, many who have had to hide their sexual identities to appease heterosexist black communities, have not been forced to question their commitment to lesbigay politics. It has been interracialists who have had to question their blackness and their commitment to black politics.

Central to a black-identified definition of blackness is having roots in "the" black community and to placing a supreme value on one's home of origin. Barbara Smith, in her introduction to *Home Girls*, warns against transforming "cultural beliefs and habits that may characterize many [Black women] into requirements and use them as proof of [their] own and others' full membership in the race" (Nicholson 1991, 106). But the selection of stories and essays in her anthology contradicts this.

All of the pieces in *Home Girls* and the other major anthologies featuring black lesbians focus on black communities.

Jewelle Gomez's review of black lesbian literature best shows this bias. She praises Audre Lorde's *Zami* because it "advances the theme of women-loving-women within a recognizable context of Black life" (Gomez, 1983). For Gomez, a "recognizable context" is one that "takes place in the bosom of the Black community which Black Lesbians recognize as the place of their beginnings" (119). This praise of Lorde's work for these reasons seems odd because in the text Lorde reveals that she opened up about her sexuality only after she moved out of the black neighborhood she grew up in and began living and socializing in the mostly white and/or lesbian spaces of Greenwich Village. Here she felt disconnected from other blacks, including other black lesbians:

> During the fifties in the Village, I did not know the few other Black women who were visibly gay at all well. Too often we found ourselves sleeping with the same white women. We recognized ourselves as exotic sister-outsiders who might gain little from banding together. Perhaps our strength might lay in our fewness, our rarity. That was the way it was Downtown. And Uptown, meaning the land of Black people, seemed very far away and hostile territory (Lorde 1982, 177).

While Gomez (1983) praises Lorde, she criticizes writer Ann Shockley, saying that her novel, *Say Jesus and Come to Me*, does not situate black lesbians in the appropriate cultural context: "The main character, the Reverend Myrtle Black, is egotistical and self-centered. She lacks any kind of anchor in Black culture. Neither her language nor her posture say anything about the complex society which spawned her" (114). Gomez claims that although Shockley does deal with black issues such as racism in the music business and the white women's movement as well as black male sexism, "[s]he skims the surface of these complicated issues and of the characters themselves, leaving no lasting literary or human sensation in her wake" (113).

Shockley (1983), in her review of representations of black lesbians in the same anthology, makes similar claims about what it means to be black. She argues that "Black women writers *live* in the Black community and *need* the closeness of family, friends, neighbors, and coworkers who share the commonality of ethnicity in order to survive in a blatantly racist society" (86). Hence, the lack of black lesbian characters in 1979, the time she wrote the essay, resulted from the tremendous pressure black women felt to conform to heterosexist black cultural norms. Because she sees "being black" as rooted in the black community, she criticizes white author Rita Mae Brown for featuring an "inauthentic" black lesbian in her novel, *In Her Day:*

> [T]he bourgeois professor Adele, a Ph.D. in pre-Columbian art, is hardly recognizable as Black...Adele talks white without any of the intentional or unintentional breaks into Black English which are commonly made by all Blacks, regardless of education, at some time or another. Adele acts white, thinks white, and apparently has no significant Black friends (Shockley 1983, 113).

For Shockley and others, a black lesbian whose primary social world, whose "home" of origin or choice has been among whites, or who has internalized Euro-American values and patterns of behavior is an impossibility. This is the case even though a growing number of blacks are living and working outside the predominantly black communities where most African Americans continue to live (Feagin and Sikes, 1994). As a result, the lives of lesbian-identified blacks are erased—as is the diversity within black communities—and a black-identified lesbian life is presented as the only viable way to be an African American lesbian.

An exception to this rule—at least to an extent—is the latest anthology to focus on black lesbian life (and the only one to do so exclusively), *Afrekete*. In their introduction to *Afrekete* (1995), Catherine McKinley and L. Joyce Delaney engage the politics of representing black lesbian identity directly. They note that as artists, their primary interest was to collect "good writing" and that "[i]dentity politics bind and frankly bore us." They also acknowledge, however, that presenting a singular vision of black lesbian identity is problematic. They are most explicit about their agenda in their discussion of the Audre Lorde character after whom they named the anthology:

> Afrekete is a black Black woman, a primal link to a history and community many of us are accused of forsaking when we "cross" over into the lesbian "nation." For many of us, Afrekete offered a comfortable, reassuring image of ourselves

and allowed for imaginings of the lovers who might be out there. She is a perfect creation of the Black lesbian feminist imagination. And yet while we need this myth and others, and at times our lovers, we need them to exist complicated by other Black lesbian lives. We cannot afford...single representations of Black lesbians or a handful of generally recognized texts that portray Black lesbian lives (McKinley, 1995).

This uneasy balance between de-essentializing black lesbian identity while having a favored one is reflected in the writings McKinley and Delaney include in the anthology. Most of the writings in *Afrekete* center on black-identified lesbians. Several stories, however, focus on women whose lives intersect in various ways with the mostly white lesbigay community, the mostly heterosexual black community, and/or the black lesbigay community. What is interesting about them, however, is that they focus primarily on the encounters these women have with other blacks in mostly black spaces.

An example is Melanie Hope's "Dare," a defense of interracial relationships. In it, she attempts to dispel stereotypes about blacks involved in interracial relationships. Primary among them is the myth of black self-hatred. She notes that when growing up, although her parents encouraged her to have nonblack friends, "Our home [was] a place where Blackness [was] celebrated" (265). She did not grow up hating her Afrocentric features or various black cultural traditions, and she continues to value them. She also argues that being in an interracial relationship does not make one a "traitor to the race." She points to black gays and lesbians such as Pat Parker, Audre Lorde, and James Baldwin as people who, while they were in interracial relationships at various points in their lives, made significant contributions to black culture and politics. From Hope's perspective, "in no way did their concern for the world's treatment of Black people lessen because of the intimate relationships they shared with people who are not black" (265).

Hope also subverts the idea of black self-hatred by examining her concerns about being accepted by other blacks, particularly her family and other black lesbians. The message she received from them was that black people should not "deal in snow" (263). Clearly, these are the people whose acceptance she wants. Nowhere does she mention being concerned about acceptance by whites because of her interracial relationships, even though such relationships are commonly taboo among them as well.

This emphasis on black acceptance is also evident in the anthology's other writings that focus on women whose lives link them to multiple communities. Jocelyn Maria Taylor's "Testimony of a Naked Woman" also examines the politics of interracial relationships. That is not, however, her primary theme. Like Jamika Ajalon in "Kaleidoscope," she focuses on other kinds of black lesbian behavior that some blacks read as being "white" or antiblack.

Taylor writes of her interest in exploring other ways of expressing black female sexuality, such as through exhibitionism, public nudity, and public sex, while avoiding racist sexual stereotypes. In one of her attempts to do this, however, other black lesbians rebuked her. When she bared her breasts while dancing in a mostly black women's gathering, they laughed at her and called her a freak. That is, she was one of those women "who have no sexual boundaries and who are 'indiscriminate' about their sexual encounters" (37). In essence, they accused her of reinforcing racist sexual stereotypes in the one setting where she felt they would understand that what she did was a political act designed to reclaim black women's eroticism. One of the guards told her if she did not put her top back on, she would be thrown out: "She asked that I put my shirt back on for the sake of my 'sisters.' Her tone implied that I was not conducting myself in a way that was appropriate for a Black woman" (39). Reinforcing this, most of the women in the club who had decided to follow her lead and bare their breasts were part of the white minority.

Ajalon, through the character of Latto, also examines the politics of "appropriate" behavior for black lesbians. In one scene, a mostly heterosexual group of Afrocentric black poets throw a party for Latto, who is concerned that she and her so-light-she-could-pass-for-white date "wouldn't pass their 'Blackability' test" (132). That they live in and adopt/adapt some of the cultural styles of the mostly white community (lesbigay and straight) in the East Village section of New York City enhances her uneasiness: "We stuck out in our semi-grunge wear that people related with the East Village, our haircuts mocking theirs. I was painfully aware that the shaved parts of my head in some people's eyes disqualified the dreadlocks up front" (132).

As with the anthology's other writings, emphasis is placed on how black lesbians' construction of black identity marginalizes them from the blacks from whom they seek acceptance. This fits right in with McKinley and Delaney's overall goal of the anthology: to privilege yet problematize black-identified constructions of lesbian identity. They do this, however, by choosing (consciously or not) writings that emphasize an engagement with other blacks rather than also including writings in which there is an engagement with white or other nonblack lesbigays.

In contrast to black lesbian anthologies, those that focus on the lives of black gay men generally use the black nationalist "blacker-than-thou" rhetoric to discredit gay-identified black men. Gay-identified blacks either do not have roots in black communities or have severed their connection to them. Also, many of them prefer whites in sexual relationships. Because of this, others portray them as being oblivious to the racism that exists in white gay culture and as hating their blackness. For example, in his description of an interracialist, Joseph Beam writes, "Maurice has a propensity for white people, which is more than preference—it's policy. He dismisses potential Black friendships as quickly as he switches off rap music and discredits progressive movements. He consistently votes Republican. At night he dreams of razors cutting away thin slivers of his Black skin" (1986, 240).

While some interracialists may fit these characterizations, it is a mistake to attribute these qualities to most of them. If the essays and stories in *Black Men/White Men*, the only major anthology of interracialist experiences produced thus far, are any indication, interracialists are only too aware of the racism that exists in the "home" they have chosen. The sexual stereotyping; the discrimination in bars, baths, employment, and housing; the prevalence of white male standards of beauty; the racist personal ads that appear in gay newspapers; and the gay white gentrification that has displaced lower-income blacks—all pervade the pages of the anthology. Interracialists are no less aware of white gay racism than Afrocentrists and other black-identified gays are of straight black heterosexism, a theme that pervades their work.

Both groups are aware of the limitations of the primary communities they have chosen, and of the ones they have not. It is ironic that black-identified gays have used black nationalist rhetoric to discredit interracialists, since many heterosexual black nationalists have used the same rhetoric to discredit them. Homosexuality is a "white thang," according to them, and those blacks who practice it have "sold out." Haki Madhubuti, for example, has argued that getting black men to practice homosexuality is one way in which whites systematically "disrupt black families and neutralize black men" (Simmons 1991, 215).

Ultimately, choosing a primary community when you do not have access to one that accepts both your racial/ethnic and sexual preference identities is an intensely personal decision that, for many, centers around these questions: Which do you find more oppressive or important politically, racism or heterosexism? Which identity is more important in your social life: race/ethnicity or sexual preference? How much value do you place on your home of origin? Which community is more conducive for having sexual relationships with those who have the qualities you desire? The answers to these questions will depend upon, among other things, each black lesbigay's personal history, the meanings they have attached to their experiences, whether their home of origin is a black community, the nature of their sexual desires, and their politics. The answers to these questions may also change over time. Because of this, interracialist black lesbigays should not be made to feel they are not really black simply because they prefer white lesbigay communities as their home of choice. In fact, as Jordan (1990) has argued, having black lesbigays in both cultures can be politically beneficial. Many lesbigay-identified blacks have battled racism among white lesbigays, just as many black-identified lesbigays have challenged heterosexism in black communities (25).

CONCLUSION

Black-identified lesbigays must de-essentialize their idea of what it means to be black. As black cultural critics have argued, while distinct black cultural characteristics do persist over space and time, "[t]hey do not, however, form the basis of a black racial or cultural essence. Nor do they indicate *the* meaning of blackness will be expressed in a quality or characteristic without which a person, act, or practice no longer qualifies as black" (Dyson 1993, xxi).

The essentialist notion of blackness promoted by black-identified lesbigays is that interracialists and other lesbigay identified blacks to question the authenticity of their black identity. And for those who find aspects of what has been promoted as "being black" by other blacks to be problematic, some decide not to forge a new kind of black identity, but to reject what they perceive as "being black" altogether. Reginald Shepherd, the token tortured interracialist in *In the Life*, writes about this dilemma in relation to the anti-intellectualism promoted in the black neighborhoods in which he grew up:

Too much of what I've seen of black society simply assumes that black people should have no interest in these words [of culture and education], that these words are irrelevant to or destructive of "black culture".... I've had notions, negative each one, images of what it is to *seem* black: to look black, to talk black, to dress black.... The language of culture and education was not among these seemings. I've shaped for myself a manner of appearing quite other than those seemings (Shepherd, 1986).

As a result, Shepherd and others like him are forced to live a contradiction. On the one hand, they have the physical characteristics generally associated with blacks, and hence, others interact with them as such. At the same time, they have a sense of themselves as being something other than black because they or others perceive them as not exhibiting the "right" cultural characteristics. And the ones they do exhibit are usually associated with whites. While black lesbigay identity must be de-essentialized, this does not mean that various socially constructed definitions of blackness should be immune to criticism. All meanings of blackness have social, cultural, and political implications, and these implications change depending on their historical context; they must continually be reevaluated and reshaped.

The silences and "blacker than thou" rhetoric that has characterized the conflict between Afrocentric and interracialist black lesbigays needs to be cast in different terms. What should be at issue is not who is or is not "really" black, but the social, cultural, and political implications of adopting various definitions of blackness. This changes the debate in several ways: (1) Emphasis is placed on exploring which qualities are desirable or undesirable in various definitions of blackness rather than on racial essence; (2) It acknowledges there are a multiplicity of potentially valuable black lesbigay identities, rather than just one "right" one; (3) It recognizes that there are advantages and disadvantages to all potential definitions of blackness.

This does not, however, resolve the issue of who decides the content of and benefits the most from the political agenda for African American lesbigay America. L. Lloyd Jordan correctly notes that a central part of the debate about primary community choice is "who gets to call the shots, lobby the politicians, get funding, and mug for the media in *your* name" (1990, 25). Efforts by lesbigay-identified blacks to end racist practices perpetuated by white lesbigay cultural institutions such as bars and the press may not be a major concern for black-identified lesbigays since they do not participate in these cultural spaces. Similarly, many lesbigay-identified blacks may not see linking black lesbigay issues to those of the larger African American community as being most important. We need to recognize that African American lesbigays have multiple and often conflicting values and political agendas. But with contending groups of African American lesbigays battling over limited resources, who is going to be listened to by those who control the resources?

Another danger exists: being in one community or the other. In both, African American lesbigay voices risk being usurped, co-opted and/or silenced to serve the ends of the larger communities. This is evident, for example, in the sole anthology that focuses on interracialist experiences, *Black Men/White Men*. The editor, Michael J. Smith, is a white gay man and one of the founders of the interracialist organization Black and White Men Together. Because he edited the book, black gay men were not in a position of power to control how they were represented in an anthology that was primarily supposed to be about them. If the anthology centers on "the Black and interracial gay experience in White America," (Smith, 1983) why did not blacks, at the least, share editorial control over how these experiences were to be represented? And why are a significant number of the articles about blacks written by whites? Regardless of whether his representation is "fair" or "accurate," the fact that he uses his white male privilege to speak for and about African American gays at a time when there are so few speaking for themselves is problematic.

Both black-identified lesbigays and lesbigay-identified blacks must be aware of and deal with the paternalism, racial essentialism, and other kinds of power relationships that exist—both among themselves and between them and the larger black and lesbigay communities within which they are marginalized. Only then can there be a constructive dialogue on black lesbigay identity. The goal is not to have a social world in which all black lesbigay identities are equally valid; that is neither possible nor desirable. It is not possible because we cannot ignore history and existing power relationships. Through historically determined power relationships, some discourses on and cultural meanings of black lesbigay identity are more dominant than others. That is, they are more widely available, believed by more people, and asserted with greater authority (either through persuasion or force). Such a goal is not desirable because there are some constructions of black lesbigay identity that should be discouraged, such as those rooted in internalized racism or heterosexism. The goal, then, is to have a multiplicity of nonoppressive black lesbigay identities that takes into account the diversity among us.

REFERENCES

Ajalon, J. (1995). "Kaleidoscope." In *Afrekete*, edited by Catherine McKinley and L. Joyce Delaney. New York: Anchor Books.

Beam, J. (1986). "Brother to Brother: Words From the Heart." In *In the Life*, edited by Joseph Beam. Boston: Alyson Publications.

—(1986). (Ed.). *Brother to Brother*. Boston: Alyson Publications

Combahee River Collective. (1986). "The Combahee River Collective Statement." In *Home Girls*, edited by Barbara Smith. New York: Kitchen Table Press.

D'Emilio, J. (1993). "After Stonewall." In *Making Trouble*. New York: Routledge.

Dyson, M. (1993). *Reflecting Black*. Minneapolis: University of Minnesota Press.

Feagin, J. B. & Sikes, M. P. (1994). *Living With Racism: The Black Middle-Class Experience*. Boston: Beacon Press.

Gomez, J. L. (1993). "A Cultural Legacy Denied and Discovered: Black Lesbians in Fiction by Women." In *Home Girls: A Black Feminist Anthology*, edited by Barbara Smith. New York: Kitchen Table Women of Color Press.

Hemphill, E. (1991). *Brother to Brother*. Boston: Alyson Publications.

hooks, b. (1989). "Homophobia in Black Communities." *In Talking Back: Thinking Feminist, Thinking Black*. Boston: South End Press.

Hope, M. (1995). "Dare." In *Afrekete*, edited by Catherine McKinley and L. Joyce Delaney. New York: Anchor Books.

Horowitz, P. (1988). "Beyond the Gay Nation: Where Are We Marching?" *Out/Look* 1 7-21.

Hunter, B.M. (Ed.). (1993). *Sojourner: Black Gay Voices in the Age of AIDS*. New York: Other Countries.

Johnson, C. A. Robinson, C. Taylor. (Eds.). (1988). *Other Countries: Black Gay Voices*. New York: Other Countries.

Johnson, J.M. (1982). *Influence of Assimilation on the Psychosocial Adjustment of Black Homosexual Men*. Ann Arbor: UMI.

Johnson, M.L. (1982). *Influence of Assimilation on the Psychosocial Adjustment of Black Homosexual Men*. Ann Arbor: University of Michigan.

Jordon, L. L. (1990). "Black Gay vs. Gay Black." *BLK* 2, no. 6, 25-30.

Loiacano, D. K. (1989). "Gay Identity Issues Among Black Americans: Racism, Homophobia, and the Need for Validation." *Journal of Counseling and Development* 68, 21-25.

Lorde, A. (1982). *Zami: A New Spelling of My Name*. Freedom, CA: The Crossing Press.

McKinley, C. E. & Delaney, L.J. (Eds.). (1995). *Afrekete*. New York: Doubleday.

Moraga, C. and Anzaldua, G. (Eds.). (1983). *This Bridge Called My Back.*. Watertown, MA: Persephone Press. New York: Kitchen Table Press.

Nicholson, J. (1991). "Dear Sisters." In *Piece of My Heart,* edited by Makeda Silvera. Toronto: Sister Vision Press.

Peterson, J. L. (1992). "Black Men and Their Same-Sex Desires and Behaviors." In *Gay Culture in America*, edited by Gilbert Herdt. Boston: Beacon Press.

Riggs, M. (director). *Tongues Untied*. 55 min. Frameline, Inc., 1989. Videocassette.

Robinson, C. (1988). Introduction to *Other Countries: Black Gay Voices*, edited by C. Johnson & T. Taylor. New York: Other Countries.

Shepherd, R. (1986). "On Not Being White." In *In the Life*, edited by Joseph Beam. Boston: Alyson Publications.

Shockley, A. A. (1983). "The Black Lesbian in American Literature: An Overview." In *Home Girls: A Black Feminist Anthology*, edited by Barbara Smith. New York: Kitchen Table Women of Color Press.

Silvera, M. (Ed.). (1991). *Piece of My Heart*. Toronto: Sister Vision Press.

Simmons, R. (1991). "Some Thoughts on the Challenges Facing Black Gay Intellectuals." In *Brother to Brother*, edited by Essex Hemphill. Boston: Alyson Publications.

Smith, B. (Ed.). (1983). *Home Girls*. New York: Kitchen Table Press..

Smith, M. (Ed.). (1983). *Black Men/White Men*. San Francisco: Gay Sunshine Press.

Soares, J. V. (1979). "Black and Gay." In *Gay Men: The Sociology of Male Homosexuality*, edited by Martin P. Levine. New York: Harper & Row.

Taylor, J.M. (1995). "Testimony of a Naked Woman." In *Afrekete*, edited by Catherine McKinley and L. Joyce Delaney. New York: Anchor Books.

Thomas, Don. "Liberty and Justice for All." *The Advocate*, 5 Oct. 1993, 5.

Tinney, J. S. (1986). "Why a Black Gay Church?" In *In the Life*, edited by Joseph Beam. Boston: Alyson Publications.

Can the Queen Speak? Racial Essentialism, Sexuality, and the Problem of Authority

Dwight A. McBride

The gay people we knew then did not live in separate subcultures, not in the small, segregated black community where work was difficult to find, where many of us were poor. Sheer economic necessity and fierce white racism, as well as the joy of being there with black folks known and loved, compelled many gay blacks to live close to home and family. That meant, however, that gay people created a way to live out sexual preferences within the boundaries of circumstances that were rarely ideal, no matter how affirming. In some cases this meant a closeted sexual life. In other families, an individual could be openly expressive, quite out....

Unfortunately, there are very few oral histories and autobiographies that explore the lives of black gay people in diverse black communities. This is a research project that must be carried out if we are to fully understand the complex experience of being black and gay in this white-supremacist, patriarchal, capitalist society. Often we hear more from gay people who have chosen to live in predominately white communities, whose choices may have been affected by undue harassment in black communities. We hear hardly anything from black gay people who live contentedly in black communities.

—bell hooks, *Talking Back*

I speak for the thousands, perhaps hundreds of thousands, of men who live and die in the shadows of secrets, unable to speak of the love that helps them endure and contribute to the race. Their ordinary kisses of sweet spit and loyalty are scrubbed away by the propaganda makers of the race, the "talented tenth."

The black homosexual is hard-pressed to gain audience among his heterosexual brothers; even if he is more talented, he is inhibited by his silence or admissions. This is what the race had depended on in being able to erase homosexuality from our recorded history. The "chosen" history. But the sacred constructions of silence are futile exercises in denial. We will not go away with our issues of sexuality. We are coming home.

It is not enough to tell us that one was a brilliant poet, scientist, educator, or rebel. Whom did he love? It makes a difference. I can't become a whole man simply on what is fed to me: watered-down versions of Black life in America. I need the ass-splitting truth to be told, so I will have something pure to emulate, a reason to remain loyal.
—Essex Hemphill, *Ceremonies*

The fundamental question driving this essay is: Who speaks for "the race," and on what authority? In partial answer, elsewhere I have argued that African American intellectuals participate, even if out of political necessity, in forms of racial essentialism to authorize and legitimate their positions in speaking for or representing "the race." This essay is in some ways the culmination of a three-part discussion of that argument. Of course, the arguments made here and in those earlier essays need not be limited solely to the field of African American intellectuals. Indeed, the discursive practices described in these essays are more widely disseminated. Nevertheless, because I am familiar with African American intellectualism and am actively invested in addressing that body of discourse, it makes sense that I locate my analysis of racial essentialism in the context of a broader discussion of how we have come to understand what "black" is.

My essay moves from an examination of African American intellectuals' efforts to problematize racial subjectivity through black antiracist discourse to a critique of their representation, or lack thereof, of gays and lesbian in that process. I further examine the political process that legitimates and qualifies certain racial subjects to speak for (represent) "the race," and excludes others from that possibility. I use three exemplary reading sites to formulate this analysis. First I examine bell hooks's essay, "Homophobia in Black Communities." I then move to an exchange, of sorts, between essays by the controversial black psychiatrist Frances Cress Welsing and the late black poet, essayist, and activist Essex Hemphill's "The Politics Behind Black Male Passivity, Effeminization, Bisexuality and Homosexuality" and "If Freud Had Been a Neurotic Colored Woman: Reading Dr. Frances

Cress Welsing," respectively. Finally, I consider two moments from the documentary *James Baldwin: The Price of the Ticket.*

In her now oft-cited intervention into the 2 Live Crew controversy of a few years ago, "Beyond Racism and Misogyny: Black Feminism and 2 Live Crew," Kimberlé Williams Crenshaw asserts that the danger in the misogyny of the group's lyrics cannot simply be read as an elaborate form of cultural signifying, as Henry Louis Gates, Jr. argues in his defense of 2 Live Crew. On the contrary, Crenshaw maintains that such language is not mere braggadocio. Those of us concerned about the high rates of gender violence in our communities must be troubled by the possible connections between such images and violence against women. Children and teenagers are listening to this music, and I am concerned that the range of acceptable behavior is being broadened by the constant propagation of antiwoman imagery. I am concerned too about young black women who together with men are learning that their value lies between their legs. Unlike that of men, however, women's sexual value is portrayed as a depletable commodity: By expending it, girls become whores and boys become men (Crenshaw 1993, 30).

My concerns are similar to those of Crenshaw. Having come of age in a small rural black community where any open expression of gay or lesbian sexuality was met with derision at best and violence at worst; having been socialized in a black Baptist church that preached the damnation of "homosexuals"; having been trained in an African American studies curriculum that provided no serious or sustained discussion of the specificity of African American lesbian and gay folk; and still feeling—even at this moment of writing—the overwhelming weight and frustration of having to speak in a race discourse that seems to have grown all too comfortable with the routine practice of speaking about a "black community" as a discursive unit wholly separate from black lesbians and gay men (evidenced by the way we always speak in terms of the relationship of black gays and lesbians to the black community or to how we speak of the homophobia of the black community, etc.)—all of this has led me to the conclusion that as a community of scholars who are serious about enacting political change, healing black people, and speaking truth to black people, we must begin the important process of undertaking a more inclusive vision of "black community" and of race discourse. Any treatment of African American politics and culture, any theorizing of the future of black America, any black religious practice or critique of black religion that does not take seriously the lives, contributions and presence of black gays and lesbians (just as we take seriously the lives of black women, the black poor, black men, the black middle class, etc.) or any critique that does no more than to render token lip service to black gay and lesbian experience is a critique that not only denies the complexity of who we are as a representationally "whole people," but denies the very "ass-splitting truth" that Hemphill refers to so eloquently and appropriately in *Ceremonies*.

I mean this critique quite specifically. Too often African American cultural critique posits an essential black community that serves as a point of departure for commentary. In other cases it assumes a kind of monolith when it calls upon the term *black community* at all. Insofar as the position of such a construct might be deemed essential to the critical project, it is not that gesture to which I object. Rather, what is most problematic is the narrowness of the vision for what constitutes that community. If we accept that the term *community*, regardless of the modifier that precedes it, is always a term in danger of presuming too much, we must make sure that our use of the term accounts for as much of what it presumes as possible.

At present the phrase *the black community* functions as a shifter, or floating signifier. That is, its meaning shifts in accordance with the context in which it is articulated. At the same time, the phrase is most often deployed in a manner that presumes a cultural specificity that works as much on a politics of exclusion as it does on a politics of inclusion. Many visions and versions of the black community are posited in scholarly discourse, popular cultural forms, and political discourse. Rarely do any of these visions include lesbians and gay men, except perhaps as an afterthought. I want to see a black antiracist discourse that does not need to maintain such exclusions to be effective.

Insofar as there is a need to articulate a black antiracist discourse to address and to respond to the real and present dangers and vicissitudes of racism, essential to that discourse is the use of the rhetoric of community. Perhaps in the long term it would be best to explode all of the categories relating to the notion of "black community" and all of the inclusions and exclusions that come along with it. I will be among the first to applaud the advent of such a project. However, in the political meantime, my aim is to take seriously the state of racial discourse, especially black antiracist discourse and the accompanying construct of "the black community," on the irksome terms in which I have inherited it.

As I think again on the example of the exchange between

Crenshaw and Gates over the misogyny charges against 2 Live Crew, it occurs to me that similar charges of homophobia or heterosexism could be waged against any number of rap or hip-hop artists, though this critique has been paid little attention. If similar charges could be made, could not, then, similar defenses of heterosexism be mounted as well? The argument would go something like this: What appears to be open homophobia on the part of black rap and hip-hop artists is really engaged in a complicated form of cultural signifying that needs to be read not as homophobia but in the context of a history of derisive assaults on black manhood. This being the case, what we really witness when we see and hear these artists participate in what appears to be homophobia is an act involved in the project of the reclamation of black manhood that does not mean the literal violence it performs. This is, in fact, similar to the logic uses by bell hooks in her essay "Homophobia in Black Communities," when she speaks of the contradiction of openly expressed homophobia among blacks:

> Black communities may be perceived as more homophobic than other communities because there is a tendency for individuals in black communities to verbally express in an outspoken way antigay sentiments. I talked with a straight black male in a California community who acknowledged that though he has often made jokes poking fun at gays or expressing contempt as a means of bonding in group settings, in his private life he was a central support person for a gay sister. Such contradictory behavior seems pervasive in black communities. It speaks to ambivalence about sexuality in general, about sex as a subject of conversation, and to ambivalent feelings and attitudes toward homosexuality. Various structures of emotional and economic dependence create gaps between attitudes and actions. Yet a distinction must be made between black people overtly expressing prejudice toward homosexuals and homophobic white people who never make homophobic comments but who have the power to actively exploit and oppress gay people in areas of housing, employment, etc. (hooks 1992, 122).

Hooks's rhetoric is to be commended for its critique of the claims that blacks are more homophobic than other racial or ethnic groups, and to be critiqued as an apology for black homophobia. For hooks to offer as rationale for black homophobia as in her anecdote of the "straight black male in a California community," the fact that "bonding" (since it is unspecified, we can assume both male and racial bonding here) is the reason he participates in homophobic "play" is both revealing and inexcusable. This is precisely the kind of play that, following again the logic of Crenshaw, we cannot abide given the real threats of discrimination and violence against gays and lesbians. While hooks may want to relegate systematic discrimination against gays and lesbians to the domain of hegemonic whites, antigay violence takes many forms—emotional, representational, and physical—and is not a practice exclusive to those of any particular race. Furthermore, it seems disingenuous and naïve to suggest that what we say about gays and lesbians and the cultural representations of gays and lesbians do not, at least in part, legitimate—if not engender—discrimination and violence against gays and lesbians.

The rhetorical strategy she employs here is an old one, wherein blacks are blameless because they are "powerless." The logic implied by such thinking suggests that because whites constitute a hegemonic racial block in American society that oppresses blacks and other people of color, blacks can never be held wholly accountable for their own sociopolitical transgressions. Since I am treading sensitive and volatile territory, let me take extra care to ensure that I am properly understood. I do not mean to suggest that there is not a grain of truth in the reality of the racial claims made by hooks and sustained by a history of black protest. However, it is only a grain. And the grain is, after all, but a minute particle on the vast shores of discursive truth. For me, any understanding of black oppression that makes it possible—and worse, permissible—to endorse at any level that sexism, elitism, or heterosexism is a vision of black culture that is ultimately not politically consummate with liberation. We can no more excuse black homophobia than black sexism. One is as politically and, dare I say, morally suspect as the other. This is a particularly surprising move on the part of hooks (1990) when we consider that in so many other contexts her work on gender is so unrelenting and hard-hitting. So much is this the case that it is almost unimaginable that hooks would allow for a space in which tolerance for black sexism would ever be tenable. This makes me all the more suspect of her willingness not just to tolerate but to apologize for black homophobia.

There is still one aspect of hooks's argument that I want to address: her creation of a dichotomy between black gays and lesbians who live in black communities and those who live in predominately white communities. It is raised most clearly in the epigraph with which I begin this essay. She laments that "often we hear more from black gay people who have chosen to live in predominately white communities, whose choices may have been affected by undue harassment in black communities. We hear hardly anything from black gay people who live contentedly in black communities" (hooks 1990, 122). This claim about the removal of black gays and lesbians from the "authentic" black community is bizarre for a number of reasons. Is to say that those who remain in black communities are not "unduly harassed"? Or is it that they can take it? And is undue harassment the only factor in moves by black gays and lesbians to other communities? Still, the statement is problematic beyond these more obvious curiosities in that it plays on the kind of authenticity politics under critique here.

Hooks faults many black middle-class gays and lesbians and many of her colleagues in the academy who live in "white communities" in a way that suggests they are unable to give us the "real" story of black gays and lesbians. What of those experiences of "undue harassment" that she posits as potentially responsible for their exodus from the black community? Are those narratives, taking place as they do in hooks's "authentic" black community, not an important part of the story of black gay and lesbian experience, or are those gays and lesbians unqualified because of the geographical locations from which they speak? It appears that the standard hooks ultimately establishes for "real" black gay commentary is a standard that few black intellectuals can comfortably meet—a by-product of the class structure in which we live. In most cases the more upwardly mobile one becomes, the whiter the circles in which one inevitably finds oneself circulating—one of the more unfortunate aspects of American society.

The logic used by hooks in regard to black homophobia is dangerous not only for the reasons I have articulated, but also because it exists on a continuum with thinkers such as Frances Cress Welsing. They are not, of course, the same, but each does exist in a discursive field that makes the other possible. Therefore, hooks's implied logic of apology played out to its fullest conclusion bears a great deal of resemblance to Welsing's own heterosexist text.

Welsing's (1991) sentiments exemplify and grow out of a black cultural nationalist response to gay and lesbian sexuality, which has most often read homosexuality as "counter-revolutionary." She begins first by dismissing the entirety of the psychoanalytical community, which takes its lead from Freud. Welsing dismisses Freud immediately because the psychoanalyst was unable to deliver his own people from the devastation of Nazi Germany. This "racial" ineffectualness for Welsing renders moot anything that Freud (or any of his devotees) might have to say on the subject of sexuality. The logic is this: Since the most important political element for black culture is that of survival and Freud didn't know how to do that for his people, nothing that Freud or his devotees could tell us about homosexuality should be applied to black people. The idea of holding Freud responsible for not preventing the Holocaust is not only laughable, but also denies the specific history which gave rise to that event. Furthermore, if we use this logic of victim blaming in the case of the Jews and Freud, would it not also follow that we should make the same critique of slavery? Are not black Africans and the tribal leaders of West African, then, responsible for not preventing the enslavement of blacks? This sort of specious logic makes an articulate Welsing difficult and frustrating when one tries to take her seriously.

But take her seriously we must. Welsing continues to speak and to command a following among black cultural nationalists. We have to be concerned, then, about the degree to which Welsing's heterosexist authentication of blackness contributes to the marginalization of black gays and lesbians. For Welsing, black Africa is the site of an "originary" or "authentic" blackness. At the beginning of her essay, Welsing says:

> Black male passivity, effeminization, bisexuality and homo-sexuality are being encountered increasingly by Black psychiatrists working with Black patient populations. These issues are being presented by family members, personnel working in schools, and other social institutions, or by Black men themselves. Many in the Black population are reaching the conclusion that such issues have become a problem of epidemic proportion amongst Black people in the U.S., although it was an almost nonexistent behavioral phenomenon amongst indigenous Blacks in Africa (Welsing 1991, 81).

From the beginning, Welsing describes homosexuality in a language associated with disease. It is a "problem of epidemic proportion" that seems to be spreading among black people. This rehearses a rhetorical gesture I mentioned earlier by speaking of the black community as an entity wholly separate from homosexuals, who infect its sacrosanct authenticity. Of course, it goes without saying that Welsing's claim that homosexuality "was an almost nonexistent behavioral phenomenon amongst indigenous Blacks in Africa" is not only supported by anthropological study (Caplan, 1987) but also suggests the biological or genetic link, to use her language, that nonindigenous blacks have to indigenous black Africans. Welsing more than adopts an Afrocentric worldview in this essay by positing Africa as the seer of all real, unsullied, originary blackness. In this way she casts her lot with much of black cultural nationalist discourse, which is heavily invested in Afrocentrism. For further evidence of this, we need look no further than Welsing's own definition of "Black mental health":

> The practice of those unit patterns of behavior (i.e., logic, thought, speech, action and emotional response) in all areas of people activity: economics, education, entertainment, labor, law, politics, religion, sex and war—which are simultaneously self- and group-supporting under the social and political conditions of worldwide white supremacy domination (racism). In brief, this means Black behavioral practice which resists self- and group-negation and destruction (Caplan 1987, 82).

Here, as elsewhere, Welsing prides herself on being outside of the conceptual mainstream of any currently held psychiatric definitions of mental illness. She labels those the " 'European' psychoanalytic theories of Sigmund Freud" (Caplan 1987, 82). Welsing seems to want to be recognized for taking a bold position solidly outside any "mainstream" logic. This is because all such logic is necessarily bad because it is mainstream, which is to say, white. One then gets the sense that homosexuality too is a by-product of white supremacy. And further, that if there were no white supremacy, homosexuality would not, at best, exist, or at worst, be somehow OK if it did. The overriding logic of her arguments is the connection between white supremacy and homosexuality. The former is produced by the latter as a way to control black people. Hence, it follows that the only way to be really black is to resist homosexuality.

From this point on, Welsing's essay spirals into a deepening chasm from which it never manages to return. For example, she argues that it is "male muscle mass" that oppresses a people. Since white men understand this fact and the related fact of their genetic weakness in relation to the majority of the world, who happen to be women of color, they are invested in the effeminization and homosexualization of black men (83-84). She also states that the white women's liberation movement—white women's response to white males' need to be superior at least over them—has further served to weaken the white males' sense of power, "helping to push him to a *weakened* and *homosexual* stance" (my emphasis; the two are synonymous for Welsing). Feminism, then, according to Welsing, leads to further "white male/female alienation, pushing white males further into the homosexual position and...white females in that direction also" (85-86). Finally, she suggests that black manhood is the primary target of racism, since black men, of course, are the genetically superior beings who cannot only reproduce with black women but also with white women. And since the offspring of such unions, according to Welsing's logic, are always black (the exact opposite of the result of such sexual pairings for white men and black women), black manhood is the primary target of a white supremacist system. Welsing's words are significant enough here that I quote her at some length:

Racism (white supremacy) is the dominant social system in today's world. Its fundamental dynamic is predicated upon the genetic recessive deficiency state of albinism, which is responsible for skin whiteness and this the so-called "white race." This genetic recessive trait is dominated by the genetic capacity to produce any of the various degrees of skin melanation—whether black, brown, red, or yellow. In other words, it can be annihilated as a phenotypic condition. Control of this potential for genetic domination and annihilation throughout the world is absolutely essential if the condition of skin whiteness is to survive. "White" survival is predicated upon aggressiveness and muscle mass in the form of technology directed against the "nonwhite" melanated men on the planet Earth who constitute the numerical majority. Therefore, white survival and white power are dependent upon the various methodologies, tactics and strategies developed to control all "nonwhite" men, as well as bring them into cooperative submission. This is especially important in the case of Black men because they have the greatest capacity to produce melanin and, in turn, the greatest genetic potential for the annihilation of skin albinism or skin whiteness (Welsing 1991, 83).

This passage demonstrates the critical hazards of privileging the category of race in any discussion of black people. When we give "race," with its retinue of historical and discursive investments, primacy over other signifiers of difference, the result is a network of critical blindness that prevents us from perceiving the ways in which the conventions of race discourse become naturalized and normativized. These conventions often include, especially in cases involving, though not exclusive to, black cultural nationalism, the denigration of homosexuality and the accompanying peripheralization of women. Underlying much of race discourse, then, is always the implication that all "real" black subjects are male and heterosexual. Therefore, in partial response to the query with which I began this essay, only these such subjects are best qualified to speak for or to represent the race.

Unfortunately, Welsing does not stop here. She continues her discussion of black manhood to a point where what she means by the appellation for-and-above exceeds her mere genetic definition. Though she never clearly defines what she intends by black manhood, we can construct a pretty clear idea from the ways in which she uses the term in her argument. Welsing proclaims:

The dearth of black males in the homes, schools and neighborhoods leaves Black male children no alternative models. Blindly they seek out one another as models, and in their blindness end up in trouble—in juvenile homes or prisons. But fate and the dynamics of racism again play a vicious trick because the young males only become more alienated from their manhood and more feminized in such settings (1991, 89).

In this statement black manhood is set in opposition to femininity and is retarded by the influence of women, especially in female-headed households. She describes the effect of effeminizing influences on black men as the achievement of racist programming. This achievement is, in part, possible because of the clothing industry as well, according to Welsing: "The white-run clothing industry is all too pleased to provide the costumes of feminine disguise for Black male escape. However, they never would provide uniforms or combat gear if customers were willing to pay $1000 per outfit" (1991, 89). Welsing also faults television as "an important programmer of behavior in this social system" that "plays a further major role in alienating Black males (especially children) from Black manhood" (1991, 89). The examples she cites are Flip Wilson's persona Geraldine and Jimmy Walker's character J.J. on the 1970s television series *Good Times*. "These weekly insults," she maintains, "to Black manhood that we have been programmed to believe are entertainment and not direct racist warfare, further reinforce, perhaps in the unconscious thinking of Black people, a loss of respect for Black manhood while carrying that loss to even deeper levels" (1991, 90). Most telling, perhaps, is that the clinical method she endorses for "disorders" of "passivity, effeminization, bisexuality, homosexuality" is to have the patients "relax and envision themselves approaching and opposing, in actual combat, the collective of white males and females (without apology or giving up in the crunch)" (1991, 91-92). Again, there is an essence to what black manhood is that never receives full articulation except implicitly. But what is implied could be described as monstrous, combative, even primitive. There is certainly no room for a nurturing view of manhood here. To be a man is to be strong. And strength, in Welsing's logic, is the opposite of weakness, which can only signify at best effeminacy or passivity and at worst bisexuality or homosexuality. Still another of the vexatious implications of this logic is that in a world devoid of racism or white supremacy, there would be no black male homosexuality. In this way, Welsing reduces black male homosexuality to a by-product of racist programming. Once again, this is the function of an argument that privileges race discourse over other forms of difference in its analysis of black oppression.

Let me turn my attention now to Essex Hemphill's response to Welsing's troublesome essay. Hemphill's rhetoric demonstrates how even in an astute and well-wrought "reading" of Welsing—and it is fair to say Hemphill "reads" her in both the critical and the more campy sense of the word—the move is never made to critique the structure (and by *structure* I mean the implied rules governing the use of) and function of race discourse itself. As argued earlier this is precisely what is missing from hooks's logic, which under-girds her discussion of homophobia in black communities as well. Hemphill's response to Welsing is thoughtful, engaging, and identifies the faulty premises upon which Welsing bases her arguments. Still, Hemphill's own essay and rhetoric falls prey to the conventions of race discourse in two ways.

First, to combat Welsing's homophobia and heterosexism, Hemphill feels the pressure to legitimize and authorize himself as a speaker on race matters by telling his own authenticating anecdote of black/gay experience at the beginning of his essay:

> [In] 1974, the year that Dr. Frances Cress Welsing wrote "The Politics Behind Black Male Passivity, Effeminization, Bisexuality, and Homosexuality," I entered my final year of senior high school. By that time, I had arrived at a very clear understanding of how dangerous it was to be a homosexual in my Black neighborhood and in society...Facing this then-limited perception of homosexual life, I could only wonder, where did I fit in?...
>
> Conversely, I was perfecting my heterosexual disguise; I was practicing the necessary use of masks for survival; I was calculating the distance between the first day of class and graduation, the distance between graduation from high school and departure for college—and ultimately, the arrival of my freedom from home, community, and my immediate peers....
>
> During the course of the next 16 years I would articulate and politicize my sexuality. I would discover that homo sex did not constitute a whole life nor did it negate my racial identity or constitute a substantive reason to be estranged from my family and Black culture. I discovered too that the work ahead for me included, most importantly, being able to integrate all of my identities into a functioning self instead of accepting a dysfunctional existence as a consequence of my homosexual desires (Hemphill 1992, 52-53).

While Hemphill's personal anecdote demonstrates his access to the various categories of identity he claims, it does not critique of the idea of the categories themselves. In fact, he plays the "race/sexuality" card much in the way Welsing plays the "race" card.

Secondly, while Hemphill's critique of Welsing is thorough and extremely insightful, it does not move to critique the methodological fault Welsing makes in her analysis—that is, the fact that much of what is wrong with Welsing's argument results from the privileging of "race" over other critical categories of difference. Instead, Hemphill treats Welsing's heterosexism as the critical disease instead of as symptomatic of a far more systematic critical illness.

A noteworthy thing about Hemphill's anecdotal testimony is that while it insists, and rightly so, upon the integration of what Welsing has established as the dichotomous identities of race and homosexuality, it also participates in a familiar structural convention of race discourse in its necessity to claim racial identification as a position from which even the black homosexual speaks. In other words, part of the rhetorical strategy Hemphill enacts is to claim the category of racial authenticity for himself as part of what legitimizes and authorizes the articulation of his corrective to Welsing's homophobic race logic. The net result is the substitution of heterosexist race logic with a homo-positive or homo-inclusive race logic. Still, the common denominator of both positions is the persistence of race as the privileged category in discussions of black identity.

The first clue to Hemphill's failure to identify the larger systematic problem of Welsing's argument occurs when he compares Welsing to Shahrazad Ali:

> Dr. Welsing is not as easily dismissable as Ali, author of the notorious book of internal strife. By dismissing the lives of Black lesbians and gay men, Ali is clearly not advocating the necessary healing Black communities require; she is advocating further factionalization. Her virulently homophobic ideas lack credibility and are easily dismissed as incendiary (Hemphill, 1992).

Welsing is much more dangerous because she attempts to justify *her* homophobia and heterosexism precisely by grounding it in an acute understanding of African American history and an analysis of the psychological effects of centuries of racist oppression and violence (54).

While Hemphill's reading of Welsing is astute, it does not go far enough: Ali is not more easily dismissable than Welsing. In fact, Ali's ideas are rooted in a history of sorts as well, a history shared by Welsing's arguments—that is, the history of race discourse itself which, in its privileging of the dominant category of analysis, has always sustained the derision or exclusion of black gays and lesbians. Another such moment in Hemphill's essay comes when he identifies what he understands as the central problem of Welsing's text:

> Welsing refutes any logical understanding of sexuality. By espousing Black homophobia and heterosexism—imitations

of the very oppressive forces of hegemonic white male hetero-sexuality she attempts to challenge—she places herself in direct collusion with the forces that continually move against Blacks, gays, lesbians, and all people of color. Thus, every time a gay man or lesbian is violently attacked, blood *is* figuratively on Dr. Welsing's hands as surely as blood is on the hands of the attackers. Her ideas reinforce the belief that gay and lesbian lives are expendable, and her views also provide a clue as to why the Black community has failed to intelligently and coherently address critical, life-threatening issues such as AIDS (Hemphill 1992, 55).

Welsing's logic does imitate that of the oppressive forces of white male heterosexuality that she tries to refute. The difference is that Welsing does not view the latter category as crucial to her analysis. But the problem with Welsing's argument does not end where Hemphill suggests it does. Much of race discourse, even the discourse of racial liberation, participates in a similar relationship with hegemonic antigay forces. This is especially the case, and some might even argue that it is inevitable, when we consider the history and development of black liberations or antiracist discourse with its insistence on the centrality of black masculinity (in the narrowest sense of the term) as the essential element of any form of black liberation. If racial liberationist discourse suggests at best the invisibility of homosexuality and at worst understands homosexuality as racially antagonistic, Dr. Welsing radically manifests one of the more unseemly truths of race discourse for blacks: the demonization of homosexuality.

The critical blindness demonstrated by Hemphill does not alone express the extent of what happens when a gay black man takes up the mantle of race discourse. Another example worth exploring is that of James Baldwin. I would like to call attention to two moments in the 1989 documentary *James Baldwin: The Price of the Ticket*. The first is a statement made by Amiri Baraka; the second a statement made by Baldwin himself in interview footage from *The Dick Cavett Show*. I turn to these less literally textual examples to demonstrate that in our more casual or less scripted moments, our subconscious understanding of the realities of race discourse often is laid bare more clearly.

The film documents well Baraka's regard for Baldwin. Baraka discusses how Baldwin was "in the tradition" and how his early writings, specifically *Notes of a Native Son*, affected him profoundly and spoke to an entire generation. In an attempt to describe or to account for Baldwin's homosexuality, however, Baraka falters in his efforts to unite the racially significant image of Baldwin that he clings to with the homosexual Baldwin with whom he seems less comfortable. Baraka says, "Jimmy Baldwin was neither in the closet about his homosexuality, nor was he running around proclaiming homosexuality. I mean, he was what he was. And you either had to buy that or, you know, *mea culpa*, go somewhere else."

The poles of the rhetorical continuum that Baraka sets up here for his understanding of homosexuality are telling, and recall the earlier dichotomy set up by bell hooks between homosexuals who live somewhat closeted existences in black communities and those who do not. To Baraka, one can either be in the closet or "running around proclaiming homosexuality" (the images of the effete gay man or the gay activist collide here). What makes Baldwin acceptable to enter the pantheon of race men for Baraka is that his sexual identity is unlocatable. It is neither here nor there, or perhaps it is everywhere at once, leaving the entire question undecided and undecidable. And if Baldwin is undecided about his sexual identity, the one identity to which he is firmly committed is his racial identity. The rhetorical ambiguity surrounding his sexual identity, according to Baraka, makes it possible for Baldwin to be a race man who was "in the tradition."

Baldwin himself was aware of the dangers of the "price of the ticket" for trying to synthesize his racial and sexual identities. He understood that his efficacy as a race man was, at least in part, owing to limiting his activism to his racial politics. The frame of the documentary certainly confirms this in how it represents Baldwin's own response to his sexuality. In one interview, he says:

> I think the trick is to say yes to life.... It is only we of the 20th century who are so obsessed with the particular details of anybody's sex life. I don't think those details make a difference. And I will never be able to deny a certain power that I have had to deal with, which has dealt with me, which is called love; and love comes in very strange packages. I've loved a few men; I've loved a few women; and a few people have loved me. That's...I suppose that's all that's saved my life.

Interesting to note is that while Baldwin makes this statement, the camera pans down to his hands, which are fidgeting with a cigarette and cigarette holder. This camera move undercuts the veracity of Baldwin's statement. It suggests what I think of as a fair conclusion about his statement. That is, Baldwin himself does not quite believe all of what he is saying. From the 1949 essay "The Preservation of Innocence," which he wrote and published in *Zero*, a small Moroccan journal, Baldwin knows just how important sexuality is to discussions of race. But Baldwin's apparent desire to render it as secondary to recognize. When we understand this statement as spoken in a prophetic mode, it imagines a world in which the details of a person's sex life can matter as part of a person's humanity, but does not need to usurp their authority or legitimacy to represent the race. If Baldwin's statement raises the complications of speaking from a complex racial/sexual identity location, the following excerpt from his interview on *The Dick Cavett Show* illustrates this point all the more clearly:

> I don't know what most white people in this country feel, but I can only conclude what they feel from the state of their institutions. I don't know if white Christians hate Negroes or not, but I know that we have a Christian church which is white and a Christian church which is black. I know, as Malcolm X once put it, "The most segregated hour in America is high noon on Sunday." That says a great deal to me about a Christian nation. It means that I can't afford to trust most white Christians and certainly cannot trust the Christian church. I don't know whether the labor unions and their bosses really hate me. I don't know if the real estate lobby has anything against black people, but I know the real estate lobby keeps me in the ghetto. I don't know if the board of education hates black people, but I do know the textbooks they give my children to read and the schools that we go to. Now this is the evidence! *You want me to make an act of faith risking myself, my wife, my woman, my sister, my children on some idealism which you assure me exists in America which I have never seen.* [emphasis added]

Interesting for both the rich sermonic quality and the vehement tone for which Baldwin was famous, this passage is also conspicuous for the manner in which Baldwin assumes the voice of representative race man. In the last sentence, when Baldwin affects the position of race man, part of the performance includes the masking of his specificity, his sexuality, his difference. And in race discourse, when all difference is concealed, what emerges is the heterosexual black man "risking [himself], [his] wife, [his] woman and [his] children." The image of the black man as protector, progenitor, and defender of the race—which sounds suspiciously similar to the image fostered by Welsing and much of black cultural nationalism—is what Baldwin assumes here. The truth of this rhetorical transformation—the difficult, worrisome truth—is that to be a representative race man, one must be heterosexual. And what of women? They would appear, in the confines of race discourse, to be ever the passive players. They are rhetorically useful in that they lend legitimacy to the black male's responsibility for their care and protection, but they cannot speak any more than the gay or lesbian brother or sister. If these are part of the structural demands of race discourse, the erasure of subtlety and black difference, it is time to own up to that truth. As black intellectuals and cultural workers, we have to demand, insist upon, and be about the business of helping to create new and more inclusive ways of speaking about race that do not cause even good, thorough thinkers such as hooks, Hemphill, and Baldwin (and many others), to compromise their/our own critical veracity by participating in hegemonic race discourse. Race is, indeed, a fiction, an allegory, if you will, with an elaborate linguistic court. Knowing that, more needs to be done to reimagine race; to create new and inclusive mythologies to replace the old, weather-worn, heterosexual masculinity-centered ones; to reconstitute "the black community" as one that includes our various differences as opposed to the monolith to which we inevitably seem to return.

For far too long the field of African American/Afro-American/Black Studies has thought about race as the primary category of analysis for the work that proceeds from the field. The problem with such work has always been, and continues to be, that African Americans and the African American experience are far more complicated than this. And it is time to begin to understand what that means in the form of an everyday critical and political practice. Race is not simple. It has never been simple. It does not have the history that would make it so, no matter how much we may yearn for that degree of clarity. This is a point I have argued in a variety of venues. The point being, if I am thinking about race, I should already be thinking about gender, class, and sexuality. This statement assumes the very impossibility of a hierarchy or chronology of categories of identity. The point is not just one of intersection—as we have thought of it for so long—it is one of reconstitution. That is, race is already more than just race. Or put another way, race is always already everything it ever was, though some of its constitutive aspects may have been repressed for various nefarious purposes and/or for other strategic ones. Either way, it is never simple, never to be taken for granted. What I say is not revolutionary or revelatory. The theory, in this way, has gotten ahead of the critical practice. Almost all good race theorists these days recognize the merit of this approach; the point is that the work we produce has not fully caught up. That explains why it is still possible to query: What does a race theory of which all of these identity categories are constitutive look like? And more importantly, how do the critiques, the work informed by such theory, look different from what now dominates the field? I have great hope for the future works of scholars such as Lindon Barrett, who are beginning to theorize racial blackness in relationship to the category of value with all the trappings of desire, commodification, and exchange inherent in that operation. This may be just the kind of critical innovation needed to help us to reconstitute our ideas about "race" and race discourse.

Of course, I am not suggesting that there are not good heterosexual "race men" and "race women" on the scene who offer progressive views about sexuality and are "down" with their gay and lesbian brothers and sisters. In fact, quite the contrary. In many instances, it adds an extra dimension of cachet and progressivism to hear such heterosexual speakers being sympathetic to gays and lesbians. As long as they are not themselves gay or lesbian, it would appear on the open market to enhance their "coolness" quotient. The issue that needs more attention exists at the level on which we authenticate our authority and legitimacy to speak for the race as representational subjects. In other words, there are a number of narratives that African American intellectuals employ to qualify themselves in the terms of race discourse to speak for the race. And while one routinely witnesses the use of narratives of racial discrimination, narratives of growing up poor and black and elevating oneself through education and hard work, narratives about how connected middle-class black intellectuals are to "the black community" or "the hood," we could scarcely imagine an instance in which narrating or even claiming one's gay or lesbian identity would authenticate or legitimate oneself as a racial representative. And as we see in the case of James Baldwin, when black gays and lesbians do don the racial representational mask, they often do so at the expense of effacing (even if only temporarily) their sexual identities.

Given the current state of black antiracist discourse, it is no wonder that even now that there is only one book-length critical literary investigation of the work of James Baldwin; it is no wonder that Langston Hughes's biographer even in 1986 felt the need to defend him against the "speculation" surrounding his homosexuality; it is no wonder that even to this day we can still say with Cheryl Clark and bell hooks that there exists no sustained sociological study of black lesbians and gays; and it is no wonder that among the vanguard of so-called black public intellectuals there is the notable near absence of openly gay and lesbian voices. Lamentable though this state of affairs may be, we cannot deny that part of the responsibility, for it has much to do with the limits of black antiracist discourse—that is, what is still considered appropriate to say about race and the policing of who speaks for the race.

Let me thank Bob E. Myers (UCLA), Darieck Bruce Scott (Stanford) and Prof. Toni Morrison (Princeton) for listening to and responding to these ideas in their even more unfinished conversational form. I also wish to thank Professors Arthur Little (UCLA), Prof. Jonathan Holloway (UCSD), and Prof. Chris Cunningham (UCLA) for reading and responding to an earlier draft of this essay. And finally let me acknowledge the careful and instructive readings of Kara Keeling (U Pittsburgh) and of Professors Eric Clarke (U Pittsburgh) and Lindon Barrett (UCI).

REFERENCES

Ali, S. (1989). *The Blackman's Guide to Understanding the Blackwoman*. Philadelphia: Civilized Publications.

Caplan, P. (Ed.). (1987). *The Cultural Construction of Sexuality*. London and New York: Tavistock.

Crenshaw, K. (1993). "Beyond Race and Misogyny: Black Feminism and 2 Live Crew." In *Words That Wound*, edited by Mari J. Matsuda, et. al. Boulder: Westview Press.

"Cornel West and the Rhetoric of Race Transcending." *Harvard Black Letter Law Journal* (Spring 1994): 155-68.

Eldridge. C. (1998). *Soul On Ice*. New York: McGraw-Hill.

Hemphill, E. (1992). *Ceremonies: Prose and Poetry*. New York: Plume.

hooks, b. (1992). *Black Looks: Race and Representation*. Boston: South End Press.

— (1990). *Essays in Yearning: Race, Gender, and Cultural Politics*.Boston: South End Press.

— (1989). *Talking Back: Thinking Feminist, Thinking Black*. Boston: South End Press.

Welsing, F.C. (1991). *The Isis (Yssis) Papers: The Keys to the Colors*. Chicago: Third World Press.

Safety Among Strangers: The Million Man March

Townsand Price-Spratlen

Abstract

This article considers three queer dimensions of the Million Man March (MMM): 1) homoerotic desire in the moment of the march; 2) acts of remembrance; and 3) the praxis of atonement in our daily lives thereafter. Each dimension contributes to a greater understanding of the interaction between desire, mourning, and collective identity, and influence of this interaction on the formation and sustenance of a proactive pedagogy of cultural place. Because the "erotic functions...in several ways, [including] providing the power which comes from sharing deeply any pursuit with another person" (Lorde 1984, 56), the erotic has both sexual and nonsexual expressions. Both were a part of the MMM.

Praxis is here defined as the active cultural process of negotiating legacies and seeking our viable action steps through which those legacies are celebrated by enacting social change (Price-Spratlen, 1996; from Freire 1985, 1970). The pedagogy of place (Haymes, 1995) is the manner in which the uses of the erotic and the praxis of atonement converge. I build from Minister Louis Farrakhan's chosen theme of atonement during his MMM keynote speech to clarify aspects of the spiritual, so central to the event itself. The praxis of atonement can build on the recognition that individual empowerment and collective liberation are possible end points to the pedagogy of place, and on the pursuit of realizing a vision of sustainable safe space(s) one day at a time.

"Black men loving Black men is a call to action, an acknowledgement of responsibility. We take care of our own kind when the night grows cold and silent. These days the nights are cold-blooded and the silence echoes with complicity." —Joseph Beam, 1986

First Steps

How should one give meaning to the phrase *our own kind* in this quote? How might we better understand the breadth of Black men loving Black men? What tasks does the acknowledgment of responsibility make necessary? These were among the thoughts that occurred to me as I stepped off the Washington, D.C., metro train and walked up the staircase to the street. I was struck by how isolated I suddenly felt in the midst of this "day of absence," this celebration of collective Black make identity, labeled the Million Man March (MMM). I had come to the MMM to ensure that my voice was one of the many that would be heard cheering and shouting in the news reports that would surely misrepresent this historic day. One aspect I thought unlikely to be mis-represented was a compulsory heterosexism that would surely be a part of the gathering. To qualm any concerns of sexual identity among the many brothers who had responded to the call to bring together a million men of African descent, the need to be clearly heterosexist would be magnified, I expected. Much of the MMM's pre-event rhet-oric was presented in gendered terms celebrating a stereotypically masculine identity while simultaneously leaving out any questions of the meanings and consequences of such terms.

One reason I felt isolated on the steps of the metro that I chose to wear a promotional T-shirt for a performance piece by the gay African American theater group PomoAfroHomos. The T-shirt says FIERCE LOVE in broad, capital letters, along with the phrase STORIES FROM BLACK GAY LIFE. Just above these words is a picture of the three group members, heads adorned with polka-dot–covered pillbox hats; quirky, endearing smiles are on their faces. *Fierce Love* was almost totally ignored by the African American press and was blocked from many African American venues (Murray, 1996). I wore the T-shirt as an individual mini-protest to challenge the MMM's likely heterosex-ism. I did so knowing that such an individual act of rebellion is always risky, especially when it can easily be perceived as "indicting" not only the wearer of the T-shirt as gay or gay-friendly but many other persons as well.

Quite often people are not interested in engaging in a dialogue that may critique their assumptions and clarify what the act wearing such a T-shirt may or may not represent to each of us, and how those mean-ings might seem to be in contention. Gay bashing is about group behav-ior in a moment and the need to brutally affirm the validity of the het-erosexist norm; my perceived susceptibility to being victimized sudden-ly became quite real as many of the other men around me looked quizzically at my shirt. I was challenged by being stigmatized within an in-group, Black men, to which I unquestionably belonged. I was, if only minimally, testing the boundaries within which the intended unity of the day would be understood. Wearing the T-shirt during the MMM was a critical aspect of a "subjective transformation of my consciousness" as a proud gay man of African descent, not unlike historical, racialized expressions that increased confidence in the possibility of successful resistance to previously accepted stigmatization of African Americans (McAdam, 1982).

Clearly, many of the million-plus men who participated in the MMM were (and are) gay, and many others who might reject such a term as representing them are men who have (or have had) sex with men. Despite this (probably) silent representation among the march participants, there was a profound sin of omission that this paper attempts to rectify: the absence of an acknowledged presence of visibly gay-identified men and the importance of discussing the truths of the erotic related to the MMM. In short, many aspects of the march were indeed quite queer. One may begin to examine the queerness of these aspects by considering the MMM as an intense expression of homoerotic desire in light of the roles that places play in the process of affirming identity.

This essay is about the meaning that special events in special places provide, and the places in which meaning is defined and refined in the ongoing process of collective and individual identity. A person's answer to the question "Who am I?" rests in part in where they have been and the significance they have attached to those places. The question's answer is about meaning, location, and participation; it lies in a few select aspects of the MMM. Given that "cultural action for freedom is characterized by dialogue, and its pre-eminent purpose is to conscientize the people, (and) cultural action for domination is opposed to dialogue and serves to domesticate the people" (Freire 1985, 85), the MMM was a cultural act intended to challenge domination; as a result, our understanding of it should be marked by an ongoing dialogue—a dialogue to which this paper attempts to contribute. For "even as we identify strategic conflicts and problems, we also have to identify the location of our joys" (hooks 1991, 58). For many reasons considered below, the MMM was one such location.

CONSIDERING THE QUEER

At various times in the recent past, Washington, D.C., has earned the dubious label of being the murder capital of the country, if not the world. A large proportion of the city's murders involved men of

African descent as both perpetrator and victim. In stark contrast to this potentially unsafe context, more than a million African American men (and women) came to the nation's capital, and, if only for a weekend, created—and sustained—a safe space, an environment of caring in which an understanding of the potential for creating a diverse yet common destiny was realized. The MMM was an event in which men of African descent gathered together and "began to truly listen to and touch each other's hearts" (Madhubuti 1996, 3). The march was at once a concentration of male love, a density of male intimacy, and a focused intense expression of male desire. The male love or "other brother" sensibility in which the MMM was grounded (and which was practiced throughout the day) expressed inclusive, intersectional, and multiple possibilities.

While "it was clear that each man came for *different* and for the *same* reasons" (Madhubuti 1996, 3), the MMM was grounded in the theme of atonement, seeking "satisfaction or reparation for a wrong or injury. It means to make amends," (Farrakhan 1996, 15). Individuals had come to Washington, D.C., to participate in an affirming environment, to help broaden the salience of the sociopolitical and cultural statement such an event would invariably make, and to collectively acknowledge that as diverse Black men, we must stand together, learn from, love, and protect each other "in contributing to a better tomorrow for all" (Madhubuti 1996, 4).

The queerness of the March is rooted in the concept that "locations in gender, class, race, ethnicity, and sexuality complicate one another and not merely additively" (Smith and Watson 1992, xiv). The instigators of the march, Minister Farrakhan and the Nation of Islam, reached out to the broad heterogeneous Black community, successfully using a strategy of inclusion. And, much to Farrakhan's credit, the strategy of inclusion resulted in a great deal of diversity, including many gay participants. But beyond the mere presence of gay-identified men, the march was rooted in at least three queer dimensions: 1) the presence of homoerotic desire in the moment of the march; 2) the meaning given to acts of remembrance throughout the day; and 3) the praxis of atonement thereafter in the daily lives of march participants.

HOMOEROTIC DESIRE IN THE MOMENT OF THE MARCH

Audre Lorde (1984, 56) stated that "the erotic functions for me in several ways, and the first is in providing the power which comes from sharing deeply any pursuit with another person." During the day of the MMM, multiple expressions of homoerotic desire appeared in the moment of the event. Consistent with Lorde, if we are to understand the erotic as having *both* sexual and nonsexual expressions, the entire day was grounded in a homoeroticism, (i.e., same-sex, passion-centered longing for change.) Regardless of the sexual identity of the participants, we were all a part of a concentration of male love and an intense expression of male-centered desire. Those million-plus men shared in a social movement community, having created "a network of individuals and groups loosely linked through an institutional base, multiple goals, and actions, and a collective identity that affirms members' common interests in opposition to dominant groups" (Taylor and Whittier 1992, 107).

The sexual dimension of the erotic, narrowly defined, was expressed by the overflowing crowds at clubs catering to a predominantly gay African American clientele during the weekend preceding the march and in the multiple levels of "cruising" that took place during and after the march itself. The *nonsexual* erotic was expressed in many ways as well, given at least four ways in which the erotic informs human choice: by 1) providing the power that comes from sharing deeply any pursuit with another person; 2) affirming an open and fearless underlining of one's capacity for joy; 3) providing energy to pursue genuine change within our world; and 4) affirming the bridge between the spiritual and the political (Lorde, 1984). As previously stated, the MMM was, at base, a concentration of male love, a density of male intimacy, and a focused intense expression of male desire. By forging an intersection among these things, each of the components of the erotic was simultaneously celebrated.

An implicit aspect of erotic affirmation presented in the MMM is the process of reifying collective identity. Taylor and Whittier (1992) have identified three components of this process, whereby individuals 1) see themselves as part of a group when some shared characteristic becomes salient and is defined as important; 2) achieve a (sustainable) consciousness (i.e., the goals, means, and environment of action); and 3) participate in direct opposition to the dominant order. In short, the process of affirming collective identity works hand in hand with the uses of the erotic. Since the day was rooted in a homoerotic desire for change, there was an explicit (and implicit) queerness in the march itself. In the midst of the MMM, I felt I needed to assert my difference as a gay man to challenge the conception of "the dominant order" held by other march participants. The basic definition of the dominant order during the day was "white folks." We are "other" relatives to whites, and it is therefore essential for us to understand them as the opposition. However, missing from that racialized definition is a recognition of other components of the dominant order, including heterosexism. In celebrating *Fierce Love*, I attempted to make visible an otherwise invisible aspect of my identity, and provided a visual reminder to myself and others that the dominant order must be understood outside of just racial terms.

Another aspect of the homoerotic moment of the march rests in the brilliant poetry of the late Essex Hemphill. Hemphill, a gay man of African descent and a D.C. native, helped to forge a new understanding of the multiple meanings a given location can provide and the negotiations that are a part of attaching significance to place (Gilroy, 1991; Haymes, 1995). Three stanzas of the poem "Tomb of Sorrow" illustrate aspects of this process:

> Gunshots ring out above our heads
> as we sit beneath your favorite tree,
> in this part called Meridian Hill,
> called Malcolm S, that you call
> the "Tomb of Sorrow"
>
> (and claim to be its gatekeeper);
> in the cool air lingering after the rain,
> the men return to the Wailing Wall
> to throw laughter and sad glances
> into the fountains below...
>
> Slouching through Homo Heights,
> I came to the Tomb of Sorrow
> seeking penetration and Black seed
> My self-inflicted injuries occurred
> when I began loving you
> and trusting you.

These stanzas exemplify the process of "place-making," or the means by which African American "urban communities resist white supremacists' urban meanings and urban forms by constructing alternative images and representations of place" (Haymes 1995, 9).

Hemphill considers an African American neighborhood's choice to refer to a D.C. park officially named Meridian Hill as "Malcolm X Park." This symbolic renaming is one aspect of place-making in that it renders the park more relevant, both to community residents and visitors, given the immediate, named link to an African American sociopolitical and spiritual icon. It provides a direct link between place and resistance, given that even "though Malcolm was more famous for his scathing critique of whites, his call for unity among blacks was actually the dominant theme of his ministry" (Cone 1991, 105). Within the imagery of the poem, Hemphill extends the place-making beyond its racialized parameters by linking it to homoerotic sexual desire. He does so by emphasizing the multiple dangers to which that place is subject: potential urban violence, the risks of public sexual pursuit, and the pain from realized or unrealized desire.

While the MMM did not take place adjacent to Malcolm X Park geographically, it did so spiritually. My association of D.C.'s intersection as place, symbolic resistance, risk, and homoerotic desire was linked with the imagery of Hemphill's poem. These connections were further reinforced when Dr. Betty Shabazz spoke and I was reminded of her husband, the late freedom fighter Malcolm X. Since "places are significant because we assign meaning to them in relation to our specific projects" (Haymes 1995, 10), by invoking Malcolm's name, Dr. Shabazz again brought to life the park and its sexual significance, even if only implicitly, and only to add to the homoerotic subtext of the day. The reinforcement of homoerotic desire in the moment of the march and the raising of multiple meanings through the name "Malcolm X" extend in part from the multiple projects with which his name has become linked, including a D.C. park bearing his name.

Viewing homoerotic desire as a part of the core of the MMM is not intended to legitimize the sexual myths of this culture surrounding men of African descent. The African American male has historically been perceived as the bearer of a bestial sexuality, as the savage "walking phallus" that poses a constant threat to an idealized white womanhood and thus to the entire U.S. social order (Harper, 1993). "A structure of sociosexual relations that confers an inordinately threatening status upon black men remains very firmly in place in the United States" (Harper 1993, 261n. 20). Beyond the narrowly sexual, it is essential to understand that the uses of the erotic are grounded in a nonsexual expression of the capacity for collective joy, providing us with "the energy to pursue genuine change within our world" (Lorde

1984, 59). To focus purely on the sexual is to trivialize the breadth of the passion-centered desire shared by all the speakers and participants in the march. But to deny the presence of the erotic is to reinforce a fictive distance between passion-centered desire, spiritual affirmation, and social activism.

ACTS OF REMEMBRANCE

The Queerness also rests in the centrality of the celebration of history and the acts of remembrance in the march. Many of the sentiments conveyed by the speakers emphasized the crucial link between participation in the MMM and aspects of the broader historical context into which the march should be placed. In doing so, the speakers challenged Eurocentric definitions of various symbols and structures on the Capitol Mall and beyond, "constructing a counterhistory in which desire and mourning and identity can interact" in a much more complete fashion than is typical of historical associations (Gates 1993, 235).

As Minister Farrakhan (1996) stated, "We are standing in the place of those who couldn't make it here today. We are standing on the blood of our ancestors...[and] on the sacrifice of the lives of those heroes, our great men and women that we today may accept the responsibility that life imposes upon each traveler who comes this way." The queerness of this counterhistorical narrative was a product more of omission than of inclusion. First, when the 1963 March on Washington was celebrated, the significance of the contribution of Bayard Rustin, a gay African American man, was brought to mind. Minister Farrakhan in effect recreated the role of Mr. Rustin, instigating the idea for the march, bringing together the people who would organize the content and logistics of the day, and helping to manage the multiple and varied personalities and ideologies to be represented. A more complete acknowledgment of Mr. Rustin's role would have necessitated a celebration of the bridge between the two men. Farrakhan's intentional omission of their link is partially rooted in the often homophobic and "exclusionary obsessions of (some expressions of) the Black nationalist movement" (Gates 1993, 235). But in many ways such an exclusionary act makes the link between the two men pronounced and further affirms the queer historical dimension of the MMM itself.

Second, through the participation of numerous church figures, the MMM emphasized the critical link between the history of the African American church as an environment in which religious and spiritual expression were linked to social protest and political activism. "The Black-church context, though ostensibly hostile to homosexuality and gay identity, nevertheless has traditionally provided a means by which Black men can achieve a sense of themselves as homosexual" (Harper 1993, 251), and the explicit omission of this connection on the part of the speeches from the state galvanized the link by striving to ignore such an obvious and sustained truth. It has long been held that "from the African understanding of religious priorities, the confusion of identity in the world of the living must of necessity reverberate in the world where the spirits of the departed continue their existence after death" (Lincoln 1996, 99). Thus the queerness of the MMM is partially grounded in the prevalence of religious participation, the significance of a gay-identified presence in African American church history, and the framing of the MMM as an act of remembrance.

Third, by bringing together a somewhat diverse group of speakers, MMM organizers helped to represent the diversity of issues and sentiments seen as central to the march itself. This was perhaps most clearly illustrated in the number of women who spoke and the varied contributions they chose to make. I considered whom I would have liked to see and hear on stage. This was itself an act of remembrance, as late lesbian-feminist poet and activist Audre Lorde, poet Essex Hemphill, and filmmaker Marlon Riggs came immediately to mind. Thus the queerness of this intended omission (i.e., the lack of an openly queer-identified speaker) was rooted in a "reevaluation of and a dialogue with the past in the light of the present" (Hutcheon 1989, 19). The voices I desired and idealized spoke to me through the power of Maya Angelou's poem and the "what ifs" it instigated; yet I wanted to hear the words of Lorde or Riggs or Hemphill. This is not to imply that there are not numerous lesbians and gays of African descent who are alive and well and could have and should have been on the podium. Nor is it intended to take away from Dr. Angelou's elegance and strength of verse. It is simply to acknowledge that this spiritual resonance of mourning and loss was a part of what I, and perhaps many others, experienced in the moment of the march.

Another example of acts of remembrance within the queerness of the MMM rests in the cultural symbols of being on the Capitol steps, or in the shadow of the Washington Monument and the "cultural capital" these symbols of icons represent. Affirming the understandably numerous references to the 1963 March on Washington, the MMM was marked by a strong legacy of celebrated icons, represented in the living contribution of Ms. Rosa Parks, viewed by many as the mother of the modern civil rights movement. For many, this celebration of icons and the collective identity they affirm is linked with the loss of friends and mentors to AIDS, including two of the icons I would have liked to hear, Marlon Riggs and Essex Hemphill. Through the chosen speakers, other acts of remembrance occurred, as one was reminded of many other men and women of African descent who would have liked to have been at the march but who were prevented because of AIDS. Here again, the *Fierce Love* T-shirt was chosen to be inclusive of the queer legacy and our critical contribution to prior expressions of the

FIGURE 1

CIRCLES OF OUR MUTICULTURAL SELVES
seeing ourselves in more than one circle,
dancing in between center and margin

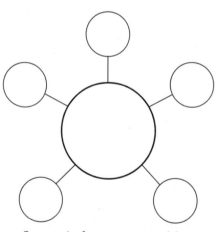

Some circles are created by:
religion, race, profession, workplace, physical appearance, gender, age, financial status, hobby/pastime, ethnic group/country of origin, family role, friendship, sexual orientation, college affiliation, political views, belief/ideology, geographic location, neighborhood, language, state of health, self-help groups, community service

Naming ourselves in more than one circle acknowledges the dance that our life is...in between/within circles.

movement upon which the MMM was built, a movement "in which desire and mourning and identity can interact in their full complexity" (Gates 1993, 235). The interaction between these three is crucial to the process of negotiating legacies that allow the full complexity of their interaction to be realized by seeking out viable actions through which legacies of greatness are celebrated by enacting social change (Price-Spratlen, 1996).

THE PRAXIS OF ATONEMENT IN OUR DAILY LIVES THEREAFTER

Another aspect of the queerness of the MMM rested in giving meaning to a "praxis of atonement," extending from the sentiments conveyed by Minster Farrakhan in his speech. First, in the moment of the march, this praxis meant sharing in the collective strength of reciting the MMM Pledge. The pledge reinforced that "the African individual is always more than merely an individual: He or she is always located within an expanding system of relationships which ultimately link them to God" (Lincoln 1996, 100). It was an act of spiritual connectedness among the participants, and it reinforced the importance of both an introspective search to clarify one's individual role in a collective struggle and the necessity to act with conscious vision to participate in bringing about a broadened justice.

Second, the praxis meant affirming the strength of weak ties among and between march participants with the hugs we shared after reciting the MMM Pledge (see Granovetter 1973). In doing so, we affirmed our individual value to the collective by physically sharing in bonds that exist between us and the unique contributions we can each make, given the strength those bonds provide. By our contributing to the greater good of our collective destiny in this way, both sexual and nonsexual homoerotic dimensions were part of this shared affection between strangers. The queerness extended from "a genuine spiritual affirmation is discovering [that] magic can arise between strangers—magic that in most of our waking moments we train ourselves not to see" (Browning 1993, 23), affirming a meaningful intimacy that can, at times, occur instantly.

Third, and perhaps most importantly, beyond the moment of the march there is the need for multiple expressions of individual community development, or actively participating in the process to "Africanize or to liberate this system from its exclusively Euro-american model" (Madhubuti 1994, 23). One queer example of that at the march was the open, organized participation of members of the National Black Gay and Lesbian Leadership Forum (NBGLLF). They marched together with the million other participants that day, acknowledging the diversity involved in "striving to improve [one]self spiritually, morally, mentally, politically, and economically" (Farrakhan 1996, 29). Beyond the march itself, this praxis in the day-to-day includes, among many things, participating in queer-identified organizations such as NBGLLF, and/or being out in nonqueer ones (e.g., Alpha Phi alpha Fraternity, Inc., and NAACP). Additional aspects of this praxis are considered below.

Praxis, Collective Identity, and the MMM

The MMM was an event of collective action in which men of African descent heeded the call of Minister Farrakhan and shared in "an act of humility, spiritual growth, inclusion, and political insight" (Madhubuti 1996, 2). It should perhaps best be understood as an act of praxis, a complex activity by which individuals create culture and society, and (re-)create themselves as human beings (Young, 1976). Moments of praxis occur when one's consciousness is changed through a unity of action and reflection, a unity "between practice and theory in which both are constructed, shaped, and reshaped in constant movement from practice to theory, then back to a new practice" (Freire 1985, 124). These moments are inclusive of five dimensions of praxis: self-determination, intentionality, sociality, creativity, and rationality (Young, 1976). Each individual who came to the Mall of Washington, D.C., on October 16, 1995, was acting, and insight was illustrated by sharing in a special day representative of "the struggle of the black masses to achieve identity [which] has been a gut struggle in the pursuit of group recognition and dignification" (Lincoln 1996, 106). Perhaps the most salient power of the MMM as a moment of praxis rests in the diversity of purposes and levels of insight represented among the many participants.

The intentionality of the act was a result of all the participants engaging in the "mental act by which one participates in the organization of one's own behavior" (Young 1976, 63), the act of affirming one's values through choice and collective practice. Perhaps chief among the components of praxis is sociality, because one achieves self-realization when the needs of other human beings are met at the same time. Among the central values of the MMM was allowing an acknowledged coming together of the multiple needs shared by (at least) all those who fall under the label "Black men." This need was based in the value of acknowledging a diverse yet common destiny and in the critical importance that participation in the MMM represented in moving us proactively toward the destiny. Finally, in praxis, rationality is activity linked to the achievement of human purpose in which the organization of resources makes predictable outcomes possible (Young, 1976). Purposeful action, which is intended to create a more achievable social justice borne of individual motivation and tied closely to the growth and sustenance of a health community, ties these dimensions in the process of praxis.

The MMM centered on a theme of atonement. For atonement to be given an operational meaning, conscientious praxis is necessary. Relating to acts of remembrance, the most comprehensive meaning of praxis can be effectively framed within the context of a legacy fulfilled and unfulfilled—the knowledge that many people who would have loved to be in the march had passed away due to AIDS (among many other causes), and a part of the reason of their passing rests in the consequences of the (often) strong link between gayness and shame. And gay visibility was, in many ways, the best of praxis, simultaneously challenging oppression both within and outside the movement for a broader social justice in the moment of its pronouncement.

As stated, my participation in the MMM was centered on my wanting to bring about a moment "in which *desire and mourning and identity* can interact in their full complexity" (Gates 1993, 235). For me, that meant acknowledging the presence of the erotic in all its diverse expressions. As a gay man who lovingly affirms all manners of respectful interaction among men of African descent, being surrounded by a million-plus Black men affirmed the erotic in the extreme. "The erotic is a measure between the beginnings of our sense of self, and the chaos of our strongest feelings. It is an internal sense of satisfaction to which, once we have experienced it, we know we can aspire. For having experienced the fullness of this depth of feeling and recognizing its power, in honor and self-respect we can require no less of ourselves" (Lorde 1984, 54). The meaning and expression of erotic desire was far more whole than what the sexual alone can sustain. Central to the praxis of atonement is desire, the want for various kinds of change and the motivation to contribute to its realization. The more intense the desire, the more complete the consequences of atonement may be. By recognizing our deepest feelings, "we begin to give up of necessity, being satisfied with suffering and self-negation and with the numbness which so often seems like their only alternative in our society. Our acts against oppression become integral with self, motivated and empowered from within" (Lorde 1984, 58). So the praxis of atonement can be viewed, in part, as an expression of homoerotic desire, i.e., same-sex, passion-centered longing for realized change that may or may not be sexually focused.

PARTNERSHIPS OF COLLECTIVE IDENTITY

The collective act of coming together to form a functional—albeit temporary—coalition was a transformative opportunity in which the common, uniting bonds of race and gender needed to be understood both within the context of oppression or a "partnership of misery," and within the context of praxis of atonement for a broadened social justice or "partnership for change." To focus on atonement means that a clearer understanding of the ways in which both partnerships function together should be pursued. An acknowledgment of contested meaning becomes central to this because it is in negotiation through the praxis of atonement, beyond the single-day mobilization or event that can effectively fuel and further a partnership for change (Tessman, 1995). The contested meaning rests in celebrating diversity and collective identity simultaneously.

Minister Farrakhan used atonement as the central theme of his MMM keynote speech to articulate the importance of the march's primary intention, that of "Black men choosing to come together in love to affect change in their situation; to impact positively on their representative villages" (Jackson 1996, 17). And acknowledging diversity, both within the places to which the participants have returned and among the march participants themselves, while obvious, remains an important task, lest one legitimize the fiction of the whole of the march's million-plus men as a solitary homogenous "moral community." We were not. Fundamental to an understanding of the MMM is the need to recognize the significance of differences among the march participants and the many aspects of difference that were overtly embraced, overtly dismissed, or covertly ignored.

Within any group there is at least as much invisible diversity as visible (Style, 1995), and a coming together under a label as broad as "Black men" is certainly going to be representative of this truth. Figure 1 on page 53 provides a heuristic that "reveals that we all are multicultural, carrying more than one group identification. Basic literacy (diversity literacy) about our own multiple roles and the skills needed for role and code switching ought to inform any meeting" (Style 1995, 68), including the MMM. The "circles of Our Multicultural Selves" provide a starting point from which familiarity with others is built through a sharing of both visible and "invisible" affiliations that make up the process of moving between circle and margin. The circles may lead people to think beyond standard "us/them" dichotomies by recognizing and embracing the breadth of their internal private diversity and affirming the link between that internal diversity and the public choices we make every day.

Any mobilization such as the MMM is principally organized around the production of meaning, desire, affect, and identity (Haymes, 1995). Historically, African American mobilization is viewed by many as the first to expand the concerns of politics to the social, to the terrain of everyday life (Omi and Winant, 1986). Thus the most effective expressions of the praxis of atonement require working at becoming aware of significant invisible territory (Style, 1995) in our daily lives, by acknowledging shared and unshared desire in the process of affirming both individual and collective identity. Oliver and Marwell (1988) have found that "the positive effect on collective action of the size of a population with grievances increases both with group heterogeneity and with overlapping social circles" (cited in Murray 1996, 54). Thus, the acknowledgment of *invisible* diversity can beneficially effect the potential impact of collective action based on a shared characteristic of *visible* diversity. In other words, the movement toward queer visibility is to the potential benefit of the praxis of atonement in our daily lives as men of African descent, regardless of sexual identity.

The potential praxis benefit of acknowledging visible and invisible diversity results from a reciprocity between critical mass, subcultural formation/diversity, subcultural intensity, and the broadening of the critical mass (Fischer 1975, 1982). In a single expression of collective identity, challenging invisibility becomes an important expression of the "fund of necessary polarities" (Lorde, 1988) to the benefit of increased, visible intensity and subsequent collective action. One aspect of the praxis of atonement is to make invisible diversity visible. The act of *Fierce Love* was an affirmation to those kept silent by the heterosexist compulsories and the invisibility they affirm. The visible participation of the NBGLLF's "call to action" did the same thing collectively. Other brothers, who in isolation or within a social network or through force-fed shame keep their sexuality invisible needed to realize "that even the other person also opposes the (heterosexist) 'consensus' greatly [which] increases the likelihood of enunciating contrary views" (Murray 1996, 54). This too is a part of the process of enhanced visibility and acknowledging diversity within any given individual, and within the subculture en masse.

CIRCLES AT THE STARTING LINE

In carrying out the praxis of atonement, the circles of one's multicultural self need to be recognized as "starting point identities" (i.e., points from which the process of affiliation and seeking community affirms the meanings, desires, and effects one understands to be representative of themselves). And within the context of collective action, the circles recognize the interlocking of oppressions and that "separation along one line of difference ignores that the self is constituted in more than one community" (Tessman 1995, 64). The MMM was a collective act of resistance, an action intended to further galvanize and motivate the creation of resistant communities. The creation of these communities requires an act of identifying, to realize how individual starting point identities of those involved have been formed under oppression, and that these identities are never "finished." The ever-present motion toward a "finish line" becomes a crucial goal for the praxis of atonement, by furthering a *resistant* identity.

Even amidst an environment of perpetual oppressions such as the U.S., when identity seems to be something imposed or given by the oppressive system, a resistant identity can be claimed or created within a coalition that transforms identity rather than accepts it as given by the oppressive system (Tessman, 1995). It is this resistant identity that is crucial to the development of an participation in a praxis of atonement. Crucial to this praxis, both within the moment of the mobilization as well as actions in the day-to-day thereafter, is that "the idea of solidarity must be constructed so that there is still room for noticing one's differences from those with whom one is solidary" (Tessman 1995, 80). Making the otherwise invisible visible, or "queering the MMM," serves as one such example, affirming the malleability of identity and the process of participating in a selective solidarity. Detailed below, it is a process of participating in the "pedagogy of place" (Haymes, 1996) that the MMM exemplified.

A PEDAGOGY OF PLACE AND THE MMM

The praxis of atonement and the formation of a resistant identity, the uses of the erotic and the queer dimensions of each, can perhaps best be understood within the context of a "pedagogy of place" for the MMM. "A crucial pedagogy or urban place and struggle...must take up how the manufacturing of urban meanings structures our perceptions about different living spaces and the political and ethical consequences of those meanings on both the spaces and the people that live in them" (Haymes 1995, 3). The MMM was a mobilization intended, in part, to redefine how we view the nation's capital, Black men, and the power of the legacy left relating one to the other. It was a mobilization that took up the task of making homeplace by constructing a safe space where African American people could affirm one another and, by doing so, move toward a healing of the many wounds inflicted by racist domination (hooks, 1990). By creating a moment in which a million-plus men of African descent could simultaneously come together and feel safe among strangers, the MMM challenged the "murder capital" label, affirming the ability to share time and place with one another outside the context of violence and exploitation (Marcuse, 1969). As a result, this mobilization affirmed a proactive pedagogy of cultural place.

This proactive pedagogy of cultural place is linked with the queerness of the MMM and is rooted in the diversity of march participants, the meaning of the march's location, and the imagery of Essex Hemphill and in acts of remembrance relating the three to one another. In fusing these conceptual relationships, the MMM can be recognized as a mobilization to move beyond a narrowly defined communitarian unity (i.e., single category affiliation) idealized by Minister Farrakhan. The insistence of such an ideal can act against the potential for achieving a diverse unity of resistant identities by systematically marginalizing those who do not fit conveniently within a dominant group to the exclusion of all other individual group affiliations. Such an ideal directly challenges the potential of a pedagogy of place. By moving against an illusory or fictive communitarian unity, acts of remembrance and the praxis of atonement can be truly transformative. They can affirm identity and are tied to the process of place-making and to progressive, just definitions of a diverse self, a diverse community, and the relationship between them. As Haymes (1995) states:

> It is within this context that place making is tied to the idea that places are significant because we assign meaning to them in relation to our specific projects. [Place making] is linked with self-definition or identity formation, [and] projects are

shaped by experiences in everyday life, so that within black urban communities place making and therefore the production of public spaces is linked with day-to-day survival...[and] a [diverse] consciousness and politics of resistance (10-11).

Community must be understood to be far more than "a territorial base with primary institutions serving a residential population" (Hooker 1961, 356). Crucial to any understanding of the term is giving importance to the "community of memory," as geographic and perceptual spaces which "tell painful stories of shared suffering that sometimes creates deeper identities than success...[because when] history and hope are forgotten and community means only the gathering of the similar, community degenerates into lifestyle enclave" (Bellah et al. 1985, 153-54). As a gay man of African descent, for example, one's community of memory relative to the MMM may, in part, be shaped by poet Essex Hemphill's reflections of growing up in D.C. as a child, as well as his adult experiences. The performance piece *Fierce Love* also reinforces that community of memory and links with the image making of Hemphill to affirm a bridge between the geographic location of the MMM and the place-making context central to one's understanding of the meaning of the march.

In short, "place and identity are bonded together, and culture is the glue that bonds them" (Haymes 1995, 89). Among the more useful cultural components that act to strengthen the glue is the alternative images and representations of place that are crucial to our construction of social identity as African Americans. And it is this place-making process that "has been significant in forging a politics of struggle or resistance" (Haymes 1995, 9-10). Thus, the MMM for me was inherently queer because of the place-making narratives formed by PomoAfroHomos and Hemphill's imagery, the contextualization of the meaning of D.C., and the gathering of more than a million men of African descent sharing in a diverse unity that was inherently homoerotic, both sexually and nonsexually.

By understanding the proactive pedagogy of cultural place, participating in a mobilization such as the MMM should perhaps most effectively "be linked to how individuals and collectives make and take up culture in the production of public spaces in the city, with particular emphasis on how they use and assign meaning to public spaces within unequal relations of power in an effort to 'make place' " (Haymes 1995, 3). The power imbalance is rooted in the racist domination that is the cultural history of African peoples in the Americas. This power imbalance was symbolically challenged by gathering amidst the physical structures paying homage to significant, sociopolitical white men of this country. The power imbalance also roots itself in heterosexist domination (along with its gender and class corollaries). This power imbalance was symbolically challenged in collective, visible participation of the NBGLLF and in individual acts such as my wearing the *Fierce Love* T-shirt.

These symbolic challenges acknowledge both individual and collective power, since cultural and historical images have *as much* influence on the spatial form of the city as do economics (Castells, 1983; Saunders 1986; Langer, 1984). While this view is debatable, urban settings are often made up of many different voices and living spaces that together define the cultural and historical images of influence. The MMM provided an environment in which individuals affirmed resistant cultural images, proactively investing "in the experimentation and practice of new cultural models, forms of relationships, and alternative perceptions of the world." In this way, the march was itself the message, "a symbolic challenge to the dominant codes" of cultural oppression in the U.S." (Melucci 1989, 60).

Following Omi and Winant (1986), Tessman (1995, 58) observes that "members of categories have the lived experience of shaping their identities in relation to (or within histories and communities of) other members of that category or group and in contradistinction from members of other groups." Essential to the place-making process and the queerness of the MMM is that the intersection of oppressions must be visibly acknowledged within the moment of an event because "if different forms of oppression are seen as isolated and stratified, one is left with an identity politics that erases the nonprimary elements of identity" (Tessman 1995, 61). Participation in such mobilizations, then, is a matter of group representations, carried out through caucuses based on social groups (i.e., the praxis of atonement) whose interests and perspectives might otherwise be ignored. In this way, it is possible to participate in the transformation of identity that "takes place by asserting identity as a collective and contested political commitment" (Tessman 1995, 76), transforming partnerships in misery and oppression into partnerships for proactive change.

COLLECTIVES AND A POSSIBLE FUTURE

Essential to an understanding of the MMM is the recognition of the multiple, layered, and fluid concentrations of identity that express themselves through the praxis of atonement. What varies across the multiple specifications of identity (i.e., circles of the multicultural self) is their relative malleability, permeability, and density/volume. The MMM celebrated one set of concentrations to the (intended and potentially detrimental) exclusion of several others. The *explicit inclusions* were gender and race/ethnicity (i.e., "Black men"). Clearly, the *implicit inclusions* of the MMM were age, physical ability, physiognomy (e.g., skin color, hair texture, height and weight). The *questionable inclusions* were class and sexuality. Among the key points to acknowledge here is that any praxis, and pedagogy, is, by definition, selective. The "pedagogy of the oppressed" that Paulo Freire (1970) wrote of clearly and intentionally privileges those who fall under the label "oppressed." This privileging is true of any other dimension of collective identity. What must be understood is that the movement forward from the MMM will—in fact, must—exhibit privileged concentrations via selective participation in terms of both individual and collective praxis, linked simultaneously with other individuals and groups lying outside those privileged concentrations.

Just as there are constraints on power, there are consequently constraints on pedagogy, praxis, and identity. Perhaps most importantly, there are also constraints on virtually every dimension or concentration of identity, and the proactive pedagogy of cultural place following from the MMM selectively challenges these constraints. In challenging the restrictive nature of those constraints (i.e., affirming resistant cultural images and resisting single category affiliation), a critical lesson of the MMM can occur by carrying a piece of the spirit of the march forward in day-to-day praxis. And it is through heeding a call to action, acting on an acknowledgment of responsibility that Joseph Beam wrote of, that one can constantly reaffirm and recharge within the spirit of the MMM by reinforcing a reciprocity between choice and spirit, negotiating legacies with each choice.

At the end of the march, after the MMM pledge had been recited and in the midst of sharing hugs with men who were otherwise complete strangers prior to that moment, an African American woman and I approached each other and shared a hug. "Thank you so much for sharing in this very special day," I said as we broke our embrace and held hands for a brief moment. She responded by saying, "I celebrate you, my brother, the million other brothers and sisters that were here, and the power and potential that lies within us as we move forward together." I then went to a nearby restaurant, where I met a gay man of Puerto Rican descent who had also been at the march. We talked at length of potential alliances and the meaning of the march beyond its affirmation of Black men narrowly defined.

These two personal incidents, which occurred directly on the heels of the MMM, helped me to recognize the many possibilities the march held in the instigation of "communicative action" (Habermas, 1989) that contribute to cross-group cooperation by striving for a "consensus against the background of a set of norms agreeable to the negotiating partners involved" (Holub 1992, 187). Such communicative actions are both large (e.g., the MMM itself) and small (e.g., sharing a "cross-group" hug), and can affirm our multicultural selves in unique and powerful ways. It is a uniqueness that can be affirmed without condescension and within a power borne of movement beyond a restrictive communitarian unity.

Such actions are representative of living against the grain in ways that can "keep alive the possibility [of no longer being] obsessed with sexuality and fearful of each other's humanity" (West 1993, 131). These actions strengthen the ongoing dialogue crucial to cultural action for freedom (Freire, 1985). While I began the day of the MMM with cautious steps beyond the metro train, I ended the march with a sentiment of powerful possibilities. This sentiment will be with me individually, and with this culture for some time to come.

References

Beam, J. (1986). *In the Life: A Black Gay Anthology.* Boston: Alyson Publications.

Bellah, R.; Madsen, R; Sullivan, W.M.; Swidler, A.; Tipton, S.T. (1985). *Habits of the Heart.* Berkeley: University of California Press.

Browning, F. (1993). *The Culture of Desire: Paradox and Perversity in Gay Lives Today.* New York: Crown Publishers, Inc.

Castells, M. (1983). *The City and the Grassroots.* Berkeley: University of California Press.

Cone, J. H. (1991). *Martin & Malcolm & America: A Dream or a Nightmare.* Maryknoll, New York: Orbis Books.

Farrakhan, L. (1996). "Day of Atonement." *Million Man March/Day of Absence: A Commemorative Anthology,* edited by Haki R. Madhubuti and Maulana Karenga. Chicago: Third World Press.

Fischer, C.S. (1982). *To Dwell Among Friends: Personal Networks in Town and City.* Chicago: University of Chicago Press.

Fischer, C.S. (1975). "Toward a Subcultural Theory of Urbanism." *American Journal of Sociology* 80: 1319-1341.

Freire, P. (1985). *The Politics of Education: Culture, Power and Liberation.* South Hadley, MA:

Bergin & Garvey Publishers, Inc.

Gates, H.L, Jr. (1993). "The Black Man's Burden." In *Fear of a Queer Planet: Queer Politics and Social Theory,* edited by Michael Warner. Minneapolis: University of Minnesota Press, 230-238.

Gilroy, P. (1991). *"There Ain't No Black in the Union Jack": The Cultural Politics of Race and Nation.* Chicago: The University of Chicago Press.

Granovetter, M.S. (1973). "The Strength of Weak Ties." *American Journal of Sociology* 78: 1360-1380.

Habermas, J. (1989). *The Theory of Communicative Action.* Boston: Beacon Press.

Harper, P.B. (1993). "Eloquence and Epitaph: Black Nationalism and the Homophobic Impulse in Responses to the Death of Max Robinson." In *Writing AIDS,* edited by T. Murphy and S. Poirier. New York: Columbia University Press, 117-139.

Haymes, S.N. (1995). *Race, Culture, and the City: A Pedagogy for Black Urban Struggle.* Albany: State University of New York Press.

Hemphill, E. (1992). *Ceremonies: Prose and Poetry.* New York: Plume.

Holub, R. (1992). *Antonio Gramsci: Beyond Marxism and Post-Modernism.* New York: Routledge.

Hooker, E. (1961). "The Homosexual Community." In *Perspectives in Psychopathology,* edited by J. Plamer and M. Goldstein. New York: Oxford University Press, 354-64.

hooks, b. (1990). *Yearning: Race, Gender, and Cultural Politics.* Boston: South End Press.

— (1991). "Cornel West Interviewed by bell hooks." In *Breaking Bread: Insurgent Black Intellectual Life,* edited by bell hooks and Cornel West. Boston: South End Press, 27-58.

Hutcheon, L. (1989). *The Politics of Postmodernism.* New York: Routledge.

Jackson, J. (1996). "Remarks Before One Million Men." In *Million Man March/Day of Absence: A Commemorative Anthology,* edited by Haki R. Madhubuti and Maulana Karenga. Chicago: Third World Press, 32-36.

Langer, P. (1984). "Sociology—Four Images of Organized Diversity: Bazaar, Jungle, Organism, and Machine." In *Cities of the Mind: Images and Themes of the City in Social Science,* edited by Rodwin and Hollister. New York: Plenum Press, as cited in Haymes (1995).

Lincoln, C. E. (1996). *Coming Through the Fire: Surviving Race and Place in America.* Durham, NC: Duke University Press.

Lorde, A. (1988). *A Burst of Light.* Ithaca, NY: Firebrand Books.

— (1984). *Sister Outsider: Essays and Speeches.* Trumansberg, NY: Crossing Press.

— Madhubuti, H. (1994). *Claiming Earth: Race, Rage, Rape, Redemption: Blacks Seeking a Culture of Enlightened Empowerment.* Chicago: Third World Press.

— (1996). "Took Back Our Tears, Laughter, Love, and Left a Big Dent in the Earth." In *Million Man March/Day of Absence: A Commemorative Anthology,* edited by Haki R. Madhubuti and Maulana Karenga. Chicago: Third World Press, 2-4.

Marcuse, H. (1969). *An Essay on Liberation.* Boston: Beacon Press.

McAdam, D. (1982). *Political Process and the Development of Black Insurgency, 1930-1970.* Chicago: University of Chicago Press.

Melucci, A. (1989). *Nomads of the Present: Social Movements and Individual Needs in Contemporary Society*. Philadelphia: Temple University Press.

Murray, S. O. (1996). *American Gay*. Chicago: The University of Chicago Press.

Oliver, P. E. and Marwell, G. (1988). "The Paradox of Group Size in Collective Action: A Theory of Critical Mass II." *American Sociological Review* 53: 1-8.

Omi, M. & Howard W. (1986). *Racial Formation in the United State: From the 1960s to the 1980s*. New York: Routledge.

Price-Spratlen, T. (1996). "Negotiating Legacies: Audre Lorde, W.E.B. DuBois, Marlon Riggs, and Me." *Harvard Educational Review* 66: 216-30.

Saunders, P. (1986). *Social Theory and The Urban Question*. New York: Holmes & Meier Publishers, Inc.

Smith, S. and Watson, J. (Eds.). (1992). *Decolonizing the Subject: The Politics of Gender in Women's Autobiography*. Minneapolis: University of Minnesota Press.

Style, E. J. (1995). "In Our Own Hands: Diversity Literacy." *Transformations* 6: 64-84.

Taylor, V. and Whittier, N.E. (1992). "Collective Identity in Social Movement Communities: Lesbian Feminist Mobilization." In *Frontiers in Social Movement Theory*, edited by Aldon D. Morris and Carol McClurg Muller.. New Haven: Yale University Press, 104-129.

Tessman, L. (1995). "Beyond Communitarian Unity in the Politics of Identity." *Socialist Review* 24: 55-83.

West, C. (1993). *Race Matters*. New York: Vintage Books.

Young, T.R. (1978). *Red Feather Dictionary of Socialist Sociology*. San Francisco: Red Feather Institute.

Homophobia in Black Communities

BELL HOOKS

Recently I was at home with my parents and heard teenagers expressing their hatred of homosexuals, saying they could never like anybody who was homosexual. In response I told them, "There are already people who you love and care about who are gay, so just come off it!" They wanted to know who. I said the "who" is not important. If they wanted you to know, they would tell you. But you need to think about the shit you've been saying and ask yourself where it's coming from.

Their vehement expression of hatred startled and frightened me, even more so when I contemplated the hurt that would have been experienced had our loved ones who where gay heard their words. When we were growing up, we would not have had the nerve to make such comments. We were not allowed to say negative, hateful comments about the people we knew who were gay. We knew their names, their sexual preference. They were our neighbors, our friends, our family. They were us, a part of our black community.

The gay people we knew did not live in separate subcultures, not in the small segregated black community where work was difficult to find, where many of us were poor. Poverty was important; it created a social context in which structures of dependence were important for everyday survival. Sheer economic necessity and fierce white racism, as well as the joys of being there with the black folks known and loved, compelled many gay blacks to live close to home and family. That meant, however, that gay people created a way to live out their sexual preference with the boundaries of circumstances that were rarely ideal no matter how affirming. In some cases this meant a closeted sexual lifestyle. In other families, an individual could be openly expressive, quite out.

The homophobia expressed by nieces and nephews coupled with the assumption in many feminist circles that black communities are somehow more homophobic than other communities in the United States, more opposed to gay rights, provided the stimulus for me to write this piece. Initially I considered calling it "Homophobia in the Black Community." Yet it is precisely the notion that there is a monolithic black community that must be challenged. Black communities and urban and rural experiences create diversity of culture and lifestyle.

I have talked to folks who were raised in Southern communities where gay people were openly expressive of their sexual preference and participated fully in the life of the community. I have also spoken with folks about the opposite.

In the particular black community where I was raised there was a real double standard. Black male homosexuals were often known, were talked about, were seen positively, had played important roles in community life, whereas lesbians were talked about solely in negative terms and the women identified as lesbians were usually married.

Often, acceptance of male homosexuality was mediated by material privilege. That is to say that the homosexual men with money were part of the materially privileged ruling black group and were accorded the regard and respect given that group. They were influential people in the community. This was not the case with women.

In those days homophobia directed at lesbians was rooted in the deep religious and moral belief that they denied their womanness by not bearing children. The prevailing assumption was that a lesbian was unnatural because one would not be participating in childbearing. There were no identified lesbian parents, even though there were gay men known to be caretakers of other folks' children. I have talked with black folks who recall similar circumstances in their communities. Overall, a majority of older black people I spoke with, raised in small, tightly knit Southern black communities, suggested there was tolerance and acceptance of different sexual practices and preferences. One black gay male I spoke with felt that it was important for him to live in a supportive black community, where his sexual preferences were known but not acted out in an overt public way, than live in a gay subculture where this aspect of his identity could be openly expressed.

Recently I talked to a lesbian from New Orleans who boasted that the black community has never had an orange person like Anita Bryant running around trying to attack gay people. Her experience coming out to a black male roommate was positive and caring. But for every positive story one might hear about gay life in black communities, there are also negative ones. Yet these positive accounts call into question the assumption that black people and black communities are necessarily more homophobic than other groups in this society. They also compel us to recognize that there are diversities of black experience. Unfortunately, there are very few oral histories and autobiographies that explore the lives of black gay people in diverse black gay communities. This is a research project that must be carried out if we are to fully understand the experience of being black and gay in this white-supremacist, patriarchal, capitalist society. Often we hear more black gay people who choose to live in predominantly white communities, whose choices may have been affected by undue harassment in black communities. We hardly anything from black gay people who live contentedly in black communities.

Black communities may be perceived as more homophobic than other communities because there is a tendency for individuals in black communities to verbally express in an outspoken way antigay sentiments. I talked with a straight black male in a California community who acknowledged that though he has often made jokes poking fun at gays or expressing contempt as a means of bonding in group settings, in his private life he was a central support person for a gay sister. Such contradictory behavior seems pervasive in black communities. It speaks to ambivalence about sexuality in general, about sex as a subject of conversation, and to ambivalent feelings and attitudes toward homosexuality. Various structures of emotional and economic dependence create gaps between attitudes and action. Yet a distinction must be made between black people overtly expressing prejudice toward homosexuals and homophobic white people who never make homophobic comments but have the power to actively exploit and oppress gay people in areas of housing, employment, etc. While both groups perpetuate and reinforce each other and this cannot be denied or downplayed, the truth is that the greatest threat to gay rights does not reside in black communities.

It is far more likely that homophobic attitudes can be altered or changed in environments where they have not become rigidly institutionalized. Rather than suggesting that black communities are more homophobic than other communities and dismissing them, it is important for feminist activists (especially black folks) to examine the nature of that homophobia, to challenge it in constructive ways that lead to change. Clearly religious beliefs and practices in many black communities promote and encourage homophobia. Many Christian black folks (like other Christians in this society) are taught in churches that it is a sin to be gay, ironically sometimes by ministers who are themselves gay or bisexual.

In the past year I talked with a black woman Baptist minister who, although concerned about feminist issues, expresses very negative attitudes about homosexuality because, she explained, the Bible teaches that it is wrong. Yet in her daily life she is tremendously supportive and caring of gay friends.

When I asked her to explain this contradiction, she argued that it was not a contradiction—that the Bible also teaches her to identify with those who are exploited and oppressed and to demand that they be treated justly. To her way of thinking, committing a sin did not mean that one should be exploited or oppressed.

The contradictions, the homophobic attitudes that underlie her attitudes, indicate that there is a great need for progressive black theologians to examine the role black churches play in encouraging persecution of gay people. Individual members of certain churches in black communities should protest when worship services become a platform for teaching antigay sentiments. Often individuals sit and listen to preachers raging against gay people and think the views expressed are amusing and outmoded, and dismiss them without challenge. But if homophobia is to be eradicated in black communities, such attitudes must be challenged.

Recently, especially as black people all over the United States discuss the film version of Alice Walker's novel *The Color Purple* as well as the book itself (which includes a positive portrayal of two black women being sexual with each other), the notion that homosexuality threatens the continuation of black families seems to have gained new momentum. In some cases black males in prominent positions, especially those in the media, have helped to perpetuate this notion. Tony Brown stated in one editorial, "No lesbian relationship can take the place of a positive love relationship between black women and black men." It is both a misreading of Walkers's novel and an expression of homophobia for any reader to project into this work the idea that lesbian relationships exist as a competitive response to heterosexual encounters. Walker suggests quite the contrary.

Just a few weeks ago I sat with two black women friends eating bagels as one of us expressed her intense belief that white people were encouraging black people to be homosexuals so as to further divide black folks. She was attributing to homosexuality the difficulties many professional heterosexual black women have finding lovers, companions, and husbands. We listened to her and then the other women said, "Now you know we are not going to sit here and listen to this homophobic bull without challenging it."

We pointed out the reality that many black gay people are parents, hence their sexual preference does not threaten the continuation of black families. We stressed that many black gay people have white lovers and that there is no guarantee that were they heterosexual they would be partnered with other black people.

We argued that people should be able to choose and claim their sexual preference that best expresses their being, suggesting that while it is probably true that positive portrayals of gay people encourage people to see this as a viable sexual preference or lifestyle, it is equally true that compulsory heterosexuality is promoted to a far greater extent. We suggested that we should all be struggling to create a climate where there is freedom of sexual expression.

She was not immediately persuaded by our arguments, but at least she had a different perspective to consider. Supporters of gay rights in black communities must recognize that education for critical consciousness that explains and critiques prevailing stereotypes is necessary for us to eradicate the notion that homosexuality means genocide for black families.

And in conjunction with discussions of this issue, black people must confront the reality of bisexuality and the extent to which the spread of AIDS in black communities is connected to bisexual transmission of HIV.

To strengthen solidarity between black folks irrespective of our sexual preference must be discussed. This is especially critical as more and more black gay people live outside black communities. Just as black women are often compelled to answer the question: Which is more important? Feminist movement or black liberation struggle? Women's rights or civil rights—which are you first, black or female? Gay people face similar questions. Are you more identified with the political struggle of your race and ethnic group or gay rights struggle? This question is not a simple one. For some people it is raised in such a way that they are compelled to choose one identity over another.

In one case, when a black family learned of their daughter's lesbianism, they did not question her sexual preference (saying they weren't stupid, they had known she was gay) but the racial identity of her lovers. Why white women and not black women? Her gayness, expressed exclusively in relationships with white women, was deemed threatening because it was perceived as estranging her from blackness.

Little is written about this struggle. Often black families who acknowledge and accept gayness find interracial coupling harder to accept. Certainly among black lesbians the issue of black women preferring solely white lovers is discussed, but usually in private conversation. These relationships, like all cross-racial intimate relationships, are informed by the dynamics of racism and white supremacy. Black lesbians have spoken about the absence of acknowledgment of one another at social gatherings where the majority of black women present are with white women lovers.

Unfortunately, such incidents reinforce the notion that one must choose between solidarity with one's ethnic group and those who share sexual preferences, irrespective of class and ethnic differences in political perspective. Black liberation and gay liberation are both undermined when these divisions are promoted and encouraged. Both gay and straight must work to resist the politics as experienced in sexism and racism that lead people to think that supporting one liberation struggle diminishes one's support for another or stands one in opposition to another. As part of education for political consciousness in black communities, it must be continually stressed that our struggle against racism, our struggle to recover from oppression and exploitation are inextricably linked to all struggles to resist domination and gay liberation struggle.

Often black people, especially nongay folks, become enraged when they hear a white person who is gay suggest that homosexuality is synonymous with the suffering people experience as racial exploitation and oppression. The need to make gay experience and black experience of oppression synonymous seems to be the one that surfaces much more in the minds of white people. Too often it is seen as a way minimizing or diminishing the particular problems people of color in a white supremacist society, especially the problems encountered because one does not have a white skin. Many of us have been in discussions where a nonwhite person—a black person—struggles to explain to white folks that while he can acknowledge that gay people are all harassed and suffer exploitation and domination, we also recognize that there is a significant difference that arises because of the visibility of dark skin. Often homophobic attacks on gay people occur in situations where knowledge of sexual preference is indicated or established—outside of gay bars, for example. While it in no way lessens the severity of such suffering for gay people, or the fear it causes, it does mean that in a given situation the apparatus of protection and survival may be simply not identifying as gay. In contrast, most people of color have no choice. No one can hide or mask dark skin color. White people, gay and straight, could show greater understanding of the impact of racial oppression on people of color by not attempting to make their oppressions synonymous, but rather by showing the ways they are linked and differ. Concurrently, the attempt by white people to make synonymous the experience of homophobic aggression with racial oppression deflects attention from the particular dilemma that nonwhite gay people face as individuals who confront both racism and homophobia.

Often black gay folk feel extremely isolated because there are tensions in their relationship with black communities around issues of homophobia. Sometimes it is easier to respond to such tensions by simply withdrawing from both groups, by refusing to participate or identify oneself politically with any struggle to end domination. By affirming and supporting black people who are gay within our communities as well as outside our communities, we can help reduce and change the pain of such isolation. Significantly, attitudes toward sexuality and sexual preference are changing. There is greater acknowledgment that people have different sexual preferences and diverse sexual practices. Given this reality, it is a waste of energy for anyone to assume that their condemnation will ensure that people do not express varied sexual preferences. Many gay people of all races do not express varied sexual preferences. Many gay people of all races, raised within this homophobic society, struggle to confront and accept themselves, to recover or gain the core of self-love and well-being that is constantly threatened and attacked both from within and without. This is particularly true for people of color who are gay. It is essential that nongay people recognize and respect the hardships, the difficulties black gay people experience, extending the love and understanding that is essential for the making of an authentic black community. Once we can show our care is vigilant protest of homophobia, by acknowledging the union between black liberation struggle and gay liberation struggle, we strengthen our solidarity, enhance the scope and power of our allegiances, and further our resistance.

Sexuality and the Black Church

Is Homosexuality the Greatest Taboo?

Delroy Constantine-Simms

The title of this book is based on the notion that homosexuality is the greatest sexual taboo within the African Diaspora, especially the United States, the Caribbean, and the United Kingdom. According to Walter Wink (2000), issues of sexuality are tearing apart the Christian community as never before. He argues that the issue of homosexuality threatens to fracture entire communities and churches as the issue of slavery did 150 years ago. What he doesn't realize is that homosexuality isn't just tearing apart the African American churches; it is also affecting Black churches worldwide. But as bell hooks writes, "The Black community has always found a role for the ever-growing numbers of gay and lesbians becoming more open and active in the role they play with the African American Church." It is important, though, to recognize that there are other sexual taboos that society does not emphasize as greatly. Interpreting the Bible, however, is a task in itself, which begs the question: Should the Black community use the Bible to sort out our confusion about homosexuality? Should people such as Buju Banton and Shabba Ranks be allowed to advance the idea that homosexuals deserve crucifixion, especially when they themselves are womanizers, spilling more seeds outside of marriage than many heterosexuals have ever done? Should Caribbean governments maintain their homophobic laws based on their interpretation of the Bible? As Wink (2000) has made clear, some Bible passages that have been advanced as pertinent to the issue of homosexuality are, in fact, irrelevant. One is the story of attempted gang rape in Sodom (Gen. 19:1-29), since it features ostensibly heterosexual males intent on humiliating strangers by treating them "like women," thus demasculinizing them. (This is also the case in a similar account in Judges 19-21.) However, nationalists such as Frances Cress Welsing (1991), Eldridge Cleaver, and Amiri Baraka would argue that this passage is important in that homosexuality is now being used to effeminize Black men.

Wink (2000) correctly argues that the brutal behavior in this Bible passage has nothing to do with whether genuine love expressed between consenting adults of the same sex is legitimate. Are these not the very types of behavior that supposedly heterosexual men display in prisons? In single-sex schools or other single-sex environments? Are these individuals ever labeled gay? If so, would they accept that they were? Indeed, many heterosexual brothers at historically Black universities have chosen to participate in these same practices as part of fraternity pledge rituals.

Another area of contradiction relates to heterosexual individuals who prostitute themselves homosexually for money. One only has to venture to the Caribbean to find self-proclaimed hard-core antihomosexual Black men selling their wares to the highest bidder. One only has to go to Britain's Leicester Square or New York's Time Square or 42nd Street and the Village to discover that heterosexual Black men are increasingly selling homosexual sex as never before. However, Deuteronomy 23:17-18 must be pruned from the list of Bible passages condemning homosexuality, since according to Wink (2000) it refers to a heterosexual male prostitute involved in Canaanite fertility rites that have infiltrated Jewish worship; the King James Version inaccurately labels him a "sodomite." Several other texts are ambiguous. It is unclear whether 1 Corinthians 6:9 and 1 Timothy 1:10 refer to the "passive" and "active" partners in homosexual relationships or to homosexual and heterosexual male prostitutes. In short, it is unclear whether the issue is homosexuality itself or promiscuity and "sex-for-hire."

UNEQUIVOCAL CONDEMNATIONS

One thing is for certain: The following references as cited by Wink (2000) unequivocally condemn homosexual behavior. Leviticus 18:22 states this principle: "You [masculine] shall not lie with a male as with a woman; it is an abomination," while Leviticus 20:13 adds the penalty: "If a man lies with a male as with a woman, both of them have committed an abomination; they shall be put to death; their blood is upon them." In the Bible, such an act is regarded as an "abomination" for several reasons.

The Hebrew prescientific understanding was that male semen contained the whole of nascent life. With no knowledge of eggs and ovulation, people assumed that the female body merely provided an incubating space. Hence the spilling of semen for any nonprocreative purpose—in coitus interruptus (Genesis 38:1-11), male homosexual acts, or male masturbation—was considered tantamount to abortion or murder. If my interpretation is correct, then it looks as if nearly half the human race should be sentenced to death for the act of spilling those seeds by virtue of masturbation, using a condom, and even having wet dreams.

Female homosexual acts, however, were not as seriously scrutinized and are not mentioned at all in the Old Testament (but see Romans. 1:26). This is telling in that it follows the hidden convention among heterosexual men that lesbianism is more acceptable than male homosexuality among African Americans (Herek, 1990). In addition, when a man acted sexually like a woman, male dignity was compromised. It was degradation not only with regard to himself, but for every other male. According to Wink (2000), the patriarchalism of Hebrew culture shows its hand in the very formulation of the commandment, since no similar structure was formulated to forbid homosexual acts among females. And the repugnance felt toward homosexuality was not just that it was deemed unnatural but also that it was considered un-Jewish, representing yet one more incursion of pagan civilization into Jewish life. In addition, nationalists could argue that homosexual White people are asserting their uncivilized tendencies against Africans (Welsing, 1991). On top of that is the more universal repugnance heterosexuals tend to feel for acts and orientations foreign to them.

In line with the punishment meted out by the Jamaican prisoners who killed a total of 16 suspected gay inmates in their prison 1997, and the punishment recommended by Buju Banton and Shabba Ranks, persons committing homosexual acts are to be executed. This is the command of Scripture. The meaning is clear: Anyone who wishes to base his or her beliefs on the witness of the Old Testament must be completely compliant with its prescriptions and demand the death penalty for everyone who performs homosexual acts. (This may seem extreme, but some Christians today actually urge this.) Even though no tribunal is likely to execute homosexuals ever again, a shocking number of gays are murdered by heterosexuals every day in America alone.

These Old Testament texts have to be weighed against those of the New. Consequently, Paul's unambiguous condemnation of homosexual behavior in Romans 1:26-27 must be the focal point of discourse. The Bible text also suggests that the women who exchanged natural intercourse for unnatural, and in the same way also men, giving up natural intercourse with women, were consumed with passion for one another. Men committed shameless acts with men and received their due penalty for their error.

But according to Wink (2000), Paul was unaware of the distinction between sexual orientation, over which one has apparently very little choice, and sexual behavior, over which one does. He seems to assume that those whom he condemns are heterosexual and are acting contrary to nature, "leaving," "giving up," or "exchanging" their regular sexual orientation for that which is foreign to them. Paul knew nothing of the modern psychosexual understanding of homosexuals as persons whose orientation is fixed early in life, or perhaps even at birth in some cases. For such persons, having heterosexual relations would be acting contrary to nature, "leaving," "giving up" or "exchanging" their natural sexual orientation. Wink (2000) also suggests that the relationships Paul describes are heavy with lust; they are not relationships of genuine same-sex love. They are not relationships between consenting adults who are committed to each other as faithfully and with as much integrity as any heterosexual couple.

As discussed in the work of West (1996), some people believe that venereal disease and AIDS are divine punishment for homosexual behavior; we know it as a risk involved in promiscuity of every stripe, homosexual and heterosexual. In fact, around the world the vast majority of people with AIDS are heterosexuals. If AIDS is divine punishment, why are nonpromiscuous lesbians at almost no risk of contracting the virus? Moreover, Wink argues that Paul believes that homosexuality is contrary to nature, whereas today it is a documented fact that other animal species practice homosexuality (but not solely) under the pressure of overpopulation. He also mentions that homosexuality appears to be a natural mechanism for a species to preserve itself. He accepts, however, that we cannot decide human ethical conduct solely on the basis of animal behavior or the human sciences, but in Romans 1:26-27 Paul argues from the standpoint of nature, as he himself says, and new knowledge of what is "natural" is therefore relevant here.

HEBREW SEXUAL TABOOS

According to the Bible, homosexuality is still a major taboo. Moreover, the Bible clearly prohibits homosexual activity. This does not, however, solve the problem of how Scripture is to be interpreted—because in reality, homosexuality is not the only sexual taboo. It is clear, though, that society is selective about the types of sexual behavior it stigmatizes. The Old Testament law strictly forbids sexual intercourse during the seven days of a woman's menstrual period (Leviticus 18:19; 15:19-24), and anyone in violation was to be "extirpated" or "cut off from their people" (*kareth*, a term in Leviticus 18:29, refers to execution by stoning, burning, strangling, or to flogging or expulsion; Leviticus 15:24 omits this penalty). If making love during menstruation results in extirpation, a lot of men are in serious trouble. The punishment for adultery was death by stoning for both the man and the woman (Deuteronomy 22:22), but here adultery is defined by the marital status of the *woman*. According to the Old Testament, a married man who has intercourse with an unmarried woman is not an adulterer. Does this mean a man is allowed to have affairs with women as long as she is not married? Does it mean a man cannot commit adultery against his own wife?

If you examine the entire issue of fidelity, the Bible goes so far as to suggest that it is taboo for a bride not to be a virgin; therefore, if she is discovered, she must be stoned to death (Deuteronomy 22:13-21). Male virginity at marriage, however, is never an issue. Considering the current debate on sexuality, it is evident that adultery, which creates far more social havoc, is considered less "sinful" than homosexual activity. Is this because there are more heterosexual adulterers than gays and lesbians in congregations? I'm sure some churches would like to bring back stoning as punishment for a number of "sins," but I haven't seen anyone line up to cast the first stone, despite the Scripture's clear commands, which Buju Banton and Shabba Ranks cite as the foundation of Biblical beliefs.

Another example: In Judaism, nudity was regarded as reprehensible (2 Samuel 6:20; 10:4; Isiah. 20:2-4; 47:3). When one of Noah's sons beheld his father naked, he was cursed (Genesis 9:20-27). This taboo probably even inhibited the sexual intimacy of husbands and wives to a great extent. We may not be prepared for nude beaches, but are we prepared to regard nudity in the locker room or in the privacy of one's home as an accursed *sin*? The Bible does. So here we sin again, every time we go for a sauna or a swim. Well, it appears that I have been sinning on a weekly basis every time I go swimming. I'll just have to watch out for those stones in between my strokes.

Polygamy and concubinage were regularly practiced in the Old Testament. Neither is condemned in the New Testament (with the questionable exceptions of 1 Timothy 3:2, 12, and Titus 1:6). Jesus' teaching about marital union in (Mark 10:6-8) is no exception, since he quotes (Genesis 2:24) as his authority, and this text was never understood in Israel as excluding polygamy. A man could become "one flesh" with more than one woman through the act of sexual intercourse. We know from Jewish sources that polygamy continued to be practiced within Judaism for centuries following the New Testament period. So if the Bible allows polygamy and concubinage, why don't we? Why disobey the Bible now?

A form of polygamy was the Levitate marriage. When a married man in Israel died childless, his widow was to have intercourse with each of his brothers in turn until she bore him a male heir. Jesus mentions this custom without criticism (Mark 12:18-27). As Christians, regardless of sexuality, would you want this law to be obeyed? Why is this law ignored, and the one against homosexuality preserved?

According to Wink (2000), The Old Testament does not explicitly prohibit sexual relations between unmarried consenting heterosexual adults as long as the woman's economic value (bride price) is not compromised; that is to say, as long as she is not a virgin. There are poems in the Song of Songs that eulogize a love affair between two unmarried persons, though commentators have often conspired to cover up the fact with heavy layers of allegorical interpretation. In various parts of the Christian world, quite different attitudes have prevailed about sexual intercourse before marriage. In some Christian communities, proof of fertility (that is, pregnancy) was requisite for marriage. This was especially the case in farming areas where the inability to produce children-workers could mean economic hardship. Today many single adults, the widowed, and the divorced are reverting to "biblical" practice while others believe that sexual intercourse belongs only within marriage. Both views are scriptural. Which is right?

The Bible lacks accurate terms for the sexual organs, content with euphemisms such as "foot" or "thigh" for the genitals and other euphemisms to describe coitus, such as "to know her." Today most of us regard such language as puritanical and contrary to a proper regard for the goodness of creation. In short, we do not follow Biblical practice.

Semen and menstrual blood rendered unclean all who touched them (Leviticus 15:16-24). Intercourse rendered one unclean until sundown; menstruation rendered the woman unclean for seven days. Today most people regard semen and menstrual fluid as natural and only at times "messy," not "unclean." It is interesting to note that while many men claim they do not make love to their partners during the menstrual cycle, they in fact do. If they say otherwise, they are in serious denial. I say this because menstruation is the one time of the month when you can more or less guarantee that a woman won't get pregnant. This is especially true for those men who are reluctant users of any form of male contraceptive.

In the Old Testament, social regulations regarding adultery, incest, rape, and prostitution are determined largely by considerations of male property rights over women. Prostitution was considered quite natural and necessary as a safeguard of the virginity of the unmarried and the property rights of husbands (Genesis 38:12-19; Joshua. 2:1-7). A man was not guilty of sin for visiting a prostitute, though the prostitute herself was regarded as a sinner. Paul must appeal to reason in attacking prostitution (1 Corinthians 6:12-20); he cannot lump it in the category of adultery (vs. 9). Today we are moving, with great social turbulence and at a high but necessary cost, toward a more equitable, nonpatriarchal set of social arrangements in which women are no longer regarded as the chattel of men. We are also trying to move beyond the double standard. Love, fidelity, and mutual respect replace property rights. We have, as yet, made very little progress in changing the double standard with regard to prostitution. As we leave behind patriarchal gender relations, what will we do with the patriarchalism in the Bible?

Jews were supposed to practice endogamy—that is, marriage within the 12 tribes of Israel. Until recently a similar rule prevailed in the American South in laws against interracial marriage (miscegenation). We have witnessed, within the lifetime of many of us, the nonviolent struggle to nullify state laws against intermarriage and the gradual change in social attitudes toward interracial relationships. Sexual taboos can alter quite radically even in a single lifetime. The law of Moses allowed for divorce (Deuteronomy 24:1-4); Jesus categorically forbids it (Mark 10:1-12; Matthew 19:9 softens his severity). Yet many Christians, in clear violation of a command of Jesus, get divorced. Why, then, do some of these very people consider themselves, but not homosexuals, eligible for baptism, church membership, communion, and ordination? What makes one a much greater sin than the other, especially considering that Jesus never mentioned homosexuality but explicitly condemned divorce? Yet we ordain divorcees. Why not homosexuals?

The Old Testament regarded celibacy as abnormal, and (1 Timothy 4:1-3) calls compulsory celibacy a heresy. Yet the Catholic Church has made it mandatory for priests and nuns. Some Christian ethicists demand celibacy of homosexuals, whether or not they have a vocation that requires celibacy. One argument is that since God made men and women for each other in order to be fruitful and multiply, homosexuals reject God's intent in creation. Those who argue this must explain why the apostle Paul never married—or, for that matter, why

Jesus, who incarnated God in his own person, was single. Certainly heterosexual marriage is *normal*, else the race would die out. But it is not *normative*. Otherwise, childless couples, single persons, priests, and nuns would be in violation of God's intention in their creation—as would Jesus and Paul. In an age of overpopulation, perhaps a gay orientation is especially sound ecologically.

In many other ways we have developed different norms from those explicitly laid down by the Bible: "If men get into a fight with one another, and the wife of one intervenes to rescue her husband from the grip of his opponent by reaching out and seizing his genitals, you shall cut off her hand; show no pity" (Deuteronomy. 25:11f). We, on the contrary, might very well applaud her. The Old and New Testaments both regarded slavery as normal and nowhere categorically condemn it. Part of that heritage was the use of female slaves, concubines, and captives as sexual toys or breeding machines by their male owners, which (Leviticus 19:20f., 2 Samuel. 5:13, and Numbers. 31:18) permitted—and as many American slave owners did some 130 years ago, citing these and numerous other scripture passages as their justification.

THE PROBLEM OF AUTHORITY

According to Wink (2000) These cases are relevant to our attitude toward the authority of Scripture. Clearly we regard certain things, especially in the Old Testament, as no longer binding. Other things we regard as binding, including legislation in the Old Testament that is not mentioned at all in the New. What is our principle of selection here? For example, modern readers *agree* with the Bible in rejecting incest, rape, adultery, and intercourse with animals, but we *disagree* with the Bible on most other sexual taboos. The Bible *condemned* the following behaviors, which we generally *allow:* intercourse during menstruation, celibacy, endogamy, naming sexual organs, nudity (under certain conditions), masturbation (Catholicism excepted), and birth control (Catholicism excepted). And the Bible regarded semen and menstrual blood as unclean, which we do not. Likewise, the Bible *permitted* behaviors that we today *condemn:* prostitution, polygamy, Levitate marriage, sex with slaves, concubinage, treatment of women as property, and very early marriage (for the girl, age 11-13).

And while the Old Testament accepted divorce, Jesus forbade it. Why then do people appeal to proof texts in Scripture in the case of homosexuality alone, while they feel perfectly free to disagree with Scripture in regard to most other sexual issues? Obviously, many of our choices in these matters are arbitrary. Mormon polygamy was out-lawed in this country despite the constitutional protection of freedom of religion, because it violated the sensibilities of the dominant Christian culture. Yet no explicit biblical prohibition against polygamy exists. The problem of authority is not mitigated by the doctrine that the *cultic* requirements of the Old Testament were abrogated by the New, and that only the *moral* commandments of the Old Testament remain in force. For most of these sexual taboos fall among the moral commandments. If we insist on placing ourselves under the old law, then, as Paul reminds us, we are obligated to keep *every* commandment of the law (Galatians 5:3). But if Christ is the end of the law (Romans 10:4), if we have been discharged from the law to serve, not under the old written code but in the new life of the Spirit (Romans 7:6), then all of these biblical sexual taboos come under the authority of the Spirit. We cannot then take even what Paul says as a new law. Fundamentalists themselves reserve the right to pick and choose which laws they will keep, though they seldom admit it.

Judge for Yourselves

The crux of the matter, it seems, is that the Bible has no sexual ethic. *There is no biblical sex ethic.* Instead, it exhibits a variety of sexual taboos, some of which changed over the 1,000-year span of biblical history. Taboos are unreflective customs accepted by a given community. Many of the practices prohibited in the Bible we allow, and many that it allows, we prohibit. *The Bible knows only a love ethic, which is constantly being brought to bear on whatever sexual taboos are domi-nant in any given country, or culture, or period.* The notion of a "sex ethic" reflects the materialism and fractured state of modern life, in which we increasingly define our identity sexually. Sexuality cannot be separated from the rest of life. No sex act is "ethical" in and of itself, without reference to the rest of a person's life, the patterns of the cul-ture, the special circumstances faced, and the will of God. What we have are simply sexual taboos that change, sometimes with startling rapidity, creating bewildering dilemmas. Within the span of just a life-time we have witnessed the shift from the ideal of preserving one's vir-ginity until marriage to couples living together for several years before getting married. The response of many Christians is merely to long for the hypocrisies of an earlier era.

Wink (2000) argues that our moral task, rather, is to apply Jesus' love ethic to whatever sexual taboos are prevalent in a given culture.

We might address younger teens, not with laws and commandments whose violation is a sin, but rather with the sad experiences of so many of our own children who find too much early sexual intimacy overwhelming, and who react by voluntary celibacy and even the refusal to date. We can offer reasons, not empty and unenforceable orders. We can challenge both gays and straights to question their behaviors in the light of love and the requirements of fidelity, honesty, responsibility, and genuine concern for the best interests of the other and of society as a whole. Christian morality, after all, is not a iron chastity belt for repressing urges, but a way of expressing the integrity of our relationship with God. It is the attempt to discover a manner of living that is consistent with who God created us to be.

For those of same-sex orientation, being moral means rejecting sexual taboos that violate their own integrity and that of others, and attempting to discover what it would mean to live by the love ethic of Jesus. Morton Kelsey goes so far as to argue that homosexual orientation has nothing to do with morality as such, any more than left-handedness. It is simply the way some people's sexuality is configured. Morality enters at the point of how that predisposition is enacted. If we view it as a God-given gift to those for whom it is normal, we could move beyond the acrimony and brutality that have so often characterized the un-Christian behavior of Christians toward gays.

Approached from the point of view of love rather than that of law, the issue is at once transformed. Now the question is not "What is permitted?" but rather "What does it mean to love my homosexual neighbor?" Approached from the point of view of faith rather than works, the question ceases to be "What constitutes a breach of divine law in the sexual realm?" and becomes instead "What constitutes integrity before the God revealed in the cosmic lover, Jesus Christ?" Approached from the point of view of the Spirit rather than the letter, the question ceases to be "What does Scripture command?" and becomes "What is the Word that the Spirit speaks to the churches now, in the light of Scripture, tradition, theology, psychology, genetics, anthropology, and biology?"

In a little-remembered statement, Jesus said, "Why do you not judge for yourselves what is right?" (Luke 12:57). Such sovereign freedom strikes terror in the hearts of many Christians; they would rather be under law and be *told* what is right. Yet Paul himself echoes Jesus' sentiment immediately preceding one of his possible references to homosexuality: "Do you not know that we are to judge angels? How much more, matters pertaining to this life!" (1 Corinthians 6:3). The last thing Paul would want is for people to respond to his ethical advice as a new law engraved on tablets of stone. He is himself trying to "judge for himself what is right." If new evidence is in on the phenomenon of homosexuality, are we not obligated—no, *free*—to reevaluate the whole issue in the light of all the available data and decide, under God, for ourselves? Is this not the radical freedom for obedience in which the gospel establishes us?

It may, of course, be objected that the Wink (2000) analysis has drawn our noses so close to texts that the general tenor of the whole Bible is lost. The Bible clearly considers homosexual behavior a sin, and whether it is stated three times or 3,000 is beside the point. Just as some of us grew up "knowing" that homosexual acts were the unutterable sin, though no one ever spoke about it, so the whole Bible "knows" it to be wrong.

The issue is precisely whether that biblical judgment is correct. The Bible sanctioned slavery as well and nowhere is it attacked. Are Africans in the diaspora prepared to argue that slavery today is biblically justified? One hundred and fifty years ago, when the debate over slavery was raging, the Bible seemed to be clearly on the side of slaveholders. Abolitionists were hard-pressed to justify their opposition to slavery on biblical grounds. Yet today, if you were to ask Christians in the South whether the Bible sanctions slavery, nearly everyone would agree that it does not. How do we account for such a monumental shift? What happened is that the churches were finally driven to penetrate beyond the legal tenor of Scripture to an even deeper tenor, articulated by Israel out of the experience of the Exodus and the prophets and brought to sublime embodiment in Jesus' identification with harlots, tax collectors, the diseased and maimed and outcast and poor. It is that God sides with the powerless. God liberates the oppressed. God suffers with the suffering and groans toward the reconciliation of all things.

In the light of that supernal compassion, whatever our position on homosexuality, the gospel's imperative to love, care for, and be identified with their sufferings is unmistakably clear. In the same way, women are pressing us to acknowledge the sexism and patriarchalism that pervades Scripture and has alienated so many women from the church. The way out, however, is not to deny the sexism in Scripture, but to develop an interpretive theory that judges even Scripture in the light of the revelation in Jesus. What Jesus gives us is a critique of domination in all its forms, a critique that can be turned on the Bible itself.

Wink (2000) correctly argues that the Bible thus contains the principles of its own correction. We are freed from bibliolatry, the worship of the Bible. It is restored to its proper place as witness to the Word of God. And that word is a person, not a book. With the interpretative grid provided by a critique of domination, we are able to filter out the sexism, patriarchalism, violence, and homophobia that are very much a part of the Bible, thus liberating it to reveal to us in fresh ways the in breaking, in our time, of God's domination-free order.

Special thanks to Walter Wink, professor of biblical interpretation at Auburn Theological Seminary in New York City.

REFERENCES

Allport, G. (1954). *The Nature of Prejudice*. New York: Addison Wesley.

Amiri, B./Jones, L. (1979). *Selected Poetry*. New York: William Morrow.

Eldridge C. (1968). *Soul On Ice*. New York: McGraw-Hill.

Herek, G. M. & Capitanio, J. P. (1995). "Black Heterosexuals' Attitudes Toward Lesbians and Gay Men in the United States." *Journal of Sex Research* 32 (2): 95-105.

Welsing, F. C. (1991). *The Isis (Yssis) papers*. Chicago: Third World Press.

West, C. (1996). *Race Matters*. New York: Vintage Books.

Wink, W. (2000). "Homosexuality in the Bible." www.bridges-across.org/ba/wink.htm

Feeling the Spirit in the Dark: Expanding Notions of the Sacred in the African American Gay Community

E. Patrick Johnson

"Darkness falls as the gay male subculture gets to work, late. The thick blanket of darkness is a cover, a protector of anonymity and an erotic focus: a mantle of oppression and opposition. It heightens the danger as it provides the pleasure. This tension between pleasure and danger, dream and nightmare, is a major source of its eroticism."
—Tim Edwards, *Erotics & Politics*

"Spirit in the Dark" is one of many songs recorded by the "Queen of Soul" diva, Aretha Franklin, that blurs the boundaries between the sacred and the secular—both through its lyrics and its musical composition. Fueled with the vocal melismas and rhythmic syncopation found in gospel and blues, Franklin's song uses the sacred notion of "spirit" as a metaphor for sexual ecstasy as she sings, "It's like Sally Walker, sitting in her saucer. That's how you do it. It ain't nothing to it. Ride, Sally, ride. Put your hands on your hips and cover your eyes and move with the spirit in the dark." While some listeners might argue that the reference to spirit in this song is symbolic of the "holy" spirit, those of us who hear the double entendre know that Franklin's use of this word is much more fluid. Indeed, she endows Sally Walker, the innocent and chaste little girl of the famous children's nursery rhyme, with sexual agency as Franklin encourages Sally to "ride" the spirit in the dark.

"Spirit in the Dark" also highlights the dichotomy of body and soul within the black church, the belief that to be "saved" means not to yield to temptations of the flesh. Within the context of the black church, feeling the spirit in the secular/sexual sense is an act of transgression, a symptom of the "sinsick" soul. And in the most fundamentalist interpretations of the Bible, the sin of the flesh will pave a slippery road to the fiery gates of hell and into everlasting darkness. Although this split of the spirit and flesh is continually preached from the pulpit, it is rarely practiced by the deliverer of the message and the congregants who listen. But this denial of the flesh encourages an unhealthy and unrealistic view of sexuality and the body in general. Indeed, feeling the spirit under these conditions may only happen under a shroud of darkness because the spirit and flesh never unite, never become one incarnation through the body of Christ.

This essay focuses on how African American gays have attempted to reconcile the spirit and the flesh by moving from "place to space." Drawing heavily upon Michel de Certeau's formulation of place and space, Vivian M. Patraka (1996) argues that "place refers to a prescripted performance of interpretation, while space produces sites for multiple performances of interpretation, which situate/produce the spectator as historical subject" (Patraka 1996, 100). In their attempt to be closer to God and to express their sexuality, black gay men transgressively unite body and soul by moving from the prescripted "place" of the black church into the ambiguous "space" of the gay nightclub. Thus the notion of feeling the spirit in the dark engenders a celebration of the black gay body as well as a communion with the Holy Spirit. Precisely because the black gay and Christian body are highlighted in performance, the veil of darkness dividing body from soul in the "place" of the black church is lifted in the darkened "space" of the gay nightclub.

BODY AND SOUL

In her song, Aretha Franklin, daughter of Reverend C.L. Franklin, embodies the blurring of sacred and secular boundaries found in many African American expressive traditions from spirituals and gospel to blues and folk preaching. The reasons for such blurring are multiple. One reason is that African Americans' notion of the sacred is connected to the reality of their daily lives. For instance, it is not uncommon to find African Americans who party all night on Saturday but never fail to miss Sunday school the next morning (in some instances the same musicians who play in nightclubs are those who also provide the music for the church); or who, like Franklin, use sacred or biblical language to comment on everyday life, as is the case with phrases such as, "The Lord don't like ugly, so He must hate you," used to comment on someone's unattractiveness rather than their sinfulness. And even more generally, the black church has always been a site of social transgression, from the days of slavery when folk preachers drew upon the signifying tradition to encode sermons about a better life in heaven with messages of insurrection and directions for how to escape to the North to ministers such as Martin Luther King Jr., who used the church as a site of political activism during the Civil Rights Movement. In fact, at every significant moment in African American history, the church has been a centralizing and galvanizing force for social and political change. Thus the black church has always served a dual role within the black community: It has served as place to worship God and a place to address the social and political needs of its constituents.

The church has been less willing to blur the secular and the sacred when it comes to sexuality, however. According to minister and cultural critic, Michael Dyson,

> "Sex...is a difficult subject to treat in the black church, or for that matter, in any church. This is indeed ironic. After all, the Christian faith is grounded in the Incarnation, the belief that God took on flesh to redeem human beings. That belief is constantly being trumped by Christianity's quarrels with the body. Its needs. Its desires. Its sheer materiality. But especially its sexual identity (Dyson 1996, 80)."

When the church does address sexuality, it does so by exhorting the glories of sexual expression between heterosexuals within the institution of marriage (and usually for the purpose of procreation as opposed to recreation). Single members of the congregation are expected to remain celibate until marriage. And although many heterosexual members of the church—married and single—engage in out-of-wedlock, multipartnered, and even anonymous sex, the condemnation these members receive (if they are condemned at all) is tempered by the fact that the sex in which they engage is still *heterosexual*. Indeed, a certain amount of heterosexual loose play is accepted as a normal part of the church community—even, or especially, among its anointed.

Thus African American folklore consistently depicts preachers as lovers of women, money, cars, chicken, and liquor—in essence, as pimps. One of Daryl Dance's folktales, collected in her book, *Shukin' and Jivin'*, provides a perfect example:

> Say John came in and his wife hadn't cooked or nothin'. And say all at once, she jumped up. She spied a chicken out in the yard. Say she jumped up and started runnin' after the chicken. Her husband say, "What in de worl' you runnin' dem chickens like dat for?" Say, "You ain't even cooked no supper or nuttin'."

She say, "De preacher want chicken."
He say, "Fuck de Preacher!"
She say, "I done did dat, but the Preacher *still* want chicken"
(Dance 1978, 55).

Such a story clearly reflects the congregation's need to ridicule an authority figure: The black preacher's historically high position within African American communities makes him only too vulnerable to ridicule and satire. Moreover, the lore of the minister/pimp calls attention to the hypocrisy of the black preacher. Michael Dyson (1996) offers a firsthand account of the minister who does not practice what he preaches. After delivering a sermon that encourages sexual propriety and condemns promiscuity, a visiting minister, along with four other clergy, including Dyson, meet in the pastor's office. There the visitor asks the host pastor about a woman in the congregation:

"Revrun, I need to ask you something," the visiting preacher begged the pastor. "Who is that woman with those big breasts who was sitting on the third aisle to my left?" he eagerly inquired. "Damn, she kept shouting and jiggling so much I almost lost my concentration."

"She *is* a fine woman now," the pastor let on.

"Well, Doc, do you think you could fix me up with her?" the visiting preacher asked with shameless lust.

"I'll see what I can do, Revrun," the pastor promised
(Dyson 1996, 81).

Dyson is shocked by this pastor's blatant display of lust, particularly after having admonished the congregants to "stop [their] rovin' eyes":

The fact that he [the visiting pastor] could seek an affair less than an hour after he had thundered against it offended my naïve literal sense of the Christian faith. I thought immediately of how angry I'd been in the past when I heard preachers justify their moral failings, especially their sexual faults. Such ministers chided their followers with a bit of theological doggerel dressed up as a maxim: "God can hit a straight lick with a crooked stick."

The point to be made, however, is that while the prevalence of the minister in folklore suggests that lusting preachers are unacceptable, the black church tolerates the obvious paradox of their behavior in a way that nonetheless makes heterosexuality normal. Consequently, those heterosexual church members who "yield to the flesh" are rarely, if ever, asked to leave the church.

But whether embraced by its constituents or not, the black church has always been a site of contradictions where sexuality is concerned. In fact, one might argue that the body is the one organizing site of multiple and competing signifiers within the black church service. Congregants perform the black body and inspire performance in others through the various rituals of the service, Dyson writes:

> The black church...is full of beautiful, boisterous, burdened, and brilliant black bodies in various stages of praising, signifying, testifying, shouting, prancing, screaming, musing, praying, mediating, singing, whooping, hollering, prophesying, preaching, dancing, witnessing, crying, faking, marching, forgiving, damning, exorcising, lying, confessing, surrendering, and overcoming. There is a relentless procession, circulation, and movement of black bodies in the black church (Dyson 1996, 88).

As seen in Aretha Franklin's song, these black bodies in motion conjure and inspire not only a "holy" spirit, but also a sensuous and sexual one. When congregants "feel the spirit," their bodies are flung into motion in ways that transform the sacred body into a very secular body, a body that weds the spiritual with the sexual. Within the context of the sacred "place" of the church, however, the sexual/sensual body is both invisible and foregrounded, shunned and gazed upon, denigrated and enjoyed. The black body is theologized as a "temple of the Lord," as a vessel that should be kept pure and "clean." However, when church members try to put this doctrine into practice, both in and outside the context of the church, their guilt about their carnal thoughts reinforces the false dichotomy between the spirit and the flesh.

Nowhere is this false dichotomy foregrounded more than within the traditional African American worship service. The entire church service may be likened to a sexual encounter: There is flirting, petting, foreplay, orgasm, and postcoital bliss. Indeed, "the black worship experience formed the erotic body of black religious belief, with all rites of religious arousal that accompany sexual union" (Dyson 1996, 91). Every aspect of the black church service is centered around the preacher's message; and at its height, a preacher's sermon may galvanize a congregation into a state of spiritual ecstasy that coalesces with feelings one experiences during orgasm: "It requires no large sophistication to tell that something like sexual stimulation [is] going on" (Dyson 1996, 1991).

Secular Bodies/Sacred Spaces

Commenting on the performance "place" of the black church from a queer perspective, African American gay writers often highlight the sexual tension present in the black church worship service. Moreover, these writers expand upon the folkloric figure of the lusting minister, which rests uneasily beside the minister's homophobic attitude. Thus, these writers deftly demonstrate how insidious and oppressive the place of church is. Alternatively, African American gay writers attempt to transgress the performance place of the black church by queering the gaze of the worshiping body. In his first novel, *Go Tell It On the Mountain,* James Baldwin calls attention to the sensuality and sexuality of the black worship service. In the novel, Baldwin worries about the distinction between the spirit and flesh by embellishing not only the eroticism but also the homoeroticism implicit in the black church worship service. Early in the book, for instance, Baldwin describes a typical worship service at The Temple of Fire Baptized as seen through the eyes of John, the novel's protagonist, who throughout the course of the novel tries to come to terms with his homosexuality by reconciling it with his faith. In the following passage the reader glimpses not only the sensuality of the black worship service, but also how the black body becomes eroticized when overcome by the Holy Ghost. Through John, we specifically see the eroticism evoked by Elisha's body, the object of John's gaze:

> At one moment, head back, eyes closed, sweat standing on his brow, he sat at the Piano, singing and playing; and then, like a great, black cat in trouble in the jungle, he stiffened and trembled and cried out. *Jesus, Jesus, oh, Lord Jesus!* He struck one last wild note and threw up his hands, palms upward, stretched wide apart. The Tambourines raced to fill the vacuum left by his silent piano, and his cry drew answering cries.

Then he was on his feet, turning blind and congested, contorted with his rage, and muscles leaping and swelling in his long, dark neck. It seemed that he could not breathe, that his body could not contain the passion that he would be, before their eyes, dispersed into the waiting air. His hands, rigid to the very finger tips, moved outward and back against his hips, his sightless eyes looked upward, and he began to dance. Then he closed his fists, and his head snapped downward, his sweat loosening the grease that slicked down his hair; and rhythm of all others quickened to match Elisha's rhythm; his thighs moved terribly against the cloth of his suit, his heels beat on the floor, and his fists moved beside his body as though he were beating his own drum. And so, for a while, in the center of the dancers, head down, fists beating, on, on, on unbearably, until it seemed the walls of the church would fall for very sound; and then, in a moment, with a cry, head up, arms high in the air, sweat pouring from his forehead, and all his body dancing as though it would never stop. Sometimes he did not stop until he fell—until he dropped like some animal felled by a hammer-moaning, on his face. And then a great moaning filled the church (15-16).

In this passage, Elisha's body becomes the site of both sexuality and spirituality. Consumed by the generative power of the Holy Ghost, Elisha "stiffened and trembled"; his muscles were "leaping and swelling" and his "body could not contain the passion." The passage builds into a climax until Elisha drops "and a great moaning filled the church." After only a paragraph break, the text moves from orgasmic language to public scorn accorded the carnal thoughts of Elisha and his girlfriend, Ella Mae Washington: "There was sin among them. One Sunday, when regular service was over, Father James had uncovered sin in the congregation of the righteous. He had uncovered Elisha and Ella Mae. They had been 'walking disorderly' " (16). Therefore, Baldwin calls attention to the irony of Elisha's sexuality both as it manifests itself in the act of worship and as it expresses itself toward another.

Ultimately, Baldwin challenges the split between the spirit and the flesh, between spirituality and sexuality, especially given that our sexuality is preached as something "God given" and integral to our humanity. Florence, the only character in the novel whose name is not derived from the Bible, remarks that "what's in you is in you, and it's got to come out" (180). Florence's words reflect the common saying in the black church that one should not try to "quench the spirit." But in the context of the novel, Florence is specifically referring to her brother Gabriel's "chasing after women and lying in the ditches, drunk" (180), which implies that "what's in you" is also sexual and that too must be made manifest. Baldwin's critique of religion, then, rests on the premise that the body and soul are one and neither should be denied. Moreover, Baldwin reveals through the gayness of John's gaze upon Elisha's worshipping body that the Christian body may also be a queer body.

If the church holds a contradictory and duplicitous attitude toward sexuality in regard to its heterosexual members, the same is true for its attitude toward its gay and lesbian members. Even though they comprise a large majority of those who hold positions in the church—from usher to preacher—African American gays are not afforded the same latitude in terms of expressing their sexuality (or spirituality) as their heterosexual counterparts. Though they might express "femininity"—a gender role stereotypically associated with gayness, but nonetheless tolerated by church members—African American gay men are rarely if ever out of the closet. Such a blatant expression of one's sexuality would be an affront to the fundamentalist conventions of the church, even though this attitude embodies a double standard in terms of who can and cannot express sexual agency within the black church.

Indeed, in the "place" of the church, heterosexual members maintain a hierarchy intent on hiding their own sins of the flesh, creating not a sacred "space" (a site that invites multiple acts of interpretations)—but a sacred "place" (a site prescripted and narrativized in advance). Again, African American gay critics and writers observe the limitations of the church performance place through personal testimonies, memoirs, poems, novels, and short stories. In particular, these writers depict a place in which heterosexual members treat gayness as an illness. As with other forms of "sinsickness," the church's answer to homosexuality is exorcism. For example, when Johnny Rae Rousseau, the protagonist in Larry Duplechan's novel *Blackbird* comes out to his pastor, rather than affirm Johnny's gay identity and reassure him of God's love irrespective of sexual orientation, the minister dismisses Johnny's confession as temptation by Satan and proceeds to lay his hands on him. Johnny tells the reader:

What Daniel did was wrinkle his one great eyebrow and

assure me...that I was indeed not a homosexual at all, but that Satan had planted this wild notion in my mind to test the steadfastness of my Christian commitment.

"Satan will often suggest (ahem) certain ungodly desires to the minds and hearts of Christian young people," said Daniel....

Daniel then proceeded to lay hands on me and pray for my speedy deliverance from these unnatural and ungodly desires, instructed me to pray likewise daily, assured me that of course this entire matter was strictly between the two of us, and sent me on my way (150).

This pathologizing of homosexuality as "unnatural" and "ungodly" creates a hostile, oppressive, and homophobic environment for gays and lesbians—an environment that is, according to Christian doctrine, supposed to foster community and acceptance through Christ. Instead, "the homosexual dimension of eroticism remains cloaked in taboo or blanketed in theological attack. As a result, the black church, an institution that has been at the heart of black emancipation, refuses to unlock the oppressive closet for gays and lesbians" (Dyson 1996, 105).

Another example of the church condemning homosexuality as a sinsickness to be exorcised is found in Craig G. Harris's short story "Cut Off From Among his People" in which the story's narrator, Jeff, remembers the funeral of his lover who has died of AIDS. Homophobia pervades the service; the minister's eulogy insidiously equates AIDS with homosexuality, contending that the disease is a sickness of the soul for which the only cure is an exorcism of the sin of gayness. The preacher proselytizes:

In Leviticus, Chapter 20, the Lord tell[s] us: If a man also lie with mankind as he lieth with a woman, both of them have committed an abomination: they shall surely be put to death; their blood shall be upon them. There's no cause to wonder why medical science could not find a cure for this man's illness. How could medicine cure temptation? What drug can exorcise Satan from a young man's soul? The only cure is to be found in the Lord. The only cure is repentance, for Leviticus clearly tells us, "...whoever shall commit them shall be cut off from among their people (66).

Indeed, black gay men are "cut off from among their people" when those people—family, friends, church members—fail to provide an affirming and supportive environment in which their humanity is acknowledged, particularly during times of bereavement. Later in the same story, the undertaker is the only member of the church to extend compassion to the mourning lover. Recalling the pain of losing his own lover to AIDS three months earlier, the undertaker elaborates on the continual dismissal of the black gay body by the church:

> It's been very difficult—living with these memories and secrets and hurt and with no one to share them. These people won't allow themselves to understand. If it's not preached from a pulpit and kissed up to the Almighty, they don't want to know about it. So I hold it in, and hold it in, and then I see you passing, one after the other—tearless funerals, the widowed treated like nonentities, and these 'another faggot burns in hell' sermons. My heart goes out to you, brother. You got to let your love for him keep you strong (67).

The undertaker captures well the hurt and pain inflicted by those who preach love and compassion but whose practice of such virtues is limited to specific members of the church and the African American community at large.

Most insidious about the church's denouncement of homosexuality, however, is its exploitation of its gay members. As with Elisha in *Go Tell It On the Mountain*, who serves as the church pianist, the church exploits the musical talents, financial savvy, and leadership abilities of gays. At the same time that it denies homosexuality as a valid form of black Christian sexuality—and denies the homosexual his/her rightful place among the "saints"—it uses the black gay body to bring others to Christ. Dyson writes:

> One of the most painful scenarios of black church life is repeated Sunday after Sunday with little notice or collective outrage. A black minister will preach a sermon railing against sexual ills, especially homosexuality. At the close of the sermon, a soloist, who everybody knows is gay, will rise to perform a moving number, as the preacher extends an invitation to visitors to join the church. The soloist is, in effect, being asked to sing, and to sing his theological death sentence. His

presence at the end of such a sermon symbolizes a silent endorsement of the preacher's message (Dyson 1996, 105).

Dyson's scenario rings true for many gay men who use their musical talents in the church but who, ironically, are called to affirm a theology of hate rather than of love and acceptance. In the church performance "place," however, the gay man's complicity in his own oppression is common, for not only is a performance place "linked to a single narrative; it is a single performance of interpretation elicited by that narrative...Moreover, our bodies are implicated in the task by performing the required movement" (Patraka 1996, 100). How then, does the black gay Christian affirm his fellow heterosexual brothers and sisters in Christ? Indeed, how does he go about "feeling the spirit"? One answer to these questions is the move from place to space, the church to the club—"the liberating move that allows [them] to understand experience of everyday life" (Patraka 1996, 100).

Removed from the homophobic, guilt-ridden, and self-hating rhetoric of many black churches, the gay nightclub has become an alternative space in which African American gay men can express their spirituality as well as their sexuality. By incorporating sacred traditions found in African American culture and infusing them in the secular space of the gay nightclub, African American gay men have created a self-validating environment in which they possess sexual agency on the one hand, and are possessed by the spirit on the other.

"Hold My Mule"

It is well-known throughout black gay communities that Washington, D.C., is a gathering place for black gay men during Memorial Day weekend; alternatively, Atlanta is the hottest spot during Labor Day weekend. On these two holidays in these two respective cities, African American men from around the country gather to celebrate their blackness and their gayness (both cities have a high black and gay population), to meet potential life partners, to "hook up" for the weekend, and to commune with one another.

It's Labor Day weekend, 1995. I take a trip to Atlanta to visit friends, to escape from my mostly white New England environment, and to return home to the South to find refuge amongst my black queer peers. During my stay my friends take me to a number of gay nightclub; some are predominately white, some racially mixed, others predominately African American. One of the more popular African

American clubs we visit is called "Tracks" or "The Warehouse," though it is a gay venue only on Fridays and Saturdays. We go to Tracks on Saturday, arriving just past midnight. Located about a mile and half from downtown Atlanta, Tracks is indistinguishable from the other warehouses in the industrial district—indistinguishable, that is, except for the line of people that coils around the side of the building and down the block. While standing in line, we overhear the catty yet playful conversations of those in front and back of us: "She [he] think she cute. Too bad she ain't" (laughter); "Chile, I ain't tryin' to be standin' in this line all night—not with these pumps on!"; "Look, Miss Thing. I ain't got no other ID. Miss Thing at the door better not try to be shady. I'll cut her ass." In general, we cruise and get cruised, negotiate sexual deals. We're all men on a mission. I know I'm home.

Inside, the club is sparsely decorated, which makes it appear even larger than its 3,500 square feet. The entrance is on the second level, which overlooks the dance floor and resembles the second floor of a shopping mall. Around the edge of this level are booths, dimly lit by red votives. Above each booth are pictures taken of scantily clothed or naked black men from the "Brothers" 1995 Black Gay Men's Calendar. Some of the models are at the club taking pictures with patrons and signing the calendars. The first floor has two bars on each side of the dance floor and a raised stage at the far end of the room. On the edge of the stage, on each corner, are two huge column speakers that rise about ten feet in the air. Colored moving lights don the ceiling along with a mirrored disco ball.

My friends and I squeeze down the staircase and descend into the sea of bodies and onto the dance floor. There is barely enough room to breathe, let alone move. Every inch of the space is filled with a body: fat bodies, thin bodies, hard bodies, soft bodies, warm bodies, sweaty bodies, every body imaginable. Clearly, the body is on display: drag queens in skintight hot pants and platform shoes; "butch" men donning black leather jackets, lining the wall like two-by-fours holding the structure together; "queens" in tight black jeans and black chiffon blouses unbuttoned to their navels, constantly pursing their lips while looking over the tops of their retro cat's-eye shades; older men (in this club anyone over 45) sitting on barstools, dressed conservatively in slacks and button-up shirts sipping their scotch and sodas while looking longingly at the young bodies sauntering across the dance floor.

The hip-hop contingent is sprinkled throughout the club in baggy jeans, ski caps, sneakers, and black shades, some sucking on blow pops while others sip Budweisers. And then there are those like me and my friends who are dressed in designer jeans (Calvin Klein) and tight span-dex muscle shirts, performing middle class (acting bourgeois)—as if we actually have two nickels to rub together! You can smell us coming because we sprayed and resprayed cologne behind our ankles, on the small of our backs, and, of course on the front of our chests and all around our necks. We're beyond reproach. We manage to dance—spoon fashion—the seemingly thousands of flying arms, legs, and butts.

I dance with the same man all night—Kevin—a friend of a friend. Kevin and I don't mean to be exclusive dance partners; it just works out that way. We dance close. Every now and then we back off from one another as far as we can and then come together again. We kiss. We bump booties. We hold on to each other for dear life as the beat of the music, the smells of Drakkar, Cool Water, Eternity, Escape, and CK one, the sweat drenching our shirts, and the holy sexual spirit that pre-sides works us into a shamanistic euphoria. Time stands still.

Around 5 A.M. the mood of the club shifts, and there is a feeling of anticipation in the air. The music shifts to—No, it couldn't be!—what sounds like the "shout" music played in my church back home. Kevin and I stare at each other with carnal intensity as the driving rhythm of the music makes us grind harder. Before long the DJ, a 300-pound African American man dressed in a flowing white shirt, blue jeans, high-top sneakers, a thick gold chain, glittering rings on either hand, a baseball cap, and diamond-trimmed sunglasses appears on the stage and begins a roll call of different locations:

"We got any L.A. in the house? Show your hands if you're from the gay mecca of D.C.! How about the northern children from Ms. New York City? Detroit! Chicago! We got any Boston children up in here? And last, but not least, let me see the children from Hotlanta!" We cheer and wave our hands in the air when our city is called. Then, intermittently dispersed throughout the music, are sound bites from gospel singer Shirley Caesar's song "Hold My Mule": "It's just like fire!"; "Somebody say yes (yes), say yes (yes), yes (yes)"; "If you don't stop dancing!"; "You come to tell me that I dance too much!"; "I'm gonna shout right here!" While this musical interlude continues, the DJ begins to testify:

"Thank Him! For how He kept you safe over the dangerous high-ways and byways. Thank Him, because you closed in your right mind!"

"Somebody say yes (yes), say yes (yes), yes (yes)."

"Look around you. Somebody that was here last year ain't here tonight! Look around you! Somebody that was dancing right next to you ain't here tonight! Look around you! Somebody's lover has passed on! Look around you! Somebody's brother, somebody's sister, somebody's cousin, somebody's uncle done gone on to the Maker. Sister Mary has passed on tonight! Brother Joe has gone on to his resting place! But Grace woke you up this morning! Grace started you on your way! Grace put food you your table! How many of you know what I'm talking about?!"

"It's just like fire! It's just like fire! It's just like fire. Shut up in my bones."

"If He's been good to you, let me see you wave your hands."

"Somebody say yes (yes), say yes (yes), yes (yes)."

Kevin and I, along with others, dance to the beat of the music, waving our hands, crying, kissing, and shouting "Yes!" A drag queen appears from nowhere and begins to walk around the side of the dance floor beating a tambourine to the beat of the rhythm. The house music swells as the DJ sermonizes in the manner of an African American folk preacher, embodying the chant-like cadence and rhythm of the preacher's voice. He chants the old folk church song "Ninety-nine and a Half Won't Do," to get his message across. Thus, to the rhythm of the music he sermonizes:

"Twenty-two just won't do; 33, just look at me; 44, I need some more; 55, I'm still alive; 66, I'm in the mix; 77, on my way to Heaven; 88, got my business straight; 99, I'm still climbing; 99 won't do; 99 won't do; 99 won't do."

The DJ's preaching, along with the repetitive beat of the music, works us into a frenzy. The echoes of my Southern Baptist minister's sermons consume my thoughts...yield not to temptation...I dance on... something got a hold on me...Kevin pins me against the wall...it's just like fire!. . I consume his tongue..."There was sin among them."...I feel the tears well up in my eyes..."It seemed that he could not breathe, that his body could not contain this passion"...I dance on...Somebody say yes (yes), say yes (yes), yes (yes)...A drag queen sobs silently with her hands stretched upward..."Whoever shall commit any of these abominations, even the souls that commit them, shall be cut off from among their people"...It's just like fire!...Thank you, Jesus!...We dance on ..."and the rhythm of all the others quickened to match Elisha's rhythm"...You come to tell me that I dance too much!...I'm aroused by his touch...For I have touched the hem of His garment..."his thighs moved terribly against the cloth of his suit"...99 won't do...his fists moved beside his body as though he were beating his own drum"... my body seeks joy...It's just like fire!..."and then, in a moment, with a..." Thank Him!... I'm gonna shout right here..."head up, arms high in the air...You come to tell me that I dance too much...If a man lie with mankind....My groin aches..."sweat pouring from his forehead, and all his body dancing as though it would never stop"... I weep...Hold my mule... Dancing... "he dropped like some animal felled by a hammer... Kevin holds me up...Hold my mule...I dance too much...Kevin wipes my tears... Hold my mule... "moaning on his face"...abomination... Hold my mule Say yes (yes), say (yes), say (yes)...How many of you know what I'm talking about?...Hold my mule.. we feel the spirit... Hold my mule..."a great moaning filled the church...Hold my mule....

MOVING TOWARD THE LIGHT

In the event described above, body and soul coalesced—flesh and spirit were wed. In other words, feeling the spirit in the dark became a process through which the spirit was made manifest through the flesh or through an enactment of what Cherrie Moraga and Gloria Anzaldua call a "theory in the flesh." They define this theory as "one where the physical realities of our lives—our skin color, the land or concrete we grew up on, our sexual longings—all fuse to create a politic born out of necessity" (23). The "politic borne out of necessity" is that of sexual expression and affirmation, the conjoining of the physical realities of being black and gay with those of being Christian. The performance "space" of the nightclub makes this union possible. Indeed, "this performance environment ...[allowed] us to experience our subjectivity in unusual ways..." (Patraka 1996, 101) as we celebrated our spirituality and our sexuality by publicly displaying our eroticized black gay bodies. As spectators of eroticized gay bodies that are simultaneously *Christian* bodies, black gay men in the nightclub space both witness and become witnesses for the union of body and flesh. In turn, this witnessing forges a sense of community and belonging among the nightclub patrons—a sense of community denied them in the performance "place" of the black church.

In the nightclub space black gay men draw upon the rich vernacular of African American folklore, a discourse that has always been used as a weapon against oppression. Therefore, Shirley Caesar's folk narrative that precedes her song becomes a metaphor for the plight of African American gay men and their experience in the black church.

Caesar's song could be subtitled "I Feel Like Praising Him," for those are the lyrics that are actually sung. In fact, "Hold My Mule" is the theme of the narrative Caesar tells before she sings the song. "Hold My Mule" tells the story of an 86-year-old man named Shoutin' John, who joins a church that does not allow "dancin'." Caesar testifies:

"I just wanna take time to tell you a story about a man called Shoutin' John. John joined a dead Church. They didn't believe in shoutin'. They didn't believe in dancing and speaking in tongues. But when they opened the doors of the church, John joined that church. Well. And when John joined that church, he came in dancing. Everything, everything got disturbed, because John was dancing all around the church. The deacons ran and sat him down; he jumped back up. They tried to hold his legs, his hands would go. When they turned the hands a loose [loose], the FEET WERE GOIN' / IT'S JUST LIKE FIRE! / IT'S JUST LIKE FIRE! Shut up in my bones. Well. They did everything they could to stop old John from shoutin' and when they couldn't finally stop him, they made up in their minds, 'We got to go out to John's house, y'all, for something is wrong with him. DOESN'T HE KNOW! We don't act like that in our church. DOESN'T JOHN KNOW! We've got dignitaries in our church. We're goin'. We're goin'. We're goin' to John's house.' Well. When they got out there, they found this old 86-year-old man, him and an old beat-up mule, plowin', plowin' in the field. They drove up, all of the deacons; they got out of their fine cars; they walked over to John. John looked around and said, 'Hold, mule.' He walked over to them and said, 'Brethren, I know why you've come out here. You've come out here to tell me that I praise the Lord too much. You've come out here to tell me that I dance too much.' One of the deacons told him, 'IF YOU DON'T STOP SHOUTIN'! IF YOU DON'T STOP DANCIN'! WE GONNA PUT YOU OUT OF OUR CHURCH!' [chanting] Somebody say yes (yes), say yes (yes), wave your hand and tell God, yes. JOHN said to them, 'WELL PUT ME OUT! I can't hold my peace. DID YOU SEE ALL THAT LAND YOU JUST DROVE UP OVER?' He said, 'GOD GAVE ME ALL THAT LAND! But you don't want me to dance in your church. LOOK AT MY SONS AND DAUGHTERS,' said, 'GOD GAVE ME ALL OF MY CHILDREN! NOT ONE TIME, HAVE I BEEN TO THE COUR-THOUSE. NOT ONE TIME, HAVE I HAVE I BEEN TO THE CEME-TERY. BUT YOU DON'T WANT ME TO DANCE IN YOUR CHURCH.' Then he said, 'LOOK AT ME. I'M 86 YEARS OLD. I'M STILL ABLE TO WALK DOWN BEHIND THAT OLD MULE. I'M

STILL ABLE, TO HARVEST MY OWN CROP. BUT YOU DON'T WANT ME TO DANCE IN YOUR CHURCH. LISTEN BROTHER DEACONS, IF I CAN'T SHOUT IN YOUR CHURCH, HOLD MY MULE, I'M GONNA SHOUT RIGHT HERE!' SAY YES! SAY YES! SAY YES! OH LORD! Hold my mule. Hold my mule. Hold my mule."

Caesar follows the story of John by singing, "I feel like praising, praising Him. I feel like praising, praising Him. Praise Him in the Morning. Praise Him all night long. I feel like praising, praising Him."

John's relationship with the "dead" church is similar to African American gay men's relationship to the church in general. Despite John's perception that the church is "dead," he decides to join, hoping he might be able to put some "life" into it. But John soon discovers that the church is not only dead—it is spiritless. Indeed, the members work hard to "quench" the spirit in him and in the church in general. The members of John's church try to constrain him, denying him freedom to express his faith in God in his own way.

The church fails to practice the doctrine of "whosoever will let him come." Similarly, the black church condemns the African American gay male's sexuality, denying him the opportunity to be out within the context of the church. But as John reminds the deacons who visit him, something as powerful as the spirit cannot and must not be quenched. Like the spirit, sexuality too, is "just like fire, shut up in [the] bones." But the black church fervently opposes a reconciliation of the body and soul because "the mind-body split...flourishes in black theologies of sexuality" (Dyson 1996, 91). If this split creates all kinds of paradoxes in the sexual expression of heterosexual Christians, it is hardly surprising that attitudes toward homosexuality would be oppressive. Ironically, the common formulaic expression "just like fire shut up in my bones" implicitly links the spirit and the flesh, body, and soul. Continuously repeated throughout house music, this phrase encourages the expression of both spirituality and sexuality, as clubgoers acknowledge both through their sexual dancing as well as cries of praise to God.

Moreover, if the spirit is real, it may be made manifest in or outside the church: "Where two or three are gathered in my name." Indeed, contrary to the beliefs of many churchgoers, the "House of the Lord" is not always defined as what we call a "church." The "House of the Lord" is wherever the spirit resides. As John demonstrates, he can express his faith anywhere, even in a field with a mule. Likewise, because the church cannot and will not provide an affirming environment for African American gay men to express their sexuality as well as their spirituality, the night-club becomes an alternative "sanctuary." In Hartford, Conn., for instance, "Sanctuary" is the name of a gay nightclub, publicly trans-gressing what that place traditionally signifies.

It is also significant that the song chosen by the DJ is titled "Hold My Mule," which resonates with phallic and sexual imagery. Shoutin' John's request that the deacons "hold his mule" while he shouts in the field is his way of dismissing them and standing his ground. Within black street vernacular, however, "hold" is a euphemism for "suck," in which case John's verbal response would reflect the verbal put-down "suck my dick." While John's signifying is nonsexual, it nonetheless evokes a duplicitous meaning. In the nightclub the title is also imbued with double meaning. On the one hand, similar to how it functions within the story of John, "Hold My Mule" reflects a political stance against the oppression of the church's condemnation of homosexuality. On the other hand, the title draws attention toward the sexual conno-tations of the song, in which the "mule" becomes a metaphor for the penis. The song, as an anthem in the nightclub, thereby celebrates sex-uality and, more importantly, homosexuality, by inviting an erotic focus on the body engaged in same-sex oral sex.

FROM PLACE TO SPACE

Although I seem to romanticize the communion between spirituality and sexuality, I am more intent upon calling attention to the transgres-sion implicit within the move from place to space. The "sacred" place of the church where the rhetorical discourse of the service censures and confines the body is revisioned within the secular space of the nightclub so as to liberate the body. As I've described, people on the dance floor are sexualized in their movements, as couples grope each other to the beat of the music and to the sound of the preaching, as arms, legs, and hands fling in sensual and provocative motion. The space secularizes the whole notion of the "shout" or the "holy dance"; in turn, a sexu-alized body is offered in praise of God. The result is that the dancer affirms both the sexual and the spiritual.

Certainly the sexualized body exists within the church, even as "the black church has aimed to rid the black body of lascivious desires and to purge its erotic imagination with 'clean' thoughts" (Dyson 1996, 91). Thus, for example, many black churches have "nurses" who cover the legs of women who have "passed out" from the spirit, there-by ensuring that no one can see up their dresses. Such modesty and carefulness suggests the churchly knowledge of the possibility of these women's bodies as objects of a sexual rather than "holy" gaze. Within the church as place, the performance of the body is already scripted, prescribed as a "holy" rather than "sexual" body, "narrativized in advance, soliciting [its members] to perform the script that is organized for and given to [them]" (Patraka 1996, 100). And within the nightclub as space the body is provided with "a site that invites multiple acts of interpretation" (Patraka 1996, 100). Accordingly, black gays incorporate the "tools" of the black church worship service—i.e., gospel music and preaching—in the club space, but use them toward a different end. Indeed, when black gay men move black Christian discourse into the space of the dance floor, they forge alternative epistemological frames of reference. That is to say, they create new ways of understanding the linking of body and soul or sexuality and spirituality. Black gay men transform the supposedly solely secular, solely sexual, wholly sinful, utterly perverse club into a space where the identities of African American, homosexual, and Christian no longer compete.

In the same vein, the move from the church performance place to the gay nightclub performance space creates a sense of community that the church fails to provide. I do not wish to suggest that black gay men do not find community within the church; only that the church community does not affirm the homosexual, thereby limiting the ways in which gay men may commune. In the space of the club, however, sexuality invokes spirituality and thus community. This coming together of mind, body, and spirit is neither coerced nor enshrouded in guilt and shame. Love, desire, and spirit are all celebrated in a space that facilitates that celebration. The club provides a space where those who share same sex desire may also celebrate their knowledge of the Lord and vice versa.

Finally, the club as performance space calls into question interpretive authority and power. In this space "interpretation itself becomes a kind of complex performance, a way of experiencing subjectivity" (Patraka 1996, 100). In the performance space of the nightclub, the DJ is the central figure who embodies this interpretive authority and power and who shepherds the nightclub goers toward subjectivity. Indeed, the DJ appropriates the role of the black preacher. He dismantles the meaning of gospel music and black sermonic rhetoric as one "truth," and in its place offers a truth that is constructed and named depending on the interpreter. In doing so, the DJ corroborates Elizabeth Bell's stance that "we don't discover truth through/in performance; rather, we invent truth in performance." Bell maintains that this formulation of truth in/through performance is also an enactment of power. The DJ's authorial and interpretive power is reflected not only in the way he reinterprets black Christian discourse, but also in the way in which he "moves" those who are in the club.

Similar to those preachers who step down from the pulpit to be closer to their members, this DJ comes down from his booth to be closer to the people on the dance floor. And like a seasoned black preacher, he takes a secular concept (driving to Atlanta to go dancing) and blurs it with a sacred one (arriving at the nightclub safely by the grace of God). Even his roll call is similar to the religious lore in which God calls the names of those who will enter Heaven. The lore suggests that if you live a clean life, God will write your name on His roll to be called at judgment day. Through his roll calling, this DJ affirms that these men, these gay men, are also children of God, a position the men themselves claim when they refer to each other as "children."

BLACK QUEER THEOLOGY

Michael Dyson (1996) calls for a "theology of queerness" in the black church. That is, a theology that would use "the raw material of black social alienation to build bridges between gay and lesbian and straight black church members" (106). Historically, this kind of bridge building has not occurred within the black church. Because of its own paradoxical relationship to the black Christian body, the black church has censured to a greater extent the black gay Christian body. The censorship of black homosexuality, along with the false separation of the secular and the sacred, of the body and soul, has made the black church less a site of comfort, affirmation, and community, and more a place where "opening the doors of the church" means opening those to the closet as well. Moreover, the homophobic, guilt-ridden, and oppressive rhetoric of the black church leads to self-hatred, low self-esteem, and in some cases, suicide, for those gay members who cannot come to terms with their sexuality within the confining place of the church. In those instances where one's homosexuality is known, the church embraces that member only if he is willing to "exorcise" his gayness. This kind of backhanded acceptance maintains the hegemony of heterosexuality as Christ-like and reinforces the notion of homosexuality as an abomination. Black theology such as this refuses to imagine that the same God who can identify with other oppressed groups—African Americans, Jews, women, etc.—can also identify with gays and lesbians. "We don't have to stop being black to be saved. We don't have to stop being women to be saved. We don't have to stop being poor to be saved" (Dyson 1996, 107). So why should we have to stop being gay and lesbian?

Some members of the African American gay community have found their way out of the homophobic, closet-producing, demonizing, dark place of the black church and into the more affirming space of the nightclub. Certainly, "both place and space construct the subject as performer" (Patraka 1996, 100). But if this is the case, then it follows that the place of performance is more likely to be rigid, more about the spectacular or the quest of the Real, whereas performance space suggests multiple crisscrossing performances the possibility of interpretations that foreground the historicity of the individual subject" (Patraka 1996, 100). The "Real" body in the church is the virtuous, "pure," heterosexual body, while the body in the nightclub space is grounded as a site of performative possibilities—indeed, as a site of multiplicity and becoming—that historicizes its subjectivity inside and outside the "body" of black Christian discursive practices.

Drawing upon a longstanding tradition of blurring the sacred and the secular in African American culture, African American gay men embed their own secular traditions—house/club music, vogueing, dragging, snapping—within black sacred traditions to provide a more liberating way to express all of who they are. The result is an affirmation of their faith in God, a God who sees them as His children, and an affirmation of them as sexual agents. Like John in "Hold My Mule," they refuse to be held to the conventions of and limitations placed upon the black body in the black church. Rather, they proclaim, "I'll shout right here," in this space—this "secular" space—that I call home. In this place they enact what they already know: that one's sexuality cannot be quenched any more than one's spirituality. Indeed, they know, like Aretha, that one can "feel the spirit" in the light or the dark.

REFERENCES

Bell, E. Respondent. "Contributed Debut Papers in Performance Studies." National Communication Association Convention. Chicago, Nov. 21, 1997.

Caesar, S. "Hold My Mule." *Shirley Caesar Live in Chicago With the Reverend Milton Brunson and the Thompson Community Singers.* Word, 1988.

Dance, D. (1978). *Shuckin' and Jivin': Folklore from Contemporary Black Americans.* Bloomington: Indiana University Press.

Duplechan, L. (1986). *Blackbird.* New York: St. Martin's Press.

Dyson, M. (1996). *Race Rules: Navigating the Color Line*. Reading, MA: Addison-Wesley Publishing Company, Inc.

Edward, T. (1994). *Erotics & Politics: Gay Male Sexuality, Masculinity and Feminism*. New York: Routledge.

Franklin, A. (1992). "Spirit in the Dark." *Aretha Franklin Queen of Soul: The Atlanta Recordings*. Atlantic, R2 71063. (Sound Recording)

Harris, C. C. (1986). "Cut Off From Among His People." In *In the Life: A Black Gay Anthology*, edited by Joseph Beam. Boston: Alyson Publications.

James, B. (1985). *Go Tell It On the Mountain*. New York: Laurel.

Moraga, C. and Anzaldua, G. (Eds.). (1983). *This Bridge Called My Back: Writings By Radical Women of Color*. New York: Kitchen Table, Women of Color Press.

Patraka, V.M. (1996). "Spectacles of Suffering: Performing Presence, Absence, and Historical Memory at U.S. Holocaust Museums." In *Performance & Cultural Politics*, edited by Elin Diamond. New York: Routledge.

Tinney, J.S. (1983). "Struggles of a Black Pentecostal." In *Black Men/White Men: A Gay Anthology*, edited by Michael I. Smith. San Francisco: Gay Sunshine Press.

Their Own Received Them Not: African American Lesbians and Gays in Black Churches

Horace Griffin

Within the past two decades, the social and religious oppression of lesbians and gays has increasingly become a primary issue of focus for the Western world. Almost every social institution and religious denomination has engaged the issue of homosexuality and, in some cases, reassessed unfounded notions about lesbian and gay people. Many people, both within and outside church communities, have struggled to accept lesbians and gays as moral and equal human beings within a predominantly heterosexual society.

It is striking, however, that African Americans have often been absent from this discussion. Typically, African Americans have entered the dialogue on homosexuality begrudgingly or in reactionary ways, as was true in recent civil rights debates, including that of gays in the military and the legalization of same-sex marriage. At other times, African Americans are simply silent about homosexuality. For example, in the 1994 summer edition of the *Journal of Pastoral Theology*, a leading African American pastoral theologian did not even mention African American homosexuality in an article on African American sexuality (Wimberly 1994, 19-31).

While African Americans are not exceptional in their view that homosexuality is immoral, there are few arenas where the dread and condemnation of homosexuality is more noticeable than in black church settings. In the climate of gay visibility in religious circles, African American heterosexual voices have been some of the most intolerant and oppositional. The following is one such example.

Last spring at a United Methodist theological seminary forum, African American seminarians spoke with a united voice in an emotionally charged discussion condemning fellow lesbian and gay seminarians as immoral. The African American heterosexual professors at the seminary expressed similar views. When a European-American professor reminded the black seminarians that their response paralleled white racist theological arguments used to justify slavery and the belief

110

that black people were immoral, students fumed. An African American bishop who was present at the meeting joined the black students in a repudiation of the parallel. This became one more example of how seminary discussions on homosexuality usually happen: Black students posit themselves as heterosexuals against white lesbian and gay students. When there is a refusal to acknowledge African American lesbians and gay men by both groups, white lesbians and gays are not challenged to confront their racism and black heterosexuals are not forced to deal with their homophobia. Thus, it usually follows that an identified black heterosexual group condemns a white lesbian and gay group, using religious morality as the justification for their disapproval and rejection of lesbians and gays.

What no one addressed this day was the harassment and oppression that African American lesbians and gays continue to face in black churches. Within the past few decades, there has been silence and dishonesty about African American heterosexuals as victimizers of lesbians and gays within black churches. In this paper, as a gay African American Christian and religious academic, I assert that African American lesbians and gays should not be viewed as a problem, but rather that the problem is African American homophobia and the black church teaching that homosexuality is immoral. The homophobia I address is not just that of mere discomfort of being around lesbians and/or gays but the negative reaction to lesbians and gays and their love relationships.

There may be no greater challenge than to speak against prevailing unjust attitudes of one's blood family, church family, and primary social community. This situation places all lesbians and gay men in a particularly difficult position, unlike that faced by most oppressed groups. This is a *major* reason why African American lesbians and gays have not been more forthright in their opposition to African American antigay rhetoric. Such a challenge usually results in scourge and ridicule from other African Americans for "airing dirty laundry" in public. In Ofra Bikel's 1992 *Frontline* documentary, "Public Hearing, Private Pain: The Clarence Thomas/Anita Hill Hearings," African American feminist Paula Giddings argues that Anita Hill committed the black community's unpardonable sin by exposing the wrongdoing of a fellow African American. Those who dare to speak out often face negative labeling as "Uncle Tom," "sellout" or "traitor to the race." This labeling is a powerful weapon used to silence any African American who criticizes, in this respect, a black church system that has historically subordinated heterosexual women, lesbians, and gay men. Since much of the "sellout" labeling is a fear tactic to ensure that these groups will not speak against exclusionary practices within church settings, lesbians, gays, and bisexuals must challenge black church homophobia. While there will be those who deny the present state of gay oppression in black churches, many heterosexuals will support the validity of this claim and begin the difficult task of changing black theology and church structure that define homosexuality as immoral.

In the seminary discussion referred to above, black seminarians were outraged when racial oppression was compared to homosexual oppression. While no white lesbian or gay person has ever attempted to argue that they have suffered in exactly the same way as African American heterosexuals, lesbians and gays are correct to point out that known lesbians and gays of all races experience discrimination, ridicule, ostracism, beatings, and killings. Indeed, we must not be *too* dismissive of the common response of African American heterosexuals that homosexual oppression is not the same as racial oppression. European-American lesbians and gays have never been placed in chattel slavery. By the same token, in terms of racial oppression, black heterosexuals have never had to endure assaults from family and church members and others in their own community, as white lesbians and gays, and all gays for that matter, have had to experience because of their sexual difference. Both black heterosexuals and gays find support from blacks when faced with hostile racist attacks from society. But African American lesbians and gays, by and large, often have nowhere to turn in the midst of pain, loneliness, ostracism, and ridicule about their homosexuality, and experience the first voices of homophobia, harsh looks, and moral condemnation from family, church members, and others within black communities. However, when we divide ourselves into camps, nothing is gained. How does one decide which is worse, being denied to vote or being disowned by a parent? Ultimately, we must come to the realization that one group's attempt to establish itself as the most oppressed is irrelevant. If we could arrive at such a point, does it mean that we ignore the pain and suffering of other groups that did not win the "most oppressed" prize? The appropriate response is to recognize that the oppression of any group is wrong and must be condemned as an unacceptable human practice.

Moreover, it is questionable whether there is a formal difference between the behavior of African American Christians who use Biblical texts to categorize lesbians and gays as immoral and that of 18th- and

19th-century European-American Christians who used the same Bible to identify African Americans as a cursed people characterized by their immorality. In many discussions, African Americans have dismissed this juxtaposition by simply stating that "it is not the same," implying that one response, theirs, is an appropriate one, while the racist practices of whites were contrary to God's will. Yet, there is a clear dichotomy between, on the one hand, the historical black church as an agency opposed to religious and scriptural support of slavery and racial oppression and, on the other hand, the contemporary black church as an institution that enforces oppression and church exclusion of African American lesbians and gays through its religious teachings and scriptural support of homosexuality as immoral.

In an attempt to distance homosexuality from African Americans, many Afrocentric thinkers have claimed that homosexuality is a perverse sexual practice, unknown to Africans until it was imposed on them by Europeans. No historical support exists for such a generalization, and this assertion reflects the human tendency to attribute stigmatized behavior to a despised culture. Research indicates instead that homosexuality existed in Africa, as in the rest of the world, prior to European colonialism.

Since homosexuality is a part of human sexuality, identified in various forms on all continents by anthropologists and sociologists, it is a racist claim to state that Africans do not express themselves with same-sex love or sexual activity like other humans. African American sociologist Robert Staples asserts that African homosexual practices have existed for centuries. In *Black Masculinity* he argues that given the pattern of sex divisions in African cultures, homosexual expression was probably quite common (Staples 1983, 87). However, despite the presence of homosexual expression in African and European countries, most of Europe, prior to and during the African slave trade, did not accept same-sex sexual practice. In fact, Europeans were generally sex-negative and antihomosexual.

Thus, European Christian missionaries and slave traders who went into African cultures were more prone to condemn homosexual practice rather than condone or encourage it. When European missionaries arrived in this country and witnessed the acceptance of homosexuality in some Native American tribes and communities, they expressed disgust and outrage (Williams 1986, 133). In contrast to European Christian missionaries who viewed homosexuality as immoral, as historian Robert Baum (1993) states "in many Native

American communities, [homosexuals] were regarded as sacred people, chosen by gods and given special powers that could benefit the community." These findings reveal: 1) the majority of Europeans neither accepted homosexuality nor influenced other cultures with same-sex practice; and 2) contrary to the assertions of many Afrocentrists, some nonwhite religious people have viewed homosexuality as a moral sexual expression. Even if Africans had uniformly opposed homosexuality, African Americans do not construct a moral code or ethos strictly based on African religious and cultural traditions. By and large, African and African Americans practice different religions and have organized different marital structures, with the latter rightly refusing to participate in African female genital mutilation, which has caused damage and death to many African girls and women.

Two primary reasons account for African Americans' negative view of homosexuality: 1) Slaves were mainly converted to Christianity by conservative white Christians who were sex-negative and opposed to homosexuality; 2) African Americans have recognized that conspiring with mainstream society in targeting homosexuals as the "despised other" frees them from the deviant label of being sexually immoral and provides a degree of social acceptance.

African Americans are typically unaware that a large part of their sexual understanding and sense of sexual morality is a result of the English Christian social order imposed on them in this country during the last three centuries. Bill Piersen, a historian of African American culture, documents that "[Africans] found many of their standards of morality and premarital sexual mores rejected out of hand by a puritanical master class.... Many of the African American sexual relationships that appalled Christian observers as immoral deviations of monogamy were in reality attempts to blend African mores with the new social realities of American bondage" (Piersen 1993, 94). Some of these initial teachings came from slaveholding puritans who often associated immorality with sexual practice. The Baptist denomination's lack of structure in worship and de-emphasis on education eventually attracted the largest number of African Americans. Religious historian Albert Raboteau (1978) states that the traditional conservative teachings of Baptists transformed black slaves into Bible Christians. Liberal denominations have not had much success in attracting African Americans; historically, conservative denominations have attracted African Americans in greater numbers.

This embrace of conservative white Christianity is ironic, since a majority of conservative European-American Christians also turned to scripture to justify slavery. In light of scriptural sanction of slavery, European-American Christians emulated biblical slaveholders such as Abraham. White Christian ministers, missionaries, and masters supported slavery by appealing to scriptural passages such as Ephesians 6:5: "Slaves be obedient to your masters" (Raboteau 1994, 73). Some of the strongest proponents of the theological view that it was God's will for African Americans to be slaves were Baptist ministers and congregants. Pro-slavery Baptists differed so strongly with some Baptists that they organized a separate denomination in 1845, the Southern Baptist Convention, which is presently the largest Protestant denomination (Handy 1976, 190). Historian Benjamin Quarles informs us that they argued that "race determined mental and moral traits. The Negro as a member of an inferior race, was meant to be a slave, his normal and *natural* condition." In light of historical and contemporary discussions about whether homosexuality is "natural," it is important to understand that such language was also used to support the horrific institution of slavery. In other words, appeals to the "natural" were used to justify human subjugation, in this case, slavery.

Although the master-slave structure clearly appeared in the Bible, the overwhelming majority of African American slaves refused to accept these scriptures as authoritative. Raboteau (1994) notes "as early as 1774 American slaves were declaring publicly and politically that they thought Christianity and slavery were incompatible." Such a paradox moved black Methodist minister Richard Allen out of the white St. George's Methodist church in 1787 into the black Bethel church which gave rise to the first African American denomination, the African Methodist Episcopal church. Since African American slaves understood God as just, scriptures that demanded domination of some people by others created conflict for many slaves. Howard Thurman's grandmother, Nancy Ambrose, provides a perfect example. In *Jesus and the Disinherited*, Thurman documents his grandmother's clever response to Paul's writings: "During the days of slavery...master's minister would occasionally hold services for the slaves. Always the white minister used as his text something from Paul. Slaves be obedient to your masters as unto Christ. Then he would go on to show how if we were good happy slaves, God would bless us. I promised my maker that if I ever learned to read and if freedom ever came, I would not read that part of the Bible" (Thurman 1945, 30-31).

The attitude of Thurman's grandmother typifies the response of the overwhelming majority of African American Christians: to disregard scripture that supports slavery. Despite Raboteau's description that African Americans are Bible Christians, history has shown us that African American Christians have been able to move beyond the simple belief that all scripture is authoritative.

Depictions of blacks as inferior to whites were also supported by referring to African Americans as sexually deviant. African Americans were viewed as being obsessed with sex, sex predators with uncontrollable desires (Herton 1988, 5). Such views led white men to justify their sexual lust for and rape of black women and lynching of black men, arguing that lynching was practiced to protect white womanhood (Herton 1988, 57-58). Gay men have shared aspects of this history. Gay bashing and the killing of gay men have been justified as also protecting the society from sex predators. While black heterosexual men were defined as having a constant sexual desire for white women, gay men, on the other hand, were defined by antigay heterosexual men as preoccupied with sexual desire for boys. Predominant social and religious attitudes defined both groups as sexually immoral.

In an attempt to avoid accusations of immorality and prove their moral worth, African American heterosexuals continue to distance themselves from gays while increasing their antigay rhetoric. Throughout the last three decades of the lesbian and gay civil rights movement, African American heterosexual ministers have become more hostile in their condemnation of homosexuality. In addition to the homophobia that has played itself out in countless sermon, ministers have also taken their message that homosexuality is immoral to black families, college and seminary classrooms and political arenas. They have been active in opposing the civil rights of lesbians and gays in Boston, Chicago, Cincinnati, Nashville, Philadelphia, and Washington, D.C. Keith Boykin refers to a prominent Washington, D.C., pastor who boasts of his reference to homosexuality as an abomination, citing Paul's passage in Romans (Boykin 1996, 129).

Despite claims from many black heterosexuals that the black church is tolerant toward gays, it is a fact that black gays and lesbians are not treated equally with heterosexuals. Some heterosexuals attempt to support a tolerance and acceptance claim by acknowledging that gays have been allowed to remain in churches. However, mere acknowledgement of lesbians and gays in black churches is not equivalent to full acceptance of them. Moreover, since the church community benefits from the leadership and music ministry of many gays and lesbians, removing lesbians and gays would be detrimental to the worship and life of the church. Like blacks who accepted a place of inferiority in order to stay within white racist churches and institutions, black lesbians and gays must stay in a place of inferiority to remain in black churches. They are allowed to stay within the institutions if they are willing to play by the rules of listening to statements that homosexuality is sinful and immoral and gays are in need of change.

Gays and lesbians endure sermons that define them as sick people and never expect to have their relationships recognized and affirmed verbally or in a ceremony. Gays and lesbians are also denied ordination. Gay men who desire to be a part of the ordained ministry must deny their gayness and pretend to be heterosexual, even if it means marrying. Since the majority of black churches deny women in general ordination, unlike gay men, lesbians who conceal their sexual attraction are still denied ordination. Lesbians and gays who dare to speak out quickly learn the extent of black church tolerance.

This practice runs counter to the claim that the black church has been a place of liberation, an agent against injustice and oppression. Black liberation theology calls for justice and equality for all members within the community (Cone 1975, 147). A true practice of justice would allow all members within black churches to experience treatment based on moral character as Christian people, not on gender and sexual differences. This practice would focus on scriptural passages of love and liberation found within the ministry of Jesus and reach the conclusion that any scripture which supports the oppression of a group is antithetical to the spirit of Jesus and the Gospel. Given that there is not a focus on homosexuality within the Bible (a total of six references), it is clear that the Bible is used as a convenient tool to support religious and social bigotry against lesbians and gay men. The majority of African American heterosexual Christians have not only refused to adhere to scriptures supporting slavery, but they have likewise ignored scriptures which require the obedience to all civil laws (Romans 13), the relinquishing of wealth (Matthew 19:21) and greeting everyone with a kiss, including those of the same sex (Romans 16:16 and 1 Corinthians 16:20). This lack of consistency in the treatment of scripture points to heterosexuals' ability to accept God's will outside the limitations of scripture that support their supremacist notions of heterosexuality.

Because black churches continue to fail lesbian and gay Christians like Richard Allen and his cohorts, some have started their own churches for other marginalized lesbians and gays. The increasing number of African American lesbians and gays who are leaving mainline black churches challenges the notion that black churches have been tolerant. One often hears that whites can never speak for black people due to the fact that they do not experience nuances of racial denigration. Likewise, African American heterosexuals are not in the position to speak for lesbians and gays by claiming that the black church is tolerant of gays. Homophobia must ultimately be defined by those who have written about and spoken against homophobic black attitudes and practices are Dr. Renee Hill, Dr. Elias Farajaje-Jones, Rev. Irene Monroe, Rev. Leonard Patterson, Rev. Sandy Robinson, and Dr. James Tinney. This is not to say that heterosexuals cannot and should not speak out against heterosexuals who impose hateful attitudes, bigotry and discrimination against the lesbian and gay people. To the contrary, heterosexuals ought to stand and be in solidarity with lesbians and gays and speak against the atrocities that are heaped on them in black church and social communities.

Another antigay argument used by many black heterosexuals is that lesbians and gays are a threat to black families and black communities. The Genesis command "to be fruitful and multiply" is conveniently used to invalidate lesbian and gay sexual relationships. However, African American heterosexuals do not use this scripture to invalidate nonprocreative heterosexual sexual relationships. Considering that there is presently an abundance of black children within society as well as those waiting to be adopted (after having been given up by their heterosexual parents), procreation is an unnecessary concern; a recent study showed that of children who are waiting to be adopted, up to 90% are children of color (Woog 1978, 70).

In addition, African American lesbians and gays do not in any way pose a threat to black communities or the common god. In terms of generativity, African American lesbians and gays are a part of the intergenerational process, which includes the maintenance of African American culture, the education of and recreational activities for our young, healthcare for our elderly, and nurture of our families. We are members of black communities and the wider society and provide leadership in black organizations, agencies, and churches. Thus it is clear that the antihomosexual religious and social message under the guise of a concern for the black community has all to do with a problem with gay sex. To make a claim that lesbians and gays "severely undermine the heterosexual family," as Howard Divinity School ethics professor

Cheryl Sanders states, is to identify gays and lesbians as the culprit to heterosexual family problems (Waddle 1998, 2b). Moreover, such a claim does not speak favorably or convincingly to the stability of and attraction to heterosexuality.

Many heterosexual ministers, along with many community leaders, continue to focus on lesbians and gay men as a problem instead of the problems that seriously threaten the survival of African American people. Are claims that gays and lesbians threaten the black family and community in reference to the violent crimes committed against African Americans? Are there studies that can support that gay men are the primary culprits in the emotional and financial neglect of children, violent physical and sexual abuse of children and rape of and violence against women? Moreover, is there any evidence that African American gay men are remotely responsible for most of the murders of innocent women, children and men through drive-by shootings, carjackings and other acts of violence? Until such evidence shows that lesbians and gays play a significant role in the above problems that clearly destroy black families and communities, I find the position that "African American lesbians and gays are a threat to the black family" to be meritless. Rather than using lesbians and gays as a scapegoat or a diversion from the problems, there is a need for African American heterosexual ministers to address the above problems being committed by many heterosexuals who threaten black families and the common good of black communities.

Many African American heterosexual female ministers have been reluctant to conspire with their heterosexual male counterparts in gay religious oppression. They are too familiar with a similar use of scripture and rhetoric used to justify women's subjugation to men and the exclusion of women from ministry. Since they realize scripture and tradition do not legitimize women ministers, they too have been unwilling to accept these unjust scriptures as part of Divine will. They have identified the common link between these oppressions in black churches.

The present message of homosexuality as immoral also creates an inescapable feeling of unworthiness and low self-esteem in African American lesbians and gay men. The continued antihomosexual attitude creates a climate of denial that can develop into rage and hostility by those who experience psychic pain. In an attempt to find acceptance, lesbians and gay men often marry the opposite sex and begin to live an unfulfilled life. This opens the door for many problems, including health concerns and fidelity issues for their spouses (Isay 1996, 90-95).

Moreover, the message of homosexuality as immoral keeps heterosexuals hostile to the understanding and acceptance of lesbians and gay men who are their own family members and friends (Jung and Smith1993, 94). An otherwise happy family can turn into a place of shame, anger, and pain. Many heterosexual family members have estranged and disowned responsible and caring lesbian and gay family members simply because they consider them perverse and sinful individuals in need of change. Within black congregations, many lives are damaged because of homophobia. African American lesbians and gays, like our heterosexual counterparts, simply seek the freedom to establish and maintain our own sexual relationships and families without the burden of heterosexual harassment, ridicule, and restriction.

In conclusion, I argue that a revision of the present stance on homosexuality is necessary for a true liberation theology for black churches. This process can begin by obliterating the view that lesbians and gays and our relationships are inherently bad and inferior to heterosexuals and their relationships. Like the black seminarians, black Christians are failing to learn from history. The slavery example is powerful because it has taught us that Paul was incorrect in his understanding that certain humans should be slaves to others. Even ruling out white racists' use of those passages to justify African American slavery, we would still conclude today that slavery and oppression of any human being lacks moral justice and is therefore contrary to Divine will.

Finally, whether the black church community should accept homosexuality among its members becomes an unnecessary and irrelevant question. Homosexuality is part of human sexuality, just as African Americans are part of the human race. Thus, there will always be African American lesbians, gays, and bisexuals within and outside of church communities. The question therefore becomes whether African American heterosexuals are going to practice justice toward their daughters and sons, sisters and brothers, mothers and fathers, other relatives, friends, colleagues, and fellow Christians who are lesbian and gay.

Just as African Americans have been able to be critical in their analysis of Christianity and race, they must also begin the critical process regarding Christianity and homosexuality. Paul's first-century prescientific mind could not have known the fullness of human sexuality in general and homosexuality in particular. In light of this, we would all be better served if we followed the wisdom of Nancy Ambrose in her response to Paul's slavery passages and promise our maker that when it comes to Paul's scriptures on homosexuality, we will no longer read that part of the Bible.

References

Baum, R. (1993). "Homosexuality and the Traditional Religions of the Americas and Africa." In *Homosexuality and World Religions*, edited by Arlene Swidler. Valley Forge, Pennsylvania: Trinity Press.

Benjamin, Q. (1987). *The Negro in the Making of America*. New York: Macmillan Publishing Co.

Boykin, K. (1996). *One More River to Cross: Black and Gay in America*. New York: Anchor Books.

Saunders, C. "The Black Church and Homosexuality." (Presented February 21, 1998 at a confer ence sponsored by the Carpenter Program in Religion, Gender, and Sexuality at the Kelly Miller Smith Institute of Vanderbilt Divinity School.) The quote is cited in the above paper and taken from "The Tennessean," ed. Ray Waddle (February 13, 1998, p. 2b).

Cone, J. (1975). *God of the Oppressed*. San Francisco: Seabury Press.

Greenberg, D. (1988). *The Construction of Homosexuality*. Chicago: The University of Chicago Press.

Handy, R (1976). *A History of Churches in the United States and Canada*. New York: Oxford University Press.

Herton, C. (1988). *Sex and Racism in America*. New York: Anchor Books.

Isay, R. (1996). *Becoming Gay: The Journey of Self-Acceptance*. New York: Henry Holt and Co.

Jung, P. and Smith, R. (1993). *Heterosexism: An Ethical Challenge*. New York: State University of New York Press.

Nero, C. (1991). "Toward a Black Gay Aesthetic." In *Brother to Brother*, edited by Essex Hemphill. Boston: Alyson Publications, 1991.

Piersen, W. (1988). *Black Yankees*. Amherst: University of Massachusetts Press.

Raboteau, A. (1978). *Slave Religion*. New York: Oxford University Press.

Staples, R. (1983). *Black Masculinity*. San Francisco: Black Scholar Press.

Wimberly, E. (1994). "African American Spirituality and Sexuality: Perspectives on Identity, Intimacy and Power." In *Journal of Pastoral Theology* 4, summer: 19-31.

Woog, D. (1998). "Adopting a Family." *The Advocate,* issue 750/751: 70.

Homosexuality in Africa

Heart of Lavender

Eugene J. Patron

We will never know if Lucy was a lesbian. The discovery of the famous skeleton in Ethiopia in 1974 by Dr. Richard Leaky was the clearest proof to date that human evolution began on the African continent. Carbon dating revealed that Lucy lived some 3 to 3.7 million years ago. Yet whether she ever lusted after other female Australopithecines is a secret that will remain hers for eternity.

Lucy is not the only one with secrets. The recorded knowledge about sexuality in African societies is far from encyclopedic. Little more than anecdotal attention has been paid to departures from procreative sexual practices in traditional cultures. The issue of individual desires rarely makes it into a body of anthropological literature dominated by the analysis of the collective. At best, homosexuality is consigned to little more than a footnote in any discussion of sexuality in Africa.

If anthropologists and other researchers needed an excuse to avoid the subject, they've had only to point to widespread denial of homosexual practices by Africans themselves. Along with so many other unwanted social conditions, homosexuality is often thrown onto the pile of artifacts left over from the legacy of European and Arab colonialism.

Nowhere did such sentiment present itself as vocally as in South Africa and the 1991 trial of Winnie Mandela and members of the "football team," who were convicted of kidnapping and murdering a 14-year old boy. Defending herself both in court and in the press, Mandela argued she was actually trying to protect a number of local youths from the homosexual overtures of a white priest.

Rachel Holmes, writing about the trial in *Defiant Desire: Gay and Lesbian Lives in South Africa,* notes that "the defense case attempted to connect homosexual practice with abuse in terms of it being an exploitation of the vulnerability of disadvantaged people" (Holmes 1995, 288). Winnie Mandela's supporters, no strangers to effectively utilizing media attention, displayed for the cameras placards declaring HOMOSEX IS NOT IN BLACK CULTURE.

Today, South Africa is the only country in the world to include a sexual orientation clause in its bill of rights (section 8, part 2). Given

South Africa's sordid history of negating the human rights of millions of its citizens, the recognition that "people's sexual nature is fundamental to their humanity," as Archbishop Desmond Tutu put it, is a remarkable turn of events.

Still, the celebrated sexual orientation clause in the country's interim constitution (awaiting a two-thirds ratification by the constitutional assembly) does not necessarily translate into approval of homosexuality by the majority of the population. The existence of the clause is closely linked to a camaraderie among oppressed peoples under the apartheid regime, one fostered by the socialist idealism of the African National Congress. That homosexuals were even invited into the family of the oppressed by the South Africa liberation movement is partially rooted in the pragmatic recognition by the ANC that many overseas antiapartheid groups had adopted a gay-positive stance.

Perhaps it is because the South African liberation struggle lasted so long that the liberation movement was able to achieve a level of maturity that recognized the necessity of full and genuine inclusion of all minorities in society. In neighboring Zimbabwe this past August the government of President Robert Mugabe threatened to withdraw its financial support of the Zimbabwe International Book Fair because of the inclusion of a booth by GALZ (Gays and Lesbians of Zimbabwe). Moralizing about the need to protect societal values from corruption, Mugabe's ensuing antihomosexual comments fit what Dr. Neville Hoad of Columbia University labels "the homophobic strictures of European discourse which are mobilized by anticolonial agents in national liberation struggles."

The ensuing international outcry included statements from Nadine Gordimer and Wole Soyinka supporting GALZ's right to free speech as well a motion filed with the United Nations by an American human rights activist seeking to censure Zimbabwe for violating the spirit of various human rights declarations. Not surprisingly, the government played upon nationalist sympathies and helped feed the populist notion of homosexuality as something being forced upon Zimbabwe by external forces.

COMING OUT FROM BEHIND THE MASK

The growing body of evidence supporting a biological root to homosexual behavior presents a strong case to argue that homosexuality is to some extent innate in all races and cultures. Yet even if homosexual desires are innate to a percentage of any population, cultural boundaries clearly regulate the opportunities for expressing such desires.

Anthropologist Evelyn Blackwood, editor of *The Many Faces of Homosexuality* (1986), cites Ross and Rapp to emphasize the historical-cultural construction of sexuality.

> Sexuality's biological base is always experienced culturally, through a translation. The bare biological facts of sexuality do not speak for themselves; they must be expressed socially. Sex feels individual, or at least private, but those feelings always incorporate the roles, definitions, symbols and meanings of the worlds in which they are constructed (Blackwood 1986, 5).

Many traditional African cultures are based upon extended families and clan structures. But a misconception widespread in popular views of sexuality and even in anthropology is to place homosexuality in a position of opposition to procreation. Homosexuality can indeed be viewed through an economic perspective whereby a society must be able to afford an individual the choice not to have children. However, the idea that the economic interdependence of members of an extended family or clan is a deterrent to homosexuality addresses behavior but not desire. Moreover, there is anthropological evidence showing that a number of African cultures exhibit a degree of accommodation to homosexuality.

Some of the best known work exploring homosexuality in Africa is that of E.E. Evans-Pritchard and his studies of the Azande of present-day Zaire beginning in the 1920s. Evans-Pritchard found repeated examples of adolescents prior to the age of 17-18 serving as "boy wives" to older men. They were expected to help their "father-in-law" and "mothers-in-law" to cultivate the fields, build huts and would often sleep with their fathers-in-law.

According to Evans-Pritchard, "if a (Azande) man has sexual relations with a boy, he is not unclean. The Azande say, 'A boy does not pollute the oracle.'" Moreover, the boy wife and his father-in-law would often refer to each other as "my love" and "my lover."

Accounts of homosexuality in traditional African cultures often find similar practices accepted among adolescents but discouraged among adults. Tessemann, writing in the 1913 about the Fang of West Africa, states:

> In adults such conduct is regarded as something immoral and

unnatural, simply unheard of. In reality, however, it is frequently heard of that young people carry on homosexual relations with each other and even older peoples who take boys...readily console them by saying, "we are having fun, playing a game, joking." Adults are excused with the corresponding assertion, "He has [the] heart (that is, the aspirations) of boys," which is, of course, by no means flattering to them.

The findings of Evans-Pritchard and Tessemann, along with those of many other researchers, read as mixed messages when one tries to draw a line between what sexual practices various African societies will and will not accept. The hetero-homosexual split so entrenched in Western societies becomes even harder to peg to African cultures when one considers cases of gender display that are out of sync with an individual's biological sex.

In traditional Zulu culture women are the spirit diviners. As females, able to give birth, it is through their bodies that spirits may cross from one world to another. However, men who display female gender characteristics are also allowed to be spirit diviners. Moreover, a man who becomes possessed, no matter what his gender identity, is considered a woman. While not conclusive, this may well relate to the widespread belief in southern Africa that homosexuals are, in fact, hermaphrodites.

Probably the best-documented cases of homosexuality in Africa are among the mine workers of South Africa. Living in all-male compounds and separated from girlfriends and wives for months at a time, it is very common for adolescent boys to visit these compounds and provide sexual service to its inhabitants. Such can be thought of as situational homosexuality based upon the extenuating circumstances of an all-male setting.

Yet far less consideration has been given to those miners and their partners who admit to enjoying sexual contact with other men beyond obtaining sexual release in the absence of women. Writing in *Defiant Desire*, Linda Ngcobo and Hugh McLean interviewed 20 African men who have sex with other men about gay sexuality in the townships around Johannesburg.

"A *Skesana* is a boy who likes to get fucked," explains Ngcobo, himself one of the first black gay men in South Africa to publicly declare his homosexuality. "An *injongo* is the one who makes the proposals and does the fucking" (McLean 1995, 164-165). Much of the sex between miners and those who service them is "thigh sex," an accepted practice between members of the same sex in many African cultures. Yet, the authors argue, anal sex is far from unknown. Moreover, the definition of what constitutes "sex" for African men who have sex with other men is anal penetration. "Remember that *skesanas* who 'play with each other,' even to the point of orgasm, do not consider this to be sex. Sex happens when *amanjonga wa kwabo bab-ayinela*, when their *injongas* penetrate them" (McLean 1995, 167).

Corresponding to the large-scale migration of men in Southern Africa seeking work are the close relationships and support networks developed by women. Again, the situation-specific explanation of these relations, exhibited both emotionally and sexually, must be considered along with other evidence.

In exploring the "mummy-baby" relationship between adolescent Basotho women in Lesotho, Judith Gray found that not only were young girls "gradually socialized into adult female roles and relationships by slightly older and more experienced girls," but that "sexual intimacy is an important aspect of these relationships." Over the time the women grow older and start to raise a family, the sexual nature of these relationships lessens, but the support network formed and the deep emotional attachment among women remain. Gray theorizes:

The fact that close physical and emotional relations between women often have a significant place, even after heterosexual relations have begun, suggests that the growing recognition of bisexuality in psychosexual studies may find support in studies of non-Western societies. As one Mosotho woman said about the physical side of these relationships: "It is not wrong. It's just another side of life" (Gray 1986, 111).

HEAR NO EVIL, SEE NO EVIL

What could be said of many cultures around the world is that they have little problem with homosexuality; it is *homosexuals* that are not tolerated. When President Mugabe calls on "churches and other custodians of human rights" to help Zimbabweans "observe their culture and traditional values," homosexuality is catapulted beyond being an issue of sexual practice. The supposed do's and don'ts of morally proscribed behavior are rooted deeper in earthly struggles for power than in heavenly sanctity.

Invoking the authority of the Catholic Church to protect traditional African culture is one of the many strange twists in the history of how European-exported systems of belief and governance became rooted on the continent. When asked about homosexuality, a Ghanaian-born editor of an African affairs publication was quick to blame its existence on missionaries and their schools. Such a perception, very widespread throughout Africa, is directly related to the mixed message colonialism brought; missionaries who came to save souls, and armies that came to steal the land and everything on it.

The very denial of indigenous homosexuality in African cultures plays into the hands of racism. Historian Wayne Dynes, in the introduction to a list of 84 references to homosexuality in Africa, notes that "Europeans have often held that 'sodomy' is a vice of advanced, even decadent civilizations. The Africans, being innocent 'children of nature,' must be exempt from such corruption" (Dynes 1983, 20-21).

The idea of Africans as "innocent children" of nature corresponds to European views that African sexual practices were primal and devoid of emotion. Likewise, homosexuality has also been vilified in Western thought as being incompatible with intimacy and true romantic notions of love. As viewed from a defensive position, the ascription of homosexual behavior to Africans can be regarded as doubly denying the emotional component of their sexual lives. It is not surprising, then, that the popular view in Africa is that homosexuality is, in Dynes' words, "a 'white vice' forced on healthy people to drag them down."

Black nationalism in Africa and elsewhere, paired with Afrocentrism, has tended to perpetuate the notion that homosexuality is removed from the "true" African experience. As with so much else relating to Africa, the issue is informed by attitudes outside the continent as much as by those of Africans themselves.

In the United States, homosexuality is often viewed with hostility by African Americans when placed in the sphere of a civil rights struggle. Homosexuals are seen as undeserving claimants to the same civil rights victories African Americans have struggled for. A posting on Net Noir, an African American Internet section of America Online, reflects the aforementioned:

> I am utterly insulted that the gay movement has degraded the struggles of minority groups in America, especially Blacks, by comparing their struggle to ours. Despite what pop psychology and many liberal whites may want us to believe, sexual orientation is a choice. The Black community has enough problems; do not further our problems by forcing us to accept the

lifestyle. Let's work on keeping crack, crime, illiteracy, and gay lifestyles out of our neighborhoods.

New York–based African American lesbian activist Jackie Bishop explains the consequences of such attitudes as "being de-raced. In being a lesbian, I'm not Black" (Bishop, 1995). Bishop points to Black Nationalism as being essentially misogynist and homophobic. Homosexuality is regarded as an external influence that weakens the link between African Americans and their African roots.

The popular idea of a lost "pure" Africa that existed prior to colonialism is an exclusionary one, built as much around Judeo-Christian ideals as traditional African ones. Yet the persuasiveness and influence of such a concept are extensive. In discussing the experiences of a gay man from Nairobi with a member of a university African Studies department, the professor proceeded to dismiss the man's experiences as a product of the "breakdown of the traditional family structure" in the postcolonial urban environment of Africa.

Who gets to speak for the "traditional family structure" in Africa, who best represents a "pure" African perspective on life, is an ongoing power struggle not unlike the battle over "family values" in the United States. In both cases, reality based on history is being swept aside in favor of easily salable constructions of nationalistic and racial identity. The disheartening result, according to Jackie Bishop, is that, "We [as people of African descent] still have yet to really reconstruct our history. We need to uncover and recreate our own stories" (Bishop, 1995).

There is at best a handful of openly gay social and gay rights groups in Africa, but to what extent homosexuals in Africa should organize along the models of western gay organizations is a pertinent question. Nearly 20 years ago Sylvanus Maduka, a Methodist minister in Nigeria, on hearing of a "gay church" in the United States contacted the offices of the Universal Fellowship of Metropolitan Community Churches. He then proceeded to establish an MCC church in Imo state, hiding nothing of MCC's mission to welcome all peoples—including homosexuals.

According to the Reverend Kavar, who used to administer World Extension for MCC churches, there are more than 20 MCC churches in Nigeria, as well as MCC churches in 16 other African countries. "What Maduka established are mostly village churches serving husbands, wives and children. They are subsistence farmers and receive very little from the government. MCC helped them build a clinic.

Nothing about MCC's focus on serving gays and lesbians is hidden from them. It's not an issue. Asked about the sexuality of his congregates, Maduka once said, "If you want us to be homosexual we will be; it doesn't matter to us" (Kavar, 1995).

Reverend Kavar admits to reading between the lines in Maduka's letters to him, trying to determine if Maduka himself was gay. But the answer is largely immaterial. The nonjudgmental inclusion that MCC offered responded to the needs of the people Maduka sought to help.

Idealism that may seem fanciful in the West can be downright practical when one is faced with the poverty of choices that someone like Maduka faced. Cycles of war and famine in Africa have created the terrible impression, even among Africans themselves, that the people of the African continent cannot afford to be humane to one another. Yet to deny anyone their dignity and rightful place in African society for reasons of ethnic background, sexuality, or race is to continue to rob Africa of its complete humanity.

REFERENCES

Bishop, J. (1995). Interview by Eugene J. Patron.

Blackwood, E. (Ed.). (1986). *The Many Faces of Homosexuality*. New York: Harrington Park Press.

Dynes, W. "Homosexuality in Sub-Saharan Africa." *Gay Books Bulletin*. Spring/Summer 1983: 20-21 .

Evans-Pritchard, E.E. (1970). "Sexual Inversion Among the Azande." *American Anthropologist,* vol. 72: 1428-34.

Gray, J. (1986). "Mummies and Babies" and "Friends and Lovers in Lesotho." In *The Many Faces of Homosexuality*, edited by Evelyn Blackwood. New York: Harrington Park Press, 1986.

Holmes, R. (1995). "White Rapists Made Coloreds (and Homosexuals). In *Defiant Desire,* edited by Mark Gevisser and Edwin Cameron. New York: Routledge.

Rev. Kavar (1995). Interview by Eugene J. Patron.

McLean, H. and Ngcobo, L. (1995). "Abangibhamayo bathi ngimnandi." In *Defiant Desire,* edited by Mark Gevisser and Edwin Cameron. New York: Routledge.

Ross, E. and Rapp, R. (1981). "Sex and Society: A Research Note From Social History and Anthropology." *Comparative Studies in Society and History* 23: 51-72.

Hearing Voices: Unearthing Evidence of Homosexuality in Precolonial Africa

Cary Alan Johnson

Until recently, African scholars and politicians have asserted that homosexuality is a Western phenomenon and not an indigenous element of African culture. In 1984 Angola's ambassador to The Hague stated that "the evil of homosexuality does not exist in our country." Even within African literature, one finds the acute stigmatization of homosexuality as an unequivocally external phenomenon (Dunton, 1989).

This article makes two assertions: 1) Male homosexuality has long existed within African culture. It was not imported to the continent by any outside forces, as some argue, but has its roots in traditional African social patterns; and 2) Among some ethnic groups, male homosexuality and bisexuality have been viewed as acceptable sexual alternatives. Homosexual males have played important and integral roles in a number of African societies. The discussions that follow seek to support these statements with evidence from diverse regions of the continent. Working with established models, this paper also attempts to further develop a number of categories for understanding male homosexual orientation in an African context, utilizing both traditional and contemporary examples.

According to Foucault, homosexuality, like other sexual variations, was accepted without much controversy in Western Europe until the Victorian period and the rise of a world market economy. "For was the transformation of sex into discourse not governed by the endeavor to expel from reality the forms of sexuality not amenable to *strict economy of production*" (Foucault, 1978). Fortunately, the resulting homophobia has been unable to silence the evidence of homosexuality and bisexuality as acceptable, if not preferable alternatives in a number of societies, most notably in ancient Greece. This is primarily due to the wealth of written material that is the legacy of that society. Our knowledge of homosexual tradition in African cultures is limited by the absence of such material. Lacking firsthand accounts, we are forced to rely upon oral history and the written documentation of foreign social scientists, mainly Europeans and Americans.

The stigmatization of homosexuality in modern Western culture has had a detrimental effect on its examination in cross-cultural contexts. Information regarding homosexuality in both traditional and contemporary African cultures is buried under a pile of both Western and African bias. Western anthropologists have gone to Africa wearing blinders, not seeing homosexual behavior when it existed or imputing to it a negative societal response when there was none. Homophobic filters caused Metraux to declare that "*abnormal* sexual relationships between women (were) tolerated and *accepted* on Easter Island," a strange contradiction in terms for a supposedly unbiased observer (Blackwood, 1986).

Fear of being marginalized within the academy also prevents open-minded researchers—lesbian, gay and otherwise—from undertaking studies designed with a consciousness of homophobic bias. Competition for grants, publication in journals, and tenured positions at prestigious universities function as strong disincentives for those interested in exploring issues perceived as sensitive or controversial.

One cannot, however, discount the role of European missionaries in helping to suppress a free-flow of unbiased information regarding homosexual behavior in Africa. One of the oldest accounts of male homosexual behavior in southern African can be found in Junod's *The Life of a South African Tribe*. While providing important data on male-male marriages in South African mining camps during the first decade of the century, the Swedish missionary can barely contain his disgust. He writes that "these immoral customs [onanism and sodomy] were entirely unknown in the Thonga tribe before the coming of *civilization* [emphasis added]. Unhappily it is no longer so" (Junod 1962, 98).

While noting that traditional marriage customs, including the payment of bride wealth, are maintained in this "disgusting parody of Bantu marriage," and ignoring the likelihood that the Thonga word denoting the male-wives in such relationships developed outside of the camps, in the workers' home villages, Junod posits that such a custom cannot possibly have roots in pre-European society.

Another bias clouding the horizon of research on homosexuality in Africa lies in the unqualified use of psychoanalytic theory. The weak father/dominant mother model, which Freud described as the root of male homosexuality, may have limited value outside of a Western cultural context. Polygamy, extended families, matrilineality, age groups, initiation rituals, and other unique systems make "normal" family life and social development quite different in Africa than in the West. In his work on Zulu spirit mediums, Beattie spends a great deal of time attempting to categorize the type of "hysteria" afflicting male mediums rather than devoting more space to their important role in that society.

Both (Morris, 1965) and (Roberts, 1975) attempt to construct a theory of latent homosexuality in their historical analysis of early 19th-century military leader Shaka of the Zulus. Shaka, born to an unwed mother, was rejected by his father, a Nguni prince, and developed an extremely close relationship with his mother. During his frequent and lengthy military campaigns, he refrained from intercourse, presumably to protect his strength, and demanded that his warriors do the same. Though he maintained a large seraglio, he referred to women of the royal kraal as his sisters, not as wives, and produced no heir to the Zulu throne (Roberts 1975, 86). Morris goes as far to say, "[h]e was unquestionably a latent homosexual, and despite the fact that his genitals had more than made up for their previous dilatoriness, so that he always took great pride in bathing in full public view, he was probably impotent" (1965, 46). Without more concrete evidence, however, we must place this information in the category of interesting but unsubstantiated historical gossip.

Reticence on the part of Africans to openly discuss behavior that runs the risk of being negatively construed by outsiders further, complicated the drawing of a more complete picture of homosexual behavior in Africa. Those who have conducted field research know that oft-studied subjects prove quite adept at discerning the unspoken values of western social scientists. Judith Gay noted in her study of sexual play among girls and young women in Lesotho that "privacy...is an essential aspect of these relations, and points out the women's fear of condemnation by an outsider" (Blackwood, 1986). Linton also takes note of the reticence of the Tanala (Madagascar) to discuss transvestitism and homosexuality in their culture with foreigners (Linton 1933, 229).

In arguing against the existence of homosexual behavior among the Sebei, Walter Goldschmidt writes:

> [T]he Sebei would clearly regard homosexual behavior as
> *sokoran* (illegal taboo), if they practiced it. Sebei informants
> know about homosexuality from other people, but they
> absolutely deny that it occurs among the Sebei, either now or
> in the past, and I am convinced that they are correct in this

assertion. They made no effort to deny transvestism or other acts they know are repugnant to Western society, or to hide the following case, which was reported as a unique (and amusing) item:

"I heard that two men of Kapsumpata were sleeping in the same house and while one was asleep the other had intercourse on him. That man, when he woke up, knocked down the other fellow and had intercourse on him. Old Marakan told me about this" (Goldschmidt 1967, 136).

The author vouches for the veracity of his informant by explaining that the latter would have learned about homosexuality at European-operated boarding schools. It is quite possible that the informant may have also taken into account European ambivalence toward homosexual behavior and colored his comments regarding his own society accordingly. It is also quite remarkable that the author uses an actual example of a homosexual encounter to refute the existence of such activity within the society.

The obstacles to serious scholarship on this topic are numerous and daunting. The sum of material on homosexuality in Africa amounts to brief references to homosexual behavior in ethnographic studies, a few journal articles, and cross-cultural material on sexuality, which may have a paragraph or two, devoted to African realities. Many of the references to Africa are hopelessly out of context. Without having conducted firsthand research on such a complex and hidden phenomenon, this article can only hope to survey the existing material and make a few general observations.

To clearly explain male homosexual behavior in Africa, I have borrowed and expanded a set of categories from Martin Duberman, et al (1989, 9): Type 1: between adults and youths (initiatory); Type 2: between men and biological males who have "female" or "feminine" male status; Type 3: between men of different races or classes; and Type 4: between mean of equal age, status, and class. While these categories are meant to be exhaustive, they are not mutually exclusive.

MALE-WIVES/BOY-WIVES

Institutionalized intergenerational sexual contact among men is nearly as old as civilization itself and is documented in material on ancient Greek, Chinese and Byzantine civilizations (Adam qtd. in Blackwood, 1968). Evans-Pritchard has provided documentation of bisexual behavior in

Azande (Zaire). The Zande warrior class in particular engaged in inter-generational homosexual activity exemplary of Type 1 behavior:

> Many of the young warriors married boys and a commander might have more than one boy-wife. When a warrior married a boy, he paid spears, though only a few, to the boy's parents as he would have done had he married their daughter (Evans-Pritchard 1971, 199).

"He gave the boy pretty ornaments; and he and the boy addressed one another as *badiare*, "my love" and "my lover.""

"The boy fetched water for his husband, collected firewood and kindled his fire, bore his shield when traveling and also a small bag containing wava leaves" (Evans-Pritchard 1970, 1430).

A similar pattern of male-male marriages is found among the ancient Berber culture of Siwa (Egypt) where "men and boys entered into alliances ...with family approval and these alliances had many of the traits of formal marriage"(Adam 1968, 24). In the 20th century, after the military function of the warriors had faded, Siwi clubhouses became known for their hedonistic style, which included music, dancing, drinking, and sexual practices described as "orgiastic" (Adam 1968, 25).

Among both Zande and Siwi, boy-wives were eventually married to women, their former husbands paying the bride price. The new husbands subsequently took boy-wives of their own, making for a society of male interaction that was cyclically bisexual at its core. Though it has not yet been documented by sustained field study, personal observation leads this author to assert that there exists a similar pattern of intergenerational male homosexuality among the Swahili people of the East African corridor, possibly magnified by the Arab/Bantu cultural confluence in that area.

In both of the above cases, boys maintained their male identities both during and after the marriage to the older male. Among, the Bara, Bitsileo and Tanala of Madagascar, there were also marriages of males to other biological males, but in these societies homosexual transvestitism is quite common, pointing to the relevance of Type 2 behavior in this part of Africa. In field research conducted during the early colonial period, Linton (1993) observed that the Malagasy *berdache*, who were "rather numerous" and known among the Bara as *sarombavy*, wore women's clothes, hairstyles, and practiced weaving and other traditionally female activities (298). *Sarombavy* could become fully accepted secondary wives and "seemed to command considerable respect" (298).

Kardiner remarked that the "societal attitude toward this institution is completely natural. The Tanala take it for granted" (1962, 265). Marriage to men provided instant status and an acceptable role in the community for homosexual males, just as it does for young girls entering womanhood.

Male marriages (as well as other manifestations of male homosexuality) were also elements of African societies in the diaspora. In his *Autobiography of a Runaway Slave*, Esteban Montejo gives a first-hand account of these relationships in a 19th-century Cuban slave *barracoon*. Commenting on the scarcity of marriageable women, Montejo writes:

> Some men did not suffer much [from delayed marriages to women], being used to this life. Others had sex between themselves and did not want to know anything of women. This was their life—sodomy. The effeminate men washed the clothes and did the cooking too, if they had a "husband." They were good workers and occupied themselves with their plots of land, giving the produce to their "husbands" to sell to the white framers. It was after the Abolition that the term *effeminate* came into use, for the practice persisted. I don't think it could have come from Africa, because the old men hated it (Montejo 1968, 21).

Montejo was a Cuban-born slave, a *criollito*. Evidence of male-marriages presented here above and elsewhere refute his assertion that this practice was non-African. It is possible, though, that the custom was either foreign or distasteful to the particular groups that were present on Montejo's plantation. Homosexuality may have existed as a marginal or maligned alternative in these cultures, but one that was tolerated nonetheless, just as it was on the plantation. As an aside, it would be interesting to examine whether there is a higher incidence of same-sex behavior in cultures which, due to famine, poverty, warfare, or other causes, must delay marriage for particular individuals or age groups.

Though this paper makes no attempt to address female marriages in any depth, the practice was common and continues to some extent in Dahomey (Benin) among the Nandi, the Lovedu, and other southern Bantu groups (Oboler, 1980). In Nandi tradition, the inheritance of property was an exclusively male right. Some women who had produced no male heir initiated these marriages in order to have a son to whom they could bequeath their share of a male-husband's property. The older woman would betroth—complete with the traditional payment of bride wealth—a younger woman who would take a male consort and produce heirs; the children would belong to the clan of the female-husband's male husband. Though it would appear to an outsider that women were tacitly forced into the role of female-husbands to satisfy patriarchal restrictions on property inheritance, many women, both older and younger, reported that they preferred these marriages as they gave them greater autonomy in their daily lives. These marriages are not reported to have been sexual in nature, but further sensitive study might reveal interesting information on African female sexuality.

Thus it appears that many Africans societies show remarkable flexibility in accommodating divergent sexuality, mainly in the assignment of gender roles. Sexual genitalia at birth is merely one determinant of the gender-linked roles an individual will play throughout his or her life. Inheritance customs, societal patterns regarding initiation cycles in the case of boy-wives, and sexual desires are other important determining factors.

Priests, Witches, and Mediums: Spirituality and the African Homosexual

In many cultures a strong link exists between homosexuals and spirituality. This phenomenon is not unique to Africa but is found in ethnographic material from around the world. The religious role of "berdache" biological groups has been well documented. *Winkte* were respected and powerful member of Lakota Sioux societies, famous for their curative and clairvoyant abilities (Williams 1986, 192). Homosexual men were temple priests in ancient China (Karlen, 1971) and heavily represented among the ranks of the devotees in the monasteries of medieval Europe.(Boswell 1989, 28).

Beattie has documented the role of male transvestites within Zulu (southern Africa) and Lugbara (Uganda) spirit cults. While the majority of Zulu spirit mediums were women, most of the men who experienced possession and subsequently joined the cults evidenced homosexual orientation. Spirit possession usually occurred when a man was still young and unmarried. Possessed males dressed as women, often spoke in high-pitched tones, and reported dreams that were homosexual in nature. "Usually the dreamer was passive and was being attached, sexually or aggressively, by another male, sometimes his own male ancestors" (Beattie 1969, 143).

In societies which, as a result of low birth rates, high infant mortality or agrarian labor requirements place a high value on reproductive ability, we might surmise that exclusively homosexual males were unlikely to have high status, even if there existed the option for self-actualization through becoming "male-wives." Spirit mediums, on the other hand, are "shrewd, intelligent, and accepted members of their communities" (Beattie, xxiv). They provide the important services of divining, recommending cures, and appeasing ancestors. Membership in a spirit cult, or recognition as a skilled medium, offered a route to social empowerment for men who couldn't or wouldn't follow the traditional avenue for marriage and fathering.

Besmer (1983) makes a similar point in his description of homosexual males in Hausa *bori* possession cults. Homosexual males and others "whose status identity is somewhat ambiguous" being integral and regularized through cult membership (122).

All of the associations of homosexuality to magic are not wholesome ones. Among the Nyakyusa (Tanzania and Zambia), homosexual relations between boys, and even between boys and men, constitute fairly acceptable behavior. Forcing another boy into homosexual relations, however, is classified as witchcraft (*bo bulosi*) (Wilson 1951, 196).

Evans-Pritchard (1937) noted Zande men's fear of lesbian sex, which was commonly practiced, especially in the royal courts. Respondents described homosexual women as "the sort who may well give birth to cats and be witches also" (56). The bisexuality of Sande men, however, is viewed quite differently, as discussed earlier.

A recent article in a commonly read Nigerian magazine shows that the spiritual connection to homosexuality continues to the present day:

> One bizarre yet interesting feature of homosexuality in the country is that it is cult-oriented and is making millionaires out of those who belong...after every love session, Q [magazine] learnt, the big shots who normally play the aggressor role, rush home keeping mum. At home, they wash with some charms in a bowl and perform a ceremony...its success is said to bring about a windfall of money (Egbi, 1988).

Following this connection into the diaspora, Peter Fry and others have found that sexually passive homosexual men, or *bichas*, play leadership roles in cult houses in the Blem region of Brazil. In describing this phenomenon in Afro-Brazilian religion, Fry explains:

> Whatever the proportion of males ascribed either real *bicha* [queen] or incubated *bicha* [closet queen] status in the cults, the fact remains that most people believe that the two roles are linked. No one, however, has gone so far as to say that all males who danced in the *terreiros* were *bichas*. Nevertheless, a large number of the most expressive and important *pais de santo* in Blem fall into the category (Fry 1986, 143).

A connection can be drawn between African homosexual mediums, their counterparts among the *bicha* of Brazilian Umbanda cults, and "church queens," African American gay men prominent as ministers, choir leaders, and gospel singers in the black Protestant churches of contemporary North American life.

What is it about homosexuals that promotes the carving out of these roles? Why do societies sometimes view them as closer to the metaphysical world? This can partially be explained by a perception of such individuals as having both male and female essences, of being *obaa banyin* (female men), as they are described by the Akan.

All social actors have a need to achieve status in their societies. Becoming a "male-wife" is one means of achieving status while embracing important roles in the community's spiritual life is another, be these roles ascetic as in European and American monasteries, or flamboyant as in African and Brazilian cults. Fry notes:

> Both homosexuality and the possession cults share a common reputation as deviant in relation to dominant Brazilian values...to be defined by society as defiling and dangerous is often a positive advantage to those who practice a profession which deals in magical power. Persons who are defined and who define themselves as homosexuals find themselves classified as "perverts" and "deviants" and thus live on the margins of the formal social structure (Fry 1986, 139).

HOMOSEXUALITY AND LANGUAGE IN AFRICA
Many African cultures use words that Western linguists have translated as "homosexual" (see Fanti, Hausa, Swahili dictionaries). Most

often, however, these words indicate some sort of androgyny or a combination of male and female characteristics, arguing that individuals described by such terms are not viewed as different with regard to sexual orientation in the Western sense, but within the arena of gender. "Realist extremists...assume that lexical equivalence betokens experiential equality, and that the occurrence of a word that 'means' *homosexual* demonstrates the existence of 'homosexuality' as the modern realist understands it, at the time the text was composed" (Boswell 1989, 22).

The Akan (Ghana) were quite familiar with homosexuality, but viewed it in culturally relevant terms as indicated by the expressions for such individuals in Fanti language. Described by a western anthropologist, "There is the life principle (*okra*), the blood principle (*mogya*), and what might be called the personality principle (*sunsum*).... In this sense, *sunsum* is not an entity; it is, rather, a manner of being" (Wiredu 1990, 224).

"A 'light' *sunsum* is characteristic of a woman, while an extroverted female, or one with homosexual tendencies, thus having a 'heavy' *sunsum* is referred to as *obaa banyin* (female man) ...Similarly, males with 'light' *sunsum* are the cowards, the sexual deviants, or those of retarded mentality who usually stay around the house in the company of women, and are referred to as *banyin obaa*, 'male woman' " (Christensen 1954, 92).

The term that describes homosexual transvestites in Lango, a Nilotic agricultural people living along the banks of the White Nile in East Africa, is *Jo Abioch*, or "the impotents." Driberg says that such individuals are believed to have been born "ruined" and have adopted the female role out of necessity:

> Being impotent, they have all the instincts and nature of women...They wear the characteristic facial and bodily ornaments of a woman ...they wear their hair long, dressing it in ringlets like women's hair, and take women's names.... They appear in all respects to be mentally sound and are most industrious. Being women, therefore, in all except physical characteristics, they are treated as such, and live with a man as his wife without offending against Lango law (Driberg 1923, 210).

The process of becoming a woman is expressed in Langi by the term *dano mulokere, mudoko dako*, supporting the notion that among the Lango, gender, while being definite, was not definitive. Africans, or the gods who rule them, seem to have considerable flexibility in determining gender at different stages of the life cycle.

SAME-SEX ENVIRONMENTS

Jails and other facilities for detention did not exist in traditional African systems. Modern African prisons, like their Western counterparts, are same-sex environments in which consensual sex between males, homosexual prostitution, and rape are found. Role differentiation in this environment appears to be quite strong, with those accepting the passive sexual position being viewed as "wives" (Tanner, 1969).

Age-group segregation creates another set of single-sex environments worth investigating. Wilson documented sexual play, including fellatio and anal intercourse, among preinitiated boys and young men in Nyakyusa age-villages (Type 4 behavior). Elders considered such activity to be relatively harmless as long as it was consensual (190).

Homosexual liaisons occurring in South African mine camps present an interesting example of Type 1 (initiatory), and Type 2 (gender-differentiated) homosexual behavior. Several studies have described the relationships between older and younger mine workers. Such relationships were quite common and at least partially predicated on the grounds that "Mature men with authority...are entitled to regular sexual activity. The gender of the partner seems of less import than the overriding right to sexual congress" (Moddie 1989, 124).

Preparation for these marriages included the payment of bride wealth to the elder brother of the betrothed boy in certain instances (Junod 1962, 493). In addition to sexual availability, the boys' duties included fetching water, cooking food, and doing odd jobs, traditionally the jobs of females in village settings. For the "boys," who were really younger men in their early 20s, the benefits of such relationships included financial assistance, preferential job assignments, and immediate acceptance through their husband, or *sibonda*, into the hierarchical structure of the camp life. These relationships, which remain a feature of mine life today, usually involve penetration between the thighs, but according to one informant, "when they got drunk, men kissed each other openly" (Moddie 1989, 416).

Unlike those mining diamonds, men working in the gold mines did have access to the outside world and to women, so it is not wholly correct to classify such environments as "gender-closed." Some miners, it appears, preferred the life of the camps. As one Pondo respondent explained:

> I had an *induna* as my best friend who took me to the township.
> Again I had a boy, and the *induna* had one too. In the township
> we both had girlfriends. We left the boys in the compound when
> we went to town, but we never spent the night in the township.
> We just spent a few hours with our girlfriends and then returned
> to our boys. We loved them better (Moddie 1989, 420).

The camps provide an environment in which men with homosexual orientations are able to express hidden desires, to "come out," in the Western sense. "Such men (who preferred other men) either became fixtures on the mines, often puppets of mine management, or they left the mines for urban employment or to join criminal gangs" (Moddie 1989, 421).

Some transvestitism in the camps has been witnessed, particularly on special occasions such as holidays or feasts. In 1912 Junod recorded parades involving "*tinkhontshana*, boys who have placed on their chests the breasts of women carved in wood, who are going to the dance in order to play the part of women" (Junod 1962, 492). These "wives of the mines" were, however, simultaneously mine workers, many playing traditionally male roles in their work lives. In their mid 20s young men grew too old for their roles as wives. Many who returned to the mines for additional contracts took boy-wives of their own.

The instances, both historical and contemporary, of male-male marriage in South African mine camps, in Azande, Siwa, and elsewhere on the continent, encourage a reevaluation of notions of family by anthropologists and social historians. The African men described above are using relationships with other men to improve their economic situations much in the same way that southern Malawian women from *anjira* bonds with other women (which have not been recorded as sexual) to survive famine, illness, and other periods of economic hardship (Vaughn, 1983). Without a better understanding of male relationships, those looking at family structures among groups in which such liaisons were common may be missing an important piece of the puzzle.

"IN THE LIFE": THE EMERGENCE OF AN AFRICAN GAY COMMUNITY

Modern Western assumptions of homosexual lifestyles (exclusive of predominant same-sex object choice, childlessness, independence from traditional family structures) are antithetical to traditional African values (which emphasize reproductive fertility and responsibility to an extended family). Contrary to the ideals of individuals and personal rights that have come to characterize Western society, an African worldview tends to emphasize rights and duties equally.

Asmarom Legesse claims that "no aspect of Western civilization makes an African more uncomfortable than the concept of the socialized individual whose private wars against society are celebrated." Denolt Ngom further contends that Africans have no notion of private (individual) life; even lovemaking has a ritualized, public nature to it. Olusola Ojo agrees that "the Africans assume harmony, not divergence of interests...and are more inclined to think of their obligations to other members of society rather than their claims against them" (Howard 1990, 162).

African communalism, however, is not nearly as harmonious a concept as these scholars argue. Individualism and personal rights, including the right to protection from one's own group, are becoming increasingly valued in Africa and ingrained in national constitutions and regional human rights treaties.

The views of African leaders are slowly beginning to reflect changing attitudes toward homosexuality. The application for UN Economic and Social Committee consultative status submitted in 1991 by the International Lesbian and Gay Association, though unsuccessful, was supported by delegates from both Ethiopia and Lesotho. The Ethiopian representative stated, "[T]his is an example of the problems confronting minorities. The United Nations should be the last place to exercise discrimination." The representative from Lesotho went further, advising his colleagues that a positive vote was "a chance for us to liberate ourselves" (qtd. at ECOSOC NonGovernmental Organizations Hearing, 22 January 1991). In its proposed constitution for a new South Africa, the African National Congress has declared discrimination on the grounds of sexual orientation to be unlawful.

Nevertheless, men and women known to engage in homosexual behavior face significant prejudice in Africa. Though increasingly visible in urban areas, those seeking to live outside of traditional roles face a variety of responses from their communities, including disbelief, ridicule, and contempt. And despite the allegations of African politicians that homosexuality is a purely Western phenomenon, most African nations have laws that prohibit sexual contact between men, statutes adopted mainly from the jurisprudence of the former colonial powers. The need for laws to regulate behaviors which do not exist has not yet been explained.

We have argued that homosexual men have been present as important actors in many African societies. It is only in modern history, however, and in urban settings that we can begin to identify a "gay" community, by Western definitions. We refer here to the social networks, formal and information, in which homosexual and bisexual men meet, entertain, seek and provide information and support, and enter into relationships with other men. Though these networks are often clandestine and virtually invisible to an outsider, they are fast becoming an undeniable element of urban African life.

Just as the development of gay and lesbian political organizations and social networks in the West have evolved over time, similar institutions are emerging with their own particular forms and styles in Africa. Traditional roles of all kinds are being questioned, discarded, and retooled in African cities throughout the continent. If the available historical literature is representative, it is only now that we are beginning to experience more Type Four consensual age/status–equal sexual behavior between adult males.

Bars frequented by African male homo/bisexuals have existed in the last ten years in Abidjan, Ivory Coast; Dakar, Senegal; Lagos, Nigeria; and Nairobi. In North Africa, *hammams,* or bathhouses, serve as meeting grounds for homosexual and bisexual men. Gay and lesbian organizations are currently functioning in Ghana, Zimbabwe, and South Africa. Liberia's gay organization had over 75 members prior to the recent political shredding in that country. According to Nigeria's *Quality* magazine, homosexuals, "are getting more and more aggressive and courageous by the day and are made up of the top brass in the society—successful lawyers, doctors, swanky businessmen, military men, ex-politicians, diplomats, and university undergraduates—all with a passion for men" (Egbi 1988, 10).

While this may be something of a paranoid response to the increased visibility of homosexually identified men in Africa, allegations of homosexuality were used in 1990 against Nigerian head of state Ibrahim Babangida as an excuse for the stating of a military coup to unseat him, indicating the willingness of the Nigerian populace to acknowledge the existence of homosexuals within the highest ranks of their society ("Successful Coup Announced," *FBIS* 23, April 1990, 20).

Our discussion of homosexuality in contemporary Africa would not be complete without reference to the influence of foreign gays, particularly Europeans and North Americans, who play a pivotal role in urban homosexual male subcultures. Unfettered by the traditional values and societal pressures that tend to silence Africans, the homes of Europeans become headquarters for homosexual nexus. Male prostitution (Type 3 behavior) emerged in African cities, as it did elsewhere in the developing world, to service the appetites of an expatriate homosexual elite and the burgeoning tourist trade. (See V.S. Naipaul's "In a Free State," Spartacus' *Gay Guide to the World*.) Homosexual relationships between expatriates and Africans are also common, many having an informal financial component. White gays, be they missionaries, businessmen, or Peace Corps volunteers, have helped to disseminate the Western concept of homosexuality in Africa.

Homosexuality, however, remains heavily stigmatized, and African males who engage in homosexual relationships lead secretive lives. Most are partners in heterosexual marriages, playing the roles modern society demands of them, that of father and breadwinner, thus maintaining their community's ignorance of their homosexual activities. According to one young activist,

> Here in Ghana, gay life is very hard. I mean, since it is not legalized, all of our activities are behind closed doors. Though we are as many as one can imagine, each and every one of us is afraid to come out of his/her shells, be vocal. Besides, the people take homosexuality as a taboo and therefore a disgrace to a family. Gays are absolutely neglected in the system. If one is found to be gay, he can easily lose his job and any social gatherings, he is neglected. But among ourselves, we are happy because though we are not legalized, we have free movement, by organizing parties, going to beaches and the like. But the next problem is how to get the people educated on the issue of homosexuality.... (Anon, 1990).

African literature, while still maintaining a significant bias against homosexuality, has at least begun to include some homosexual characters. Novels such as Yulisa Amadu Maddy's *No Past, No Present, No Future*, published by the prestigious African Writers Series, and more recently Thomas Mpoyi Buatu's *La Réproduction*, are paving the way for a more enlightened treatment of the subject by African intellectuals.

The evidence in this essay demonstrates that homosexuality is not new to Africa, but is located within a rich tradition of accommodation to diversity. Through the institutions of boy-wives, spirit mediumship, and male initiation rituals, homosexuality was indeed a regular part of the sexual patterns of many African ethnic groups. But why was homosexuality accepted in some cultures, but marginalized or rejected in others? Given the integral role of homosexuals in some African cultures, is there a corollary tolerance for urban gays in the cities to which such ethnic groups migrated? If not, what are the roots of modern intolerance, and how can it be combated? These and other questions are raised for future scholarship.

Two Akan maxims seem relevant in concluding the very beginning of this important discussion, which must be taken up by other social scientists:

"Everyone is the offspring of God; no one the offspring of the earth." (Everyone has the right to pursue their unique destiny, and no one is a lesser person.)

"Nobody was there when I was taking my destiny from God." (Despite the strong sense of African communalism, everyone has a right to privacy and to negotiate their own destiny within their moral conscience) (Wiredu, 1990).

The moral basis for a gay rights movement in Africa is already in place. It need only be further elaborated through an open-minded examination of African attitudes toward diversity. The historical basis is also available, but needs further unearthing by enlightened scholars, particularly Africans, who can dig through the cultural biases, their own and those of others, to amass a body of serious scholarship on homosexuality in African.

REFERENCES

An-Na'im, A.A. (Ed.). (1990). *Human Rights in Africa: Cross Cultural Perspectives*. Washington, D.C.: The Brookings Institution.

Anon. "Letter to Author." Nov. 1, 1990.

Beattie, J. (1969). *Spirit Mediumship and Society in Africa*. New York: Africana.

Besmer, F. (1983). *Horses, Musicians, and Gods: The Hausa Cult of Possession-Trance*. South Hadley: Bergin and Harvey.

Boswell, J. (1989). "Revolutions: Universal and Sexual Categories." In *Hidden From History: Reclaiming the Gay and Lesbian Past*, edited by Martin Duberman, et al. New York: Meridian.

Christensen, J. B. (1954). *Double Descent Among the Fanti*. New Haven: Yale University.

Driberg, J.J. (1989). *The Lango: A Nilotic Tribe of Uganda*. London: Adelphi Terrace.

Dunton, C. (1989). "'Wheyting Be Dat?': The Treatment of Homosexuality in African Literature." *Research in African Literatures* 3: 422-448.

Egbi, R. "Men With a Passion for Men." *Quality*, June 16, 1988: 10-15.

Evans-Pritchard, E.E. (1970). *Sexual Inversion Among the Azande*. Oxford: Clarendon.

— (1971). *The Azande*. Oxford: Clarendon.

— (1937). *Witchcraft Among the Azande*.

Foucault, M. (1978). *The History of Sexuality*. New York: Pantheon Books.

Goldschmidt, W. (1978). *Sebei Law*. Berkeley: University of California Press. In *Homosexual Behavior*. New York: Harrington Park Press.

Howard, R.E. "Group Versus Individual Identity In the African Debate on Human Rights." In *Human Rights in Africa,* edited by Abdullahi Ahmed An-Na'im. and Francis Deng. Washington, D.C.: Brookings Institute.

International Gay Association. (1984). *Pink Book: A Global View of Lesbian and Gay Oppression and Liberation*. Amsterdam: International Association of Lesbians, Gay Women, and Gay Men.

Junod, H. A. (1962). *Life of a South African Tribe*. New York: University Books.

Kardiner, A. (1962). *The Individual and His Society*. New York.

Karlen, A. (1971). *Sexuality and Homosexuality: A New View*. New York: Norton.

Linton, R. (1933). *The Tanala: A Hill Tribe of Madagascar*. Chicago.

Montejo, E. (1968). *Autobiography of a Runaway Slave*. London: The Bodley Head Ltd.

Moodie, T.B. (1989). "Migrancy and Male Sexuality and the South African Gold Mines." In *Hidden From History: Reclaiming the Gay and Lesbian Past,* edited by Martin Duberman, et al. New York: Meridian.

Oboler, R. S. (1980). "Is the Female Husband a Man?: Woman/Woman Marriage Among the Nandi of Kenya." *Ethnology* 19: 69-88.

Roberts, B. (1975). *The Zulu Kings*. New York.

Tanner, R.E.S. (1969). "The East African Experience of Imprisonment." In *African Penal Systems,* edited by Alan Milner. New York: Praeger.

Vaughn, M. "Which Family ?: Problems in the Reconstruction of the History of the Family as an Economic and Cultural Unit." *Journal of African History* 24, 1983.

Walter L. Williams. (1986). "Persistence and Change in the Berdache Tradition Among Contemporary Lakota Indians." In *The Many Faces of Homosexuality,* edited by Evelyn Blackwood. New York: Harrington Park Press.

Wilson, M. (1951). *Good Company: A Study of Nyakyusa Age Villages*. London.

Wiredo, K. (1990). "An Africa Perspective On Human Rights." In *Human Rights in Africa,* edited by Abdullahi Ahmed An-Na'im and Francis Deng. Washington, D.C.: Brookings Institute.

Mati-ism and Black Lesbianism: Two Idealtypical Expressions of Female Homosexuality in Black Communities of the Diaspora

Gloria Wekker

Summary

There are different ways in which black women in the Diaspora have given expression to their erotic fascination with other women. In this article two idealtypical expressions of black female homosexuality and the outlines of their underlying cosmologies are sketched: *mati*-ism and black lesbianism. *Mati* (or *matisma*) is the Sranan Tongo word for women who have sexual relations with other women but who typically also will have had or still have relationships with men, simultaneously. More often than not they will also have children. While both types can only be understood via a constructionist view of homosexuality, the institution of *mati*-ism will be shown to have retained more Afrocentric, working-class elements, while black lesbianism has more middle-class, Eurocentric features.

Introduction

In this article I focus on the experience of black women and the ways in which their erotic interest in those of their own gender have taken shape. I shall begin by giving a résumé of the historical and social factors that enable us to think of the black female experience in the Diaspora as a unitary, though multifaceted, process. I shall then indicate that ideas about female homosexuality in black communities in the Diaspora are anything but uniform. By presenting a large excerpt from a public discussion with two black women poets, I hope to elucidate the contours of two idealtypical cosmologies as far as female homosexuality is concerned. I am assuming that their views are representative of those held by larger groups of women in black communities in the United States, Suriname, and the Netherlands. These cosmologies may be indicated as *mati*-ism and black lesbianism. My argument will make clear that both types can only be understood via a constructionist view of homosexuality.

Mati-ism and Black Lesbianism

You Are the Offspring of Slaves

Black women of the Diaspora share a terrible history involving the slave trade based in Africa, a history of being transported like cattle across the Atlantic Ocean, of rootlessness in the "New" World, of centuries of living under a system of slavery, of various degrees of retention in their communities of African elements, and after abolition (Suriname 1863; USA 1865), of living in sexist and racist societies, based on class.

Originating from West Africa, an area that stretches from Senegal to Angola and extending far into the interior, slaves belonged to various tribes with hundreds of different languages and dialects, different systems of family relationships, and many habits and customs. For centuries slaves of both sexes in the Americas were forbidden to learn how to read and write and had few opportunities to develop their creative and artistic gifts. The list of prohibitions to which they were subjected was extensive: No marriages were permitted without the consent of their masters nor other relations among themselves; they had no control over children born to such relationships; their children were the property of the mother's owner; they had no right to own property or to wear shoes and no protection against cruel and unreasonable treatment by the master class.

For both the North American and the Surinamese slaves, one of the things that enabled them to maintain themselves in their new environment was their African culture, which they endeavored to keep intact in the given circumstances and which, in the unshakeable misery of their existence, gave them a sense of having something to which they belonged and that afforded them some foothold. In the days of slavery and later on, the role women played in preserving, communicating, and developing elements of African culture was of inestimable importance. Recent scholarship indicates that the principal residue of the African cultural heritage in the Diaspora should be explored in the realm of social values and orientations to reality rather than in more or less concrete sociocultural forms (Mintz and Price, 1976).

Important differences between the history of black women in the U.S. and that of black women in Suriname can be pointed to. Some of these differences affected the degree to which retentions—especially orientations to reality—were able to continue almost unharmed. One of these differences concerns the ratio of blacks to whites that existed during a great part of the 18th and 19th centuries in the (former) British and Dutch colonies. In North America whites have always significantly outnumbered blacks. The ratio in 1780 was, for example, 15 to one (Price 1976). On the estates of the Surinamese colony, on the other hand, a handful of whites endeavored to exert control over an immense number of slaves. The ratio there ranged from one to 25 in the urban area, to one to 65 in the plantation districts further removed from the capital (Van Lier, 1949).

It was partly due to this numerical relationship that a different cultural policy toward slaves took shape in the two colonies. British colonists succeeded in forbidding their slaves to speak their original African languages. As a result, Black English with a grammar, a syntax, and a lexicon of its own developed. In Suriname, on the other hand, slaves were left free to develop their own tongue, a creole called Negro English (now Sranan Tongo), for centuries. They were also allowed to elaborate and work out their own cultures. Government policy in the colony until abolition and after, until 1876, was aimed at creating as wide as possible a geographical, cultural, and psychological gap between the colonists and the slaves. The ban on speaking Dutch was only one of an endless series of ordinances designed with this view in mind.

Generally speaking, Surinamese slaves had more freedom than their North American partners in misfortune, and for a longer period of time they were able to cultivate their languages and ways of life and thought, as long as these did not conflict with the interests of the planter class. That the African constituent in the Surinamese orientation to reality must have been considerable for many centuries is emphasized by the fact that the importation of so-called "saltwater negroes" (i.e., slaves newly transported from Africa) was a continuing necessity until the official ban on the slave trade in 1808. In contrast to the situation in North America, where the capacity of female slaves to produce children was encouraged and in certain periods even subjected to coercion, Surinamese planters preferred to force as much labor from the slaves as possible in the space of a few years. The mistreatment, undernourishment, and murder of slaves repeatedly saw to it that within a few years the entire body of slaves could be "written off." Surinamese female slaves hardly reproduced. Whereas at the end of the U.S. Civil War there were 4 million blacks, the Surinamese census only counted 50,000 ex-slaves at the time of abolition, while roughly the same number of slaves (350,000 to 400,000) had been imported over the past two and a half centuries (Van Lier, 1949). The world the slave owners created in Suriname was one which one left as soon as one could, with one's pockets loaded with money.

Despite the differences between North American and Surinamese history, the correspondences are so marked that one can speak of a unitary, though multi-faceted, experience of black women in the Diaspora.

Considering the Roots, Surinamese Style

In describing the history of black women in the Diaspora, I have made no distinction between the history of black women in general and "lesbian" women in particular. There are various reasons for this. First, black "lesbian" women have for the greater part of the time they have been in the Diaspora played an integral part in their communities; they were subject to the same orders and prohibitions as other women in these communities. Secondly—this is important in regard to their position in their own circles—they often had simultaneous relationships with men and had children. The earliest information about *mati*-ism in Suriname dates from the beginning of this century, 1912, and refers precisely to its being embedded in the culture of the ordinary Creole population. A.J. Schimmelpenninck van den Oye, a high ranking Dutch government official, remarks in a memorandum on the physical condition of the "underprivileged":

> Speaking about the physically weak condition of so many young women, in addition another reason should be mentioned. I am referring to the sexual communion between women themselves (*"mati* play"), which immorality has, as I gather, augmented much in the past decades, and, alas!, penetrated deeply into popular customs. It is not only that young girls and unattached women of various classes make themselves guilty of this, the poorest often going and living together in pairs to reduce the cost of house rent and food for each of them, but women who live with men, and even schoolgirls, do the same, following the example of others (Ambacht 1912, 98-99).

Somewhat later, in the 1930s, *mati* culture had taken on such proportions that another reporter, Th. Comvalius, expressed his disturbance about:

> the unusual relationships among women in Suriname, which

were not dependent on social rank, intellectual development, race or country of origin. Love brought women and young girls of very different walks of life together as intimate friends. While this in itself could be called a "sociological misconception," there is another, dark side to it, the discussion of which is no concern of ours. Probably it was blown over here from the French West Indies (Comvalius n.d., 11).

In hindsight, it is possible to state that the institution of *mati* relationships did not just fall out of the blue sky. Linguistically, two explanations for the word *mati* are offered: It can be traced to the old Dutch *maatje*, meaning *buddy, mate*; the other explanation is more convincing and links it to the Hausa terms *mata* or *mace*: *woman, wife*. It is now known that in a number of West African regions from which slaves were taken—for example, Ashanti and Dahomey—that female homosexuality was practiced in times long past and that it was not burdened with negative sanctions prohibiting it. Anthropologists Herskovits reported that in Dahomey a woman could formally marry another woman and that offspring born to the one woman were regarded as the children of the other woman (Herskovits, M. and F. Herskovits 1938). Female slaves who were carried off to the "New" World were therefore familiar with the phenomenon. Elsewhere it is stated about the Saramaka Maroons, the descendants of the runaway slaves who formed viable societies in the rain forests of Suriname from the 17th century on, that in Saramaka society,

> *Mati* is a highly charged volitional relationship, usually between two men, that dates back to the Middle Passage— *mati*s were originally "shipmates," those who had survived the journey out from Africa together; *Sibi* is a relationship of special friendship between two women. As with the *mati* relationship, the reciprocal term of address derives from the Middle Passage itself: *Sibi* referred to shipmates, those who had experienced the trauma of enslavement and transport together (Price and Price 1991, 396; 407).

The word *sibi* does not occur with this meaning in Sranan Tongo, the coastal creole; here the term *mati* covers all modalities. It may very well be that, encapsulated in the Sranan Tongo *mati*, there may at one time also have been the notion of shipmates who had survived together, but at present that connotation is no longer there.

Features of *mati* culture mentioned in older sources have been preserved to this day. There were, for example, female couples who wore *patweri*: the same dress; women who embroidered handkerchiefs with loving texts in silk for each other: *lobi kon"*(love has come) and *lobi n'e prati* (love does not go away); women who courted each other by means of special ways of folding and wearing their *eanyisa,* head cloths; and finally, the widespread institution of *lobi singi* (love songs). In these songs women sing the praises of their *mati*, in metaphorical language and enlarge the faults of their rivals (Comvalius n.d.; Herskovits 1936). One such text is sung as follows:

> *Roos e flauw* (The rose is weak)
> *A de fadon* (It has fallen down)
> *Roos e flauw* (The rose is weak)
> *A de fadon* (It has fallen down)
>
> *Ma stanvaste* (But steadfast)
> *Dat e tan sidon* (That stays upright.)

Mati relationships in 1990 are a very visible feature of Afro-Surinamese working-class culture. Spokespersons speak of "one big family," in which everyone knows each other and older women clearly predominate. But women and men of younger age groups are also present. Many female couples have a marked role division, in which one partner will play a "male" role and the other a "female" role. It is, furthermore, important to note that a *mati* career, for most women, is not a unidirectional path; thus it is possible that a woman may take a man for a lover after she has had several relationships with women. It is also not unusual for a woman to have both a female and a male lover at the same time. Nor does *mati* life necessarily imply restriction to one partner. As one 35-year-old informant told me:

> I never have just one lover at the same time. I have my *tru visiti* ("steady girlfriend") and then two or three other lovers. If my "steady" is a Creole woman, I take care that the others are of different ethnic origin or just over here on vacation from Holland, because Creoles aren't likely to take this arrangement easily. I handpick my lovers; I don't take just anybody. Because it takes a lot of time to find a "Ms. Right," I can't

afford to begin looking after me and my steady have broken up. So I keep them in reserve.

AN AFRICAN AMERICAN ANGLE

The literature of black North American women writers, which began to appear in a rich variety of forms from the beginning of the 1970s, makes it clear that the societies they describe would have been unthinkable failing the strong ties of love and eroticism among women. The literature also reveals a certain tolerance of homosexuality in working classes, as long as it does not bear a name, and this corresponds with the situation in Suriname. I want to illustrate this by a single fragment from the biomythographical novel *Zami, A New Spelling of My Name* by Audre Lorde. In this fragment the North American black communities of the 1950s are discussed and Lorde describes the attitude of Cora, a factory worker and mother of Zami's first woman lover, Ginger:

> With her typical aplomb, Cora welcomed my increased presence around the house with the rough familiarity and browbeating humor due another one of her daughters. If she recognized the sounds emanating from the sunporch on the nights I slept over, or our haggard eyes the next day, she ignored them. But she made it very clear that she expected Ginger to get married again. "Friends are nice, but marriage is marriage," she said to me one night as she helped me make a skirt on her machine.... "And when she gets home don't be thumping that bed all night, neither, because it's late already and you girls have work tomorrow" (Lorde 1982, 142).

LESBIANISM, SAY WHAT?

In addition to the established custom of women having relationships with other women and the degree of tolerance for this in black communities, there is another reason for my choosing not to make a sharp distinction between the history of black women in general and "lesbian" women in particular. There are strong indications that the Western categories of "homo," "bi," and "hetero" have insufficient justification in some black situations. The concept of "homosexuality" introduces an etic category that is alien to the indigenous emic system that exists in some sections of black communities.

Sexuality cannot be considered independently from the social order in which it exists. Ross and Rapp state rightly that the biological basis of sexuality is always experienced and interpreted according to cultural values. The simple biological facts of sexuality are not self-explanatory; they require social expression. The image they employ for the universal rootedness of sexuality in larger social units such as family relationships, communities, national and world systems, is that of the union. One may have the illusion that by peeling off one layer after another, one comes nearer to the core of sexuality, after which one realizes that all the different layers together form its essence (Ross and Rapp, 1983).

How societies precisely give form to sexuality remains relatively obscure. I am not claiming to describe all the different layers of the emic system of sexuality to which *mati*-ism belongs. I would, however, like to sketch the outlines of two idealtypical sociohistorical structures, situating two differing cosmologies, as far as female homosexuality in black communities is concerned.

In summer 1986, black women in Amsterdam had the good fortune to be witnesses to and participants in a public discussion between two eminent women poets, true children of the black Diaspora, Audre Lorde and Astrid Roemer. While many subjects were addressed during this discussion, the burning question, which also aroused a passionate interest among the audience, proved to be the matter of name-giving/nomenclature: How important is it that black women who love other women should call themselves "black lesbians"?

Two Idealtypical Expressions

ASTRID ROEMER: I do not call myself lesbian, and I do not want to be called lesbian either. Life is too complex for us to give names not derived from us, dirty, conditioned words, to the deepest feelings within me. If I were to call myself a lesbian, it would mean that I should be allowing myself—on the most banal, biological level—to be classed as one who chooses persons who also have female genitals. If I love a woman, I love that one woman and one swallow does not make a summer.

People have a masculine and a feminine component in them, and these two components constantly seek to come into equilibrium with each other and with the rest of the world. Who is to say whether I shall not love a man in my later life? The result of that search for equilibrium is not a constant. I should be terribly ashamed as a human being were I to know in advance that for the rest of my life I should love only women. It would, moreover, conflict with feminism, for feminism also insists that men can change.

AUDRE LORDE: First of all, I want to make clear what I understand by a lesbian. It is not having genital intercourse with a woman that is the criterion. There are lesbian women who have never had genital or any other form of sexual contact with another woman, while there are also women who have had sex with other women but who are not lesbian. A lesbian is a woman who identifies fundamentally with women as her first field of strength, of vulnerability, of comfort lies in a network of women. If I call myself a black feminist lesbian, I am acknowledging by that that the roots of my strength, and of my vulnerability, lie in myself as a woman. What I am trying to achieve in the first place is changes in my awareness and that of other women. My priority does not lie with men.

There are two reasons only why I call myself a black lesbian. It makes me aware of my own strength and shows my vulnerability too. In the '60s we could do anything we wanted to as long as we did not talk about it. If you speak your name, you represent a threat to the powers that be, the patriarchate. That's what I want to be too. The price I pay for that and the vulnerability it makes me aware of are no greater than what I feel if I keep it a secret and let others decide what they want to call me. That also perpetuates the positions of inferiority we occupy in society.

The other reason I consider it important is that there may be a woman in my audience who, through this, may see that it is possible to speak your name and to go on living. If we, who are in a relatively more secure position enabling us to come out for what we are, if we fail to do so that will only perpetuate the vicious circle of inferiority."

ASTRID: I think your definition of a lesbian is interesting. In that sense, all Surinamese women are lesbian, because they draw their strength to carry on from women. All the same, I do not see why it is necessary to declare oneself a lesbian. In the community from which I come, there is not so much talk about the phenomenon of women having relations with other women. There are, after all, things which aren't to be given names—giving them names kills them. But we do have age-old rituals originating from Africa by which women can make quite clear that special relations exist between them. For instance, birthday rituals can be recognized by anyone and are quite obvious. Also, when two women are at a party and one hands the other a glass or a plate of food from which she has first tasted herself, it is clear to everybody and their mother what that means. Why then is it necessary to declare oneself a lesbian? It is usual there. Surinamese women claim the right to do what they want to do. They can love women, go to bed with men, have children. We distinguish between the various levels of feeling and experiencing which life has to offer and allow ourselves the opportunity to enjoy these things in a creative manner. This is different from the situation in the Netherlands, where you are shoved into a pigeonhole and find your opportunities restricted. My not wanting to declare myself a lesbian is certainly not prompted by fear. I also want to remain loyal to the ways in which expression has been given from of old in my community to special relationships between women. Simply doing things, without giving them a name, and preserving rituals and secrets between women are important to me. Deeds are more obvious and more durable than all the women who say they are lesbian and contribute nothing to women's energy.

AUDRE: I respect your position and I recognize the need and the strength that lie behind it. It is not my position. I think it necessary for every woman to decide for herself what she calls herself, and when and where. Of course, there have always been rituals and secrets between women and they must continue. But it is important to make a distinction between the secrets from which we draw strength and the secrecy, which comes from anxiety and is meant to protect us. If we want to have power for ourselves, this secrecy and this silence must be broken. I want to encourage more and more women to identify themselves, to speak their name, where and when they can, and to survive. I repeat: and to survive.

Finally, I think it important to state my essential position as follows: It is not my behavior that determines whether I am lesbian, but the very core of my being.

TOWER OF BABEL

So much for the burning discussion among the black poets. The positions taken up here are shared by large groups of women in the black communities of the Diaspora and are typical of two idealtypical cosmologies where female homosexuality is concerned. The position defended by Audre Lorde is a prototype of that held by groups of black lesbians within the U.S., Suriname,and the Netherlands. In the attitudes adopted by Roemer, features can be discerned of the *mati* paradigm, whose protagonists are also to be found everywhere in the Diaspora yet who, almost by definition, attract less attention.

Perhaps it is unnecessary to say that in practice numerous intermediate positions and hybrid forms exist. Without wishing to force people into one camp or the other, or to question the legitimacy or "political correctness" of either position, I seek to throw light on the outlines of these two idealtypes. Exchanges around the theme of name-giving often give rise to heated discussions that aren't particularly fruitful because, as in a true tower of Babel, people speak in mutually unintelligible tongues.

Central to my thinking on the matter is the fact that orientation to reality—which includes the meaning given to and the form taken by homosexuality in black communities in the Diaspora—is more or less colored by the cultural heritage from Africa. In the cosmology of *mati*-ism more African elements have been preserved, while the black lesbian groups have drawn more inspiration from Western influences. *Mati*-ism is characterized by a centripetal, a comprehensive and inclusive movement, whereas in the black lesbian world a centrifugal, exclusive spirit seems to be present. This is reflected in the attitudes in various circles to relationships with men. While in the lives of many *mati* women men play a role, among the black lesbians this must generally be regarded as excluded. Children in the lives of black lesbians are either a residue from a former lifestyle or a conscious choice within a lesbian relationship. Neither circumstance necessarily asks for continued emotional and/or financial commitment from the father to the child or the mother. The part played by men in the life of *mati* women, apart from possible economical support for children, is underscored by the fact that motherhood is regarded as a rite of initiation into adulthood and by many as a sign of being a woman.

Besides displaying a differential level of African elements, *mati*-ism and black lesbianism are exponents of two different class cultures. *Mati* typically are working-class women whose claims to social status lie in their capability to mobilize and manipulate kin networks. Indeed, according to Janssens and van Wetering, *matisma* can be seen as entre-preneurs, who through their extensive kin networks with women and men, try to build up social and real capital (Janssens and van Wetering, 1985). While in Suriname, middle- and higher-class black lesbians are largely invisible, obviously not having found appropriate models to style their behavior, in the U.S. and in the Netherlands, they have increasingly come out of the closet. Through their education, income, and, often, professional status, they are insulated against some of the survival hazards of working-class black lesbians.

A further difference distinguishing *mati* relationships from black lesbian connections is the often wide age gap between *mati* partners, while in the latter circles "equality" along many dimensions, including age, seems to be an aspiration. It is not at all unusual, in the *mati* world, to find a 20-year-old (*yong' doifi*, young dove) having a rela-tionship with a 60-year-old woman. For the young woman, the emo-tional and financial security of the older woman, who will typically have raised her children and receive financial support from them, is an important consideration. The older woman, for her part, now as almost sixty years ago when it was first recorded (Herskovits, M. and F. Herskovits, 1936), will demand unconditional loyalty and faithful-ness from her "young dove" in return for indulging and spoiling her with presents, notably gold and silver jewelry. Ideally, she teaches her young dove "*a mati wroko*" (the *mati* work) and she "trains" her the way she wants the young woman to be.

A further differentiation would seems to lie in the underlying self that organizes all of life's experiences, sifts through them, and inte-grates them into manageable material. Though this issue awaits further elaboration, the self of *matisma* would seem to be a sociocentric phe-nomenon, while the self of black lesbians could be characterized as an egocentric, individualistic entity. Among *matisma*, sociocentrism is evi-dent not only in the zeal with which human capital is constantly being mobilized but also in the perceptions of what a person is. Linked with the folk religion *Winti*, persons are perceived to be built up out of sev-eral components: *kra* (= *jeje*), *djodjo*, and several *winti* or gods, who each have their specific characteristics. *Kra* with its male and female component can be understood as the "I"; *djodjo*, also male and female, are like guardian angels, acquired at birth. The different *winti,* or gods, are divided into four pantheons: those of the Sky, the Earth, the Bush, and the Water. Male homosexuals are often believed to have a female *Aisa,* the (upper) goddess of the Earth, who is said to be frightfully jealous of real women the man may get involved with. Female homosexuals are perceived to be "carried" by a male bush god, *Apuku,* who cannot bear to see the woman connected, on a long-term basis, with a flesh-and-blood male.

Black lesbians' personhood, on the other hand, seems more aptly characterized by Western notions of individuality, persons as self-contained "islands" with their own motivations and accountabilities.

An additional distinction between *matisma* and black lesbians is that concentration on women for the latter is a political issue aimed at male-dominated society. In their own communities they often wage war on sexism and homophobia. While they experience their sexual choice as a matter of politics, *matisma* tend to see their behavior as a personal issue. A typical response is: *"Mi na wan bigi uma f' mi eygi oso. No wan sma e gi mi njan,"* (I am a big woman in my own house. Nobody gives me food), meaning it's nobody's business but my own with whom I sleep. In a small scale society such as Suriname (400,000 inhabitants), this can be seen as a rather defiant survival posture.

Lastly, one could posit that *matisma* display lesbian behavior, while black lesbians have a lesbian identity. I assume that the *matisma* unwillingness to declare oneself can, functionally, be explained with reference to this point. In a society in which the avenues to status for working-class women are limited, it would not seem wise to declare oneself openly and thereby alienate potential personnel, men and women, from one's network.

EPILOGUE

Within black communities there are many different ways of giving expression to erotic relationships between women. The biological basis of sexual desire takes form in various sociohistorical structures, underpinned by differing cosmologies. *Mati*-ism and black lesbianism are two of these structures. Lesbians have not always existed in black communities. In some sectors today they still do not exist. But this statement is not a complaint about the lack of sexuality between those of the same gender in the black communities of the Diaspora. Rather it is a statement, which tells us more about the socio-historical structure of the concept *lesbian.*

Mati-ism and Black Lesbianism

References

Ambacht. (1912). Rapport van de commissie benoemd bij Gouvernementsresolurie van. 13 janu ari 1910. Suriname: Gouvemement.

Comvalius, Th. (n.d.). Krioro: Een bijdrage tot de kennis van het lied, de dans en de folklore van Suriname. Deel I. Paramaribo.

Herskovits, M. and Herskovits, F. (1936). *Suriname Folklore*. New York: Columbia.

Herskovits, M. (1938). *Dahomey: An Ancient West-African Kingdom*. New York.

Janssens, M. and Van Wetering, W. (1985). "*Mati* en Lesbiennes. Homosexualiteit en Ethnische Identiteit bij Creools-Surinaamse Vrouwen in Nederland." *Sociologische Gids5/6*.

Lorde, A. (1982). *Chosen Poems, Old and New*. New York: W. W. Norton & Co., Inc.

— (1982). *Zami: A New Spelling of My Name*. New York: The Crossing Press.

Mintz, S. and Price, R. (1976). *An Anthropological Approach to the Afro-American Past*. Philadelphia: Ishi.

Price, R. (1976). *The Guiana Maroons: A Historical and Bibliographical Introduction*. Baltimore: The Johns Hopkins University Press.

Price, R. and Price, S. (1991). *Two Evenings in Saramaka*. Chicago/London: The University of Chicago Press.

Ross, E. and Rapp, R. (1983). "Sex and Society: A Research Note From Social History and Anthropology." In *Desire: The Politics of Sexuality,* edited by A. Snitow, et al. London.

Van Lier, R. (1949). Samenleving in een Gronsgebied. Een sociaal-historische Studie van Suriname. Amsterdam: Emmering.

Van Lier, R. (1986). Tropische Tribaden. Een Verhandeling over Homosexualiteit en Homosexuele Vrouwen in Suriname. Dordrecht/Providence: Foris Publications.

Wooding, C. (1988). *Winti*. Een Afro-Armerikaanse Godsdienst. Rijswijk: Eigen Beheer.

Institutionalizing Sexuality: Theorizing Queer in Post-Apartheid South Africa

Vasu Reddy

"The Black homosexual is hard-pressed to gain audience among his heterosexual brothers: even if he is more talented, he is inhibited by his silence of his admissions. This is what the race has depended on in being able to erase homosexuality from our recorded history. The chosen history. But these sacred constructions of silence are futile exercises in denial. We will not go away with our issues of sexuality. We are coming home."

—Essex Hemphill, 1991

Introduction

It would seem appropriate to begin this essay with a reference to a film, which intertextually underscores the theme of the session at which a version of this essay was first presented. In 1995 at the University of Cape Town, South Africa, brief history was made when the first gay and lesbian studies colloquium was held on African soil. The theme of the session in question, "Queers in Africa: A White Man's Disease?" cogently encapsulated the views of some prominent African leaders, many of whom undoubtedly need no naming as they have notoriously defined themselves over the years. To return to the film, *And the Band Played On*, despite its strengths in highlighting the scientific and medical vendettas during the early years of the AIDS epidemic, introduces a double bind in framing Central Africa in the first shot. This shot has the following comment: The Ebola fever outbreak was contained before it could reach the outside world. It was not AIDS. But it was a warning of things to come. The shot is also significant, for in as much as it marks the public consciousness and demonstrates once again the semiotic link between disease, nationality, and race, it also opens up a further field of inquiry. Although the Africa in question here is more than a geographical location, the ideological implications of this reference should not be underplayed. Simon Watney (1989, 37) situates HIV infection, AIDS, and Africa in "terms of a long racist legacy of colonial connotations of supposed depravity, dirt, and disease." If sexuality and sexual orientation are added to the list, the issue is further problematized: In this manner "African AIDS" becomes another version of the "white man's burden," rather than a catastrophe for Africans themselves, who are reduced to the status of potential "AIDS carriers" (Carter and Watney, 1989).

The shot in question and the comments by Watney and Carter seem to confirm the view that there is a link between disease, nationality, and race. This plays into the popular imagination of Africans who claim that homosexuality is an alien Other that has infected the nations of Africa. More recently, Gevisser (1994, 70-71) has shown that the attitudes of senior South African political figures such as Ruth Mompatie (African National Congress), Strini Moodley (Azanian People's Organization), and Khoisan X (Pan Africanist Congress) may be influential in shaping popular opinion, thereby also mobilizing a homophobic following. According to Gevisser (1994, 57), the PAC and the ANC viewed "gay issues as bourgeois frivolities and irrelevancies." He mentions that political leaders were willing to offer their support on paper but reluctant to attend any functions of gay groupings for fear of losing support from their electorate who some leaders have claimed were homophobic.

In 1999 the leader of the Pan Africanist Congress, Methodist minister Dr. Stanley Mogoba, denigrated homosexuality as un-African, and then when the press caught up with him, he downplayed his statements by stating that he was misquoted. Ironically, during constitutional lobbying, Dr. Mogoba took a courageous stance against the African Christian Democratic Party in support of lesbian and gay rights. In his letter to the Constituent Assembly (the body that drafted the Constitution of post-apartheid South Africa), he said, "I appeal to you to resist any attempt to limit the recognition of the rights of all people, which is the genius of the proposed Constitution, and to retain the 'sexual orientation' clause" (*Equality* June 1999, 13). It should be recalled that in 1993 Dr. Mogoba was the leader of the Methodist Church in South Africa; in 1999 he was leading the PAC in South Africa's second general election.

What is at stake here is the metaphoric link between disease and sexual orientation: queers and disease thereby becoming signifiers for a pathological deviance. In his critique of the pathological discourse at work, and as precursor to Sontag's more influential twin study *Illness as Metaphor/AIDS and Its Metaphors*, Weeks (1985, 46) made the following comment (somewhat dated but nevertheless pertinent):

> AIDS is a metaphor that has come to symbolize...the identity between contagion and a kind of desire. In the fear and loathing that AIDS evokes there is a resulting conflation between two plausible, if unproven theories, that there is an elective affinity between disease and certain sexual practices, and that certain sexual practices cause disease and a third, that certain types of sex are diseases.

Similarly, in *Policing Desire: Pornography, AIDS, and the Media* (1987), Watney suggests how this classification precipitated a hegemonic attempt to rehomosexualize, or remedicalize, the gay identity through the popular press (qtd. in Keane 1993, 459). Not coincidentally, though, the *Star* (a Johannesburg newspaper) featured the following headline in 1985: GAY PLAGUE SPREADS TO THE TOWNSHIP. In a different light, Susan Sontag reminds us that AIDS was a gift to the old South African regime when the Foreign Minister (Pik Botha) reportedly stated at the time, "The terrorists are now coming to us with a weapon more terrible than Marxism: AIDS" (1991: 148). The very same foreign minister from the apartheid government today openly supports the African National Congress, led by the present State President, Thabo Mbeki. Significantly, a central thread in these representations is language and terminology. This essay concerns the broader aspects of sexuality, sexual orientation, and the politics of homophobia. And the politics of language is only one underlying aspect of this field, and therefore the issues raised so far suggest that the discursive interests that underlie the territory of sexuality can be refracted through the lens of the notion of disease. In a sense, AIDS and HIV infection foreground at one level a specific "sexual practice," locating subjects within a certain "risk group," a "community of pariahs" as Sontag (1991, 111) calls it. On another level it calls into question images of deformity that are linked to infirmities. The so-called "dual metaphoric genealogy" (102) of AIDS, described in military metaphors as a "clinical construction, a progressive disease of time" (107), the "gay cancer," or better still, the "gay plague," as it was known in the early '80s, stems directly from the ideological construction of AIDS as an alien Other.

In representing the viewpoints of the homophobic dominant fiction, I hope to corroborate my own position that those in control of the cultural and political apparatus hegemonically produce images of themselves and others through which they can misrecognize their legitimacy. And those who are disenfranchised by lack of access to signifying production are forced to recognize, or at least painfully negotiate, the contradiction between technologies of legitimacy and technologies of illegitimacy (Keane 1993, 457). Within this configuration, the concept of sexuality is irreducibly discursive, particularly in terms of the many and varied truths it espouses. Much that is central to the interpretation (rereading?) of sexuality that most recent research provides stems from a committed attempt to unsettle codified notions of sexuality and sexual orientation.

Within this rubric this essay seeks to assess the cleavages of a discourse on sexuality in post-apartheid South Africa. And while I understand sexuality (as concept) to be complex and problematic, my use of the term in this argument has more to do with sexual orientation, in particular homosexuality, but more specifically gay identity. If, as Michel Foucault argues in *The Order of Things* (1970), the modern is indeed the age of history, then the discourses generated by sexuality are historically grounded and logically must occupy a privileged position in the South African episteme. And like Foucault, in his seminal *The History of Sexuality* (1990), I agree it is not whether societies say yes or no to sex, or whether they permit or prohibit, but that both of these positions are part of the way in which sex is put into discourse. In effect, the issue is the representational and symbolic quality of sexuality that to me take on new *meanings* in South Africa, post-1990.

This new context in South African history began February 2, 1990, because it was on this day that the last apartheid President, F.W. de Klerk, unbanned the liberation organizations and signaled his government's intention to transform. This date may well be a legitimate signifier for scholars in this part of Africa. However, in conceiving the contradictions of institutionalized racism, I would like to stress that apartheid also provides us with a context in which gay and lesbian sexuality could be renegotiated, reevaluated, and theorized in new contexts in a way that does not assume that we have transcended apartheid. In suggesting a possible synchronic trajectory, I do not mean an exclusion of the histories that preceded apartheid. What significantly complicates any study of sexuality in our context is the notion of racial alterity and difference, which is located in the nexus of a historicized tropology. While I agree that feminist historiography has opened the space for the expanded treatment of social and historical construction for sexual identity and experience of women, little if anything exists in the area of gay and lesbian identities.

According to Fuss (1994, 20), the politics of identification is embedded in a colonial history that poses serious challenges for contemporary recuperations of a politics of identification Given the specific nature of colonialism in South Africa (which is not the project of this essay), we should not merely isolate significant historical events but also interrogate historical genealogies that could lead us into precolonial times. Colonialism on its own is a limited historicized signifier that points to a specific historical existence.

Certainly one might argue that an effect of reworking the binary opposition of sexuality follows from an attempt to tap into the memory of people to access subjectivity. The territory of queer studies in South Africa therefore cannot ignore the crucial question of identity formation, especially in the light of homosexuality's being constrained by oppressive attitudes in major parts of Africa.

If the title of this essay, "Institutionalizing Sexuality," seems to suggest a return to the regime of the regulation of discourses on sexuality, then it does so, within an epistemological dynamic, to expose some silences, challenge prohibitions, and problematize oppressive constructions. Perhaps the more immediate relevance of the title is displayed by the jargon of this essay, which is cast in the mold of the discourse of the academy. The concern here is to examine critically the notion of gay rights and race as it may be operating in our present context. And I would like to link this to the academic study of sexuality.

In broaching the subject I do so with a full awareness of my sexuality as a gay person of color, my position as a citizen of Africa's youngest democracy, and my involvement in an understanding of gay liberation politics. In delineating these conditions in no order of importance, I find my sexuality to constantly resurface as an important marker.

This inflection does confirm that private acts are connected to institutions, which regulate them. For what we nominate antiracist, antisexist, or antihomophobic, the central concern within such image analysis is often that of the stereotype, which is often prioritized in literary criticism, particularly in challenging negative constructions of given preconstituted models. Meanings, therefore, are not necessarily the properties of the components of a signifying system, but their associations are established by particular conventions. In this regard there exists some obtrusive presence of ambivalence and ambiguity in the way language is implicated in gay and lesbian politics. What we are faced with, then, is a discontinuity between the ways in which sexuality is apprehended and the way we (re)make meaning of it. With this statement I do not suggest that gay and lesbian oppression is simply a species of language, but rather that both are inextricably linked and are deeply entrenched in history. This leads me to the second part of the title.

MOFFIES AND QUEERS

In South Africa, as I assume is the case elsewhere in the world, there is a vocabulary operating within the social logic of scandal to pervert homosexuality. In addition to our own unique South African concept of the *moffie*, which has a fashionable currency in some quarters, we are also familiar with the derogatory slant that the word *queer* has come to signify, with its original meaning of eccentricity and oddity somewhat blurred. While *moffie* is an Afrikaans word, often used as a word of defiance by white, Indian, and colored gay men, other words exist in other African languages. For example, many black gay men, particularly among Zulu speakers, use the word *isitabane* as a form of defiance; the word is a negative description for both male and female homosexuals. But the word *queer* has a unique history, and its etymology clearly shows how its semantics have changed. On the etymology of the word *moffie*, see Jean Branford's *A Dictionary of South African English* (1987), the glossary in Isaacs and McKendrick's *Male Homosexuality in South Africa* (1992), and *Defiant Desire* (1994) by Gevisser and Cameron. For her part, Anna Marie Smith (1993, 21) considers the political strength of the word *queer*; the self-articulation of *queer* with pride, strength, and activism similarly harnesses the forces of disgust and terror and redirects that tremendous energy right back against its bigoted source.

The homosexual appropriation of the word *queer* from homophobic discourse signals a change in usage. It is not simply an eccentric word for a suspicious individual, but its reappropriation implies that it transforms bigoted language into a statement of defiance, and we may even read it as a less gendered alternative (Woods 1994, 10). In keeping with this trend, De Lauretis (1991, iv) employs the term *queer* as opposed to *gay* and *lesbian* to mark a certain critical distance from the latter since these terms foreground gayness and homosexuality. Inasmuch as she justifies her use of the word by claiming to refine existing distinctions in discursive protocols, she prioritizes a theoretical focus at the expense of their ideological liabilities (1991, v). In problematizing the categories gay/lesbian, she seems to ascribe homosexuality only to the conceptual mystifications of logocentric power (Blau 1987, 112), while political accountability does not percolate her argument.

I employ De Lauretis's terminology not as a specific methodological and conceptual field as she does, but as a politically relevant construction used to problematize issues surrounding gay and lesbian sexuality and to reframe some questions from a South African perspective. This polarized codification of sexuality has emerged from the work of a nonhomogenous group of cultural and literary theoreticians associated with the concept of queer theory. Sex is not now grounded in the family, or in morality, nor is it simply a function of capitalism, but is grounded in the hetero-and-homo binary. These critiques have delivered important insights for our understanding of the historical context whereby perversity and the norm are mutually dependent and reinforcing. But like the 1960s account of Victorianism, they also carry with them the burden of a binary reading of modern sexual regimes. Queer theory elevates the principle of sexual dissidence as the epistemology of sexuality in such a way that the perverse versus the normative becomes the motif of sexuality (see also Bland and Mort for a more detailed exposition of this issue, 1997, 17-31).

But the point I want to make in this essay is framed in a skeptical question, which De Lauretis asks, and one that may possibly conflate our different positions. She asks: Can our queerness act as an agency of social change and our theory construct another discursive horizon, another way of living the racial and the sexual? (De Lauretis 1991, x-xi). A first response to this question would be in the affirmative, but we need to address the specificities of social change as an all-embracing term, which subsumes the important categories of race and sexuality. Given the pariah status South Africa correctly earned in the heydays of grand apartheid, it is no exaggeration to reemphasize the issue. In fact, it seems logical to consider that race, particularly in the South African context, continues to be central, stands at the intersection of many discursive universes.

Race, Culture, and Sexuality

Race continues to be a category most often examined in conjunction with sexuality. The notion of "racialized sexualities," to borrow the phrase from Fuss (1994, 3), complicates any intervention into gay and lesbian politics in South Africa. With the institutionalization of racism, which was formalized through apartheid, and the rise of the police state in the '60s, which was primarily characterized by surveillance of left-wing politics, race and sexuality could be seen to bear an unacknowledged bond to the larger framework of South African cultural history. In this regard, interrogations of sexuality are only beginning to emerge, which significantly challenge not only the many misconceptions about homosexuality but confirm specifically the notion that homosexuality in Africa is not a Western import but a fundamental part of a nation's culture and history.

This is evident in the increasing number of openly gay and lesbian people of color who are assuming leadership positions in government and in the corporate world. Indeed, if homosexuality is viewed by conservative African leaders and the fundamentalist religious right as disease and sin, then the only cutting-edge rationale guiding this view is an attempt to deny its existence. In fact, Robert Mugabe of Zimbabwe, Sam Nujoma of Namibia, Daniel Arap Moi of Kenya, Federick Chiluba of Zambia, and most recently, Yoweri Museveni of Uganda, are in agreement that homosexuality is a "scourge" that defies Christian teachings and African traditions. The style of condemnation is shared by all: Homosexuality is un-African and against the teachings of the Bible. The threats too remain; they are couched in a performative and declaratory language: Homosexuals must be arrested and removed from society. And while these leaders may be the heroes of their postcolonies, their tirade against homosexuality is uncritically couched in contradiction, for they use the very same colonial laws that criminalized homosexuality to claim that it is foreign, colonial, and by implication, alien. And it is also becoming increasingly clear that it is not homosexuality that these leaders fear but primarily the attack on patriarchal dominance presented by gay relationships. If anything, homosexuality could possibly also dispel certain patriarchal myths. For many African leaders it may be strategic to also hide behind oppressive institutions in the name of culture. And perhaps one way to do this is to demonize homosexuality to maintain a power base for themselves or possibly also create a popular front against homosexuality as a way of countering their own repressed sexualities.

Another irony in Robert Mugabe's 1995 outburst is not his homophobia or the racial connections between homosexuality and white Western decadence, but the confirmation of the existence of same-sex desire in his country. His tirade brought world attention to his demonization of homosexuals and has prompted gay and lesbian leaders in Zimbabwe to establish political links with their world counterparts. Harassment is of such a nature in Zimbabwe that a black 25-year-old man who applied for refugee status in Australia in 1993 was granted a protection visa by the Australian government. The man in question faces ostracization and charges under the Unnatural Offenses Act if he returns to Zimbabwe. Such a scenario corroborates the Foucauldian notion, in his critique of Western sexuality, in which he argued that legal sanctions were effected to curtail unreproductive activities, with the intention to propound a norm of sexual activity that was defined (Foucault 1990, 36). Similarly, this idea, in another interpretation, is echoed in Halifax's 1988 observation that gay sexuality challenges the idea of the monogamous family. But according to him, sexuality is not a private affair regulated by the traditions and prejudices of the community, as it has been in precapitalist societies, but a public matter for the state to regulate and restrict.

In a 1995 article on black homosexuality in Zimbabwe, H.M. Tirivanho, a black Zimbabwean, argues that coming out is crucial to dispel the assumption that black homosexuality is borne out of white homosexuality. The notion of coming out is fraught with ambiguity but is a useful strategy to mobilize a political and sexual identity. We know that "coming out" is never really about dispelling the "closet," but as the defining structure of oppression, the image of coming out regularly interfaces with perversion and decadence. To even talk about homosexuality is a form of coming out, because by bringing the supposed unknown into the public realm is also a problem for some African leaders. This issue primarily plagues Mugabe and most recently was experienced by the Ugandan leader.

In a bid to legitimate the existence of homosexuality, Tirivanho (1995, 18) argues against the three common misconceptions that plague Zimbabwe (if not all African countries). First, homosexuality is anathema to African/black culture; homosexuality is therefore traceable to a Western way of living. Second, homosexuality is a recent development in Zimbabwe; it is a postindependence (1980) phenomenon. Third, there is no black lesbianism in Zimbabwe; the homosexuality that exists is among blacks who are forced into it due to poverty.

What all of the above provide is a map with which to navigate the territory of sexuality in the Zimbabwean context, and with a bit of refinement this could be extended to other African countries. It also highlights the need to reorganize perceptions of sexuality from an oppositional stance in the voice of the very people who are denigrated as sexual perverts in their own country. Furthermore, on a theoretical level, many other incoherences continue to exist, especially in the work of Frantz Fanon, an important critic of the colonial world. To many scholars in African Studies, Fanon is the African intellectual equivalent of Foucault. Notwithstanding the merits of his work, significant contradictions appear in his theorizing and understanding of homosexuality. Fuss (1994) offers a cogent critique of Fanon's oppressive reading of homosexuality. The point here is the apparent contradiction of Fanon's anticolonialist argument, and Fuss's (1994) thesis essentially critiques his inability to think beyond the presuppositions of colonial discourse to examine how colonial domination works through the social institutionalization of misogyny and homophobia.

Therefore, in disentangling the complexities of identity formation and sexual politics, there is a need to challenge all structures of homophobia. The manner in which race is imbricated in social, economic, and political systems, and the contradictions that exist in newfound political systems with a colonial legacy, pose many problems. Recently, in her critique of the gay military setup in the U.S., Lane (1994) attempted to uncover the shortcomings of gay activism, the military, and the question of race. According to Lane (1994, 1077-1078), the most important outcome of many gay advocates' strategies is that they neutralized race as a real issue of concern. She makes the further point that white gay men's experiences of discrimination were presented as the paradigmatic experiences, the ones that fully articulated what it means to be a gay or lesbian in the military.

Such a scenario has its limitation, and may not be totally relevant to the South African context. However, we can read aspects of this observation into our context, but we cannot displace the paradox it presents. It not only underscores the exclusion of Africans from the South Africa Defense Force (during the apartheid era) but also proposes that racialized codes are clearly implicated in gay liberation politics, which often are naturalized. Furthermore, Smith's (1993) somewhat prophetic statement, one which is particularly relevant to post-apartheid South Africa, could also be easily read into our context: We white queers have to deal with our racism, and we have to transform our entire political agenda if we want black queers to commit themselves to the very difficult labor of working in white-dominated organizations. More recently, the empirical social-work perspective of crisis in sexual identity study by Isaacs and McKendrick, *Male Homosexuality in South Africa* (1992), addressed a range of issues but gave cursory attention to questions of race and sexuality. Where this study reveals shortcomings of the former, *Aliens in the Household of*

God (1997) presents a haunting analysis of the role of the Christian faith in the lives of homosexual men and women in South Africa. And the study is equally sensitive to questions of race and sexuality in Christian theological debates.

GAY LIBERATION AND ACTIVISM

Expanding the contours of sexuality to the realm of politics, we find an interesting anchoring point for queer identification. If the storming of the Stonewall Inn precipitated gay liberation internationally and supported the coming-out technology in the U.S., Australia, and Britain, or if European gay liberation revealed itself during the dark night of Nazi oppression, then it would seem South African gay liberation politics display a marked shift from the experience of our Western counterparts. In fact, what has characterized the West in the early '70s in terms of queer activism—and in the U.S. this was closely connected to other social and political factors (such as the peace, anti-Vietnam, and civil rights movements)—is not justifiably comparable to South African activism. My contention is that queer activism is possibly articulated on a very light scale or at its best is closely aligned with national politics in South Africa. Quite correctly, in my opinion, some of the major activists in gay politics in South Africa have been imprisoned or detained for antiapartheid activities, as opposed to sexual offenses. One of the most prominent of these prisoners was the late Simon Tseko Nkoli (imprisoned Nov. 26-30, 1998).

It may be worth observing that if queer activism in South Africa is to be distinguished from its Anglo-American equivalent, then the distinguishing signifier is the broad antiapartheid coalition which may have subsumed gay rights into its agenda in terms of the broader democratic struggle. In a sense, the implication of politics in the deployment of gender and sexuality in the context of post-apartheid South Africa would need to foreground the significance of activism in what I would term the political construction of our sexuality. Ultimately, gay liberation is a struggle by gay and lesbian people to free themselves from patriarchal oppression. While a political strategy, it offers a form of resistance to almost all oppressive structures. In the South African post-apartheid context, gay liberation is intimately connected to fundamental human rights (we celebrate Human Rights Day on March 21 each year), but it is also about the affirmation of homosexuality not simply as a nondiscrimination issue, but also as an equality issue. And the South African gay and lesbian movement continues to assert equality as a nonnegotiable right of all its citizens.

THE GAY AND LESBIAN MOVEMENT IN SOUTH AFRICA

While the assertion that there is a clearly defined movement in South Africa may be misleading, it is correct to assert that the '90s witnessed the emergence of a progressive gay and lesbian politics in South Africa. This history is yet to be documented, but its origins are partially documented in Gevisser's 1994 study. What seems to guide the gay movement in South Africa is the large-scale social, political, and economic changes that have taken place since April 27, 1994. This date officially marked the post-apartheid era; it closed the chapter on the apartheid past and marked Nelson Mandela's entry into government from prison. It signaled what will be known as the transitional period of South African political history: the period in which South Africans were to reconcile themselves with each other in the light of the country's turbulent racial history.

In essence, democracy and its fundamental precept, human rights, seemed to guide the recapitilization of our sexuality in the hope that politics would not deform but consolidate such virtues of civil society as recognizing the freedom to practice sexuality. On a basic level then, we witnessed the politics of inclusion and equality, notwithstanding that the bureaucrats responsible for including a clause on sexual orientation were reluctant to do so. Yet on another level, by framing sexual orientation rights in the bill of rights and the working draft constitution (adopted in 1996), we witnessed, in the words of Herbert Blau (1987), homosexuality as "a political style and body of thought." In this sense queer activism in South Africa took on an international dimension, especially in terms of its mandate to decriminalize homosexuality and to decontaminate some of its diseased signifiers. While gay rights are logically implicated in the agenda of the gay movement in South Africa, gay liberation plays itself out largely in decriminalization campaigns. And this I would argue has been one of the remarkable achievements of the movement in South Africa.

But out of this observation is another glaring paradox: Does a grammar of legitimization necessarily signify gender equality? It is important to consider this contradiction, for it helps to explain why women in this country are not simply content with equal rights but insist on equal representation in all institutional structures. This description complicates and possibly militates against the imperatives of a legal sanction, since representation in the sense of visibility appears to be a more viable mechanism of defining and protecting equality. The way women have negotiated this strategy is bound to have major significance on the way in which queers reconcile their homosexual behavior, sexual identity, and human rights in terms of visibility within a nation-state. In response to a question on human rights and sexuality, Foucault states, "Human rights regarding sexuality are important and are still not respected in many places. I think we have to go a step further. Not only do we have to defend ourselves, but also we have to affirm ourselves; not only affirm ourselves as an identity but as a creative force" (Gallagher and Wilson, 1987, 27).

By visibility, I do not mean a celebration of the queer subject as revealed by gay pride, and according to Blau (1987, 109), this more often than not amounts to a reflection of the kinkier pleasures of a specific fringe as an experimental index of self-chosen identity. It could be argued, however, that the foregrounding of the visualization of sex in gay pride may have compromised its radical (activist?) potential in the sense that queers may have contoured their behaviors and identities in ways that generate voyeuristic desire rather than challenge and neutralize the illusions of a homophobic ethos. I am not suggesting this is a futile vantage point above the discursive traffic.

On the contrary, the importance of pride marches cannot be overemphasized: Queers may have positioned themselves in a space to deploy the power of representing identity and unity as a form of consciousness raising for the queer community. Yet even as I acknowledge this point, a further weariness sets in. Is a common front or political alliance of queers not a contradictory enterprise? If we acknowledge that sexual orientation is only a symptom of more deep-rooted differences, is the notion of a united lobby not evidence of a refusal to acknowledge the disparities and divisions in South African queer communities?

And this brings me to some of my criticisms of a recent historiographic study on gay and lesbian lives in South Africa, aptly titled *Defiant Desire* (1994) and edited by two distinguished individuals. Mark Gevisser is one of the best journalists in the country, and Edwin Cameron is a champion of Human Rights issues and a judge in the Constitutional Court who went public about his HIV status. Given the book's seminal contributions and status as the first representative study of queer communities in South Africa, I would like to critically assess two points raised in this text. Utopian or not, the motivating ideal in the *Defiant Desire* is a res publica, and it prioritizes and urges a united lobby for gay and lesbian rights at this moment of profound constitutional change (Gevisser 1994, 82). That moment of great social change has come and gone. South Africa is now in its second phase of its post-apartheid context with President Mbeki at the helm. The task of this presidency has little to do with reconciliation and more to do with a consolidation of democracy by speeding up its delivery to the people.

Returning to *Defiant Desire*, is it correct to assume, as Gevisser points out (33), that gay liberationists in South Africa might have found their manifesto within the African National Congress's Freedom Charter? For if Gevisser assumes that a document predicated on democratic principles has the potential to attract queers who would compromise their political allegiance for sexual liberation, it would appear we queers would be one happy family. On the subject of alliances with political parties, Smith (1993, 23) offers an important perspective on the British context, and her comments resonate in most democracies: We cannot predict the ways in which multiple identities will be combined together in taking a position on one particular subject. For example, just because the Labor Party tends toward leftist positions, such as the defense of the national health system or the defense of the trade unions, does not mean it will naturally take a progressive position on lesbian and gay issues.

Alliances with political parties may seem to be a short-term goal if anything is to be achieved. My contention is that political parties are often interested in securing a constituency. If this entails turning a temporary blind eye to issues they may not passionately believe in (such as sexual orientation) in order to secure power, then forging an alliance may well be likened to Dr. Faustus's bargain with the devil. While I would rather stress the discontinuities and ambiguities that lend alliances their shortcomings, I would like to believe that in the field of AIDS education there may well be a more successful alliance, particularly in Africa where the disease has reached epidemic proportions. The point to be emphasized about a united lobby is that it possibly also naturalizes divisions and differences that exist in queer communities. In fact, divisions are so rife that it is hardly possible to live up to that progressive ideal of speaking with one voice. But whatever the problems, building movements for social change is crucial.

This problematic is central to any theorization of queer historiography. While the Gevisser book prioritizes pertinent questions, which may be absent from the Isaacs and McKendrick study, both fail to assess fully the cleavages that exist. In her 1991 article, "Theorizing Deviant Historiography," Jennifer Terry explores the theoretical possibilities for the development of a queer historiography as a strategy to map the complex discursive and textual operations at play in the emergence of queer identity. Terry also notes that the idea of a coherent, full identity that is marked only by homosexuality is unsettled by its cultural production of lesbians and gay men of color, whose work enacts the multiplicities and contradictions of living at the intersection of many different marginal subjectivities. In assessing the relevance of this statement to queer communities and the gay movement, we should consider the political, economic, and racial divisions, which in my opinion are underemphasized. We have learned that the reactionary politics of the predominantly (now defunct) white male middle-class Gay Association of South Africa (GASA) occupies a central place in South African gay and lesbian history. Its downplaying of race and failure to challenge apartheid led to its membership being withdrawn from the International Gay and Lesbian Association. We also saw the formation of more progressive queer organizations such as GLOW (Gay and Lesbian Organization of the Witwatersrand), whose members are primarily black working- and middle- class men and women.

In retracing this to the race issue Gevisser (1994) notes—and this may well be viewed as a critique of GASA—that whites were more interested in material interests and comforts and ignored issues of discrimination and oppression. Also important is the question of whether queer rights and unity are being used by a racial minority within gay groups and placed on the agenda to protect their own material interests at the expense of more crucial issues such as economics, race, ethnicity, gender, age, and class. Especially pertinent in this instance, and in the intellectual context of feminism over the past two decades, is that we have increasingly seen perhaps one crucial flaw: The divisions between gay men and lesbian women corroborate the view that chauvinist attitudes may not be restricted to straight men.

So we must ask, in returning to alliance politics: Is it a useful strategy to argue for queer rights by setting up a dialogue with previous liberation movements now turned political parties? Is it also strategic to position ourselves within a broad post-apartheid coalition? If the tactic is to negotiate a relationship with the big fish, do we have any guarantees that these rights, at the moment a grammatical construction, will be recognized in the future constitution?

Ultimately, for any movement, this will be the litmus test.

What is apparent is that consciousness raising, sexual identity, and gay liberation cannot only be fixed in the locus of social practice. Rights are not simply normative guarantees that tell us more about humanity and what it is to be human. The task confronting us, therefore, is to begin to interpret and redefine these rights on a practical and theoretical level. While it is crucial to prioritize issues such as legalizing homosexual partnerships and queer adoptions, extending tax rights to partners, and ending job discrimination, it is equally important to invest energy in and initiate academic discussions on issues concerning queer sexuality. In a sense decriminalization has come a long way in South Africa. Sodomy is now legal, and the recent finding of the Cape High Court included the provision that all immigrant same-sex partners of permanent and lawful residents of South Africa (including the applicants) be granted exemption until the government changed the Alien Control Act. It was given 12 months in which to do so.

Also, the first gay and lesbian studies colloquium (held in 1995, at which a version of this paper was first presented), must therefore be viewed as positive for queer studies. The implied connection between gay studies and the gay movement is again telescoped by the political: Our intervention in the field is an attempt to deghost contradictory representations of homosexuality.

THE NATIONAL COALITION FOR GAY AND LESBIAN EQUALITY (SOUTH AFRICA)

The National Coalition for Gay and Lesbian Equality (NCGLE) was founded on December 2, 1994, at a conference called by the University of Witwatersrand Center for Applied Legal Studies. Approximately 80 lesbians and gay men from across South Africa were present at its formation. The NCGLE has grown from 36 affiliated organizations at its founding conference to a current 73 organizations. As a nonpartisan body committed to equality and justice for all South Africans, the NCGLE identified several of its objectives. At its founding conference, the following objectives were identified: 1) To lobby successfully for the retention of sexual orientation in the Equality Clause of the final Constitution; 2) to campaign for the decriminalization of same-sex conduct; 3) to initiate constitutional litigation challenging discrimination against same-sex relationships; 4) to train a representative gay and lesbian leadership on the basis racial and gender equality. And the scope of the NCGLE during the past six years has shown major strengths and weaknesses. These aspects are the subject of further study and therefore will not be interrogated here.

In the 1995 Interim Executive Committee report of the National Coalition for Gay and Lesbian Equality (NCGLE), the struggles of the international lesbian and gay movement for legal and social reforms and, in particular, the lobbying campaign of the local National Coalition, were highlighted. Although the report foregrounded the gains made by the retention of the sexual orientation clause in the South African constitution, especially the claim that the inclusion of sexual orientation in the equality clause gave lesbian and gay people full citizenship, the idea nevertheless has to be approached with some trepidation. Citizenship, which stands metonymically for the nation, and logically, nationality, may present a blurred picture of democracy. What is worrisome about this conflation is not the optimism displayed in the rhetoric but the assumption that equal rights is a guarantor of citizenship. Citizenship, similar to nationhood/nationality/nationalism is a problematic construct, and as such, will have to be interrogated with some degree of caution. Central to the definition of nationhood is the recognition of identity, which we know by now is fraught with contradiction. If we view nations in Benedict Anderson's phrase as imagined communities, we see as McClintock (1995, 353) argues, nationalism becomes, as a result, radically constitutive of people's identities through social contests that are frequently violent and always gendered. This notion of a gendered nationality perhaps unmasks some potential insecurities of an invented unity, which is being prioritized. Also relevant is a linguistic mapping that dominates the notion of a united front. On the level of language then, the "we" extends beyond the boundaries of a pronoun to resemble a sign of how the contours of culture are delineated. As a rhetorical device the "we" effects a politics of inclusion frames positions, allegiances, and group identifications but simultaneously constitutes a covert (perhaps coercive) universal, and in retarding this authority, the gay and lesbian "movement" could show more sensitivity to confronting these differences.

Despite these criticisms and in the light of its gains, the NCGLE at its 1999 national conference decided to transform itself into a nongovernmental organization and at the same time secure the option to recall the coalition should there be a threat to gay and lesbian equality.

FEMINISM, GENDER, AND GAY AND LESBIAN STUDIES: PEDAGOGICAL INITIATIVES

Feminist discussions and research prove useful in facilitating a more cogent critique of a representative and inclusive gendered field. While we cannot deny the impact women's organizations and feminists have on a phallocratic society, similarly we cannot dismiss the reluctance, ignorance (and possibly an overt homophobia) some have displayed to contextualize fully the imperatives of a "gender" discourse. In fact, the concept of "gender" is a relatively recent development in South Africa. If "gender studies" existed in South Africa, it has displayed an institutional bias toward women's studies. As a category that subsumes all aspects of sexuality, gender has come to signify women's rights and "womanness" in South Africa. If one examines, especially from a literary perspective, the research that is being done, it is not surprising to find that special issues on feminism or women in academic journals ordinarily prioritize the representation of women. For example, several anthologies on South African women's writing, all of which prioritize women, not gender, have been published. Some include Cherry Clayton's *Women and Writing in SA* (1989), Cecily Lockett's *Breaking the Silence: A Century of South African Women's Poetry* (1990), Annemarie van Niekerk's *Women's Stories* (1990). The first anthologized publication on gay and lesbian writing, *The Invisible Ghetto: Lesbian and Gay Writing from South Africa,* edited by Matthew Krouse, was published in 1993. The Gevisser and Cameron text also contains a limited selection of creative writing.

The field of gender studies, despite its institutional bias toward aspects of gay and lesbian studies, is undergoing some changes in the light of the new political context. There appears to me to be a deeper commitment from feminists to be representative in designing curricula and courses. Despite the positive developments, I doubt if gay and lesbian studies will be constituted as a separate discipline at our universities: The best option could be its integration into a gender program. The canon debate that flourished in the '80s is not entirely far removed from the project of gay and lesbian studies. Changes to existing curricula are brought about largely through a process of struggle and by social pressures and new demands for new knowledge and for the reorganization and reconceptualization of what we already know (D'Emilio 1992, 163). Given this scenario, the following question arises: What does gay and lesbian studies (or queer studies) signify if we intend constituting it as a field of academic study at our universities? I will attempt to address some of these issues (some of which have been discussed elsewhere in this essay) in an indirect way by drawing on the insights of Piontek (1992), who in an excellent article situates the debate within the locus of activism and academia. He argues that the gay studies scholar should be viewed as a mediator between the cultural branch of a gay movement and the academy (141). If we strip activism from its narrowly defined categorization as political action that functions at grassroots level, and if we acknowledge that academia is not a totally privileged location that is resistant to social change, we may go places. Piontek questions the belief that a dichotomy exists between activism and academia as the two are not mutually exclusive, and the existing gap is not the result of inherent differences and therefore is not entirely insurmountable. Perhaps I should add at this point that my faith in the discipline of gay and lesbian studies does not necessarily signify that the study of queer culture should be restricted to queer scholars. Part of the contradiction lies in that those who support the establishment of such a field of study are also in the process of working out their sexual identities. Identity, as we have come to understand it, is marked by differences and is constantly developing in terms of an individual's articulation.

We should not rule out, however, the possibility of setting up formal interdisciplinary courses to teach, research, and problematize crucial aspects of queer sexuality. While this may be already happening in the West, it is not occurring in African universities. In fact, at some universities the infrastructure and resources exist, but we should remember that institutional prejudices run deeper. Consider Fuss's (1991) observation: Supporters of gay studies, a recently emergent interdisciplinary yet autonomous field of inquiry, must grapple with many of the same issues its predecessors confronted, including the vexed question of institutionalization and the relation of gay and lesbian communities to the academy. Similarly, Piontek argues that we need to remember that our selection of objects of study is not merely a matter of personal choice: What we study and write about—and what gets published—is subject to many institutional pressures (1992, 133).

Here are more specific implications. Apart from the hostilities of the academic establishment (not to mention certain individuals, their cartels and clubs at our universities), gay studies should not be simply construed as a political project. More specifically, it should not be viewed as a pseudo- or nonacademic special interest project (Piontek 1992, 138). There is a reluctance on the part of some to see the academic strengths of queer sexualities and also a reluctance to fund queer courses. Bureaucrats at our universities who underfund departments on outdated and vague formulas need to consider the academic potential of this emerging field of inquiry. In fact, the very notion of queer may well have a Western bent to it, but there is simultaneously something distinctly queer about being African queers, and perhaps this is what scholars should investigate.

CONCLUSION

Narratives of knowledge that constitute what we label experience may be used to reconcile the internal, formal, and private structures of sexuality with its external, referential, and often homophobic effects. It matters little whether we present a humane picture of sexuality or an anti-homophobic defense. The recurrent debate (especially in academic studies) is predicated on seriously questioning the way in which we (re)make meaning of ourselves as queer people, and one way of achieving this is to demystify the psychology of oppression with all its attendant signifiers, in both theory and praxis. If queer theory is a fashionable and politically sound concept, this essay may have made visible some flaws in aspects of queer sexuality in South Africa. What I have attempted to propose is not only a way of reading the topos of homosexuality against the grain of history and homophobia, but also a way of conceptualizing aspects of gay historiography from a South African perspective, if "South African" is simply meant an awareness of geography. Some of the variables—such as race, activism, and difference—have profound implications for understanding ourselves as African queers facing a 21st century that Thabo Mbeki calls the "African Century." While the political importance of this vision cannot be overlooked, I am equally keen to see how African queers are viewed in this century.

REFERENCES

Bland, L. and Mort, F. (1997). "Thinking Sex Historically." In *New Sexual Agendas,* edited by L. Segal. London: Macmillan.

Blau, H. (1987). *The Eve of Prey: Subversions of the Postmodern.* Bloomington and Indianapolis: Indiana University Press.

Branford, J. (1987). *A Dictionary of South African English.* Cape Town: Oxford University Press.

Carter, E. and Watney, S. (Eds.). (1989). *Taking Liberties: AIDS and Cultural Politics.* London: Serpent's Tail.

De Lauretis, T. (1991). "Queer Theory: Lesbian and Gay Sexualities, An Introduction." *Differences* 3(2): iii-xviii.

D'Emilio, J. (1992). *Making Trouble: Essays on Gay History,Politics, and the University.* New York: Routledge.

Edelman, L. (1994). *Homographesis: Essays in Gay Literary and Cultural Politics.* New York: Routledge.

Edwards, T. (1994). *Erotics & Politics: Gay Male Sexuality, Masculinity, and Feminism.* New York: Routledge.

Foucault, M. (1970). The Order of Things. London: Tavistock.

Foucault, M. (1990). *The History of Sexuality: An Introduction.* London: Penguin.

Fuss, D. (Ed.) (1991). Inside/Out: Lesbian Theories, Gay Theories. New York: Routledge.

Fuss, D. (1994). "Interior Colonies: Frantz Fanon and the Politics of Identification." *Diacritics* 24 (2-3): 20-42.

Gallagher, B. & Wilson, A. (1987). "Sex and the Politics of Identity: An Interview with Michel Foucault." In *Gay Spirit: Myth and Meaning,* edited by Mark Thompson. New York: St. Martin's Press.

GALZ (Gay and Lesbian Organization of Zimbabwe). Newsletter, November 1995.

Germond, P. & de Gruchy, S. (1997). *Aliens in the Household of God: Homosexuality and Christian Faith in South Africa.* Cape Town & Johannesburg: David Philip.

Gevisser, M. & Cameron, E. (1994). *Defiant Desire: Gay and Lesbian Lives in South Africa.* Johannesburg: Ravan Press.

Halifax, N. (1988). *Out Proud and Fighting: Gay Liberation and the Struggle for Socialism.* London: Socialist Workers Party (a Socialist Workers Party pamphlet).

Halperin, David M. (1995). *Saint Foucault: Toward a Gay Hagiography.* New York and Oxford: Oxford University Press.

Harwood, V. et.al. (Eds.) (1993). *Pleasure Principles: Politics, Sexuality,y and Ethics.* London: Lawrence & Wishart.

Isaacs, G. and McKendrick, B. (1992). *Male Homosexuality in South Africa: Identity, Formation, Culture, and Crisis.* Cape Town: Oxford University Press.

Keane, J. (1993). "AIDS, Identity, and the Space of Desire." Textual Practice 7 (3): 450-464.

Lane, A. J. (1994). "Black Bodies/Gay Bodies: The Politics of Race in the Gay/Military Battle." *Callaloo* 17(4): 1074-1088.

McClintock, A. (1995). *Imperial Leather: Race, Gende, and Sexuality in the Colonial Contest.* New York and London: Routledge.

Miller, N. (1993). *Out in the World: Gay and Lesbian Life from Buenos Aires to Bangkok.* London: Penguin.

Morton, D. (1993). "The Politics of Queer Theory in the (Post) Modern Moment." *Genders* (17): 121-149.

National Coalition for Gay and Lesbian Equality. (1995). "We Must Claim Our Citizenship!" Report of the Interim Executive Committee (IEC) of the NCGLE: December 1994- Dec. 1995: 1-100.

National Coalition for Gay and Lesbian Equality. (1999). *Equality,* Issue 4.

National Coalition for Gay and Lesbian Equality. (1999). *Equality*, Issue 5.

Piontek, T. (1992). "Unsafe Representations: Cultural Criticism in the Age of AIDS." *Discourse* 15(1): 128-153.

Sedgwick, E. K. (1994). *Epistemology of the Closet*. London: Penguin.

Sontag, S. (1991). *Illness as Metaphor/AIDS and Its Metaphors*. Harmondsworth: Penguin.

Terry, J. (1991). "Theorizing Deviant Historiography." *Differences* 3(2): 55-74.

Tirivanho, H.M. (1995). "Black Homosexuality in Zimbabwe." *GALZ*. Nov. 1995: 18-19.

Weeks, J. (1985). *Sexuality and its Discontents: Meanings. Myths & Modern Sexualities*. New York: Routledge.

Woods, G. (1994). "Aimless Snippets" (review of Patrick Higgin's *A Queer Reader*). *Times Literary Supplement*. Feb. 25: 10.

Homosexuality and Heterosexist Dress Codes

How RuPaul Works: Signifying and Contextualizing the Mythic Black [Drag Queen] Mother

Seth Clark Silberman

How is it that RuPaul Andre Charles, a 6-foot-5 black gay drag queen ("but with hair, heck, and attitude, honey, I am through the roof!"), became a media darling in the United States in the summer of 1993? And how is it that she has not quite suffered the fate of so many one-hit wonders before her, never completely fading from public view? The mainstream popularity of RuPaul—the June 26, 1993 issue of *TV Guide* instructs us to "add another leggy looker to the pack of super-models...who are taking over TV," as if mere mention in *TV Guide* alone does not signal RuPaul's mainstream arrival in and of itself—is not quite as radical as it may suggest. RuPaul's hit single "Supermodel (You Better Work)," which peaked at No. 45 in *Billboard* magazine and sold nearly 500,000 copies, marked no grand societal shift to embrace transgendered individuals. Though, as Michael Musto sardonically notes, "an army of nocturnal cross-dressers continues to step over each other's bound feet in hopes of becoming the next Ru" (Musto 1996, 50). RuPaul's success did remind the entertainment industry that drag can be a marketable commodity, as the recent successful films *To Wong Foo, Thanks for Everything! Julie Newmar* and *The Birdcage* confirmed; especially in the safe distance a movie theater offers and especially when the actors who portray drag queens profess their heterosexuality. How then did Ru attain her crossover appeal? Savvy self-promotion and her clever signifying on the myth of the black mother. Signifying on the cultural mythology of the archetypal black mother, RuPaul invokes an "unthreatening," instantly recognizable black image to overlap with the potentially threatening image of the black gay drag queen, one that Sheri Parks argues is "founded upon Western attitudes toward women, caste/class, blackness, and fierce matern[ity]." Innumerable media images, including those of *Gone with the Wind* and *Ghost* (and is it any coincidence that Hattie McDaniel and Whoopi Goldberg are the only two black women to win an Academy Award for these "black mother" roles?) remind us that the black mother is the redeemer, the enabler, the nurturer.

She is the knower of secrets, the mystic. She solves contradiction. In popular narratives she often serves as a bridge between black and white communities, often (but not always) to provide a happy ending for the narrative's white characters. Both Western and Afrocentric creation stories describe the mother of the world as black. As Parks illustrates, the mythic black mother has been most prominent during periods of economic and social unrest, when the status quo conceptualizations of class, gender, and race have been threatened as members of disenfranchised groups pushed for change. Her popularity has peaked during the periods of the Civil War, the depression, and the postindustrial age, when she has been used as the mythical figure of transformation and deliverance from chaos back to order. Only she who knows the uncontrollable can conquer it.

Ru heralds her own arrival during her April 8, 1993 appearance on Black Entertainment Television's *Video Soul* with a similar proclamation: "In the '90s things are really happening. It's a great time to be alive, and I think things are coming to the forefront. You know, people are having to find out how they feel about their sexuality, how they feel about their parents, how they feel about whatever. And you know, this is one thing people are having to deal with." Ru includes herself in everyone's self-realization narratives, as if she acted as a conduit for that realization, for that movement "from chaos back to order." Immediately after her serious assessment of why she has become popular, however, she humorously glows, with her eyes open wide, first staring at *Video Soul* cohost Donnie Simpson then slowly turning to the camera, "I'm not going anywhere. I will not be ignored!... Fear of a drag planet!" She punctuates her retort with her stage laugh, effectively softening—while not retracting—the political significance of what she has just said. Herein lie the real transgressive qualities of RuPaul's media presence, to firmly entrench the political in entertainment in a way that displaces neither. After all, as Ru claims, "every time I bat my eyelashes, it's a political act" (Trebay, 1993).

Ru rarely lets the political significance of her success go unnoticed. In the *Los Angeles Times,* she explains, "We're entering the new era of glamour, and actually, I'm heralding it. Glamour is a response to the bleak '80s and a response to the whole Reagan-Bush era. That's why there's a sexy Democrat in the White House and we're returning to what's fun and loving and...beautiful and full of color" (Sigmund, 1993). RuPaul even signifies upon her need to invoke the black mother to navigate U.S. racial politics: She playfully points out her "unthreatening" posturing at the end of her *Video Soul* appearance when she says to Donnie Simpson, "You know, in America a black man can't get a hand until he puts on a pair of high heels and a wig!" Or, as she explains a few months before the release of "Supermodel," "I'm accessible as a black woman. Our society doesn't know what to do with a black man" (Skinny 1992, 28). Invoking such a prominent cultural myth allows her public an unthreatening way to identify with her and her music, a safe and accessible way to "work the runway, sweetie!" Invoking myth offers an instantly recognizable narrative with which to interpolate the audience's identification with—if not temporarily suspend their recognition of—a black gay drag queen. The cover of *Out* magazine's January 1994 issue, which includes Ru in their "media bombshells of 1993," encapsulates this strategy in one image: her lips are parted with great sass while a naked baby rests on her hip. She can serve it up and take care of her baby, thank you very much.

RuPaul is able to (re)fashion the mythic black mother to work for her because, like any mythic type, the myth of the black mother is not a fixed or essential type (even though racial types like the mythic black mother are used to essentialize black women). Part of its very structure and prevalence is to be adaptable. Myth, Roland Barthes illustrates, is the raw material that creates the "ideas-in-form" that shape culture. Myth is "a mode of signification ...not defined by the object of the message, but by the way in which it utters this message" (Barthes 1972).

Or as Ru advises, "It's not what you wear, but how you wear it!" Ru may not be a "real" black woman, but she plays one on TV; the utterance of the nurturing, wise, and sassy black mother is all Ru needs to invoke her. Signifying on the expectations held for the mythic black mother in an über–Oprah Winfrey manner, RuPaul offers her audience (her) drag as a transformative rehabilitator so they can nurture themselves. As Ru often explains, "You're born naked, and all the rest is drag." Ru fashions herself and the power of drag as an American success story: She proclaims in *Wigstock: The Movie,* filmed on Labor Day in 1993, "When I started out, right here in this neighborhood, they told me I couldn't make it. They said wasn't no big black drag queen in the pop world, and you ain't gonna do it. Well, look at the bitch now!" Because of her own success, Ru instructs on *Video Soul,* "If RuPaul can do it...you can write your own ticket."

RuPaul's first foray onto MTV in fall 1992, and thus her first introduction to a mass U.S. audience, crystallized her self-help-trans-formation message. *MTV News* sent reporter Alison Stewart with RuPaul to a New Jersey mall to discuss the phenomenon of RuPaul and the club success of the just-released "Supermodel." And, of course, to do a little shopping. MTV's choice of the mall was intentionally sym-bolic, meant to enact how their projected demographic—suburban white youths for whom a mall is a common denominator—would interpolate the image of a gargantuan black drag queen singing about the supermodels of the fashion industry. The segment's displacements of Ru are archetypal: first, the displacement of Ru from the host and potential audience; and second, the displacement of the social taboos most commonly associated with the black drag queen, homosexuality and prostitution. The segment opens and closes with Alison Stewart and RuPaul arriving and leaving the mall in a white limousine in order to reinforce Ru's "otherness": She is familiar with, does not come to, and thus is not part of the community of this mall since MTV is bring-ing her here. While MTV's artist profiles are often done either in per-formance situations—backstage, somewhere around or inside a per-formance venue, or in a recording studio—or somewhere personal—at the artist's house, a favorite hangout—Ru's artist profile was filmed in a mall, ostensibly because any personal or performance setting would not be as "accessible" to their demographic. It's OK to talk about Ru's own transgendered body (it was on this segment that Ru premiered her classic sound bite about her height, "with hair, heels, and attitude, I am through the roof!"), and to demonstrate how "different" it is from "ours" (on this segment Ru shops for size 14 women's shoes, of course, to no avail), but to see her within the context of the gay or drag com-munity, in which she had been performing for years prior to her Tommy Boy Music contract, would "reveal" too much. Instead, the segment provides images of Ru's transformative powers. Starting what became, and still is, a RuPaul convention, Ru instructs willing female mall volunteers on how to walk and serve attitude, a spiritual trans-formation to unleash the "all-powerful queen" within their own "everyday" bodies.

Part of the continued repetition of this transformation is to emphasize the skill of her drag: "I've been in the business for 11 years but am still learning new tricks. I discovered the push-up bra last year and it changed my life!" or "Let's face it, in this business you need a shtick. Offstage I wear jeans and a T-shirt; onstage, I look damn good in a pair of pumps and a blond wig" (*TV Guide*, June 26, 1993). Ru insists upon her drag as a cultivated and studied performance, akin to vaudeville or shtick, a liminal comic release, to de-emphasize the oft-assumed association of drag with a queer identity. She also displaces any references to drag queen culture and her own "drag queen authenticity" onto Jennie Livingston's 1991 documentary of the drag balls in Harlem, *Paris Is Burning*. Ru professes that she "stole" the title of her album from Octavia St. Laurent, an interviewee in the film who admits she wants to become the "supermodel of the world."

RuPaul's strategic displacement of drag authenticity and her initial avoidance in naming her sexual identity are not, however, closeted maneuvers; they illustrate the potential of what Peggy Phalen urges is the freedom from the overdetermined and reductive association of "identity politics" with visibility: "There is real power in remaining unmarked" (Phalen 1993, 6). By not overstating the obvious, RuPaul was able to speak to a number of communities at the same time. She was able to create and address an audience she characterizes in *USA Today* as "mostly young, black and white kids who've never experienced real glamour and outrageous, unadulterated fun" (Jones 1993, D1). Even with this seemingly innocuous statement, however, Ru demonstrates how she leaves her sexuality unmarked but not hidden. Glamour is often her signifier. As she proclaims her everydayness, she points toward her "natural" abilities: "I'm just an ordinary Joe. I just have the unique ability to accessorize." Her May 28, 1993 appearance on *The Arsenio Hall Show* illustrates her linguistic signifiers. Before her live interview, Hall introduces a taped segment they filmed together shopping for lingerie. While shopping, Ru explains, "I'm just like anybody else, Arsenio. I put my panty hose on one leg at a time!" When Hall asks, "What size do you wear?" Ru replies "Honey, I wear queen-size." Her linguistic substitutions and displacements may seem at odds with her over-the-top appearance—on *Video Soul* Ru concedes to cohost Sheri Carter that people are shocked by her "and for good reason"—but this juxtaposition shows what Ru did learn from watching *Paris Is Burning* and witnessing its subsequent critical acclaim. Ru's juxtaposition shows she better understands the pop potential of what Peggy Phalen calls the "hyper-visibility" of the ball walkers in *Paris Is Burning* than does Phalen. Phalen explains the significance of what she claims is the essence of what the "aping" of the ball's "realness" categories ostensibly promotes with the following reading:

> As one of the informants explains, to be able to look like a business executive is to be able to be a business executive. Within the impoverished logic of appearance, "opportunity" and "ability" can be connoted by the way one looks. But at

the same time, the walker is not a business executive, and the odds are that his performance of that job on the runway of the ball will be his only chance to experience it. The performances, then, enact simultaneously the desire to eliminate the distance between ontology and performance—and the reaffirmation of that distance (Phalen 1993, 9).

Neither categories nor the ball, however, enact a desire to eliminate or reaffirm the distance between ontology and performance—no one in *Paris* ever denies the material realities of being a poor black queen in New York City or claims that the balls can change those realities. No one "confuses" the balls with reality. Dorian Corey, in particular, is very conscious and critical of the ball's functions within the community as well as its representational politics. What Livingston's informants continually affirm is that the balls and their categories are a site of conscious fantasy. They are a means to usurp—albeit for one night—the very real implications race has on ontology and performance, on "opportunity" and "ability," in the U.S. For some ball walkers, these "performances" are not simply for the balls; these "categories" are a means of survival; Corey instructs that "femme realness" occurs when after the ball the contestant can get home on the subway in one piece, when no one has detected that she is "really" a he.

The positive critical reception of the film showed Ru what effect the fantasy of "realness" could have outside the ball communities too, what Jean LaPlance and Jean-Bertrand Pontalis argue, that "Freud always held [to be] the model fantasy: the reverie, that form of novelette, both stereotyped and infinitely variable, which the subject composes and relates to himself in a waking state" (Laplance and Pontalis 1986, 22). The "reverie" of the balls—detached from the real struggles of ball participants—speaks to many audiences, each writing their own fascination with the ball onto their explanation of the film; as Terrence Rafferty of *The New Yorker* explains: "The material [in the film] is almost too rich, too suggestive. Everything about *Paris Is Burning* signifies so blatantly and so promiscuously that our formulations—our neatly paired theses and antitheses—multiply faster than we can keep track of them, and the movie induces a kind of semiotic daze" (Rafferty 1991, 72). Ru simply turns up "the semiotic daze" and wraps it in a recognizable package for a pop audience. With the "stereotyped [yet] infinitely variable" script of the mythic black mother, Ru offers herself as tabula rasa, one that "the [audience] composes and relates to himself [as if] in a waking state." One way she and Monica Lynch, president of Tommy Boy Music, who offered RuPaul her historic record contract, the first—and so far the only—major label contract for a drag queen, accomplished this was to add a new wig to Ru's routine, a platinum blond one. Before signing with Tommy Boy Music, Ru was best known for her "starbooty" persona, very blaxploitation, very Pam Grier, very Tamara Dobson; but such a look, Lynch must have feared, would not be widely accessible. Making Ru blond, the eternal signifier of glamour, a look Ru calls "total glamour, total excess, total Vegas, total total," (Trebay, 1993) was Lynch's way to make Ru harmless. Ru explains succinctly, "I'm like Monica's full-size Barbie doll" (Musto 1992, 26). As if to model herself for Ru's audience, Lynch admits "to nabbing vicarious thrills through Ru's über-glamour."

Maintaining the reverie of über glamour, keeping the tabula rasa blank, necessitates the deft deflection of questions about sexual identity. Fixing her sexual identity would prevent her audience from being able to script whatever 'reverie" necessary to "nab vicarious thrills" through her glamour. The following excerpt from RuPaul's April 8, 1993 appearance on *Video Soul* illustrates how adroitly Ru navigates any questions of cohosts Sheri Carter and Donnie Simpson that aim to "fix" her:

Sheri Carter: Now what would you call yourself? If you had to describe yourself, what would you say?

RuPaul: My look today is sort of a retro. I got my Daisy Dukes on, first of all. I want everybody to know I got my Daisy Dukes on. Did you see my Daisy Dukes?

SC: No, I didn't.

R: Well, the '70s are back with a vengeance, of course. And everybody's wearing Daisy Dukes, like little hot pants.

SC: Oh, OK, well, they would have called them hot pants.

R: Well, we call it...like the song "I Got My Daisy Dukes On." So we're featuring Daisy Dukes today. But I am doing a neo-black hooker look today [SC and Donnie Simpson laugh], which is always fun. When I first starting doing drag, you know, I was enamored—just like Dolly Parton—with hookers. I mean, hookers wear the best clothes, don't they?

DS: [SC and DS laugh] I don't know about that.

R: I think so. I love them. They are the backbone of the American Trade Association! [SC and DS laugh]

SC: I bet there's a lot of politicians that would agree with you [more laughter]. Now, you mentioned that you said that you are in drag. What does that mean? Does that mean you're gay? Does that mean that you really want to be a woman? Or that you just enjoy dressing up as a woman? [R laughs as she asks the questions]

R: I'm laughing because, you know, I've been doing these interviews for a long time now.

SC: Don't they always ask you that, though? Don't they always ask you that?

R: It's the same questions but, you know, it's fine. You know, I don't want to be a woman. Dressing in drag is just that. I mean, everybody is in drag. Any time you step out of the shower and put something on, you're going to get into drag [turns to DS, who looks stunned]. You know what I'm saying?...You're mesmerized by my eye lashes, aren't you? [both R and DS laugh]

DS: No, I'm trying to understand this "get out of the shower and I'm in drag thing." What do you mean?

R: No, well, you're born naked and the rest is drag.

Ru skillfully deflects personal questions to offer the audience familiar context(s) within which to understand her: fashion and fads, popular black music, Dolly Parton's affection for hookers. All of these contexts displace herself from "real" drag queens. Evoking Parton's admiration in particular demonstrates Ru's savvy acknowledgment and deflection of people's reactions to her. Above she playfully acknowledges the spectacle drag can be when teasing Donnie Simpson for staring at her. She caps her navigation with one of what some call her New Age truisms, truisms she repeats with the demeanor of a preacher so that the next time you see her, you know how to chime in. Ru leads her common sermon on the show, asking the viewing audience to place their hands on their television sets, then commanding, "Everybody say love!" She punctuates her call with the following lesson: "It's all about love, baby, 'cuz if you don't love yourself, how the hell you gonna love anybody else? Can I get an amen in here?" The *TV Guide* article echoes what Ru says on *Video Soul*. "There's a message behind the makeup, insists the singer. 'People ask me, "Should I call you he or she?" I say,

"You can call me he, she, or Regis and Kathie Lee." It's what's inside that counts' " (1993, 2).

Ru's message of love, however, was not always received as openly or as positively as it was on *Video Soul*. Ru's appearance during MTV's 1993 spring break programming, with both the tension and adulation she inspired, shows how critical Ru's charismatic navigating was in creating and maintaining her audience. Filmed live in Daytona Beach, Fla., in front of a large audience of college students who had come to party, Ru was a guest on the spring break edition of MTV's *Chillin' With the Weez,* one of the network's highest-rated shows at the time, starring comedian Pauly Shore. Ru also performed "Supermodel" on "Beauty and the Beach," a beauty contest for both women and men for which she later served as a celebrity judge. While the mostly white, mostly heterosexual crowd of "Beauty and the Beach" bopped and waved their hands in the air along with her as she shantayed down the runway during her performance of "Supermodel," Pauly Shore appeared not as comfortable with Ru. For the interview, Shore dressed in comic drag to illustrate, as he later explains to Ru that although he "does a chick on his show," he hasn't "gone the distance" like Ru. Throughout Shore's almost hostile interview, he continues to ask, "What are you, a transsexual?" Unfaltered, Ru counters, "It's all about fun," again invoking her preacher demeanor, proclaiming, "I am a drag queen! Can I get an amen in here?" Later in the interview she looks to the audience and adjusts, saying, "I am a big ol' black man wearing women's clothes!"

Ru's call-and-response deflection of "fixing" her identity is what saved her from Shore's assault, and what ultimately maintained her crossover appeal. Even after she later became more visibly "out," Ru's über-glamour remained (for the most part) transcendent. As Lynch echoes, "There's something about RuPaul that transcends being a drag queen. People just gravitate toward Ru, regardless of age, race, gender, whatever" (Decaro, 1992). Ru elaborates, "The one thing I do that no one else does better than me is, I communicate somehow. I plug into a frequency that other people understand. When people see me onstage and I'm gorgeous, what they're seeing is a reflection of their own beautiful imagery. When they pick up on my frequency and my rhythm, they go, 'Oh, I love that. That's me' " (1993, 19).

Maintaining that frequency, however, is a difficult, often stifling job. At the beginning of the rise of "Supermodel," Ru claimed to have a handle on the stress: "At one point, when I do the thing I do, I know people are looking at me; everyone's staring. But it's not me. It's the 'thing' people are looking at. And I can stand outside it" (Trebay, 1993). But keeping that "thing" separate is taxing. In a review of *Supermodel of the World,* Vince Aletti prophesies the toll Ru's working would take:

> As a canny, playful critique of gender straitjacketing, drag's the perfect cocktail for the hot and bothered: ambivalence on ice. But drag can be a straitjacket too; unlike androgyny, which suggests all kinds of possibilities (think Jagger, Bowie, Patti Smith, Boy George, early Prince, even Sylvester, who kept his options open), full drag often seems neutering. At its sassiest and most confrontational, drag's a surprise package; but is it the best of both worlds or an empty box? (Aletti 1993, 63).

By summer 1994 drag had become an empty box for Ru, and she wanted out. She granted *The Advocate* an interview they called "RuPaul Unmasked," posing for pictures sans wig, complaining that the perfectly marketed media image of RuPaul "left me somewhere between Pee Wee Herman and Rozalla" (Yarbrough, 1994). For her new album, *Soul Food*, she promised more depth and a touch of auto-biography. To gain credibility, she even solicited the services of R&B legendary producer Nick Martinelli, who worked with divas Stephanie Mills, Phyllis Hyman, Regina Belle, Mild Howard, and Diana Ross. Martinelli spoke glowingly of legitimizing Ru as a vocalist: "I think people are going to be surprised. It's definitely a new RuPaul." Ru promised to expand upon the "Disney Ru" of the first album: "I'm just adding dimension. Fleshing the whole image out. Flapping my wings harder, you know?"

Monica Lynch, however, was not thrilled by Ru's new "dimen-sion" and subsequently clipped Ru's wings, dropping her from Tommy Boy Music. Though Lynch never publicly commented on the decision, undoubtedly she was concerned that the "kinder, gentler" RuPaul would not speak to the masses as well as her ber black mother image did. Being dropped from Tommy Boy, however, was only a minor set-back, and perhaps it clarified for Ru her pop sensibility. Soon enough, Ru picked herself—and her wig and pumps—back up and worked again. She landed the first spokesmodel contract for MAC, an elite cos-metics line popular for years with celebrities, who decided to use Ru's image when they went "commercial" with counters at Nordstrom's and other upscale chains. She published her autobiography with

Hyperion Books, *Letting It All Hang Out*; headlined a review in Las Vegas; hosted her own video show, *RuPaul's Party Machine,* on MTV-owned music video channel VH-1; hosted the morning show for New York's WKTU; has her own Web page devoted to her—she declared herself "The Queen of Cyberspace" on *Late Night with Conan O'Brien*—and has recently signed with Buena Vista to do her own talk show, which was slated to start in fall 1996. Even her long-awaited second album is also scheduled to be finished soon. She has even had small roles in major motion pictures *Crooklyn, The Brady Bunch Movie, Blue in the Face,* and *To Wong Foo*; and prime time TV shows *Sister Sister, All in the House, The Crew,* and *Nash Bridges,* as well as a cameo on the late-night. comedy show *Mad TV.* Ru has been far from idle.

Ru's lingering media presence, however, cannot be explained only by her deft drag emulation of the black mother myth. Other post-"Supermodel" attempts at a neo-Ru crossover black drag queen have failed. The ABC sitcom *On Our Own*, which centered on the older brother of an upper-middle-class black family recently orphaned by a car accident who must cross-dress and emulate his "Aunt Jocinda" to prevent social workers from displacing him and his five siblings, debuted in Fall 1994 and quickly flopped because it failed to garner an audience. NBC "retooled" its sitcom *The John Laroquette Show* to find a larger audience. Before it was changed, the show was set in an urban bus station. Laroquette, the show's namesake, personally inter-acted with a host of "urban" characters, including a prostitute and two drag queens, one black, portrayed by New York club queen Jazzmun. When the show was "retooled," Laroquette moved to a more suburban neighborhood with a white neighbor and the bus station took less prominence on the show. Jazzmun never appeared again.

These "failures" prove the importance of the uncanny timing RuPaul had for her major-label debut. While Ru continually credits *Paris Is Burning* for her *"je ne sashay quoi,"* the film that did prefigure her crossover appeal, however, was Neil Jordan's 1992 crossover art house thriller *The Crying Game.* The outrageous success of Jordan's film and the word-of-mouth fascination with Jaye Davidson's charac-ter Dil and her "secret" demonstrated the real crossover potential for the "reverie" of the black drag queen, the mainstream marketability of the fantasies the black drag queen presents. The U.S. success of Jordan's film, as its infamous marketing foreshadowed, rested entirely on audience's fascination with Dil and the revelation that "she" is a "he" when she disrobes for her "love" Fergus, a success culminating in Jaye Davidson's nomination for an Academy Award and the subsequent buzz about what Davidson was going to wear to the ceremonies since "she" was nominated for Best Supporting Actor.

Carol Cooper argues in her article, "What Angels Lack," that the recent proliferation of transgender romances such as *The Crying Game* attempts to shore against the new ambiguities of what she calls a "postgender society," the product of the new roles heterosexual women inhabit in a society in which the nuclear family and the once-corollary gender roles heterosexual marriage enforced are no longer considered attainable or desirable. Citing the following from an article by Katha Pollitt in *Glamour* magazine, Cooper argues that "when women talk among themselves... the talk is less and less frequently about how to get a man than how to do well without one... 'The collapse of the traditional middle-class marriage bargain has left both sexes bewildered and is a major cause of the much-discussed open hostility between men and women. But how can you make the sexes act as if they need each other to survive when they don't? All they need each other for is love, and love is hard to find' "(Cooper 1994, 15). Love, however, has never been hard to find in the media; and now, in this new "postgender society" where traditional gender roles are changing in the work force and at home, the media offers transgender romance as "a same-sex version of the male-dominant, female-submissive dynamic," not so subtly reproaching women who have forsaken their traditional gender roles. These romances, Cooper argues, deliver the following edict to heterosexual women: "If you no longer want to provide it, drag queens will inherit the earth" (Cooper 1994, 15).

While her article concentrates on *The Crying Game*, the most popular of the transgender romances she cites (which include *Kiss of the Spider Woman*, *M. Butterfly*, *Farewell My Concubine*, and scenes from *La Cage Aux Folles* and *Torch Song Trilogy*, Cooper does not theorize why Jordan's film garnered the most attention. The reason Jordan's anhouse film "crossed over" to mainstream success, earning over $62 million in the U.S. alone, is not just because Dil reveals her "secret" midway through the film, but because Dil is black. As Hawley Russell argues, "the film's most attractive feature is the illusion that Dil is an accessible, exotic, racialized 'feminine' body" (Russell 1994, 109). Dil's function in the film is not just as Fergus's love interest; "Dil operates to revive latent cultural dreams among American moviegoers" (110).

Even though Russell does not name this dream as such in her

article, that latent cultural dream is the dream of the black mother. Russell offers that her idea of "cultural dreaming," of the iconic significance of the bodily manifestation of that dream, is informed by Lisa Kennedy's article, "The Body in Question," in which the body she describes clearly reflects the mythic representation of the black mother. She writes that the collective body is "that phantasm with which I share blood, history, and hips...ambling, lumbering, hobbling in a monstrous mass, more male than female, urban than rural, angry than forgiving, the CB [collective body] monster is reminiscent of some creature from a '50s sci-fi flick, bigger than a house" (117). For Russell, Dil acts as this collective body because Dil reflects "the social constructions of black female sexuality [and thus] Dil serves as a gateway to a world of otherness, a world which mainstream American culture deems sexually deviant" (117).

What many assert as drag's sexual deviancy stems from the confusion surrounding locating the drag queen's penis; in fact, the first question people ask drag queens is "What do you do with it?" Anxiety over finding the penis of the drag queen is, as Freud would say, the classic reenactment of the primal scene of the boy who refuses to recognize that his mother does not have a penis. The apprehension over the absence of the penis, and the need to locate it, is the enactment of disavowal, the search for a phallic woman. It is the search for a fetish to substitute the absent penis. In the case of the drag queen, however, the penis is not absent, merely hidden. What, then, is the anxiety when the disavowal is true? How too is the anxiety of the disavowal amplified when the penis to be found is black?

Kobena Mercer interrogates these questions in "Reading Racial Fetishism: The Photographs of Robert Mapplethorpe." Mercer asserts that Mapplethorpe's "imagery opens an aperture onto the fetishistic structure of stereotypical representations of black masculinity" that draws more attention to the "landscape of the white male imaginary, the 'political unconscious' of white masculinity." The anxiety in looking for the black penis is thus also the anxiety of "the unknown" white gaze maintaining its subject position in maintaining its social control over the black body on display. It's the recapitulation of "the history of lynchings in the United States—the black man as the object of white male fear and fantasy, upon whose body history has inscribed the violence that white supremacy both abhors and yearns for" (Mercer 1994, 80).

In his book, *Love and Theft: Blackface Minstrelsy and the American Working Class*, Eric Lott demonstrates how central this repulsion and attraction are in the U.S. by demonstrating their roots in 19th-century blackface minstrelsy. Minstrelsy, he posits, "often attempted to repress the ridicule of the real interest in black cultural practices they nonetheless betrayed—minstrelsy's mixed erotic economy of celebration and exploitation" (6). As Lott demonstrates with the following minstrel song, "Astonishing Nose," minstrelsy's celebration and exploitation of black culture often provides "the occasion for a wider preoccupation with sexuality, not least homosexuality [and especially] black male genitalia":

> Like an elephant's trunk it reached to his toes,
> And wid it he would gib some most astonishing blows
> Like a dog in a fight—'twas a wonderful nose,
> An it follows him about wherever he goes.
>
> De police arrested him one morning in May,
> For obstructing de sidewalk, having his nose in de way.
> Dey took him to de court house, is member to fine;
> When dey got dere de nose hung on a tavern sign.
> (162)

This preoccupation is one of both captivation and apprehension. Here the captivation is with the nose's length; the apprehension is with the police's inability to contain it.

If the captivation and apprehension over that "astonishing nose" in *The Crying Game* revived latent cultural dreams for American moviegoers in fall 1992 and spring 1993, unearthing "the violence that white supremacy both abhors and yearns for," Jordan's film also neatly contains those impulses by the film's end. The last image of the film, after all, is of Fergus and Dil talking, separated by a glass wall. Fergus is serving a prison sentence for Dil, and we are reassured that this glass wall will separate them for at least six years. Thus, the homoerotic energy between them is contained. Depicting the consummation of their romance, however, (much as I would have loved to see it) would not necessarily fulfill the fantasy Dil enacts. As Lacan argues:

> The phantasy is the support of desire, it is not the object that is the support of desire. The subject sustains himself as desiring in relation to an ever-more complex signifying ensemble. This is apparent enough in the form of the scenario it

assumes, in which the subject, more or less recognizable, is somewhere, split, divided, generally double, in his relation to the object, which usually does not show its true face either (Cowie 1984, 71).

The "subject" in *The Crying Game*, the character with whom we're supposed to identify, Fergus, is indeed "split" in many ways: He has a split allegiance to the IRA with whom he affiliates himself with blank, patriotic duty; he has a split attraction to Dil once he sees Dil's penis, refusing to let her call him "darling" yet saving her from Jude, his former IRA girlfriend, with blank, chivalric attention. The "object," Dil, does not indeed show her "true face" initially—that is, if her big hands or Adam's apple don't give it away. The film indeed illustrates that "phantasy is the support of desire," or as Elizabeth Cowie's explains, that fantasy is "the mise-en-scene of desire, the putting into a scene, a staging, of desire" (Cowie 1984, 71). After Fergus sees Dil's penis, the film's mise-en-scène reflects Fergus's new recognition. When Fergus first follows Dil to The Metro, the drag club where she performs, it does not look like a drag club, and Dil and the other queens look alluring, "real." When Fergus returns post–penis-viewing, the lighting is harsh, and everyone in the club looks like a drag queen, dressed in tackier outfits with bad wigs. Dil, too, immediately and drastically devolves from provocative and confident to hysterical and codependent. With Fergus's fantasy of Dil marred, he now sees the "real" Dil.

The Crying Game proves "the pleasure [of Fergus's desire] is in how to bring about the consummation, is in the happening and continuing to happen: in how it will come about, and not in the moment of having happened, when it will fall back into loss" (Cowie 1984, 80) Fergus spends his moment of "having happened" puking into Dil's toilet (the longest vomit scene I can remember). The subsequent loss is the "literal" loss of the "girl" Fergus thought Dil was. Post-penis Fergus fulfills his chivalric duties, themselves a displacement for the real gay romance of the film, also a fantastic one that is staged yet never fulfilled, the one between Fergus and Jody. It is Jody, after all, whom Fergus dreams of, Jody throwing him the cricket ball. In true homosocial fashion, Fergus wants to cap the few intimate moments he shared with Jody by sharing Jody's "girl." Even the infamous penis scene with Dil simply echoes the one with Jody, when Fergus helps Jody urinate. It is Jody's penis, not Dil's, that Fergus actually touches. Ultimately, the U.S. success of *The Crying Game* was possible because of its minstrelsy-like sublimation of "a wider preoccupation with sexuality, not least homosexuality [and especially] black male genitalia."

The Crying Game proved for Ru in 1993 that drag was a highly marketable means to both heighten and mitigate the captivation with and apprehension over the black penis. In 1995 with the publication of *Letting It All Hang Out* after her "unmasking" in *The Advocate* and the loss of her Tommy Boy contract, Ru seems to recall and revel in *The Crying Game*'s lessons. With her "autobiography," part memoir, part how-to book, she restages the fantasy of the mythic black [drag queen] mother with a vengeance as well as reiterates the fascination with [what she does with] her penis. Ru repositions her own mother as both the primal drag queen and the mythic black mother, her ultimate inspiration she continues to "channel" when she performs. Ru explains that her mother was her greatest inspiration because "she was the first drag queen I ever saw. She had the strength of a man and the heart of a woman. She could be as hard as nails, but also sweet and vulnerable—all the things we love about Bette Davis, Joan Crawford, and Diana Ross. To this day when I pull out my sassy persona, it's Ernestine Charles that I am channeling" (RuPaul 1995, 32). With *Letting It All Hang Out*, Ru reclaims the mythic and spiritual role she cultivated with "Supermodel": "A drag queen is like a priest or a spirit familiar. We represent the myths, the duality of the universe" (Trebay, 1993). She reiterates the constant fascination with how she hides her penis by naming the first chapter "How to Tuck," which doubles as her own Ru creation story. (This chapter even comes before her standard autobiographical beginning, "Little Runi.") The chapter title, and even the book's title, seem to poke fun at the "delicate balance" Vince Aletti observes in Ru's popularity: "RuPaul can't take the risk that Dil took in *The Crying Game* and dangle the goods in our face; even if the meat is metaphorical, it's sure to upset the delicate balance between subversion and diversion here" (Aletti, 1993).

Of course, as Ru knows from her many interviews, people's interest in "tucking" is not always so delicate; as Pauly Shore so eloquently poses, "What happened to the dong? Did you bail the dong?" What Ru does with her "business" has always been seen as the transformation Ru takes. With "How to Tuck," Ru restages the captivation and apprehension with her penis as the self-help transformation message of drag for herself, tautologically proving it with the narrative of the mythic black [drag queen] mother.

Ru's description of her own transformation, in fact, is a camp version of the first Western black mother myth, the Sumerian genesis narrative, "Inanna's Descent to the Nether World." In the myth the white queen of heaven, goddess Inanna, must pass through the chaos of the underworld, the realm of the dark Erieslikigal, the goddess of death, decay, and renewal, to be reborn. As Sheri Parks explains the Sumerian myth, "Inanna had to face Erieslikigal before she could become a fully functional goddess." So, too, Ru has to pass through pain in to transform into "what people expect of me—nothing less than perfection":

> It's gonna take nothing short of a miracle for [my transformation] to happen in just three short hours, and that's what a queen is—a miracle worker. The first thing I do is say a little prayer. I go to my vanity and pray to the gods of Charles Revlon, Max Factor, Flori Roberts, and all the other patron saints of beauty. Then I run a hot bubble bath with gorgeous bath oils from Origins—because I'm a natural queen. I unplug the phone, light some incense (Jasmine Extravaganza), and select the music that I will be listening to: something by Diana Ross, Donna Summer, or Barbra Streisand. This particular night I will be listening to Cher's *Greatest Hits*, which includes, "Save Up All Your Tears," my fave Cher song of all time. It has become the theme song for my transformation. All that pain and suffering for great beauty. It hurts, but you mustn't grumble and mustn't cry—big girls don't cry.
>
> After testing the temperature with my toe, I tell my faithful intern Juan, "No matter what happens, or what you hear, do not open this door for the next three hours. Then I lock and double-bolt the door and slowly begin to shed my manly disguise. I toss the clothes into a corner, where they watch discarded and miserable, unable to believe the transformation they are about to witness as the Goddess is born. I slip into the tub and before I move another muscle I soak for a good 15 minutes. Then very slowly I take my loofah sponge and scrub my skin. The skin must be clean and supple, with every pore exfoliated, every dead skin cell removed before I can begin the process of shaving" (RuPaul 1995, 2-3).

While she comically refers to it, the process of Ru becoming RuPaul, the entertainer, is a painful renewal—literally exfoliating her dead skin and shaving her hair from her body to enable her to easily don her supermodel guise does hurt, but as she explains, "all that pain and suffering [is necessary] for great beauty." Her renewal is also a feminine one, with the obvious birthing metaphor of the water of the bathtub; and considering the ultimate drag queen she channels is her mother, it's also a black feminine one.

RuPaul's creation story here, in fact, retreads Ru's brilliant homage to her mother in the song "Back to My Roots." With "Roots," Ru wields the fantasy and narrative of the mythic black [drag queen] mother both for crossover appeal and as a celebratory black cultural signifier. Unlike "Supermodel," which only alludes to a clearly fictional childhood, the "Supermodel" video enacts Ru's rise to fame in the guise of a rags-to-riches fable about a 1-year-old girl spotted by an *Ebony* fashion fair talent scout. To heighten the camp value of Ru's performance, the video for "Back to My Roots" focuses entirely on a fantastic childhood, one deliberately archetypal, with LaWanda Page cast as Ru's mother, who owns a hair salon. While no less fictional than "Supermodel," "Roots" is set in and thus highlights the love and warmth Ru feels from her black family and community (Laughlin and Schuler, 1995), echoed by a chorus of black people singing along with the chorus. The all-black communal settings of the video—Ru's mother's kitchen, her hair salon, the infomerical for black hair care products Ru hosts—illustrate the sources of Ru's inspiration. As the autobiographical assumption the video promotes, Ru's ability to become the Supermodel of the World is inspired by her mother's creative and nurturing skill of doing hair in the kitchen. The first lines of the song cement this assumption: "This a special shot going out to my Mama, Miss Ernestine Charles. Mama used to do people hair in the kitchen—pressin' curls, hot curlers, everything. I love you, Mama!" (RuPaul, 1993). The familial glee of the song's homage to Ru's mother emulates what Manthia Diawara calls "the black good-life society":

> At a literal and crucial level, the black good life society refers to black people's right to a good life, i.e., the right not to have one's life-world colonized by systems that emancipate others. The black good-life society emphasizes the necessity for a productive space which is accompanied by consumption, leisure, and pleasure in black people's relation to modernity (Barr et al, 1993).

The productive space that Ru envisions with Mama's hair salon on

Auburn Avenue in Atlanta, is again an example of how Ru "walks the line," how Ru leaves her sexuality unmarked yet not hidden. At its representational heart, Mama's hair salon is a revolutionary black and gay space, a space "accompanied by consumption, leisure, and pleasure," one that at its center is empowered by Mama's love, as the framing of Ru and LaWanda Page's smiling faces together at the end of the video posits when Ru "comes home" (with a fried chicken bucket in tow) to the salon. Mama's salon, like Ru's description of her transformation into the goddess, signifies "the work of self-presentation and self-invention" (White, 1993), and like the duality of the universe that Ru argues drag signifies, like the dual referents of drag that Ru navigates in her public appearances, "Back To My Roots" also navigates two cultural traditions. Obviously grounded in black cultural practices, as the song's refrain "Black hair is a revolution!" emphasizes, the video also connotes gay cultural practices in its camp association of Ru and hairdressing.

While the video is about Ru's mother's renowned ability as a hairstylist, Ru is equally a part of this celebration; Ru's centrality in the celebration of her mother is emphasized by their mirrored appearances at the end of the video (both Ru and her mother wear large blond wigs that connote drag). Even though Ru never fixes anyone's hair in the video—and while the audience may know that Ru's stylists, Mathu and Zaldy, actually do her hair, makeup, and sometimes her clothes—her hair does change 14 times during the video. Thus the assumption within the video narrative is that Ru does her own hair since, as the song professes, her mother's artistic abilities are what inspired her. While doing people's hair in the kitchen is commonplace for black working-class women, and certainly a part of RuPaul's childhood, hairdressing also has an implicit gay connection or camp connotation—as if Ru changing her hair 14 times in a single video in true diva style weren't campy enough. Richard Dyer argues that "gay men have made certain 'style professions' very much theirs (at any rate by association, even if not necessarily in terms of the numbers of gays actually employed in these professions)—hairdressing, interior decoration, dress design, ballet, musicals, revue" (1992, 138). Thus, hairdressing both celebrates African American cultural practices and points to Ru's sexuality without naming it. Despite Ru's unnamed sexuality in the video, however, the song and video act as powerfully positive and obvious representations of a black gay man coming home to his family and community, as the chorus of the song implies: "I'm going back, back, black to my roots / where my love can be found and my heart is true / I'm going back, back, black to my roots / to the time and the place, coming back to you."

Ru foreshadows this when she appears Video Soul discussing the idea for the video, grounded in her recent experience going and performing at a family reunion. Ru says, "I wanted to go back for the kids in the family to show them that this is their family too. A lot of people, you know, are exiled from their families and it's important for the family to know what's going on." What's going on, at least what the video envisions should go on, is the celebration of black gays and lesbians reuniting with their families. In the context of Ru and her video family, such a connection is forged through the mother's and drag queen son's craft, their ability to fix hair. Herein lies the revolutionary potential that the song's refrain implies. "Black hair is a revolution" thus connotes both the sociopolitical consciousness that black hair styles embody and the potential bond between a queen, her mother, and community.

Ru's most "daring" mainstream manipulation of the fantasies of the mythic black [drag queen] mother, one with the most explicit evocation of a drag community and of a drag queen's autonomy, is her recent appearance on Nash Bridges, the CBS police drama starring Don Johnson. While Ru did not write the part, the part was clearly written with her in mind, and some of Ru's lines clearly indicate that she was allowed to ad lib. The ways in which the officers relate to Ru, and the fantasy of the black drag queen, are clearly influenced by Ru's media presence. The role is also much more radical than other recent black drag queen characters on ER and Chicago Hope, who are both "tragic queens," HIV-positive, and die by the end of the episode (Hope's queen is nonetheless played with verve by the African American Giancarlo Esposito). Ru's character, Simone DuBois, reenacts what David Finkle argues is the "new stage personage." RuPaul's success has invigorated "the black drag queen who, bluntly reading everyone in the vicinity, is the voice of reason." RuPaul's presence on Nash Bridges, however, does not function as comic release, or as Steven Bochco explains the role of drag in Pubic Morals, his upcoming comedy about a vice squad, "I figure that in a situation where there are six-foot transvestite prostitutes, there's a lot of built-in absurdity" (Hass 1996, H30).

Ru's Nash Bridges character, Simone DuBois, is a six-foot transvestite prostitute, but is by no means absurd. The star of the secondary plot line of the "Javelin Catcher" episode in which Nash Bridges tracks down an antitank weapon ("the javelin") stolen from the military,

DuBois comes to the precinct to report some hate crimes to Bridges's lieutenant. After she is unable to find the assailant in the mug shot books, the lieutenant introduces DuBois to his officers as a representative of the gay/lesbian/transgender communities to set up an undercover operation. He explains the hate crimes as "a rash of beatings on Polk Street. Three transvestite prostitutes have filed reports since January." DuBois interrupts: "Excuse me, that's transgendered sex workers." The camera cuts to a close-up of her face as she corrects the lieutenant. Even though DuBois replicates the standard "tell it like it is" caricature of the black mother for sassy comic relief—at the beginning of the episode RuPaul says to another transgendered sex worker who is also searching though mug shot books, "Child, this ain't no date book. What you think this is, the *Love Connection*?"—her terminological correction here is not punctuated with a laugh track and the lieutenant earnestly apologizes, correcting himself.

The resolution of DuBois's complaint in some ways adheres to the self-help transformation message Ru used to market herself as *Supermodel*. Despite DuBois's nods to ameliorating the black drag queen, however, her role in *Nash Bridges* does not (simply) function as unthreatening camp or as the nurturing black mother. One way DuBois's transformative effect differs from *Supermodel* is that DuBois transforms a man, the officer DuBois selects *for* the undercover assignment, and that the officer's transformation does not detract from his heterosexual masculinity or implicate him in any homocontingent behavior. Of course, Officer Evan Cones is reluctant to don a dress. But unlike Pauly Shore's comic display of transformative drag, Cones's cross-dressing rehabilitates his relationship with his girlfriend, Stephanie. Yet while Cones's rehabilitation seems at the hands of DuBois (she coaches him and selects his outfit), she has no direct hand in his relationship; DuBois does not (like the mythic black mother) act as a bridge between the two. Cones's transformation into "Dorothy," the name he selects for his undercover persona, does offer DuBois ample opportunity to shoot catty one-liners (when Cones complains that his first outfit is too *Showgirls*, DuBois snaps, "Please, what do you think, you're going to the White House to have tea with Hillary Clinton?"—but her retorts do not simply allow DuBois to tell him "like it is." They articulate her autonomy. When Cones again complains that the assignment is not for him, DuBois spouts, "Let me tell you something, I'm doing this for the girls. I'm not getting paid for this. I'm doing this for the girls. Not for you." Her resistance to putting Cones "at ease" here contradicts the mythic black mother narrative and fore-shadows what happens later in the episode once they are "on assign-ment." Most interesting about Cones's transformation is the way the archetypal tensions of drag are displaced from DuBois onto Cones; clearly RuPaul was needed to be DuBois to serve as an identifiable reference point of what Eric Lott elucidates is the wide "preoccupation with sexuality, not least homosexuality [and especially] black male genitalia," but she is not exploited in her role. Cones's transformation takes place in the precinct bathroom, a common site of tension echoed throughout Ru's interviews," but the anxiety over locating the penis in drag is on Cones, not DuBois. Once Cones dons his outfit, a curly blond wig, a black dress crowned by a black-and-white full-length fur, and black pumps, and "completes" his transformation, DuBois is not in the frame. Cones looks into the sink mirror alone. Nash Bridges then enters the bathroom with the lieutenant and gushes, "Wow, that's hot. No kidding, seriously, that's good." Cones asks Bridges advice as they both use the urinals; but Bridges is distracted by the sight of Cones in drag at the urinal. Bridges even gives Cones the once-over, gazing at his penis. When DuBois does return into the frame (punctuating an entrance from a stall with the flushing of her toilet, no less!) and intro-duces herself to Bridges, inviting him to come down to Polk Street, Bridges does not stare at DuBois in the way he did Cones. He looks from DuBois to Cones and advises, "Good luck, ladies" as he leaves.

Centering drag on Cones is cemented by the show's ending, when, still in drag, he returns from his assignment to his apartment where Stephanie awaits. He enters the bedroom apologetic for being out all night. When she sees his outfit, however, she no longer cares; in fact, his outfit cures the trouble in their relationship: his inability to sexual-ly satisfy her. She is aroused by him in a dress, and the scene ends with the two kissing on their bed, Cones still in drag. While this resolution reduces Cones's drag to sexual fetish, it heterosexualizes it. Moreover, it does not ridicule his drag: the reconciliation of Cones and his girl-friend is not comic. Cones even keeps the "uniform" after the assign-ment. And again DuBois plays no role in Cones's reconciliation and new appreciation of drag.

DuBois, in fact, does not even assist Cones undercover as planned because he slanders her. When the first car passes them on Polk Street, DuBois shouts to the car, "Let me be your fantasy," and Cones timidly waves. DuBois instructs, "What you think you are, Miss Princess Diana? You can't be wavin'." Cones then retorts, "Look, I'm sorry, all right? This is my first night out here. Maybe when I've been here like, you know, working the street for like ten years like you, then maybe I'll have it down." In response, DuBois spits, "You should have not gone there, sister. Forget it." Even though Cones apologizes, DuBois crosses the street and never reappears during the show. No celebration with Cones once he does catch the assailant, no reconciliation, no DuBois-directed movement from chaos back to order. DuBois, after all, is in service to no one but "the girls" on Polk Street, where she leaves Cones to fend for himself.

While such a radical narrative that gives such autonomy to a black transgendered prostitute may be ready for prime time within the guise of a police drama, where ultimately every featured narrative succumbs to the constants the show offers, where all featured narratives ultimately further the character development of the show's stars, RuPaul's stellar performance points to the possibilities of black drag dramatic roles that fulfill the mainstream need for drag as spectacle but also present an autonomous drag queen character. Unlike her cameo in Spike Lee's *Crooklyn* as a salacious bodega woman or her TV cameos on *Sister Sister* or *The Crew,* where she plays "herself," her role on *Nash Bridges* demonstrates Simone DuBois is her own woman after all.

Whether or not the United States is ready for RuPaul to be her own woman on her forthcoming Buena Vista-produced talk show, or on her forthcoming second album, now dubbed *Snatched for the Gods,* remains to be seen. For the recent *RuPaul's Party Machine,* VH-1 took no such chances, sanitizing Ru's shtick for her to become, as the announcer introduces her, "the beautiful, the glamorous, the indisputable queen of your small screen."' Taped before a live audience, Ru's opening monologue is identical to her routine at the beginning of her *Supermodel of The World* tour, which she also replicated at the beginning of her 1993 British Christmas special, *RuPaul's Christmas Ball.* Shortly after she walks on stage, she asks the audience if they like her outfit, showing them first the front then the back, to which the audience cheers. On *Party Machine* Ru replies, "Oh, you're just saying that" followed by canned laughter. On *Christmas Ball* she replies, "Oh, you're just saying that. I bet you say that to all the queens." For a mass audience, VH-1 proffers, *queen* can only be used as a double entendre, not divorced from its regal denotation. Her VH-1 script continues to work "Disney Ru"'s black-mother shtick; with a rural accent, she informs the audience, "Now they don't know what they'd done gone and did by giving me my own show, child. Honey, the lunatics have taken over the asylum." VH-1 also recreates the power of drag as an American success story. In a pretaped segment called "And God created RuPaul," a collection of photographs, video images, and a Ru voice-over tell Ru's success story. After the tape is over, Ru reiterates the story, adding that she is "hostessing my very own show here on VH-1. Dreams do come true."

Of course, repetition is no stranger to Ru; it is how she established her *Supermodel* familiarity. It is with her familiarity that Ru, as Vince Aletti explains, "pulls off something of a coup" (Aletti 1993, 63). With her repeated displacements and contextualizations Aletti illustrates that she becomes "a looming icon of sexual blur [and] manages to both disappear into his drag and parade it like a coat of armor. His persona may be a triumph of realness—a supremely successful but quite transparent masquerade—but his performance is, against all odds, mighty real." Her unmarked but unhidden presence may be harder to pull off now that she has come out; but no doubt Ru's new project will savvily manipulate the fantasy and narrative of the mythic black mother for her own ends. With such a familiar narrative to contextualize her, Ru should have no problem continuing to garner reactions such as Armond White's in 1993: "This brother's image isn't so much female as joyful and free" (White 1993).

I would like to thank Sheri Parks and Craig Seymour for their help in guiding this essay. Part of this essay was delivered as "Looking for the Black Penis: The Spectacular Logic and Erotics of Racial Fetishization in United States Popular Culture" at The Dynamics of Change, the 20th Annual Conference of Literature and Film at Florida State University, January 27, 1995.

REFERENCES

Aletti, V. "Mr. Queen." *The Village Voice* (July 6, 1993): 63.

Barthes. R (1972). *Mythologies*. Trans. Annette Lavers. 1957. New York: Hill and Wang, 1972.

Cooper, C. "What Angels Lack." *The Village Voice*. (Jan. 4, 1994): 15.

Cowie, E. (1984). "Fantasia." 1249 : 71.

DeCaro, F. "Latest Supermodel? RuPaul, Y'all." *New York Newsday* (Dec. 1, 1992).

Dyer, R. (Ed.). (1992). *Only Entertainment*. New York: Routledge.

Finkle, D. "The Uses of Drag: I." *The Village Voice* (Aug. 30): 83.

Hass, N. "Bochco Gets a Chance to Try a Laugh Track." *The New York Times* (July 14, 1996): 1430.

Hawley, R. (1994). "Crossing Games: Reading Black Transvestism at the Movies." *The Journal of Women Gender and Culture* 8.1: 109.

James, T and Jones, W. "RuPaul, 'Supermodel' With His Own 'Je Ne Sashay Quoi.'" *USA Today* (30, 1993): Dl.

Laplance, J. and Pontalis, J.B. (1986). "Fantasy and the Origins of Sexuality. " In *Fans of Fantasy,* edited by Victor Burgin, James Donald, and Con Kaplan. New York: Methuen.

Mercer, K. "Fear of a Black Penis." *Artforum* (April 1994): 80-1.

Musto, M. "Mondo." *The Village Voice* (Nov. 24, 1992): 26.

Parks, S. (1995). "My Mother's House: Black Feminist Aesthetics, Television, and *A Raisin in the Sun.*" In *Theatre and Feminist Aesthetics,* edited by Karen Laughlin and Catherine Schuler. Madison: Fairleigh Dickinson University Press.

Parks, S. *Lion Mother of the American Soul: The Black Matenzal Fire in Popular Culture.* Unpublished manuscript.

Phalen, P. (1993). *Unmarked: The Politics of Performance.* New York: Routledge.

Rafferty, T. "The Current Cinema: Realness." *The New Yorker* (March 25, 1991): 72.

RuPaul. "Back to My Roots." *Super Model of the World.* Tommy Boy Music, 1993.

RuPaul. "From Sister to Sister: Confessions, Obsessions, Revelations, and Proclamations by RuPaul." *Sister 2 Sister* 5.6 (June 1993): 19.

RuPaul (1995). *Letting It All Hang Out: An Autobiography.* New York: Hyperion Books.

RuPaul's Party Machine. VH-1. (April 13, 1996).

"Same Difference." *TV Guide.* (June 26, 1993): 2.

Siegmund, H. "Dance Music's RuPaul: Poised for World Domination." *The Los Angeles Times* (Feb. 5, 1993).

Skinny, V. "RuPaul." *Thing* 6 (Summer 1992): 28.

Trebay, G. "Cross-Dresser Dreams." *The New Yorker* (March 22, 1993).

Video Soul. Black Entertainment Television (April 8 1993).

White, A. "Everybody Ain't Able, But RuPaul Is." *The City Sun.* (July 6, 1993).

Yarbrough, J. "RuPaul: The Man Behind the Mask." *The Advocate* 661/662 (Aug. 23, 1994).

CREATIONS OF FANTASIES/ CONSTRUCTIONS OF IDENTITIES: THE OPPOSITIONAL LIVES OF GLADYS BENTLEY

CARMEN MITCHELL

For many years I lived a personal hell. Like the great number of lost souls, I inhabited that half-shadow no-man's land which exists between the boundaries of the two sexes. Throughout the world there have been thousands of us furtive humans who have created for ourselves a fantasy as old as civilization itself: a fantasy which enables us, if only temporarily, to turn our back on the hard realism of life.
—Gladys Bentley

Gladys Bentley begins her autobiographical article, "I Am a Woman Again," published in *Ebony* magazine in 1952, with a harrowing, Dante-esque account of an unspoken but conspicuous homosexuality. Bentley emerged as a prominent and sensational lesbian, drag king/male impersonator, and recording artist during the intense cultural and political period known as the Harlem Renaissance. Through the coercion and constraints of "hard realism," or what I would term a form of Western hegemony that privileges white, heterosexual, male-centered experiences, Bentley continuously reconfigured and publicly changed her multiple identities.

Born August 12, 1907 in Philadelphia to a Trinidad-born mother and an American-born father, Gladys Bentley was the oldest of four siblings. As noted in her essay, Bentley transformed from an unwanted female child to the desired male-identified tomboy, from an "in-between" sexed lesbian to a female-sexed woman, and from a raunchy Black nightclub performer to ardent Black churchgoing wife. Indeed, Bentley lived a number of lives that were both resistant and complacent in a society that validated the normative operating structures of the church, family, and marriage, which in turn placed heterosexuality, whiteness, maleness, and middle- and upper-class identities as preferred signifiers in the categorization of others.

In this essay I situate the experiences and identities of Gladys

Bentley as potential trajectories toward understanding the multiple subject identities of a Black lesbian. I assert that these identities are similar in their construction, actualization, and subsequent pathologizing and regulation in dominant Western culture. First, I interrogate the constructions of race, gender, and sexuality as identities for Gladys Bentley. Second, I investigate how Bentley acted upon these realized identities by publicly asserting herself through blues and drag performance. And lastly, I explore the fluctuation of Bentley's identities as a probable result of the pathology and regulation of lesbianism and Blackness.

CONSTRUCTIONS OF IDENTITIES

In *Modernity: An Introduction to Modern Societies*, Stuart Hall presents a broad genealogy of Western theorizations of identities from the Enlightenment position that perceived of one's identity as an individualist notion of self. In other words, one was born with a static and stable essence that would flower or blossom over time. Thus, this individual identity was at the center of one's historical moment (597). Hall then delineates a turn in Western discourse on identity that recognized the influence of ideologies, structures, and social institutions such as church, school, and family on the formation of identity. In other words, a subject's identity was incumbent on interaction/contention with institutions, structures, or dominant ideologies thus created/constructed the ways in which the subject developed, actualized, and contemplated identities.

I provide the construct of racial identity to concretize this notion. Ian Haney Lopez's "The Social Construction of Race" articulates a forceful and convincing argument for the definition of race as being a consequence of collective histories and socially important events against the general assumptions of biological determinants. Thus, the author marks a race as "a vast group of people loosely bound together by historically contingent, socially significant elements of their morphology and/or ancestry. I argue that race must be understood as a sui generis social phenomenon in which contested systems of meaning serve as the connections between physical features, faces, and personal characteristics" (193).

Although apparent variations exist in skin color, hair texture, and other physical characteristics, one group of people cannot possess all or be devoid of these certain physical characteristics. An example of this can be illustrated by the false statement that all Latinos have brown skin and no Latinos have white or Black skin. Hence, Lopez invites us to view racial categorization and the subsequent results (i.e. slavery, colonization) as an outcome of "human interaction rather than natural differentiation" (Lopez 1995, 196).

Given this reading, I postulate that, like race, the categories of gender and sexualities are also social constructs. In *The Epistemology of the Closet*, Sedgwick views chromosomal sex as homo sapiens with XX and/or XY chromosomes, which can be biologically varied in terms of "genital formation, body hair growth, fat distribution, hormonal function, and reproductive capacity" (Sedgwick 1990, 250). Gender, in turn, is the value and meaning humans place upon these biological variations. The categories of male, female, transsexual, and other are turned into sites of contention and separation and/or subordination. As for sexuality, Sedgwick's asserts the centrality of marginal homosexuality, namely male, within 20th-century Western culture. She points to the Foucaultian claim that the recognized homosexual subject did not appear until the last third of the 19th century. The popularizing definition of the homosexual not only proceeded that of the heterosexual, it was also central in the categorization of subjects throughout the fields of medicine, law, literature, and psychology (Sedgwick 1990, 245).

In regard to her lesbianism, Bentley states, "It seems I was born different. At least I always thought that. In later years I learned that 'different' people are made, not born" (Bentley 1952, 96). This statement could easily support the postulation that sexualities are indeed constructs. As a Black lesbian, her racial construction of Blackness draws from the collective histories and experiences of Africans displaced in the Americas for the means of economic exploitation through slavery. Her gender formation as a woman points to the social meanings and consequences of having female genitalia and other female-identified physical characteristics in a male-dominated society. In turn, Bentley's sexual formation as a lesbian comes from the categorization of gendered subjects in contrast to the affirmed opposite-sexed couples and "the array of acts, expectations, narratives, pleasures, identity formations, and knowledges, in both women and men, that tends to cluster most densely around certain genital sensations" (Sedgwick 1990, 251).

But in terms of the concept of "Black lesbian," additional questions need to be asked. How do the constructions of Black, woman, and lesbian identities conflict or coexist with one another in regard to their formations? In what ways are these constructions of multiple identities fostered in particular historical moments?

I turn to the perspectives of critical race theory to probe these inquiries. Derrick Bell's edited version of the *Dred Scott v. Sanford* case was a seminal court decision that arose concerning the actual humanity of slaves (mainly Blacks) in the United States. The court ruled that Dred Scott, a Black slave, could not sue any party for his freedom or utilize any services of the court. Being a slave, he was deemed property, Black chattel. He was not human and certainly not an American citizen, therefore no rights, privileges, or freedoms could be afforded to him. This "legal" proclamation signaled the inhuman fate of all enslaved Blacks in the United States wishing to use any type of legislative methods to challenge and contest the oppressive and violent operations of slavery. If Black slaves were not human, a deep and secretive contradiction arises when the discourse of sexuality and gender enters this framework. Abdul R JanMohamed's 1992 essay, "Sexuality on/of the Racial Border: Foucault, Wright, and the Articulation of a 'Racialized Sexuality,' " notes that if enslaved Africans in America were not human, what can be said of the white master's sexual desire and longing for Black bodies? He writes:

> The master's rape of the female slave was an "open secret." The need to deny the "open secret" (through miscegenation laws and "one drop of Black blood" racial categorization) leads, moreover, to the formation of an internally contradictory juridical discourse around racialized sexuality...the necessity for this "open secret" can be traced to the white master's sexual desire for a slave. Since this desire implicitly admits the slave's humanity, it undermines the foundation of the border—the supposed inhumanity of the Black other" (JanMohameds 1992, 104).

Thus, the construction of a racialized sexuality for African Americans (mainly women) was predicated by the uncontrolled desires of white slave masters. The result was children of mixed race, along with the denial and silence of white desire for Black bodies through the legal discourse of miscegenation laws and the "one drop of Black blood" criteria for Blackness. Out of this construct involving multiple identities, I would like to draw inferences to the alteration of this construct for African Americans after emancipation. Angela Davis asserts that the role of sexuality in the aftermath of slavery was critical. It was the first time freed Black people could love and live with whomever they chose as opposed to either forced or secretive sexual and romantic relationships with and between Black slaves (249).

For Black gay men, lesbians, bisexuals, and transgendered people, the constructs of these subject identities have altered throughout certain historical moments. A more racialized view of Black homosexuality appeared during the Black Power movement of the 1960s according to Cheryl Clarke's essay "The Failure to Transform: Homophobia in the Black Community." Numerous male figures in the Black Power movement crusaded for the essentialist notions of an inherently heterosexual African American community. Hence, their outdated heterosexist presumptions about Black homosexuals veered toward the claim that this "sexually deviant behavior" was promulgated by white Europeans to Black communities with the creation and perpetration of capitalism. Given this later construction of a racialized homosexuality, Alycee Jeanette James's *Homosexuality and the Crisis of Black Cultural Particularity* notes that to be a Black homosexual meant that one was not authentically Black, according to some leaders in the Black Power Movement (12-13).

However, the historicity of Black homosexuality during Gladys Bentley's life was somewhat different. The space of a northern urban environment such as Harlem provided Black gays, lesbians, and bisexuals, who might have been closeted in small towns or other cities, an opportunity to meet one another in clubs, on street corners, and in storefront churches (Garber 1990, 318). Hence, Black heterosexuals interacting, living next to, and working with Black lesbians, gay men, and bisexuals was inevitable. Accordingly, Lillian Faderman concludes that during the 1920's, homosexuality in Harlem was disdained but tolerated (Faderman 1991, 73). In fact, one could create a roster of the known and unknown Black gay men, lesbians, and bisexuals of the Harlem Renaissance (Frommer 1998, 1).

ACTUALIZATION AND CONTEMPLATION OF IDENTITIES

I would like to proceed to the ways identity constructs are actualized and contemplated. In other words, how did the actualization of the subjected identities of race, gender, and sexuality inform Bentley and others during that particular historical moment of the Harlem Renaissance? Illustrated through the construction of a racialized sexuality, all of the identities Bentley embodied were interdependent and interrelated to one another. They may have been employed in various fashions, be they conflicting or in conjunction with one another. One way or another, they came to the forefront with Bentley's celebrity entrance into the Harlem Renaissance. Davis notes that after emancipation, autonomously decided Black relationships, with all the heartbreaks and happiness, were musically articulated through blues music (1998, 249). This musical agency for Black bisexual and lesbian women was boldly articulated through entertainers such as Bessie Smith, Ma Rainey, and Bessie Jackson (Faderman 1991, 77). Because they and other Black women were the first successful blues singers, Bentley, being a blues entertainer herself, was able to take advantage of this musical opportunity. She publicly and boldly actualized herself as a Black lesbian through blues and drag performance during the Harlem Renaissance.

Following the availability of thousands of jobs before and after World War I, the arduous trek of many African Americans to the northern United States had transplanted their musical traditions of the spirituals, gospels, and blues within newly industrialized urban centers. Within African American musical traditions, however, the schism between sacred music, gospel and spirituals, and the secular, blues and jazz, did not necessarily signal a sharp distinction between the two in regard to performance and audience participation. Instead, this separation was witnessed through the context of space: The church was sacred while the nightclubs and private rent parties were reserved for the secular. It was in these cites, away from the blatant homophobia and racism, that many Black gays, lesbians, and bisexuals felt most comfortable and affirmed (Garber 1990, 321).

Tolerant attitudes toward homosexuals and exciting musical opportunities proved to be inviting for Bentley, who sang and played piano. At the age of 16 Bentley left home and, according to Laurence Frommer, "Like many African Americans of her generation she ended up in New York City's Harlem, the capitol of 'the New Negro.' For Gladys, her lesbianism made her need to strike out on her own all the more urgent" (Frommer 1998, 1). It was the early 1920s, the heyday of the Harlem Renaissance. Bentley states that, with luck, she was able to secure a recording gig in New York City and was on her way to success and stardom. She applied to be a nightclub pianist at Connie's Inn, and from there she became the toast of the town with her raunchy nightclub act. Later on Bentley was the regular lounge act in Harlem's premier gay-friendly club, The Clam House. Eric Garber, in his essay "A Spectacle in Color: The Lesbian and Gay Subculture of Jazz Age

Harlem," describes Bentley as "a 250-pound, masculine, dark-skinned lesbian who performed all night long in a white tuxedo and top hat. Bentley, a talented pianist with a magnificent growling voice, was celebrated for inventing obscene lyrics to popular contemporary melodies" (324).

Another actualization of Bentley's identities as a Black lesbian was performed through drag. In her article, "Mack Daddy, Superfly, Rapper: Gender, Race and Masculinity in the Drag King Scene," Judith Halberstam (1997) defines the drag king as

> a performer who pinpoints and exploits the (often obscured) theatricality of masculinity. The drag king can be male or female; she can be transgendered; she can be butch or femme. The drag king might make no distinction between her offstage and onstage persona or she may make an absolute distinction; she may say that on and offstage personae bleed into each other in unpredictable and even uncontrollable ways (105).

According to this broad definition, Bentley's performance as a drag king was already evidenced in her most of her life. In her autobiographical essay in *Ebony*, Bentley notes that she felt more comfortable in boys' clothes than in dresses and skirts. As an act of childhood sibling rivalry she stole her younger brothers' suits and wore them to school (Bentley 1952, 96). Always sporting suits and male attire, Bentley, "wore men's clothes on and off the stage for most of her life" (Garber 1992, 278). Bentley's "drag-kinging" (Halberstam 1997, 117) was both the creative resistance to racial and sexual hegemony *and* the incarnation of Bentley as a spectacle and phenomenon to her audiences. I assert that one can read her drag king performance as a possible spoof on privileged white masculinity and skin privilege (Halberstam 1997, 110). In fact, Lois Sobel, a prominent entertainment columnist of the day, wrote about the marriage ceremony announced by Gladys Bentley to her white female lover in New Jersey (Frommer 1998). As Bentley dressed in a tuxedo for the event, her public declaration of lesbianism as a Black woman, through a marriage ceremony to a white woman, contested white patriarchal ownership of white women. It may have been a mere publicity stunt, but Bentley and her mannish appearance nonetheless "attracted celebrities like flies" (Faderman 72). Bentley recalls the fame and notoriety she attained through her nightclub acts. Numerous Harlemites, celebrities, and VIP guests gushed with delight at her lively performances. Despite this positive recognition from her audience, the contradiction of their admiration was bellied by homophobia. Bentley states:

> I have violated the accepted code of morals that our world observes but yet the world has trumped to the doors of the places where I have performed to applaud my piano playing and song styling. These people came to acclaim me as a performer and yet bitterly condemn my personal way of living. But even though knew me as a male impersonator, they could still appreciate my artistry as a performer (93).

The musical endeavors of African Americans have historically been held in high regard by white dominant Western culture. The popularity of jazz and blues attests to this. Despite the lauds of the dominant society for African Americans in this sphere, the political and economic oppression of this marginalized community outweighed any admiration (Shaw, 1986). From this paradoxical relationship, I pose the following questions: How did African Americans relate to the dominance of white supremacy, norms, and social standards? How did this community exist within or challenge spaces, institutions, and dominant ideologies that did not recognize and affirm their existence? Contemplation on the identity of African Americans was hypothesized and metaphorically symbolized by W.E.B. DuBois's concept of the double consciousness. DuBois recognized the two distinct worlds within and between which descendants of Africans in America lived. One was a world of white dominance in America, the other world as a "Negro," the descendant of people from Africa (DuBois, 615).

The particular experiences of Gladys Bentley evoke DuBois's contemplation of the African American double consciousness, but hers may have been a *twofold* double consciousness as a African American situated as a lesbian "between the boundaries of the two sexes" (Bentley 1952, 93). Again, additional but similar questions must be asked. How did gay men, lesbians, bisexuals, and transgendered people relate to the hegemonic and social institutions that affirmed heterosexism? In what ways did this marginalized community endure within or contest sites of heterosexual supremacy? Bentley offers a response with this observation:

> Somewhere along the line after we discover that we are fascinated by a way of life different from that approved by society,

we attempt to analyze ourselves. All about us we hear the condemnation of our kind...The censure which rages all about us
has the effect of creating within us a brooding self-condemna-
tion, a sense of not being as good as the next person, a feeling
of inadequacy and impotence.... Of course we all reach varying degrees of adjustment. Some of us, on the face of things,
accept our predicament and defiantly try our best to live with
it. Others, by guilt or grudgingly, but if drawn by some mag-
netic force, give in to our way of life. But forever the majority
of us are trying to find excuses, alibis, answers to the eternal
why. Almost all of us live in a restless constant search for happiness (93).

This particular passage echoes the process of Bentley's actualizing
of sexual identities in her own life as a condemned Black lesbian and
later with her identification as an accepted heterosexual housewife. I
look to Amina Mama's *Beyond the Masks: Race, Gender, and
Subjectivity* and consider how Bentley's process initially resembles
Nigrescence, a model defined by Black psychologist William Cross,
that explains how the self-hating Negro proceeds through the course of
becoming a positive Black person (Mama 1995, 59). Unfortunately, the
similarities between Bentley's process and Nigrescence are rather limited. In Bentley's time and location, there had been no method or process
to *become* an affirmative gay, lesbian, bisexual, or transgendered person, since an inherent sexually perverse, indecent, and immoral label
had been placed on these communities and people. Furthermore, like
Thomas Parham, another Black psychologist who critiqued the Cross
model of Nigrescence as being too unilateral and unchanging (Mama
1995, 61), Bentley's own life attested to the notion that one's identity
could change though space and time.

PATHOLOGIZING AND REGULATION OF SUBJECT IDENTITIES

Again I turn to Amina Mama to discuss the influential ways in which
African American racial identity has been situated in a pathological
context. In other words, because of white racism, the entire identity of
African Americans was psychologically traumatized and damaged (47).
These essentialist pathology theories passed through medical and academic discourse into mainstream society, which used these notions to
rationalize the plight, misery, and inferiority of African Americans (47).

Conceivably, presented with this information, Bentley may have interpreted her situation as an African American *and* lesbian woman as twice as psychologically and socially harmful. She states, "Mine has been a story of what sociologists and psychiatrists would have perhaps termed extreme social maladjustment" (Bentley 1995, 96). She further illustrates her unnamed lesbianism as a sin, a crime, a deviation, and "a hell as terrible as dope addiction" (96). Bentley rationalizes that her parents could have possibly curtailed her deviance from the heterosexual norm. In fact, Bentley's family moved out of the neighborhood and took her to various doctors because of her growing "fascination" with wearing boys' clothes and fantasizing about a particular female teacher. Bentley writes:

> What my family did not know was that I didn't need a doctor but love, affection, and healthy interests to supplant the malignant growth festering inside me. This is the tragedy in the relationships between many parents and their children once the secret of "being different" is out. Who knows what my whole would have been if I had been handled differently? Certainly my parents meant well. They just didn't know how to cope with a situation which was to them was at once startling and disgraceful (96).

In her essay *Compulsory Heterosexuality and Lesbian Existence*, Adrienne Rich notes that the pathologizing of the lesbian includes bizarre penis envy and unusual man-hating impulses (Rich 1983, 36). Some forced heterosexist results of this afflicted lesbianism are "physical torture, imprisonment, psychosurgery, social ostracism, and extreme poverty" (36). For Bentley, the historical moment of the Harlem Renaissance and the Roaring '20s may have appeared to placate overt and violent oppression of lesbians, gays, bisexuals, and transgendered folk. Despite some level of reluctant tolerance, Black lesbians were feared and demonized, as evidenced in this 1920s account from a Harlem newspaper, *The New York Age*:

"One of the rent parties a few weeks ago was the scene of a tragic crime in which one jealous woman cut the throat of another, because the two were rivals for the affections of a third woman. The whole situation was on a par with the recent Broadway play [about lesbianism, *The Captive*], imported from Paris, although the underworld tragedy took place in this locality. In the meantime, the combination of bad gin, jealous women, a carving knife, and a rent party is dangerous to the health of all concerned" (Garber, 321).

In 1937, after the excitement of the Harlem Renaissance died down with the onset of the Great Depression (Garber 1990, 330), Bentley moved to Los Angeles to live with her mother. Because of the migration of lesbians and gays men to West Coast cities such as San Francisco, Los Angeles, and San Diego during and after World War II, Bentley managed to successfully perform in her signature drag-king attire throughout California (Frommer 1998, 2). With the passage of time, the eroding of tolerance toward sexual difference peaked with the sex-panic frenzy of McCarthyism in the 1950s. Thus, the forced heterosexist results Adrienne Rich named above were applied to all assumed nonheterosexuals during the McCarthy-era witch-hunts (Jennings 1994, 151). Frommer notes the peculiar situation in which Bentley found herself: "Bentley, who for so long been one of THE most open [regarding] her homosexuality, was of course a sitting duck for persecution. Out of desperate fear for her own survival (particularly with an aging mother to support) Gladys Bentley started wearing dresses, and sanitizing her [nightclub] act" (Frommer 1998, 2).

Frommer maintains that Bentley wrote the 1952 *Ebony* article to protect herself from public prosecution during the McCarthy era. He contests much of the article as fabrication. Whether or not the article is true, untold numbers of lesbians and bisexual women led similar paths toward more accepted heterosexual lives to avoid ridicule, economic hardship, threats, and alienation (Rich 1983, 37). Therefore, it is interesting to interrogate the possible regulation and eradication of sexual identities through medicine and marriage.

Even before her illustrious career as a drag king, Bentley recalls a warning issued from a friend to avoid auditioning for a pianist job at a nightclub because of male bias. She retorted, "There's no better time for them to start using a *girl*," (Bentley 1952, 94). Although she dressed in boys' clothes and "the secret of 'being different' was out," the teenage Bentley allied herself with the gendered construction of a girl. Important too is Bentley's statement that she soon became aware that "different" or nonheterosexuals were "made" or constructed even though she was later "cured" by a medical doctor who injected her with female hormones. Despite these contradictions, they regress to the notion of the damaged subject, both for African Americans and lesbians as well as gay men, bisexuals, and transgendered people.

Blackness as an identity, however, was seen either through an essentialist lens that remained unchanged and fixed or could be reached by entering the process of becoming a self-loving Negro. On the other hand, homosexuality and bisexuality were viewed primarily as sexual acts or desires that could be morally controlled, regulated, and held in check.

From the title of her article "I Am A Woman Again," Bentley presumably ceased being a woman when she publicly proclaimed her lesbianism through her performance practice as a blues drag king on and offstage. Later, as Bentley claimed, the construct of her womanness was regained through her identification with heterosexual desires, social institutions such as marriage, and the assistance of medicine. According to Bentley, her doctor stated, "Now I can tell you what I have known for a long time. Your sex organs are infantile. They haven't progressed past the stage of those of a 14-year-old child." Note that the construct of "girl" is invoked even in Bentley's experience with medical treatment. Although I assert Bentley had coexisted as both a lesbian and woman, the regulation of lesbian desire employed by medicine signaled the supposed blossoming of Bentley's girlhood of earlier years into an essential womanhood.

In a passage hauntingly familiar to the opening of Bentley's essay, where she finds people like her are constantly in a restless search for happiness, Bentley states that she parted from her first spouse, newspaper columnist J.T. Gibson, to take another husband, Charles Roberts. Some allegations have been made about the authenticity of these marriages (Frommer 1998, 1), while others claim that Bentley was bisexual and not strictly lesbian (Faderman 1991, 72). Despite these observations, Bentley became an active and devoted member of The Temple of Love in Christ, Inc. near the end of her life. Bentley had even planned to become an ordained minister. Unfortunately, she passed away from a flu epidemic at the age of 52 in 1960 (Frommer 1998, 3).

CONCLUSION: LEARNING FROM OPPOSITIONAL LIVES

This essay has illustrated the relationship and commonalties of subjected identities through their construction, actualization, and subsequent pathologizing and regulation. The lives of Gladys Bentley have provided a fascinating example to engage the discourse on the multiple identities of a marginal Black lesbian in America. In addition to helping us to understand these identity relations, the interchangeability of

Bentley's identities can inform our current historical moment between the modern and postmodern. In a postmodern framework one can have diverse identities that contradict and/or consolidate one another. The main polemics for postmodern identities encompass the transformations and uprootedness of common social structures, institutions, and ideas. This in turn signals a decentering or "crisis of identity" (Hall, 596). Following Stuart Hall's historicity of identity from essentialist Enlightenment notions to the sociological constructions of stable identities to the crisis of identity in postmodern times, Bentley's lives can be seen as a postmodern moment within modernity.

Regardless of Bentley's retreat to the very norms she began to contest, her other diametrical life upset social norms and structures by her publicly proclaiming her lesbian identity, her visible Blackness within social nightlife and clubs, and notions of gender within her performative practice of blues and drag. It is extraordinary to realize what Bentley had accomplished decades before the civil rights, women's, and gay and lesbian movements. The inconspicuous meanings behind Bentley's public rejection of her past lesbian life still remain something to uncover. Consequently, her story can inform current historical moments by depicting the power and influence of the closet, acts of silence, and repression of one's sexual self. Despite the public retraction of her nonconformity to heterosexuality, Gladys Bentley remains a potent Black lesbian icon who performed her identities within the spotlight and outside the afterglow. Audre Lorde, in *Uses of the Erotic: The Erotic As Power,* illustrates this intrinsically erotic past life of Bentley and the reverence *and* indignation that ensued:

> For once we begin to demand from ourselves and from our life pursuits that they feel in accordance with that joy which we know ourselves to be perfectly capable of. Our erotic knowledge empowers us, becomes a lens through which we scrutinize all aspects of our existence, forcing us to evaluate those aspects honestly in terms of their relative meaning within our lives (150).

REFERENCES

Bell Jr., A. (1980). "Dred Scott v. Sandford." In *Civil Rights: Leading Cases.* Boston and Toronto: Little, Brown and Company.

Bentley, G. "I Am a Woman Again." *Ebony.* Aug., 1952: 92-98.

Butler, J. (1993). *Bodies That Matter: On the Discursive Limits of "Sex."* New York : Routledge.

Carby, H.V. (1984). "It Jus Be's Dat Way Sometime: The Sexual Politics of Women's Blues."
    SAGE: A Scholarly Journal on Black Woman, vol. 1, no.2: 8-22.

Clarke, C. (1983). "The Failure to Transform: Homophobia in the Black Community." In *Home
    Girls: A Black Feminist Anthology*, edited by B. Smith. New York: Kitchen Table: Women of
    Color Press.

Davis, A. (1998). *Blues Legacies and Black Feminism: Gertrude "Ma" Rainey, Bessie Smith, and
    Billie Holiday*. New York: Pantheon.

DuBois, W.E.B. (1903). "Of Our Spiritual Strivings in the North." In *Anthology of African
    American Literature*, edited by H.L. Gates, N.Y. McKay et al. New York: W.W. Norton,
    1997, 612-619.

Faderman, L. (1991). *Odd Girls and Twilight Lovers: A History of Lesbian Life in Twentieth-
    Century America*. New York: Columbia University Press.

Frommer, L. (1998). "Gladys Bentley: The Bulldagger Who Sang the Blues!"
    http://members.tripod.com/~laurencefrommer/celebrity/celebrity2bentley.html.

Garber, E. (1990). A Spectacle In Color: The Lesbian and Gay Subculture of Jazz Age Harlem. In
    Hidden From History: Reclaiming the Gay and Lesbian Past, edited by Martin Duberman,
    et al. New York: Meridian.

Garber, M. (1992). *Vested Interests: Cross-Dressing and Cultural Anxiety*. New York: Routledge.

Halberstam, J. (1997). "Mack Daddy, Superfly, Rapper: Gender, Race, and Masculinity in the
    Drag King Scene." *Social Text 52/53*, Vol. 15, Nos. 3 and 4, Fall/Winter 1997: 104-131.

Hall, S. (1996). "The Question of Cultural Identity." In *Modernity: An Introduction to
    Modern Societies*, edited by S. Hall, et al. Malden, Mass.: Blackwell Publishers, 596-632.

Haney Lopez, Ian F. (1995). "The Social Construction of Race." In *Critical Race Theory: The
    Cutting Edge*, edited by R. Delgado. Philadelphia: Temple University Press.

JanMohommed, A. R. (1992). "Sexuality on/of the Racial Border: Foucault, Wright, and the
    Articulation of Racialized Sexuality." In *Discourses of Sexuality: From Aristotle to AIDS*,
    edited by D.C. Stanton. Ann Arbor: The University of Michigan Press.

Jennings, K. (Ed.). (1994). *Becoming Visible: A Reader in Gay and Lesbian History for High
    School and College Students*. Boston: Alyson Publications.

Lane, A.J. (1997). *Homosexuality and the Crisis of Black Cultural Particularity*. Los Angeles:
    University of California Los Angeles.

Lorde, A. (1991). "Uses of the Erotic: The Erotic As Power." In *An Intimate Wilderness: Lesbian
    Writers on Sexuality*, edited by J. Barrington. Portland: The Eighth Mountain Press.

Mama, A. (1995). *Beyond the Masks: Race, Gender, and Subjectivity*. New York: Routledge.

Niles, B. (1931). *Strange Brother*. New York: Harris Publishing.

Rich, A. (1983). "Compulsory Heterosexuality and Lesbian Existence." In *Lesbians, Gay Men,
    and the Law*, edited by W. B. Rubenstein. New York: The New Press.

Rubin, G. S. (1993). "Thinking Sex: Notes for a Radical Theory of the Politics of Sexuality." In
    The Lesbian and Gay Studies Reader, edited by H. Abelove, M.A. Barale, D. Halperin. New
    York and London: Routledge.

Sedgwick, E. K. (1990). "Axiomatic." In *The Cultural Studies Reader*, edited by S. During. New

York: Routledge, 1993, 243-268.

Shaw, A. (1986). *Black Popular Music in the America: From the Spirituals, Minstrels, and Ragtime to Soul, Disco, and Hip-Hop*. New York: Schirmer Books.

Van Vetchen, C. (1930). *Parties: Scenes From Contemporary New York Life*. New York: A.A. Knopf.

Black Men in the Mix: Badboys, Heroes, Sequins, and Dennis Rodman

Lindon Barrett

It is an understatement to claim that the anomaly in sports and popular culture that is Dennis Rodman has grown into an equally peculiar national phenomenon and Rodman's perhaps most notable form of sedition—his brands of cross-dressing both on and off the NBA court—places him in a controversial spotlight he shares with no other sports celebrity and, arguably, no other African American man in 20th-century post–civil rights culture. RuPaul may come to mind, but RuPaul does not occupy a national spotlight as a "man" as that designation is commonly taken. Rodman, on the contrary, by virtue of being a highly competitive and successful professional athlete, does present himself and is perceived as a "man." Thus, one of the most startling aspects of the phenomenon of Dennis Rodman is the attention he draws to his unashamedly wearing sequined halter tops, women's leggings, or leather shorts, or marking his body by conspicuously tattooing himself, dying his hair, and painting his fingernails even as he pursues and collects NBA championship rings. He remains in the popular mind neither a drag queen nor one of the innumerable and easily assimilated comedians or actors who make their living by drawing on long and various traditions of male drag in the West. Dennis Rodman—to employ a cliché—is "something else."

The primary sense of this cliché connotes, of course, that Rodman is clearly and highly individual. But on closer examination, an argument can be made that one of the upshots of his unusual public position is a demonstration of ways in which the notion of the individual proves inadequate to fully understanding the peculiarities of post–civil rights U.S. culture. This analysis proposes the obsolescence of the notion of the individual for assessing Rodman's phenomenal position, and for assessing the potent conjunction of racial, commercial, gendered, and moral economies in the peculiar figure of Rodman. The proposal is that important facets of post–civil rights U.S. culture suggest a fracturing of the "individual" not entirely calculable by recourse to that concept. And this fracturing, as one must suspect of market cultures, occurs through mechanisms aimed at channeling desire and pleasure. In Rodman's self-reflections such fracturing is evident in key rhetorical ploys as well as inconsistencies between his sexual imaginary and exploits. The claim here is that these "individual" instabilities reflect always incomplete attempts on the part of hegemonic cultural orders to contain desire and pleasure. What amounts to the characteristically and strictly rationalized dynamics of post–civil rights U.S. culture do not always remain so strict or so rational. The resulting eccentricity, however, is not unique to Rodman but endemic to post–civil rights U.S. culture itself.

Rodman's state of publicity, in other words, seems to underscore Kobena Mercer's sense that

> Black struggles over access to the means of representation in the public sphere, in cultural and political institutions alike, require an analysis that is not exclusively centered on individualizing or psychologizing theories of subjectivity but which acknowledges the contingent social and historical conditions in which new forms or collectivity and community are also brought into being as agents or subjects in the public sphere (Mercer 1994, 296).

The concept of the individual is sometimes most remarkable for the abiding insistence placed on it rather than its utility or relevance, and Rodman's most extended statements on Rodman, his Delacourte autobiography *Bad as I Wanna Be*, foregrounds this circumstance. It becomes clear that—despite the awkward configuration of *Bad as I Wanna Be* as an extended monologue to a reader/confidant, its almost unthinkable repetitiveness, and its structural skirting with incoherence—many of the perplexities of Rodman's rehearsal of his 30-some years of blackness, maleness, athleticism, travails, and insecurities are not merely the result of what must have been the impatience of a publisher and hasty work with his cowriter Tim Keown. These perplexities also arise from Rodman's sometimes shrewd critical remove concerning the incidental circumstances as well as the not-so-incidental corporate, market, and media forces that careened him to a moment in his life when eager audiences seek his autograph, await the latest gossip concerning his comings and goings, embrace his self-proclaimed revisionary style of NBA basketball, and make *Bad as I Wanna Be* (1996) a national bestseller. As a result of this critical stance and cynical remove and its disclosures, the autobiographical persona and the seemingly singular trajectory Rodman aims to construct for himself splinters into irreducible but functional points of identification.

Any proposal of a splintered or decentered autobiographical subject is not a startling one. In the contemporary intellectual climate, assaults on "the metaphysics of subjectivity" (Watson 1993, 57) are common in autobiographical criticism, humanist discourses, and cultural criticism in general. For instance, Candace Lang in 1982—to mention only one of numerous possible examples in autobiographical criticism—marshals Roland Barthes and deconstructive analyses to dismiss the "entirely unskeptical acceptance of the unified, autonomous subject ...[as well as reluctance] to ponder the consequences of a total rejection of that notion of the subject" (Lang 1982, 5). She aims her reprove at less theoretically intent critics James Olney, Georges Gusdorf, etc., even as they already work with various concepts of a somewhat split autobiographical subject. One might construe it as remiss, then, not to discover an analogous autobiographical subject in *Bad as I Wanna Be*. But what remains most intriguing is the particular way Rodman's critique of the circumstances in which he finds himself produces irreducible points of self-identification never quite readable as a composite or refracted "individual." The routine exorbitance of the individual is overwhelmed in the text—even as Rodman dramatically appeals to the symmetry of the individual; "Everybody wants to stop Dennis Rodman" (122)—and this has everything to do with the convergence of blackness, masculinity, and a market with a moral imaginary for which each of the three, to greater or lesser degrees, may form the convergence of these four concerns, as little as it is noted, and prove indispensable to the political economy of the NBA, which is maintained, Rodman states, by "taking these young guys who come into the league and marketing the hell out of them until they become stars...[who] show the NBA in the most positive light so everybody buys jerseys with their names on them and votes them into the All-Star game" (94). In the same way Rodman's flamboyant and unorthodox appearance troubles a libidinal circuit undergirding but virtually unexamined within U.S. culture, so does this characterization of the NBA. What Rodman exposes as indispensable to the NBA is its "struggle over the relations of representation" (Mercer 1994, 296) and systems of representation and desire as Butler adeptly demonstrates, mirror one another in a "strangely necessary" relation (Butler 1993, 374). Both are premises not only on "displacement, but also [on] an endless chain of substitutions" (380). Displacements and an endless chain of substitutions are readily apparent in Rodman's characterizations. Still, what is of particular interest, for the purposes of this analysis, is the fact that Rodman details how these principles are actualized in the NBA by transforming (primarily African American) "young guys" into heroic figures, who are fixed implacably "in the most positive light," then introduced for profit in a variety of forms into the *residences and imaginations* of a mass of enthusiasts. How is it that post–civil rights U.S. culture arrives at a situation in which it nimbly negotiates the allowance to take routine unbridled pleasure in African American "young guys"?

The significance of the phrase "in the most positive light" must be scrutinized to recognize fully the libidinal configuration in which both Rodman's arresting physical appearance and the political economy of the NBA as he characterizes it share parallel but irreconcilable interests. While Rodman does so only reluctantly or intermittently, and on very different terms, the NBA traffics indefatigably in heroism made to conform to the most proprietary standards. Heroism, as it is carefully and lucratively managed by the NBA, as well as U.S. moral and commercial culture, entails a proprietary appeal that, above all, enforces market-driven colonizations of desire (and representations). These colonizations—given their way—would reduce desire in all its material, imaginary, and symbolic manifestations to a narrow set of calculable, idealized civilities, and affabilities ultimately resolving themselves in "the heterosexual domestic space...as an inviolate sanctum" (Alexander 1996, 167). When all is proprietary—that is, when idealized moments and sites of the social imaginary are fully appreciated—culturally and economically circulating displacements and substitutions find their origins and terminations in the equation of certainty with heterosexual domestication. The flex translation of heterosexual couplings into aseptic domestic wards is privileged as the singular calculus laying claims—impossible to construe as controversial or untoward—on what stands in and as "the most positive light."

Heroism is an idealized form of subjectivity, and the subjectivity Dennis Rodman would claim, both discursively and in terms of the palpability of his body, is decidedly not colonized by "the heterosexual domestic space...as an inviolate sanctum," in Elizabeth Alexander's apt phrase. The subjectivity he would claim is one in which the prerogatives of heterosexual desire are in no way averse to considering or displaying "[t]he feminine side of Dennis Rodman" (Alexander 1996,

166) nor to fittingly resolving themselves, for instance, in the improvisa-
tional zest of Madonna "stroking [his] shaft and getting into it ...[so
that] before long [he] was insider, he and [they] were fucking" (184). The
cultural logic willfully proposing national order (and all human order)
as an aggregate of domestic sanctums refuses such prerogatives. And, as
best it can, it refuses to imagine or—better yet—to imagine even the
imagining of such prerogatives. This logic is given the shorthand of
"family values" and is deeply implicated in the economic fortunes of the
NBA, corporate culture, and the powerful representations they under-
write. An enormous financial return for the NBA depends on the win-
some introduction of (primarily African American) "young guys" into
what U.S. culture insists on regulating as demure domestic wards.
Rodman's unusual appearance and cynicism, on the other hand, interrogate these presumptions. They query the NBA's economic/entertainment
monopoly, the equally suspect monopoly of moral/ethical discourse in
the U.S., and the imperatives of those "people in this league who allow
themselves to be controlled by the image the league wants to project...the
ones who are scared they might say the wrong thing and get punished"
(56). Reward and punishment, of course, have to do with lucrative player contracts as well as potentially much more lucrative commercial and
corporate sponsorships, as "the market extends daily into hitherto neglected areas and niches of opportunity" (Herman 1995, 3).

Rodman is antagonistic toward the political economy of the NBA
and its direct ties to a moral/ethical economy in which "Charles
Barkley got crucified for saying he isn't a role model" (102). Embracing
the tumultuous position in which he is placed vis-à-vis these aggressively promoted interests, Rodman states, "I'm not either. I'm not trying to be a role model" (102). He continues:

> Is it fair for me to pretend I can give you the leadership the
> guidance, and the direction just because I can play this game?
> How did you function before I got here? How did you make
> it to work or school or where you go before I came along? Did
> you have a great life or a bad life and now—just because you
> found somebody you really love, idolize, and emulate—you
> want to trademark yourself as that person? Do you really
> want to wear that person's jersey and pretend you're him just
> because he can play a game? (104)

Rodman's queries expose how his league as well as a pervasive moral/ethical refrain are not responsive, in fact, to those they claim to service, but are, instead, disingenuous and even abusive. Fans of the NBA are led to believe that the on-court antics and projected off-court affability and urbanity of "young guys" known for their sportsmanship can and should have directive force on their self-conception and conduct. What is most often unappreciated, Rodman implies, is the fact that such a belief merely ranks amongst a vast number of "products being created to fill any and every 'need' " (Herman 1995, 4).

Rodman's style of making these disclosures is inflected by antinomian acknowledgments of race, class, and sexual enthusiasm not sanctioned by the prevailing structures of desire. His style and the disclosures contravene interpolated market agendas creating and disavowing, through national and international campaigns, communities where, in Rodman's words, "[d]rugs are running wild, like a fucking river down the street. Girls are getting pregnant younger and younger, and AIDS doesn't give a shit how old you are" (105). In one of the initial and only sustained images of *Bad as I Wanna Be*, Rodman symbolizes these communities through his recollection of generations of black kids in Dallas who would "walk five miles through a sewage tunnel to get [in]to the state fair" free (13). Given this striking redaction of U.S. social reality, it is almost unspeakably peculiar that select African American men are directly introduced into the material and libidinal economy of a national "sanitary normativity" (Wiegman 1995, 142), for "sanitary normativity" in the United States relies on the representation of African American men and women as paramount threats to its dispensation. This recollection and Rodman's cynicism trouble, then, an extraordinary set of historical circumstances, in which post–civil rights U.S. culture performs the seemingly impossible incorporation of African American "young guys" within structures of desire to which they are characteristically considered alien. Whereas these structures of desire are defined by the notion that the "sanitary normativity of all the sexual roles within the...family is a necessary precondition for [the family's] function as the emotional and moral rehabilitative center" (142) of social life, African Americans as a collective are most fully understood as agents antithetical to any "emotional and moral rehabilitative center."

In other words, within the structures of desire detailing "sanitary normativity," the very concept of racial blackness articulates a crisis that would seem to preclude—even if market-driven—the nimble negotiations on which the NBA depends. Moreover, the crisis, on close examination, proves libidinal. Race, since it is not a genetic reality, might be more assuredly characterized as a series of prohibitions on social desire and sexual practice, prohibitions stabilizing and ensuring the transmission of identifying phenotypical traits from generation to generation. Race amounts foremost to a set of fundamental prohibitions on the discharge of sexual energies. The family, of course, is the most routine and acceptable instrument for the management of sexual energies, with the result that from the vantage of hegemonic racial whiteness those "[i]ndividuals who are designated black have the ability, through the mechanisms of their heterosexuality, to destroy the white identity of white families and...individuals" (Zack 1993, 27). If race proves to destroy, at bottom, a set of practices worrying over the coding and dissemination of visible but unstable physical traits, then it is ineluctably insinuated into the notion of heterosexual domestication itself, the matrix of wards and libidos Rodman's league seeks deftly to manipulate. Insofar as the "sanitary normativity of all the sexual roles within the ...family" remains an implicit element of the NBA's commercial interests and an explicit element of the aggressive monopoly on moral discourse in the U.S., it is imperiled, according to its own logic, by the massive introduction of African American "young guys" into the *residences and imaginations* of the populace of U.S. consumers.

The antinomian rendition in *Bad as I Wanna Be* of being in the rough-and-tumble mix of professional play in the nation's arenas and the coercive mix of the cultural politics poised around those gamed highlights the heady mix of African American men within unprecedented arrangements of desire in the United States. In this mix, the figure of the "individual" is more a cipher for processes of acquisition and accumulation than anything else—processes both capital (financial) and corporeal (racial). In this mix, collectives of select young black men are gingerly transformed into "loci of visual pleasure and spurs to consumption" (Solomon-Godeau 1995, 74). Perilously, whatever market reflex enacts this unprecedented cultural allowance for African American men in the post–civil rights U.S. is a reflex both mutating and mirroring the libidinally charged "process" that is race itself. That is, race as a prohibition on the discharge of sexual energies exceeds the individual, not in the sense of simply connoting an aggregate of individuals but in the sense of a process that, ad infinitum, superintends structures of desire that support the idealized and highly exploitable domestic sanctum. The connection, then, between this dynamic eccentric to (rather than concentric with) the individual and the way

Rodman's narrative also belies the dynamics of the individual becomes highly instructive for understanding the meaning of what amounts to the irrationalism of Rodman's national appeal.

Nonetheless, the mix in which Rodman is caught is seductive and, despite all his cynicism, even Rodman is seduced; he is seduced by his very reliance on the symmetry of the individual. For, as taken as he is with dismissing the cultural order proposed by the NBA, he is equally taken by a fascinated disbelief in the great fortunes of his "whole crazy life" (83). An important motif of *Bad as I Wanna Be* is a rags-to-riches, boy-makes-good narrative, with the result that a significant strand of the text remains invested in at least one brand of heroism, or idealized subjectivity, agreeing in many ways with the cultural order closely supervised in the NBA. Rodman muses, "I was beaten up and given up for dead, but I made it back to shock the whole world" (86). The logic of this strand of *Bad as I Wanna Be* seems to propose that individual perseverance, fortitude, and luck afford a binding resolution to the social straits, redacted in the image of a "tunnel that got real narrow [and put] sewage right in our noses" (13). Rodman writes with no cynicism whatever:

> There are thousands of kids out there in the projects and the cities, thinking they're going to work hard and get a basketball scholarship. They're going to use the game to get out. I say great. I say go for it. A lot of people will tell you it's a lie, that you can't get out that way. They say nobody does. They have statistics and all that, but I say why not go for it? I got out that way, and as long as there is a living example of the dream, kids are going to chase it (79).

Rodman's assessment and encouragement are acutely short-sighted, because they leave intact "projects and the cities" teeming with straitened circumstances. Rodman merely imagines the return of select "young guys" with enough perseverance, fortitude, and luck to U.S. urban life with greatly enlarged bank accounts and some measure of local or national celebrity. His pronouncement in no way challenges a social and cultural order, in the same way as does a 6-foot-6, 220-pound professional athlete (regularly projected into U.S. homes) matter-of-factly stating "[c]ross-dressing is just like everything else in my life: I don't think about it, I just do it" (178). The persona of a 6-foot-6, 220-pound professional athlete unashamedly proclaiming the pleasures of cross-dressing dismisses the relevance of "sanitary normativity" in a way in which the implied heroism of rags-to-riches notion of individual rehabilitation does not. This is not to say Dennis Rodman should not rejoice in his unique and unlikely accomplishments, but it is to say that the Dennis Rodman who would do so in this manner and the Dennis Rodman wielding an iconoclastic critical remove are not strictly reconcilable in *Bad as I Wanna Be.*

One might go so far as to say that Rodman's repeated fascination with a rags-to-riches characterization of his rise to the national spotlight aligns him with one of the essential and most aggressively championed myths of U.S. exceptionalism, the fable of the U.S. as a vast site of opportunity. This is a fable that the very league that Rodman critiques shares, insofar as it seems to substantiate it. The NBA not only furnishes exciting athleticism for rapt national spectatorship but also equally spectacular opportunities for any individual (i.e. young guy) with the wherewithal to seize them. This myth, like the fast-paced professional action itself, is highly suitable for consumption within the matrix of domestic wards and libidos sponsored by the cultural order.

Indeed, Rodman's simple fascination with his own rags-to-riches fable at times renders his autobiographical persona similar to African American cultural figures such as Diana Ross, who in 1993 published her autobiography, *Secrets of a Sparrow.* In her long career Diana Ross powerfully upholds conventions of gender, sexuality, race, and deportment that Rodman revels in obliterating. All the more irreconcilable, then, is that Rodman shares as sharp a fascination with the rags-to-riches mythology endemic to U.S. lore as does Ross. To move momentarily to hyperbole, and as astounding as the thought might seem, one might for a moment lose sight in *Bad as I Wanna Be* and *Secrets of a Sparrow* of which D.R. is which.

In any case, since Rodman shares this significant site of pleasure with the order against which he positions himself, one begins to see in the contradiction that his text accommodates no individual Dennis Rodman but—to employ the cliché again—is "something else." This peculiarity is apparent in additional ways. It is difficult not to come to the same conclusion concerning Rodman's rehearsal of his very public relationship with Madonna, for instance. The chapter recounting this relationship follows what might be considered the most controversial chapter of the book, "Man on Man," in which Rodman discusses his cross-dressing, his affinity for gay clubs and communities, his sexual curiosities concerning other men, and the homoerotic dimensions of the male camaraderie displayed in the mix of fervor and athleticism on and around NBA basketball courts. "Man on Man" disregards the usual decorum and purview of the discourse of professional sports. It has unapologetic regard, instead, for provocative and fulfilling sexual license. This regard anthropologist Gayle Rubin codifies as a "concept of benign sexual variation" (1995, 15). Desire and the pleasures accruing from desire are matter-of-factly unfixed from their customary moorings in "Man to Man."

As one might anticipate, however, matters are not so easily settled. Even having made his striking series of provocative statements in "Man on Man," Rodman just as matter-of-factly seems to forget them when he writes in the next chapter: "Everybody thinks she would have the greatest, wildest sex in the world, and *every gay wants* to sleep with Madonna" (96-7; emphasis added). There is no trace in this statement of the multiple avenues and permutations of sexual desires and identities contemplated at length in the previous chapter. Rather, there is implied a singularity of sexual desire and identity—according to the logic of which Rodman must be mercilessly ostracized for having made his previous statements. The cultural order in which he lived and which he chafes against is one that claims to be certain about what *every gay wants* and as a result does, in fact, prescribe what every man and woman wants. In this offhanded description Rodman aligns himself perfectly with this cultural imaginary. How might one account for the dissonance between what Rodman is trying to say and what he actually states? What, in fact, is he trying to say about the public perception of Madonna and why is it recorded in such a doubtful fashion?

Given the daring stance of "Man to Man" and much of the rest of the book, the reasons Rodman provides for his reluctance to ultimately follow through with his relationship with Madonna raise similar questions:

> In the end it didn't work because I didn't want to be known as Madonna's playboy, her boy toy. I didn't want people to think of me as Madonna's quack-quack duck in the bathtub....I know she didn't think of me that way, but a lot of people looked at it like I was. That bothered me. I admit it. Normally, I don't give a shit what other people think about me.... Maybe I gave in to appearances on that, but I think being Mr. Madonna would have been a tough thing to overcome. I didn't want what I had created on my own to be mixed up with what being with her would have created (200).

The emotional calculations of this point of crisis in Rodman's life revolve around gauging public perceptions, a pointedly ironic turn of events in a text and for a figure repeatedly scorning public perceptions and elaborate machinations undertaken to groom them. These concessions to public perceptions are made by an autobiographical figure who, in the previous chapter, devoted an entire page to one sentence set in enormous bold type: DON'T LET WHAT OTHER PEOPLE THINK DECIDE WHO YOU ARE (175). The irreducibility of these postures could be no more glaring, and an important answer to the puzzle lies, as before, in the understated logic of Rodman's statements. Normative prescriptions of the cultural imaginary loom large. Notwithstanding his usual philosophy abrogating conventional standards of sexuality and gender, Rodman's assurance that he would not be able to brook the idea of "being Mr. Madonna" arises, one supposes, because that arrangement explicitly skews gender relations. For, if the prevailing "social construction of masculinity ...[entails] the stereotype of the ideal man [as] forceful, militaristic, hyper-competitive, risk-taking, not particularly interested in the culture and the arts, protective of his woman, heedless of nature, and so on" (Delgado and Stefanic 1995, 211), then the "man" cannot be subordinate to a female partner so that he is publicly situated as having to take "her" name: "Mr. Madonna." The thought of this arrangement seems insurmountable, notwithstanding Rodman's usual in-you-face iconoclasm: "I can't change anybody's mind, so they can think what they want" (211).

The profundity of Rodman's self-contradiction requires elaboration: Presiding notions of gender, with their direct ties to monopolized notions of sexuality and propriety in general, are routinely dispelled by Rodman. For instance, when writing of the virtual circus of sexual possibilities attendant to life in the NBA, he muses: "Don't get me wrong. I've bought my share of magazines. I've bought my share of movies. I've had my share of lonely nights with Judy (my right hand) and Monique (my left hand). I'm not going to deny that. I'm guilty of that as much as the next guy" (157). In these comments, gender is exposed as a system of merely arbitrary and convenient placeholders. Gender identifications function in the description only to reiterate the reflexively presumed dominance, inexorability, and certainty of heterosexual desire, pleasure, domestication. "Judy" and "Monique" do not exist, except as part of a seemingly requisite imaginary. A flippant naming of left and right hands at one level camouflages the knowledge that both bodily and fantasized pleasured need not conform to standardized notions of heterosexual couplings. Moreover, it camouflages the knowledge that individual desires and pleasures *with notable frequency do not*. The humor of the statements resides in teasing symmetry; it might as satisfactorily result from solitary performances or sexual couplings far exceeding two. Isn't it funny to think so? This rather than any sexual performance, is the real performance of "Judy" and "Monique." "Judy" and "Monique" are discursive surrogates for an abeyant heterosexual in the enterprise at hand—one might say. And one might only imagine further the aberrant performances—sexual and otherwise—that might result had Rodman named his hands *John* and *Roger* or, for that matter, *Rashid* and *Jamal*.

What is made emphatically clear, in any case, is the tenuous cast of gender normally understood as obdurate and impermeable. All the more reason that Rodman's pronouncements on his relationship with Madonna are puzzling, a relationship openly admitted as one of the most intense and important romantic/sexual relationships of his life. If gender imperatives, as they are symbolized by "Judy" and "Monique" are insubstantial, then, strangely, these imperatives appear overwhelmingly substantial as they are rehearsed in "An Old-Fashioned Tale of Romance." Again, there seems to be no individual position here, so that rather than contained by the boundaries of "individualizing or psychologizing theories of subjectivity" (Mercer 1994, 296), the issue is really lodged in the diffuse and insinuating rationalizations of heterosexual domestication.

More relevant than an essentialism of the individual is a series of transactions played across and over the figure of the individual. What is in evidence are the warring trajectories of a variety of appeals to social meaning, which vie with each other through the figure of the individual, and which do not necessarily find coherent resolution in any singular configuration or body. The inconsistency or incoherence in question is not so much Rodman's as it is indicative of perpetual productions of desire constantly inviting self-identifications to ensure corresponding and equally perpetual material/economic transactions.

One must not underestimate on this point the role of desire. Desire seeks pleasure(s) it can never fully attain, which is to say it is oddly "condemned to figure that beyond"—which is its sought-after object—"again and again within its own terms" (Butler 1990; 1995, 374), and the perpetual loop of this movement is crucial to the profitability of the spectacles staged by the NBA and even more generally to grooming a population of consumers on which such profitability depends.

However, the processes of strict rationalization involved in these perpetual transformations of "individual" self-identifications into the rapid circulation of commodities seem also to require with some regularity gestures at abandoning the strict rationalism of this perpetual loop. The culture paradoxically seems to invite the population in the way of constant consumption to imagine themselves in ways without and abrogating the straitened structures of desire and order to which they are overpoweringly confined. Rodman in his outrageousness is a paradigmatic figure of this abrogation and herein lies, it seems, so much of his appeal, even as he himself exhibits the resulting inconstancy and vacillation that may be more rightly a common feature of the cultural order than a sign of being "something else."

Although the production and harnessing of desire is marked in this way by extreme rationalism and irrationalism, they by no means cancel each other out. The rationalism is pronounced and lucrative: Throughout the contests staged by the NBA, the specular pleasure of professional play is translated, via regularly aired commercials, into anticipatory identification with some further moment of pleasure objectified in the form of a "readily" acquired product and image. As stated earlier, this circuit centered "around the theme of consumption" Jhally (1987, 142) entails the extremely unlikely combination of blackness, masculinity, the market, and the acute moral imaginary. Moreover, the circuit formed by this unlikely combination is most effective and most rationalized when particularly adulated players in the mix of NBA competition also occupy the narratives of exchange punctuating the play. In the most economical versions of NBA events, indispensable catalysts of this phantasmatic production of desire are select physically adept African American "young guys" spectacularized within the acrobatics of the NBA as well as proliferating within the commercial narratives underwriting the broadcast. To identify with these figures in their technological displacement from basketball courts to vignettes of available consumption and new pleasures is to be bound up in an extremely economical set of manipulations. It is to be beckoned, on one level, to equate one's residence with one's imagination, for the NBA and other commercial interests count on the fact that when one sits down with the notion to watch NBA games, one also sits down with the notion to figure one's "place" through imagining what one might acquire in and for it. When one sits down with the notion to watch NBA games, one is situated in relation to the infinitely desirable marketplace through the translation of African

American "young guys" into crucial figures in the articulation of one's desires.

The trouble with this unlikely arrangement arises from the fact that the dynamics of racialization and the circuit of NBA spectatorship stand as antagonistically bipolar imperatives of desire, pleasure, and self-regard:

> This schism is played out daily in the popular tabloid press. On the front page headlines black males become highly visible as a threat to white society, as muggers, rapists, terrorists and guerrillas: their bodies become the imago of savage and unstoppable capacity for destruction and violence. But turn to the back pages, the sports pages, and the black man's body is heroized and lionized; any hint of antagonism is contained by the paternalistic infantilization of [black men] to the status of national mascots and adopted pets—they're OK because they're "our boys" (Mercer 1994, 178-79).

The identification and desires channeled through this precarious equipoise of racialized meanings might very easily—and in the most untoward ways—overwhelm the closed circuits in which they would be fixed. The employment of African American young men in the production and exploitation of desire in late capitalism marks an enormous potential threat to "sanitary normativity," given that "the only viable models of black male sexuality trafficked in the mainstream economy are variations on outlaws and gladiators" (Alexander 1996, 160). For, at its most proprietary, the specular network of relations sponsored by the NBA parallels in rationalization—not only in the point of reception—the closed economy of heterosexual domestication. Rationalization is a key term in this context, because heterosexual domesticity seeks to make characteristically unruly and treacherous sexual impulses unquestionably rational insofar as it renders them *objective*, that is, insofar as it would place them in the vehemently acknowledged service of one incontrovertible goal: utter satisfaction and dissipation in procreation. The economy of sensual intimacy codified by heterosexual domesticity and the economy of vicarious investment sponsored by the NBA would ideally correspond to each other in the extremely rational efficiency and reserve of their independent circuits.

The irrational or wayward, in this scheme, amounts to any fantasy or practice confounding or circumventing these sparring systems of expenditure and return. Yet, strangely enough, this is precisely what happens whenever the correspondence between the two circuits proves too impeccable. To patently confuse libidinal urges of sexual desire with commercial urges of consumerism is to compromise the stated objectives of both sexuality and consumerism (though more patently of the first). Yet, to have this troublesome conflation refracted and exacerbated through proliferating figures of African American "young guys" is, without a doubt, much more unsettling. (For African Americans are assumed to be agents of desire not easily nor fully subsumable within the customary equations of either the market or heterosexual domesticity.) Energies that should return to starkly economical circuits become lodged elsewhere, caught not in a fully mediated circuit or longing but a more puzzling one in which first "[b]lacks are looked down upon and despised as worthless, ugly and ultimately unhuman...[then] in the blink of an eye, whites look up to and revere black bodies, lost in awe and envy as the black subject is idolized as the embodiment of...[a momentary] ideal" (Mercer 1994, 201). Indeed, Rodman writes of his own position in a popular imaginary: "When it comes to sex, I think I've heard it all. The wildest thing I get is from married couples. They'll come up to me in a bar or after a game, and the man will tell me he wants me to fuck his wife. He wants me to do her while he watches. It's her fantasy, and the man's too" (156).

What clearer statement could there be of what the NBA and U.S. cultures—racial, masculine, market, and moral—*must* not stand for? What more emphatic representation could there be of the potential specter of adulated African American "young guys" being anomalously introduced into the residences and imaginations of a rapt U.S. populace? The infelicities of this proposition underscore the imbalance that, if propriety and its "most positive light" come only in one form, conversely, impropriety comes in many. From the perspective of the "most positive light," the improprieties are prodigious: If race is, at bottom, a series of fundamental prohibitions on the discharge of sexual energies aimed at the transmission of valenced physical traits, it is severely reputed. If masculinity is, at bottom, one of two requisite placeholders guaranteeing heterosexual symmetry, then it is severely ruptured as well. If the market depends foremost on simplifying and exploiting virtually all orders of the imagination, then it is exceptionally eluded. If the U.S. moral imaginary enshrines demure domestic wards above all, then it is defied to its core.

This is a moment that, one might suspect, Rodman would relish (whether or not he obliges). But he professes incredulity: "The first time I got this proposition was in a club in Dallas. I couldn't believe it. I was blown away. Since then, it's happened many times—a bunch of times in a rest room, for some reason. The husband will follow me in there and ask me to do it. They actually want me to do this" (156).

Plainly, Rodman is not the only badboy to emerge in the aptly titled *Bad as I Wanna Be.* What should be the occasion for an unremarkable bodily function becomes an occasion, instead, for the airing of highly remarkable, surreptitious longings. The relief sought is not from routine physiological pressures but from the convergence of parallel, yet ideally separate, market-sponsored circuits of vicarious investment and sensuous intimacy. Apparently, to be as bad as one wants to be is to overreach and thwart constantly naturalized cultural orders and their rationalizations. It is to fail to domesticate or groom desire so that *pleasure* is willfully translated into the installed as the *pleasant.* One embraces, instead, what passes as the unseemly and unthinkable. The pressures at hand, so to speak, are much more complex than those of any physiological commonplace and much more difficult and hazardous to relieve, and Rodman's reported response in this situation points up those perils:

> I look at the guy and say, "OK. You want to see me fuck your wife? I'd like to see the expression on your face if I ever *did* fuck your wife. How would you feel when your wife likes it? I think you'd be standing there saying, "Oh, shit." And then what if she comes up to me and says, "I want to do it again, without my husband knowing about it"? (156)

Rodman unearths the powerful irrationality of the request. He acknowledges that actually granting it would be strangely incompatible with its structures of desire and the spirit in which it is made. His response plays on the fact that the proposition irreconcilably both disrupts and reinforces the premises of heterosexual domesticity. In terms of its mathematics as well as its explicit masturbatory voyeurism, the proposed encounter exceeds prescribed heterosexual coupling yet, at the same time, ultimately returns these illicit pleasures to a domestic symmetry only momentarily abrogated—and strengthened, supposedly, for its brief abrogation. The husband and wife seek an encounter that would momentarily nullify, or stand in for, their own sexual coupling but that, nevertheless, allows them subsequent enjoyment of that nullification as a re-articulated couple. The economy of their unseemly desires is not nearly as strict or sparing as prevailing cultural prescriptive would have it but still returns to the terms of enshrined heterosexual domesticity, and Rodman's quip plays precisely on the potential derailment of this errant circuit: Whereas the fantasies to be realized in this encounter are too delightful, what might, in fact, be placed overwhelmingly in peril is the unproblematic rearticulation of the couple so anxious to exceed their own coupling. Unanticipated desires might arise that could not be contained within the terms of heterosexual domesticity. Desire might play itself out in no prescribed terms, no terms except those of its own treacherous and unruly drives. Rodman unearths the untenable position in which the men facing him in rest rooms place themselves vis-à-vis their own daring—their desires to be as bad as they want to be.

Significantly, however, such a contrary position is ironically the position Rodman also occupies throughout *Bad as I Wanna Be,* as shown, for example, in his odd rhetorical resemblances to Diana Ross, or his rendition of his relationship with Madonna. Both Rodman and the husbands he faces in rest rooms share a muddled position both within and outside the cultural orders they appear to disregard, and the upshot of the resemblance is not an exposure of comparable stances of ironically similar individuals but, quite differently, an exposure of the usually unacknowledged irrationalities of prevailing cultural orders—cultural orders never fully able to contain all the energies they invoke.

This paradox is certainly all too evident in the realm of the NBA when citywide celebrations of national championships turn raucous and violent despite all "reasonable" pleas to the contrary. The city of Chicago, in anticipation of Rodman's 1996 championship win with the Bulls, spent 4 million dollars on security measures and deployed hundreds of city policemen and state officers in efforts to preempt and contain what turned out to be a relatively mild spree of looting and vandalism yielding about 100 arrests—timorous unrest compared to previous championship years. This crisis attests to the strength of the appeals that the NBA makes to its zealous consumers as well as to the force those appeals exert on a populace otherwise posturing themselves within or seeming to accede to the most positive light of "sanitary normativity." It is a crisis on the part of a populace generally able to answer charges to contain itself.

The appropriate container, of course, is that of the "individual" and, in accordance with ideally rational economies of desire, one can only assume that more exemplary responses might be moderate and circumscribed gestures—a sanguine toast, a reckless grin, an outburst of absorbed applause—followed by a return, with equanimity, to matters of business, romance, child rearing or, say, any other number of commodified and televised pleasures consumable at leisure.

This is to say that, above all, a series of penetrating appeals and their trajectories through a population figures as consumers prove the most substantive and viable principles of the cultural order. Either as a concept or lived term, the "individual" is more functional than substantive within the idealized rationalisms of the prevailing social disposition—irrelevant, more than anything else, except perhaps as a point of uninvited crisis. Ideally and foremost, the individual is overwhelmed by processes aimed at accruing commodified "[s]urplus-value ...which can only be made real (realized) through the sale of those commodities" in which it is lodged, since "a lengthy period of circulation reduces cash flows, reduces the turnover of capital, and thus reduces the annual surplus value" (Jhally 1987, 116). In short, Rodman and the men he teases in rest rooms are fixed in situations in which desire, self-regard, and the "individual" correspond in no enduring way to the cultural systems sponsoring a vested principle, a fetish through which other fetishes are refracted. As his interactions in rest rooms reveal, individuals are no more than loci for productions of desire to be harnessed, irrespective of how desire might resolve itself, even if only as an aporia that, "[I]n contrast to the claims of academic deconstruction ...is rarely experienced as a purely textual event ...[but] rather [as] the point where politics and the contestation of power are felt at their most intense" (Mercer 1994, 202).

Rodman, in his cross-dressing, his iconoclasm, his retorts to sexual propositions, his unruly cultural exhibitions, exposes a discordant system of interlocking fetishes. In his astute study, *The Codes of Advertising: Fetishism and the Political Economy of Meaning*, sociologist Sut Jhally works through the crucial role of advertising and the media in this system and, drawing ultimately on Marx and Freud, defines fetishism as "seeing the meaning of things as an inherent part of their physical existence when in fact that meaning is created by the integration into the *system* of meaning" (29). This definition proves useful in the context of Rodman's narrative because, more than any singularity of identity, *Bad as I Wanna Be* reveals a political economy of the individual. Insofar as he fashions his body as an inscrutable cipher, and insofar as he revels in his reckless adventures, Rodman exposes that one's *person* is an incoherent entity largely because meaning invested in one's *person* is neither one's own nor "individual." In ways sometimes analogous to surplus value, self-identification is produced and extracted within the flows of daunting social forces: race, gender, capital, morality, or any combination of these with other factors. Such an exposure challenges sedimented views of the individual as, on the contrary, upholding or moving through the flows of social forces. The exposure does not suggest, however, that actual individuals do not exist. Of this there is incontrovertible physical evidence. It only reveals that, as confirmed by the anomalous figure of Rodman, the meaning of individual personhood is "questionable." Starkly removing the individual from "the most positive light" of U.S. culture amounts to one critical way of questioning—even to the point of dispelling—the individual.

Nevertheless, the moments when Rodman faces down sexually titillated admirers in rest rooms disclose more than the questionability of the "individual." These moments also go a long way toward answering the conundrum of how African American young men come to figure so crucially in some public arenas of post–civil rights U.S. culture. It would be remiss, that is, to overlook the glaring homosociality of the scene; indeed, much of the threat of Rodman's reply to his overardent admirers is that it returns the acute homosociality of their propositions to a preemptive heterosexuality: Were the perils of Rodman's reply to come true, what would come to an end is the titillating "intercourse" occurring between the men.

Numerous feminist scholars have theorized the role of male homosociality in structuring heterosexual paradigms and, among them, Laura Doyle writes: "The heterosexual relation for a man often emerges not as the end but as the means to a relationship with another man or men. Heterosexuality becomes secondary to the homosocial intercourse it makes possible" (Doyle 1994, 82). In short, even those facets of cultural life one would least suspect remain subordinate to relations "strictly between men, attesting once more to the extraordinary difficulty men have—not in speaking *through* or *for* women to each other—but in *addressing* women" (Bersani 1995, 70). Rodman's reply cuts discordantly to the center of this relationship because, by invoking a heterosexual encounter that would disrupt rather than reinforce the homosociality of the moment, the reply forecloses the homosocial stance that would couple Rodman with his admirer.

Homosocial regard is not by any means new, as recent feminist scholarship also makes clear, but the type of open regard described by Rodman, in fact, is. Indeed, rather than an overwhelming contestation of homosocial privilege itself, one substantial outcome of the cultural upheavals of the 1950s and 1960s is the nominal expansion of the circle of homosocial regard. Such an understanding of recent historical events does not dismiss important gains made by a variety of feminist movement associated with or renewed in the 1950s and 1960s, but remarks the daunting challenge facing them. U.S. culture—as it is also does in terms of "whiteness," "heterosexuality," or "class"—continues fundamentally to imagine itself as a male domain, with both material and psychic resources accruing primarily on the male side of the gender divide. Thus, interracial homosociality is not extraordinary in the post–civil rights United States. In many ways, the signal turn of events of the 1950s and 1960s seems to be the limited admission of nonwhite men into the most public circles of homosocial regard and, particularly, the most intense arena of homosocial appeal—professional sports. Sut Jhally's (1990) understanding of select gender-based imperatives of contemporary capitalism is useful for gauging the import of these changes. Jhally redacts the collective concerns of manufacturers, advertisers, and broadcasters in the appreciation of the fact that:

> the audience for sports includes a large proportion of adult males whom advertisers of high-price consumer articles (such as motor cars) are anxious to reach. To reach 1000 males advertisers of those products will be willing to pay more than to reach 1000 female viewers through prime-time advertising...It is exactly this type of reasoning that has resulted in the huge expansion of televised sports in the last 20 years (Jhally 1990, 78-79).

The appeal men have to and for each other cannot be underestimated as a factor in determining the dynamics of commercial and material cultures in the United States nor those rituals U.S. culture celebrates most conspicuously. African American men, after the social upheavals defined as the civil rights movement, emerge as indispensable to U.S. economies of commerce and spectacle insofar as they lend masculine prowess to certain public homosocial events. On closer consideration, then, Rodman's anecdote is not nearly as eccentric as it first seems: With all their homosocial suggestiveness, men's rest rooms are patently appropriate, if not symbolic, sites for extreme admiration of him.

Still, rest rooms are by no means the most common venues for celebrating Rodman in a culture and a market that, for more reasons than usual, should refuse him. John Edgar Wideman's shrill admiration of Rodman in the "Black in America" issue of *The New Yorker* (April 29 and May 6, 1996) provides a more customary, if equally telling, example. In Wideman's (1996) brief, "Playing Dennis Rodman," Rodman's homosocial appeal is in no way understated. The article opens with astonishingly masculinist bravado:

> I knew the word *'tain't*. Old people used it, mainly; it was their way of contracting 'it ain't' to one emphatic beat, a sound for saying "it is not" in African American vernacular.... But I'd never heard it used to refer to female anatomy—not the front door or the back but a mysteriously alluring, unclassifiable, scary region between a woman's legs (" 'Tain't pussy and 'tain't asshole, it's just the *'tain't*," to quote Walter Bentley) until a bunch of us were sitting on somebody's stoop listening to Big Walt, a.k.a. Porky, discuss with his cousin Donald some finer points of lovemaking (Wideman 1996, 94).

The resemblance between Wideman's recollections and the propositions recalled by Rodman requires little elaboration. In both instances, the homosocial site of heterosexual esteem is unmistakable. What does call for elaboration is the manner in which Wideman postures an absent Rodman within the scene on the porch and, on the other hand, the manner in which he postures the scene on the porch within the playing of Rodman.

Wideman's reader, as the very first order of business, is asked to consider the "mysteriously alluring, unclassifiable, scary" *'tain't* as somehow representative of Rodman's peculiarity. *'Tain't*, as it is defined here, is to be taken as a metaphor for Rodman himself: "Porky's crude connoisseur's riff on *'tain't* returns when I think about Dennis Rodman, the professional basketball player, and his gotta-have-it rebound jones" (Wideman 1996, 94). The initial equation, however, is soon forgotten; Wideman contradicts it as quickly as he invokes it. One is not asked, in fact, to imagine Rodman in terms of the *'tain't* itself but, more fully, in terms of a masterful, heterosexual (and homosocialized) masculine gaze and tactility discovering, naming, and possessing female anatomy. Rodman is likened to a number of young men Wideman has seen on the playgrounds of Pittsburgh:

> The best we could say about a guy like that was "cockstrong": "The brother's cockstrong." Which meant all the above plus the insinuation that he wasn't getting much love action, so all

the energy he should be using up in some sweeter place got dropped on you. "Cockstrong" meant a guy was a load. And loaded (Wideman, 1996).

As it turns out, Rodman is not identified with female body parts at all but with what is emphatically presented as the more readable male sexual organs. He is not the *'tain't,* even though introduced as such, but the "irresponsible" male principle that would be its connoisseur. Curious. Again Rodman is "something else"—an exceptionally exceptional anomaly. But, as is the case with Rodman's encounters in rest rooms, the dynamics of the paradox exceed the terms of any individual figure. The irrationalities in question are more far-flung. One witnesses, as with Rodman's other extreme admirers, Wideman dramatically failing to reconcile a "heteronormative vision" (Thomas 1996, 66) with an explicit homosocial appreciation of Rodman (and, in this case, other men on the playgrounds of Pittsburgh). The incoherence of Wideman's divergent appeals might be masked by recourse to either configuration individually, but becomes plain when they are employed concomitantly. His laudatory gestures prove so irreconcilable that what becomes enigmatic is the obvious pleasure Wideman takes in seeing or thinking about Rodman playing.

What is clear, however, is that whatever this pleasure may be, it invites expression in explicitly sexual terms: The terms *cockstrong* and *cocksure* appear eight times in three paragraphs, with usually only a few words separating them. This virtual chant suggests, at the very least, that Wideman is delighted to take Rod/man's name very seriously. While similar fantasies might well be possible in their cases, it is unimaginable that a similar chant could be taken up so effortlessly in nationally disseminated encomiums to, say, Grant Hill or Michael Jordan. One begins to understand that Rodman, as a result of his flagrant eccentricity, enlists enthusiasms that lay bare the inherent and equally peculiar eccentricities of the circuits of market and imaginative forces shaping the U.S. population of cultural consumers. Yet, at all costs, even the cost of consistency, these forces would be defined by a "heteronormative vision," while a "heteronormative vision" is starkly inadequate in capturing Rodman and his flamboyance. Hence, the paradox is that Rodman's extraordinary unlikely eccentricities remain the essence of his extreme appeal. Even Wideman acknowledges as much:

Cross-dressing, cross-naming himself (Denise), frequenting

gay nightclubs, going AWOL from his team, head-butting a referee, winning four rebounding titles in a row, painting his hair, dating Madonna, challenging the NBA commissioner to suspend him, bad-mouthing the men in suits who pay his salary, Dennis Rodman, though not voted onto this season's All-Star team, verges on media superstardom (Wideman 1996, 95).

The phenomenon of Rodman's national celebrity unearths eccentricities much greater and much more remarkable than his own. It highlights irrationalities endemic to the normative configurations of personhood and the normative ploys of self-identification most widely sponsored and routinely indulged in. Rodman's eccentricities call forth a kind of national attention and admiration that should be impossible given the particular colonizations of desire idealized in the culture. The matters that place Rodman on the verge of "media superstardom" should exile him from public admiration altogether, because they result in self-promotion on Rodman's part betraying cherished visions of normalcy and, in particular, enshrined heterosexual domesticity. One might say, then, it is the culture Rodman stands athwart, more than Rodman himself, that is really—and grudgingly—"something else," a culture patently beside itself. For, although Rodman is taken as representative of energies uncontainable in starkly economical circuits of desire, he is celebrated precisely for this reason by a culture of desire. These enormous inconsistencies no doubt account for the astonishing recklessness of Wideman's "Playing Dennis Rodman," especially its (darling?) opening gambit. And, like the larger culture itself, Wideman never fully fathoms his own recklessness.

Beyond the opening disquisition on the term *'tain't*, Wideman refers to women only two other times: once in parenthetical mention that "now...more women show up on outdoor courts" (1996, 94), and once in acknowledgement of his "daughter playing in the regional finals of the NCAA" (1996, 95) Both references seem to imply a social progressiveness characterized by greater inclusiveness and parity. Basketball is a field of endeavor and a point of concern, like many facets of post–civil rights U.S. culture, in which women (or choose any other group you wish) now receive more generous and overdue recognition. The primary tenor and logic of "Playing Dennis Rodman" overwhelming these references, however, only admits women in a profoundly different light than that of increasingly equal participants in an intricate and artful endeavor. Given the provocativeness of Wideman's introduction and subsequent unmistakable equation of basketball with exhibitionist male heterosexuality, it would seem that the only way any woman (*even* a daughter) might enter this discourse is in terms of the distracting bodily topography of the *'tain't* and the attendant masculinity only barely able to contain itself in conceptualizing the *'tain't*. In a public statement openly styling itself on the order of male homosocial sites of heterosexual esteem, the appearance of a daughter is strikingly troublesome, for undifferentiated female flesh is the medium that Wideman imagines Rodman (and men like him) either exercising their ingenuity upon or in desperate need of exercising their ingenuity upon. Given the force of Wideman's introduction and his subsequent attention to which men are or are not "cocksure," the mention of any particular woman remains necessarily subordinate to an overarching characterization of women as undifferentiated flesh open, so to speak, to the execution of "the finer points of [ingenious male] lovemaking."

Stated differently, Wideman's mention of a daughter is strikingly out of place given the logic and tenor of his encomium, because the reference infers to him a paterfamiliar stance he can in no way sustain legitimately or credibly given both the specifics of the enthusiasms in question and usual understandings of paterfamilial postures. That is, although reference to a daughter signals on some level (in the midst of much homoerotic discourse) normative heterosexual congress, it also alludes to heterosexual domesticity greatly at odds with the enthusiasms unfolding. Heterosexual domesticity has more to do with prohibitions on sexual enthusiasms than homosocial esteem of "the finer points of lovemaking." Binding arrangements that would contain or domesticate male libidinal energy are not of the moment in "Playing Dennis Rodman" but, very differently, the mouth and hands and penis and scrotum as agents of pleasurable distraction and even disorder. In Wideman's reflections, the acute pleasures imagined in, through, and around sexual activity are broached—as in the instances in the rest rooms—through the imagination of another man's sexual prowess, an act, whether in imagination or fact, exceeding the proscribed mathematics of heterosexual domesticity as well as its rationalization of libidinal energies (marked here by reference to a daughter). In short, Wideman goes the men in the rest room one better.

The arresting images of Rodman on the jacket of *Bad as I Wanna Be* provides a fitting, powerful rendition of these dynamics. On the dust jacket Rodman sits naked astride an imposing Harley Davidson, his long, muscled legs akimbo contrasted against the black metal and chrome of the motorcycle, his torso lean and erect, his tattooed arms in open display, as is the left cheek of his butt and as are five basketballs in close proximity—three on the ground next to the Harley, one pinned by a knee against the bike, the other in his crotch, a forearm resting casually across it. The lighting of the shot directs one's attention to this final detail. On the back cover Rodman stands fully upright, his bare buttocks to the camera, the muscles of his butt and back prominently displayed, his legs stretched to their full length, as are his upreaching arms, a shading of other body parts barely visible through his open legs, six basketballs in proximity this time—four on the ground between or around his legs, two in the open palms of his hands. Thus, in addition to the invitation to see Rodman as having a powerful, brooding instrument between his legs that almost dwarfs the rest of him, the dust jacket poses the invitation to imagine, as do Wideman and innumerable others, that Rodman has balls. Big tan brown ones that are striped and so big and unwieldy they fit in your hand only one at a time. All of this at the same time that Rodman must also be imagined as just one of the guys. All of this at the same time that one is never invited to see in these images the incapabilities—glaringly evident—of keenly promoted systems of order making exacting colonizations of desire, pleasure, and self-regard.

By what startling set of imaginative feats readily practiced in the culture is Wideman able to see the cross-dressing, cross-naming Dennis Rodman simply as one of the boys and simply to see one of the boys in Rodman's play? The mix of appeals, metaphors, and postures elicited by the elite mix of men on the basketball court, a mix the NBA struggles to put in "the most positive light," is so compelling that it seems overwhelming that its crises are generally overlooked, even in the unseemly antics of its most critical proponent. For these reasons, perhaps even more than it is about any individual, *Bad as I Wanna Be* seems more rightly about a compound crisis. Wideman and innumerable others are eager to imagine not just what the title, but also the dust jacket, of the book boldy proclaims. There exists an eager population of cultural consumers willing to undertake the highly profitable fantasy (both antagonistic to and in compliance with the cultural order) that Rodman has balls. Balls all the more intriguing and open to public consideration because they draw attention to themselves not only on the basketball court, but at the site of sexual energy itself with its perilous crush of racial, gendered, domestic, and commercial prohibitions and imperatives. What a mix-up.

REFERENCES

Alexander, E. (1996). "We're Gonna Deconstruct Your Life!: The Making and the Unmaking of the Black Bourgeois Partriarch in *Rochchet.*" In *Representing Black Men,* edited by Marcellus Blount and George P. Cunningham. New York: Routledge.

Bersani, L. (1995). *Homos.* Cambridge, MA: Harvard University Press.

Butler J. (1990); (1995). "Desire." In *Critical Terms for Literary Study,* edited by Frank Lentricchia and Thomas McLaughlin. Chicago: University of Chicago Press.

Delgado, R. and Stefanic. J (1995). "Minority Men, Misery, and the Market Place of Ideas." In *Constructing Masculinity,* edited by Maurice Berger, et al. New York: Routledge.

Doyle, L. (1994). *Bordering on the Body: The Racial Matrix of Modern Fiction and Culture.* New York: Oxford.

Herman, E.S. (1995).*Triumph of the Market: Essays on Economic, Politics, and the Media.* Boston: South End Press.

Jhally, S. (1990).*The Codes of Advertising: Fetishism and the Political Economy of Meaning in the Consumer Society.* New York: Routledge, 1987.

Lang, C. (1982). "Autobiography in the Aftermath of Romanticism." *Diacritics* (Winter 1982): 2-16.

Mercer, K. (1994). *Welcome to the Jungle: New Positions in Black Cultural Studies.* New York: Routledge.

Rodman, D. (with Tim Keown.) (1996). *Bad as I Wanna Be.* New York: Delacourte.

Ross, D. (1983). *Secrets of a Sparrow.* New York: Villiard Books.

Rubin, G. (1995). "Thinking Sex." In *The Gay and Lesbian Studies Reader,* edited by Henry Abelove, et al. New York: Routledge.

Solomon-Godeau (1995). "Abigail: Male Trouble." In *Constructing Masculinity,* edited by Maurice Beger, et al. New York: Routledge.

Thomas, K. (1996). "Ain't Nothing Like the Real Thing: Black Masculinity, Gay Sexuality, and the Jargon of Authenticity." In *Representing Black Men*, edited by Marcellus Blount and George P. Cunningham. New York: Routledge.

Weigman, R. (1995). *American Anatomies: Theorizing Race and Gender.* Durham, NC: Duke University Press.

Wideman, J.E. (1996). "Playing Dennis Rodman." *The New Yorker* (29 April and 6 May 1996): 94-95.

Zack, N. (1993). *Race and Mixed Race.* Philadelphia: Temple University Press.

Iconic Signifiers of the Gay Harlem Renaissance

Lighting the Harlem Renaissance Afire!!: Embodying Richard Bruce Nugent's Bohemian Politic

Seth Clark Silberman

Most Harlem Renaissance scholars are familiar with Richard Bruce Nugent. Poet, painter, short story writer, dancer, playwright, sketch artist, actor, and novelist, Nugent was an accomplished Renaissance man who was friends with and a partial member of the "elite" of the New Negro movement in Harlem during the 1920s and 1930s. Because he was one of the longest-living survivors of the movement, Nugent's recollections of the "elite" have been immortalized in many books, including David Levering Lewis's *When Harlem Was in Vogue*. Yet while Nugent figures prominently in numerous histories of the Renaissance, he is included only as a witness. Nugent as writer is only mentioned as historical anecdote; his infamous short story "Smoke, Lilies, and Jade," was the much-ballyhooed controversial focus of the "otherwise noteworthy" journal *Fire!!: Devoted to the Younger Negro Artists,* the first of many "failed" projects by Wallace Thurman. Nugent's life and work are often relegated to the shadows of most scholarship on the New Negro movement, in part because Nugent was a bohemian in every sense of the word. He was unabashedly flamboyant, a fact most scholars will never let you forget: In his recent pictorial Renaissance survey, Steven Watson depicts Nugent as "the perfumed orchid of the New Negro movement" (Watson 1995, 90); poet Albert Rice describes him as "the bizarre and eccentric young vagabond poet of High Harlem" (Watson 1995, 216); and Claude McKay's biographer, Wayne F. Cooper, explains that Nugent "enjoyed an active social life [and] frankly admitted that he was a dilettant in all the arts save painting and that he enjoyed the role" (Cooper and McKay, 1987).

Such characterizations are not altogether false. Nugent was noticed at Harlem's elite parties because he often aimed to shock. White gay writer and patron Carl Van Vechten noted the following about Nugent's appearance at a party in a letter to Langston Hughes:

As I went out, William Pickens caught my arm to ask me who the "young man in the evening clothes" was. It was Bruce Nugent, of course, with his usual open chest and uncovered ankles. I suppose soon he will be going without trousers" (Kellner 1987, 96).

Nugent's story, "Smoke, Lilies, and Jade," the first extant published story by an African American that openly depicted homosexuality, *did* shock the Harlem community when *Fire!!* was distributed in November of 1926. But there is much more to say about Richard Bruce Nugent and his work, though most scholars stop here. While scholars agree that initial negative reactions to *Fire!!* were hasty—Rean Greaves from *The Baltimore Sun* referred to it as "Effeminate Tommyrot"—scholarly reappraisal of *Fire!!* merely examines the contributions by Langston Hughes, Countee Cullen, Zora Neale Hurston, and the cover drawing by Aaron Douglas. "Smoke, Lilies, and Jade" is still discounted. Acclaimed Harlem scholar David Levering Lewis describes Nugent's story as "a montage of pederasty and androgyny...prose dissolving into pointillistic soft pornography" (Lewis, 1917).

The notion of "disembodied" politics to attain civil rights in the 1920s, proposed by the black gay Renaissance ideologue Alain Locke, is one that philosopher Jurgen Habermas investigated nearly 40 years later in *The Structural Transformation of the Public Sphere*. Locke's prescriptions for Negro fiction prefigure Habermas's for social change, in which the disembodied people of what Habermas calls "the bourgeois public sphere" can manifest change in public opinion through the written word. Locke's thesis that aesthetic blackness would be easily digestible to a white audience was correct—the Renaissance and all it was associated with were a hit with those who wanted to "slum" for a night north of 125th Street— but his assertion that such an aesthetic appreciation would foster civic change did not instantly materialize. As the popularity of 19th-century minstrelsy proved, the performance of aesthetic blackness (via music, dance, even blackface) could be easily accepted by white audiences and could just as easily be disassociated from the experiences of actual black people. The acceptance of the *presence* of black people by whites—as lynching cases proved at the time, and as police brutality cases continue to remind us—is another issue entirely.

Nugent's *presence* as a black gay man in Harlem and the *pres-*

ence of homosexuality in his fiction is in part a protest against Locke's disembodied directives for Negro fiction. As opposed to creating mythic pastoral fictions, Nugent crafted ones refracted from everyday life in the phenomena and spectacle of Harlem itself. Nugent looked around him for the inspiration for his fiction, crafting his protagonists from his own life. He emphasized this corporeal connection to his work by writing almost exclusively in a roman-à-clef style. What distinguishes Nugent's work from most of the canonized Harlem Renaissance fiction, however, is its construction of a relationship to its audience. Nugent's collapse of boundaries between author and audience, between fiction and fact, stems from his suspicions of the conscious marketing of "New Negroes" for, and popular among, white audiences. While this difference could partly be explained by Nugent's marginal interest in pursuing a *career* as a writer in the way that Hughes or Hurston did—because he had the "freedom" to write "to himself" and without the constraints of publishing, he *could* be critical of white publishing houses—such an explanation does not adequately explain Nugent's narrative strategy. Nugent's conspicuous construction of audience deliberately highlights the presence of the reader, and thus how black fiction and black authors are spectacles in the aestheticizing, celebrating, and marketing of Harlem's New Negro.

To embody the black gay Harlemite within the context of the disembodied New Negro was Nugent's design; "Smoke, Lilies, and Jade" was his tour de force. "Smoke" was also the apogee of *Fire!!* itself intended to attack Locke's constraining New Negro image. Not only did Nugent's unprecedented and unashamed sexual narrative complicate the debates over (how) race matters, the journal—complete with Thurman's story about prostitution, "Cordelia, the Crude," and defense of white gay writer/patron Carl Van Vechten's inflammatory novel *Nigger Heaven*—confounded Locke and others. Yet they did not have to worry about *Fire!!* for long. Aided by an accidental (yet ironic) fire that destroyed the majority of the first and only printing of *Fire!!*, Locke and others discovered the best way to extinguish *Fire!!*'s assault on the New Negro: to ignore it completely. Shortly after it was published, *Fire!!* was rarely mentioned. Such a reaction not only demonstrates the weight Locke's New Negro ideal carried, but also demonstrates how effective *Fire!!* and Nugent ultimately were.

Nugent echoes the importance of the embodiment of the

bohemian in "Smoke, Lilies, and Jade," not simply the *representations* of homosexuality, when he responds to the often-asked question: How could he have written such a *gay* story in 1926? Nugent replied, "I didn't know it was gay when I wrote it" (Beam 1986, 24). Indeed, *gay* is not the proper term for the sexuality Nugent explores in "Smoke, Lilies, and Jade." Nugent says of his short story:

> I've never been able to make anybody understand that Langston and I said there should be a magazine where we could say whatever we wanted to. Harlem was very much like the village. People did what they wanted to do with whom they wanted to do it. You didn't get on the rooftops and shout, "I fucked my wife last night." So why would you get on the roof and say, "I love prick." You didn't. You just did what you wanted to do. Nobody was in the closet. There wasn't any closet (Kisseloff 1989, 288).

Whether there actually was no "closet" in Harlem could be argued, but what Nugent does demonstrate is the problem in naming the black gay men and lesbians of Harlem during a time when *homosexuals* were believed only to be white. As Jeanne Flash Grey, a resident of Harlem in the 1930s, remembers, "There were many places in Harlem run by and for black lesbians and gay men, when we were still bulldaggers and faggots and only whites were lesbians and homosexuals" (Duberman 1989, 331).

Despite the notion that no African Americans were *homosexuals*, there were many bulldaggers and faggots in Harlem. Despite the lack of the official homosexual label, people knew who they were; and Nugent was not the only one. Other black gay men and women in Harlem—Wallace Thurman, Gladys Bentley, Countee Cullen, Harold Jackman, George Hannah, Bessie Smith, Claude McKay, Alain Locke, Angelika Weld Grimke, Alice Dunbar-Nelson, Augustus Granville Dill, and Alexander Gumby, among others—all participated and contributed to the bohemian culture from which Nugent drew in his work. Still, Nugent became *the* signifier for homosexuality in Harlem, despite another public scandal shortly after the publication of *Fire!!*, the arrest of Augustus Granville Dill for indecent exposure in a public rest room (Kellner 1984, 100).

Dill was no stranger to the Harlem Renaissance. A Harvard graduate, he was active in the NAACP and edited a magazine for children,

Brownie Book, with Jessie Fauset. Dill was also a close associate and employee of W.E.B. DuBois, acting as the business manager of *The Crisis.* When he was arrested for having sex with a man in a public rest room, DuBois immediately fired him but forever regretted it:

> In the midst of my career there burst on me a new and undreamed-of aspect of sex. A young man, long my disciple and student, then my cohelper and successor to part of my work, was suddenly arrested for molesting young men in public places. I had before that time no conception of homosexuality. I had never understood the tragedy of an Oscar Wilde. I dismissed my coworker forthwith, and spent heavy days regretting my act (Lester 1971, 730).

In the March 1928 issue of *The Crisis* DuBois writes glowingly of Dill, who was "by nature and training, *the sensitive artist*" for his "loyal and efficient service," yet he writes "it is with deep regret" that Dill left *The Crisis* "with the good wishes of all" (DuBois 1928, 96).

Why this public scandal did not overshadow the one surrounding Nugent and *Fire!!* is directly connected to publication. While Dill certainly fit the description of the dandy—Bruce Kellner writes that Dill's "personal flamboyance brought him north" to Harlem, and that he was "something of a dandy...recognized by the bright chrysanthemum he wore in his buttonhole" (Kellner 1984, 100)—Dill's scandal did not carry as much weight because his scandal did not occur within what Habermas would call the Harlem public sphere. Because Nugent offered a *fictional representation* of homosexual desire, as opposed to an arrest that pointed toward his own homosexuality, Nugent interjected sexuality into the public sphere of the Harlem Renaissance, within the body of its published literature; and thus, unlike Dill's foible, fiction, as Habermas argues, is a powerful medium that implicitly involves—and implicates—its readers. Fiction necessitates "intimate mutual relationships between [the author and reader who] "talked heart to heart" (Habermas 1991, 50). Writing such a "gay" story provided a visceral entry into the psyche of the protagonist of "Smoke, Lilies and Jade," Alex, a black gay man in Harlem. Because of the importance of fiction to the sociopolitical goals of the Harlem Renaissance—outlined by Locke in his movement-defining 1925 anthology *The New Negro*— "Smoke, Lilies, and Jade" was more than merely a story. It was an outright attack on the goals of the Renaissance itself.

In *The Structural Transformation of the Public Sphere*, Habermas explores much of what Locke wrote about the sociopolitical potential of fiction. For Habermas, the significance of the ideological power of fiction lies in the sociopolitical conditions that fostered the birth and popularity of the novel in Western Europe. "The novel refined the role of the narrator through the use of reflections by directly addressing the reader, almost by stage directions [so that] the novel [would] place a final veil over the difference between reality and illusion. The reality as illusion that the new genre created received its proper name in English, "fiction": It shed the character of the *merely fictitious*. The psychological novel fashioned for the first time the kind of realism that allowed anyone to enter into the literary action as a substitute for his own, to use the relationships between the figures, between the author, the characters, and the reader as substitute relationships for reality" (Habermas 1991, 50).

With the creation of characters, the reader has a heightened sense of interaction—and individual freedom—through the genre of fiction. Because of the assumed intimacy of the form, these readers' sense of themselves grew increasingly tied to their intention with it; and this these readers became *sujets de fiction*. As Habermas summarizes, readers of fiction "formed the public sphere of a rational-critical debate in the world of letters [which], by communicating with itself, attained clarity about itself" (Habermas 1991, 51). Because fiction represented and manipulated both the private sphere (the individual) and the public sphere (public opinion, political action), Habermas argues, its political intentions were sometimes obscure. It is, however, precisely this indecipherability between fact and fiction that makes fiction such a powerful ideological tool. This indecipherability makes it possible to proffer a "simple" narrative, a perfected view of reality, that despite its perceived apolitical aesthetic argues its sociopolitical ideals through representation.

Like Habermas, Locke saw the potential of fiction as the key medium for Negroes to "attain clarity about themselves," to celebrate their culture. Locke views fiction as a reflection of both public and private spheres: The foreword to *The New Negro* explains, "this volume aims to document the New Negro culturally and socially—to register the transformation of the *inner and outer life* of the Negro in America that have so significantly taken place in the last few years" (Locke 1925, xv). Fiction is also a means to affect public opinion, or to educate; it is "the truest social portraiture [for] who[m]ever wishes to see the Negro in his essential traits, in the full perspective of his achievement and possibilities, [for those who] must seek the enlightenment of...the present developments of Negro culture." Like Habermas's public sphere, Locke explains that for this cultural fiction to be produced and disseminated,

> culture must develop an elite that must maintain itself upon the basis of standards that can move forward but never backward. In the pursuit of culture one must detach himself from the crowd...Culture likewise is every inch representative of the whole personality when it is truly perfected (Locke 1925, 180).

Locke's notion of cultural fiction, "every inch representative of the whole personality" of Negro culture, is necessarily disembodied not only because Locke's New Negro (once disembodied) could enter ongoing rational-critical debate to promote racial uplift but also because Locke's mission was to separate blacks from racist ideologies and myths that tied blacks to conceptions about their bodies. Locke hoped to dissociate racist ideology from biological determinism. His solution was to create new "positive" Negro literature to celebrate the distinct aesthetics of Negro culture that were not linked with stereotypes about black bodies, either by looking to Africa as a source of race pride or by exalting Africanisms evident in the black folk tradition.

Although the celebration of difference from white people may not seem a "disembodied" enterprise, the celebration of "the folk"— whether it is Langston Hughes's emulation of jazz rhythms in his poetry, Zora Neale Hurston's anthropological capturing of black Southern vernacular in her fiction, or Jean Toomer's pastoral portraits of country life in *Cane*—fulfills a "disembodied" politic because, as Chip Rhodes explains, any representation of "the primitive, spontaneous approach to life [that characterizes "the folk"] is always already a representation, always already a feeling evoked, not a reality encountered" (Rhodes 1994 195). The folk's representation is first and foremost a product of the imagination, and thus it can be imagined by both blacks and whites. Rhodes concludes that "the whole vogue of the Negro in the '20s [then] is not the 'otherness' of blacks that so intrigued whites. Rather, it is the ultimate identity, the ultimate sameness, among all people."

Locke's *New Negro* was his own account of the ultimate sameness among all people. It aimed to fulfill what James Weldon Johnson had asserted four years before, that "nothing will do more to change the mental attitude [of society] and raise [the Negro's] status than a demonstration of intellectual parity by the Negro through the production of literature and art" (Lewis, 149). *The New Negro* celebrated the entrance of the Negro into a Habermasian public sphere by not only providing fiction, poetry, and essays, but also bibliographies that chronicle the Negro in literature, drama, music, art, folklore, and politics. Part anthology, part reference book, *The New Negro* was also a manifesto. It encapsulated Locke's philosophy of racial uplift. Locke, as Jeffrey Stewart argues, "approached race as Karl Marx had analyzed class—as the vortex of modern social relations.... For Locke, modern races resulted from the praxis of modern imperialism, which defined as "inferior" those races...who were unable to free themselves from colonial subordination" (Jeffries 1925, xxvi-xxvii). To recognize racism as social praxis irreconcilable with biological determinism was Locke's strategy to move beyond what he felt was racism's ideological hold on African Americans.

This shift, for Locke, had to take place at the ideological level, since it was at this level that race theories were grounded in biological determinism. Locke's New Negro, after all, was not just to celebrate Negro life in Harlem in the '20s, but to replace the "Old Negro," who was "a creature or moral debate and historical controversy [who] has been a stock figure perpetuated as an historical fiction partly in innocent sentimentalism, partly in deliberate reactionism." To erase this "historical fiction," then, the New Negro had to create fiction that, to borrow from Habermas, had to "shed the character of the merely fictitious,"(Locke 1925, xv) fiction that implicitly followed his doctrine for racial uplift.

The New Negro was Locke's symbol for "Negro life...finding a new soul [as well as] a fresh spiritual and cultural focusing." The "usual outburst of creative expression" during the Renaissance was Locke's heralding sign that the New Negro Movement was of historic importance. For this reason Locke carefully delineated the responsibilities for "the intelligent Negro of to-day [who] is trying to hold himself at par, neither inflated by sentimental allowances nor depreciated by current social discounts" (Locke 1925, 8). The responsibilities he did outline recall the ideals for "Negro talent" posed in Alexander Crummell's lecture, "Civilization, the Primal Need of the Race," delivered 28 years earlier at the first meeting of the American Negro Academy in 1897.

Like Locke's *New Negro*, Crummell's address is a call to arms to the black leaders who were gathered before him. Crummell (1922) commends his audience for their gathering to inspire "the civilization of the Negro race in the United States, by the scientific processes of literature, art, and philosophy, through the agency of the cultured men of this same Negro race" (Crummell 1922, 285). The attainment of civilization for Crummell is paramount for blacks because without civilization, with which he equates art, science, philosophy, and scholarship, blacks will never succeed in the United States, blacks will never "hold our place in the world of culture and enlightenment," because "to make *men* you need civilization; and what I mean by civilization is the action of exalted forces, both of God and man."

The etiology of Crummell's exalted forces, however, does not exactly stem from formal Christian doctrine. While Crummell grounds his doctrine in religious metaphor, he equates social and civil progress with civilization, art, nationality, culture, and enlightenment. Crummell even anticipates Locke in his reliance on disembodied fictions to achieve racial uplift:

> Neither property, nor money, nor station, nor office, nor lineage, are fixed factors, in so large a thing as the destiny of man; that they are not vitalizing qualities in the changeless hopes of humanity. The greatness of peoples springs from their ability to grasp *the grand conceptions of being*. It is *the absorption* of a people, of a nation, of a race, in large majestic and boding things which *lifts them up to the skies*" (Crummell 1922, 286, emphasis added).

Crummell's spiritual renewal rebuts materialist methods for racial uplift by embracing the grand conceptions of being, which he defines as the "height of noble thought, grand civility, a chaste and elevating culture, refinement, and the impulses of irrepressible progress" (Crummell 1922, 287). For Crummell spirituality is often used metaphorically "to transform and stimulate the souls of a race or a people, a work which will require the most skilled resources and the use of the scientific spirit" (Crummell 1922, 287).

Crummell suggests that these conceptions can only be interpreted by the scholars, thinkers, and philosophers of the race who must also be philanthropists so that they can "employ their knowledge and culture and teaching and to guide both the opinions and habits of the crude masses" (Crummell 1922, 287). While the dogmatic aspect of Crummell's solution to "uplift all the latent genius...of this neglected Race" clearly influenced DuBois's "Talented Tenth," and Locke's exalted "New Negro," Crummell even prefigures Habermas in portraying what for Habermas is the "feeling that first gave rise to the replacement of the earlier cultural stratum with its roots in the middle class by the social group that we call the 'intelligentsia. " (Crummell 1922, 174).

Locke's philosophy also retained Crummell's metaphoric religiosity. Locke writes of the New Negro: "By shedding the old chrysalis of the Negro problem we are achieving something like a spiritual emancipation." Yet for Locke such a spiritual emancipation is either connected with the divinity of Africa and the emulation of African tradition in art, or is used as a marker for disembodiment, in contrast with the material realities of race relations. When he argues that "for generations the Negro has been the peasant matrix of that section of America which has most undervalued him," he concludes that the Negro "has contributed not only materially in labor and social practice, but spiritually as well." Locke often equates spirituality with self-expression or community effort: "If in our lifetime the Negro should not be able to celebrate his full initiation into American democracy, he can at least...celebrate the attainment of a significant and satisfying *new phase of group development, and with it a spiritual Coming of Age*" (Locke 1925, 15).

Despite the veiled or silent protests over *Fire!!*, it too was born from "a spiritual Coming of Age," though not quite like the one Locke intended. The coming of age that *Fire!!* aimed to document was that of the younger Negro artists who rebelled from Locke's strict definitions for Negro art. *Fire!!* was meant to be the forum for their concerns. Eleonore van Notten (1994) argues that at the time

the separation between art and propaganda [was] a major concern. Harlem's younger generation took the position that the role of the artist was neither moral nor political. They aspired to an autonomous and unfettered art in which literary quality was not linked to the moral stature or exemplary lifestyle of either the author or fictional characters in the work. Unlike Harlem's old guard who, in an effort to demonstrate their parity with the white cultural elite, focused almost exclusively on the artistic treatment of the well-educated and respectable black middle class, the younger generation turned to the lower social strata, concentrating specifically on those elements they considered to be still uniquely black and racially distinct" (Van Notten 1994, 131).

While Van Notten's distinction between art and propaganda mirrors age-old debates over the function of African American fiction—debates that exist merely as an excuse to formalistically devalue any literature the critic wants to rebuke, and does not adequately represent the need that *Fire!!* attempted to fill—she does isolate the political attributes of *Fire!!*, despite her definition to the contrary. While Van Notten claims that "unfettered" art focusing on "the lower social strata" is necessarily apolitical, it is precisely here that *Fire!!*'s political assault lies. By embodying "the lower social strata," by focusing on the body with Nugent's "Smoke, Lilies and Jade" and Thurman's "Cordelia, the Crude," *Fire!!* aimed to contradict Locke's ideals for Negro fiction. *Fire!!* concentrated on "uniquely black and racially distinct" characters that could not be disembodied in order to be co-opted by whites as proof of "the ultimate sameness among all people."

Locke's ideals were foremost in the minds of Nugent and Langston Hughes the night they met at a salon hosted by Georgia Douglas Johnson in Washington, D.C., the night *Fire!!* was conceived. Nugent recalls the evening in Jeff Kisseloff's *You Must Remember This: An Oral History of Manhattan from the 1890s to World War II:*

There was a woman in Washington who was fantastic. She was a very good poet, Georgia Douglas Johnson, and she had salons. I met Langston at her home.... That's the night *Fire!!* was born. Hall Johnson, at whose house I was living, had written a spiritual called "Fire!"

> *Fire, fire, Lawd fire burn my soul.*
> *Fire, fire, Lawd fire burn by soul.*
> *I ain't been good. I ain't been clean.*
> *I been stinkin' low down mean.*
> *But fire, fire, Lawd fire burn my soul.*

Both Langston and I were very fond of that. As we were walking back and forth, I think it was Langston who said we—by *we*, I mean blacks—should have a magazine of our own, in which they [sic] could have art, in which they [sic] could express themselves however they felt (Kisselhof, 1999).

Having "a magazine of our own," a forum for young black writers in which to speak their mind "however they felt," was for Nugent and Hughes an ideological challenge to Locke's New Negro. Given both Hughes's and Nugent's close association with the "talented tenth" that Locke led and their inclusion in *The New Negro*, their desire to publish *Fire!!* was not simply one to create "unfettered" art, as Van Notten might argue. Hughes biographer Arnold Rampersad claims that Hughes's interest in creating *Fire!!* was sparked by the violently negative reaction to Carl Van Vechten's *Nigger Heaven* and by his own essay, "The Negro Artist and the Racial Mountain" (Rampersad 1990, 134).

Certainly Hughes's essay outlines the ideological battles *Fire!!* wages. Hughes's essay opens with the recounting of an exchange he had with an unnamed Negro poet:

"I want to be a poet—not a Negro poet," meaning I believe, "I want to write like a white poet"; meaning subconsciously, "I would like to be a white poet"; meaning behind that, "I would like to be white." And I was sorry the young man said that, for *no great poet has ever been afraid of being himself* (Hughes 1941, 167).

Hughes later echoes this sentiment of self-pride when he praises "the low-down folks, the so-called common element" of Harlem, those people who "have their nip of gin on Saturday nights and are not too important to themselves or the community, or too well-fed, or too learned to watch the lazy world go round":

And perhaps these common people will give to the world its truly great Negro artist, *the one who is not afraid to be himself*. Whereas the better-class Negro would tell the artist what to do [Alain Locke, et al], the people at least tell him alone when does appear. And *they are not ashamed of him*—if they know he exists at all. *And they accept what beauty is their own without question* (168, emphasis added).

Perhaps Hughes's sentiments about what the younger Negro artist should do and be is both why he and Nugent hit it off so famously (it was also during this first night they met that Hughes convinced Nugent to move to New York), and why, as Nugent recounts, Hughes "had a very strange kind of unnecessary envy of" Nugent (Kisselhof 1989, 288).

Perhaps Hughes envied Nugent because Nugent embodied a carefree spirit Hughes wanted to emulate. Nugent's fiction certainly embodied everything they wanted *Fire!!* to accomplish. "Smoke, Lilies, and Jade," an experimental short story written in a series of sentence fragments connected by ellipses, follows the thoughts of 19-year-old artist Alex as he discovers he is attracted to a man he meets, sleeps with him, ponders what this attraction could mean, and finally resolves that "one *can* love" a man if he wants. By focusing on the body, by exploring not just the erotic but what Alex's new erotic discoveries could mean vis-à-vis his identity, and by setting his story in contemporary black urban Harlem, Nugent broke every rule Locke had for Negro fiction and its black authors to enter a disembodied public sphere. Not content to place his fiction in an imagined, idyllic Negro past, Nugent's "Smoke" explores the epistemologies of a black and gay identity, thus boldly complicating Locke's effort to transcend race matters. As opposed to creating easily marketable characterizations of Negro life, Nugent shows what Harlem Wallace Thurman writes of in 1928, a Harlem that is "a dream city pregnant with wide-awake realities" (Thurman 1999, 91). Closing "Smoke" with Alex's bold acceptance that "one *can* love" a man, Nugent audaciously questions the aims and ends of Locke's transcendent racial uplift when it does not incorporate the "uplift" of every part of black people's lives.

"Smoke" clearly realizes Hughes's goals for the Negro artist and demonstrates that Nugent was certainly someone who was "not afraid to be himself." Nugent's story follows Hughes's intimations about Negro literature the closest. In "Smoke," Alex literally "accept[s] what beauty is [his] own without question": He calls the man he sleeps with "Beauty." "Smoke" is an experimental, linguistic climb up "the racial mountain" about which Hughes writes in his essay, one that expects and includes the reaction such literature usually garners into its narrative. Hughes explains:

> The road for this serious black artist, then, who would produce a racial art is most certainly rocky and the mountain is high. Until recently he received almost no encouragement for his work from either white or colored people. The fine novels of [Charles W.] Chesnutt go out to print with neither race noticing their passing. The quaint charm and humor of [Paul] Dunbar's dialect verse brought to him, in his day, *largely the*

same kind of encouragement one would give a sideshow freak
(A colored man writing poetry! How odd!) *or a clown.* How
amusing! (Hughes, 169).

The "quaint charm and humor" of the "racial art" of Nugent's
"Smoke" lies in its celebration of (what people will refer to as) its own
"freakishness." By calling attention to its "freakishness," "Smoke" also
implicates its readers. After all, it is the reader who must recognize the
story's "freakishness" for what it is because Nugent never explicitly
names the import of Alex's self-questioning. For the reader to recognize
"Smoke" as a story about a black homosexual means that he or she
must already know experimentally what a black homosexual is. Thus
the reader is implicated in Alex's search to name his sexual identity.

Because of the story's implications, however, not everyone celebrated the "freakishness" it inspires, as Nugent recalls:

We had done an unspeakable thing when we published. There
were things in *Fire!!* that you didn't talk about, like the story
about a prostitute or homosexuality. It was a scandalous magazine that didn't really have enough weight to be a scandal. So
many people hated it. I remember soon after it appeared,
Wallie and I went up to a restaurant in Sugar Hill, and there
was Paul Robeson and his wife sitting there. She didn't like it
at all, and Paul didn't want to say anything in front of her. He
just turned his head toward us and gave us a wink. I think
everybody was upset who hadn't done it who thought they
should have, like DuBois. I remember DuBois did ask, "Did
you have to write about homosexuality? Couldn't you write
about colored people? Who cares about homosexuality?" I
said, "You'd be surprised how good homosexuality is. I love
it" Poor DuBois (Kisselhof 1989, 288).

The responses of Robeson and DuBois represent the range of reactions Nugent inspired. Negative reactions, however, quickly passed. As
many of the initial copies of *Fire!!* were destroyed by fire, the commotion over Nugent's story also seemingly went up in smoke.

To seal *Fire!!*'s fate, neither *The Crisis* nor *The Opportunity,* the
two most popular and influential black magazines of Harlem, reviewed
the journal. This absence is almost inconceivable considering *Fire!!*'s
impressive editorial board (Wallace Thurman, Langston Hughes, Zora

Neale Hurston, Gwendolyn Bennett, Aaron Douglas, John Davis, and Nugent), *Fire!!*'s impressive list of contributors (including the editors, Countee Cullen, Arna Bontemps, and Helene Johnson), and *Fire!!*'s influential patrons (Carl Van Vechten, Arthur Huff Fauset). Bennett and Cullen each had columns in *Opportunity*. Nugent often contributed drawings and even guest-wrote Cullen's column in *Opportunity* 11 months after *Fire!!*'s publication. Hughes contributed regularly to both *Opportunity* and *The Crisis*. Fauset's sister, Jessie Redmon Fauset, worked closely with W.E.B. DuBois, editor of *The Crisis*. Cullen too had a close relationship with DuBois. DuBois even spoke with Nugent about his story. Yet no review appeared in print.

Despite this attempt to silence, the infamy of the journal and Nugent smolder on. Not only does a relentlessly bohemian image of Nugent appear in general discussions of the Renaissance, and in recent analyses of sexuality in the Renaissance, but also he commands a presence in scholarship that is ostensibly about someone else, like Arnold Rampersad's biography of Langston Hughes:

> Hughes's favorite among the regulars was probably Richard Bruce Nugent, a willowy, intelligent, but rebellious nineteen-year-old of Italianate coloring and good looks, who hoped vaguely to make a career of painting and acting. Meanwhile, Nugent aimed mainly to shock. From the black upper class (one distant relative may have been Blanche K. Bruce, a United States senator during Reconstruction and later Register of the Treasury), Nugent nevertheless sometimes dispensed with wearing socks in public, sometimes with shoes; only a few years later, when he had more fully developed his personality, he would be remembered as "a soft young fellow with a purr, like a cat's, and little gold bead in one ear." In a culture that shrank from the mention of homosexuality, Nugent at 19 was already openly gay, a fact that cost him many friendships—but not one with Hughes (Rampersad 1986, 106).

Nugent's caricaturization as "the enfant terrible of Washington and Harlem," however, is not as playful as it may seem. It is a strategic way to keep Nugent and what he represents marginalized. This marginalization is an example of what D.A. Miller calls "the open secret" of homosexuality, one with Habermasian implications, a secrecy that functions as the subjective practice in which the oppositions of private/public, inside/outside, subject/object are established and the sanctity of their first term kept inviolate. And the phenomenon of the "open secret" does not, as one might think, bring about the collapse of those binarisms and their ideological effects, but rather attests to their phantasmic recovery.

The "phantasmic recovery" of the "open secret," afforded in both the literature of and scholarship about (homosexuality in) the Harlem Renaissance comes in the brief mention of Nugent within studies of the Renaissance. Often the way he is mentioned has more to do with the writer Nugent than with Nugent himself. Nugent was aware of the effect his work had on the way people interacted with him, the way his work became conflated with his person. Nugent's unpublished poem "Who Asks This Thing?" explores the effect his spectacular display of bohemianism often accorded him:

I walk alone and lone must be
And wear my love for all to see:
It matters not how close our hearts appear to be—

Since I tell my love for all to know
It matters not how close our hearts may seem to grow;
Love must not be blind or small or slow:

But that I wear my heart for all to see
Means I am bound while you are, sadly, free:
He walks alone who walks in love with me.

Nugent's open expression of "the love that dare not speak its name," that he wear his heart for all to see, is what binds him more so than any other black gay artist of the Harlem Renaissance. Nugent, of course, was not the only black gay or lesbian artist who included homosexual desire in his or her work: Wallace Thurman's *The Blacker the Berry...* (1928) and *Infants of the Spring* (1932), Nella Larsen's *Passing* (1929), Claude McKay's *Home to Harlem* (1928), and the love lyrics of Angelina Weld Grimke (1927), all explicitly express gay desire. Others also included homosexual desire implicitly; and much work is now being done to reclaim this gay subtext.

Gregory Woods's article, "Gay Re-Readings of the Harlem Renaissance Poets," is an example of such a study that

explore[s] various gay reading strategies [for the poems of Langston Hughes, Countee Cullen, and Claude McKay] to suggest to contemporary readers likely subtexts which had to be kept concealed at the time of their writing—concealed, that is, from hostile readers, but always accessible to perceptive, sympathetic readings (Woods 1993, 128).

Woods (1993) suggests that "to turn these poems into 'gay poems' one must take the simple, and entirely excusable, step of isolating them from the rest" (Woods 1993, 129). Beneath this strategy of "rereading" and "isolating," however, is a modern assumption that gay writers of the Harlem Renaissance were "hiding" simply because they did not use terms "properly" to name homosexual desire. In this light, Woods applauds Nugent's prose poem "Sahjdi," included in Alain Locke's The New Negro, and "Smoke": Nugent was not included. When reading the writers of the Negro Renaissance we should not expect, nor be disappointed by the lack of, the kind of openness we now reasonably demand of gay writers." Woods's article forwards the assumption that "the kind of openness we now reasonably demand" is the only "true" or "positive" gay representation possible. His final condolences that even though "Harlem writers may have had to remain closeted...they were no less gay for that" (Woods 1993, 140) follows a spectacular logic that offers a qualitative scale placed on "gayness," one that locks the history of (re)presentations of "homosexual desire" within an illusionary narrative of progress but makes the search for the "most" gay paramount in any historical gay research.

Such a search also dislodged "gayness" from the people and historical period its (re)presentation is a product of. Robert Padgug warns against this in his article, "Sexual Matters: Rethinking Sexuality in History":

...in any approach that takes as predetermined and universal the categories of sexuality, real history disappears. Sexual practice becomes a more or less sophisticated selection of curiosities, whose meaning and validity can be gauged by that truth—or rather truths, since there are many competitors—which we, in our enlightened age, have discovered (55).

The assortment of "sexual practice [as] more or less sophisticated selection of curiosities" follows the ideology behind D.A. Miller's "open secret." The notion that we scholars and readers need to snoop through old poetry and prose to "discover" its hidden homosexuality keeps its (re)presentations of homosexuality in the closet even as we proclaim its existence. We comply with the ideology that "free" expression of homosexual desire is predicated upon its expression in terms that reflect a contemporary gay experience (i.e., queer, gay, lesbian, bisexual, transgender, etc.).

Not acknowledging and appreciating "homosexualities" of different times and cultures within their own social spheres discounts the visibility those "homosexualities" may have entertained. Nugent often attests to the visibility of people "in the life" in Harlem in interviews. In his article about Nugent, Charles Michael Smith writes:

> Being a gay man in 1920s Harlem caused him little, if any disapproval from the community. Nugent's attitude at the time was that he thought everybody he met was "in the life," especially if he found them physically attractive. He went around Harlem with the belief that "if you can't take me the way I am, it's your problem. It's certainly not mine" (Smith 1986, 209).

Nugent's attitude illuminates the real "problem" in the (re)presentations of homosexual desire: people's homophobic reactions to them. "It is homophobia," D.A. Miller concurs, "not homosexuality, that requires a closet, whence it characteristically makes its sorties only as a multiply coded allusion, or an unprovable, if not improbable connotation" (215). As Miller asserts, the "coded allusion" of "the closet" often accorded to "homosexual desire" actually represents homophobic reactions to any expression of that desire.

Reactions to Nugent then and now prove that Nugent and his work do not need to be "reread" to discern a (re)presentation of homosexuality—and I assert that the work of Cullen, McKay, Hughes, et al, also do not need to be "reread"—simply "read" on their own terms. Deprecatory reactions to "Smoke" prove the story's central importance in any Harlem Renaissance literary historiography. Despite the insistence of many scholars, the significance of "Smoke" is not simply in its forthright representation of homosexual desire, but in Nugent's affront to the ideological assumptions between Alain Locke's "New Negro," and consequently the import and implications of the "racial uplift" directive Locke proclaimed for Negro literature.

I would like to thank Craig Allen Seymour, Carla Paterson, and Thomas Wirth for their assistance with this ongoing project.

References

Cooper, W.F. (1987). *Claude McKay: Rebel Sojourner in the Harlem Renaissance.* New York: Schocken.

Crummell. A (1922). "Civilization, the Primal Need of the Race." *Destiny and Race: Selected Writings, 1840-1898, Alexander Crummell*, edited by Wilson Jeremiah Moses. Amherst: University of Massachusetts Press.

DuBois, W.E.B. "Postscript by W.E.B. DuBois." *Crisis* (March 1928): 96.

Dyer, R. (1993). *The Matter of Images: Essays on Representations.* New York: Routledge.

Garber, E. (1989). "A Spectacle in Color: The Lesbian and Gay Subculture of Jazz Age Harlem." In *Hidden From History: Reclaiming the Gay and Lesbian Past*, edtied by Martin Duberman, et al. New York: Meridian Books, 331.

Habermas, J. (1991). *The Structural Transformation of the Public Sphere: An Inquiry into a Category of Bourgeois Society.* Cambridge: The MIT Press.

Kellner, B. (1984). *The Harlem Renaissance: A Historical Dictionary for the Era.* Westport: Greenwood Press.

Kellner, B. (Ed.). (1984). *The Harlem Renaissance: A Historical Dictionary for the Era.* Westport: Greenwood Press.

— (Ed.). (1987). *Letters of Carl Van Vechten.* New Haven: Yale University Press.

Kisseloff, J. (1989). *You Must Remember This: An Oral History of Manhattan From the 1890s to World War II.* New York: Schocken Books.

Lester, J. (Ed.). (1971). *The Seventh Son: The Thought and Writings of W.E.B. DuBois.* vol 2. New York: Vintage.

Lewis, D.L. (1997). *When Harlem Was in Vogue.* New York: Penguin.

Locke, A. "The Ethics of Culture." In *The Philosophy of Alain Locke,* edited by Leonard Harris, 180, 183.

— (1925). "Introduction." *The New Negro.* New York: Atheneum, 1977: xv.

Nugent, B. and Thurman, W.H (1996). "Reclaiming Black Male Same-Sexualities in the New Negro Movement." *In Process* 1.1.

Rampersad, A. (1986). *The Life of Langston Hughes: Volume I: 1902-1941: I, Too, Sing America.* New York: Oxford University Press, 130.

Rhodes. C. (1994). "Writing Up the New Negro: The Construction of Consumer Desire in the Twenties." *Journal of American Studies* 28.2: 195.

Smith, C.M. (1986). "Bruce Nugent: Bohemian of the Harlem Renaissance." In *In The Life: A Black Gay Anthology,* edited by Joseph Beam. Boston: Alyson Publications, Inc., 1986: 24.

Van Notten, E. (1994). *Wallace Thurman's Harlem Renaissance.* Atlanta: Rodopi.

Watson, S. (1995). *The Harlem Renaissance: Hub of African American Culture, 1920-1930.* New York: Pantheon.

Woods, G. (1993). "Gay Re-Readings of the Harlem Renaissance Poets." In *Critical Essays: Gay and Lesbian Writers of Color,* edited by Emmanuel S. Nelson. New York: Harington Park Press.

THE LIVES OF RICHMOND BARTHÉ

MARGARET ROSE VENDRYES

African America welcomed into the New Negro fold the young, handsome, and articulate artist Richmond Barthé when his work received positive reviews at Chicago's 1927 *Negro in Art Week*. Barthé exhibited two portrait heads, both sculpture studies assigned by Albin Polasek for his Art Institute of Chicago School studio class. The clay heads were exceptional for a part-time painting student's first attempts at sculpture and marked a turning point in Barthé's artistic career. Within two years of this small but significant exhibition, Barthé received a scholarship to attend his final year at the Art Institute School full-time, followed by a Rosenwald fellowship to create enough sculpture for a one-man exhibition scheduled for June 1930. Under the guidance of black American philosopher and arbiter of taste Alain Locke, Barthé moved to Harlem in 1929 in search of inspiration from and inclusion in the Negro Arts Renaissance already well under way. Harlem, then the nucleus of urban African America, was the epicenter of black American creative arts. Encouraged by Locke and actor/author Richard Bruce Nugent, whom he met in Chicago, Barthé was convinced that not only did black artists flourish in Harlem, but that men like themselves, who preferred the company of men, also made their home in the largest black community in the country.

Shortly after finding a suitable space to live and work, Barthé found that Harlem had some unfortunate limits. His inclusive goals reached well beyond the scope of the New Negro Arts movement that focused on breaking down negative stereotypes with straightforward social realism or what was a form of early Afrocentricism. Integration into mainstream art circles was paramount to the level of success Barthé hoped to enjoy.

As a sculptor with a respectable academic art education, Barthé felt authorized to incorporate the loftiest themes his medium and mentors encouraged. Within a short time, nudes surfaced as Barthé's signature genre; male nudes often overtly influenced by European masterworks.

Barthé hoped that moving to Manhattan would offer him autonomy.

He was, for the first time in his life, out of the South and free from the interference of well-meaning family and friends. Although Barthé had acquired some urban savvy from years of residence in Chicago, he boarded with an aunt who kept family informed of his progress. Discretion with respect to his sexual orientation was nothing new to Barthé, but he was not prepared to be a "race man," or respond to the advances of marriageable women drawn to his good looks and professional respectability. With their high expectations and prying scrutiny, Harlem's striving literati and elite classes loomed large as surrogate family.

Before we take a closer look at Barthé's art, some early biographical information provides a useful foundation for understanding his mature work. Barthé's interest in male anatomy surfaced at an early age and remained a lifelong passion. As a youth, Bernarr Macfadden's *Physical Culture* magazine was Barthé's favorite source for figure drawing models. Copying from *Physical Culture* (with a clear conscience that "decent" people could worship the body) marked the adolescent beginning of Barthé's fascination with the nude. Physically frail throughout his life, Barthé rightly admired the robust bodies pictured in Macfadden's magazine. Dedicated to bodily health, *Physical Culture* contained scantily dressed or completely naked men photographed performing fitness exercises (women in full leotards appeared less often). Although gay men bought the magazine for the bodies in much the same spirit that bodybuilding publications are consumed today, Macfadden promoted a healthy attitude toward nudity. In his opinion, "nastiness exists in the minds of those who view it [nudity], and those who possess such vulgar minds are the enemies of everything clean, wholesome, and elevating" (Chauncey 1994).

Barthé ended his secondary education at age 14. Two years later he acquired his first permanent job as a house servant in New Orleans. His mother's family, the Raboteaus and Rochons, and the Barthés were devout Roman Catholics with deep roots in Louisiana. His position as a domestic lasted seven years, which Barthé remembered affectionately. His rich fantasy life was fueled by New Orleans's lavish street fetes as much as his employers' literary and artistic taste for 19th-century romanticism.

In 1919, at age 18, Barthé met Lyle Saxon, a journalist and amateur artist who would play a significant role in his young adult life. Saxon had impeccable taste in fashion, design, and deportment. He was a notorious Southern dandy embraced by New Orleans' elite as an eccentric historian and stalwart advocate for the restoration of the city's fragile historic districts. Locally respected as a writer, Saxon was also notorious for his sexual exploits with men (Harvey, 1980). The bohemian French Quarter, where elicit goings-on behind courtyard gates were legendary, was his home. Although Saxon was a heavy drinker, he remained steadfastly discreet. Barthé's sincere interest in painting and literature endeared him to Saxon, who earnestly investigated possibilities for his formal art instruction. Unfortunately, Saxon's clout could not defy the color line. No art schools were open to African Americans in New Orleans. In an effort to offset this injustice, Saxon modeled for Barthé, offered criticism, and lent him books from his extensive library. It was here that Barthé was first exposed to Lord Byron and Walt Whitman. As he was a mature artist, a taste for the exquisite and antique was one of Barthé's notable character traits.

Barthé was undoubtedly aware of Saxon's homosexuality, and his ease with Saxon points toward an affinity to the elder's lifestyle. At the threshold of manhood, Barthé became acquainted with the codes and conduct of homosexual men when he entered Saxon's confidence. In a moment of levity, Barthé recalled that during his years in New Orleans Saxon treated him as an equal. Despite their age difference, the two men built a relationship upon shared interests and similar creative urges. The level of intimacy in their friendship remains unknown. Nevertheless, Saxon's fellowship was key to Barthé's development because the older man opened an avenue into well-heeled society within which Barthé would later travel with relative ease.

New York's homosexual networks stretched across cultures, races, genders, and classes, overturning the heterosexist, black American myth that homosexuality was a "white man's disease" (Mercer, 1994). Facts notwithstanding, associating with white gays was blamed for African America's "loss" of a number of black American artists. For some artists, it was preferable to live with racism among whites who tolerated homosexuals than among African Americans who ostracized them. Artistic men functioning "in the life" or on the margins of it, such as Nugent, Locke, Wallace Thurman, Claude McKay, Langston Hughes, Ellis Wilson, and Beauford Delaney were working-class African Americans placed in the ranks of the elite Talented Tenth. Ranking as professionals was relatively new for artists. Before historically black institutions of higher education formed art departments shortly after World War I and black American artists' visibility increased with exhibitions such as those sponsored by the Harmon

Foundation, black American artists were isolated minimum wage–earners who made art in their spare time waiting for that elusive lucky break. Race solidarity was a state of mind for most artists whose primary concern was freedom to express themselves in whatever way their creative energy dictated. These and other artists revered the pains and triumphs of African Americans but were disinterested in limiting their art to service what black American community leaders deemed appropriate portrayals of African America. These were the kind of men bell hooks cites as having willingly "shunned a ready-made patriarchal identity and invented themselves" (hooks 1992). Each in their own way skillfully used art as an autobiographical tool.

With heterosexuality as a formidable decoy, alternative sexual orientations have remained invisible for generations. Further, the demands of making art exempted dedicated men from the typical roles of husband and father. When asked why he never married, Barthé claimed to have spared any potential wife the grief of being married to a devoted professional artist. His art was always given priority, and Barthé's family made a pat answer of "he was married to his art" to that most intrusive question for homosexual men. The number of major contributors to the New Negro arts movement now being revealed as homosexuals continues to grow as scholars explore the role sexuality plays in the creation of art. Barthé effortlessly veiled his homosexuality with his race and reverent spirituality, even though a number of his most successful sculptures were clearly homoerotic. Common knowledge dictates that no God-fearing black man could be queer, therefore, a religious black man need not construct his closet—it is ready-made. Deviations from established norms challenge but may never change those norms.

Barthé came of age at a time when difference was tolerated, while not necessarily accepted, in avant-garde circles. Homosexuals found a relatively safe haven in bohemian urban enclaves. Barthé relocated his studio residence downtown to the outskirts of Greenwich Village since Harlem limited his visibility and accessibility to collectors. At least that was how he explained the move. Leaving Harlem to Harlemites, Barthé finally gained a measure of that most desirable autonomy. The list of visitors to his studio was impressive as random social calls turned into formal interviews for the likes of *Artnews* and *Time* magazine. Networking was essential to the art market, and Barthé attracted key players to his fifth-floor cold-water walk-up in Union Square.

In carefully guarded social circles, black and white gays supported each other emotionally and economically. White gay contemporaries such as Carl Van Vechten, Kenneth Macpherson, and Alfred Kauffman Jr., were financially and socially well-situated patrons who, over time, became friends. Like Barthé, their right to remain closeted was respected without question. Loosely structured "communities" fostered a sense of normalcy and wholeness for individuals otherwise stigmatized by society. As he was a spirited and graceful black man, white men and women anxious to experience life beyond their own confined social circles undoubtedly fetishized him. However, finding common ground with influential and wealthy gay men had tangible advantages for a struggling artist. The onerous social and criminal reprisals that threatened Barthé's generation created support systems and communal bonds between homosexuals that at times transcended race prejudices. Once he settled downtown, Barthé found that his male figures had the potential to be potboilers as much as commissioned portraits because homosexual men favored them.

Social scientists found gays useful as case studies for self-disclosure behaviors because gays, like other "stigmatized individuals," invented codes in order to safely identify each other (Ringer, 1994). Laws prohibiting homosexual practices made coding necessary, even though most were short-lived because vice police and the more ominous civilian blackmailers made it their business to crack them. With this in mind, art historian Jonathan Weinberg argues that the formation of a singularly gay iconography was hindered by social instability. Art critic Allen Ellenzweig disagrees with Weinberg, citing what he called "an iconography of the homoerotic" as evidence of gay communal aesthetics. Ellenzweig asserts that privileging the subjective reception of art "clues us into the puzzle of same-sex relations without violating a given era's social conventions" (Ellenzweig, 1992). Barthé's art was many things to many people. Some believed that intense race pride was *the* point of his figures. Others were convinced that arresting movement at the optimum moment was Barthé's triumphant intent. Still others shared in the desire they felt radiating from sensually detailed limbs and moving expressions on his portrait-quality faces. Perhaps Barthé's work was all of the above. He remained mute about his intentions so that his art could be specific to each viewer no matter the time or circumstances surrounding their encounter.

Intelligence and talent did not guarantee financial solvency, nor did it undo racial prejudices. Although Barthé was embittered by his inability to circulate independently in white society (inclusion was a privilege afforded only when in the company of his white friends), he accepted his "token" status as beneficial even if flawed. Being the only black person in a room was normal for Barthé and preferable for the sale of his art. Exclusivity was key. Once other black American artists began jockeying for market attention as the ranks of American artists were made more inclusive under the 1930s Works Progress Administration art programs, exclusivity, and Barthé's claim to it, were threatened.

Barthé's search for an intimate domestic relationship with another black man was lifelong and unfruitful. In his study of homosexuality and the creative process, psychiatrist Paul Rosenfeld found that denial of "romantic fulfillment" inhibited personal growth, and that romance was creativity's "most essential instrument" (Rosenfeld, 1986). Although his family knew and remained silent in respect for his privacy and/or fear of damaging his reputation, Barthé's feelings for men were important in his life and art. Unfortunately, his fleeting romantic partnerships were unable to survive for any appreciable length of time. Like Winslow Homer before him, or Nugent in his time, the intimate details of Barthé's life were not for public consumption. Nevertheless, his work is punctuated by highs and lows caused, in part, by imagined or actual partners—found, lost, or invented. At times his work was a substitute for human interaction; each figure represented an idealized lover. Desire, and its satisfaction, accounts for the intensity of popular figures such as *Stevedore* or *Feral Benga*. Although he rarely spoke of anything other than platonic love, Barthé was passionate about and appreciative of those who knew him and allowed him to be himself.

Formal studio photographs portray Barthé as a clean-cut and serious intellectual. With a somewhat smug expression, the impeccably dressed and groomed Barthé literally was, using the epithet of the 1960s race-pride movement, young, gifted, and black. Despite the demands of a notoriously fickle and racist art market, Barthé's talent with the human figure gained enough notice in New York to afford him financial stability at certain intervals. Most of the time he survived with the help of concerned friends and patrons who helped him maintain his elitist profile, at least when out in the open. Reserved in public, Barthé depended upon his self-confident figures to speak for him. As meticulous about the finish on his work as his haberdashery, the surfaces of his sculptures retain delicate traces of the sculptor's hand, even after casting. Patina was carefully monitored in the foundry, and plaster casts that Barthé executed himself in his studio were given faux finishes that imitated bronze and marble with amazing accuracy.

Barthé's art contains specific autobiographical notes, some more apparent than others. Many can never be retrieved. He reveled in the freedom of his imaginative noncommissioned works. These figures offer the most poignant clues to who he was and how he fit into his time. Barthé admired from afar vibrant and erotic dancers on the professional stage, vital youths as he faced midlife, and massive, working-class men in glorification of a physical presence he could never hope to attain. His two known self-portraits (both lost to us, save a few faded photographs) exposed Barthé's fragile psychological state at key moments in his career. The second of the two, created at the height of his popularity around 1939, was a mask, jagged at the edges and mounted on a post. It appeared like a death mask, as if lifted from life, yet only an empty impression. As his notoriety grew, Barthé wore an invisible mask to protect himself from his celebrity. The impressive technique and daringly sensual compositional choices that dazzled audiences were conceived in his studio where the mask could be removed. Barthé was drawn to and feared the attention, always uncertain about where it was rooted; in his race or his talent. He knew celebrity could vanish at any moment. Interest in "blackness" had waned by 1940 and, as abstraction found favor in American art markets, his ability to deftly model a figure held less currency than it had only a decade earlier.

Unlike Augusta Savage, a gifted colleague who took naturally to teaching, Barthé had not considered teaching until 1936, when Langston Hughes introduced him to a young Ralph Ellison, then interested in becoming a sculptor (Rampersad, 1986). Working steadily at commissions, Barthé enthusiastically took on the role of mentor. He advocated rigorous and uncompromising academic exercises that must have contributed to Ellison's change of heart about sculpture. Consequently, Ellison's apprenticeship under Barthé was tumultuous and short-lived. Shortly thereafter, Ellison turned to creative writing. Since the particulars of their relationship remain undocumented, it appears as if the two men never met.

A few years later, Savage sent the aspiring sculptor John Rhoden downtown to Barthé because of his strong interest in the human figure. Barthé's second student, 17 years his junior, was willing to learn sculpture Barthé's way. Within a short time, a friendship formed that transcended the initial student-mentor arrangement. Rhoden remembered how Barthé swore by rigorous drawing assignments that taught him more than he cared to know about human anatomy. Barthé hoped their friendship would eventually mature into a life commitment, but shortly after Rhoden moved into the studio, he made it clear that their relationship would remain platonic.

Barthé accepted Rhoden's decision with grace, but his deeply felt disappointment irrevocably damaged the friendship. Thereafter, Rhoden kept his distance, and after his marriage in the mid-1950s, the relationship between the men dissolved. Today Rhoden is a well-known and respected sculptor. His sumptuous and fluid female nudes possess sensuous qualities that, while uniquely his own, carry the mark of his early anatomy training with Barthé.

The years that Barthé shared his studio with Rhoden were some of his most productive. The nudes invented during this time reflect a light-hearted whimsy missing in earlier works. *Boy With a Flute* is a superlative example from this period. The model for this piece was Allen Meadows, a boy in his early teens who was probably spotted on the street and propositioned by Barthé to model. Very little is known about Meadows's background, but for a time he circulated among the likes of illustrator Prentiss Taylor, Carl Van Vechten, and Barthé (Kellner, 1987). Van Vechten photographed Meadows shortly after he posed for Barthé. Those photographs, both camp and pornographic, document Barthé's penchant for idealization of the body and his complicity with Van Vechten's often tasteless portrayals of black sexuality. While the artistic merit of Van Vechten's photographs provokes debate, they are indispensable traces of an era seen through the eyes of a contemporary aesthete who gained access to the most elite sectors of African America. Picturing blacks was so steeped in sociopolitical commentary that Van Vechten's photograph of Meadows tied to a tree in a forest setting with arrows between his legs denoting the gay icon St. Sebastian evoked upsetting lynching imagery. No manner of fantastical dramatics or theatrical props overpower the sadomasochistic display of a naked black body in bondage. Yet when Barthé received prints from Meadows's sessions, he complimented Van Vechten, wishing that Meadows had been more relaxed before the camera.

In contrast, Meadows, a rough-around-the-edges pubescent with gangly limbs, was transformed by Barthé into a broad-shouldered, Pan-like imp with enviously defined tapered legs. This was Barthé's second and last life-size nude completed shortly after the tragically limp figure in *The Mother*. Unlike the lynched victim in *The Mother*, *Boy With a Flute*'s was lively and sensual. Barthé hollowed out the eyes, creating a penetrating and mysterious void that offset the mischievously carefree demeanor. Positioning Meadows as a flute-playing nude was an open reference to Arcadian scenes favored by 19th-century artists such as F. Holland Day and Thomas Eakins. Further, Barthé's reference to Pan, the mythological figure repeatedly rejected because of his ugliness (and from whose name *panic* was derived), was an astute remark on how Eurocentric standards of beauty destroy African Americans' ability to sense their difference as attractive. For, even as we enjoy the aesthetic qualities of *Boy With a Flute,* pleasure is taken in the art object and not the blackness it represented.

Like Barthé, *Boy With a Flute* also wore a mask. The boy brings to mind a satyr; an idyllic deity of Greek mythology devoted to Dionysian merrymaking. To temper the figure's eroticism, Meadows's genitals were minimized, and by rendering his hands slightly oversized and animated over the unusual flute, our attention was directed upward. A voracious reader, words often moved Barthé with a force equal to visual signs. He, and several of his circle, read *Dark Rapture: The Sex-Life of the African Negro* by Felix Bryk, essentially a work of literary pornography published as pioneering research on African peoples in 1939. The book caused quite a stir among black American gays because it contained information about homosexuality in so-called "primitive" societies. This was an odd kind of ancestral confirmation that homosexuals were a part of black history and genealogy. Barthé was most likely acquainted with the book. In 1942 he exhibited the head of *Boy With a Flute* at Chicago's Southside Community Center as *Dark Rapture.* Perhaps it was merely a coincidence that the book *Dark Rapture* contains a section devoted to homosexuality accompanied by a photograph of an African boy playing a flute, or that Beauford Delaney, a fellow black American gay artist also titled his long-limbed, black nude *Dark Rapture* in a painting from 1941 (Leeming, 1998).

From the onset of his career, Barthé tested the limits of an American art market whose interest in African America's artistic endeavors fluctuated up and down throughout his lifetime. He took a compositional gamble and lost when he made the exhibition version of *Boy With a Flute* life-size. *Boy With a Flute,* although recognized in 1940 as "highly illusory," was brushed aside as a mere "exercise in the anthropomorphic." The figure, flaunting its undeniably agreeable eroticism, is unengaged with its audience much like Barthé's self-absorbed *Black Narcissus* (1929). Its gaze is inwardly directed. This fanciful snake charmer was out of step with acceptable black images such as those Locke published in his 1940 survey. Although *Boy With a Flute* was featured in the 1939 Whitney Annual, the 20-inch maquette was cast in bronze and sold while the larger work, with an unabashedly sexual aura that demanded considerable physical and empathetic space, was eventually destroyed.

Even as he narrated his life with his sculpture, Barthé's public had limited knowledge about him. The tenderness with which Barthé addressed male sensuality was overtly homoerotic, but remained unacknowledged until the late homosexual writer Eric Garber mentioned, in passing, that a "gay sensibility was evident throughout [Barthé's] work" (Duberman et al, 1989). Does one need be a homosexual to recognize this gay sensibility Garber referred to? What it means to be "in the life" is not yet common knowledge, but today the nuances of gay and lesbian experience are more than ever out in the open. Barthé's work made homosexuals proud of his artistic talent and titillated by his audacity at a time when silence was golden.

Are there distinct homosexual cultures? Is there a recognizable homosexual aesthetic? There is no point in debating the fact that, historically, a significant number of artists have been and continue to be homosexual. Prior to the increased visibility of homosexuals in the last two decades of this century, sexual orientation was considered inconsequential to cultural development or aesthetic experience. Sexuality (read: heterosexuality) was an intangible feature in relation to the visibility, and hence viability, of race or ethnicity to identity development. Historian James Saslow cited this culture debate as a major obstacle to the academic advancement of gay and lesbian studies as a viable discipline (Saslow, 1986). Scholars such as Gregory Woods and Emanuel Cooper supported Saslow's work by documenting the existence of a unique gay aesthetic. Among the many figures in art and literature that have attracted male homosexual admiration, Saint Sebastian and Walt Whitman are consistently cited as important icons.

The cult status of Saint Sebastian and Whitman among gay men translates across race, class, ethnicity, and even nationality. It betrays a widespread cohesion among gay men concerning the specificity of certain images to their community. Saint Sebastian appealed to a genteel class of men. The martyr's popularity with 15th and 16th-century Renaissance masters (Reni, Ribera, Mantegna, and Botticelli, among others) fostered a high-art profile for Sebastian, even though these artists merged his Christianity with overt sadomasochistic eroticism. Whitman, in contrast, was the quintessential American poet of the working classes. Democratic, egalitarian, patriarchal, and accessible, his *Leaves of Grass* (1860) personified what has been described as a "common language" known to homosexual men (Groff and Bermann, 1996). A mention of interest in Whitman's writing was one of the safest and most enduring homosexual codes. *Leaves of Grass* has been illustrated by generations of male artists, among them Rockwell Kent, Charles Cullen, Edward Weston, and most recently, photographer Frank Yamrus. These artists visualized "manly love" as undeniably homoerotic. Barthé kept a framed reproduction of Thomas Eikens's portrait of Whitman on his bureau and created representations of Saint Sebastian, both overt and veiled, beginning while still in art school.

Barthé found he was quickly forgotten shortly after expatriating to Jamaica in 1949. While living on the island he composed his final portrayal of Saint Sebastian. This was one of several paintings executed in 1957 when Barthé returned to two-dimensional mediums after 20 years of sculpting. This Saint Sebastian has a particular autobiographical significance. More alone in Jamaica than at any other point in his life, Barthé had time and solitude to contemplate his life. The picture of Saint Sebastian was painted when Barthé was mentally and emotionally unstable. The years of rejection by African America, he felt, unjustly inflicted upon him, weighed heavily on his mind. While we can sense the artist as a voyeur outside the two earlier works in sculpture, here artist and model became one. In isolation, the artist separated himself into two distinct people: Richmond, the man and Barthé, the artist. He was both executor and executed.

Barthé's disconnection in Jamaica was self-imposed, and the arrows in his painting of Saint Sebastian represented self-inflicted wounds. After painting this last Saint Sebastian, Barthé inserted a sliver of wood—a pin carefully positioned in a voodoo fetish doll—under the canvas as if into exposed flesh. At one and the same time, his art was keeping him sane *and* driving him mad. With head thrown back and away from the viewer, Sebastian accepted his fate no longer anticipating salvation from death. Throughout his life, Barthé went about uncovering what eluded the common eye. He portrayed actors as saints and gardeners as prophets in hopes that his art would speak not only for itself, but also tell his story.

Art historians have interpreted the classical nude as noble and natural. Modern life, more outspoken and honest, sexualized the nude. In African America, nudity and nakedness are synonymous; nakedness denotes either poverty or fornication. black American people still suffer from a debilitating loss of agency. Regardless of European classical tradition, wounds inflicted centuries ago by slavery remain unhealed going into the new millennium. The unclothed black body cannot be nude—it is a naked, deprived, unbearably lacking image. The unclothed black body belongs behind closed doors. As a consequence, black American artists committed to the depiction of their people have avoided the nude.

Barthé revealed his homosexuality from the beginning of his career when he exhibited his boldly composed male nudes. He stands out as the singular black American artist of his generation who centered his work on the nude. Because the artist never spoke out about his sexual orientation, we will never know if this thematic choice was a conscious, revelatory effort. But, as art critic David Martocci made plain in his essay for *The Male Nude*, "Being nude is an act of rebellion. Artists, consciously or unconsciously, declared their independence from societal restraint through the depiction of the nude body" (Martocci, 1980). While enduring inequitable and, at times, demoralizing treatment, African Americans understandably cherish all liberating experiences. The nude liberated Barthé.

Writers concerned with African America hesitate consulting psychoanalysis or other progressive methods of reading art because distancing black issues from Eurocentric theories to preserve the virtuous profile of black role models remains paramount to black American revisionist history. Arnold Rampersad correctly assessed that analysis, based on progressive Freudian theories, has the power to destroy cherished myths spun around African America's heroes, specifically that they were "centrally impelled in their careers by a desire to champion the race" above and beyond all other concerns (Rampersad, 1989). Few outsiders read Barthé's childhood interests in Macfadden's magazines or his obvious disinterest in marriage as signs of homosexuality. Homosexuals, even in the face of progressive research and media exposure of positive contributions made by gays and lesbians, continue to be regarded by the majority of heterosexuals as disturbed and unnatural.

Just as race made Barthé's homosexuality invisible to the general public, being a sculptor made his eccentricities excusable. Contrary to popular theories that self-hatred doubles when race and sexual orientation are combined, Barthé identified positively with his homosexuality even though he concealed it. He thrived in an encouraging and inspiring atmosphere among like-minded people. This positive identification held the artist together at times when negative forces threatened his sanity.

Sustained participation in black American communities was not necessary for Barthé to be counted among the accomplished few. During his early years in the public eye, relationships with men such as Saxon and Van Vechten made Barthé a target for those who resented his popularity with white society. His friendships with homosexuals fueled rumors he eventually learned to ignore. While most knew he was homosexual, his homosexuality was never used against him in public. He was perceived as a member of the significantly entitled black American elite whose idiosyncrasies were tolerated because of their model status in society at large. African America could not afford to ignore the good works of such an accomplished and highly visible black man. As long as Barthé remained discreet, he was honored and revered. Silence was all that was required of him, just as silence is used today to placate a homophobic America. Barthé did not leave a silenced legacy. Look a bit closer at his art. The real story is there for the taking.

References

Ames, W. "Contemporary American Artists: Richmond Barthé." *Parnassus* (March 17, 1940).

Barthé to Van Vechten, 21 March 1940, *Carl Van Vechten Papers*, Beinecke Rare Books and Manuscript Library, Yale University, New Haven.

Chauncey, G. (1994). *Gay New York: Gender, Urban Culture, and the Making of the Gay Male World, 1890-1940*. New York: Basic Books.

Cooper, F.W. (1987). *Claude McKay: Rebel Sojourner in the Harlem Renaissance*. Bloomington: Indiana University Press.

Crump, J.F. (1994). "Holland Day: 'Sacred' Subjects and 'Greek Love'." In *History of Photography*, vol. 18, no.4 (Winter): 322-366.

Duberman, M.B. et al. (Eds.). (1989). *Hidden From History: Reclaiming the Gay and Lesbian Past*. New York: New American Library.

Edgar, T. (1994). "Self-Disclosure Behaviors of the Stigmatized: Strategies and Outcomes of the Revelation of Sexual Orientation. In *Queer Words, Queer Images*, edited by R. Jeffrey Ringer. New York: New York University Press..

Ellenzweig, A. (1992). *The Homoerotic Photograph: Male Images from Durieu/Delacroix to Mapplethorpe*. New York: Columbia University Press.

Garber, E. (1939). "A Spectacle in Color: The Lesbian and Gay Subculture of Jazz Age Harlem,." In *Felix Bryk, Dark Rapture: The Sex-Life of the African Negro*. New York: Walden.

Groffmann, D. and Berman, R. (Eds.). (1996). *Whitman's Men: Walt Whitman's Calamus Poems Celebrated by Contemporary Photographers*. New York: Universe Publishing.

Harvey C. (1980). *Lyle Saxon: A Portrait in Letters, 1917-1945*. Tulane University. Unpublished Ph.D. dissertation.

hooks, b. (1992). *Black Looks: Race and Representation*. Boston: South End Press.

Kellner, B. (Ed.). (1987). *Letters of Carl Van Vechten* New Haven: Yale University Press.

Leeming, D. (1998). *Amazing Grace: The Life of Beauford Delaney*. New York: Oxford University Press.

Martocci, D. (1980). *The Male Nude* (ex. cat., Massachusetts: Sterling and Francine Clark Art Institute). (n.p.)

Mercer, K. (1994). *Welcome To The Jungle*. New York: Routledge.

Rampersad, A. (1986). *The Life of Langston Hughes,* Vol. 1. New York: Oxford University Press.

Rampersad, A. (1989). "Psychology and Afro-American Biography." *The Yale Review*, vol. 78, no. 1: 1-18.

Rosenfeld, P. (1986). *Homosexuality: The Psychology of the Creative Process*. New York: Libra Publications.

Saslow, J. (1986). *Ganymede in the Renaissance: Homosexuality in Art and Society*. New Haven: Yale University Press.

Watson, S. (1995). *The Harlem Renaissance: Hub of African Culture, 1920-30*. New York: Pantheon.

Weinberg, J. (1993). *Speaking For Vice: Homosexuality in the Art of Charles Demuth, Marsden Hartley and the First American Avant-Garde*. New Haven: Yale University Press.

Heterosexism and Homophobia in Popular Black Music

Any Love:
Silence, Theft, and Rumor in the Work of Luther Vandross

Jason King

Lonely house, lonely me!
Funny with so many neighbors. How lonely it can be!
Oh lonely street! Lonely town!
Funny you can be so lonely with all these folks
around.

The night for me is not romantic.
Unhook the starts and take them down.
I'm lonely in this lonely house
In this lonely town.
                        —"Lonely House," words by Langston Hughes,
                                       music by Kurt Weill

A chair is still a chair, even when there's no one sitting
there
But oh, a chair is not a house,
And a house is not a home when there's no one there
to hold you tight
And no one there you can kiss good-night...
                        —"A House Is Not A Home,"
                  words by Hal David, music by Burt Bacharach

1947: Langston Hughes writes the lyrics to Kurt Weill's classical opera, *Street Scene* (based on Elmer Rice's play of the same name). The show's most captivating arioso is "Lonely House," in which a young male tenor cries out for a romantic partner to "fill" the emptiness of his house. Though it has now become a jazz standard, "Lonely House" is a rare sentimental song about male romantic longing within the context of domestic space. Although critics of the era make mention of the unique collaborative effort between its Negro lyricist and its German-American composer, few catch the complex portrayal of male sexuality so effortlessly tucked into Hughes's lyrics.

1992: filmmaker Isaac Julien directs the independent short *Looking for Langston*. Nonlinear in narrative and abstract in concept, the film fastidiously opposes the way Hughes has been memorialized in mainstream culture as heterosexual, and attempts to reclaim the literary icon as a gay artist. Julien declares that he intended the project to redefine the closet as "an era of *knowledge* especially in black popular culture" (my italics, qtd in Grundmann 1995, 30). Yet the controversial film ultimately "outs" Hughes to the mainstream public, and Julien ends up in a legal wrangling with the relatives in charge of the poet's estate. As a critical project, however, the film invites a reevaluation of the Hughes canon. What does it mean that the lyrics to "Lonely House" may have been composed by a black gay man? What's more, *Looking for Langston* asks its audiences to reconsider African American cultural and collective memory as a field of ethical and political contestation: Who do we remember? How do we remember, and why?

1981: Luther Vandross debuts on the R&B scene with another song of male domestic yearning, "A House is not a Home." A stunning reworking of Dionne Warwick's 1964 original (penned by Burt Bacharach and Hal David), the song helps bring Vandross worldwide success, and it still stands, in the eyes of many of his fans, as the defining artistic triumph of his career. Although Vandross releases, over the 1980s and 1990s, a bevy of platinum and double platinum albums chock full of original material, he is perhaps most cherished for his remakes of popular songs of the 1960s and 1970s. Although critics tend to praise Vandross's body of work, few have addressed the complex issues surrounding male sexuality and desire that constitute his musical achievements and star discourse.

Although parallels between the work and life of Hughes and Vandross seem rather explicit, even from a comparative reading of the epigraphs with which I open this paper, I am not aware of any writer yet who has openly claimed Vandross in terms of his contribution to queer cultural politics (as Julien did with Hughes). I want to note up front that I have no interest per se in Vandross's "real" offstage sexual identity, if only because there is no "real" Vandross that can be ascertained or ever truly known. His discourse, like that of all celebrities, is a collection of images, ideas, representations, artistic and informational data, advertisements, clues, and conversations, that in the end do not amount to any integral knowledge that could be claimed as "authentic." Sorry, I have no low-down information to pass along about

Vandross's offstage sexual practices. Nor am I interested in the practice of "outing," a cynical and last-ditch tactic that lately has become almost procedural and commonplace.

Yet despite Vandross's preeminence as a conduit of romantic ideals, the singer has remained remarkably cryptic about his sexuality in the public realm. Unlike most celebrities, the public Luther Vandross has yet to be "attached" romantically to anyone, nor has he publicly specified the gender of his object choice. During his June 27, 1990 appearance on *Oprah,* Vandross is asked by an audience member if there is "one specific person" who inspired his romantic ballad "Here and Now." Vandross deflects the question by replying simply: "Well, yes. Next question."

I believe it is possible to wrestle over the meanings of such ambiguity toward a "queer" reading of Vandross's reconstructions of old, sentimental pop songs. In this essay I use *queer* not exclusively in the sense of gay or homosexual, nor in the sense of "odd" or "weird" (although certainly these terms are inextricably folded, and most welcome, within the connotative meanings of *queer* itself). Instead I draw upon the term *queer* mindful of the way it is mobilized by John Hguyet Erni when he says, "the queer body is an adventure in *surplus representations*" (my italics, Erni 1998, 161). The surplus in Vandross's work—all the residual effects that lie outside of assumed intentions and "official" meanings proscribed to the music—is what positions the singer as a queer icon. Further, it could be argued that the experience of being colored in modernity itself is an adventure in surplus or excess representations. I would then propose that Vandross's cover of "A House is Not a Home," in the context of his body of artistic work and his celebrity discourse, can be reasonably imagined as an act of creative expression that is borne from the state of being both black and gay.

Many black gay and lesbian cultural critics have demonstrated how problems of silence and invisibility in black communities might foreclose the possibility of a progressive cultural politics (Riggs 1989; Hemphill 1992; Julien 1992; Mercer and Julien 1994; Goldsby 1995; Harper 1996; Rowell 1996). With respect to this pioneering work and its contributions, I want to bring attention to the way certain forms of representational silence might actually produce the possibility for the transformation of racialized gender and sexuality. Compounded by his proximity to discourses of—and artistic conventions associated with—femininity, and the circulation of rumor within queer communities that decidedly posits the singer as gay, Vandross's refusal to disclose his sexuality may have inspired, in ways that have yet to be explored, the reconstruction of sexual politics in the black communities.

I would argue, then, that Vandross's ambiguous star text is polysemous, in the sense that it generates a number of different and equally persuasive meanings for a variety of cultural readers. At the same time, Vandross's work calls for a rethinking of how audiences cognitively understand—and then make use of—cultural texts. Through an analysis that seeks to redress the value of silence, theft, and rumor in regard to popular representation and readership, this essay considers Vandross's impact on queer communities of color in terms of his implicit role in the (re)construction and (re)articulation of male sexualities in and beyond the early 1980s. Zeroing in on a reading of "A House is Not a Home," this essay aims toward three ends: to reclaim the political effects of black sentimentality; to demonstrate the value of black cultural practices that are reconstructive in nature; and to reconsider the power of silence at this historical moment in which the imperatives of identity politics surrounding visibility and representation threaten to obscure more complicated processes of how identities are manifested and negotiated in everyday experiences.

RECONSTRUCTING A HOUSE

"I lived for the love of music. Maybe that's why when everyone was forming couples and falling in love, when romance was all around me, I missed out. I was distracted. My passion was in the headphones. My life was in the headphones. It might have been lonely in there, but I had no choice. By then, music was an obsession. It still is" (Luther Vandross quoted in Ritz 1990, 80).

The song "A House is Not a Home" appears on Luther Vandross's 1981 debut album, *Never Too Much* (Epic Records). Before his emergence as a solo artist, Vandross worked as a songwriter of modest success, a jingle singer for television commercials and radio, and as a backup singer for artists as diverse as Roberta Flack, Bette Midler, Todd Rundgren, and David Bowie. Near the outset of Ronald Reagan's first presidential term, Vandross found himself in the throes of success: first with the infectious title track and later with the towering release of his version of "A House Is Not a Home."

The 1964 original is one of the many songs written by the famous songwriting team of Burt Bacharach and Hal David that helped catapult Dionne Warwick to success in the 1960s. Although she is unfortunately known in many circles these days as "the psychic lady" as a result of her hugely successful telephone network, Warwick publicly emerged in the throes of the Civil Rights movement as a stunning emblem of black femininity and crossover potential.

Substantive yet light and pure, Warwick's stylish voice, in the 1960s, was mannered but emotionally charged. (It's dropped from a mezzo-soprano to a contralto since then.) Performing Bacharach's and David's intensely musical—if melodramatic—material, Warwick's early sound seemed hard to pin down in terms of musical style. Was it gospel? R&B? Pop? All three? (Twenty years later, Warwick's niece, Whitney Houston, would rise to superstar status by drawing on the same strategy of stylistic ambiguity.) The "newness" of this melange of styles brought Bacharach's and David's material a tremendous amount of crossover appeal that it might not have otherwise received. To boot, the very visibility of crossover icons such as Warwick and Diana Ross and the Supremes seemed, in the mid 1960s, to provide new possibilities for racial integration. If one could cross over on the charts, perhaps one might cross over in everyday life too—or so the argument seemed to portend.

Yet crossover music, and its emphasis on mannered style, has always maintained a tenuous relationship to black nationalist projects. If the public ascendance of icons such as Warwick seemed to signal changes in processes of exclusion by race, the overt sentimentality of her music and lyrics (not to mention the visibility of Warwick's close relationship with two white songwriters) might have seemed to challenge, in certain circles, possibilities for a radical black and/or feminist consciousness. While it may be too ambitious to imagine that every pop cultural production has to be somehow related to progressive politics, it's equally hard to deny how distant the original "A House is Not a Home" was from the racially charged turbulence of 1960s America. "A House Is Not a Home" is wrapped up in the silence of what it can't say, or couldn't say, about the era in which it was produced. Moreover, the lyric comes out of a crusty tradition in which lyricists (usually men) imagine women as passive, waiting at home for a lover to return. In the liner notes to a recent Warwick musical retrospective, the writer asks "Were Warwick, Bacharach, and David mirroring the times in their many hits, reflecting a social reality that generally regarded women as being at the mercy of men? Or did they just work their magic best when the theme was unrequited love?" (Widner 1989)

Warwick's early stardom should also be considered in its historical context of the 1960s in relation to certain "countercultural" icons such as Abbey Lincoln, Nina Simone, and Odetta. These black female singer-songwriters were perceived by many at the time, and certainly in contemporary times, to have a more explicit and contemplative relationship to the politics of black revolution. In contrast, Warwick's "A House is Not a Home" stands within, rather than outside of, a tradition of conventional narratives allotted to females in pop and R&B. In the end, there's a limited radicality to the original "A House Is Not a Home." Even by the early 1970s Bacharach and David's schmaltzy musical style, which had taken the charts by storm just ten years earlier, was widely considered trite, kitsch—the laughing stock of a bygone moment in American popular culture.

Although the historical, sociocultural, and political context in which "A House is Not a Home" emerged cannot be easily removed from the distributional effect of the song itself in 1964, I am not attempting to enforce any singular, fixed meaning on the song. Instead, I am interested in redeclaring consumer agency by demonstrating the valuable results that emerge from the restoration of pop cultural materials that have been publicly memorialized, and derided, as kitsch. Vandross's resplendent 1981 cover of Warwick's saccharine 1964 hit single must be considered from this angle. Cultural critic Manthia Diawara has previously argued that Afro-Kitsch, in its promotion of "mass identifications through authenticity, repetitions, sequels and imitations," bears a strained relationship to revolutionary politics in the black public sphere (1992, 285-91). "Can kitsch make new?" Diawara asks. While the author seems to respond no, the question remains, for the most part, largely unanswered.

Vandross's seven-minute, seven-second version of "A House is Not a Home" engages but surpasses traditional processes of restoration in cultural practice. His version is more than a rereading, a term that tends to imply an artist's unusual or unconventional take on an original text. It's far from a remake, a term which calls to mind a mimetic or only slightly altered copy of the original. Not a misreading, either, which occurs when an artist's improper and unfulfilled reading of an original allows certain meaning to performatively circulate outside of that artist's intent (see Lipsitz 1994, 158-170). I would be willing to consider Vandross's version as a sort of overreading of Warwick's original, which would, without implying any faulty work on the part of the artist, mean that the reading explodes the containment of meaning in the original, thereby engendering any number of surplus and unintentional readings (see Martin 1998). Yet I would more readily classify

Vandross's version as a reconstruction, which would imply that he restructures the original in ways that reorient both the melodic and lyric foundations of the original as well as its performative cultural and political effects.

The term *reconstruction* also links my reading of his text to a crucial history of strategic positionings, identifications, and redressings of minority groups in modernity and commodity capitalism. Over the 1980s and 1990s, Vandross has become especially famous for his reconstruction of popular songs, including Marvin Gaye's "If This World Were Mine," The Carpenters' "Superstar," and Major Harris's "Love Won't Let Me Wait." (His 1994 *Songs* failed largely because the album consisted of songs mostly from the 1960s and 1970s, including "Always and Forever" and "The Impossible Dream," which were well-produced, but less reconstructions than plain-Jane remakes.) Vandross's reconstructive efforts, including "A House Is Not a Home," have been previously described in such celebratory fashion: with "pastel washes of strings, riffing piano arpeggios, elaborate but intimate backup vocals, and gently propulsive rhythm tracks, the arrangements turn songs of no particular literary distinction into emotional landscapes that constantly change color" (Holden 1982, H21).

Despite his ability to craft original up-tempo tunes, Vandross's greatest success is his definitive skill as a sentimental balladeer. I would argue that he is, preeminently, a skillful reconstructor of black pop cultural artifacts. In this light, Vandross is not merely a musical artist but an archivist. As exemplified in *Looking for Langston,* the process of archival reconstruction occurs through subjective processes of critical memory. Vandross's tendency toward reconstruction in his art shows once again that the making of human history is dependent on the excesses of the creative imagination. All access to history is interpreted through subjective eyes. It is the same mix of historical fact and imaginative speculation that allows me to propose a queer reconstruction of Vandross's celebrity even though his sexuality remains something of a secret.

If Warwick's "A House is Not a Home" can be likened to a club soda, Vandross's version is more like an expensive glass of sparkling champagne. (The class polarity of that metaphor is crucial to this discussion.) Arranged by Vandross and Leon Pendarvis, the 1981 version begins with a series of cascading and descending keyboard arpeggios, backgrounded by a timpani's promise of rhythm. There's a brimming quality of "liveness" about the recording, right from its opening moments, and a sense of virtuoso mastery behind the arrangement. (In time, Vandross would come, of course, to be known as a masterfully perfectionist singer in live concerts, able to recreate—no, reconstruct—the sound of his recordings in live arenas. What's more, the low-key video for "A House is not a Home" simply films the singer lip-synching the track in a recording studio. The direction of the video seems to attempt to recover the liveness of Vandross's star image in spite of the canned music and the partial disappearance of presence frequently assumed in recorded mediums, video and audio alike. As the harp, bass, acoustic guitar, ascending strings, and drums flood the track, Vandross's lithe, airy vocal comes into the foreground, scatting the melody as if he were attempting to separate the air.

The tempo is decidedly slower, more deliberate, and more rubato than Warwick's chugging original, although the sense of explosive possibility is retained in Vandross's project. The extended scat intro is added here, along with the intermediary a tempo measures, and the extended vamp ending in which Vandross improvises, both melodically and lyrically, off the final phrase "still in love with me." There is a refined majesty about Vandross's version, a quality that is present in Warwick's production, but only skates on the outer perimeter. Indeed, the drama and the intentional stakes of Vandross's version seem higher, more explicit, as the domestic melodrama becomes amplified. The additional musical silences in the 1981 version—spaces for breath, if you will—open up pauses and breaks in the lyric so that each phrase maintains a greater sense of urgency, critical importance. In other words, the "emptiness" of the house seems complete in the 1981 version.

That emptiness, in turn, foregrounds the control and stillness of Vandross's vocal instrument. An idiosyncratic singer with a large palette of vocal colors, tinctures and textures, Vandross is known for his contemplated and controlled—yet not cold—delivery and interpretation. His reconstructive impulses begin, and take wondrous flight, in his voice. Taking notes at the outset of Vandross's career, Stephen Holden describes how Vandross's vocal delivery reflects a rupture in the short history of black masculine performance in soul music:

Mr. Vandross, who calls himself a "second tenor," has extended this tradition by romanticizing and toning down the physically aggressive style of such soulful belters as Levi Stubbs of the Four Tops and Teddy Pendergrass. Along with even harder-edged soul men such as Wilson Pickett and James Brown,

Mr. Stubbs and Mr. Pendergrass have equated the flexing of vocal muscle with soulfulness: Generally, the louder they sing, the truer and deeper the emotion. But Mr. Vandross, who commands the same massive vocal power, eschews their machismo. Even in passionate moments, Mr. Vandross retains a coherent sense of lyric line, and in emotional climaxes, instead of belting, he draws out key phrases in elaborate, florid melismas, sometimes repeating the same phrase over and over until he's exhausted its emotional possibilities (1982).

Holden is astute to recognize that Vandross's smoothly performed masculinity is profoundly different from that of the singer's peers within black popular music. Yet it's not quite clear from his critique how Vandross's masculinity expresses itself, other than through vocal performance; nor is Holden particularly interested in the effects that such reconstructed masculinity might portend for the communities who buy Vandross's records. For I must state the obvious: What precisely differentiates Vandross's song from the Warwick's original is his maleness. Like Langston Hughes's "Lonely House," "A House is Not a Home" paints a portrait of a sensitive narrator who longs for—quite simply put—romantic space. While Warwick's performance of the song might have redistributed, rather than reimagined, the available female narratives of passivity, Vandross's performance of the song in 1981 expands the available mainstream representations of black masculinity.

As sung by Vandross, the 1981 version becomes a narrative of male vulnerability, if not outright submissiveness. No longer actively in control of destiny, the male performer of "A House is Not a Home" must sit and wait for his partner to "turn this house into a home." While the portrayal of sensitive black men within domestic space has become old hat by the late 1990s, that project was something of a commercial risk in 1981 when "A House is Not a Home" climbed the R&B charts. Other popular black male singers of that era who professed a self-effacing, smooth and vulnerable masculinity were Lionel Richie, Frankie Beverly of Maze, Peabo Bryson, Ron Isley, Smokey Robinson, Marvin Gaye (although his return to the spotlight would not come till 1983 with "Sexual Healing" from the *Midnight Love* album), and Al Green (who had, at the time, been mostly absent from the R&B charts). Vandross's significant contribution was to reconstruct the R&B "scene" as a site where black men could perform softness to degrees previously unexplored. The success of Vandross's work, in tandem with Richie, Babyface, and others, ultimately helped generate a self-sustaining "alternative" black masculine ethic/aesthetic for black popular music, carried into the late 1990s by acts such as Maxwell, D'Angelo, and R. Kelly. While it still leans toward a conquest-oriented sexuality, this aesthetic/ethic works to redress, or at least provide an alternative to, the narratives of violent masculinity which surface in certain strains of R&B and rap.

No black male balladeer of the 1980s and 1990s has captured so many diverse audiences as Vandross, and no singer has come to so thoroughly affect practices of lovemaking, romance, and intimacy through his music. I would argue that Vandross stood apart from his peer artists in the 1980s partly as a result of his ambivalence to disclose his sexuality—heterosexual, bisexual or homosexual—and through his association with discourses conventionally associated with femininity. The accompanying expansion of black masculinity has also been understood in certain circles as a profound source of threat, and has generated a number of pressing anxieties around the feminization of black musical traditions. We all know that a man who appears too soft or too vulnerable "risks" being considered gay—but the equation is much more complicated than that. Vandross's vision of a sentimental masculinity, I would argue, cannot be separated from elitist class ideals that ruminate in both his artistic work and star discourse. These ideals, in tandem with Vandross's volitional tendency toward an ambiguous silence, begin to account for the way the performer becomes understood as queer in and among certain communities.

RUMOR AND THE IN-BETWEEN SPACE OF KINSHIP

"Loneliness is often a painful and restless time. It leaves its traces in man, but these are marks of pathos, of weathering, which enhance dignity and maturity and beauty, and which open new possibilities for tenderness and love" (Moustakas 1961, 103).

Luther Vandross can't be gay!

In the popular media, Vandross has long been publicized exclusively in terms of his contributions to heterosexual practices of romantic monogamy and lovemaking. In a general American sex survey, Vandross was declared one of the top three favorite performers whose music you'd want to make love to, behind Neil Diamond and Beethoven ("Your Secret Love Interview" on E!, November 14, 1996). One journalist writes that Vandross is specifically "known for giving women chills with his one-of-a-kind voice" (*Ebony* 1996, 94); another claims that his "style of crooning has become almost synonymous with romance and love," and we also learn that he's an "unlikely and somewhat reluctant sex symbol" (Norment 1985, 83). In 1990 Vandross found his biggest commercial hit with "Here and Now," a soaring ballad that celebrates two souls' monogamous union: "Here and now / I promise to love faithfully." Incidentally cowritten by David Elliot, Dionne Warwick's son, the song became a wedding standard, bringing Vandross his first Grammy and only major crossover single. A significant portion of Vandross's audience, based on attendance at his concerts, was composed of black women.

In these specific (and inconclusive) heterosexual contexts, Vandross's peculiar sensibilities for monogamous romance and domestic partnership extend, rather than rupture, the available representations of male sexuality and interpersonal relations in black popular culture. If we only consider in isolation his impact on cultures of heterosexual kinship, Vandross's project is not necessarily reconstructive at all. Rather, his work travels undisturbed along an evolutionary continuum of sentimental black popular culture dealing with themes of love and romance—an exclusively heterosexual continuum with long roots that became especially shot through with promise in the 1970s by popular movies such as *Lady Sings the Blues* (1972), *Claudine* (1974), and *Mahogany* (1976). In these contexts there is a limited radicality to Vandross's reconstruction of "A House Is Not a Home."

But then again—Luther Vandross can't be straight!

In the fugitive cultural spaces outside of the mainstream media, Vandross is understood to be anything but heterosexual. In a recent review, Greg Tate notes that "Luther has spent a portion of his career pooh-poohing rumors of gaiety" (Tate 1998, 68). While the singer has never denied the possibility of his homosexuality, he has never made any confirming remarks. In 1986 Vandross was at the helm of a three-car accident that killed the brother of *Star Search* singer Jimmy Salvemini (see "Fatal Car Crash" and "Luther Vandross Injured"). Outside of the mainstream media, many questioned the extent of the relationship of Vandross to his passengers. On his 1994 album *Songs*, Vandross covers Roberta Flack's 1973 ode to voyeuristic idolatry, "Killing Me Softly With His Song" without altering the gendered pronoun of the lyric and title. His 1996 hit, "Your Secret Love," from the album of the same name, also raised a number of plucked eyebrows. And a song called "Religion" from his 1998 album *I Know* (already suggestively titled) concerns a young man's tensions about his sexual desires: "Little Billy likes his best friend Jack / How in the world could he be like that / Mama and Henry wanna have a chat / Boy, you need religion." To top it all off, the singer's sexual orientation is understood to be common knowledge within many gay communities, despite his silence. Via E-mail, I recently queried a number of men who had previously identified themselves as black and gay. Thirty-four replied. Acting independent (presumably) of each other's respective knowledge, all claimed to know with certainty (and to my knowledge, none of them personally knows the singer), labeling Vandross as decidedly homosexual.

More work needs to be done on the relationship between rumor, cognition, and kinship in minoritarian communities. In the pioneering study of rumor, *The Psychology of Rumor*, the authors inform us that gossip is spread primarily by "suggestible people" and that "it is never under any circumstances safe to accept rumor as a valid guide for belief or conduct" (Allport and Postman 1947, 148). Yet in communities marginalized by race, gender, class, and other markers of identity, receptional evidence is a not a promise, but a luxury. As José Muñoz has clarified, "instead of being clearly available as visible evidence, queerness has instead existed as innuendo, gossip, fleeting moments, and performances that are meant to be interacted with by those within its epistemological sphere—while evaporating at the touch of those who would eliminate queer possibility" (Muñoz 1996, 6; also see 1999). Isaac Julien's reconstructive project on the life of Langston Hughes precisely demonstrates the critical and ethical stakes in regard to receptional evidence. Attempting to reconstruct Vandross as a queer icon is a similarly vexed project since most of the available data (magazine articles, interviews, concert videos, records, liner notes, fan letters) posit him squarely in terms of heterosexual discourses.

Despite the official silences about his sexuality, or perhaps because of them, Vandross is understood within some marginalized communities as a family member, part of the clan. When I questioned black gay male audiences via E-mail, two individuals responded with interesting claims. "He's family," said the first; and the second: "He's one of the children." The metaphor of domestic kinship enacted in these responses (*family, children*) demonstrates how racialized queer readership mandates a reevaluation of how audiences read cultural texts. *Family* and *children* are colloquial expressions in black gay communities. Yet as metaphors, these terms of endearment surpass simple notions of community to suppose an inclusive kinship among strangers.

If we are attentive, we may find a space of inclusion rather than exclusion in between contradictory interpretations of cultural texts. I refer to this space as the in-between space of kinship. Under polysemy, it is often imagined that two groups battle over different interpretations of the message of a given text. Yet black queer cultural readership demonstrates how intimate bonds unite these differing interpretations in ways outside of the critical vocabulary. These bonds may be outside of formal speech, outside of the potential for coherence and articulation—in the same way that sound carries a formal power that lies outside the valence of text. In this case, silence does not necessarily denote a lack of communication. Silence is a realm of possibility unto itself. In the supposed gap between official discourses that work to silence and make invisible public displays of queerness and those underground discourses circulated by marginalized audiences, silence becomes reconstructed not only as knowledge, but also as sentimental kinship ("one of the children"). Kinship and—if we are willing to take a leap of faith—love can offer a revisionist approach to the question of depth in cultural readership.

And yet, to be sure, Vandross's ambivalence to disclose his sexuality works in complicity with heterosexual discourses in a queer fashion. Frequently, Vandross is referred to as, simply, "the voice"—a label that could be taken as complimentary but also suggests the way the singer's talent has been disembodied by a willing public, stripped away from its sociopolitical contexts. Vandross also lacks not only the set of presignified vocal effects of singers such as Teddy Pendergrass, Otis Redding, and Prince, but also their intensely phallic eroticism. (Even Michael Jackson could make a claim to that.) The predominant male soul singer before Vandross arrived on the scene was Pendergrass, whose Gamble-and-Huff produced solo albums in the late 1970s were chart-toppers. Pendergrass's after-hours, "ladies only" concerts, where women willingly threw their underwear onstage, set a new standard for black male sexuality in performance. Vandross has no such ambitions. As one journalist says: "Proffered lingerie is obviously not the way to his heart. When one woman tossed her underwear onstage last year, he said, 'I am not flattered by that. Come and pick up your drawers' " (Karlin and Stapinski 1998, 122).

Underlying the praise for Vandross's music within heterosexual discourse is a contiguous willingness to imagine him as less than "properly" masculine. A 1986 article in *Jet* magazine claims that the "adjective most often attached to singer Luther Vandross's name is 'sensitive.' For thousands of adoring female fans he has become a brother and best friend whose easy, soothing voice is capable of calming many turbulent waters" (my italics, *Jet*, "Fatal Car Crash"). The unnamed writer first limits the possibility of Vandross's work to its effects on and for women. Then the singer is then imagined to be only capable of fulfilling an exclusively filial relationship to women: He's a "brother or best friend" rather than potential partner.

In 1986 Vandross went on a crash diet and eventually shed more than 90 pounds in six months, generating a flurry of national rumors that his weight loss was related to AIDS (*Jet* 1986, "Luther Dispels Rumors," 54). To distance himself from such rumors, Vandross went to several major media outlets to set the record straight by explicitly discussing the terms of his diet. He also successfully sued the British tabloid *Blues and Soul*. Part of the anxiety surrounding Vandross and AIDS in 1986 was related to the silence with which Vandross constructs his sexuality in public discourse. Though it may not be ethical, the impulse behind the AIDS rumors cannot be considered wholly "malicious" since it may have helped some queer communities wrestle Vandross's image and discourse away from the heteronormative impulses that so fully devour the sexual fluidity of black popular culture and representation. If AIDS was stereotypically construed as a "gay" disease in the popular discourse of 1986, then we must at least consider how rumor worked to rescue the singer back toward the surplus elements in his work.

Vandross has also been an accessory, rather than a spectator, of his own "queering." It has always been rather unorthodox for men in popular music to cover female songs. Although the practice is recurrent in drag performance (and drag, at least since the early 1990s, has become eligible for mainstream status), Vandross toys with dominant conventions of male sexuality without engaging in androgyny or explicit forms of traditionally feminine embodiment. The same could not be said, needless to say, for other dominant icons of 1980s and 1990s pop soul, such as Michael Jackson and Prince, whose careers owe a fantastic debt to the trailblazing efforts of drag.

Vandross also disassociates himself from patrilinear conceptions of artistic influence. "I acknowledge what Stevie Wonder, Donny

Hathaway, Tony Bennett, and all the fabulous male singers did,"
Vandross says, "but that's not what aroused my artistic libido" (quoted in Waldron 1985, 54). In countless interviews, he declares the extent
to which his mother Mary Ida has "subliminally" influenced and motivated his work. At the same time, he holds up Aretha Franklin, Diana
Ross and the Supremes, and Dionne Warwick as his primary inspira-
tions for being in the business. "It was the female singers who lit my
fire," he says (qtd. in Holden, 1982).

Vandross's justification for his attraction to female pop and R&B
turns into a critique of machismo and an elaboration of black masculine skilling through active listening. In one article, he says, "A lot of
the time I find male singers plowing their way through songs with this
obsession about being macho and all that. Being strong, being gruff,
being in charge and on top, etc. etc.... Whereas some of the female
singers in the structure of their songs could be questioning in the first
verse, more sure of themselves in the second, bitchy as hell in the third.
I just liked that ride better" (qtd. in Farsides, 1996). Vandross's admiration for the legendary black musical divas has influenced not only his
career choice, but also his approach to the music industry itself. By the
early 1990s Vandross became famous in public discourse for his own
diva personality—he was deemed a perfectionist, and acquired a public reputation for being relentlessly difficult with fellow artists on tour,
including En Vogue and Anita Baker.

Of all the divas in Vandross's life, Dionne Warwick is of special
importance to his career:

> The first time [Vandross] heard the good music of Dionne
> Warwick, in concert at the famed Brooklyn Fox Theater in
> 1963, he vowed to become a singer. "She wiped me out," he
> exclaims. "She knocked me down with that tone quality.
> That's when I made the decision to sing. I wanted to do to
> somebody what she did to me (Waldron 1985, 55).

The unique relationship between Vandross and Warwick calls not
only for a revision of the false binary between "passive" consumers and
"active" cultural producers but also for a revision of the value of cultural theft in minoritarian communities. One of the ways Vandross
reconstructs the 1964 "A House is Not a Home" is by wrestling public memory of the history and authorship away from both the songwriters and the original performer herself. You could say that Vandross

"steals" the song and makes it his own. As Dionne Warwick herself states in the liner notes to Vandross's retrospective collection:

> Riding one day in my car, listening to one of my constant radio stations, KJLH, the beginning of a song familiar and yet different came on. It was a song that I had not only sung many times but had recorded many years ago. Thinking it was going to be an updated instrumental, I listened intently. My thoughts were, "Oh not, not a remake!" Usually they are not anywhere near the original version.
>
> The song was Luther's version of "A House Is Not a Home," and was by no stretch of the imagination a remake. My opinion is that he has the definitive recording of that song!

Born of different generations, the two singers nonetheless became close friends by the mid 1980s. In 1985 Vandross admits that one of his "favorite pastimes is playing Pac-Man with Dionne at his New York City duplex penthouse" (Waldron 1985, 58). Warwick's praise for Vandross's work is far removed from the corporate battles and professional jealousies one hears about when new artists "steal" songs from older, more established ones. An adolescent consumer of Warwick's music, Vandross matured not only to become a cultural producer (he even produced and arranged tracks on her 1993 album *Friends Can Be Lovers*) but also to reconstruct the music that influenced him to produce in the first place. The trajectory of Vandross's career provides a welcome critique of the now-untenable binary between producers and consumers—a binary that still animates the study of performance and culture.

The public friendship of Vandross and Warwick also disavows conventional representations of gender warfare between black men and black women across differing sexualities. The in-between space of kinship—a space that exists in all interpersonal relationships, although here I am specifically referring to those between men and women—has proven most difficult for intellectuals to theorize. In this ambivalent space where love flourishes despite differences in outlook, theft no longer carries the negative resonance of malicious intent. Rather it becomes a progressive cultural technology in which people outside of traditional power structures make use of popular mainstream products to form counternarratives that allow them to better survive. Vandross's work helps illuminate the in-between space of kinship between women and men, and this brings us one step closer to understanding the value of his reconstructive impulses around black sentimental art about romance, intimacy, and love.

BLACK QUEER CROSSOVER

> "Crossing over would be nice, but I wouldn't
> put on a blond wig to do it"
> —Vandross, quoted in Ritz 1990, 77

Vandross is also made queer through his relationship to class aesthetics and aspirations. In terms of genealogical black male performance, Vandross emerges from a tradition of singers such as Nat King Cole, Billy Eckstine, and Johnny Mathis, whose mannered presentation and stylistic performance has been described as "gentlemanly." Always precise in diction and enunciation, these "crooners'"represent contentious figures in black popular culture. While their mannered delivery is seen to cut against prevailing stereotypes of black masculinity as inherently aggressive and threatening, that same delivery is seen to simultaneously erase the possibilities for an insurgent and reactionary black masculinity. The upward mobility embedded in these singers' performances certainly brought these artists greater acceptance in mainstream culture. Yet it often defined their relation to certain black communities as potential race traitors.

By the 1980s Vandross took such gentlemanly presentation to new heights. His stylized presentation borrowed expressly from the Temptations and the stable of related Motown acts. That most of Vandross's influences happen to come from the sentimental/stylistic realm of black performance in the 1960s and 1970s makes his connection to the black-crossover aesthetic complete.

The singer's taste for fashion also clarifies his relationship to upward mobility. Frequently outfitted by his "favorite" designer, the late Gianni Versace, in concert Vandross sports expensive sequined outfits and suits; and, more often than not, he wears a conservatively styled, chemically processed hairdo. The way that Vandross's flair for "low" art (besides his musical tastes for 1960s melodramatic schmaltz, he has a penchant for soap operas); (Waldron 1985) plays out in relation to his acquired tastes for "high" art is the stuff of which intriguing celebrity texts are made.

If the Supremes and Temptations aspired to more than black reception through their trials in Motown's Artist Development Unit and through their attempts to record Broadway songs and land gigs at upper-crust nightclubs such as the Copacabana, Vandross might also seem to be willing to cross over the R&B genealogy from which he emerges. Vandross's work recalls the tension and grandeur of classical European operatic performance, especially when one considers how that style of music is more or less determined by structured arrangements and live instrumentation. The privileging of instrumental effects in Vandross's music seems closely related to classical tropes.

Yet Vandross's relationship to opera runs deeper than mere appropriation—classical aesthetics are embedded symbolically in his star discourse. At times Vandross has been called by critics "The Pavarotti of Pop" (see Holden 1985). Although Vandross reportedly took the label as an insult, this comparison refers to the way the R&B singer has been constructed by the media as the supreme or best male vocalist in popular music (from the time of his debut on the scene in 1981). It also refers to Vandross's highly stylized live performances, which recall the formality of opera as well as the purity and extended tenor reach of his vocal instrument.

Yet the label "The Pavarotti of Pop" can't help but also refer to Vandross's physical size, which controversially fluctuated during the 1980s and 1990s. (When he came on the scene in 1981 he was quite wide in girth.) In the cultural imaginary, there seems to be a conflation between physical largesse and vocal ability to the extent that Vandross's vocal supremacy could possibly be understood in some relation to his physique. Might Vandross's crash diets over the 1980s and 1990s have been partly motivated by his desire to disrupt such easy conflation of size and talent? One article states that Vandross says "his fans have never objected to his weight, but he felt the music critics were focusing more on his size than his music. At one point he was so disillusioned that he stopped making television appearances because he was shy about being on camera" (Norment 1988, 85).

Vandross's immersion in classical aesthetics also plays out in his offstage domestic lifestyle. Indeed, much of the singer's offstage publicity revolves around questions of his house, and as such, I would argue that "A House is Not a Home" is a crucial song through which to understand the singer's importance as an artist. Continually, Vandross fashions himself in terms of high society connoisseur culture. Through articles in *Essence* and *Ebony*, which offer a revealing look at his $8.5 million home and lifestyle, we learn that Vandross is an esteemed artwork collector and has sophisticated, cosmopolitan tastes in interior decoration. "The fact that Vandross's California hideaway is stunning and spacious comes as no surprise to those who are familiar with the velvet-voiced crooner. Vandross is a man known for doing things in a big way, though always within the confines of good taste. And he is also known for demanding quality—in his recordings, his performances, and his work and lifestyle in general" (Norment 1989, 30).

Perhaps taking a clue from the mythical character of Superman, Vandross's favorite color is pink—certainly a welcome but unusual aesthetic choice for an individual of male gender. "If I were not singing, I'd be an interior decorator," he says. "The living room will be done with a leather sofa, carpeting and lacquered walls [all in pink, his favorite color]. It won't be a shocking pink, but a pale, pale pink because it's soothing to me," he says. "The master bedroom will be done in black, with a bathroom dominated by a square black tub complete with a whirlpool, radio, pillow, cassette player and telephone" (Norment 1985, 88). By 1998 Vandross had moved from Beverly Hills to relocate in a $9 million, 25-room mansion in Greenwich, Conn.

Through this active publicizing of the private domestic sphere, there is a kind of cross-lateralization of the singer's queer tastes and styles with his music. Vandross's immersion in royal luxury and possessive materialism explains the praises he is known to receive about his talent: "golden-throated," "silvery-voiced," "everything he touches turns to gold." And Vandross's vision of the domestic as a site for conspicuous consumption extends into the symbolic realm as well. The prime metaphors of his public text—food, love, and romance—and the lack of each, are all elements related to compulsion and consumption. How quickly they conflate: Vandross says "In the past, I'd lose [weight] when I fell in love and then, when the love failed, gain it back. Food and heartache are intertwined within me" (qtd in Ritz 1990, 80); and again: "A good relationship would make me happy. Losing weight would make me happy" (Norment 1989, 88).

Vandross's constant yearnings for stability help classify him as an "authentic" soul singer. Yet, unlike other male singers of the past, Vandross's problems tend to be wholly circulating under the aegis of domestic space, indoors. Vandross invites a critically inflammatory response from critics who still view masculinity and domesticity as sites of contradiction. One of the ways in which contemporary feminists have traditionally sought equality is by leaving the home to go to work, in the process redefining the place of men within and without of domestic space. Vandross becomes feminized in his role as a chief accessory to the reconstruction of the male domestic sphere.

Because of his relationship to crossover and because of his willingness to embody that which is not conventionally masculine, Vandross has been excoriated by a number of prominent music critics. In a 1993 article one reviewer claims that "soul singing is supposed to have sweat in it. It's supposed to be visceral and emotionally involving, and Vandross's too-smooth approach shows none of that" (Considine 1993, 77). In a 1990 article Vandross describes his disdain for one particular English journalist who wrote that the singer lacks the "perspiring passion of a true soul singer." Vandross replied, "Who ever said that you have to fall on your knees to convey emotion? I just wish Otis Redding were alive so he could tell this guy what an asshole he is" (qtd. in Ritz 1990, 80).

Both critics question Vandross's status as an authentic "soul" singer precisely because of his lack of "sweat" or "perspiration"—and I would argue that these terms are crucial to understanding the way Vandross can be read as queer. Vandross is menaced in certain critical circles by his "lack" of masculinity as it relates to his racialized class status and the terms of his artistic labor. The singer's soulfulness, the authenticity of his "blackness," come under fire because of his lack of "masculine" funk. Precisely, Vandross comes to represent the loss of funk in soul.

Nelson George has previously argued that because of the ongoing corporatization of R&B music, the early funk music genre of the 1970s became disarticulated from its political potential (1988). This disarticulation first occurs through the rise of disco, a style of music whose monotony he sees as a capitulation to corporate influences; and then through the rise of "corporate soul" or "retronuevo." Hence, George proclaims, by the late 1980s, the "death of rhythm and blues." From a more comprehensive angle, Paul Gilroy has also made claims for the loss of soul in the 1980s in terms of its disarticulation from funk: "The thing about soul which distinguishes it from funk was its relationship to the idea of embodiment and its very particular attachments to notions of bodily performance, where the voice is the dominant aesthetic issue, nor the rhythm." Later he states, "I think that soul is only soul in relation to funk and without funk it loses something of its value" (1998, 253-254).

Traveling on a less theoretical bandwagon, Brian Ward admits that the smooth new corporate soul of the 1980s, as embodied by Vandross and his peers Anita Baker and Freddie Jackson, marked an expansion of definitions of black style. Yet at the same time, the new soul mandated a hierarchical binary of "middle class audiences who could experience the lush productions and uptown image of glitzy sophistication" of singers like Vandross and the "lower-class black adults who tended to go for darker funk tones, deep soul classics and later for the rap stylings which spoke more directly to their still functionally segregated and disadvantaged black lives" (Ward 1997, 427). Ward's class binary is a conservative, racially problematic one indeed. Vandross's work—and rap too, for that matter—can be, and has been, appreciated across class.

The facts: Vandross wants us to know that his sound has no formal connection to the church. Instead we are to assume that his vocal style comes directly through the crucible of the amateur night circuit. Of course, the aesthetic relationship between amateur night and the church is much more promiscuous than Vandross might want to admit. Violent frenzy (shouting, screaming), which is commonly thought of as a universal black aesthetic, is not present in Vandross's voice. His brand of silent frenzy functions in a different fashion toward a "Quiet Storm" aesthetic. His sound is soft, flowing, smooth—not striated or rough. His music is music you make love to, but you don't *fuck* to it. Yet beyond all this, it is the way the reconstructed soul of artists such as Vandross coincides with the "problem" of black class aspiration that allows critics to express anxieties about the death or loss of soul as a black cultural tradition.

Vandross's antiperspirant performance style and his aesthetic of cool control are deeply linked to a narrative of black corporatization that, I would argue, becomes symbolically linked to anxieties about whiteness, depoliticization and, eventually, queerness. While sensitive and "feeling" singers such as Vandross and his spawns (Babyface and Tony Rich, for example) could in theory be considered key players in a broadening and extension of the possible varieties of available black masculinities, critics instead mount anxieties over the crossover potential of soul in relation to class and whiteness. A queer reading of Vandross's work is then most appropriate, since historically, in the mind of so many black nationalist critics like Eldrige Cleaver, homosexuality has been seen as "the 'extreme embodiment' of a 'racial death wish' negatively conflating homosexual desire with a literal desire for whiteness" (Ongiri 1997, 281). Vandross's upward mobility similarly represents for certain folks a desire for whiteness that would fold the political potential of a radical black consciousness.

One flaw in such critique is that it limits the possible meanings of Vandross's work into a binary of black versus white, never pausing to contemplate how the singer's music is absorbed in different racial contexts, nor across sexualities within an intraracial black context. It is possible to read into the surplus elements of Vandross's work his contribution to the progressive management of masculinities. This contribution contests both the negative evaluation of the feminine, soft aesthetic of 1980s soul that surfaces in critiques of Vandross. It also contests the dominant constructions of the singer as exclusively heterosexual within the public sphere.

ROMANCE IN HARD TIMES

"As was once said of male jazz singers, the modern era sees little necessity for male soul classicists, or more pointedly, Black men who feel very deeply" (Tate 1998, 68)

Like many, if not most celebrities, Luther Vandross has tried to divorce politics from the content of his music. This project is, of course, impossible. In fact, it is only historical and political context that gives his sentimental music social importance. Vandross emerged into visibility in 1981, right on the fading heels of disco culture. (His only two explicit adventures in disco were "The Glow of Love" and "Searching," although his first hit, "Never Too Much," distinctly carries over some of the rhythms of disco.) Vandross's job was to carry the torch of black romantic soul from not only Donny Hathaway, who committed suicide in 1979, but from Teddy Pendergrass, who ruled the R&B scene until 1981. Publicized as a macho playboy and ladies' man until his controversial car crash, Pendergrass in many ways embodies the sexual freedom that emblematized 1970s relationship culture right across the spectrum of sexualities.

Critics have well documented how many gay men in the 1970s practiced cultural politics through the performance of sexual excess and the adoption of a hard phallic machismo indexed in the rise of bodybuilding culture. Vandross not only carried on the musical torch of romantic soul: He helped evolve masculinity in a way that would serve the new, more conservative times to come in the 1980s.

It is rarely acknowledged that Vandross emerged into high visibility at the precise moment that AIDS came to awareness as a public health problem only, supposedly, for queer communities. (It would come to widespread national attention only in 1985 with the death of Rock Hudson—several years too late.) By the early 1980s the disease, which had yet to be formally named, threatened to shut down the way some men had learned to negotiate their identities through sex. Spurred on by the newly astringent homophobia toward the afflicted, AIDS also threatened to harden people's ability to even imagine how to go about cultivating romance, love, and intimacy on an interpersonal level. AIDS also placed a very dim shadow on many men's prospect of sustaining long-lasting gay relationships. The numbing impact of the disease on black gay men's lifestyles—those lifestyles specifically compounded not only by sexuality, but also by racism, poverty, and other social oppressions—continues to be especially drastic.

Vandross's music, especially his reconstruction of "A House is Not a Home," brought, as never before, emphasis to love, sensuality, and compassion at a time when these sentimental values threatened to disappear from the cultural vocabulary. Practicing unprotected sex with random multiple partners—one cause of so much queer celebration in the 1970s—had by the 1980s become the leading cause of infection. Almost in response, Vandross's music celebrated the value of utopian monogamy, while his self-effacing, mannered, and cool presentation directly cut against the grain of hypermasculine behavior that had given such a radical fervor to the performance of male sexuality in the disco era.

We need romance in hard times. What Vandross contributes to both private and public culture in 1981 is feeling, convicted sentiment. His music goes beyond the question: "Can you love in the worst of times?" but instead asks: "Can you afford not to love in the worst of times?" He rarely specifies the gender of whom one should love, only the importance of love as a universal human prescription: "Everybody needs a love no doubt, any love"—or so Vandross professes in another of his hit songs. The dire stakes of marginality demand sometimes that love is nothing less than a political act.

Knowing this, can we ever afford to say that kitsch has no value to the politics of change in black cultures? Certainly the issue is a temporal one. If Vandross released "A House is Not a Home" in today's climate, the song may not have had the impact that it has. Into the third decade of AIDS, many people are managing the syndrome more skillfully through the use of evolving medications. What's more, the highly conservative American political landscape of the early 1980s out of which Vandross's music emerged has been replaced by the relatively liberal Clinton administration. In an age in which Babyface and R. Kelly rule the R&B charts, Vandross, in his mid 40s, has not been able to sustain the level of success he garnered at the outset of his career. One reason is because in contemporary popular music, monogamy is no longer the only ethic safe and acceptable to push. In contrast, when "A House is Not a Home" was released in 1981, romantic monogamy may have been the most important ethic for queer communities, especially for those of color. Vandross's vision of monogamy could be cynically understood as a knee-jerk response to AIDS and excessiveness of male sexual behavior in the disco era. But it is worth considering the way his vision ushered in new models of male sensibilities in the way that it exploded rather than foreclosed the available representations of masculine behavior and sexuality, and in the way it began to break down the special way 1970s male cultures had begun to divide commitment and unbounded freedom rather than look for freedom in commitment itself. Through the reevaluation of the sentimental, Vandross contests how men might define themselves to themselves.

So the question must be asked once again: Can kitsch make new? Yes! Vandross's reconstructive impulses demonstrate that kitsch can make a worthwhile contribution to the politics of change, but not if kitsch has to be divorced from its partner in crime, sentimentality, and the by-product of sentimentality, love. The theme of love that runs throughout Vandross's star text provides a new lens through which we might begin to theorize black artistic practice in relationship to theft and innovation—think for example how this might redirect critical disdain over the use of "stolen" samples in rap music. I have learned that a fight becomes something else when the parties in conflict are smiling at each other, or at least winking. Love also affects what gets archived, what we remember, how we remember and why we must remember.

It goes without saying that consumers attach intense sentimental value (affect?) to various products of popular culture that have influenced them at their core (such as the love Vandross has for Warwick's early music). But this fact means that when consumers become producers—and I would argue that all consumers are in some ways producers—love is not a phenomenon that cultural critics can afford to sweep under the critical rug. Love is the political power of kitsch. What turns a house into a home—literally and metaphorically—is love. Love animates the in-between space of kinship. So, yes, kitsch makes new, not through the recirculation of the old, but through its reconstruction. Noting the minute differences between recirculation and reconstruction may take an especially tuned eye (or ear, depending on the medium)—a queer one, if you're so inclined.

I wish Luther Vandross—whose adventures in surplus representations magically lead back to the celebration of love—serenity, comfort, happiness, and blessings in his relationships and in his career.

REFERENCES

Allport, G.W. and Postman, L. (1947). *The Psychology of Rumor*. New York: Henry Holt and Co.

Bacharach, B. and David, H. (1964). "A House Is Not a Home" [song]. Largo Music. O/b/o Diplomat Music Corp.

Considine, J.D. "Audio Review: *Never Let Me Go* by Luther Vandross." *Rolling Stone*, Aug. 19, 1993: 77-78.

Diawara, M. (1992). "Afro-Kitsch." In *Black Popular Culture*, edited by Gina Dent, Seattle: Bay Press.

Erni, J.N. "Queer Figurations in the Media: Critical Reflections on the Michael Jackson Sex Scandal." *Critical Studies in Mass Communication*, June 1998: 158-180.

Farsides, T. (1996). "An Interview With Luther Vandross." http.//www.dotmusic.co.uk/ Mwtalentluther.html.

"Fatal Car Crash Causes Crisis in Music Career of Luther Vandross." *Jet*, Feb 3, 1986: 58-61.

Flanagan, Sylvia P. "Luther Vandross's Revealing Interview About His Expanding Entertainment Career." *Jet,* June 28, 1993: 34-36.

George, N. (1988). *The Death of Rhythm and Blues*. New York: Pantheon Books.

Goldsby, J. (1995). "Queen for 307 Days: Looking B[l]ack at Vanessa Williams and the Sex Wars." In *Afrekete: An Anthology of Black Lesbian Writing*, edited by Catherine E. McKinley and L. Joyce DeLaney, New York: Anchor Books.

Gilroy, P. (1998). "Question of a 'Soulful' Style: An Interview with Paul Gilroy." In *Soul: Black Power, Politics and Pleasure*, edited by Monique Guillory and Richard C. Green. New York: New York University.

Grundmann, R. (1995). "Black Nationhood and the Rest in the West: An Interview with Isaac Julien." *Cineaste*, vol. 21 no. 1-2: 28-31.

Harper, P.B. (1996). *Are We Not Men?: Masculine Anxiety and the Problem of African American Identity*. New York: Oxford University Press.

Hemphill, E. (1992). *Ceremonies: Prose and Poetry*. New York: Plume Books.

Holden, S. "Luther Vandross: Pop-Soul Pyrotechnics." *New York Times,* Oct 3, 1982: H21.

—- "Luther Vandross at Top of the Chart," *New York Times*, May 22, 1985.

Hughes, Langston. (1947). "Lonely House" [song].

Julien, I. (1992). *Looking for Langston* [film]. New York: Waterbearer Films.

Karlin, B. and Stapinski, H. 1998. "Soul Survivor." *People Weekly,* Sept. 7, 1998: 121-124.

Lipsitz, G. (1994). *Dangerous Crossroads: Popular Music, Postmodernism, and the Poetics of Place.* New York: Verso.

"Luther Vandross Dispels Rumors About Weight Loss." *Jet,* Jan. 13, 1986: 54-55.

"Luther Vandross Injured in Three-Car collision; One Passenger Killed." *Jet,* Jan. 27, 1986: 14.

Martin, R. (1998). *Critical Moves: Dance Studies in Theory and Politics.* Durham: Duke University.

Mercer, K. and Julien, I. (1994). "True Confessions: A Discourse on Images of Black Male Sexuality." In *Welcome to the Jungle: New Positions in Black Cultural Studies,* edited by Kobena Mercer. New York: Routledge.

Moustakas, C.E. (1961). *Loneliness.* New York: Prentice-Hall, Inc.

Muñoz, J.E. (1999). *Disidentifications: Queers of Color and the Performance of Politics.* Minneapolis: University of Minnesota Press.

—— (1996). "Ephemera as Evidence: Introductory Notes to Queer Acts." *Women and Performance: Queer Acts,* Vol 8:2 #16 pages 5-18.

Norment, L. "Luther Vandross: the Voice that Seduces Millions." *Ebony,* Dec. 1985: 83-88.

—— "Luther Vandross's 8.5 Million Hideaway." *Ebony,* June 1989: 30-2 +.

"Odd Jobs That Led to Fame." *Ebony,* Feb. 1996: 94-102.

Ongiri, A.A.. "We Are Family: Black Nationalism, Black Masculinity, and the Black Gay Cultural Imagination." *College Literature,* Feb. 1997: 280-294.

Riggs, M. (1989). *Tongues Untied.* [film]. San Francisco: Frameline.

Ritz, D. "State of Luxe: Premier Soul Singer Luther Vandross Resides in Class by Himself." *Rolling Stone,* Sept. 6, 1990: 74-5.

Rowell, C.H. (1996). "Signing Yourself: An Afterword." In *Shade: An Anthology of Fiction by Gay Men of African Descent,* edited by Bruce Morrow and Charles H. Rowell. New York: Avon Books, 1996.

Tate, G. "The Long Distance Soulster." *Village Voice,* Oct. 20, 1998: 68.

Waldron, C. "Luther Vandross Tells What Inspires Him as a Songwriter and Entertainer." *Jet,* June 17, 1985 : 54-6+.

Ward, B. (1997). *Just My Soul Responding: Rhythm and Blues, Black Consciousness, and Race Relations.* California: University of California.

Widner, E. (1989). Liner notes to *Dionne Warwick: Her All-Time Greatest Hits,* Rhino Records.

Hip Hop's Closet: A Fanzine Article Touches a Nerve

Touré

It's because we're so thirsty, music-wise, that we were easily distracted. Sure, Tribe's album is great, as are De La's and Nas's, but where is this summer's undeniable classic? The "One More Chance"? The "Flava in Ya Ear"? The "G Thang"? (Ubiquity does not connote "Killing Me Softly" classic, fans.) Except for a few warm spells, this summer may be as cold musically as last winter was meteorologically: Our heavyweight titleholders—Snoop, Dre, Biggie, and Wu-Tang—are basically on vacation, and of the two most-talked-about men in hip hop (Puff and Big), neither can rhyme and only one can produce to save his life. So when *One Nut Network,* a hip hop fanzine, published a profile of an anonymous MC called "Confessions of a Gay Rapper," of course we got distracted. Of course it became our hip hop "War of the Worlds."

"I learned the hard way," the artist said, "that niggas don't think that I can be hard and true to my craft if I'm putting a dick in my mouth.... Yo, that shit is like crack. One good whiff and your ass is whipped. You see, only another brother can satisfy your need.... Only a man can satisfy another man."

Who could it be? We jumped to our cellulars and found suddenly everyone knew someone who knew some MC who liked to suck dick. Suddenly everyone had gaydar.

In time, conventional wisdom declared *One Nut*'s piece a fiction. That's probably right: It was written under a pseudonym, with the intent of luring us into a guessing game rather than shielding a real person or demanding attention to the serious issues. No doubt there are MCs who represent both Myrtle Avenue and Christopher Street. But we needn't creep through hip hop's nooks and crannies to find its homosexuality and homosociality. They're out in the open, because hip hop is a very public celebration of intense black male–to–black male love.

Male Christians stand up in church every given Sunday and claim to love a God who became a man, and talk about, "I love him so!"— just incredible erotic language to express their devotion to Jesus, the

God who was a man. It's the same way in hip hop culture. The pro-
fession of male love is so deep and the bond is so profound, it forges
this deeply erotic communion that gives the lie to their own homopho-
bic passion. There's a deep homoerotic element.
—Michael Eric Dyson, Professor of Communications Studies, the
University of North Carolina, Chapel Hill

Love your niggas that you rollin' with. Love them.
—Raekwon, from Wu-Tang Clan, in *Ego Trip* magazine

Hip hop has always been some boy shit. Boys talking to boys
about things they have done, or will do, with, or to, other boys. Black
women have slid in by submitting completely to masculine desires or
muffling their femininity. Or found themselves only slightly more
accepted than white men. Even when the audience or subject is ostensibly female, the real audience and subject is the brothers. At base,
pussy getting and pussy wrecking are no different than check getting
and mike wrecking: playing fields for a boy and his dawgs.

And in a country where, historically, the center of *so much* has
been the black penis—whether motivated by violent fear, or curious
longing, or proprietary desire, or some reaction to one or more of
those, or some reactions to that reaction—black masculinity remains
equally threatening, powerful, and fragile. So it's the black male's effort
to keep up with his legendary dick, and the resulting caricaturishly
exaggerated manhood that emerged to quash even a hint of waffling,
that are the source of the homophobia grafted into hip hop.

But as in so many homosexual political fantasies, homophobia is
a mask for gayness. In hip hop we need barely scratch the surface to
find the influence of queer culture: "Rapper's Delight" and the Village
People-esque regalia of Grandmaster Flash and the Furious Five recall
the sound and vibe of the exuberantly gay disco era. Bald-headed,
black-clad, slam-dancing, cartoonishly ultramasculine Onyx borrows
the idioms of hard-core S/M, as do the Wu-Tang Clan, who feature
thinly veiled homoerotic torture scenarios on their debut album, in
which Raekwon and Method Man jokingly threaten each other's
tongues, asses, penises, and testes: "I'll lay your nuts on a fuckin' dress-
er...and bang them shits with a spiked fuckin' bat.... I'll hang you by
your fuckin' dick off a fucking 12-story building...."

Gangsta rappers en masse have much in common with drag
queens: "They're two different kinds of drag," notes Kendall Thomas,

Columbia School of Law professor and self-described black gay intellectual activist. "The very elaborate sartorial style, the stylization of the body, the sort of self-conscious deployment of sexuality as an instrument for the assertion of subjectivity, the very self-conscious representations of the male body—there are uncanny resemblances between the gangsta and the diva." And then there's egotistical diva supreme Lil' Kim from Junior M.A.F.I.A., neck and neck with Foxxy Brown for female MC of the year. In "Get Money," Kim sounds like a dominatrix, tauntingly, seductively rhyming, "Get me open while I'm comin / Down your throat and / Ya wanna be my main squeeze, nigga / Don't ya? / Ya wanna lick between my knees, nigga / Don't ya?" She invokes the type of female icons male homosexuals have showered with obsessive love: Mae West, Eartha Kitt, Grace Jones. These are observations that any unsentimental, nuanced look at our culture would turn up. Observations that, save for the taboo, would be very, very cliché.

Perhaps the primary reason behind hip hop's homosexual influences and, more importantly, its intense homosexuality—the culture's boys' clubhouse or locker-room quality—is the massive fatherlessness, de facto and de jure, of the hip hop generation, but why were those boys running the streets all night? Why were they looking to Michael Corleone (from *The Godfather*) and Tony Montana (*Scare-face*) and Goldie (*The Mack*) and Priest (*Superfly*) for the path to manhood in the first place? Because their families ran low on Y chromosomes. The lack, in a childhood home, of any significant older males at all has led many rappers, as adults, to place tremendous value on their relationships with men. "A lot of us in Wu-Tan ain't really had older brothers," Raekwon said in an interview, seemingly taking it for granted that they wouldn't have had fathers. "So now, when you got nice brothers around you, it's like the brother that I never had, the older ones that when I need somebody to talk to and shit. Can't always go to Mon duke and talk to her. You need a man's point of view.... We learned to be the father of each other."

When Raekwon and his love-fathers convene, like the assemblages of nearly all hip hop crews from the Death Row inmates to Mobb Deep's niggas on the 41st Street side of things to the GangStarr Foundation to Erick Sermon's Def Squad, it is often an exclusively male gathering in the studio. By and large, women, who account for a minority of artists and a minuscule number of producers and engineers (if any at all), are completely barred from the studio by cultural convention. In her essay "Black Texts/Black Contexts," New York

University professor Tricia Rose admits that "Even male rap producers with either very strong feminist friends or some sort of feminist ideology themselves have found that the men just don't feel comfortable if there are women interns around in the studio. They can't say all the things they would normally say because they might offend these women. And even when these women say, 'It doesn't matter. You can say whatever you want to me, I want to learn this stuff,' eventually the male creative process is challenged."

This mix of gender exclusivity and cultural innovation directly evokes ancient Greece. "Women played no part in Athenian high culture," Camille Paglia writes in *Sexual Personae*. "They could not vote, attend the theater, or walk in the stoa talking philosophy." The Stoa is the great hall where Athenian philosophers lectured. And, of course, the studio, where rappers and their crew, their personal senate, convene to talk their philosophy, is hip hop's Stoa. The parallels between hip hop and Athens continue; Paglia goes on to say, "The male orientation of classical Athens was inseparable from its genius. Athens became great not despite but because of its misogyny. Male homosexuality played a similar catalytic role in Renaissance Florence and Elizabethan London. At such moments male bonding enjoys an amorous intensity of self-assurance, a transient conviction of victory over mothers and nature."

These hip hop senates often address issues of survival, planning not only how to express themselves musically but also how to improve themselves economically, and how to protect themselves physically. In 1993 Snoop said of L.A. gangs, "Niggas will do anything for you, do time for you, take a bullet for you, kill somebody for you. You can find that kind of love on the streets." That conflation of male-to-male love and combat recalls nothing so much as ancient Greece's homosexual fighting armies. In a 385 B.C. speech, Plato opined:

> If there were...an army...made up of lovers and their loves...when fighting at each other's side, although a mere handful, they would overcome the world. For what lover would not choose rather to be seen by all mankind than by his beloved, either when abandoning his post or throwing away his arms? He would be ready to die a thousand deaths rather than endure this. Or who would desert his beloved or fail him in the hour of danger. The veriest coward would become an inspired hero, equal to the bravest, at such a time; Love would inspire him.

Within a decade Plato's vision was realized: In about 378 B.C. the general Gorgidas put together the Sacred Band of Thebes, a force of 150 pairs of lovers. Behind them, Thebes remained the most powerful state in Greece for 40 years. Asked what he could accomplish with a crew that loved him and would do anything for him, Raekwon replied, "We could run the world, man. We could rule the world."

In the music there's a strand of black unity which requires brothers to love brothers. The question there, however, is what is the nature of that love? And there, I think, hip hop gets confused. Because the extant models of love between men are inflected, unavoidably inflected, by a homoerotic component.

—Professor Kendall Thomas

In the straight mind, the gay man is defined primarily by his sexuality, by what he will and won't do with his dick. But, as with any human, the most important and powerful part of the gay body is not below the waist. Politically and romantically, the most critical organ is the heart, which gay men choose over and gain, in the face of all sorts of societal rejection and oppression, to open for a deep, intense, self-assuring love with another male.

It is that sort of love, completely selfless, not necessarily sexual, between black men that has brought on all of our culture's epic successes. Its wane—the moment male-to-male love leaves the center of hip hop or social organizations and they lose their small family quality to become small business collectives—will directly precede our final failures. Black unity is still paralyzed by the misunderstanding that unity equals uncritical acceptance, but their best, hip hop crews, those informal boy's clubs, demonstrated true functional unity. In those moments hip hop is a national, daily Million Man March, not in what is said on records, but in the work of groups of men talking, battling, rescuing, engaging, hugging, feeding, loving, uplifting, fathering.

Black men loving black men is the revolutionary act.

—Marlon Riggs

Love your niggas that you rollin' with. Love them.

—Raekwon

Bessie Smith:
One of the First Divas

Kennette Crockett

"Bessie Smith might have been a "Blues queen" to the society at large, but within the tighter Negro community where the Blues were a total way of life, and major expression of an attitude toward life, she was a priestess, a celebrant who affirmed the values of the group and man's ability to deal with chaos."

—Ralph Ellison

Bessie Smith lived and sang the blues like no other. Her intensity came across in soul-searching lyrics as well as her excessive lifestyle. An open bisexual, she lived a hedonistic life, which her music reflected. Songs such as "Gin House Blues" and "Tain't Nobody's Bizness If I Do" illustrate her rejection of societal norms": "If I go to church on Sunday / And shimmy on down on Monday / Tain't nobody's bizness if I do."

Smith's songs also reflect the issues Black women faced in the 1920s and 1930s. Although freed of the bondage of slavery, Blacks still faced social and racial inequities. Smith's music spoke to the injustices of white society as well as those suffered at the hands of the Black community. The singer did not keep intimate relations with whites, although she had many white fans. Growing up Black in the South certainly influenced her views on whites.

Smith's life, plagued with physical and emotional problems, stood as a prequel for future divas such as Billie Holiday, Aretha Franklin, Tina Turner, and Whitney Houston: Holiday abusing drugs, Franklin coping with love problems, Turner suffering spousal abuse, Houston struggling with rumors of her sexuality and a troubled marriage.

Smith's bisexuality and love for alcohol were widely known by her fans, although she did not encounter homophobia from them. In a sense she escaped the condemnation many Black homosexuals encountered in Black society. Perhaps "The Greatest Taboo" was not associated with Smith since she also had sex with men. Or maybe it was her ability to make all of the bullshit seem OK, and for a moment amidst the gin and smoke, people found relief and celebrated Smith along with her excesses.

People have always coveted the larger-than-life existences of musicians—the lure of fame, glamour, and nontraditional values captures us. Somehow societal rules in regard to work, life, sex, and relationships don't apply to musicians (Blues singer Bessie Smith having known sexual affairs with women; Little Richard strutting around onstage in women's makeup, RuPaul being RuPaul, and countless others living a lifestyle that defies the norm). Even more extraordinary, these Black artists had a great amount of freedom of expression—in America, a country that still bears racial scars.

In this culture that loves its celebrities, fantasy and escapism are our aphrodisiacs. But what if you were trying to escape something more detrimental than trudging through a boring nine-to-five, not having the right look, or enduring the commonplaceness of suburbia? What if you were running away from bigotry and poverty, sexism and homophobia? Smith ran from these demons in 1920s America when she left behind the common identity of Bessie Smith and became Bessie Smith, a.k.a. Empress of the Blues. Smith escaped a fate of second-class citizenship bestowed to many Black women of her time, which is not to say that her celebrity or divadom rendered her free of racism. It did, however, afford her the opportunity to live more on her own terms—terms that would make her a legend boldly living a life of sexual freedom as well as a hard-drinking street life, which she sang about in her music.

In 1923 her first recording, "Down Hearted Blues," was released and became an immediate success, selling more than two million copies within a year. Smith skyrocketed to fame and soon found herself the toast of Blacks and whites in the North and South. Even with booking fees running from $1,500 to $2,000, Smith's schedule was filled. She had the money, the fame, and the attitude to go after whatever and whomever she wanted.

IN THE BEGINNING

Chattanooga, Tenn., early 1900s: The South, land of cotton and tobacco, was fast becoming the birthplace of the blues. Traveling shows such as Gertrude Ma Rainey's Rabbit Foot Minstrels, which featured singers and dancers, regularly moved through small-town America. Ma Rainey would become the first black woman to sing the blues professionally. Her songs, like Smith's, focused on issues faced by Blacks: unemployment, poverty, and sexual expression. She would later be cited as discovering the young Smith, and the two eventually collaborated on much of Rainey's music. Records do not indicate if Rainey and Smith were lovers. More than likely, their closeness resulted from Rainey's being the mother Smith never knew. But perhaps the affection and favoritism Rainey bestowed on the young Smith was sexually based.

The date of Bessie Smith's birth (April 4 or April 15) is unclear; the year is placed somewhere between 1895 and 1900. (This uncertainty can be attributed to the large number of Blacks who were born at home as well as the fact that their births were not properly recorded by the U.S. government.) Like most Black women of her era, Smith was born into a life of poverty. Her father, a Baptist minister, William Smith, and his wife, Laura Smith, died while Bessie was still a child, which left the responsibility of raising her to her oldest sister, Viola. The nine-year-old Smith began to sing—accompanied by her brother, Andrew, on guitar—on Chattanooga street corners for money. Andrew would later get a job with a traveling show, and Bessie would join him as a dancer. "Bessie Smith was not just a singer, she was a complete entertainer. She could dance, act, and performed comedy routines in tents, cabarets and dance halls. Her reputation as a captivating performer grew quickly" ("Bessie Smith, Empress of the Blues").

TELLING IT LIKE IT IS

Smith captivated audiences with her powerful voice. At six feet and weighing close to 200 pounds, she was a strong woman with an equally strong voice. According to Richard Hadlock in *Jazz Masters of the '20s,* "She could project a song more forcibly to large audiences than any other blues singer in the days before microphones and audio amplification." Smith delivered the blues with what some critics describe as a strong and tender style. Her lyrics tell of poverty and love gone wrong; yet there's always a way out of it all whether it's throwing a rent party—as in Smith's "House Rent Blues"—or finding satisfaction in someone's arms. Merely having their situations voiced helped to end the isolation many people felt. In her book *Blues Legacies and Black Feminism,* Angela Davis writes about this sort of shared community, which she elaborates upon in a recent interview:

> "In a sense, both art forms [music and literature] serve the purpose of creating what Benedict Anderson refers to as imagined communities—which is to say that black women who heard Bessie Smith sing about a frustrating employment situation or a two-timing man or whatever could feel themselves a part of a larger community; the blues were a remedy

for feelings of isolation, and the process of naming ones problems—one's blues—was a first step toward acknowledging and beginning to deal with those problems" ("Angela Davis Writes About the Blues").

Smith certainly voiced her blues, and, indeed, lived the stuff that the Blues are made of: affairs with her own chorus girls; cycles of infidelity and fighting with her husband, Jack Gee; and an insatiable love for gin. At that time in America there were two worlds: one of the church and respectability and one of the juke joint and the flesh. Obviously, Smith lived in the latter. The abolishment of slavery enabled Blacks to control their sexuality and, to some extent, their lives. They were free to come and go as they wanted; they could pick and choose their sexual partners. Consequently, Smith came into her young adulthood fully aware of her choices.

In 1923, with her career rapidly taking off, Smith met and married Jack Gee, and soon after they adopted the six-year-old son of a friend. Their marriage, however, quickly devolved into a relationship based on physical and mental abuse. Witnesses tell of Smith's chasing Gee with a knife after discovering he was sleeping with another woman. Never one to beat around the bush, Smith sang of her abusive marriage in "Please Help Me Get Him Off My Mind": "It's all about a man who always kicks and dogs me around / And when I try to kill him, that's when my love for him come down."

Smith and Gee both had affairs throughout the marriage. Smith's affairs with her chorus girls were widely known, and she often frequented private establishments where one could have a variety of homosexual encounters. Smith "had a sexual appetite that extended to both genders, and she gratified it widely and regularly" (Whitney). After Gee found out about one of Smith's affairs (her longest, with a chorus girl named Lillian), he claimed she had caused him to have a nervous breakdown—which he did to gain both sympathy and money from Smith. The two finally separated in 1928. Smith continued her affair with Lillian, but that too would end.

EVEN GODS FALL
OR, NOBODY KNOWS YOU WHEN YOU'RE DOWN AND OUT

Everything has a season, and as the 1920s ended, Smith's career began to decline. Competition from other singers, her excessive use of alcohol and marijuana, her troubled affairs, and the advent of talking pictures began to kill the traveling shows upon which Smith's career relied. She attempted to break into Broadway musicals but was unsuccessful. Her income dropped suddenly from $1,500 a week to $500, and, to add to her problems, Gee took much of Smith's money to manage another women's career. When Smith threatened to sue, Gee threatened to have their son taken away from her on grounds that Smith was an "unfit" mother. Her excessive lifestyle had come back to haunt her. Being the fighter she was, Smith continued to tour and was planning a comeback when tragedy struck in 1937. A few years earlier, in 1933, she had made her final recording, with Benny Goodman, under the direction of John Hammond. Several years before her death, Smith, with Gee out of her life, turned to Richard Morgan (Lionel Hampton's uncle) for support and affection. He had a deep fondness for Smith, as he had known her from the early days of her career and had helped her with her comeback. But, while driving to Memphis for a performance, the couple's car rear-ended a truck, crushing Smith's arm and ribs and inflicting wounds which eventually caused her to bleed to death. Reports first claimed that the refusal of white hospitals to admit Smith had resulted in her death; later those reports were said to be untrue. Smith died at a Black hospital in Clarksdale, Mississippi. Witnesses claimed that the police and the ambulance just moved very slowly due to the seriousness of the accident. The attention that Smith had demanded onstage escaped her at her most needed moment.

The burial of the Empress of the Blues proved to be much like a final performance. Crowds lined up to see the woman who had given their life so much spice and meaning. Even Smith's former husband, Gee, played his part by throwing himself onto the coffin at her funeral. Sadly, at the time of her funeral, no had one bought Smith a tombstone, perhaps because everyone had been too busy fighting over her estate. Janis Joplin, another famous female singer known for voicing her blues, bought a headstone for both Smith and Juanita Green, whom Smith had hired to clean her floors when Green was a child. Smith's headstone reads: "The greatest Blues singer in the world will never stop singing."

REFERENCES

"Angela Davis Writes About the Blues." Interview with Angela Davis.

   http://go.borders.com/features/mmk98013.xcv.

"Bessie Smith." http://www.bluesonline.mathrisc1.lunet.edu/blues/Bessie_Smith.html.

"Bessie Smith, Empress of the Blues." http://www.resnet.wm.edu/~kmgri1/amst370.htm1.

BESSIE SMITH

Hadlock, R. (1998). *Jazz Masters of the '20s."* New York: Da Capo Press.

"The Life of the Great Blues Singer Bessie Smith."

   http://americanhistory.about.com/homework/americanhistory/library/weekly/aa032000a.htm.

"Part 2 of the Life of the Great Blues Singer Bessie Smith."

   http://americanhistory .about.com/library/weekly/aa032000b.htm.

Whitney, R. "Reflections of 1920's and 30's Street Life in the Music of Bessie Smith."

   www.hub.org/bluesnet/readings/bessie.html.

THE HOUSE THE KIDS BUILT: THE GAY BLACK IMPRINT ON AMERICAN DANCE MUSIC

ANTHONY THOMAS

America's critical establishment has yet to acknowledge the contributions made by gay African Americans. Yet black (and often white) society continues to adopt cultural and social patterns from the gay black subculture. In terms of language, turns of phrase that were once used exclusively by gay African Americans have crept into the vocabulary of the larger black society: Singer Gladys Knight preaches about unrequited love to her "girlfriend" in the hit "Love Overboard"; and college rivals toss around "Miss Thing" in Spike Lee's *School Daze*.

What's also continued to emerge from the underground is the dance music of gay black America. More energetic and polyrhythmic than the sensibility of straight African Americans, and simply more African than the sensibility of white gays, the musical sensibility of today's "house" music—like that of disco and club music before it—has spread beyond the gay black subculture to influence broader musical tastes.

What exactly is house music? At a recording session for DJ International, a leading label of house music, British journalist Sheryl Garratt posed that question to the assembled artists. A veritable barrage of answers followed: "I couldn't begin to tell you what house is. You have to go to the clubs and see how people react when they hear it. It's more like a feeling that runs through, like old time religion in the way that people jus' get happy and screamin'.... It's happening!... It's Chicago's own sound.... It's rock till you drop.... You might go and seek religion afterwards! It's gonna be hot, it's gonna be sweaty, and it's gonna be great. It's honest-to-goodness, get-down, low-down gutsy, grabbin' type music" (Garratt, 1986).

Like the blues and gospel, house is very Chicago. Like rap out of New York and go-go out of D.C., house is evidence of the regionalization of black American music. Like its predecessors, disco and club, house is a scene as well as a music, black as well as gay.

But as house music goes pop, so slams the closet door that keeps the facts about its roots from public view. House, disco, and club are not the only black music that gays have been involved in producing, nor is everyone involved in this music gay. Still, the sound, the beat, and the rhythm *have* risen up from the dancing sensibilities of urban gay African Americans.

The music, in turn, has provided one of the underpinnings of the gay black subculture. Dance clubs are the only popular institution of the gay black community that are separate and distinct from the institutions of the straight black majority. Unlike their white counterparts, gay black Americans, for the most part, have not redefined themselves—politically or culturally—apart from their majority community. Although political and cultural organizations of gay Afro Americans have formed in recent years, membership in these groups remains small and represents only a tiny minority of the gay black population. Lesbian and gay African Americans still attend black churches, join black fraternities and sororities, and belong to the NAACP.

Gay black dance clubs, like New York's Paradise Garage and Chicago's Warehouse (the birthplace of house music), have staked out a social space where gay black men don't have to deal with the racist door policies at predominantly white gay clubs or the homophobia of black straight clubs. Over the last 20 years the sound track to this dancing revolution has been provided by disco, club, and now, house music.

Playback: The Roots of House

Although disco is most often associated with gay white men, its roots actually go back to the small underground gay black clubs of New York City. During the late '60s and early '70s, these clubs offered inexpensive all-night entertainment where DJs, to accommodate the dancing urgencies of their gay black clientele, overlapped soul and Philly (Philadelphia International) records, phasing them in and out, to form uninterrupted sound tracks for nonstop dancing. The Temptations' 1969 hit "I Can't Get Next to You" and the O'Jays' "Back Stabbers" are classic examples of the genre of songs that were manipulated by gay black DJs. The songs' up-tempo, polyrhythmic, Latin percussion-backed grooves were well-suited for the high-energy, emotional, and physical dancing sensibility of the urban gay black audience.

In African and African American music, new styles are almost always built from simple modifications of existing and respected musical styles and forms. By mixing together the best dance elements of soul and Philly records, DJs in gay black clubs had taken the first steps in the creative process that music critic Iain Chambers interprets as a marker of disco's continuity with the rhythm and blues tradition:

> [In disco] the musical pulse is freed from the claustrophobic interiors of the blues and the tight scaffolding of R&B and early soul music. A looser, explicitly polyrhythmic attack pushes the blues, gospel, and soul heritage into an apparently endless cycle where there is no beginning or end, just an ever-present 'now.' Disco music does not come to a halt...restricted to a three-minute single, the music would be rendered senseless. The power of disco...lay in saturating dances and the dance floor in the continual explosion of its presence (Chambers, 1985).

Although the disco pulse was borne in the small gay black clubs of New York, disco music only began to gain commercial attention when it was exposed to the dance floor public of the large predominantly white gay discos. *Billboard* only introduced the term *disco-hit* in 1973, years after disco was a staple among gay African Americans, but—as music historian Tony Cummings has noted—only one year after black and white gay men began to intermingle on the dance floor.

By the mid '70s disco music production was in high gear, and many soul performers (such as Johnny Taylor with his 1976 hit "Disco Lady") had switched camps to take advantage of disco's larger market. Records were now being recorded to accomplish what DJs in gay black clubs had done earlier. Gloria Gaynor scored a breakthrough in disco technique with her 1974 album *Never Can Say Goodbye*. The album treated the three songs on side one ("Honey Bee," "Never Can Say Goodbye," and "Reach Out, I'll Be There") as one long suite delivered without interrupting the dance beat—a ploy that would become a standard disco format and the basis of house music's energy level.

As the decade progressed, disco music spread far beyond its gay black origins and went on to affect the sound of pop. In its journey from this underground scene, however, disco was whitewashed. The massive success of the 1978 film *Saturday Night Fever* convinced mainstream America that disco was a new fad, the likes and sound of which had never been seen before. White gay men latched onto the "Hi NRG" Eurodisco beat of Donna Summer's post—"Love to Love You Baby" recordings and the camp stylings of Bette Midler.

Indeed, the dance floor proved to be an accurate barometer of the racial differences in the musical tastes of white and black gays and the variation in dancing sensibilities between gay and straight African Americans. Quick to recognize and exploit the profit-making potential of this phenomenon, independent producers began to put out more and more records reflecting a gay black sound.

Starting in 1977, there was an upsurge in the production of disco-like records with a soul, rhythm and blues, and gospel feel: Club music was born. The most significant difference between disco and club was rhythm. Club rhythms were more complex and more Africanized. With club music, the gay black subculture reappropriated the *disco impulse*, as demonstrated by the evolution in disco superstar Sylvester's music.

In 1978 Sylvester had a big hit with "Disco Heat"; in 1980 he released another smash, "Fever." "Disco Heat" was a classic example of the type of disco popular among gay African Americans. At 136 beats per minute it combined the high energy aspect of white gay disco with the orchestral flourishes of contemporary soul. The song also contained the metronomic bass drum that characterized all disco. It was only the gospel and soul-influenced vocals of Sylvester and his backup singers, Two Tons o' Fun, that distinguished the music from whiter genres of disco.

"Fever," on the other hand, more clearly reflects a black/African sensibility. To begin with, the song starts with the rhythmic beating of cowbells. Sylvester also slowed the beat down to a funkier 116 beats per minute and added polyrhythmic conga and bongo drumming. The drumming is constant throughout the song and is as dominant as any other sound in it. Just as significant in terms of Africanizing the music was the removal of the metronomic bass drum that served to beat time in disco. In African music there is no single main beat; the beat emerges from the relation of cross-rhythms and is provided by the listener or dancer, not the musician. By removing the explicit timekeeping bass of disco, Sylvester had reintroduced the African concept of the "hidden rhythm."

While most black pop emphasizes vocals and instrumental sounds, club music tends to place more emphasis on a wide array of percussive sounds (many of which are electronically produced) to create complex patterns of cross-rhythms. In the best of club music, these patterns change slowly; some remain stable throughout the song. It is this characteristic of club music, above all, that makes it an African American dance music par excellence.

Like disco, club also moved beyond the gay black underground scene. Gay clubs helped spread the music to a "straight" black audience on ostensibly "straight" Friday nights. And some club artists, such as Grace Jones, Colonel Abrams, and Gwen Guthrie, achieved limited success in the black pop market.

For most of its history, though, club music largely has been ignored by black-oriented radio stations. Those in New York, for instance, were slow to start playing club music with any regularity; finally WBLS and WRKS began airing dance mixes at various intervals during the day. In the early '80s, the two black-oriented FM radio outlets in Chicago, WBMX and WGCI, began a similar programming format that helped give rise to the most recent variation of gay black music: house.

PUMPING UP THE VOLUME

The house scene began, and it derived its name from Chicago's now-defunct dance club, the Warehouse. At the time of its debut in 1977, the club was the only after-hours dance venue in the city, opening at midnight Saturday and closing after the last dancers left on Sunday afternoon. On a typical Saturday night, 2,000 to 5,000 patrons passed through its doors.

The Warehouse was a small three-story building, an abandoned warehouse with a seating area upstairs; free juice, water, and munchies in the basement; and a dimly lit, steamy dance floor in between. You could only reach the dance floor through a trap door from the level above, adding to the underground feeling of the club.

A mixed crowd (predominantly gay male and female) in various stages of undress (with athletic wear and bare flesh predominating) was packed into the dance space, wall to wall. Many actually danced hanging from water pipes that extended on a diagonal from the walls to the ceiling. The heat generated by the dancers would rise to greet you as you descended, confirming your initial impression that you were going down into something very funky and "low."

What set the Warehouse apart from comparable clubs in other cities was its economically democratic admission policy. Its bargain admission price of $4 made it possible for almost anyone to attend. The Paradise Garage in New York, on the other hand, was a private club that charged a yearly membership fee of $75, plus a door price of $8. The economic barriers in New York clubs resulted in a less "low" crowd and atmosphere, and the scene there was more about who you saw and what you looked like than in Chicago.

For the Warehouse's opening night in 1977, its owners lured one of New York's hottest DJs, Frankie Knuckles, to spin for the "kids" (as gay African Americans refer to each other). Knuckles found out that these Chicagoans would bring the roof down if the number of beats per minutes wasn't sky high: "That fast beat [had] been missing for a long time. All the records out of New York the last three years [had] been mid- or down-tempo, and the kids here [in Chicago] won't do that all night long; they need more energy" (Wiffer 1986).

Responding to the needs of their audience, the DJs in Chicago's gay black clubs, led by Knuckles, supplied that energy in two ways: by playing club tunes and old Philly songs (such as MFSB's "Love Is the Message") with a faster, boosted rhythm track, and by mixing in the best of up-tempo avant-garde electronic dance music from Europe. Both ploys were well-received by the kids in Chicago; the same was not true of those in New York.

As Knuckles points out, many of the popular songs in Chicago were big in New York, "but one of the biggest cult hits, 'Los Ninos' by Liaisons Dangereuses, only got played in the punk clubs there." *Dance Music Report noted* that for most of the '80s, Chicago was the most receptive American market for avant-garde dance music. The Windy City's gay black clubs have a penchant for futuristic music, and its black radio stations were the first in the United States to give airplay to Kraftwerk's "Trans Europe Express" and Frankie Goes to Hollywood's "Two Tribes." The Art of Noise, Depeche Mode, David Byrne and the Talking Heads, and Brian Eno were all popular in Chicago's gay black circles.

What's also popular in Chicago is the art of mixing. In an interview with Sheryl Garratt, Farley Keith Williams (a.k.a. "Farley Jackmaster Funk"), one of house music's best known DJ-producers, says, "Chicago is a DJ city.... If there's a hot record out, in Chicago they'll all buy two copies so they can mix it. We have a talent for mixing. When we first started on the radio there weren't many [DJs], but then every kid wanted two turntables and a mixer for Christmas...and if a DJ can't mix, they'll boo him in a minute because half of them probably know how to do it themselves."

What was fresh about house music in its early days was that folks did it themselves; it was "homemade." Chicago DJs began recording rhythm tracks, using inexpensive synthesizers and drum machines. Very soon, a booming trade developed in records consisting solely of a bass line and drum patterns. As music critic Carol Cooper notes, "basement and home studios sprang up all over Chicago."

DJs were now able to create and record music and then expose it to a dance floor public all their own, completely circumventing the usual process of music production and distribution. These homespun DJs-cum-artists/producers synthesized the best of the avant-garde electronic dance music (Trilogy's "Not Love," Capricorn's "I Need Love," and Telex's "Brain Washed") with the best-loved elements of African American dance cuts, and wove it all through the cross-rhythms of the percussion tracks, creating something unique to the character of gay black Chicago.

There are so many variants of house that it is difficult to describe the music in general terms. Still, there are two common traits that hold for all of house: The music is always a brisk 120 beats per minute or faster; and percussion is everything. Drums and percussion are brought to the fore, and instrumental elements are electronically reproduced. In Western music, rhythm is secondary in emphasis and complexity to harmony and melody. In house music, as in African music, this sensibility is reversed.

Chip E., producer of the stuttering, stripped-down dance tracks "Like This" and "Godfather of House" characterizes house's beat as "a lot of bottom, real heavy kick drum, snappy snare, bright hi-hat and a real driving bass line to keep the groove. Not a lot of lyrics—just a sample of some sort, a melody [just] to remind you of the name of the record" (Garrat 1986).

That's all you can remember—the song's title—if you're working the groove of house music, because house is pure dance music. Don't dismiss the simple chord changes, the echoing percussion lines and the minimalist melody: In African music the repetition of well-chosen rhythms is crucial to the dynamism of the music. In the classic *African Rhythm and African Sensibility*, John Chernoff remarks that "repetition continually reaffirms the power of the music by locking that rhythm, and the people listening or dancing to it, into a dynamic and open structure." It is precisely the recycling of well-chosen rhythmic patterns in house that gives the music a hypnotic and powerfully kinetic thrusting, permitting dancers to extract the full tension from the music's beat.

Chernoff argues that the power and dynamic potential of African music is in the gaps between the notes, and that it is there that a creative participant will place his contribution. By focusing on the gaps rather than the beats, the dancers at the Warehouse found much more freedom in terms of dancing possibilities, a freedom that permitted total improvisation.

The result was a style of dancing dubbed "jacking" that more closely resembled the spasmodic up-and-down movements of people possessed than it did the more choreographed and fluid "vogueing" movement of the dancers at other clubs like New York's Paradise Garage. Dancers at the Warehouse tended to move faster, quirkier, more individualistically, and deliberately offbeat. It's not that the kids had difficulty getting the beat; they simply had decided to move beyond it—around, above, and below it. Dancing on the beat was considered too normal. To dance at the Warehouse was to participate in a type of mass possession: Hundreds of young black kids packed into the heat and darkness of an abandoned warehouse in the heart of Chicago during the twilight hours of Sunday morning, jacking as if there would be no tomorrow. It was a dancing orgy of unrivaled intensity, as Frankie Knuckles recalls, "It was absolutely the only club in the city to go to ... it wasn't a polished atmosphere—the lighting was real simplistic, but the sound system was intense, and it was about what you heard as opposed to what you saw" (Wiffer, 1986).

No Way Back: House Crosses Over

Like disco and club, house music is rapidly moving beyond the gay black underground scene, thanks in part to a boost from radio play. As early as 1980, Chicago's black-oriented radio stations WBMX and WGCI rotated house music into their programming by airing dance mixes. WBMX signed on a group of street DJs, the "Hot Mix 5," whose ranks included two of the most prolific and important house producers/artists—Ralph Rosario and Farley Jackmaster Funk. When the Hot Mix crew took to the air on Saturday nights, their five-hour show drew an estimated audience of 250,000 to 1 million Chicagoans.

Now in Chicago, five-year-olds are listening to house and jacking. Rocky Jones, President of the DJ International recording label, points out that in Chicago, house music "appeals to kids, teenagers, black, whites, hispanics, straights, gays. When McDonald's HQ throws a party for its employees, they hire house DJs."

Outside of Chicago, house sells mainly in New York, Detroit, D.C., and other large urban/black markets in the Northeast and Midwest. As in Chicago, the music has moved beyond the gay black market and is now popular in the predominantly white downtown scene in New York, where it is regularly featured in clubs such as Boy

Bar and the World. But the sound also has traveled uptown, into the boroughs (and even into New Jersey) by way of increased airplay on New York's black radio stations; house can now be heard blasting forth from the boom boxes of b-boys and b-girls throughout the metropolitan area. It has also spread south and west to gay clubs such as the Marquette in Atlanta and Catch One in Los Angeles. Even Detroit is manufacturing its own line, tagged "techno-house."

House music has a significant public in England as well, especially in London. In reporting on the house scene in Chicago, the British music press scooped most of its American counterparts (with the notable exception of *Dance Music Report*) by more than a year. So enthusiastic has been the British response to house that English DJs (such as Goldi, Roni Size, and The Dreem Team) and musicians (both black and white) are now producing their own variety of house music, known as "acid" house.

House music, however, is not without its critics. Like disco and club, it has been either ignored or libeled by most in the American music press. In a recent *Village Voice* article hailing the popularity of rap music, Nelson George perfunctorily dismisses the music as "retro-disco." Other detractors of house have labeled the music "repetitive" and "unoriginal"(George, 1988).

Because of its complex rhythmic framework, though, house should not be judged by Western music standards, but by criteria similar to those used to judge African music. House is retro-disco in the same way and to the same extent that rap is "retro-funk."

The criticism that this music is unoriginal stems from the fact that many house records are actually house versions of rhythms found in old soul and Philly songs. Anyone familiar with African American musical idioms is aware that the remaking of songs is a time-honored tradition. As Chernoff has documented, truly original style in African and African American music often consists of subtle modifications of perfected and strictly respected forms. Thus, Africans remain "curiously" indifferent to what is an important concern of Western culture: the issue of artistic origins.

Each time a DJ plays at a club, it is a different music-making situation. The kids in the club are basically familiar with the music and follow the DJ's mixing with informed interest. So when a master DJs flawlessly mixes bits and pieces of classic soul, Philly, disco, and club tunes with the best of more recent house fare to form an evenly pumping groove, or layers the speeches of political heroes (Martin Luther King

Jr., Malcolm X, or Jesse Jackson) or funky Americans (a telephone operator's voice or jungles from old television programs) over well-known rhythms tracks, the variations stand out clearly to the kids and can make a night at the club a special affair.

To be properly appreciated, house must be experienced in a gay black club. As is true of other African music, it is a mistake "to listen" to house because it is not set apart from its social and cultural context. "You have to go to the clubs and see how people react when they hear it...people jus' get happy and screamin'." When house really jacks, it is about the most intense dance music around. Wallflowers beware: You have to move to understand the power of house.

References

Chambers, I. (1985). *Urban Rhythms: Pop Music and Popular Culture.* New York: St. Martin's Press.

Garrat, S. "Let's Play House." *The Face,* Sept. 1986: 18-23.

George, N. "Nationwide: America Raps Back," *Village Voice,* Jan. 19, 1988: 32-33.

Wiffer, S. "House Music." *I-d:* Sept. 1986.

A Feisty Female Rapper Breaks a Hip-Hop Taboo

Laura Jamison

January 18, 1998, *The New York Times*

In "Girlfriend," Queen Pen brags about luring a woman away from her boyfriend. In person, she dances around the issue of her own sexuality. The lyrics alone don't distinguish "Girlfriend," a track on the new album by the rapper Queen Pen, from other rap songs. After all, bragging about luring a woman away from her boyfriend is practically de rigueur on a hip-hop album. "If that's your girlfriend, she wasn't last night," Queen Pen taunts a cuckolded beau. What makes this rap song different is that the girlfriend stealer in it is a woman. Queen Pen, a.k.a. Lynise Walters, who in conversation remains coy about her sexual orientation, is perhaps the first recording artist to use rap, a genre known for the misogyny and homophobia of its lyrics, to depict lesbian life. Openly lesbian or bisexual artists, including k.d. lang, Melissa Etheridge, and Me'Shell Ndegéocello, have cropped up in other musical forms, but aside from the occasional derogatory reference, rap has largely stayed away from homosexuality.

"Girlfriend" has yet to be released as a single, and the album, *My Melody,* has sold only 40,000 copies since it was released on Dec. 16, but the song is being played on radio and in dance clubs in New York and Miami. And Queen Pen, 25, says she is frequently asked about the song, by colleagues and interviewers alike. "This song is buggin' everyone out right now," she said, settling down at the dining room table in her apartment in the Crown Heights section of Brooklyn. "You got Ellen, you got k.d. lang. Why shouldn't urban lesbians go to a girl club and hear their own thing?"

"Girlfriend" is a milestone for rap, says Michael Eric Dyson, author of the book *Between God and Gangsta Rap: Bearing Witness to Black Culture.* He calls the genre "notoriously homophobic." But he said it was not surprising that the first to address homosexuality in rap was a woman. "This is still going to be a bomb she's dropping," he says. "But the real thing is going to be when you get some brother coming out."

Queen Pen's producer, Teddy Riley, concurs. "I can only tell you the street mentality," he said. "It's all right for a woman. But a man?" He doubts whether a largely male rap audience "would welcome that." Nonetheless, he views the lyrics of "Girlfriend" as a challenge to males. The song's underlying message, he says, can be interpreted as a threat issued by a woman to a man: "Straighten up and fly right or I'll go the other way." At the same time, Queen Pen aligns herself with male rappers by often adopting their language and attitude. She calls women "bitches," for example, and expresses detached amusement: "She slid by me four or five times / Wantin' me to notice the rhythm of her thighs / Girls are just so funny to me." "I think she's chosen that route because she thinks it will get her over with the urban audience," said Sheena Lester, music editor at *Vibe* magazine. "But I also think the hard language and all that is real to her. I don't think she's just putting it on." Growing up in Crown Heights and Flatbush, also in Brooklyn, Queen Pen became a single mother at 16. (She has two sons, ages 8 and 9.) "I got public assistance, and I was hustling," she said, declining to elaborate on what she means by hustling except to say that she was not referring to prostitution. She also mentions that after a magazine published an interview that displeased her, "I had to get real ghetto on them," making angry telephone calls to an editor. Moreover, she says that she had just lost $5,000 earrings in a fight. Queen Pen had been performing around New York for years when Mr. Riley asked her last year to perform as a guest on the single "No Diggity" by his group Blackstreet (the song has since gone platinum). Days after Queen Pen recorded her part, Riley signed her to his new label, Lil' Man, a division of Interscope. "Ten years of paying my dues and one night in the studio with Teddy Riley, I got my record deal," she said.

Songs on "My Melody" range from domestic violence to a first crush on a boy. "Girlfriend," based on the chorus of "Boyfriend," a 1993 song by Ndegéocello (who plays bass on "Girlfriend"), is the only song about lesbianism on the album.

Queen Pen says that Mr. Riley didn't balk when she proposed the song. "I told Teddy, 'I want to do a song talking about girls,' " she recalled. "He said, 'Dissing a girl?' I said: 'No, two girls. Lesbians.' He said, 'If that's what you want to do, let's do it.' "

Riley remembers hesitating—because he was nervous about broaching the subject with his partners at Interscope—but not for long. "I respect her for it," he said of "Girlfriend." "It's not gangsta rap. It's not telling you to kill yourself. She is teaching women to be what they want to be. It's another level for the rap game."

The song includes a reference to an "ex" named Beverly, and in conversation Queen Pen speaks of frequenting "girl clubs." But realizing the potential publicity value, she is, at least for the time being, dancing around the issue of her own sexuality.

"I'm black," she said. "I'm a female rapper. I couldn't even go out of my way to pick up a new form of discrimination. People are waiting for this hip-hop Ellen to come out of the closet. I'd rather be a mystery for a minute." She added: "Even if I sat here and said, 'I'm straight,' I could be lying. If I said, 'I'm gay,' it could be a publicity stunt." (Asked if she dates women, Queen Pen asked how big this article was going to be. A little later, she said that she would talk only "in depth" about her sexuality for a front-page article.) "Two or three years from now, people will say Queen Pen was the first female to bring the lesbian life to light on wax," she says. Then she adds, seemingly having forgotten her own caginess on the issue: "It's reality. What's the problem?"

Homosexuality in Popular Black Literature

Rereading Voices From the Past: Images of Homo-Eroticism in the Slave Narrative

Charles Clifton

The defense of black masculinity and reclamation of black manhood is an intricate component of the African and African American male slave narratives. In a "quest for being" (Baker, 1980), many freemen consciously moved to accommodate Western ideas of masculinity and manhood in their "autobiographic" narratives (Steptoe, 1979). The process of recounting the experiences of slavery and freedom in written form was often complicated by the racial and sexual ideologies of 19th-century America. While seeking to narrate their personal sufferings during enslavement, narrators blended Anglo/European visible morals with an invisible African American reality. The result was the production of texts constrained by concepts of race, freedom, and manhood— each predominately influenced by interaction with Southern white men. Frederick Douglass's efforts in his narrative, *My Bondage, My Freedom* (1855), to reassert his being and manhood, are apparent in the book's opening pages. Douglass writes:

> ...it is always a fact of some importance to know where a man is born...[t]he practice of separating children from their mothers... is a marked feature of...the slave system. It is a successful method of obliterating from the mind and heart of the slave all just ideas of sacredness of *the family*, as an institution (Douglass 1855, 27, 29).

In the black male slave narratives, *freedom* took on the culturally acceptable and masculine-defined qualities of property, power, and privilege, long connected to white slave-owning men. Historian John Blassingame suggests that many scholars, in their examination of the institution of American slavery and its influence on representations of masculinity and manhood, often find themselves confronting racial stereotypes and/or sexual myths perpetuated to justify the enslavement of black Americans. Blassingame reasons that:

In many instances, historians have been misled by analyzing only one literary stereotype. The accuracy of the literary treatment of the plantation can be determined, however, only when several of the stereotypes of the slave are examined. This is all the more necessary because the legitimacy of each stereotype is tied irrevocably to the legitimacy of all the others (Blassingame 1979, 224).

While Blassingame's critical analysis of previous historiography is correct, it is limited by an absence of a discussion of slave sexuality and a reconstruction of slave culture along simplistic lines of black patriarchal dominance. Although Blassingame's project, undoubtedly influenced by political and social forces of the late 1960s and 1970s, seeks to counter historical themes of the emasculated black male or the dominating black matriarch, he fails to present a balanced perspective on the slave community. His use of terms such as *blacks* and *slaves* often results in exclusionary meanings. Historian Jacqueline Jones reasons that these "gender-neutral" terms actually signify male actions or a romanticized vision of a monolithic black community (Jones 1985). When Blassingame addresses the slave experience, he only acknowledges the heterosexist maleness attributed to the antebellum South. For example, throughout the text, experiences in slave quarters are described in the following way: "In *his* family *he* found companionship, love, sexual gratification, sympathetic understanding of *his* sufferings; he learned how to avoid punishment, to cooperate with other blacks, and to maintain *his* self-esteem" (Blassingame 1979, 151, emphasis added). Omitted from Blassingame's groundbreaking work is what *she* found, *she* understood, *she* learned, or *she* suffered, independent of and alongside *him*. In addition, Blassingame drastically erases slave sexuality from *HIStoriography*, limiting slave experience to the realm of heterosexual relations, and, more significantly, to the female slave's submissive relation to master, mate, and/or husband. bell hooks argues more forcefully against Blassingame's critique of the slave experience. She contends that for scholars "to suggest that black men were dehumanized solely as a result of not being able to be patriarchs implies that the subjugation of black women was essential to the black male's development of a positive self-concept, an ideal that only served to support a sexist social order" (hooks, 1991).

In this introductory essay, I intend to move away from this type of heterosocial analysis of slavery and slave quarters. I seek to initiate a dialogue within a predominately taboo subject—images of white/black male sexual relations and abuses, as read in the slave narratives. By (re)reading passages from various slave narratives, I posit that the author/narrator's use of intimacy, positioning of the body, and use of language, can and should be read in some instances as an attempt to disguise same-sex sexual encounters occurring during captivity. As this project is still in its early stages of development, I have purposely chosen to examine canonized slave narratives for this essay. As Carby (1987) states in *Reconstructing Womanhood,* the passages that I will refer to will not be presented as reflections of "real life," as it "was" on the plantation, but as the author's desire to privilege his experiences while being restricted to a discourse of his historical conditions. In other words, as vast amounts of historical and literary criticism on slavery have proven, what the authors of slave narratives wrote cannot be accepted at face value. An initial discussion will focus on the possibilities of same-sex sexual relations and abuses occurring in the slave quarters, and the concealment of such occurrences in the slave narratives within euphemisms surrounding the black female body and tensions of black male–white male struggles.

In connection, my aim is to explore uncharted paths in the history of black sexuality. Thus far, a vast majority of the work detailing the histories of sexuality has primarily dealt with two fascinating areas: the recovering of (white) gay and lesbian histories and redefinition of women's histories. Unfortunately, very little research has examined "nontraditional" sexuality within the slave quarter. However, this essay is not a scholarly effort to translate dynamic 20th-century theories on the emergence of the homosexual or homosexual identities onto 19th-century slave quarters or within the plantation house. However, my theorizing, within the parameters of this piece, is part of a more expansive research project, which examines the historical representations of black homosexuality and emergence of black male homosexual identity.

In addition to cross-examining the social and political ramifications of the slave narratives—what and why the authors wrote what they did, in these autobiographies, as historians using slave narratives as primary documents—we must also attempt to read (with varying degrees of difficulty) what was not overtly articulated and possibly why. Feminist historians and literary critics agree that in an attempt to affirm their newly acquired freedom, the freedman/author imitates Western white men by exploiting the sexuality and body of the black female in culturally accepted pornographic detail and represses his own private sexual experiences. In some 19th-century circles, slave narratives were regarded as acceptable Victorian pornography. Again Frederick Douglass's narrative is replete with images of savagely brutalized black women. In one such scene, Douglass describes the vicious beating of Esther, a slave girl who disobeyed her captor. Douglass writes:

> I could distinctly *see* and hear what was going on...Esther's wrists were firmly tied.... Here she stood, on a bench, her arms tightly drawn over her *breast. Her back and shoulders were bare to the waist.* Behind her stood old master, with cowskin in hand, preparing his *barbarous* work.... The screams of his victim were most piercing. He *was cruelly deliberate, and protracted the torture, as one who was delighted with the scene. Again and again he drew the hateful whip....* Poor Esther, her shoulders were *plump and tender*...Each blow...brought screams as well as *blood....* I was hushed, terrified, stunned...*the fate of Esther might be mine next* (Douglas 1855, 58-59, emphasis added).

In this passage, Douglass curiously positions himself as an observer. However, should one read this merely as the tale of a defenseless young boy witnessing another's beating, being retold by an adult who attaches to it an underlying metaphor of rape for political purposes, as theorists propose? The story appears more complicated, as Douglass symbolically positions himself in the role of a voyeur during Esther's torture. His use of language and symbols is telling, in that there is the dual aspect of excitement and fear in his voice. This leads to a second question. It is simply the fear of the whip that terrified a younger Douglass, or does he fear that the "fate" (read: rape) of Esther might be his next? Numerous Esther-like scenes, in which the bare backs of female slaves are whipped until bloody puddles form at their feet, appear in other male-generated narratives. I find it problematic that scholarship has accepted the multiplicity of contexts and voices of enslaved narrators as historical evidence and documentation of female sexual exploitation while continuing to state that such physical contact between men, however intimate or brutal, cannot certainly be read as erotic. Certainly the truth behind the exploitation of male slaves and sexual relations lies somewhere on a continuum of relations thought to be at once brutal and sexual by 19th-century standards.

And if these sexual encounters occurred, however infrequently, is it not possible that these "filthy" and "nameless" acts were encoded in the narratives?

The necessity of coding (disguising information) in slave communities to transport messages between plantations is a well-documented phenomenon. Historians scrutinizing slave existence often reference work songs and folktales as important channels of communication, within and across plantation lines. In *The Interesting Narrative of the Life of Olaudah Equiano* (1814), Equiano used terms or phrases at once recognized by free blacks and former slaves as having multiple meanings, thereby producing a text within a text and ensuring scholarly debate surrounding the religious, economic, and sarcastic meanings attached to this text. This complex method for structuring the narrative was adopted by many others and signified upon many succeeding slave narratives, including Frederick Douglass's *My Bondage and My Freedom* (1855) and Harriet Jacobs's *Incidents in the Life of a Slave Girl* (1861). However, as historians and literary critics deconstruct these slave narratives, there develops a tendency to rearticulate the messages in a heterosocial manner, whereas each "new discovery" begins to reinforce a previous finding. Literary historian Deborah McDowell argues that a dominant discourse evolves around the tendency to reshape slave life "according to normative cultural patterns of marriage and family life" (McDowell, 1993). African American literary analysis and historiography creates, with few exceptions, a language that prioritizes masculinity and ignores themes of difference.

The Interesting Narrative of the Life of Olaudah Equiano begins with Equiano's capture in Africa at the age of nine and relates the events of his life as a slave. He describes his years of captivity as an adolescent in the company of older men abroad seafaring vessels. The statements Equiano makes concerning male relationships that developed onboard the ship are a fascinating portion of the narrative. His first friendship is with Richard Baker, a young white boy about four or five years older than Equiano. Over the course of two years at sea, Baker becomes Equiano's constant companion and instructor. Equiano writes that Baker

...shewed me a great deal of partiality and attention, and in return I grew very fond of him. We at length became inseparable.... This dear youth had many slaves of his own, yet he and I have gone through many sufferings together on ship-board; and have many nights *lain in each other's bosoms,* when in great distress" (Equiano 1914, 74, emphasis added).

Equiano also describe another relationship with seaman Daniel Queen. He confesses that Queen, a man of about 40 years, "messed with me on board," and later "became very attached to me, [saying that] he and I never should part." What type of friendship develops between the young African boy and his white companion that enables them to break all societal codes of acceptable racial and masculine behavior? Not only do these friendships transcend racial lines, but also the shared intimacy places them outside of "norms" of male behavior. Vast amounts of literature exist that describe merchant vessels as communities where sailors create unique worlds that exist apart from dominant land-based institutions of family, church, and state. Jacob Hazen, a sailor on board *Columbus* in 1839, explains that the ship is "a den where...every kind of sinful vice...[is] the continual order of the day...where crimes abound of even so deep and black a dye that it fires the cheek with shame to name them" (Hazen, 1887). More often than not, these alternative sexual practices are commonly sanctioned at sea. Could living among sexually aggressive older men have been the contributing factor for the distress felt by Equiano and Baker?

The language Equiano chooses to describe his boyhood relationships and friendships while at sea is different from what Douglass uses later. In his narrative, Douglass forms a "brotherly bond" with John and Henry Harris. Douglass confides, "I never loved, esteemed, or confided in men more than I did in these.... No band of brothers could have been more loving" (Equiano 1914, 165). In this rite of passage, Douglass experiences a sexually nonthreatening brotherhood. It becomes a fine line to walk when as scholars we attempt to determine what feelings and behaviors are implied in the language of an earlier era. One historian observes that "a common error is made by the critic who, taking Equiano's announced purpose ['to promote the interest of humanity'] at face value, fails to see his creation of a self whose muted voice veils covert intentions that lie hidden behind the facade—the mask, with which he disguises himself from the very opening lines of the work" (Samuels 1993, 65). Another historian indicates that "far too long now sexuality in all-male environments...has been analyzed as 'situational homosexuality' or the exceptional product of 'total institutions' " (Maynard, 1993). As historians, I argue, we should start with the premise that all sexuality is situational and learned from social and cultural forces that vary over time and place. Historical observations of male-female sexual relations in the antebellum South are not restricted to narrowly erotic aspects; there is, therefore, no reason why the examination of same-sex relations should be.

To understand potentially subtextual homoerotic themes in slave narratives and to further expand a discussion on slave sexuality, historically limited by a heterosexist discourse, we must "reread" the era in which many of these authors wrote. While historiographers recognize the limitations of Victorian language, many of the apparent sexual contradictions in the narratives have nevertheless gone unquestioned (Marcus, 1966; Barreca, 1990; Craft, 1994). As previously suggested, it is necessary to recognize that escaped bondsmen and women had to be exceptionally careful not to overtly offend their white readers. Such public restrictions on morality and virtue forced Harriet Jacobs to assume an accommodating voice as an author when she decided to make visible her experiences as a slave:

> God knows I have tried to [live my life] in a Christian spirit...I ask nothing—I have placed myself before you to be judged as a woman whether I deserve your pity or contempt—I have another object view—it is to come to you just as I am a poor Slave Mother—not to tell you what I have heard but what I have *seen*—and what I have suffered (Jacobs 1861, xiii, 253).

Likewise, much of Douglass's text ascribes to processes of accommodation and acculturation—temperance and moral behavior, aspiring to higher education, and abiding to dominant religious doctrine. In explaining or describing the brutalities and indecencies of slavery, writers were nevertheless persuaded (often by those men and women who authenticated their texts) to express themselves in an acceptable fashion.

Douglass writes in *My Bondage* that there are "certain secluded and out-of-the-way places...where slavery, wrapt in its own congenial, midnight darkness, *can* and *does* develop all its malign and shocking characteristics...without apprehension and fear of exposure" [emphasis in original]. In addition to telling of his own physical and psychological abuse, I posit that Douglass, because of these public and political restrictions placed on his literary voice and a personal desire to reclaim his manhood, in this quotation and in other passages throughout *My Bondage,* is possibly acknowledging the experiences of sexually exploited young black men. I am not suggesting, however, that Douglass's passages used in this essay prove that he (Douglass) was involved in homosexual relations or was homosexual, as defined by contemporary literature and historiography. I do observe in these passages a familiarity with same-sex relations on the part of the authors. And these acquaintances are documented as subtextual components of the texts. I intend to further pursue this angle of research by using other slave narratives, where one can read suggestions of a "darker" side of slavery; a sexual side of slavery involving something other than a historically heterosexist past; a side that recognized same-sex relations and possibly sexually exploited male children.

In "Narrative of the Life and Adventures of Henry Bibb, An American Slave, Written by Himself" (1849), Bibb writes of being "dragged down to the lowest depths of human degradation," by experiences and abuses of enslavement. In one particular episode, Bibb places himself as the object of sadomasochistic abuses rather than positioning himself in the role of voyeur. Bibb describes one form of "punishment" whereby he is stripped naked, tied spread-eagle to the ground, and flogged by the overseer for all the slaves to witness. This form of punishment, however, goes beyond an effort to frighten other slaves. Once the overseer is finished whipping him, Bibb's master applies the paddle:

> This paddle is made of a piece of hickory timber, about one inch thick, three inches in width, and about 18 inches in length. The part which is applied to the flesh is bored full of quarter inch auger holes, and every time this is applied to the flesh of the victim, the blood gushes through the holes of the paddle, or a blister makes its appearance. The persons who are there flogged are always stripped and their hands tied together. They are bent over double, the knees are forced between their elbows, and a stick is put through between the elbows and the bend of the legs...while the paddle is applied to those parts of the body which would not be so likely to be seen.

During paddling, as Bibb sketches in the above passage, the head of the victim is often placed between the legs of the person inflicting the punishment. Scholarly evaluation ignores this in narratives. These oversights preserve the heterosexual public personas of 19th-century African American and white men and produce a monolithic heterosexist discourse. The result of this scholarship is the erasure of homosexual relations within the limited spheres of the slave quarter and plantation family.

Compare Bibb's description of his torture to that of Frederick Douglass's now-infamous struggle with the "slave breaker," Mr. Covey. "I had not been in his possession three whole days," Douglass writes of Covey, "before he subjected me to a most brutal chastisement. Under his heavy blows, blood flowed freely, and wales were left on my back as large as my little finger" (Douglass 1855, 129). During the year in which Douglass toils under Covey's cruelty, he discovers a new understanding of slavery and abuse. His year with Covey is spent struggling to not surrender to Covey's repeated attempts to break him, or, if you will, to prevent his own psychological rape. Douglass compares his relationship with the "Negro breaker" Covey as that of Douglass with the oxen. "Covey was to break me, I was to break them; break and be broken—such is life."

Scholars repeatedly emphasize the symbolism associated with Douglass's struggle against Covey at St. Michael as well as the slave's declaration of manhood, while consistently ignoring the sexual undertones of male-to-male abuse that permeate Douglass's words. During the "last flogging," Douglass's relationship with Covey is metaphorically transformed into an attempted rape scene as his stay reaches a boiling point. He refuses to strip himself of his clothes and to assume a position for punishment when ordered by Covey. "The case that I have been describing," Douglass writes, "was the end of the brutification of which slavery had subjected me" (Douglass 1855, 152). This rebuked rape and Thomas Auld's subsequent rejection of a runaway Douglass is, as Douglass biographer William S. McFeely indicates, "as close as a Victorian author could come to speaking about the sadistic abuse of males by males" (McFeely 1991, 44).

Douglass's use of language and positioning of the black body within the narrative is at times extremely contradictory. Often overshadowing Douglass's powerful imagery is his obsession with his mixed racial identity and the Auld family, especially his complex relationship with Thomas Auld. Following his failed attempt to escape from bondage, Douglass is returned to Baltimore by Thomas Auld rather than being shipped off to the deep South. Douglass declines to provide details behind the nature of his "long and intimate" relationship with Auld, choosing rather to keep the private (and sexual) side of his slave life hidden from his readers. One could argue that possibly Douglass had no sex life to speak of prior to his escape from captivity. Deborah McDowell contends, however, that Douglass's structuring of the text, shifting from the specific—when recounting black women's oppression—to the general—when reflecting upon his own experiences—is self-consciously motivated. She suggests that Douglass strives to construct "public story of a public life...signify[ing] the achievement of adult-male status in Western culture" (McDowell 1993, 47-48). In regard to Douglass's decision to abandon his mother's name, to disregard his "strong matrilineal black heritage" (citing Henry Louis Gates, Jr.), and his rejection of the feminine, McDowell questions why so few scholars "have delved underneath the surface" of Douglass's texts "to uncover their latent grammar" (McDowell 1993, 45).

In 1848, A few years after fleeing slavery, Douglass published a letter, in the *North Star,* described as "one of the strangest pieces of literature of American slavery" (McFeely 1991, 158). Addressed to Thomas Auld, a portion of it reads as follows:

> Sir—The long and intimate, though by no means friendly, relation which unhappily subsisted between you and myself, leads me to hope that you will easily account for the great livery which I now take in addressing you in open and public manner...I have selected this day on which to address you, because it is the anniversary of my emancipation.... How, let me ask, would you look upon me, were I, some dark night, in company with a band of hardened villains, to enter the precincts of your elegant dwelling, and seize the person of your own lovely daughter, Amanda, and carry her off from your family, friends, and all the loved ones of her youth— make her my slave...a degraded victim to the brutal lust of fiendish overseers, who would pollute, blight, and blast her fair soul—rob her of all dignity—destroy her virtue, and annihilate in her person all the graces that adorn the character of virtuous womanhood (Douglass 1848, 264-271).

In this public address to Thomas Auld, Douglas ignores 19th-century rules of conduct regulating interracial and sexual relations. In one reading, he affects the controversial stance of the black aggressor in the fantasy rape of Auld's daughter Amanda. No longer the voyeur, as in the "rape" of Esther, Douglass becomes the one *who would pollute, blight, and blast* female virtue. In another interpretation Douglass can be seen as taking a much more radical stance—one in which he positions the black male body (himself) in the role of female narrator who exposes the white rapist. The "I" who enters, "some dark night, in company with a band of hardened villains," is still white men. However, it is not black females (the Amandas or Esthers) who become "a degraded victim to the brutal lust of fiendish overseers," but rather young black men.

As scholarship investigates 19th-century antebellum America and sexual relations, it predominately addresses the economic, social, and political ramifications of sexuality on the heterosexual body. Due to the scarcity of surviving documents, when studies on 19th-century same-sex relations are conducted, they focus on the white body rather than the black. Limitations such as these severely hinder a proposed reading of slave narratives that would suggest any possibility of same-sex relations, as I imply in the above readings of surviving narratives. Still in an embryonic stage, gay and lesbian historiography nevertheless provides evidence of "bisexual" and "homosexual" relations among prominent members of the antebellum political and plantation elite, urban working classes, and the earliest arriving Africans.

In 1646 Jan Creoli, a "Negro" working in the New Netherland Colony (now Manhattan), was convicted and executed for committing sodomy. Although the New Dutch West India Company supplied a large number of black laborers to the colony, surviving records do not indicate whether Creoli was an indentured servant or enslaved. However, his punishment for this "crime" did not appear to be racially biased. In 1660 Jan Quisthout, a white man, was also convicted and executed in New Netherland Colony for forcible sodomy with a "boy"; his sentence was death by drowning. The following passage recorded Creoli's trial and sentencing:

> June 25. Court proceedings. Fiscal [public prosecutor] vs. Jan Creoli, a Negro, sodomy; *second offense*; this crime being condemned of God as an abomination. The prisoner is sentenced to be conveyed to the place of public execution, and there choked to death, and then burnt to ashes.... Sentence, Mango Congo, a lad ten years old, on whom the above abominable crime was committed, to be carried to the place where Creoli is to be executed, tied to a stake, and faggots [kindling] piled around him, for justice sake, and to be flogged (as cited in Katz 1976, 22-23).

Congo's name suggests an African bloodline, yet the trial documents are silent on this and whether Congo had been a willing or unwilling participant. The question becomes, then, if Congo were a willing participant in Creoli's attack, why was he not punished? It seems probable that Congo was not executed because the court believed he was too young and unable to defend himself against Creoli.

In regard to other sodomy trials, court records for the 18th century indicate no racial bias in sentencing. The majority of states laws prohibiting "buggery" required death for the participants and, in the case of bestiality, the execution and burning of the beast. However, as a "slave" became racially identifiable in America, attitudes toward black sexuality shifted. Modifications to 18th-century state laws reflect prevalent double standards of sexuality. In Pennsylvania a sodomy law read:

> ...if any person or persons shall be convicted of sodomy and buggery, provided he or they be at age of discretion, and consenting thereunto shall suffer imprisonment at hard labor during life...if any Negro or Negroes...shall commit a rape or ravishment upon any white woman...or...buggery...they shall be punished by death (as cited in Katz 1976, 125).

After discovering a series of 1826 letters written by Jeff Withers to James Hammond, for example, historian Martin Duberman concludes that homosexual relations may have been a tolerated form of behavior, like the rape of slave women, for younger white men in antebellum America. In one letter to Hammond dated May 15, 1826, Withers admits, "I feel some inclination to learn whether you yet sleep in your shirt-tail, and whether you yet have the extravagant delight of poking and punching a writhing bedfellow with your long fleshen pole—the exquisite touches of which I have often had the honor of feeling?" (qtd. in Duberman 1989, 156).

On September 24, 1826, Withers again writes:

> I fancy, Jim, that your elongated protuberance—your fleshen pole—has captured complete mastery over you—and I really believe that you are charging over the pine barrens of your locality, braying, like an ass, at every she-male you can discover...the flaming excess of your lustful appetite may drag

down the vengeance of supernal power. And you'll 'be damned if you don't marry'?" (qtd. in Duberman 1989, 156).

These men were in their early 20s when they wrote these letters. Both went on to marry and have successful careers—Withers became a lawyer, and Hammond became one of the South's "great men," serving as South Carolina senator and governor. A socially ambitious and aspiring politician, Hammond married Charleston heiress Catherine Fitzsimmons. Immediately, Hammond became economically and socially powerful as the owner of Silver Bluff, a 10,000-acre plantation on the Savannah River worked by 220 slaves (Clinton 1991). The letters written by Withers present interesting possibilities surrounding Hammond's commitment to the marriage and surrounding sexuality among young Southern men in general. Was the sexual relation between Withers and Hammond unique, or does it reveal a wider pattern of male-male relationships in the antebellum South? How often were "gay" men (or women) marrying simply to rise in the social ranks or to fulfill an obligation to family by producing heirs? As there appears to be no attempt on Withers's part to conceal any guilt or fear of discovery of his involvement with Hammond, it is possible that the frankness exhibited in Withers's letters implies that such activity was not regarded as socially problematic for young men of the same race and equal social standing so long as it was not publicly flaunted. In other words, no public sanctions were necessary if (what we now read as) homosexual encounters did not threaten the social fabric. If Withers's letters are indicative of a more widespread pattern of male-male sexual contacts, then this behavior obviously did not carry with it the social stigmatism attached to it today. Duberman's answer to whether same-sex relations were tolerated or ignored in antebellum America is more than likely closely linked to the privileges of race, gender, and social standing.

If, as retrieved sources suggest, members of the free male population engaged in homosexual activities, contributing to societal fears of sexual differences and increases in sodomy laws, how can we as historians exclude the enslaved male from this discourse of sexuality, especially when state laws directly differentiate between the races in connection to sodomy? Afrocentric scholarship tends to be embattled by that notion that Africans and African Americans were somehow exempt from same-sex sexual behavior/relations until initial contact with white Europeans, or that black men were exempt from the rape experienced by black women during slavery. Either tendency seems to be as much embedded in late 20th-century sexual insecurities as in Victorian repression, and flawed by its own set of sexual stereotypes and racial biases. A closer and less biased examination of the narratives highlights these homoerotic images, potential homosocial relations, and alternative interpretations on these same-sex friendships.

Prevalent 19th-century prejudices in the North and South against African Americans and black sexuality placed numerous restrictions on the voices that emerged from the narratives of fugitive slaves. Fugitive and/or former slaves, when establishing their position as antislavery writers, were confronted by the social and political ramifications of their previous state of subjugation. These narratives disclosed the many levels of public humiliation and oppression slaves endured. In the process of establishing their authenticity as authors, they wrote within the confines of a Victorian prose that was acceptable for their audiences. This era of Victorian literature proliferated certain standards of femininity and masculinity. The experiences of female and male slaves needed framing within appropriate terminology and guidelines, which in many instances contradicted with the reality of slavery. African American writers faced the duality of attempting to remain within the limits of Victorian literature, which demanded compromises in their texts, and establishing a voice to tell a free story.

One such compromise is apparent in many narratives written by black women, free or enslaved. These women were offered no means of legal redress for crimes of rape committed against them, or support for the children produced. Rape was but one method of physical harassment and psychological torture used in the antebellum South to dominate and control enslaved female sexuality. Female authors, however, while constructing their texts for public consumption, were often placed in a position of apologizing for not giving birth and raising their children (often biracial children) under the sanctity of marriage. The fact that many female slaves, in the struggle to retain control of their bodies, were forced into difficult sexual situations is no longer questioned by scholars. In the case of male narrators, some scholars might question why the authors would even attempt to weave suggestions of male-male sexual assaults into their stories if they feared legal penalties or social stigmas. One possible explanation might involve the complex issue of reclaiming their rights as human beings and establishing authority over their sexuality. Even though black women faced social stigmas and questions surrounding the horrors of slavery, they nevertheless filtered these violent acts into their stories. In doing so, these ex-slaves were proclaiming that they were not the lurid women being touted in pro-slavery propaganda. They were women trying to be virtuous and honorable. In the case of the male narrators, they too can be *reread* as reclaiming their sexuality and manhood—by suggesting through various forms of coding—that these same-sex abuses and/or relationships occurred on the plantations.

In his narrative, Henry Bibb, as a fugitive slave, wrote of "licentious white men" who entered slave quarters day or night, with no fear or apprehension or punishment:

> I was a wretched slave, compelled to work under the lash...and often without clothes enough to hide my nakedness...I have been dragged down to the lowest depths of *human degradation and wretchedness* by slaveholders ...which I consider to be too vulgar to be written... (64, emphasis added).

Bibb's remarkable statements about male slaves compelled to work in a state of nakedness, and of images "too vulgar to be written," again raises interesting questions concerning sexual relations between masters and male slaves. Most striking about Bibb's testimony is not that he has witnessed abuses "too vulgar to be written," but rather that he forcefully admits to being the "I." Academic indifference and ignorance toward same-sex sexual exploitation (other than the rape of black women) did not exist during the slavery era, a very unlikely supposition. Consider for example the narrative of Harriet Jacobs's, *Incidents in the Life of a Slave Girl* (1861). Jacobs provides the story of a slave named Luke and his young master, who

> became a prey to vices growing out of the *patriarchal institution*...He was brought home [from the North], deprived of the use of his limbs by excessive dissipation. Luke was appointed to wait upon his bedridden master, whose *despotic habits* were greatly increased by exasperation at his own helplessness...as he lay there on his bed, a mere degraded wreck of manhood, he took into his head *strangest freaks of despotism. Some of these freaks were of a nature too filthy to be repeated.* When I fled from the house of bondage, I left poor Luke still chained to the bedside of this cruel and disgusting wretch (Jacobs 1861, 192, emphasis added).

This passage poses a number of possibilities for scholars reclaiming a history of (homo)sexuality on the plantation. Not only is Luke (a grown man) left chained to the bedside of his master, but also, as Jacobs adds, "some days he was not allowed to wear anything but his shirt." What exactly is Jacobs suggesting to her readers? How widespread and accepted was homosexuality on the plantation? As historians, what are we to do with other personal papers, legal documents, and narratives suggesting atypical sexual or homoerotic relations? It is one thing for white men to zealously flog and physically overwork a despised black slave, but when these masters purposefully display the naked male slave body, as demonstrated in the Jacobs and Bibb examples, these images suggest elements of homoeroticism. What is the significance of white men gazing upon the naked black male body? If the reoccurring "bloody bare backs" of black females are understood as a symbol of rape by white men during enslavement, then what does the nakedness of black men symbolize? It seems more possible that on some level and in some instances desire for the black male body replaced the fear and hatred Douglass spoke of in his text.

In this essay I have drawn heavily from the canonized writings of Frederick Douglass and other narrators to further this preliminary investigation into possible variations of sexuality emerging from the narratives. This essay would not be complete if I were not to address the term *homosexual* as it is used in the construction of my theories surrounding antebellum sexuality. While making these homosexual suppositions, I would also like to add that I have not intended to presuppose that any of the narrators referenced in this essay were aware of a homosexual identity or consciousness that may have existed in the antebellum era. While I use the term *homosexual* in reference to acts and behaviors described in the enslaved narratives, I continue to ascribe to a philosophy that homosexual identity and consciousness is a 20th-century development. In the United States, identifying oneself as a homosexual or gay male has evolved from an expanding capitalistic economy that has created opportunities for changes in "traditional" family, race relations, and cultural structures. Furthermore, as feminist theorists observe, a homosexual identity is the result of an ongoing struggle to understand an ever-changing social reality in which the personal is political. What we consider homosexual today is much more complex than a description of an 18th- or 19th-century encounter in which the participants are of the same sex and sexual intercourse is involved.

Also, as I stated earlier, I do not intend to suggest that Douglass,

Bibb, or Equiano were "homosexuals." Nor is it my goal to argue that this particular study of 19th-century antebellum sexuality and slave narratives is more correct than any other analysis. Rather, I hope to have created an opening for the future explorations in gay and lesbian historiography and for a more complete understanding of black sexuality and manhood as denoted in these narratives. Exploration into the history of antebellum same-sex relations will hopefully proceed in directions that seek to provide a broader explanation for all sexualities, more realistic and less homogeneous. In future research I will continue to rely heavily on the slave narratives as primary sources and literary criticism that attributes the narratives with multiple voices and differentiating sexual plots.

This essay has posed many questions (a number unanswerable at this point) and will probably raise a few this author did not foresee. As my research continues, I hope to better defend my theories and address some of the unanswered and/or problematic issues emerging from the essay. I admit that at this point in my research I am not in a position to take on other taboo issues, such as the question of whether participants in these sexual acts were willing or unwilling. Arguments surrounding the power relations between interracial and same-sex participants dominate many scholarly debates. As the history of African American sexuality is retraced, however, we should continue to *reread* these texts, paying particular attention to "friendships" and the possibility that some "loving" relationships developed.

Lastly, my ultimate goal is to remove the veil that continues to render sexuality and black homosexuality as taboo subject matter. Literary and historical scholarship that continues to define manhood and freedom through traditional and heterosexual domestic arrangements should be challenged. I hope this paper has presented the multiplicity of *other* experiences emerging from the African American slave narrative and in regard to sexuality, that these experiences are not necessarily heterosexual. Additionally, as scholars, we must continue to question the theories of intellectuals who have positioned themselves as the African American sons of stalwart fathers. I question the long-term value of "revisionary" scholarship, seemingly locked into a circular pattern that simply signifies and reconfirms previous work in the field. Many uncharted areas of research still exist in the realm of slave sexuality, including the possibility that the brutal exploitation of slave women described in the male-authored narratives is an attempt to cast aside their own personal abuses in slavery during the process of reclaiming of their being. This complex process of rereading slave sexuality will hopefully further discussion into the myths of black manhood, slave sexuality, and their antecedent meanings for historiography and literary criticism.

REFERENCES

Abelove, H., et al. (Eds.). (1993). *The Lesbian and Gay Studies Reader.* New York: Routledge.

Abrahams, R.D. (1985). *Afro-American Folktales.* New York: Pantheon Books.

Altman, D. (1993). *Homosexual: Oppression and Liberation.* New York: New York University Press.

Andrews, W.L. (1986). *To Tell a Free Story.* Urbana: University of Illinois Press.

Asante, M.K. (1988). *Afrocentricity.* Trenton, NJ: Africa World Press.

Baker, Jr., H.A., (1980). *The Journey Back: Issues in Black Literature and Criticism.* Chicago: University of Chicago Press.

Barreca, R. (Ed.). (1990). *Sex and Death in Victorian Literature.* Bloomington: Indiana University Press.

Bibb, H. (1849). "Narrative of the Life and Adventures of Henry Bibb, An American Slave, Written by Himself." In *Puttin' On Ole Massa',* edited by Gilbert Osofsky, New York: Harper & Row, 1969.

Blassingame, J.W. (1979). *The Slave Community: Plantation Life in the Antebellum South,* New York: Oxford University Press.

Callaghan, E.B. (Ed.). (1865). Calender of Dutch Historical Manuscript reprinted Ridgewood NJ: Gregg Press, 1968, 103.

Carby, H. (1987). *Reconstructing Womanhood: The Emergence of the Afro-American Woman Novelist.* New York: Oxford University Press.

Charles T. D. and Gates, Jr., H.L. (Eds.). (1985). *The Slave's Narrative.* New York: Oxford University Press.

Chauncey, G. (1994). *Gay New York: Gender, Urban Culture, and the Making of the Gay Male World, 1890-1940.* New York: Basic Books.

Courlander, H. *A Treasury of Afro-American Folklore.* New York: Crown Publishers.

Craft, C. (1994). *Another Kind of Love.* Berkeley: University of California Press.

D'Emilio, J. (Ed.). (1988). *Intimate Matters: A History of Sexuality in America.* New York: Harper & Row.

— (1993). Sexual Politics, *Sexual Communities: The Making of a Homosexual Minority in the United States 1940-1970.* Chicago: University of Chicago Press.

Douglass, F. (1988). *My Bondage and My Freedom.* Edited and introduced by William L. Andrews. Chicago: University of Chicago Press.

— "To My Old Master, Thomas Auld." *The North Star.r* Sept. 8, 1848.

Duberman, M. (1989). "Writhing Bedfellows in Antebellum South Carolina: Historical Interpretation and the Politics of Evidence." In *Hidden From History,* edited by Martin

Duberman, et al. New York: Signet Books.

Equiano, O. (1814). "The Interesting Narrative of the Life of Olaudah Equiano, Written by Himself." In *The Classic Slave Narratives*, edited by Henry Louis Gates, Jr. New York: Mentor, 1987.

Gates, Jr., H.L., (1988). *The Signifying Monkey: Theory of Afro-American Literary Criticism*, New York: Oxford University Press.

Genovese, E. (1976). *Roll Jordan, Roll*. New York: Vintage Books.

Harding, V. (1981). *There Is a River: The Black Struggle for Freedom in America*. New York: Vintage Books.

Hazen, J (1887). *Five Years Before the Mast, or Life in the Forecastle Aboard a Whaler and a Man-of-War*. Chicago. As cited in Katz, Gay American History, 470.

hooks, b. (1991). *Ain't I A Woman*. Boston: South End Press.

Jacobs, H.A. (1987). *Incidents in the Life of a Slave Girl, Written by Herself*, edited by Jean Fagan Yellin. Cambridge, MA: Harvard University Press.

Jones, J. (1985). *Labor of Love, Labor of Sorrow: Black Women, Work, and the Family from Slavery to the Present*. New York: Basic Books.

Katalin, O. (1993). "Dominant and Submerged Discourses in 'The Interesting Narrative of the Life of Olaudah Equiano'." *African American Review*, 27 (Winter): 661-2.

Katz, J. (1976). *Gay American History: Lesbians and Gay Men in the U.S.A*. New York: Thomas Y. Crowell Co.

Katz, J. (1983). *Gay/Lesbian Almanac: A New Documentary*. New York: Harper & Row.

Madhubuti, H.R. (1978). *Enemies: The Class of the Races*. Chicago: Third World Press.

Marcus, S. (1966). *The Other Victorians*. New York: Basic Books.

Martin, R.K. (1986). *Hero, Captain, and Stranger: Male Friendship, Social Critique, and Literary Form in the Sea Novels of Herman Melville*. Chapel Hill: The University of North Carolina Press.

Martin, R.K. (1989). "Knights-Errant and Gothic Seducers: The Representation of Male Friendship in Mid-Nineteenth Century America." In *Hidden From History: Reclaiming the Gay and Lesbian Past*, edited by Martin Duberman, et al. New York: Signet Books.

Maynard, S. (1993). "Making Waves: Gender and Sex in the History of Seafaring." *Acadiensis*, 22 (Spring): 150.

McDowell, D. and Rampersad, A. (Eds.). (1989). *Slavery and the Literary Imagination*. Baltimore: John Hopkins University Press.

McFeely, W.S. (1991). *Frederick Douglass*. New York: W. W. Norton and Co.

Rotundo, E.A. (1989). "Romantic Friendship: Male Intimacy and Middle-Class Youth in the Northern United States, 1800-1900." *Journal of Social History* 23 (Fall 1989).

Samuels, W.D. (1985). "Disguised Voice in 'The Interesting Narrative of the Life of Olaudah Equiano'." *Black American Literature Forum* 19 (1985): 65

Stepto, R.B. (1979). "Narration, Authentication, and Authorial Control in Frederick Douglass's Narrative of 1845." In *Afro-American Literature: The Reconstruction of Institution*, edited by Dexter Fisher and Robert B. Stepto. New York: The Modern Language Association of

America, 1990.

— (1991). *From Behind the Veil: A Study of the Afro-American Narrative,* Urbana: University of Illinois Press.

Weeks, J. (1995). *Invented Minorities: Sexual Values in an Age of Uncertainty.* New York: Columbia University Press.

ENVISIONING LIVES: HOMOSEXUALITY AND BLACK POPULAR LITERATURE

CRAIG SEYMOUR

This essay explores the popular phenomenon of *Invisible Life* and *Just as I Am,* two contemporary novels by and about a black gay man that have been extremely popular, not only among other black gay men, but also with straight black women. In this essay, I ask what it is about each of these books that makes them so appealing to both black gay men and straight black women. I explore various theories as to why the books have so greatly galvanized their audiences, and implicitly address the ways in which popular culture illuminates the conflicts and contradictions of everyday life. I also discuss the social, cultural, political, and economic contexts within which the novels were created, marketed, and received. Finally, I examine what these various contexts reveal about the contemporary state of race and sexuality in the United States.

When E. Lynn Harris's *Invisible Life* was first released at the end of 1991, I was working at Lambda Rising, a gay and lesbian bookstore in Washington, D.C. As a black gay man, I was initially very interested in the novel, both because it was written and self-published by a black gay man and because it dealt with homosexuality and bisexuality within the black community. I was also intrigued by the immediate success of the book. Although I had never seen the book featured in any gay and lesbian periodicals, people were already asking for the book before we even had it in the store. Once we began selling the book, it became an immediate best-seller among gay and lesbian titles, occupying the Top Ten list with books that were released and heavily promoted by mainstream publishers and small gay and lesbian presses.

I was also intrigued by who was buying the book. Although its readership was almost exclusively black, this was not the same black clientele that consistently supported such black gay and lesbian writers as Essex Hemphill and Audre Lourde. Elias Farajaje-Jones, a black bisexual divinity professor at Howard University, addressed this phenomenon in his review of *Invisible Life* in *The Fire This Time,* the quarterly newsletter of the D.C. Coalition of Black Lesbians and Gay Men:

Invisible Life is a book that has been very well-received in certain quarters; one cannot help but wonder why many Black men know about it, yet have never heard of the revolutionary lesbian-womanist writers of Afrikan descent, such as Pat Parker, Audre Lorde, Barbara Smith or Jewelle Gomez, to name several (Farajaje-Jones 1992, 9).

In fact, I had never seen much of the book's initial buyers purchasing books from the store at all, much less with the verve with which they purchased *Invisible Life.*

I make this observation not to critique the reading habits of my fellow black gay brothers in D.C. I also do not want my words to be taken as insider proof of the adage that "black folks don't read" (an anachronism that has never been wholly true even in the days when black people were legally prohibited from learning how to read). I present this anecdotal evidence only to establish why I and other similarly intrigued black gay men at the time, including Ferajaje-Jones, came to ask what it was about *Invisible Life* that galvanized an entire readership of black gay men that were not so galvanized by other works in the developing field of black gay literature.

Like many others, I first turned to the text for the answers to this question. In retrospect, I am embarrassed to admit that I was unable to get through *Invisible Life* the first time around. I was put off by what I considered to be a romance-novel style of prose (even though I consistently read mainstream romance novels throughout junior high and high school). I joked to other black gay friends that every character in *Invisible Life* wore "tight-fitting jeans" (21), and had a "well-proportioned physique" (175) and "perfectly white teeth" (10).

Since I did not finish the book, I was grateful for Farajaje-Jones's detailed analysis and ideological critique of the book in the D.C. Coalition newsletter. In the review titled "Life After *Invisible Life,*" Farajaje-Jones writes:

In an era of repression, it is always encouraging when voices that have been silenced begin to speak and make themselves heard. It is even more exciting for us, as people of Afrikan descent in the life, when one of our own speaks. However, sometimes our enthusiasm blocks our ability to read critically. We are so happy to finally see something in print that reflects our lives (or our fantasies about them) that we read eagerly without raising any questions. Sometimes, though, it is necessary to pull back and examine carefully what we have just read or seen. As a writer and cultural critic, it is also my task to ask in what ways the representations being offered further or block the cause of liberation (9).

I quote extensively from this review because it provides the context for my early thinking about the book as well the background against which I rethought the book. In the remainder of this comprehensive review, Farajaje-Jones astutely traces those representations in the book that he feels "perpetuate and encourage the attitudes and behaviors of the status quo," those that "block the causes of liberation." These include the problematic representations of women who "are presented much more as foils for the men than as real, fleshed-out characters," as well as what he sees as the book's classism, "fatophobia," and "lookism" ("the attachment to certain kinds of looks") (23). In addition, Farajaje-Jones is "profoundly disturbed" that Kyle, "the one openly gay man in the book...is portrayed as being fundamentally unhappy, unstable, and bitter" (25).

For more than a year, this was the primary lens with which I viewed *Invisible Life*. Whenever someone asked my opinion of the book—which was frequent because I am often either the token black gay man or the token black intellectual/academic (i.e. I am expected to have read and have an opinion on every book by or about black gay men in existence) in several professional and social situations—I would admit that I had not finished the book (shame!) and then defer to Farajaje-Jones's review. Most of the people I spoke with had also not read the book, so they were quick to accept my take on it and, in most cases, subsequently decided not to read the book.

No problems really arose for me until I began to talking to people who had actually read the book and in many cases (gasp!) enjoyed and even loved it. This was particularly problematic for me, because I began to realize that Farrajaje-Jones's review was not only the lens with which I viewed the book, but also had become the lens with which I I viewed those who read and took pleasure in it. I felt suspicious of them because, in my mind, they were embracing these suspect representations of homosexuality, bisexuality, black women, and, arguably, black folks in general, even though the only people I had talked to who had read the book were straight black women and other black gay men.

These suspicions and contradictory feelings increased for me after

Spring 1994 when the formerly self-published *Invisible Life* was picked up by Anchor Books, a subsidiary of a Doubleday Books, which simultaneously published *Just as I Am*, the book's sequel, in hardback. E. Lynn Harris was now a mainstream publishing sensation, having gone from selling his first book out of the back of his car to being under contract with a large mainstream (read "nonblack" and "nongay") publisher. Thus the readership for both books increased, and I began to meet more and more people who had read the them.

What made me rethink my take on these books was the way that people began to approach me about them, particularly straight black women. No longer was it simply: "You're a black gay man and the book is by and about a black gay man—whattdya think?" People began to use the book as a way to make a connection with me, to signify some sort of affinity. I particularly remember an incident in which a woman, whom I had only recently met and with whom I had never specifically discussed my sexuality, began discussing the book with me. While she talked about it—how much she had personally liked it and had given it friends—it became clear to me that she was using the book to establish a context for me to "come out" to her, that through her discussion of the book she was establishing a safe space for me to disclose my own sexuality. This was hardly the pathologizing of homosexuality that I would have expected of those so tainted by Harris's problematic representations.

A friend of mine had a similar experience which he shared with me. A woman with whom he had just started working used the book in the very same way, to establish a safe space for him to come out. What struck me about this incident was that it occurred at my friend's new workplace, and new jobs are often a source of extreme anxiety for many gays and lesbians, including myself at times. I remember distinctly entering new workplaces where I would not have been protected by any gay and lesbian antidiscrimination policies. I remember anxiously waiting for signs as to the office climate, then suddenly and sometimes quite unexpectedly hearing a homophobic joke, or, in the best case scenario, meeting someone to whom it was safe to disclose my sexuality.

These are the sites that I think are sometimes forgotten in our calls for representations that further "the cause of liberation." For instance, Farajaje-Jones asks of *Invisible Life*, "Does it lead us to call into question the current order of things in a way that will help to stretch ourselves, to broaden our horizons, to challenge us to strive for a new world of justice and equality for all?" And by the end of the review, his implicit answer is no. I would argue, however, that even though the text itself often does not "question the current order of things" and, at times, even reifies "the current order," the text has been used to create safe spaces for gay men within this hostile "current order," and personally, sometimes all the justice and equality I need is to know that I can be free to make a living in an environment that is a safe space or, at the very least, has safe spaces in which I do not have to hide my sexuality.

After experiencing the way in which the books were used in these contexts, I was intrigued enough to start reading them again. Based upon my earlier experience, I expected my rereading to be more of an intellectual endurance test than a pleasurable read. Once again, however, I was taken by surprise. I started *Invisible Life* again, but this time I could not put it down [at this point, it was only right that I acknowledged my predisposition for the soap opera format; and *Invisible Life* has been called "Gays of Our Lives" (Farajaje-Jones 1992, 23). I finished it and *Just as I Am* in a single weekend.

I acknowledge this for two reasons. First of all, although many cultural critics discuss, applaud, or condemn popular pleasures, few actually own up to experiencing them, a situation that causes undue distance between the critic and her or his subject, relegating popular pleasures and those who experience them to the category of the exotic Other. I also acknowledge the pleasure I experienced in this rereading, because it illustrates how important context is to the reading of a text. When I first began reading *Invisible Life*, I was already suspicious of it, as it was published outside the "legitimate" quarters of black, gay, or mainstream presses and as its readership was different from that of other black gay and lesbian writers. When I reread the book, however, and subsequently read *Just as I Am*, I was already convinced that the books were doing good work, creating safe spaces for members of marginalized groups—black women, and gay and bisexual black men—to dialogue with each other.

I cannot help wondering if my initial reading of *Invisible Life* is analogous to how popular culture is most often studied within the academy. On the one hand, it begs to be studied because it galvanizes such a mass audience. At the same time, it is engaged in by people whom many of us socially, rhetorically, politically, linguistically, and culturally define ourselves in contrast to. Thus it makes perfect sense that many of us view these products with suspicion, these products that everybody but us knows and cares about. Because of this, I wonder how many of us are quick to make deterministic readings about what the text means rather than explore the many ways in which the text can come to have meaning.

In this paper I explore some of the various meanings that circulate within and around *Invisible Life* and *Just as I Am*. I discuss the social, cultural, and political contexts within which the books were created, marketed, and received; and in doing so, I address the ways in which popular literature (and perhaps popular culture in general) can be used to illuminate the conflicts, contradictions, and contestations which operate in everyday life.

In his article, "Fiction and Fictionality in Popular Culture: Some Observations on the Aesthetics of Popular Culture," Winfried Fluck states that "even the most determined cultural critics of popular culture" have acknowledged that "even the most conventional or stereotypical text has to take off from some real-life conflict of its audience" (Fluck 1988, 55). Many critics argue that the texts are popular because they do not disturb the reader and enable her or him "to go through the pleasant experience of a recognition and reassurance" of their own views (Fluck 1988, 53).

According to Fluck, though, this theory does not explain "why mere affirmation should provide pleasure to such an unusual degree that it is consistently sought," as is the case with many forms of popular literature (53). Fluck argues, instead, "that a text of mere reassurance would be experienced as boring or even pointless"; and that "only if the text provokes a certain amount of genuinely felt anxiety and disturbance will the reader become engaged" (53). Challenging the more traditional tropes of interpreting popular pleasure, Fluck writes:

> It is this element of disturbance that strikes me as the first essential source for the strong emotions which the popular text evokes. It can be objected, of course, that many of the disturbances created by popular texts appear rather timid or conventionalized. But we have to take into account that *disturbance* is in itself a relational term...What strikes one reader as timid may cause considerable anxieties in another (Fluck 1988, 54).

For instance, the representation of homosexuality and bisexuality is in and of itself disturbing for many readers. Harris states that black women, who are his largest audience, call his books "eye-opening," which is arguably a degree of disturbance. "Straight black men," he adds, "have told me that the books bothered them because I write so vividly, that the mere fact they can imagine what I'm writing about unnerves them" (Shahid 1994, 7D).

An analysis of popular literature in terms of disturbance, therefore, will be less interested in "merely pointing out common attitudes and values" and "much more interested in the threats to which these values have been exposed in the text" (Fluck 1988, 54). Fluck states, "Like all fiction then, popular culture is characterized, in the final analysis, by an unstable dialectic between conventionality and its disruption (57).

The following are some examples of how this "unstable dialectic between conventionality and disruption" works both within and between *Invisible Life* and *Just as I Am*. For a variety of reasons I feel it is best to study these novels as companion pieces, especially with respect to reception. The most obvious reason is that *Just as I Am* is the sequel to *Invisible Life*; but unlike many serial novels, they were published (at least by the mainstream publisher) simultaneously. (In fact, the reissued paperback version of *Invisible Life* contains the first chapter of *Just as I Am* as a teaser.) Many of the book's readers, therefore, had instance access to the other book, allowing for a more immediate experience of the dialogue between the two novels. Also, Harris himself admits that he was somewhat "inhibited" in writing *Invisible Life* and that *Just as I Am* is, to some extent, a response to criticism of *Invisible Life* (Asim 1994, 13). Thus, many views and attitudes that are initially presented in *Invisible Life* are subsequently disrupted in *Just as I Am*.

The issue of prejudice among black people in regard to skin color is one such example. In *Invisible Life*, almost all of the main characters are described as having light brown skin. The story, in short, centers around the life of a young black bisexual man named Raymond Winston Tyler Jr., following him from his first surprise sexual encounter with a man in college to his years trying to negotiate a bisexual identity while working as a lawyer in New York City. In the book his skin is described as "camel-colored," and he admits that socially and professionally he benefits from his light skin color. Sela, his girlfriend in college, is described as having a "vanilla wafer–brown complexion," "long black hair," and "almond-shaped hazel eyes"; and in New York City, his openly gay best friend, Kyle, has "a sandy-colored complexion."

Many of the characters with darker skin or more traditionally black features are pitied in some way. Janelle, or J.J., a female friend of Kyle's, whom "most people would label ...a fag hag," is described as having "paper sack–brown skin," "a small pug nose," "extremely short well-kept dreads," and "child-bearing hips." She is, Raymond states pejoratively, "attractive in her own way." Raymond also remarks about a colleague of his at the law firm, "Brayton was extremely handsome, but his features and skin color were very ethnic" (Asim 1994, 204).

Two of the only characters with dark brown skin who are not pitied are Quinn Mathis, a married man with whom Raymond has an affair, and Nicole Springer, a woman with whom Raymond has a ongoing affair. Raymond describes Quinn as having "charcoal black skin," "closely cropped coarse hair," a "full face," "large chocolate eyes," a "slightly pug nose," and "full lips," the antithesis of what are considered white-identified standards of beauty. This description is not as transgressive as it initially may seem, however, because color standards, like most other beauty standards, generally apply more to women than to men. Also, since blackness is commonly associated with hypermasculinity, hence hypersexuality, dark skin color and what are traditionally considered black features are sometimes assets for a man.

Nicole Springer, on the other hand, is described in every way to exemplify a traditionally white-identified standard of beauty expect for her dark brown skin color:

> She looked like a porcelain Barbie doll dipped in chocolate, with beautiful black shoulder-length curly hair and a lovely face with sharp facial features that made me wonder if she had been under the knife for plastic surgery. Nicole had high cheekbones and her nose and lips were perfect (Harris 1991, 123).

In *Just as I Am*, Nicole enters therapy because of events that transpired at the end of *Invisible Life*: After years of concealing it, Raymond reveals his bisexuality to her, and her best friend, Candance, succumbs to complications associated with AIDS after being involved with Kelvin, Raymond's first lover. Nicole recounts the following story in a conversation with her therapist:

> When I was a little girl, my mother would take me to downtown Little Rock to shop. It was our special time together.

Just us girls. People always thought she wasn't my mother. Me being so dark and my mother having beautiful honey-colored skin. One day these two ladies kept badgering my mother. Saying it was no way I could be her daughter. When I thought my mother had finally convinced him, they laughed and said my daddy must have had some powerful blueberry genes. My mother joined in their laughter (Harris 1994, 156).

Her therapist then asks: "Nicole, were these women black or white?" Nicole answers: "They were black. Light-skinned black women" (156). Through this and other accounts of prejudice that Nicole experienced from other black people, the skin-color standards that are reified and naturalized in *Invisible Life* are disrupted and seen as oppressive in *Just as I Am*.

There is also an overt and self-conscious dialogue between the two books with respect to Raymond's sexuality. In *Invisible Life*, Raymond is wildly ambivalent about his own sexuality. In fact, I would propose that one of the reasons the book is so popular with straight audiences is that Raymond's sexual ambivalence reflects the ambivalence many straight readers feel about homosexuality. Throughout all of *Invisible Life*, Raymond wishes to change his sexuality. At one point he states, "Maybe being gay was like being an alcoholic. That with willpower and a little counseling you could just stop, that you would still be gay but just choose not to practice...I sometimes prayed for a pill I could take to destroy my homosexual feelings. I would have taken it in a heartbeat" (212).

In a telling move, Harris expresses these same sentiments in one of his interviews, " 'If you told me that all I had to do was eat this lemon to be straight,' " he said, pointing to a yellow sliver resting on the mouth of his glass of water, "' I'd eat a dozen' " (Evans, 1994). In another interview, Harris states that he wrote *Invisible Life* "to tell the truth" about his own sexuality (Shahid 1994, 7D); "I am Ray Tyler," he says, "I wrote myself and my own feelings into those pages" (Johnson 1994, 45). Thus, *Invisible Life* can be read as Harris's exploration of his own sexual ambivalence through the character Raymond.

Many of his readers, however, especially black gay and bisexual men, criticized the character Raymond in *Invisible Life*. Much of this criticism is easily summed up by comments made by a reader on America Online's "Black and Gay" message board, simply put: "Raymond is weak!" In an interview in the *Washington Blade*, Harris comments on such criticisms: "I heard from a lot of black gay men that they wanted a protagonist who was proud to be black and proud to be gay," Harris says, "and was in a stable, healthy relationship with another black man." At that point, the author says, he knew that his work in *Invisible Life* had not been completed. "I had to satisfy a market that was hungry for positive images of black gay men" (Johnson 1994, 47).

The development of Raymond's character in *Just as I Am* can be read largely as a response to these criticisms. From the outset of the book Raymond's sexual ambivalence is seen as an obstacle to his happiness, both professionally and personally. For instance, in *Invisible Life*, Raymond discusses how his ability to "pass" as straight has helped him in his career. He tells the following story:

> There had been a time when the top student at Columbia's Law School was an unquestionably black gay guy. I heard he went on several interviews, but didn't get offers from the top firms. The day he visited our firm for an interview, I made sure I was nowhere to be found. Later I felt badly about not being there for support, but I couldn't risk the chance of being found out by being supportive (205).

At the outset of *Just as I Am*, however, Raymond loses out on a job because he is not "out." He states:

> I had originally moved to Atlanta with understanding that I would go to work for the city government, but for a few days before I was to start, I received word that a hiring freeze had been put into effect. I later found out from a friend of my father that the reason for the freeze was because someone in the mayor's office wanted the position promised to me to go to an openly gay, black attorney. Now wasn't that just the shit (2).

As *Just as I Am* opens, Raymond is also unhappy in his personal life, partly due to his continued attraction to men who are even more closeted than he is. He begins a relationship with Basil Henderson, a closeted professional football player first introduced in *Invisible Life*. Their paths cross again in *Just as I Am* when Raymond is assigned to represent Basil in a gay-bashing suit brought by a gay man whom Basil punches in a club. Against his better judgement, Raymond enters into a relationship with Basil and almost immediately pays a high price.

During a planned weekend at Basil's New Jersey home, Basil's girl-friend, Dyanna, unexpectedly shows up, forcing Raymond to hide in the bedroom closet:

> I couldn't believe what was happening as I was pushed into the closet in my underwear and with my garment bag. Once I was inside the closet and heard the door slam shut, I was sud-denly among Basil's wardrobe.... I had never felt like such a jackass in all my life.
>
> I don't remember at what point I finally fell asleep amid Basil's suits, slacks, shirts, and shoes, but I can recall just how angry I was as I sat in the dark listening to Basil and Dyanna's lively conversation and later their loud lovemaking (146-7).

Raymond only finds happiness in a relationship toward the end of the novel, with Trent Waters, a former fraternity brother of Raymond's who is now openly gay.

In addition to changing the type of men he sleeps with, Raymond also undergoes a change in respect to his personal and political stances on homophobia and gay and lesbian rights. In *Invisible Life* he effec-tively eschews these issues; in *Just as I Am* (admittedly, after defending and sleeping with a confessed gay basher) Raymond begins to confront his friends and family about their homophobia. For instance, after meeting Kyle on a visit to New York, Raymond's little brother Kirby asks Raymond, "Is Kyle soft?...You know...[a] sissy, a fag?" Raymond answers, "Don't use those words, Kirby.... They're demeaning.... Get that fag shit out your vocabulary. Do you understand?" (237).

Also, even after the embarrassing incident in the closet, Basil invites Raymond to go with him to "The Black Ski Summit" since his girlfriend cannot go because of work obligations. Raymond does not go, however, because it is in Colorado. He explains to Basil:

> "Don't you know about the boycott?"
>
> "What boycott?"
>
> "They passed an antigay law up there and a lot of people are boy-cotting the state," I explained.
>
> "Aw, Ray, that's white folks shit. Ray, white boys don't give a shit about us," Basil said.
>
> "Well, I don't disagree with you on that, but I don't think it's right...." (264).

There is also an interesting dialogue between the two books on the subject of homosexual anal sex, a topic of significant anxiety for many heterosexuals. For most of the first novel, anal sex is never specifically mentioned, yet Harris makes it clear that Raymond is not having anal sex. In *Invisible Life*, during Raymond's first gay sexual encounter in college, he exclaims somewhat awkwardly, "How would I have known that rubbing two male sexual organs together would bring such a complete feeling of ecstasy?" (17) Later in the novel, the subject explicitly comes up during a conversation between Raymond and his father:

"You didn't let them sc—" My father stopped in mid sentence and quietly stared at me, his face creased by a question that he was struggling to articulate.

"Screw me, Pops? Is that what you want to know? Would that make me more of a man in your eyes, if I'm the doer?' I felt my rage returning. Why did my father's question cause my anger to return? Should I tell him that I didn't let men enter me? Would his knowing this make my sexuality easier to digest?" (246).

The answer to this question is implicitly yes, both in respect to Raymond's father and Harris's readership. Harris admits that he made Raymond bisexual in order to attract straight readers: "I did that for a reason. It's good to have somebody in there that you know and recognize" (Asim 1994, 4). Perhaps, for the same reason, Harris makes it clear that Raymond does not engage in anal sex and, to some extent, does not understand those who enjoy it: "I used to listen to Kyle talk about the total rapture he felt when he gave himself to another man. He would describe it like a woman talking about multiple orgasms. It sounded like a dangerous addiction that I could live without" (Harris 1994, 219).

The subject of anal sex returns in *Just as I Am*. Raymond and a straight friend, Jared, have a conversation similar to the conversation that Raymond and his father have in *Invisible Life*:

"Ray, you don't let them..." He paused.
"Let them what?" I asked.
"You know," Jared said as he moved his index finger in and out of a circle he formed with his free hand.
"What are you asking me? Do I let them poke me?"
"Yeah, but you don't have to answer that," he responded shyly.

"Does it matter?"

"No!"

"You sure?"

"I'm sure."

"I will never understand the curiosity straight folks have with who is doing who" (Harris 1994, 185).

Toward the end of the novel, however, during his relationship with Trent, a surprising change occurs in Raymond's attitude about anal sex, which Raymond discusses with his therapist:

"Well, we're both virgins in a certain way," I laughed. "Neither one of us has given up the booty—but he's willing to try for me."

"Why is that funny?"

"Well, I don't know if he expects the same thing from me."

"Will that be a problem?"

"Might be. From what I can tell Trent does not have a starter-kit dick. If you get my drift."

Dr. Paul tried to prevent a smile.

"Is that just a barrier you're putting up, Raymond?"

"No, I'm serious" (Harris 1994, 328).

Harris's willingness to have Raymond engage the issue of anal sex is, perhaps, another example of him responding to earlier criticisms of *Invisible Life*.

The issues of color prejudice among black people, Raymond's sexual ambivalence, and anal sex are all subjects that Harris engages in the text. Harris both presents conventional and status quo attitudes on these subjects and disrupts them, either by exposing the pain caused by these conventional attitudes or by having the characters question and interrogate the assumptions behind these attitudes. I do not want to suggest, however, that every attitude that perpetuates the status quo is interrogated in the novels. The classism of the novels, which Farajaje-Jones describes as "overwhelming," is one such example (Farajaje-Jones 1992, 25). In *Just as I Am*, Raymond refrains from going to a large black club in Washington, D.C., opting instead for "a party where the men may be a little older, but the majority of them are homeowners and not simply owners of Metro [subway] cards" (12). In addition, on the plane ride back to Atlanta, Raymond is pleased that his economy seat is upgraded to first class: "The upgrade was a welcome relief because I could see that the coach was packed with what could only be former Greyhound Bus frequent travelers (15).

While the classism in the books is certainly objectionable, we, as critics, must be cautious not to pathologize the texts themselves or those who take pleasure in them. Instead we must, as Tricia Rose states, "incorporate them into an analysis which explores how and why they retain currency" (Ross 1993, 17). Classism, like skin-color prejudice, is just another strategy some black people have used to give value to their lives in a society that systematically devalues them.

By focusing on the disruptions in the text, I also do not want to ignore the pleasures of recognition with the texts. These pleasures are particularly relevant in respect to communities whose lives and lifestyles are seldom represented in literature, popular or otherwise. Harris states: "...my strength is in storytelling. I tell the stories that black people—and particularly black gay people—already know and want to hear more" (Farajaje-Jones 1992, 47). In both books, Harris chronicles the richness of black gay life and culture from references to black gay icons such as R&B singer Stephanie Mills to thinly veiled references to black gay bars, to national black gay and lesbian events such as the Memorial Day weekend celebration in Washington, D.C.

Harris's ability to tell what black people "already know" is also apparent in the way in which he vividly details a particular black middle class or "buppie" lifestyle that is familiar to many readers. While popular media is saturated with stories of white middle-class lifestyles, those of the black middle class are seldom represented. Thus, his books fulfill a need of many readers. One reviewer, in fact, calls *Just as I Am* "a wonderful affirmation of black social life" (Woods); and another states that, in *Just as I Am*, Harris "depicts a black society that is whole (if not unified), and self-energizing" (Birro, 1994).

One particular pleasure of recognition that I would briefly like to explore in the novels comes from Harris's many references to black music artists. The following is just one of many similar examples in both novels. Raymond states, "Suddenly the room was filled with the sounds of LTD's 'Love Ballad.' I will never forget how, just as Jeffrey Osborne was about to proclaim the depth of his love, Kelvin (Raymond's lover at the time) gently lifted the needle from the album, gazed at me and proclaimed, 'I love you' " (Lynn 1994, 35). What interests me about this and similar passages is how little it says about the music being played, completely going against that traditional literary maxim "show, don't tell." For someone unfamiliar with the seminal yet underrated '70s R&B band LTD, the passage says virtually nothing. However, for one who is familiar with LTD and their almost canonical "slow jam," "Love Ballad," the passage is incredibly evocative. The book thus privileges in-group readings in a way that could be quite pleasurable for black readers, given that we are most often "outsiders" with respect to cultural representation in literature.

I want to turn now to explore one of the most frequently written-about aspects of the books' phenomenon: those who are almost single handedly responsible for the books' mainstream success, namely, the books' black female readership. When Harris first self-published 5,000 copies of *Invisible Life* in late 1991, he sold them primarily to straight black women in beauty salons throughout Atlanta. He would ask the beauty salons to keep a copy of the book (marked DO NOT REMOVE) in their magazine rack. Each copy of the book included ordering information (De Grazia 1994). Harris sold almost 2,000 copies this way, in addition to selling it at small bookstores and at private book parties thrown by friends in Atlanta, New York, and Washington, D.C. (Farajaje-Jones 1992, 45).

The following summer, *Essence,* a glossy monthly black woman's magazine, listed *Invisible Life* as a recommended summer read ("Book," 40). Subsequently, Harris sold an additional 3,000 copies and immediately printed another 10,000—all of which he sold without the help of a major book distributor.

Once *Invisible Life* was picked up by Doubleday and rereleased simultaneously with its sequel, both books were marketed heavily to black women. For instance, the original cover of *Invisible Life* is an illustration of a man removing a mask, emphasizing the theme of self-awareness and visibility. The rereleased version, however, includes the picture of a black woman . The photograph places a black man in the center of the picture, flanked on his left by another man, and on his right by a woman. Although the man in the center is looking at the other man, the two do not touch. The woman, on the other hand, has one hand on the man's chest and the other on his shoulder. In this depiction of one of the book's many love triangles, the woman clearly has the—pun intended—upper hand.

Also, as a part of the books' marketing plan, *Just as I Am* was excerpted in *Essence* in a special "Love Reads" section in its February (i.e., Valentine's Day) 1994 issue. In the introduction to the section, which also features excerpts from three other recent books, editor Linda Villarosa (an out lesbian, by the way) writes, "This month love is in the air. And on these pages. Some of this season's best books by Black authors pay tribute to the timeless subjects of love and romance" (Villarosa 1994, 75). When writing about *Just as I Am*, the only included book about homosexuality or bisexuality, Villarosa states: "*Just as I Am* explores a different kind of love" (Villarosa 1994, 75).

I am terribly interested here in the juxtapositioning of the word "timeless" in the overall introduction to the excerpts and the word "different" in the introduction to the excerpt from *Just as I Am*. This appeal to *Essence*'s black female readership seems to work on the same "conventionality" and "disruption" model that I discussed earlier in the essay. On the one hand, love and romance are conventional, "timeless," in the words of the magazine. On the other hand, male homosexual love is "different" and disruptive to the convention. This juxtaposition is clearly meant to entice readers with notions of "difference" and "otherness" and is often used to market homosexuality and bisexuality to mass audiences. For example, the release of *Making Love,* the mainstream 1982 film about a married man who has a homosexual affair, was timed to coincide with Valentine's Day weekend, enticing viewers with a "different" take on the very conventional theme the holiday is intended to celebrate.

I find this "conventionality" and "disruption" trope a particularly useful paradigm for analyzing works like *Invisible Life*, *Just as I Am*, and *Making Love,* because it allows one to theorize as to why straight audiences would be attracted to works that address homosexuality and bisexuality—i.e., because they both reify and disrupt romantic conventions—yet it does not place a value judgment on their attraction as do theories of the gay or lesbian "spectacle" or theories of the exotic "Other." I also like the trope because it does not assume that the audience for such works is an undifferentiated mass with only one intent toward the given work. Even though large numbers of people are interested in the works, we must not assume that their reasons for being interested are all the same. Instead, as critics, we must examine the many reasons why a given audience would be attracted to such works, placing these works in the context of other discourses that circulate both within and outside the group about homosexuality and bisexuality. Through examining popular discourse on homosexuality and bisexuality that circulates throughout black women's magazines, black popular cinema, and academic journals, one finds many reasons why black women would be attracted to Harris's books.

The cover for *Just as I Am* is an interesting site from which to begin this examination. Although it features the same models as those on the cover of *Invisible Life* and is formally and aesthetically very similar, the two men in this photo are touching, while the women stands alone in the opposite corner of the frame. I would argue that the reader is supposed to identify with the woman in this picture because hers are the only eyes we see. We meet her eyes in the left side of the frame and, reading from the left to right, we eye the two men with the same suspicion and anxiety as she does. What is centered here is not the love triangle as on the cover of *Invisible Life*, but instead the gulf between the woman and the two men.

In his article "AIDS in Blackface," Harlon Dalton argues that "more than even the 'no account' men who figure prominently in the repertoire of female blues singers, gay men symbolize the abandonment of black women" (Dalton 1994, 217). This view is prevalent throughout much of the popular and academic discourse on black women and gay men. Homosexuality is most often constructed as a threat to the ability of black women to establish stable relationships with black men.

One can see this view represented in black filmmaker Spike Lee's interracial film *Jungle Fever*. In the infamous "war council" scene, in which a group of black women discusses the problems they have with black men, Nida, a character brilliantly played by comedienne Phyllis Yvonne Stickney, states, "Ain't no good black men out there. Most of them either drug addicts, in jail, homo..." Thus, homosexuality, like drug addiction, crime, and in the larger context of the movie, interracial relationships, is seen as another obstacle for black women in their quest for relationships with black men.

This attitude is so prevalent that it even finds its way into scientific literature on black homophobia. In "Condemnation of Homosexuality in the Black Community: A Gender-Specific Phenomenon?" four researchers conclude quite problematically that homophobia in the black community is largely due to the attitudes of black women. When trying to explain these conclusions, they state:

> The reasons for this gender-specific phenomenon cannot be derived from our data. However, we have interviewed several black females to explore possible explanations. The most frequent reaction to a description of our results is derived from the perceived decreasing pool of "available black

males." To summarize the reactions, hostility toward a homosexual lifestyle apparently stems from a recognition that this factor contributes to the decreasing pool of available black males already affected by integration (interracial marriages), disproportionate incarceration rates for black males, and high rates of premature death among black males from heart disease, cancer, AIDS, drug abuse, and violence (Ernst, et al, 1991, 583).

I find this passage interesting in that it restates almost to the letter the dominant discourses about the relationship between straight black women and gay black men. This is particularly interesting given that while the article makes it clear that they interviewed 2006 people for their initial study, they are suspiciously vague about how many black women they interviewed to draw their conclusions, stating simply, "several." Also, while they explicitly state the questions posed to the initial sample, they include no information as to the specific questions these "several" black women were asked, nor do they include any direct quotes from these women. This, of course, makes the conclusions that they draw from this data quite suspect.

In the popular media, homosexuality and bisexuality have also been constructed as a threat to black women with respect to AIDS. In January 1988, *Ebony* magazine ran a feature story titled "The Hidden Fear: Black Women, Bisexuals, and the AIDS Risk," featuring an ominous shadowy illustration of a black woman holding the hand of a black man who is holding the hand of another black man. This theme is also, of course, one of the themes of *Invisible Life*, in which Candance, a friend of Raymond's girlfriend, who is engaged to Kelvin, one of Raymond's former lovers, dies from complications associated with AIDS. Although it is never explicitly stated that Kelvin exposed her to HIV, it is clearly one of the possibilities that readers are led to consider.

By including these many examples of how homosexuality and bisexuality are constructed as threats for black women both in terms of AIDS and their development of relationships with black men, I do not mean to suggest that they go unchallenged. In fact, I would argue that there is a ongoing dialogue about these issues. In "AIDS in Blackface," for instance, Dalton challenges the myth that straight black women contract HIV primarily through intercourse with bisexual black men. Although he states that "the risk that a black woman will be infected by a bisexual man is 4.6 times as great as for a white woman," he also notes that

> the principal means by which women in this country contract HIV is through sharing intravenous needles and "works." A distant second transmission route is sexual contact with straight male sex partners who themselves became infected via needles. Far back in third place is sexual contact with non–drug-using bisexual males (Dalton 1994, 226).

Challenging the assumption that homosexuality and bisexuality threaten the ability of black women to establish romantic relationships with black men, *Essence* magazine published a feature story titled "Cover Girls," referring to women who were married to or in romantic and sexual relationships with gay and bisexual black men (Ruff 1992, 69). Although some of the women in the article are dissatisfied in their relationships with gay or bisexual men, others are not. Some straight black women even desire to be in a relationship with a gay or bisexual man. The following is from a letter to the editor in response to the story:

> I am a woman who for years experienced the companionship of straight males. These men had an "old-school'"mentality and felt that the woman was to be owned and the man was the "boss." Those failed relationships made me feel that there was something wrong with me. Just as I was about to give up completely, gay males came into my life. I may even eventually meet a gay male with whom I can share my life. I am especially open to the sense of truth, openness of expression, level of considerateness, and general lack of inhibition (Anonymous 1992, 9).

In *Just as I Am*, Harris interrogates the notion that black gay men are somehow abandoning black women (albeit at the expense of straight black men). On his deathbed Kyle challenges Nicole about her feelings of resentment toward black gay and bisexual men. He states, "...women ought to think about the men who really hurt them. It's not gay men who lie, cheat, beat them, and leave them alone with kids to fend for themselves. Well, sometimes these confused gay men do. But when you think about it, heterosexual men beat women down daily" (245). Harris comments on this issue in a profile as well. Shawn R.

Evans, the writer of the piece, says, "Harris wants Black women especially to know that he and other bisexual men are not 'turning their back on them.' "

I keep returning to Harris's own words and his own intentions in writing the novels because I do not want Harris, the author, to disappear from my critique. Although in much of contemporary criticism discussions of authorship are considered passé or irrelevant, it is important not to lose sight of the implications of authorship for those who have, for a variety of historical, political, sociological, economic, and cultural reasons, traditionally been excluded from claiming it. Look, for example, at how hard it was for Harris to become an author and to present his own take on black culture. The implications of his struggle and the intentions behind it should not be overlooked.

In closing, I want to discuss the reception of the works of gay and lesbian popular artists like Harris within the field of gay and lesbian studies. In my opinion, the works of these artists have been too often overlooked. In fact, one of the things that disturbs me most about the current turn to queer theory is that, as often applies, it simply provides new ways of interpreting older canonical works rather than providing the impetus for studying gay and lesbian artists whose works have been insufficiently examined.

Gordon Merrick, the late white gay popular novelist, is one such example. As with Harris's works, Merrick's books, which were published throughout the '70s and early '80s, were very popular with mainstream audiences. In 1970, just one year after Stonewall, his novel *The Lord Won't Mind* spent 16 weeks on *The New York Times* bestseller list (Rutledge 1992, 15). Yet, to my knowledge, Merrick is not included in any contemporary surveys of gay and lesbian authors or of gay and lesbian literature.

Granted, Merrick's books were not particularly well-received by critics. About *The Lord Won't Mind*, for instance, a *Publishers Weekly* reviewer writes, "Maybe the Lord won't mind, but just about everybody else will find something distasteful in this no-holds-barred novel of a homosexual affair" (74). And one *New York Times Book Review* critic writes, "It may set homosexuality back at least 20 years" (47). I have no doubt that the fact that Merrick's books have yet to be sufficiently studied within the academy is in some part due to these and other caustic critiques.

It seems to me, however, that this "queer moment" in gay and lesbian studies is the perfect time to examine the works of gay and lesbian popular artists such as Merrick and Harris. For instance, the works of both artists are not easily subsumed under the dominant political ideologies of the contemporary gay and lesbian rights movement. Similarly, the term *queer* in queer theory is used "to mark a certain critical distance" from the "ideological liabilities" inherent in such terms as *gay* and *lesbian* (De Lauretis, 1991). Thus queer theory provides an ideal site from which to study works that resist and transgress dominant gay and lesbian ideologies.

Queer theory, as applied to the study of popular culture, also provides a useful way for studying the works of artists such as Merrick and Harris, who have a large straight following. Alexander Doty, for instance, uses *queer* to refer to the pleasures that straight people have with respect to gay and lesbian texts, arguing that "a person's positioning as a spectator often does not confirm to his/her stated sexual orientation" (Ross 1993, 10).

The purpose of this essay is largely to rescue Harris from what has been Merrick's fate. I feel strongly that if the intention of gay and lesbian studies is to study the various social, cultural, and political meanings that are constructed and circulated about homosexuality, then we must study the works of gay and lesbian artists whose ideologies we may personally agree with as well as those gay and lesbian artists whose ideologies we do not agree with. As Canaan Parker states about *Just as I Am*:

> *Just as I Am* argues implicitly that a modern gay activist consciousness cannot be forced on every nonstraight person. We are either committed to individual freedom and pluralism of lifestyle, or we are not. When gays become inflexible ideologues, we play out an Orwellian scenario that will probably fare no better than Marxism" (Parker 1994, 20).

Save for the jab at Marxism, I could not agree more.

References

Anonymous. Letter. *Essence (*May 1992) 9.

Asim, Jabari. "Making the Invisible Seen." *St. Louis Post-Dispatch* (April 3, 1994): 4-13

Birro, Louis. "In Love and In Conflict" (*Rev. of Just as I Am* by E. Lynn Harris). *Quarterly Review of Black Books (*Spring 1994).

"Book Marks." *Essence* (July 1992): 40.

Dalton, H.L. "AIDS in Blackface." *Daedalus* 1994.

De Grazia, D.G. "Becoming Visible." *New City's Literary Supplement* (Apr. 14, 1994).

De Lauretis, T. (1991). "Queer Theory: Lesbian and Gay Sexualities, an Introduction." *Differences* 3.2: iii-xviii.

Ernst, F.A., et al. (1991). "Condemnation of Homosexuality in the Black Community: A Gender-Specific Phenomenon?" *Archives of Sexual Behavior* 20.6: 579-85.

Evans, Shawn R. "Author Profile." *The Atlanta Metro* (March 1994).

Farajaje-Jones, E. (1992). "Life After Life" (Rev. of *Invisible Life* by E. Lynn Harris). *The Fire This Time: A Publication of the D.C. Coalition of Black Lesbians and Gay Men* (Summer): 9-26.

Fluck, W. (1988). "Fiction and Fictionality in Popular Culture: Some Observations on the Aesthetics of Popular Culture." *Journal of Popular Culture* 21.4: 49-62.

Harris, E. L. (1991). *Invisible Life.* Atlanta: Consortium Press. New York: Anchor Books.

— (1994). *Just as I Am.* New York: Doubleday

Johnson, M.F. "E. Lynn Harris Comes Home." *The Washington Blade.* Apr. 15, 1994: 45-7.

Parker, C. "Sell the Fantasy." *Lambda Book Report* (May-Apr. 1994).

Randolph, L.B. "The Hidden Fear: Black Women, Bisexuals, and the AIDS Risk." *Ebony* (Jan. 1988): 120-6.

Rev. of *The Lord Won't Mind* by Gordon Merrick. *New York Times Book Review* (Apr. 26, 1970): 47.

Rev. of *The Lord Won't Mind* by Gordon Merrick. *Publishers Weekly* (Jan. 5, 1970): 74.

Ross, A., et al. (1993). "A Symposium of Popular Culture and Political Correctness." *Social Text* 36: 1-39.

Ruff, P.E. "Cover Girls." *Essence* (Mar 1992): 69.

Rutledge, L.W. (1992). *The Gay Decades.* New York: Plume.

Shahid, S. "E. Lynn Harris, Successfully Sharing His 'Invisible Life'." *USA Today* (August 17, 1994): 7D.

Villarosa, L. "Love Reads." *Essence* (Feb 1994): 75.

Woods, P. "Deeper Into the Black Gay World." *Atlanta Journal Constitution* (Mar. 13, 1994).

Swishing and Swaggering: Homosexuality in Black Magazines During the 1950s

Gregory Conerly

Introduction

For people who engaged in same-sex sexual behavior, or who identified themselves as preferring some level of same-sex sexual intimacy, the 1950s was a time of unparalleled institutional repression—that is, according to the stories constructed by such historians such as John D'Emilio and Barry Adam (D'Emilio 1983, 40-53; D'Emilio 1989, 226-40; Adam 1987, 56-74). They argue that those suspected of same-sex sexual intimacies were caught up in the web of anticommunist rhetoric. Government hearings were held. "Experts" testified. A report was issued. The government concluded: "[H]omosexuals and other sex perverts are not proper persons to be employed in government for two reasons; first, they are generally unsuitable, and second, they constitute security risks" (U.S. Senate 1950, 3). They purged by the thousands those suspected of sex perversion from the military and federal, state, and local government positions.

The mass media and local police departments across the country also responded to what had come to be known as the "homosexual menace." The police raided bars, cruising areas, and homes with increasing frequency in cities such as Baltimore, New Orleans, and San Francisco. They arrested or harassed hundreds. Local newspapers frequently printed the names and addresses of those arrested. And mainstream publications such as *Newsweek* claimed these people were destroying society.

In black communities during this time, there was also a heightened awareness of same-sex sexuality. This was not only because of the national rhetoric, but also because several prominent black figures were known to have had or had written about same-sex relationships: author James Baldwin, civil rights activist Bayard Rustin, and singer Little Richard. In this essay, I examine how two popular magazines aimed at African Americans, *Ebony* and *Jet*, published material on same-sex sexuality during this time. How did they construct the "truth" about black same-sex sexuality? What were the relationships between African American lesbians, gays, and bisexuals (les-bi-gays) and the larger black communities in which most were situated?

What the pages of *Ebony* and *Jet* suggest about the relationships between various social institutions and same-sex sexuality is something more complex than the monolithic repression machine the aforementioned historians have constructed. They suggest that although there was a heightened awareness of same-sex sexuality during this period, mainstream institutions such as the police, and African American institutions like the church, entertainment industry, and segments of the media, had complex and often contradictory relationships with those preferring some level of same-sex intimacy. These magazines suggest that for many blacks, male homosexuality was tolerable under certain circumstances; lesbianism was almost universally condemned.

In the first part of this essay, I present some background on *Ebony* and *Jet*, and how discourses on same-sex sexuality were reflected in their editorial policies. Then I focus on one dominant theme of this discourse, the "truth" about the relationships between same-sex sexuality and gender nonconformity, to examine the kinds of relationships black communities had with those they perceived to be les-bi-gay.

Ebony/Jet: Emerging Voices for Black America

John Johnson first published *Ebony*, a feature-oriented monthly modeled after *Life*, in 1945. His mission was to "mirror the happier side of Negro life" (Wolseley 1990, 88). And so they published many feature stories about, among other things, economically and socially successful African Americans, black social events, and ordinary folk who overcame various kinds of adversities. *Jet*, a pocket-sized weekly news digest modeled after the short-lived mainstream magazine *Quick,* was started by Johnson in 1951 to "provide Negroes with a convenient-sized magazine summarizing the week's biggest Negro news in a well-organized, easy-to-read format" (Wolseley 1990, 145). It had "serious" news, feature stories similar to those in *Ebony*, and sensational items about such things as domestic violence and the goings-on of the famous and infamous. By the end of the 1950s, both publications reached more than 400,000 subscribers, more than twice the number of their closest competitors, *Tan* (also a Johnson publication), and *Our World*, which died in 1956 (Johnson, et al, 1950-59).

Both magazines reached all segments of the black population. But a disproportionate number of *Ebony's* readers were middle-class, and this magazine generally reflected their values: the importance of social status, self-help, material consumption, and social and economic success (Frazier, 1957; Berkman, 1963; Goodman, 1968; Hirsch, 1968). This was particularly true after the 1954 recession, when the magazine stopped running feature stories about sex and sex-related issues. They used these stories to attract a mass African American audience. Starting in 1955, though, *Ebony* concentrated on subscriptions rather than newsstand sales in an attempt to stem declining circulation. *Jet* also stopped running feature stories about sex, though throughout the decade they continued to run sex stories in the form of news and gossip items. Ben Burns, executive editor of both magazines and the one responsible for the sex stories, was forced out of his position (Johnson 1989, 234-6). It is within this context that discourses about same-sex sexuality appear in these magazines.

Same-Sex Sexuality in Ebony/Jet

Most of the stories relating to same-sex sexuality in *Ebony* focused on drag queen balls, those with a same-sex sexual preference becoming "normal," people who lived part or most of their lives as one gender but whose true gender identity was discovered upon their death, or the less than "happy" side of life in places such as the black church and in prison. *Jet* ran similar kinds of stories about same-sex sexuality. But they also had news reports, especially those of individuals arrested for various same-sex crimes, gossip items about who allegedly slept with whom, feature stories about the morality of same-sex sexuality, and a large number of stories about domestic violence among same-sex couples in their "Mr. and Mrs." Section. While the vast majority of these stories did not exactly present the positive sides of same-sex sexuality— or of heterosexuality, for that matter—there was an important exception. This involved female impersonators: both nightclub performers and those men who lived part or most of their lives as women. One common construction of same-sex sexuality was the association of "homosexuals" and "lesbians" with gender nonconformity. That is, homosexual men had feminine characteristics, and lesbians masculine characteristics, in terms of clothing, walk, and mannerisms. For example, Leatrice Calloway, a Detroit woman who, according to *Jet*, shot her lover who started dating a man, was described as wearing "a well-tailored pair of trousers, a wrinkled shirt with a wilted collar, and mannish shoes" ("Strange Lover Faces Sanity Test" 1951, 52).

Gender conformists who engaged in same-sex sexual behavior were either hiding their "deviant" gender characteristics or were "bisexual." This is in contrast to the popular Kinsey reports on human sexuality, published in 1948 and 1953, which defined a homosexual according to the extent of their same-sex sexual experiences and psychological responses (Kinsey, et al 1953, 469-72). This leads to questions regarding how members of the black press appropriated the opinions of "experts" and altered them to fit the various meanings they attached to same-sex sexuality. These questions are beyond the scope of this paper. In the case of Kinsey, though, they usually appropriated statistics on the percentage of the U.S. population believed to have had same-sex sexual experiences.

While *Ebony* and *Jet* generally condemned same-sex sexuality with words such as *unnatural* and *perversion* frequently used in their stories, one kind of gender nonconformity usually associated with lesbians and gays was not condemned—if done in the proper "space." And the proper space for those—primarily male—with a same-sex sexual preference, was in the field of entertainment. Articles about female impersonators who entertained at nightclubs and yearly interracial masquerade balls were numerous. And according to these stories, the balls were not only popular among many blacks, but also received some institutional support from the police and the black church. This suggests that one major social relationship between blacks with same-sex sexual preference and those without was similar to a major social relationship between whites and blacks in the dominant culture: In mainstream America, blacks were also more acceptable to whites as entertainment than was the case in other social spaces.

PROFESSIONAL GENDER IMPERSONATORS

Coverage of these balls focused mainly on the Halloween and Thanksgiving galas in New York and Chicago. Fennie's Club, in Chicago, had been sponsoring a dance and fashion show since the late 1930s; during the 1950s, the club's Halloween show was usually held at the Pershing Hotel Ballroom. Attendance figures for contestants and guests, which differed from year to year, ranged from 2,000 to 4,000. Contestants competing for the "Academy Award" were judged by dress designers and fashion buyers, and emphasis was placed on gown design. Billie Sinclair, a white male who won the award for the second year in a row in 1952, wore a "stunning white chantung (sic) taffeta evening dress with a ballerina halter neck," trimmed with "teardrop looped pearls," and topped with a $3,000 blue mink stole ("Female Impersonators Hold...," 64).

The New York affair was usually put on at Harlem's Rockland Palace during the Thanksgiving holidays by the Fun Makers, a group of six men headed by Phil Black, a popular female impersonator. The events began in the early 1940s and had attendance figures similar to those at the Chicago ball. Judges, however, were chosen at random from the audience. And judges appraised contestants on the basis of how successfully they approximated what was considered "feminine" in terms of mannerisms, dress, and physical features.

The contestants and guests came from a variety of occupations. They were "doctors, lawyers, undertakers, truck drivers, and dishwashers" ("Female Impersonators Hold..." 64). For many of the impersonators, these events were their one big night of the year. One contestant was quoted as saying, "I wish this night would never end.... This night means more to me that any other in the year" ("Female Impersonators Hold...," 65). Another claimed, "It is the only time of the year that I can assume the role for which I am best fitted—I dress as a woman" ("The Truth About...," 31). They spent hundreds of dollars on gowns worn just for the ball. Some even made their own, often copying the patterns of famous designers. The prize money, though, usually was not enough to cover the cost of the winner's gowns ("Female Impersonators Hold...," 64-65).

Many of the contestants dressed as popular entertainers and other well-known figures. These men, who usually went by their female names when in drag, transformed into Lena Horne, Mae West, or Josephine Baker for the night. It is not clear, however, whether there was race mixing in regard to who put on the persona of whom. Some impersonators even performed as part of their act. At the 1951 Fennie's Club contest, one sang, "The Man I Love," while another did a shake dance and strip routine.

According to *Ebony* and *Jet*, the backgrounds of the audiences were as varied as those of the contestants. Both were racially mixed, even though the New York and Chicago balls were held in black neighborhoods. Audiences were generally appreciative, and were amazed at some contestants' ability to imitate women. After staring at one impersonator for several minutes, one male spectator was quoted as saying, "Say, Baby, I think you are for real" ("Female Impersonators Hold...," 63).

Sometimes, though, there was trouble. In Chicago, for example, a fight broke out after one of the impersonators flirted with a man in the audience. But the police were there to keep order, as they ignored, for the night, ordinances banning cross-dressing in public. They spent much of their time, however, making sure the drag queens went to the "correct" bathrooms, which varied depending on the city. In New York, for example, they sent the impersonators to the women's rest room.

Besides the annual balls, in cities with high black populations some nightclubs featured female impersonators. New York's 101 Ranch, Detroit's Uncle Tom's Cabin, and Chicago's Joe's DeLuxe Club were among the biggest. Sometimes other groups used female impersonators for entertainment too. For example, in 1958 a fashion show was held in Harlem to benefit the Camp Fund of the Christian Tabernacle Church ("Fashionable 'Miss,' " 31).

Ebony and *Jet* both constructed these balls as "social events." They featured many photos of men in costume adjusting stockings, applying makeup, and flirting with male spectators. *Ebony's* articles on these events stopped after March 1953, while *Jet* continued to publish them throughout the decade. The amount of space devoted to them, though, declined as the decade wore on.

One of the things the copy tended to emphasize was the degree to which the drag queens were "feminine." According to *Jet*, "in many mannerisms female impersonators are often more feminine than real women, but many others are grotesque caricatures of real women" ("The Truth About...," 27). *Ebony* especially was quick to note those contestants who needed to shave, and who had "bulging muscles," "coarse skin," hairy arms, and "masculine-looking" legs. The magazines also noted the difficulties involved in the impersonator's art. Trying to get "hefty" feet into women's shoes, walking in high heels, and trying to prevent false breasts from slipping in strapless gowns were all problems mentioned.

Ebony acknowledged the sexual preference of the impersonators, but only implicitly. They featured several pictures of drag queens dancing with, kissing, or being kissed by men. The photos suggested, however, that the dancing and kissing were innocent and playful, and that nothing "serious" was going on between the contestants and their partners. *Jet* was more explicit. In the articles that focused on the balls, they were far more likely to use, for example, puns on the words *gay* and *queen* when describing the events. Contestants at the "gay affair[s]" provided "gay entertainment," walked "gayly down the runway," were "queenly dressed," crowned "queen of queens," and took "queenly bow[s]."

In an article that focused on female impersonators, *Jet* discussed same-sex sexuality in greater detail. The unknown author noted that these men risked social disapproval by dressing as women because of "the obscure causes of homosexuality." And audiences liked to watch them because, according to some unnamed psychiatrists, of their own "latent homosexual tendencies." Some women may have liked to watch because they thought it was a joke on them. After stating that "gay" men in "drags" have been found historically in Native American and African societies, he or she mentioned some non "queer" examples of cross-dressing, such as college students taking on female roles in plays, and those who dress as women to lure men to hotels and rob them ("The Truth About...," 26-31).

In *Ebony*, letters to the editor responding to the female impersonator articles were mostly positive. All five of the published respondents were male. And except for Frank Hawkinson of Morrice, Mich., all were from the eastern part of the country. Newark, N.J.'s Dudley Marlon claimed *Ebony*'s "sophisticated manner of presentation suggests the attainment of culture popularly connected with Europe" (Marlon 1952, 12). On the other hand, Andrew Jackson of Atlanta thought the stories "only [cheapen] the magazine" (Jackson 1953, 9). Since *Jet* did not publish reader mail, I do not know how their subscribers responded to these stories.

Jet also reported on the activities of female impersonators outside of the space of entertainment. Female impersonators were subject to arrest and harassment, as many areas had laws against cross-dressing. Police officers often made themselves "available" for solicitation. In Cincinnati, for example, Eddie Ross ("Torchy") and Gene Allen ("Margo") were arrested and sentenced to 50 days in jail and ordered to pay $100 in fines for soliciting police detectives ("Female Impersonators Solicit Cops...," 24).

But even within the entertainment space there was trouble, as impersonators were often harassed by audience members. Within this space, however, there was room for resistance. And it was usually with a sharp tongue. One performer at a Chicago club was quoted as saying in response to catcalls from the audience, "Dearies, don't you take on like that with me. Where was you last night? It was no woman you was with.... I know there's plenty of you out there who wish you had the nerve to act like me" ("The Truth About...," 28).

Stories featuring professional male impersonators were less frequent and less glamorous. Some of them focused on Gladys Bentley, a well-known entertainer who once wore men's clothing as part of her act. But the discourse surrounding her was very different from that of the female impersonators. *Ebony* and *Jet* positioned her not within the discourse of entertainment, but of black self-improvement. Of course, what needed "improvement" was her lesbianism. One characteristic story was a first-person narrative for *Ebony* in which Bentley discussed her attempt to overcome her lesbianism and become a "woman" again.

In the story Bentley claimed her mother caused the sexual desires that led her to the "half-shadow no-man's land which exists between the boundaries of the two sexes" (Bentley 1952, 93). Bentley had always wanted to be a boy instead of a girl. After she was born, her mother was hostile toward her but was kind to her two brothers, who were born a little later. When Bentley was 9 or 10, she stole her brother's clothes and wore them to school. Soon she felt more comfortable in them than in women's clothes. At 16 she left her home in Philadelphia for New York and quickly joined the nightclub scene. Part of her act was cross-dressing, which became a big hit. Her career reached its peak in the 1920s, when she headlined in white clubs all over the country, met many famous people, and sold more than a few records.

But despite her success, Bentley was unhappy. Because of her "abnormal" sex life, she felt she "was traveling the wrong road to real love and true happiness" (Bentley 1952, 93). Then a couple of "miracles" happened. First, she finally began to open up to men. Second, she went to a doctor and discovered she had "infantile" sex organs and was producing too many male hormones. Both were corrected. And after one failed try, Bentley, at the time the article was written in 1952, was "happily married and living a normal existence." But, she claimed, "I am still haunted by the sex underworld in which I once lived. I want to help others who are trapped in its dark recesses by telling my story" (Bentley 1952, 94).

All of the published responses to Bentley's article were positive. Several came from other gays and lesbians, all of whom wanted to or had already reformed their sex lives. "Virginia" proclaimed she was "a happily married woman and a devoted mother." And "A Loyal Reader" thanked Bentley for "telling the world that we hate ourselves too" (Loyal Reader 1952, 9).

GENDER BENDERS IN THE "REAL" WORLD

This ambivalence about male homosexuality and intolerance of lesbianism is also evident in stories about men and women who rejected their assigned gender roles and spent most of their lives as members of another sex. For example, both *Ebony* and *Jet* featured extensive coverage of the "bizarre" and "moving drama" of Georgia Black, "The Man Who Lived 30 Years as a Woman" ("The Man Who Lived...," 23-6; Sabb 1951, 75-82).

According to the stories, Black left the harsh South Carolina farm life of his childhood when he was 15 and went to Charleston. While there, he met and had a sexual relationship with a gay man who taught him how to live as a woman. Since then, Black married twice and adopted and raised a son. He lived his life as a wife, mother, domestic servant for wealthy whites, and avid churchgoer, all without raising an eyebrow. But a doctor discovered Black's secret when he was dying of cancer. He died in Sanford, Florida, where he had spent most of his adult life, on April 26, 1951.

Ebony and *Jet* presented Black's life as being both "bizarre" and "moving." They contrasted characterizations of his life as "one of the most incredible stories in the history of sex abnormalities" ("The Man Who Lived...," 24) with descriptions of how Sanford residents felt about him. One white person whom Black had worked for declared, "I don't care what Georgia Black was. She nursed members of our family through birth, sickness, and death. She was one of the best citizens in town" ("The Man Who Lived...," 26). Others commented on her involvement in the church and other community activities. This theme is reiterated in an *Ebony* story written by Black's son, Willie Sabb, in 1953.

The ambivalence that surrounded men such as Georgia Black did not carry over to their female counterparts. *Ebony* and *Jet* generally presented these women as criminals (like Leatrice Calloway) or as needing treatment. Clearly they saw male impersonators as being much more of a threat, suggesting that during the 1950s there may have been more hostility toward women who assumed male privileges than toward men who rejected them. This was evident in one story's description of "part-time men," those women who lived as men when it suited them. These women "compete with men for jobs—and other women." The "problems" they caused were the result of hormonal imbalances and rejection by parents who had wanted boys. Thus, they presented Gladys Bentley as a shining example of how male impersonators could be "cured" ("Women Who Pass for Men," 22-24).

CONCLUSION

Ebony and *Jet* both constructed provocative "truths" about some aspects of the lives of African American les-bi-gays and their relationships with the larger black communities of the 1950s. The contradictory actions of mainstream institutions such as the police and of African American institutions such as the church, the entertainment industry, and segments of the media like *Ebony* and *Jet* toward professional female impersonators suggest that there were spaces of tolerance for black les-bi-gays. Their primary space of acceptance was in the realm of "entertainment," both as professional impersonators and as a subject in the press designed to titillate readers. It is ironic that blacks had a similar relationship to the dominant white culture during this period.

This space was also gendered. While many blacks tolerated women such as Gladys Bentley as professional entertainers earlier in the century, particularly during the 1920s (Garber 1988, 52-61), this apparently was no longer true during the 1950s. The important thing, though, is that blacks with some level of same-sex sexual preference did have access to a "mainstream" discourse about themselves and their communities, although it was contradictory and mostly negative. But it did provide some spaces for positive self-affirmation—at least for men.

REFERENCES

Adam, B.D. (1987). *The Rise of a Gay and Lesbian Movement.* Boston: Twayne Publishers.

Bentley, G. "I Am a Woman Again." *Ebony.* Aug., 1952: 92-8.

Berkman, Dave. "Advertising in *Ebony* and Life: Negro Aspirations vs. Reality." *Journalism Quarterly* 40.1 (Winter 1963): 53-64.

"Can Science Eliminate the Third Sex?" *Jet.* Jan. 22, 1953: 46-50.

D'Emilio, J. (1983). *Sexual Politics, Sexual Communities.* Chicago: University of Chicago Press.

—- "The Homosexual Menace: The Politics of Sexuality in Cold War America." (1989). In *Passion and Power: Sexuality in History,* edited by Kathy Peiss, Christina Simmons, and Robert A. Padgug. Philadelphia: Temple University Press.

"Fashionable 'Miss'." *Jet.* June 5, 1958: 31.

"Female Impersonators." *Ebony.* Mar., 1953: 64-8.

"Female Impersonators Hold Costume Ball." *Ebony.* Mar., 1952: 62-7.

"Female Impersonators Solicit Cops, Land in Jail." *Jet.* July 30, 1953: 24.

Frazier, E. F. (1957). *Black Bourgeoisie.* New York: The Free Press.

Garber, E. (1988). "Gladys Bentley: The Bulldagger Who Sang the Blues." *Out/Look* 1.1 (Spring): 52-61.

Goodman, W. "*Ebony*: Biggest Negro Magazine." *Dissent* 15.5 (September/October 1968): 403-9.

Hirsch, P. M. "An Analysis of *Ebony*: The Magazine and Its Readers." *Journalism Quarterly* 45.2 (Summer 1968): 261-70+.

Jackson, Jr., Andrew. Letter. *Ebony*. May 1953:9.

Johnson, J. (1989). *Succeeding Against the Odds*. New York: Warner Books.

Johnson, J.P.H., et al. (Eds.). (1950-9). *N.W. Ayer and Son's Directory of Newspapers and Periodicals*. Philadelphia: N.W Ayer and Son, Inc., 1950-9.

Kinsey, A.C., et al. (1953). *Sexual Behavior in the Human Female*. Philadelphia: W.B. Saunders Co.

Loyal Reader. Letter. *Ebony*. Oct., 1952: 9.

"Man Who Lived 30 Years as a Woman." *Ebony*. Oct., 1951: 23-6.

Marlon, D. Letter. *Ebony*. June, 1952: 12.

Sabb, Willie. "My Mother Was a Man." *Ebony*. Oct. 1951: 23-6.

"Strange Lover Faces Sanity Test." *Jet*. Nov. 29, 1951: 52.

"The Truth About Female Impersonators." *Jet*. Oct. 2, 1952: 26-31.

U.S. Senate, 81st Congress, 2nd session, Committee on Expenditure in Executive Departments. (1950). Employment of Homosexuals and Other Sex Perverts in Government. Washington: GPO.

Virginia. Letter. *Ebony*. Oct., 1952: 9.

Wolseley, R. E. (1990). *The Black Press, U.S.A.* Ames, IA: Iowa State University Press.

"Women Who Pass for Men." *Jet*. Jan. 28, 1954: 22-4.

THE SILENT MYTHOLOGY
SURROUNDING AIDS AND PUBLIC ICONS

Eloquence and Epitaph: Black Nationalism and the Homophobic Response to the Death of Max Robinson

Philip Brian Harper

A report published by the Center for Disease Control titled "HIV/AIDS Surveillance" states that from June 1981 through February 1991, 167,803 people in the U.S. were diagnosed as having Acquired Immune Deficiency Syndrome (AIDS). Of that number of total reported cases, 38,361—or roughly 23%—occurred in males of African descent, although black males account for less than 6% of the total U.S. population. It is common enough knowledge that black men constitute a disproportionate percentage of people with AIDS in this country—common in the sense that whenever the AIDS epidemic achieves a new statistical milestone (as it did in winter 1991, when the number of AIDS-related deaths in the U.S. reached 100,000), the major media generally provide a demographic breakdown of the figures. And yet, somehow the enormity of the morbidity and mortality rates for black men (like that for gay men of whatever racial identity) does not seem to register in the national consciousness as a cause for great concern. This is, no doubt, largely due to a general sense that the trajectory of the average African American man's life must "naturally" be short, routinely subject to violent termination. And this sense, in turn, helps to account for the fact that there has never been a case of AIDS that riveted public attention on the vulnerability of black men the way, for instance, the death of Rock Hudson shattered the myth of the invincible white male cultural hero. Or at least not until November 1991; after the body of this essay was written, pro basketball player Earvin "Magic" Johnson announced his infection with the human immunodeficiency virus, believed to be the chief factor in the aetiology of AIDS. That announcement precipitated a public response unprecedented in the history of the epidemic. While I do not address directly the nature of that response in this essay, I do believe that it was shaped largely by the set of social phenomena that I have tried to describe here.

Indeed, I would argue that the very status of the black basketball player as a sports superstar who thus warrants mass attention (in contrast, for example, to the relatively lower profile of black tennis champion Arthur Ashe, who in April 1992 announced that he had AIDS) derives mostly from the very intersection of racial, sexual, and class politics that comprise the primary subject matter of my essay. While the rapidly changing course of the epidemic may quickly render outdated the various topical observations I make here, I fear that much time will pass before the validity of my analysis, and of the general claims based on it, expires. This is not to say that no nationally known black male figure has died of AIDS-related causes, but rather that numerous and complex cultural factors conspire to prevent such deaths from effectively galvanizing AIDS activism in African American communities. This essay represents an attempt to explicate several such factors that operated in the case of one particular black man's bout with AIDS, and thus to indicate what further cultural intervention needs to take place if we hope to stem the ravages of AIDS among African Americans.

THE SOUND OF SILENCE

In December 1988, National Public Radio broadcast a report on the death of Max Robinson, the first black news anchor on U.S. network television, staffing the Chicago desk of ABC's *World News Tonight* from 1978 to 1983. Robinson was one of 4,123 African American men reported to have died in 1988 of AIDS-related causes out of a national total of 17,119 AIDS-related deaths, according to a report published by the National Center for Health Statistics. Rather than focus on the death itself at this point, I want to examine two passages from the NPR broadcast that, taken together, describe a problematic that characterizes the existence of AIDS in many black communities in the United States. The first is a statement made by a colleague of Robinson's both at ABC News and at WMAQ-TV in Chicago, where Robinson worked after leaving the television network. Producer Bruce Rheins remembers being on assignment with Robinson on the streets of Chicago: "We would go out on the street a lot of times, doing a story…on the south side or something…and I remember one time, this mother leaned down to her children, pointed, and said, 'That's Max Robinson. You learn how to speak like him.' " Immediately after this statement from Rheins, the NPR correspondent reporting the piece, Cheryl Duvall, informs us that "Robinson had denied the nature of his illness for months, but after he died…his friend Roger Wilkins said Robinson wanted his death to emphasize the need for AIDS awareness among black people." These are the concluding words of the report, and as such they reproduce the epitaphic structure of Robinson's deathbed request, raising the question of just how well any of us addresses the educational needs of black communities with respect to AIDS.

That these two passages are juxtaposed in the radio report is striking because they testify to the power of two different phenomena that appear to be in direct contradiction. Bruce Rheins's statement underscores the importance of Robinson's speech as an affirmation of black identity, made for the benefit of the community from which he sprang. Cheryl Duvall's remarks, on the other hand, implicate Robinson's denial that he had AIDS, as part of a general silence regarding the effects of the epidemic among African Americans. I would like, in this essay, to examine how speech and silence interrelate to produce a discursive matrix that governs the cultural significance of AIDS in black communities. Indeed, Robinson, news anchor, inhabited a space defined by the overlapping of at least two distinct types of discourse that, though often in conflict, intersect in a way that makes discussion of Robinson's AIDS diagnosis—and of AIDS among blacks generally— particularly difficult.

The apparent conflict between vocal affirmation and the peculiar silence effected through denial is already implicated in the nature of speech itself, in the case of Robinson. There is a potential doubleness in the significance of Robinson's "speaking voice," which the mother cited above urges her child to emulate. It is clear, first of all, that the reference is to Robinson's exemplification of the articulate and authoritative television presence—an exemplification noteworthy because Robinson was black.

Bruce Rheins's comments illustrate this particularly well: "Max really was a symbol for a lot of people.... He was a very good-looking, well-dressed, and very obviously intelligent black man giving the news in a straightforward fashion, and not on a black radio station or a black TV station or on the black segment of a news report—he was the anchorman" (*All Things Considered*). Rheins's statement indicates the power of Robinson's verbal performance before the camera, for it is through this performance that Robinson's "intelligence," which Rheins emphasizes, is made "obvious." Other accounts of Robinson's tenure as a news anchor recapitulate this reference. An article in the June 1989 issue of *Vanity Fair* remembers Robinson for "his steely, unadorned delivery, precise diction, and magical presence" (Boyer 1989, 68). A *New York Times* obituary notes the "unforced, authoritative manner" that characterized Robinson's on-air persona, and backs its claim with a statement by current ABC news anchor and Robinson's former colleague, Peter Jennings: "In terms of sheer performance, Max was a penetrating communicator. He had a natural gift to look in the camera and talk to people" (Gerard 1988, D19). A 1980 *New York Times* reference asserts that Robinson was "blessed with a commanding voice and a handsome appearance" (Schwartz 1980 27). A posthumous "appreciation" in the *Boston Globe* describes Robinson as "earnest and telegenic," noting that he "did some brilliant reporting and was a consummate newscaster"(Khan 1988, 65). James Snyder, news director at WTOP-TV in Washington, D.C., where Robinson began his anchoring career, says Robinson "had this terrific voice, great enunciation and phrasing. He was just a born speaker" (Boyer, 1989). Elsewhere, Snyder succinctly summarizes Robinson's appeal, noting his "great presence on the air." All of these encomia embody allusions to Robinson's verbal facility, which must be understood as praise for his ability to speak articulate Received Standard English, which linguist Geneva Smitherman (1977) has identified as the dialect upon which "White America has insisted...as the price of admission into its economic and social mainstream." The emphasis that commentators place on Robinson's "precise diction" or on his "great enunciation and phrasing" is an index of the general surprise evoked by his facility with the white bourgeois idiom considered standard in "mainstream" U.S. life, and certainly in television news. The black mother cited above surely recognizes the opportunity for social advancement inherent in this facility with standard English, and this is no doubt the benefit she has in mind for her child when she urges him to "speak like" Robinson.

At the same time, however, that the mother's words can be interpreted as an injunction to speak "correctly," they might alternately be understood as a call for speech, *per se*—as encouragement to *speak out* like Robinson, to stand up for one's interests as a black person as Robinson did throughout his career. In this case, the import of her command is traceable to a black cultural nationalism that has waxed and waned in the U.S. since the mid 19th century, but that, in the context of the Black Power movement of the 1960s, underwent a revival that has continued to influence black cultural life in this country. Smitherman notes the way in which this cultural nationalism has been manifested in black language and discourse, citing the movement "among writers, artists, and black intellectuals of the 1960s who deliberately wrote and rapped in the Black Idiom and sought to preserve its distinctiveness in the literature of the period" (Smitherman 1977, 12).

Max Robinson did not participate in this nationalistic strategy in the context of his work as a network news anchor. Success in television newscasting, insofar as it depends upon one's conformity to models of behavior deemed acceptable by white bourgeois culture, largely precludes the possibility of one's exercising the "Black Idiom" and thereby manifesting a strong black consciousness in the broadcast context.

We might say, then, that black people's successful participation in modes of discourse validated in mainstream culture—their facility with Received Standard English, for instance—actually implicates them in a profound *silence* regarding their African American identity.

It is arguable, however, that Robinson, like all blacks who have achieved a degree of recognition in mainstream U.S. culture, actually played both sides of the behavioral dichotomy I have described: the dichotomy between articulate verbal performance in the accepted standard dialect of the English language and vocal affirmation of conscious black identity. Though on the one hand Robinson's performance before the cameras provided an impeccable image of bourgeois respectability that could easily be read as the erasure of consciousness of black identity, he was at the same time known for publicly affirming his interest in the various sociopolitical factors that affect blacks' existence in the United States, thus continually emphasizing his African American identity. For example, in February 1981 Robinson became the center of controversy when he was reported as telling a college audience that the various network news agencies, including ABC, discriminated against their black journalists and that the news media in general constitute "a crooked mirror" through which "white America views itself" (Schwartz 1981, C21). In this instance, not only does Robinson's statement manifest semantically his consciousness of his own black identity, but the very form of the entire incident can be said to embody an identifiably black cultural behavior. After being summoned to the offices of then-ABC News president Roone Arledge, subsequent to making his allegations of network discrimination, Robinson said that "he had not meant to single out ABC for criticism" (Gerard 1988, D19), and thus performed a type of rhetorical backstep by which his criticism, though retracted, was effectively lodged and registered both by the public and by the network. While this mode of protecting one's own interests is by no means unique to African American culture, it does have a particular resonance within an African American context. Specifically, Robinson's backstepping can be understood as a form of what is called "loud-talking" or "louding," a verbal device common within many black English–speaking communities in which a person "says something of someone just loud enough for that person to hear, but indirectly, so he cannot properly respond," or so that, when the object of the remark *does* respond, "the speaker can reply to the effect, 'Oh, I wasn't talking to you.' " Robinson's insistence that he was not referring specifically to ABC News can be interpreted as a form of the disingenuous reply characteristic of loud-talking, thus locating his rhetorical strategy within the cultural context of black communicative patterns and underscoring his African American identification.

Arledge, in summoning Robinson to his offices after the incident, made unusually explicit the suppression of African American identity generally effected by the networks in their news productions; such dramatic measures are not usually necessary because potential manifestations of strong black cultural identification are normally subdued by blacks' very participation in the discursive conventions of the network newscast (Hewitt 1985, 170). Thus, the more audible and insistent Robinson's televised performance in Received Standard English and in the white bourgeois idiom of the network newscast, the more secure the silence imposed upon the vocal black consciousness that he always threatened to display. Robinson's articulate speech before the cameras always implied a silencing of the African American idiom.

Concomitant with the silencing in the network-news context of black-affirmative discourse is the suppression of another aspect of black identity alluded to in the above-quoted references to Robinson's on-camera performance. The emphasis these commentaries place on Robinson's articulateness is coupled with their simultaneous insistence on his physical attractiveness: Bruce Rheins's remarks on Robinson's "obvious intelligence" are accompanied by a reference to his "good looks"; Tony Schwartz's inventory of Robinson's assets notes both his "commanding voice" and his "handsome appearance"; Joseph Kahn's "appreciation" of Robinson cites his "brilliant reporting" as well as his "telegenic" quality; it seems impossible to comment on Robinson's success as a news anchor without noting both his verbal ability and physical appeal. Such commentary is not at all unusual in discussions of newscasters, whose personal charms have taken on an increasing degree of importance since the early day of the medium. Indeed, Schwartz's 1980 *New York Times* article, "Are TV Anchormen Merely Performers?"—intended as a critique of the degree to which television news is conceived as entertainment— underscores the importance of a newscaster's physical attractiveness to a broadcast's success; and by the late 1980s that importance became a truism of contemporary culture, assimilated into the popular consciousness, through the movie *Broadcast News*, for instance.

In the case of a black man such as Robinson, however, discussions of a news anchor's "star quality" become potentially problematic because such a quality is founded upon an implicitly acknowledged "sex appeal," the concept of which has always been highly charged with respect to black men in the United States. In the classic text on the subject, Calvin C. Hernton has argued that the black man has historically been perceived as the bearer of a bestial sexuality, as the savage "walking phallus" that poses a constant threat to an idealized white womanhood and thus to the entire U.S. social order (Hernton, 1965). To the extent that this is true, for white patriarchal institutions such as the mainstream media to note the physical attractiveness of any black man is for them potentially to unleash the very beast that threatens their power. Robinson's achievement in a professional, public position that mandates the deployment of a certain rhetoric—that of a news anchor's attractive and telegenic persona—thus also raises the problem of taming the threatening black male sexuality that this rhetoric conjures. This taming, I think, is once again achieved through Robinson's articulate verbal performance, references to which routinely accompany acknowledgments of his physical attractiveness.

In commentary on white newscasters, paired references to both their physical appeal and their rhetorical skill serve merely to defuse accusations that television journalism is superficial and image-oriented. In Robinson's case, however, acknowledging his articulateness also serves to absorb the threat of his sexuality, which is raised in references to his physical attractiveness; in the same way that Robinson's conformity to the "rules" of standard English performance suppresses the possibility of his articulating a radical identification with African American culture, it also, in attesting to his refinement and civility, actually *domesticates* his threatening physicality, which itself *must* be alluded to in conventional liberal accounts of his performance as a news anchor. James Snyder's reference to Robinson's "great presence" is a most stunning example of such an account, for it neatly conflates and thus simultaneously acknowledges both Robinson's *physical* person (in the tradition of commentary on network news personalities) and his virtuosity in standard *verbal* performance in such a way that the latter mitigates the threat posed by the former. Robinson's standard English performance, then, serves not only to suppress black culturolinguistic forms that might disrupt the white bourgeois aspect of network news, but also keeps in check the black male sexuality that threatens the social order that the news media represent. Ironically, in this latter function, white bourgeois discourse seems to share an objective with forms of black discourse, which themselves work to suppress certain threatening elements of black male sexuality, resulting in a strange reaction to Robinson's death in African American communities.

HOMOPHOBIA IN AFRICAN AMERICAN DISCOURSE

Whether it is interpreted as a reference to his facility with Received Standard English—whereby he achieved a degree of success in the white-run world of broadcast media—or as a reference to his repeated attempts to vocalize in the tradition of African American discourse the grievances of blacks with respect to their sociopolitical status in the U.S., to "speak like Max Robinson" is to silence discussion of the various possibilities of black male sexuality. We have seen how an emphasis on Robinson's facility at "white-oriented" discourse serves to defuse the "threat" of rampant black male sexuality that constitutes so much of the sexual-political structure of U.S. society. Indeed, some middle-class blacks have colluded in this defusing of black sexuality, attempting to explode whites' stereotypes of blacks as oversexed by stifling discussion of black sexuality in general. At the same time, the other tradition from which Robinson's speech derives meaning also functions to suppress discussion about specific aspects of black male sexuality that are threatening to the black male image.

In her book, *Talkin and Testifyin: The Language of Black America,* Smitherman cites, rather un–self-consciously, examples of black discourse that illustrate this point. For instance, in a discussion of black musicians' adaptation of themes from the African American oral tradition, Smitherman mentions the popular early-'60s recording of "Sagger Lee," based on a traditional narrative folk poem. The hero for whom the narrative is named is, as Smitherman puts it, "a fearless, mean dude," so that "it became widely fashionable [in black communities] to refer to oneself as 'Stag,' as in...'Don't mess wif me, cause I ain't no fag, uhm Stag' " (52). What is notable here is not merely the homophobia manifested in the "rap" laid down by the black "brother" imagined to be speaking this line, but also that the rap itself, the very verbal performance Smitherman points out, serves as evidence that the speaker is indeed *not* a "fag"; verbal facility becomes proof of one's conventional masculinity and thus silences discussion of one's possible homosexuality. This point touches upon a truism in studies of black discourse. Smitherman herself implies the testament to masculine prowess embodied in the black "rap," explaining that, "While some raps convey social and cultural information, others are used for conquering foes and women" (82); and she further acknowledges the "power" with which the spoken word is imbued in the African American tradition (as in others), especially insofar as it is employed in masculine "image-making" through braggadocio and other highly self-assertive strategies (97; see also Abraham 1962). Indeed, an entire array of these verbal strategies for establishing a strong masculine image can be identified in the contemporary phenomenon of "rap" music, a form indigenous to black male culture, though increasingly appropriated and transformed by members of other social groups, notably black women (Berlant 1988, 237).

If verbal facility is considered as an identifying mark of masculinity in certain African American contexts, however, it is only when it is demonstrated specifically through use of the vernacular. Indeed, a too-evident facility in the standard white idiom can quickly identify one not as a strong black man but rather as a white-identified Uncle Tom who must also, therefore, be weak, effeminate, and probably a "fag." To the extent that this process of homophobic identification reflects powerful cross-class hostilities, it is certainly not unique to African American culture. Its imbrication with questions of racial identity, however, compounds its potency in the African American context. Simply put, within some African American communities, the "professional" or "intellectual" black male inevitably endangers his status both as black and as "male" whenever he evidences a facility with Received Standard English—a facility upon which his very identity as a professional or intellectual in the larger society is founded in the first place. Robinson was not the first black man to face this dilemma; a decade or so before he emerged on network television a particularly influential group of black writers attempted to negotiate the problem by incorporating into their work the semantics of "street" discourse, thereby establishing an intellectual practice that was both "black" enough and virile enough to bear the weight of a stridently nationalist agenda. Thus, a strong "Stagger Lee"–type identification can be found in the poem "Don't Cry, Scream," by Haki Madhubuti (Don L. Lee): "Swung on a faggot who politely / scratched his ass in my presence. / he smiled broken teeth stained from / his over-used tongue, fisted-face. / teeth dropped in tune with ray charles singing 'yesterday' " (Madhubuti 1969, 29).

Here the scornful language of the poem itself recapitulates the homophobic violence it commemorates (or invites us to imagine as having occurred), the two together attesting to the speaker's aversion to homosexuality and, thus, to his own unquestionable masculinity. Though it is striking, the violent hostility evident in this piece is not at all unusual among the revolutionist poems of the Black Arts Movement. Much of the work by the Black Arts Poets is characterized by a violent language that seems wishfully conceived of as potent and performative—as capable, in itself, of wreaking destruction upon the white establishment to which the Black Power movement is opposed (see Baraka 1979, 106). Important to note, beyond the rhetoric of violence, is the way in which that rhetoric is conceived as part and parcel of a black nationalism to which all sufficiently proud African Americans must subscribe. Nikki Giovanni, for instance, urges, "Learn to kill niggers / Learn to be Black men," indicating the necessity of cathartic violence to the transformation of blacks from victims into active subjects, and illustrating the degree to which black masculinity functions as the rhetorical stake in much of the Black Arts poetry by both men and women (1971, 318). To the extent that such rhetoric is considered an integral element of the cultural-nationalist strategy of Black Power politics, then a violent homophobia too is necessarily implicated in this particular nationalistic position, which since the late 1960s has filtered throughout black communities in the U.S. as a major influence in African American culture.

Consequently, Robinson was put in a difficult position with respect to discussing his AIDS diagnosis. Robinson's reputation was based on his articulate outspokenness; however, as we have seen, that very well-spokenness derived its power within two different modes of discourse that, though they are sometimes at odds, both work to suppress issues of sexuality implied in any discussion of AIDS (Mosse 1985). The white bourgeois cultural context in which Robinson derived his status as an authoritative figure in the mainstream news media must always keep a vigilant check on black male sexuality, which is perceived as threatening (and it is assisted in this task by a moralistic black middle class that seeks to explode notions of black hypersexuality). At the same time, the African American cultural context to which Robinson appealed for his status as a paragon of black pride and self-determination embodies an ethic that precludes sympathetic discussion of black male homosexuality. However rapidly the demography of AIDS in this country may be shifting as more and more people who are not gay men become infected with HIV, the historical and cultural conditions surrounding the development of the epidemic ensure its ongoing association with male homosexuality, so it is not surprising that the latter should emerge as a topic of discussion in any consideration of Robinson's death. The apparent *inevitability* of that emergence (and the degree to which the association between AIDS and male homosexuality would threaten Robinson's reputation and become discursively problematic, given the contexts in which his public persona was created) is dramatically illustrated in the Jan. 9, 1989 issue of *Jet* magazine, the black-oriented weekly. This issue of *Jet* contains an obituary for Robinson that is very similar to those issued by *The New York Times* and other nonblack media, noting Robinson's professional achievements and controversial tenure at ABC News, alluding to the "tormented" nature of his life as a symbol of black success, and citing his secrecy surrounding his AIDS diagnosis and his wish that his death be used as the occasion to educate blacks about AIDS. The obituary also notes that "the main victims [sic] of the disease [sic] have been intravenous drug users and homosexuals," leaving open the question of Robinson's relation to either of these categories.

Printed next to Robinson's obituary in the same issue of *Jet* is a notice of another AIDS-related death, that of the popular disco singer, Sylvester. Sylvester's obituary, however, offers an interesting contrast to that of Robinson, for it identifies Sylvester, in its very first sentence, as "the flamboyant homosexual singer whose high-pitched voice and dramatic onstage costumes propelled him to the height of stardom on the disco music scene during the late 1970s." The piece goes on to indicate the openness with which Sylvester lived as a gay man, noting that he "first publicly acknowledged he had AIDS at the San Francisco Gay Pride March last June [1988], which he attended in a wheelchair with the People With AIDS group," and quoting his recollection of his first sexual experience, at age 7, with an adult male evangelist: "You see, I was a queen even back then, so it didn't bother me. I rather liked it."

Obviously, an array of issues is raised by Sylvester's obituary and its juxtaposition with that of Max Robinson (not the least of which has to do with the complicated phenomenon of sex between adults and children). What is most pertinent here, however, is the difference between *Jet*'s treatments of Sylvester's and Robinson's sexualities, and the factors that account for that difference. Sylvester's public persona emerges from contexts that are different from those that produced

Robinson. If it is true that, as *Jet* puts it, "the church was the setting for Sylvester's first homosexual experience" (18), it is also true that "Sylvester learned to sing in churches in South Los Angeles and went on to perform at gospel conventions around the state" (18). This is to say that the church-choir context in which Sylvester was groomed for a singing career has stereotypically served as a locus in which young black men both discover and sublimate their homosexuality, and also as a conduit to a world of professional entertainment generally considered "tolerant," if not downright encouraging, of diverse sexualities. In Sylvester's case, this was particularly true, since he helped to create a disco culture characterized by a fusion of elements from black and gay communities, and in which he and others could thrive as openly gay men. Thus, the black-church context, though ostensibly hostile to homosexuality and gay identity, nevertheless has traditionally provided a means by which black men can achieve a sense of themselves as homosexual and even, in cases such as Sylvester's, expand that sense into a gay-affirmative public persona (see Beam,1986).

On the other hand, the public figure of Robinson, as we have seen, is cut from entirely different cloth, formed in the intersection of discursive contexts that do not allow for the expression of black male homosexuality in any recognizable form. The discursive bind constituted by Robinson's status, both as a conventionally successful media personality and as exemplar of black male self-assertion and racial consciousness, left him with no alternative to the manner in which he dealt with his diagnosis in the public forum—shrouding the nature of his illness in a secrecy that he was able to break only after his death with the posthumous acknowledgment that he had AIDS. Consequently, obituarists and commentators on Robinson's death are faced with the "problem" of how to address issues relating to Robinson's sexuality—to his possible homosexuality—the result being a large body of wrongminded commentary that actually hinders the educational efforts Robinson intended to endorse.

It is a mistake to think that, because most accounts of Robinson's death do not mention the possibility of his homosexuality, it is not a problem to be reckoned with. On the contrary, since the discursive contexts in which Robinson derived his power as a public figure function to prevent discussion of black male homosexuality, the silence regarding the topic that characterizes most of the notices of Robinson's death actually marks the degree to which the possibility of black male homosexuality is worried over and considered problematic. The instances in which the possibility of Robinson's homosexuality *does* explicitly figure serve as proof of the anxiety that founds the more than usual silence on the subject. A look at a few commentaries on Robinson's death illustrate this well; examining these pieces in the chronological order of their appearance in the media especially helps us to see how, over time, the need to quell anxiety about the possibility of Robinson's homosexuality becomes increasingly desperate, thus increasingly undermining the educational efforts that his death was supposed to occasion.

In the two weeks after Robinson died, *Newsweek* magazine featured an obituary that, once again, includes the obligatory references to Robinson's "commanding" on-air presence, to his attacks on racism in the media, and to the psychic "conflict" he suffered that led him to drink ("Max Robinson: Fighting...,"65). In addition to reciting this standard litany, however, the *Newsweek* obituary also emphasizes that "even [Robinson's] family...don't know how he contracted the disease" (65). This reference to the general ignorance as to how Robinson became infected with HIV—the virus widely believed to cause the immune deficiency that underlies AIDS—leaves open the possibility that Robinson engaged in homosexual activity that put him at risk for infection, just as the *Jet* notice leaves unresolved the possibility that Robinson was a homosexual or IV drug user. Yet the invocation in the *Newsweek* piece of Robinson's "family," with all its conventional heterosexist associations, simultaneously indicates the anxiety that the possibility of Robinson's homosexuality generally produces, and constitutes an attempt to redeem Robinson from the unsavory implications of his AIDS diagnosis.

The subtlety of *Newsweek's* strategy for dealing with the possibility of Robinson's homosexuality gave way to a more direct approach by Jesse Jackson in an interview broadcast on the NPR series on AIDS and blacks (*Morning Edition* April 5, 1989). Responding to charges by black AIDS activists that he missed a golden opportunity to educate blacks about AIDS by neglecting to speak out about modes of HIV transmission soon after Robinson's death, Jackson provided this statement:

> Max shared with my family and me that he had the AIDS virus [sic], but that it did not come from homosexuality; it came from promiscuity.... And now we know that the number one transmission [factor] for AIDS is not sexual contact; it's drugs, and so the crises of drugs and needles and AIDS are connected, as well as AIDS and promiscuity are connected.

And all we can do is keep urging people not to isolate this crisis by race, or by class, or by sexual preference, but in fact to observe the precautionary measures that have been advised on the one hand, and keep urging more money for research immediately because it's an international health crisis and it's a killer disease.

A number of things are notable about this statement. First of all, Jackson, like the *Newsweek* writer, is careful to reincorporate the discussion of Robinson's AIDS diagnosis into the nuclear family context, emphasizing that Robinson shared his secret with Jackson *and his family*, and thereby attempts to mitigate the effects of the association of AIDS with male homosexuality. Second, Jackson invokes the problematic and completely unhelpful concept of "promiscuity," wrongly opposing it to homosexuality (and thus implicitly equating it with heterosexuality) in such a way that he actually appears to be endorsing it over that less legitimate option, contrary to what he must intend to convey about the dangers of unprotected sex with multiple partners; and, of course, since he does not actually mention safer sex practices, he implies that it is "promiscuity," *per se*, that puts people at risk of contracting HIV, when it is, rather, unprotected sex, with however few partners, that constitutes risky behavior. Third, by identifying IV drug use over risky sexual behavior as the primary means of HIV transmission, Jackson manifests a blindness to his own insight about the interrelatedness of various factors in the phenomenon of AIDS, for unprotected sexual activity is often part and parcel of the drug culture (especially that of crack use) in which transmission of HIV thrives, as sex is commonly exchanged for access to drugs, as cited in the NPR Series, *AIDS & Blacks, All Things Considered*, April 7, 1989. Finally, Jackson's sense of "all we can do" to prevent AIDS is woefully inadequate: To "urge people to observe the precautionary measures that have been advised" presupposes that everyone is already aware of what those precautionary measures are, for Jackson himself does not outline them in his statement; to demand more money for research is crucial, but it does not go the slightest distance toward enabling people to protect themselves from HIV in the present; and to resist conceptualizing AIDS as endemic to one race, class, or sexual orientation is of extreme importance (though it is equally important to recognize the relative degrees of interest that different constituencies have in the epidemic), but in the context of Jackson's statement this strategy for preventing various social groups from being stigmatized through their association with AIDS is utilized merely to protect Robinson from speculation that his bout with AIDS was related to homosexual sex. Indeed, Jackson's entire statement centers on clearing Robinson from potential charges of homosexuality, and his intense focus on this homophobic endeavor works to the detriment of his attempts to make factual statements about the nature of HIV transmission.

Jackson is implicated as well in the third media response to Robinson's death that I want to examine, a response that, like those discussed above, represents an effort to silence discussion of the possibility of Robinson's homosexuality. In a June 1989 *Vanity Fair* article, Peter J. Boyer reports on the eulogy Jackson delivered at the Washington, D.C., memorial service for Max Robinson. Boyer cites Jackson's quotation of Robinson's deathbed request: "He said, 'I'm not sure and know not where [sic], but even on my dying bed...let my predicament be a source of education to our people' " (1989, 84). Boyer then asserts that "two thousand people heard Jesse Jackson keep the promise he'd made to Robinson: 'It was not homosexuality,' [Jackson] told them, 'but promiscuity,' implicitly letting people know that Robinson 'got AIDS from a woman'" (84). Apparently, then, the only deathbed promise Jackson kept was the one he made to ensure that people would not think Robinson was gay; no information about how HIV is transmitted or about how such transmission can be prevented has escaped his lips in connection with Robinson's death, though Peter Boyer, evidently, has been fooled into believing that Jackson's speech constituted just such substantive information. This is not surprising, since Boyer's article itself is nothing more than an anxious effort to convince us of Max Robinson's heterosexuality, as if that were the crucial issue. Boyer mentions Robinson's three marriages; comments extensively on his "well-earned" reputation as an "inveterate womanizer"; and emphasizes his attractiveness to women, quoting one male friend as saying, "He could walk into a room and you could just hear the panties drop," and a woman acquaintance as once telling a reporter, "Don't forget to mention he has fine thighs" (74). Boyer also notes that "none of Robinson's friends believe that he was a homosexual" (84); and it cites Robinson's own desperate attempt "to compose a list of women whom he suspected as possible sources of his disease" (84), as though to provide written corroboration of his insistence to a friend, "But I'm not gay" (82).

From early claims, then, that "even Robinson's family" had no idea how he contracted HIV, there developed an authoritative scenario in which Robinson's extensive heterosexual affairs were common knowledge and that posits his contraction of HIV from a female sex partner as a near certainty. It seems that, subsequent to Robinson's death, a propaganda machine was put into operation to establish a suitable account of his contraction of HIV and of his bout with AIDS, the net result of which was to preclude the effective AIDS education that Robinson reputedly wanted his death to occasion, as the point he intended to make became lost in a homophobic shuffle to "fix" his sexual orientation and to construe his death in inoffensive terms.

To ensure that this essay not become absorbed in that project, then, which would deter us from the more crucial task of understanding how to combat the AIDS epidemic, it is important for me to state flat out that I have no idea whether Robinson's sex partners were male or female or both. I acknowledge explicitly my ignorance on this matter because to do so, I think, is to reopen sex in all its manifestations as a primary category for consideration as we review modes of HIV transmission in African American communities. Such a move is crucial because the same homophobic impulse that informs efforts to establish Robinson's heterosexuality is also implicated in a general reluctance to provide detailed information about sexual transmission of HIV in black communities; indeed, a deep silence regarding the details of such transmission has characterized almost all of what passes for government-sponsored AIDS education efforts throughout the U.S.

SINS OF OMISSION: INADEQUACY IN AIDS EDUCATION PROGRAMS

Even the slickest and most visible print and television ads promoting awareness about AIDS consistently thematize a silence that has been a major obstacle to effective AIDS education in communities of color. Notices distributed around the time of Robinson's death utilized an array of celebrities—from Ruben Blades to Patti LaBelle—who encouraged people to "get the facts" regarding AIDS, but did not offer any, merely referring readers elsewhere for substantive information on the syndrome. A bitter testimony to the inefficacy of this ad campaign is offered by a 31-year-old black woman interviewed in the NPR series on AIDS and blacks. "Sandra" contracted HIV through unprotected heterosexual sex; the child conceived in that encounter died at ten months of age from an AIDS-related illness. In her interview,

"Sandra" reflects on her lack of knowledge about AIDS at the time she became pregnant:

> I don't remember hearing anything about AIDS until either the year that I was pregnant, which would have been 1986, or the year after I had her; but I really believe it was when I was pregnant with her because I always remember saying, "I'm going to write and get that information," because the only thing that was on TV was to write or call the 1-800 number to get information, and I always wanted to call and get that pamphlet, not knowing that I was going to have firsthand information. I didn't know how it was transmitted. I didn't know that it was caused by a virus. I didn't know that [AIDS] stood for *Acquired Immune Deficiency Syndrome*. I didn't know any of that (*All Things Considered*, April 4, 1989).

The AIDS awareness ad campaign of the late 1980s falsely homogenized the concerns of people of color and glossed over the complex nature of HIV transmission among them, which, just as with whites, implicated drug use *and* unprotected sexual activity as high-risk behaviors. The ease with which middle-class blacks can construe IV drug use as a problem of communities that are completely removed from their everyday lives (and as unrelated to high-risk sexual activity in which they may engage) makes an exclusive emphasis on IV drug-related HIV transmission among blacks detrimental to efforts at effective AIDS education.

To the extent that Robinson hoped that his death would occasion efforts at AIDS education in black communities, we must consider ad campaigns that utilize the logic manifested in Richard Harris's NPR report as inadequate to meet the challenge Robinson posed. The inadequacy of such efforts is rooted, as I have suggested, in a reluctance to discuss issues of black sexuality that is based simultaneously on whites' stereotyped notions (often defensively adopted by blacks themselves) about the need to suppress black [male] sexuality generally, and on the strictness with which traditional forms of black discourse preclude the possibility of the discussion of black male homosexuality specifically. Indeed, these very factors necessitated the peculiar response to his own AIDS diagnosis that Robinson manifested—initial denial and posthumous acknowledgment. I suggest at the beginning of this essay that Robinson's final acknowledgment of his AIDS diagnosis—in the form of his injunction that we use his death as the occasion to increase blacks' awareness about AIDS—performs an epitaphic function. As the final words of the deceased that constitute an implicit warning to others not to repeat his mistakes, Robinson's request has been promulgated through the media with such a repetitive insistence that it might as well have been etched in stone. The repetitive nature of the request ought itself to serve as a warning, however, since repetition can recapitulate the very silence that it is meant to overcome. As Debra Fried has said, regarding the epitaph, it is both

> "silent and...repetitious; [it] refuses to speak, and yet keeps on saying the same thing: Refusal to say anything different is tantamount to a refusal to speak. Repetition thus becomes a form of silence.... According to the fiction of epitaphs, death imposes on its victims an endless verbal task: to repeat without deviation or difference the answer to a question that, no matter how many times it prompts the epitaph to the same silent utterance, is never satisfactorily answered" (Fried 1986, 615).

In the case of Max Robinson's death, the pertinent question is "How can transmission of HIV, and thus AIDS-related deaths, be prevented?" The burden of response at this point is not on the deceased ,but on us. We must create educational programs that offer comprehensive information on the prevention of HIV transmission. To do so, we must break the rules of the various discourses through which black life in the United States has traditionally been articulated. A less radical strategy cannot induce the widespread behavioral changes necessary in the face of AIDS, and our failure in this task would mean sacrificing black people to an epidemic that is enabled, paradoxically, by the very discourses that shape our lives.

REFERENCES

Abrahams, R.D. (1976). *Talking Black*. Rowley, MA: Newbury House.

Abrahams, R.D. and Mitchell-Kernan, C. (1962). "Playing the Dozens." *Journal of American Folklore*, 75 (July-Sept.): 209-220.

Amiri B./ Jones, L. (1979). *Selected Poetry*. New York: William Morrow.

"Black Gay Men in Boston Organize." *Gay Community News*. 15:46 (June 12-18 1988, 3, 9.1): 27-31.

Beam, J. (Ed.). (1986). *In The Life: A Black Gay Anthology*. Boston: Alyson.

Boyer P.J. (1989). "The Light Goes Out." *Vanity Fair*. June 1989: 68-84.

Bracey, Jr., J.H; Meier, A.; Rudwick, E. (Eds.). (1970). *Black Nationalism in America*.

Indianapolis and New York: Bobbs-Merrill.

Centers for Disease Control. *HI V/AIDS Surveillance Report.* March 1991: Table 7, p. 2.

Crimp, D. (1987). "How to Have Promiscuity in an Epidemic." *AIDS: Cultural Analysis/Cultural Activism.,* 43 (Winter): 237-271.

Fried, D. (1986). "Repetition, Refrain, and Epitaph." *ELH* 53:3 (Fall): 615-632.

Full-page display ad about youths raping jogger in Central Park, paid for by Donald Trump. *New York Times.* May 1, 1989: A13.

Gerard, J. (1988). "Max Robinson, 49, First Black to Anchor Network News, Dies." *New York Times.* Dec. 21, 1988: D19.

Giovanni, N. (1971). "The True Import of Present Dialogue: Black vs. Negro." In *The Black Poets,* edited by Dudley Randall, New York: Bantam.

Hernton, C.C. (1966). *Sex and Racism in America.* New York: Doubleday.

Hewitt, D. (1985). *Minute by Minute.* New York: Random House.

Kahn, J.P. (1988). "Max Robinson: Tormented Pioneer." *Boston Globe,* Dec. 21, 1988: 65, 67.

Kochman, T. (1969). "Rapping in the Black Ghetto." *Trans-action* 6 (Feb.): 26-34.

Lauren, B. (1988). "The Female Complaint," *Social Text* 19/20 (Fall): 237-259.

Madhubuti, H.R. (1969). *Don't Cry, Scream.* Detroit: Broadside Press.

"Max Robinson: Fighting the Demons."*Newsweek.* Jan. 2, 1989: 65. Cited in a report from the NPR series *AIDS & Blacks, All Things Considered,* Apr. 7, 1989.

"Max Robinson, 49, First Black Anchor for Networks, Dies of AIDS Complications." *Boston Globe.* Dec. 21, 1988: 51.

"Max Robinson, First Black National TV News Anchor, Succumbs to AIDS in D.C." *Jet.* Jan. 9, 1989: 14-15.

Mosse, G. (1985). *Nationalism and Sexuality: Respectability and Abnormal Sexuality in Modern Europe.* Madison, WI: University of Wisconsin Press.

National Center for Health Statistics. (1990). *Health, United States, 1989.* Hyattsville, MD: Public Health Service.

National Public Radio's *Morning Edition.* The report was part of the NPR series, *AIDS & Blacks: Breaking the Silence,* broadcast on *Morning Edition* and *All Things Considered* the week of Apr. 3-9, 1989.

"On Cultural Nationalism." (1970). In *The Black Panthers Speak,* edited by Philip S. Foner. New York: Lippincott, 1970.

Schwartz, T. "Are TV Anchormen Merely Performers?" *New York Times,* 27 July 27, 1980: II 1, II 27.

Schwartz, T. "Robinson of ABC News Quoted as Saying Network Discriminates." *New York Times.* Feb. 11, 1981: C21.

"Singer Sylvester, 42, Dies of AIDS in Oakland, CA." *Jet.* Jan. 9, 1989: 14-15, 18.

Smitherman, G. (1977). *Talkin and Testifyin: The Language of Black America.* Boston: Houghton Mifflin.

Wolff, C. (1989). "Youths Rape Jogger on Central Park Road." *New York Times.* Apr. 21, 1989: B1, B3.

Containing AIDS: Magic Johnson and Post-Reagan America

Cheryl L. Cole

It's patriotic to have the test and be negative.
—Gory Servaas, Presidential Commission

*AIDS is God's judgment of a society
that does not live by His rules.*
—Jerry Falwell

The Bodies of the Condemned in the Age of AIDS

As AIDS became news during the mid 1980s, it acquired the status of the extraordinary in popular consciousness. Mainstream media routinely characterized AIDS as evidence of immoral behaviors and lifestyles that denoted identity categories: homosexuals, intravenous drug users, and prostitutes. Moreover, the meanings and values already attributed to these stigmatized groups shaped both the media coverage and popular reception of AIDS. Overall, mainstream news coverage served as a ritual of confirmation of the identity of the general public defined through familial heterosexuality and a ritual of condemnation of all of those who were HIV-positive, excepting those who had been infected through "no fault of their own." Not surprisingly, prostitutes, intravenous drug users, and, most prominently, homosexuals, were represented as threats to the general public rather than communities threatened by a devastating crisis. In general, the person with AIDS was represented as an "AIDS victim" who was portrayed as guilty, diseased, contagious, isolated, threatening, and deteriorating. By 1990 the cultural common sense of AIDS had become fairly well sedimented in the national imaginary, while in general, AIDS became "old news" and receded to the background.

At 4 P.M. on Nov. 7, 1991, major and local networks interrupted their scheduled programming to cover what has been called "the saddest press conference in sport history": Earvin "Magic" Johnson's announcement that he would immediately retire from the National

Basketball Association (NBA) because he had tested positive for HIV antibodies. The enormous amount of media coverage that followed Johnson's announcement, especially that which expressed public sympathy, compassion, and loyalty, is a clear indication of Johnson's profile in national popular culture. As Jack Kroll depicted Magic's popularity, he "has a constituency that a presidential candidate would kill for. From toddlers to doddlers, from blacks to whites, from machos to mothers, from underclass to the overrich, Americans were overwhelmed by the statement of his plight.... There's no gender gap, there's no age gap, there's no race gap in Magic's ability to inspire affection" (Kroll 1991, 70). Johnson was glorified for his position in the development and success of the NBA, his economic investments and successes, and the courage he displayed by announcing to the world that he was HIV-positive. America embraced and proclaimed its support for the first HIV-positive African American superstar. Thomas Boswell of the *Washington Post* depicted America's relation to Johnson through the most intimate and desirable of units: "Magic became part of almost every American family. And now we can't get him out of the family. He's everybody's brother or son who may get AIDS. For Magic Johnson, it's that single indigestible word *tragedy*" (Boswell 1991, D6).

Johnson's HIV status was framed by the mainstream media as a personal tragedy, an athletic tragedy and a tragedy for the sport world, with the United States narrated as a compassionate and caring nation. Pat Riley, former coach of the Los Angeles Lakers and current coach of the New York Knicks, announced the "tragic news" at Madison Square Garden that night. Tears in his eyes, voice cracking, he called for a "moment of silence" and then led the crowd and teams in the Lord's Prayer. Johnson's disclosure was made into a story of heroism (even by the Bush Administration) that was explained, to a great extent, by his characteristically courageous handling of the situation—his ability to flash "his trademark smile" even in a moment of personal crisis. And given Magic's popularity with youth, Johnson, unlike previous HIV-positive figures who were represented as threatening to children, was portrayed as a model AIDS educator who could reach those "youth" and communities depicted as having been resistant to AIDS education in the past. In general, the response to Johnson seemed to break from the earlier and more common reaction to those who identified as HIV-positive. Who could not help but be struck and touched by the public outpouring of sympathy and compassion for this national icon, especially in light of the previous media coverage of AIDS? How do we account for the apparent differences between the narration of compassion and previous narrations of condemnation that pathologized and demonized people living with aids (PLWAs)? Whereas the prominent AIDS image figured PLWAs as evidence of moral decline and threat to the family and nation, Johnson was a familiar and friendly figure whose meanings were consistent with the dominant values of America. Even as Johnson made visible his HIV antibody status, his family and proper sexuality were prominently displayed as his pregnant wife Cookie was positioned visibly behind him as he disclosed his serostatus at the November press conference.

Perhaps the apparent discrepancy between the narratives of compassion and condemnation can be attributed to a shift in the popular perception of AIDS. "Popular consciousness" surrounding AIDS had apparently been raised in 1985 through Rock Hudson's death from HIV-related complications, as indicated by the increased media coverage of "heterosexual AIDS" in 1986. But if national consciousness had indeed been raised, how do we account for the thousands of inquiries directed to national and local AIDS information hotlines and the Centers for Disease Control (CDC), in response to Johnson's press conference, about *who* was at risk? Local AIDS information lines reported receiving at least three times their usual number of calls in response to Johnson's announcement. The CDC, which typically gets 3,000 calls daily, reported receiving 40,000 calls between 5 P.M. and midnight on the day of Johnson's press conference.

Just as popular knowledges of AIDS are *imagined* through national press and television discourses and the modern categories that restrict that imagination, most Americans *imagine* they know "Magic Johnson." Although the narration of Johnson and AIDS is a media event in that the narration is produced at the intersection of multiple media narratives, in this essay I use the narrative of Magic and AIDS as a case study that offers the opportunity to interrogate the continual reinvention of the cultural imaginary. I argue that the "Magic narrative" provides an opportunity to render visible the concealed strategies and operations of power whose effects are rendered visible through modern identity categories and understandings of the body. These modern identity categories and understandings of the body enable, limit, and constrain the cultural imaginary. Given this, I argue that despite the apparent distinction between the narrative of compassion and the narratives that pathologize and police deviance, both narratives are implicated in and bound by the same normalizing logic that structure the discursive formation around AIDS. In the first section of the essay, I draw on the work of Michel Foucault and Jacques Derrida to outline the conceptual grid that guides my interpretation of the narrative generated around Johnson. I argue that the narration of Johnson, and that of AIDS more generally, is structured through a logic of containment in which the bodies of others are marked in order to define and contain the general public. I consider how the corporeal identities generated and regulated through modern logics of sexuality and race shape our understandings of Magic and AIDS and how those identities gain force and momentum through the complex political forces and conditions of Reagan and Bush America. Here I examine how "family values," defined by the Reagan and Bush administrations as the most important domestic issue of the 1980s and early 1990s, serves as a normalizing lens through which the identity of the general public is stabilized as various sexualities and behaviors are criminalized. I argue that the narration generated through Johnson's announcement relies on emblematic figures codified and circulated by the mainstream media's construction of AIDS and the inner city through a politics of lifestyle that converts social problems to a characterological moral poverty. Finally I examine how the identity of the general public is reconstituted through the dispersion of deviance.

POWER/KNOWLEDGE/BODY AND AIDS

Subject to the gaze of the camera, the body became the object of closest scrutiny, its surface continuously examined for the signs of innate physical, mental, and moral inferiority. From this science of corporeal semiotics there emerged new forms of knowledge about the individual and new ways of mapping depravity.

—David Green

The AIDS epidemic—with its genuine potential for global devastation—is simultaneously an epidemic of transmittable lethal disease and an epidemic of meanings or signification.

—Paula Treichler

Because AIDS *made visible* and was *made visible through* homosexuals, intravenous drug users, and prostitutes, HIV and AIDS were taken up in the popular imaginary as "visible" evidence of secret and inner depravity, pathologized bodily acts, and corresponding identities. Although the identity categories seem descriptive, self-evident, and self-contained, *what* and *who* we see as well as *how* we see them are the effects of these received categories. That is, the identity categories function as optics (*how, what, who we see*) that enable and constrain our sense of morality, conduct, our selves, and others; and by extension shape the cultural common sense of AIDS.

Keeping this in mind, the significance of the question "Why Magic?" repeatedly played out under the guise of compassion takes on new meaning. To ask "Why Magic?" is to ask *who* Magic *is*. The question of "who" is a question of identity, and carries with it presuppositions about free will, responsibility, and guilt. To ask "Why Magic?" underscores the perception that serostatus is understood to reveal more than HIV antibody status—it is understood to reveal an identity bound to presumptions about character and moral worth. Although multiple dyads (central/not central; body/antibody; deviant/normalized; contained/leaky) structure AIDS narratives, I argue that the dyad of act/identity dominates the others. Corporeal identities, then, have become central to the organization of the discursive formation surrounding AIDS.

In this section I outline a framework that brings together genealogical (Foucault) and deconstructive (Derrida) logics to render visible the mechanisms and strategies of power that elide the historical contingency of *corporeal identities* that underlie the popular cause-and-effect understanding of risk groups and AIDS. Both genealogical and deconstructive logics present challenges to Western reason and the modern subject (the subject of liberal humanism, the unitary, self-authorial subject) and the constant policing required to maintain boundaries that mark the deviant in order to produce and maintain the norm.

Foucault (1979, 1980a) views the invention of the homosexual and the addict as predicated upon the modern epistemic regime in which particular acts and behaviors such as sodomy and drug use were transformed into criminalized and pathologized bodies/identities through the positive effects of power. The modern regime organized itself through a division between the normal and the pathological. The normal and abnormal are mutually dependent categories: The self's border is produced through a social process of producing and policing the other. As Foucault explains, the shift from acts to identities is an effect of a modern epistemic regime that produces, locates, and contains "what" and "who" are threatened and threatening in order to produce and stabilize the norm. The strategies and operations of modern power are concealed, but work to produce and render visible the deviant, the pathological, the delinquent. Deconstruction asserts that meaning is produced through *differance:* the double process of difference and deferral (Derrida, 1976). Meaning is deferred in the sense that it is produced temporally, through the trace, and produced through difference (in that each unit derives its meaning through its difference from others). While Western logic at once depends upon a phantasmatic center, it continuously relies on its periphery to establish the center. Because it is relational, Western thought cannot posit any central self-identical ideal upon which it is founded. Identity, then, is never simply self-identical or self-contained, but depends on what it negates. Deconstructionist strategies emphasize the transgression already taking place at the border of binary terms and examine the constant motion and policing required to maintain boundaries between binary terms.

For example, the terms that organize the discourse of addiction are *free will* and *compulsion*. Terms that are apparently primary to *logos*, such as *free will*, parasitically rely on the terms that precede and oppose them (for example, *free will* relies on *compulsion*). *Free will* requires continual policing to firm up its boundaries because *free will* requires limits, borders, and the marginal. Because deconstructionists emphasize the transgression always already taking place at the border, deconstruction examines the force relations between the terms: the constant exertion of pressure at their boundaries, the policing required to maintain those boundaries, the incompleteness of the category of the will and the violence it does. In Foucault's terms, the construct of *free will*, partly constitutive of the normal, is dependent upon what it excludes: the marking of the compulsive, abnormal, and the deviant.

As it is has been articulated in the United States, AIDS narratives, like narratives of drug use, turn on a logic of addiction, a logic that depends on "free will" and locates insufficient free will in the bodies of Others. Both AIDS and illicit drug use narratives rely on a cultural logic that produces and distinguishes between the deteriorating/nonproductive body and the hard healthy body of the general (heterosexual-patriotic) public.

Drawing on Foucault and Derrida, I suggest that the national imaginary is continuously reinvented through the logic of containment and the identities made available through its dynamics. Containment functions by establishing limits around semantic-social possibilities, but since that limit can always be transgressed, containment is an ongoing project of marking transgression on new bodies and identities. The strategy of containment depends on turning bodily acts into bodily identities—making visible and containable that which is neither, marking the Other to that presumed to be self. The limit will always have to change and readdress itself. Certain bodies/identities become understood as transgressive of certain institutions; bodies become the place of transgression while the site of transmission of HIV is always between bodies. But the momentum and force accrued by bodies/identities are always related to the effects and affects achieved through historically specific economic, political, and cultural forces.

POST-REAGAN AMERICA

There can be no possible exercise of power without a certain economy of discourses of truth, which operates through and on the basis of this association. We are subjected to the production of truth through power and we cannot exercise power except through the production of truth.... In the end, we are judged, condemned, classified, determined in our undertakings, destined to a certain mode of living and dying, as a function of the true discourses, which are the bearers of the specific effects of power.

—Michel Foucault

"AIDS," then, can be understood as strategy of power and a normalizing practice that functions to assign visible character and form to acts of transgression through identity categories. The shift from acts that the body is capable of doing to the solidification and codification of that act into identity allows for the cultural common sense fantasy of the family (Watney 1987, 1990). AIDS narratives function to assign identities to the acts of transgression that threaten the mythic stable family: The act of transgression is figured (and contained) in the homosexual, the addict, and the prostitute. As Watney explains:

> The family at the heart of AIDS commentary is an ideological unit, as yet supposedly unaffected, but held to be threatened by the "leakage" of HIV infection, which, like nuclear fallout, is widely and erroneously perceived to be everywhere about

us, a deadly miasma of contagion and death…. [T]he family enjoys absolute centrality for modern policy makers and their enforcement agents. It is presented as that which precedes them—their object, that on which they work, invested with the full ideological weight of Nature (Watney 1990, 174).

The normalizing optic of the mythic family gained momentum and force in a conjunctural moment dominated by the forces (political, moral, cultural, economic) defining Reagan/post-Reagan America. Reaganism, the signature of an alliance-backlash politics, was characterized by the revival of a conservative patriotism generated and legitimated around *bodies* and a related series of racist, antigay, antifeminist, pro–nuclear family, pro-life, antisocial welfare, and anti–affirmative action positions. Under Reagan, America's economic and social problems were, to a great extent, attributed to the breakdown of the nuclear family and the moral fabric of the nation. As articulated by the New Right, the "family values agenda" denied the relation between the economy and nuclear family and created the imaginary space from which to individualize social problems, legitimate Reagan's pro-business policies, and justify the erosion of social welfare programs.

The articulation of sexual deviance and AIDS, especially the articulation of homosexuality and HIV, brings to the fore the central trope of AIDS and the central trope of Reaganism: the construction of bodies (the healthy hard body of the general public) over and against antibodies. During the Reagan and Bush years, the body/antibody trope was a discourse on the loose, marking (and unmarking) patriotism, sexuality, race, poverty, contamination, and threat by producing an affective economy of images populated by AIDS bodies, crack bodies, criminal bodies, welfare bodies, hard bodies, and productive bodies.

Although addiction became most visible in and through the figures produced and circulated by mediated moral panics imbricated in the war on drugs, the logic of insufficient free will underlies the figures produced through the moral panic around AIDS. The Reagan administration capitalized on the logic of free will, redeploying an amplified individualism and will that located America's decline and uncertain status in individual bodies and their character failings and deviance. In response to and as part of the New Right's profamily politics and war on drugs, U.S. culture became saturated with images of criminal, threatening, and out-of-control, nonproductive homosexual and black bodies (primarily black male youth) that contrasted sharply with a national masculinity—defined by a prosthetic, hard, muscular (white) body (Rambo, Robocop, etc.).

Repathologized homosexual bodies and racially coded images of drug use became inextricably bound with everyday lived experience and fears: threat and fear were heightened through the image of criminal masculinities inscribed on the bodies of homosexuals and black male youth. Such images worked to conceal the multiple effects of late capitalism: the heightened poverty produced through hyper-industrialization, globalization, and Reagan's defunding and repressive policies and their corresponding logic of insatiable consumption. As racial inequalities and tensions escalated in America's urban areas, inner cities reinvigorated their economies by promoting an urban, world-class lifestyle (restaurants, shopping districts, stadiums, sport events, and sport superstars). As the Los Angeles Lakers would have it, it was showtime in America's inner cities. The NBA claimed prominent places in national culture and in our everyday lives, and images of black athletes (*Just Do It*) and (drug and sex) addicts (*Just Say No*) remained intertwined in the national imaginary organized around a familial heterosexuality.

MAGIC JOHNSON: PROMOTIONAL CULTURE, RACE, BODIES

> *Magic is here. Magic is now. Magic is us.*
> —Leigh Montville, journalist

> *So on Nov. 7, 1991, when I listened to Magic Johnson announcing his retirement from the Lakers because he'd tested HIV-positive, I had to ask, Who's Magic Johnson?*
> *Of course, I found out right away.*
> —Douglas Crimp, AIDS activist, queer theorist

Given that the NBA, NBA players, and the products they endorse saturate the contemporary cultural landscape, it is difficult to imagine the complex and contradictory politics played out in the cultural spaces they generate and territorialize. The complexity of those politics are embedded in the NBA's attempts to overcome its stigmatized identity that was generated through its merger with the American

Basketball Association in 1977. The NBA's limited popularity and financial struggles during the late 1970s and early 1980s can be understood, to some extent, through the racial coding of the NBA as a deviant space associated with an urban black masculinity depicted as threatening. The racial inflection of deviance was codified through style of play and a politics of lifestyle depicted through excessive consumption, especially "epidemic cocaine use." Indeed, "numerous players were suspended, placed in rehabilitation programs for positive drug tests, and charged with drug crimes" (Reeves and Campbell 1994, 38). The struggles faced by the NBA in the early 1980s were serious enough to suggest that basketball would become the first major professional sport in the United States to fail (Katz 1994). Sport can be conceptualized as an apparatus that organizes and is organized by the normalizing practices and strategies of science, technology, and the media; a technology that produces multiple bodies (raced, classed, gendered, heterosexualized, prosthetic, pure, patriotic, etc.) in the context of an image-dominated consumer culture (Cole 1993). Professional sport is one of the most prominent sites for the production of the prototypical masculine body. A (hyper)heterosexual masculinity is displayed through a series of practices embedded in a "politics of lifestyle" marked by the semipublic sexual exchange of a conspicuously displayed network of adoring, supportive female fans, girlfriends, and/or wives: It is a masculine lifestyle meant to be embraced, admired, envied, and consumed. But the relationship between sport and masculinity is always already complicated by race. The historical codifications that locate the black body as closer to nature (inscribing and searching for causes of enhanced performance) and as hypersexual require that the black masculinity in sport be configured in ways that distance it from the codes of threatening black bodies (Gray, 1989; Jackson, 1994).

The black masculinity associated with the NBA was reordered and managed, in part, through the rivalry between Magic Johnson and Larry Bird *and* through the marketing of particular players' personalities. In this case, race was not displaced, but remained a dynamic force that organized and was organized through the Johnson-Bird rivalry. Johnson's marketability was established through promotional strategies that articulated Magic as the embodiment of an acceptable, nonthreatening face of masculinity, of having a personality and character consistent with the values of what Cindy Patton (1992) has called the "Africanized Horatio Alger trope of athletics": family, modest beginnings, discipline, determination, loyalty, and social mobility. Additionally, Johnson's popularity was secured through his public personality, an image designed to make "us" feel better and more comfortable with racial difference, described in terms of affability, generosity, and boyish enthusiasm for the game.

As Peter Jackson explains, the spectator's acquired knowledges of popular personalities and character function to "suppress the more threatening aspects of a stereotypically anonymous and rapacious black male sexuality," allowing black bodies "to work as objects of envy and desire" rather than provoking dread (Jackson 1994, 50, 56). The positioning of Johnson (through his physicality, outstanding character, and celebrity status) as the embodiment of the American dream, athletic hero, and AIDS hero, not only suggests a racially harmonized country, but also positions the white spectator as allied with or complicit in the heroic performance. Perhaps this explains, at least in part, the willingness to extend, through a popular discourse, love and compassion to Magic that had been denied to most HIV-positive individuals in the past.

Despite the displacement of racism and its related issues through representations of racial progress (embedded in individualism) and racial harmony circulated through sport personalities, "racial meanings" are not settled. The narration of the superstar personality is implicated in the narration of a more ordinary threatening black masculinity. That is, the narration of the African American superstar is used to promote a vision that simultaneously undergirds the illusion of meritocracy and denies racism as it inscribes blackness as a negation of the social order. In other words, the figures of the superstar and of threatening black masculinity can be understood as effects of knowledges and powers that make race *matter* and *visible* through trouble, deviance, and danger.

In this case, I want to draw attention to the strategies and operations of power that codify deviance in response to Johnson's transgression to make visible the criminal in the black body while a white familial heterosexuality is simultaneously constructed and rendered invisible yet normative. Most specifically, homosexuality and race are imagined and marked through the familiar optic of the family and repetitive and racially inflected figures (the drug addict, the Black church, and the hypersexual black man) that work to locate and contain the possibility of "African American AIDS" within the homosexual and African American communities.

MECHANISMS OF CONTAINMENT

*The insistence that AIDS is somehow a mark of perversions
transforms infected persons into "queers,"
regardless of their exposure route.*

—Cindy Patton

In a quote that exemplifies the attempt to resituate Johnson and AIDS, Malcolm Gladwell and Alison Muscatine suggest that: "the two worlds with which he [Magic Johnson] is most clearly identified—sports and the African American community—have long been among the most resistant in American society in acknowledging the disease (1991, A1).

The explicit appeal to these two apparently self-evident, contained geographical spaces (the African American community and professional sports) is a rhetorical strategy that brings to the fore racial identity to locate and contain Johnson and the possibilities of the "disease." Although racial differences in regard to HIV infection are acknowledged, the higher rate of infection among African Americans is narrated through a logic of addiction (that inscribes recklessness, compulsion, and insufficient free will on bodies) that simultaneously structures and makes visible the failed authority of the black community through the figure of the Black church. As the most prominent surrogate for the black community, the Black church is positioned as having neglected its authoritative role, allowing homophobia to interfere with its education of the black community. The narration of the negligent African American community—depicted as irrational, homophobic, in denial, and resistant to drug and safer-sex education—simultaneously produces an imaginary, superior "Middle America" outside the frame of scrutiny. The frame of community responsibility is articulated through the logic of "private community," accomplished under Reagan to legitimate defunding practices during the 1980s. The privatized logic confined individual responsibility within local community and, by extension, liberated Middle America (suburban America) from its identification with and responsibility for inner-city poverty and urban decay (Reeves and Campbell, 1994).

Not surprisingly, the logic of containment is amplified through the media's surveillance of the (racially coded) professional world, to which the media almost exclusively directs its gaze to imagine the possibility of Johnson's HIV infection. The public scrutiny of Johnson *and* the black male athletic body by and through the mainstream media marks a narrative shift from superstar to the more ordinary and threatening black masculinity. Stuart Alan Clarke (1991) has referred to this as the "black men misbehaving" narrative, a narrative that simultaneously "expresses, affirms, and authorizes popular fears, pleasures, and anxieties in ways that shape the experience of race and ethnicity in both personal and public spaces" (Cole and Andrews 1994). In this case, race *matters*: An out-of-control black sexuality in need of regulation is rendered visible.

FRAMING THE "LOSS" OF THE PRODUCTIVE BODY

Tinged with the stigma of illness that dramatically destroys the body, what was usually absent from representation becomes spectacularly and consistently visible.
—Timothy Landers

Consistent with the fatalist discourse of AIDS, which equates sex, HIV infection, AIDS, and death, eulogizing articles, structured through "where were you?" moments ranging from John F. Kennedy's assassination to John Lennon's murder on the street in New York, were produced in response to Johnson's confession. The line drawn from moments of national distress (Kennedy's assassination and Lennon's murder) to Johnson suggest an attempt to capture (and produce) America's compassion and loyalty. The narration of "loss" appeals to economic loss: The superstar narration celebrates progress through the economy and the productive body. In this case, Johnson was celebrated for elevating the economic position of the NBA (locally and globally), his investments, and his worth. The narrative of compassion and loss is racially inflected through the repetitious appeal to the figure of Len Bias (an African American college basketball player who died from a cocaine overdose within 48 hours of being drafted to play for the Boston Celtics), a figure that captures cultural anxieties around African American excessive consumption and addiction as well as moralistic fascination with the loss of the productive body. Both Bias and Johnson are depicted as African American athletes whose lives end through excess and contagion, whose tragedies are framed as individual career tragedies.

Although Johnson's body, the figure of the NBA superstar, potentially disrupts the knowledge/power relations that converge on and render visible HIV-infected bodies and the conflation of HIV and AIDS, the figure of the homosexual and the trope of HIV as evidence of inner and secret depravity are repetitiously invoked to maintain the visual border of HIV and AIDS in the popular imaginary. A quote from Leigh Steinberg, a prominent sports agent, exemplifies the attempt to undermine the stereotype of AIDS as a "gay disease": "It's like a slap in the face to people stereotyping AIDS as a gay problem. It shows the universality of the threat and the imagery of this virile, tough, married, athlete being infected by HIV is extremely dramatic" (cited in Gladwell and Muscatine 1991).

The contrast between the homosexual body with that of the "virile, tough, married, athlete" with its appeal to disease and deviant sexuality relies on the repathologized homosexual body and the before/after narration of HIV infection. Johnson's body was placed under an immediate, *retroactive* surveillance that attempted to make visible earlier evidence of HIV (as signs of inevitable death). One article suggests that Johnson had suffered from a case of shingles in October 1985 (Almond and Cimons, 1991), others cited a flu-like illness at the beginning of the 1991-2 basketball season that forced Johnson to miss three games. Chick Hearn, a radio-television announcer, said he knew as early as October 25, 1991, when Magic failed to play in the last two exhibition games before the beginning of the opening of the regular season (Howard-Cooper, 1991).

As the media refrained Johnson, photographers kept him under constant surveillance waiting to document the hidden sexualities and/or sexual practices as they became visible on the body. The now widely circulated image of Johnson seated on the bench, bleeding, after being scratched in an exhibition game against the Cleveland Cavaliers during November 1992, which accompanied the media's announcement of his second retirement from the NBA, might be understood as providing visual evidence of "threat" seeping out of the once hard and contained body, legitimating the discourse of risk, danger, and fear circulated by the media.

VISUALIZING DEVIANCE: THE PROMISCUOUS (HETEROSEXUAL) WORLD OF SPORT

Before I was married, I truly lived the bachelor's life. I'm no Wilt

Chamberlain, but as I traveled around NBA cities, I was never at a loss for female companionship.... There were just some bachelors almost every woman in L.A. wanted to be with: Eddie Murphy, Arsenio Hall, and Magic Johnson. I confess that after I arrived in L.A. in 1979, I did my best to accommodate as many women as I could—most of them through unprotected sex.

—Magic Johnson

As I've suggested, Johnson's HIV status immediately brought into question his sexuality, which remained an ongoing object of scrutiny despite his implication that he had contracted HIV through "heterosexual sex" and corroborating statements by his doctor, Michael Mellman, and the Lakers' PR department. Johnson reasserted his heterosexuality in *Sports Illustrated* ("I've never had a homosexual encounter. Never.") and the *Arsenio Hall Show* ("I'm far from being homosexual. You know that. Everybody else who's close to me understands that."), where his statement was met with enthusiastic cheering and applause. Under the cover of a recognition of a courageous political statement ("heterosexuals get AIDS too"), the applause is more properly understood as a homophobic display—and as an attempt to make visible, prove, and contain that which cannot. The popular fixation on Magic's sexual practices motivates a series of strategies meant to situate Magic and HIV outside of the general public. Under headlines such as "Johnson's HIV Caused by Sex: 'Heterosexual Transmission' Cited; Wife Is Pregnant" (Cannon and Cotton 1991, A-14) we reread the multiple codifications embedded in "heterosexual transmission," which simultaneously initiate the production of Johnson as "family man" and "tragic figure" while appealing to the seemingly stable and mutually exclusive categories that organize the logic of "heterosexual/homosexual transmission." Typical of the framing of post-1985 AIDS, the heterosexual AIDS narrative simultaneously asserts and destabilizes its possibility—thus the endless repetition of "AIDS is not just a gay disease." In this case, Magic's sexuality is made suspect, and skepticism is invited by invoking the authorial voice of science and the statistical AIDS imaginary to suggest taken-for-granted transmission patterns. Those studies, recast by the dominant media, are summarized in the following quote: "The fraction of heterosexuals now infected is very much smaller than that of homosexuals," and therefore, "the risk of it happening is far lower than in homosexual contact" (Cannon and Cotton 1991, A14). In other words, the possibility of finding a partner who is infected is quite low—with the major exception of prostitutes, a large percentage of whom are infected. It is also believed that the odds of an infected man passing the virus to a woman are far greater than those of an infected woman passing it to a man. If a man has another venereal disease, such as herpes, his odds of being infected are vastly higher (Cannon and Cotton, A14). In addition:

> The primary risk groups for infection are gay men and intravenous drug users. The Centers for Disease Control said that, through August, 6% of the people with AIDS had been infected through heterosexual transmission. Fewer than one-sixth of those cases— less than 1% overall—involved men who said they had been infected through intercourse with women. Studies of husbands of women who were infected by blood transfusions showed that the men who did not practice safe sex had a 3% chance a year of developing an AIDS infection (Kolata 1991, A12).

These studies, again recast by the media, exemplify the knowledge/power nexus that simultaneously asserts and unsettles "heterosexual AIDS" by raising doubts about its possibilities. As Watney explains it, heterosexual identity is not self-identical, but is defined over and against what it is not: "[T]he figure of the gay man interrupts yet also reinforces the social and psychical boundaries of desire, and the relations of gender which are inscribed within them. Straight society needs us. We are its necessary 'Other.' Without gays, straights are not straight" (Watney 1987, 26). Such "stabilizing" strategies include a popular construction of "heterosexual sex" as monolithic and "missionary" through the repetitive displacement of the multiplicity of sexual possibilities. Sodomy (homosexuality) is made the predominant figure of unsafe sex in the cultural imaginary (Watney 1987, 31).

Yet the attempt to contain the identity of the general public turns to the familiar trope of promiscuity and the hypersexual African American man. Most explicitly, "guilt" is displaced onto the body of sexually active women in a metonymical slip, which places them as figures for the "promiscuous world of sport."

As Michael Wilborn describes the sport world, "Sex and sports are as inseparable as the pick and roll.... If you've ever left an NBA arena late...or followed a team back to the hotel....you understand that the players don't have to go looking for sex; it's staring most of them in the face (Wilborn 1991, D3). One more time, "it," the act of sex, that is "staring most of them in the face," becomes an identity, specifically that of women. It is under headlines such as "What It Boils Down To Is Playing With Fire" (Callahan 1991, D3) that women, necessarily, re-enter the sport world to reestablish its heterosexuality. But in this case, women enter in the position of villain, victimizing athletes, signifying threat and contagion to the family. The duplicitous heterosexual AIDS discourse reappears, displacing the statistics invoked earlier by the mainstream media to problematize the possibility of female-to-male transmission, and to destabilize both Johnson's sexuality and the possibility of heterosexual AIDS. In the genre of "the promiscuous world of sport," there are no doubts: Women are resurrected as the familiar outlaws and the polluting agents, their bodies marked as contagious and dangerous.

The trope of promiscuity figures women who are sexually active outside of the prescriptions of Christian monogamy as prostitutes (Watney, 1987), whose bodies have been historically depicted "as so contaminated that [they] are…'always dripping,' virtual laboratory cultures for viral replication" (Treichler 1988, 207). The prostitute is viewed as self-destructive "rather than someone who has herself been infected by a man" (Watney 1987, 85). Additionally, these women are portrayed as looking for "the million dollar baby," trying to "set up professional athletes for paternity suits." Professional basketball player Eddie Johnson comments, "Women know if they do get pregnant, they do get paid" (*Outside the Lines*). The message in the popular press was clear: "The sex may be free, but there *is* a price to pay for the lifestyle" (Elson 1991, 77). At the same time women are portrayed as prostitutes and villains, male athletes are positioned through racially inflected codes that build on the trope of the compulsive, reckless, and absent inseminating black male repopularized through Reagan's familial politics and the war on drugs. In a shift back to the positioning of the male athlete as necessarily hypersexual, Wilborn continues:

> I'm not suggesting for one millisecond that athletes are the only people who take potentially deadly risks.... But no group of men, with the exception of high-profile rock musicians, goes through life being as sexually tempted and as frequently as professional athletes.... Not only is it not easy to say no, it's almost impossible. To abstain, we're talking about a level of

self-control that I certainly, for one, would not have under similar circumstances (Wilborn 1991, D-3).

As discussed earlier, the discursive construction of heterosexual AIDS remains destabilized, but heterosexuality is stabilized through its articulation of family values and the body that produces a pure heterosexual whose risk is determined by having sex outside the "home." Little attention is given to safer-sex practices without appealing to and supporting abstinence; instead, the narrative draws on the repetitive policing of desire: It is "multiple partners (who) put you at risk" (Cannon and Cotton 1991, A14). Once again act is conflated with identity; it is multiple partners rather than unprotected sex with someone infected with HIV that presents risk. Just say no.

While Johnson's infection is explained through the normalizing construct of promiscuity, his sexuality is now understood to be regulated through the nuclear family, but repetitive appeals to Wilt Chamberlain's 1991 autobiography, *A View From Above*, in which Chamberlain claims to have slept with more than 20,000 women, situates Chamberlain as the surrogate for and embodiment of an excessive, dangerous black sexuality attributed to the African American man. The strategies of observation and the representation of this "lifestyle" render visible the pathological culture of professional sport attributed to a dangerous lifestyle. The sports world is structured through the availability, "quality," and/or quantity of sex (or excess in general), embedded in a ritual of a fast-track lifestyle (i.e., "life on the edge") where "drugs are becoming a problem too," a politics of lifestyle that all too clearly intersects with the lifestyle of insatiable sexuality, orgies, and polluted poppers attributed to gay men to explain their vulnerability to HIV infection. The opening segment of ESPN's *Outside the Lines: Men and Women, Sex and Sports,* outlines the conflicts and questions that frame the narrative that transforms Johnson's seropositivity into an optic that allows "us" to *see* racially coded transgressions: "Do some athletes live dangerous sexual lives?" (Here we see the image of a remorseful Magic Johnson wiping a tear from his cheek.) "Do they feel entitled to grab whatever they can?" (Cut to a police-escorted, handcuffed Mike Tyson, followed by a sound bite from Nigel Clay, former Oklahoma football player convicted of rape.) "From the earliest there can be unreality in an athlete's life." (Cut to white basketball player Daemon Bailey surrounded by the press and fans.) "Later a barrage of material pleasure and privilege" (Cut to a close-up of post-gambling scandal, Michael Jordan in

dark glasses, sitting in what we are to assume is a high-priced car.)...
"Have athletes changed their behavior since the shocking announcement that Magic Johnson has the AIDS virus?" And, we are told by Bob
Ley, the host of the report, that "The games people play extend beyond
the playing fields," after which he asks, "At what cost is pleasure
indulged without consequence?"

The visual images, ordered as apparent responses to the questions raised in the voice-over, feature prominent African American
athletes involved in well-known and publicized scandals or crimes
articulated to give physical form and identity to the dangerous sexuality, excess, and criminality that apparently saturate the world of
professional sport. The ESPN report, like the coverage that generates
the "promiscuous world of sport" more generally, is a narrative of
moral outrage and normalization, organized through the optic of
family values that renders visible and inscribes immorality and danger. "Threat" is generated through the repetitive figure of the black
man as criminal/rapist and a slippage that operates through the logic
of addiction: an escalation of desire and entitlement that moves from
promiscuity (Magic Johnson) to rape (Mike Tyson). Since media
accounts do not racially specify the bodies of the athletes'
"groupies," the enormous amount of media attention focused on the
professional athlete's lifestyle can be understood as a connotation of
cultural anxieties around miscegenation.

In this genre, mechanisms of containment work to racially codify
and pathologize the lifestyle of professional athletes and the culture of
professional sport, described by Bob Ley as a "closed society" that is
"testosterone-rich" (*Outside the Lines*). Social psychologist Chris
O'Sullivan speaks in this report as an expert to explain professional
male athletes: "They sort of don't belong to society. They belong to a
separate society, this outlaw society. And women have no place in that
society—they certainly have no respectful place in that society. How
are they going to relate to women? They don't fit into this world at
all." Male athletes are represented as a "special breed, who develop an
unrealistic sense of 'entitlement.' " We are told in a voice-over by Ley
that the male athlete is "impervious to all discipline" and is a "social
creature of his physical success" as we watch an African American man
as he is escorted through a prison. Johnson, initially positioning himself as an advocate for safer sex, subsequently embraces a position that
suggests that it was sex outside of the family that created the possibility for his infection. In his 1992 autobiography, *My Life*, Johnson's

dedication line, which apparently captures both his love and regret, reads, "For Cookie, You were right. I should have married you sooner." Watney argues that Magic has been positioned in the final discursive space of the AIDS agenda: the AIDS victim. "Crushed, submissive, he or she accepts and justifies the 'punishment' of AIDS for the unforgivable capital offense of daring to live beyond the narrow and sadistic intelligibility of familial consciousness" (1990, 184). This aspect of the Magic Johnson story reproduces identities and invests in familial ideology. It is a neat sin and salvation through the normalizing optic of the sustained by tidy story of family.

CONCLUSION

> SILENCE=DEATH
>
> *When I first saw this poster I believed it said* SCIENCE=DEATH. *I had no doubt that this is what I had read. When the poster became a button, a T-shirt, the key symbol of the anarchistic resistance to a pogrom masquerading as a disease, I was sure the slogan had been changed.... But the dyad silence/science was no mistake. Straight people find this slip funny. Gay people do not.*
>
> —Cindy Patton

In this essay I have argued that multiple dyads (central/not central; body/antibody; deviant/normalized; contained/leaky) structure AIDS narratives and that these dyads function as mechanisms of containment. The cultural logic of modernity insists on rendering AIDS visible and *seeing* it operate: The modern logic of converting act into identity enables and constrains the cultural imaginary.

If normalization is continuously undermined by the invisible operation of HIV and the lack of a referent behind AIDS, disciplinary categories and the (apparent) discrete bodies to which they correspond (the addict, the homosexual, the prostitute) function to erase that which AIDS (its effects) continuously introduces: the transgression of boundaries (that of nation, family, and the modern subject)— the in-betweenness of bodies that science cannot perceive. The irony is not lost in the relationship between science and "Magic": In this case, Magic becomes the AIDS sign while AIDS becomes a magical sign. As the project of Enlightenment thought, science is embedded in the hope of eliminating magic and the unseen—the mind and verifiability remain at its center. As in the 16th century, magic stands at and as the limit of modern science—both engaged in a contest where each maneuvers around the other.

AIDS, then, like magic, designates a collection of *effects*. The complexity of knowledges, the effects of power, that classify and mark the body of the PLWA are condensed in and authorized through the visual images written into the AIDS narrative. Visual technologies that sight and render visible a virus by assigning it a corporeal identity are particularly powerful mechanisms of management because they conceal their production, perspective, and location through the codes of objectivity. As Watney explains, "AIDS is thus embodied as an exemplary and admonitory drama relayed between the image of the miraculous authority of clinical medicine and the faces and the bodies of individuals who clearly disclose the stigmata of their guilt" (Watney 1988, 78).

In the case of Magic, the narration of AIDS, or, more accurately, a virus, organized through familial politics and racial dynamics, assembles truths about America and "enemies within" that organize our cultural imaginary and everyday lived experience and everyday fears. While promotional figures such as Johnson are distanced from the threatening codes of black masculinity that dominate the racist imaginary, Johnson's HIV status is used to make visible and contain "threat." Most specifically, threat is rendered visible through the homosexual, women who are sexually active outside the family, and African American men through the optic of the family and the trope of body/antibody that structure both the discursive formation around AIDS and the broader reactionary politics that define post-Reagan America. These mechanisms of containment simultaneously function to conceal the government's failure to address AIDS; the racism, sexism, and homophobia of science; and the pharmaceutical industry's interests in AIDS while authorizing defunding strategies and repressive policies.

REFERENCES

ACT UP/NY Women's Book Group. (1990). *Women, AIDS, and Activism*. Boston: South End Press.

Almond, E. and Cimons, M. "More Issues Than Answers Are Surrounding HIV." *Los Angeles Times*. Nov. 8, 1991: C4.

Andrews, D.L. (1997). "Deconstructing Michael Jordan: Popular Culture, Politics, and Postmodern America." Ph.D. dissertation, University of Illinois, Urbana-Champaign, Illinois.

Bhabha, H. (1983). "The Other Question: The Stereotype and Colonial Discourse." *Screen*, 24 (6): 18-36.

Bordowitz, G. (1994). "Dense Moments." In *Uncontrollable Bodies: Testimonies of Identity and Culture,* edited by Rodney Sappington and Tyler Stallings. Seattle: Bay Press.

Boswell, T. "His Burden Is Everyone's." *Washington Post.* Nov. 8, 1991: D1.

Brown, C. "A Career of Impact, A Player With Heart." *New York Times.* Nov. 8, 1991: B-i, B13.

Callahan, T. (1991). "What It Boils Down to Is Playing With Fire." *Washington Post.* Nov. 10, 1991: D-3.

Cannon, L.and Cotton. A. (1991). "Johnson's HIV Caused by Sex: 'Heterosexual Transmission' Cited; Wife Is Pregnant." *Washington Post.* Nov. 9: A-14.

Carroll, J. (1992). "Love in the Time of Magic: A Chronicle of Risk and Romance on the Sidelines of the NBA." *Esquire.* April, 1992: 136-42.

Carter, E. and Watney. S (1989). *Taking Liberties: AIDS and Cultural Politics.* London: Serpent's Tail.

Clarke, J. (1991). *New Times and Old Enemies: Essays on Cultural Studies and America.* London: Harper Collins Academic.

Clarke, S.A. (1991). "Fear of a Black Planet: Race, Identity Politics, and Common Sense." *Socialist Review,* 21 (3-4): 37-59.

Cole, C. L.; Loy, J.W.; and Messner, M.A. (Eds). (1996). *Exercising Power: The Making and Remaking of the Body.* Albany: SUNY Press.

Cole, C. L. and Andrews, D. (1994). "Fear of a Black Planet: Look Who's Misbehavin' Now." Paper presented at the Gregory I. Stone Society for Symbolic Interactionism Conference, University of Illinois.

— (1993a). "Resisting the Canon: Feminist Cultural Studies, Sport, and Technologies of the Body." *Journal of Sport and Social Issues,* 17 (2): 77-97.

— (1993b). "Technologies of Deviant Bodies: The Ensemble of Sport and (Re)territorializing Practices." Paper presented at the annual meetings of the North American Society for the Sociology of Sport, Ottawa.

Connell, R. (1992). "An Iron Man: The Body and Some Contradictions of Hegemonic Masculinity." In *Sport, Men, and the Gender Order,* edited by Michael Messner and Donald Sabo. Champaign-Urbana, Ill.: Human Kinetics Press.

Coontz, S. (1992). *The Way We Never Were: American Families and the Nostalgia Trap.* New York: Basic Books.

Corea, G. (1993). *The Invisible Epidemic: The Story of Women and AIDS.* New York: Harper Collins.

Crimp, D. "Accommodating Magic." In *Media Spectacles,* edited by Marjorie Garber, Jann Matlock, and Rebecca L. Walkowitz. New York: Routledge, 1993.

— with Adam Rolston. (1990). *AIDSDEMOGRAPHICS.* Seattle: Bay Press.

— (Ed.). (1988). *AIDS: Cultural Analysis/Cultural Activism.* Cambridge: MIT Press.

— "Portraits of People with AIDS." In *Cultural Studies,* edited by Lawrence Grossberg, Cary Nelson, and Paula Treichler. New York: Routledge, 1993.

D'Emilio, J. and Freedman, E. (1988). *Intimate Matters: A History of Sexuality in America*. New York: Harper & Row.

Derrida, J. (1976). *Of Grammatology*. Baltimore: John Hopkins University Press.

— (1993). "The Rhetoric of Drugs: An Interview. *Differences* 5 (1): 1-25, trans. M. Isreal. (1989 French original published in *Autrement*, 106).

Elson, J. "The Dangerous World of Wannabes: Magic Johnson's Plight Brings Fear Into Locker Rooms Across the Country and Spotlights the Riskiest Athletic Perk: Promiscuous Sex." *Time*, Nov. 25, 1991: 77-8.

Epstein, S. (1991). "Democratic Science? AIDS Activism and the Contested Construction of Knowledge." *Socialist Review*, 21 (2): 34-65.

— (1993). "Impure Science: AIDS Activism, and the Politics of Knowledge." Ph.D. dissertation, University of California, Berkeley, California.

Ewen, S. (1988). *All Consuming Images: The Politics of Style in Contemporary Culture*. New York: Basic Books.

Featherstone, M. (1991). *Postmodernism and Consumer Culture*. London: Sage.

Fee, E. and Fox, D.M. (Eds.). (1988). *AIDS: The Burdens of History*. Berkeley: University of California Press.

Foucault, M. (1973). *The Birth of the Clinic: An Archaeology of Medical Perception*, trans. A. S Sheridan. New York: Vintage Books.

Foucault, M. (1979). Discipline and Punish: *The Birth of the Prison*, trans. A. Sheridan. New York: Vintage Books.

— (1980). *The History of Sexuality* (Volume I: An Introduction), trans. R. Hurley. New York: Vintage Books.

— (1981). "Two Lectures." In *Power/Knowledge: Selected Interviews and Other Writings, 1972-1977*. New York: Pantheon.

Gladwell, M. and Muscatine, A. "Legend's Latest Challenge: Sport's Hero's Message May Resonate." *Washington Post*, Nov. 8, 1991: A-i.

Gooding-Williams, R. (Ed.). *Reading Rodney King/Reading Urban Uprising*. New York: Routledge.

Gray, H. (1989). "Television, Black Americans, and the American Dream." *Critical Studies in Mass Communication*, 6 (4): 376-86.

Green, D. (1985). "On Foucault: Disciplinary Power and Photography." *Camerawork*, 32.

—"Veins of Resemblance: Photography and Eugenics." In *Photography/Politics: Two*, edited by Patricia Holland, Jo Spence, and Simon Watney. London: Comedia Publishing Group, 1986.

Grossberg, L. (1992). *We Gotta Get Out of This Place: Popular Conservatives and Postmodernism*. New York: Routledge.

Gruneau, R. and Whitson, D. (1993). *Hockey Night in Canada*. Toronto: Garamond Press.

Hall, S. (1991). "Cultural Studies and Its Theoretical Legacies." In *Cultural Studies*, edited Lawrence Grossberg, Cary Nelson, and Paula Treichler. New York: Routledge.

Hammonds, E. (1990). "Missing Persons: African American Women, AIDS, and the History of Disease." *Radical America*, 24 (2): 7-23.

Haraway, D. (1985). "Manifesto for Cyborgs: Science, Technology, and Socialist Feminism in the 1980s." *Socialist Review,* 15 (2): 65-108.

Haraway, D. (1989). *Primate Visions: Gender, Race, and Nature in the World of Modern Science.* New York: Routledge.

Haraway, D. (1988). "Situated Knowledges: The Science Question in Feminism and the Privilege of Partial Perspective." *Feminist Studies,* 14 (3): 575-99

Harris, S. "Announcement Hailed as a Way to Teach the Public." *Los Angeles Times.* Nov. 8, 1991: A32.

Heisler, M. "Magic Johnson's Career Ended by HIV-Positive Test." *Los Angeles Times.* Nov. 8, 1991: A-i, A33, A34.

"Hero Watch: Magic's Best Hour." *Los Angeles Times,* Nov. 8, 1991: B6.

Hoberman, J. (1992). *Mortal Engines.* New York: The Free Press.

Howard-Cooper, S. "Teammates Past and Present Are Hit Hard." *Los Angeles Times.* Nov. 8, 1991: C4.

Jackson, P. (1994). "Black Male: Advertising and the Cultural Politics of Masculinity." *Gender, Place, and Culture,* 1 (1): 49-59.

Jay, M. (1993). *Downcast Eyes: The Denigration of Vision in Twentieth-Century French Thought.* Berkeley: University of California Press.

Jeffords, S. (1994). Hard Bodies: Hollywood Masculinity in the Reagan Era. New Brunswick: Rutgers University Press.

Jhally, S.and Lewis. J. (1992). *Enlightened Racism: The Cosby Show, Audiences, and the Myth of the American Dream.* Boulder: Westview Press.

Johnson, E. with Johnson, R.S. "I'll Deal With It." *Sports Illustrated,* Nov. 18, 1991: 21-2.

Johnson, E. with Novak, W. (1992). *My Life.* New York: Random House.

Kastor, E. "The Question We Fear: How Did Magic Get the Virus? And Why Do We Have to Know?" *Washington Post,* Nov. 8, 1991: G-i, G7.

Katz, D. (1994). *Just Do It: The Nike Spirit in the Corporate World.* New York: Random House.

King, S. (1993). "The Politics of the Body and the Body Politic: Magic Johnson and the Ideology of AIDS." *Sociology of Sport Journal,* 10 (3): 270-85.

Kolata, G. "Studies Cite 10.5 Years From Infection to Illness." *New York Times.* Nov. 8, 1991: A12.

Kornheiser, T. "A Hero's Message of Hope." *The Washington Post.* Nov. 8, 1991: C-i, C4.

Kroker, A. and Kroker, M. (1988)."Panic Sex in America." In *Body Invaders: Panic Sex in America,* edited by Arthur Kroker and Marilouise Kroker. New York: St. Martin's Press.

Kroll, J. "Smile, Though Our Hearts Are Breaking." *Newsweek.* Nov.18, 1991: 70.

Landers, T. (1988)."Bodies and Anti-bodies: A Crisis in Representation." In *Global Television,* edited by C. Schneider and B. Wallis. New York: Wedge Press.

Levin, D.M. (Ed.). (1993). *Modernity and the Hegemony of Vision.* Berkeley: University of California Press.

Marshall, S. (1990). "Picturing Deviancy." In *Ecstatic Antibodies: Resisting the AIDS Mythology,* edited by Tessa Boffin and Sunil Gupta. London: Rivers Oram Press.

May, E. T. (1988). *Homeward Bound: American Families in the Cold War Era.* New York: Basic Books.

Mercer, K. (1986). "Imaging the Black Man's Sex." In *Photography/Politics: Two,* edited by Patricia Holland, Jo Spence, and Simon Watney. London: Comedia Publishing Group.

Mercer, K. (1994). *Welcome to the Jungle.* New York: Routledge.

Messner, A. (1992). *Power at Play.* Boston: Beacon Press.

Miller, J. (Ed.). (1992). *Fluid Exchanges: Artists and Critics in the AIDS Crisis.* Toronto: University of Toronto Press.

Montville, L. (1991). "Like One of the Family." *Sports Illustrated.* Nov. 18, 1991: 44-5.

Mulligan, T. "The Magic Touch: What Now?" *Los Angeles Times.* Nov. 8, 1991: D-i, D6. New York: Vintage Books.

Outside the Lines: Men and Women—Sex and Sports. (1992). Television report. ESPN.

Patton, C. (1985). *Sex and Germs: The Politics of AIDS.* Boston: South End Press.

Poovey, M. (1988). *Uneven Developments: The Ideological Work of Gender in Mid-Victorian England.* Chicago: University of Chicago Press.

Reeves, J.L. and Campbell. R. (1994). *Cracked Coverage: Television News, the Anti-Cocaine Crusade, and the Reagan Legacy.* Durham, NC: Duke University Press.

Riggs, M. (1991). *Color Adjustment.* San Francisco: California Newsreel.

Rochell, A. "CDC: Heterosexual AIDS Rising Sharply." *Atlanta Journal,* Mar. 11, 1994: A6.

"Rock Hard." (1992). Keynote paper presented at the annual meetings for the *North American Society for the Sociology of the Sport,* Toledo, Ohio.

Rogin, M. (1987). *Ronald Reagan: The Movie and Other Episodes of Political Demonology.* Berkeley: University of California Press.

Sedgwick, E. K. (1990). *Epistemology of the Closet.* Berkeley: University of California Press.

—— (1992). "Epidemics of the Will." In Incorporations, edited by Jonathan Crary and Sanford Kwinter. New York: Zone.

Seidman, S. (1992). *Embattled Eros: Sexual Politics and Ethics in Contemporary America.* New York: Routledge.

Stacey, J. (1990). *Brave New Families: Stories of Domestic Upheaval in Late Twentieth Century America.* New York: Basic Books.

Terry, J. (1990). "Lesbians Under the Medical Gaze: Scientists Search for Remarkable Differences." *Journal of Sex Research,* 27 (3): 317-39

Treichler, P.A. (1987). "AIDS, Homophobia, and Bio-Medical Discourse: An Epidemic of Signification." *Cultural Studies,* 1 (2): 263-305.

Treichler, P.A. (1988). "AIDS, Gender, and Bio-Medical discourse: Current Contests for Meaning." In *AIDS: The Burden of History,* edited by Elizabeth Fee and Daniel M. Fox. Berkeley: University of California Press.

Treichler, P.A. (1992). "Beyond *Cosmo:* AIDS, Identity, and Inscriptions of Gender." *Camera Obscura,* 28: 21-78.

Wacquant, L. (1992). "The Social Logic of Boxing in Black Chicago: Toward a Sociology of Pugilism." *Sociology of Sport Journal,* 9 (3): 22 1-54.

Watney, S. (1990). "Photography and AIDS." In *The Critical Image: Essays on Contemporary Photography*, edited by Carol Squires. Seattle: Bay Press.

—- (1987). *Policing Desire: Pornography, AIDS, and the Media.* Minneapolis: University of Minnesota Press.

—- "The Spectacle of AIDS." (1988). In *AIDS: Cultural Analysis/Cultural Activism,* edited by Douglas Crimp. Cambridge: MIT Press.

Wernick, A. (1991). *Promotional Culture: Advertising, Ideology, and Symbolic Expression.* London: Sage.

Wilborn, M. "Available at Your Peril." *Washington Post.* Nov. 10, 1991: D1, D3.

Wills, G. (1987). *Reagan's America: Innocents at Home.* New York: Doubleday.

Wilson, J.Q. and Hernstein, R. (1985). *Crime and Human Nature.* New York: Simon Schuster.

Epilogue: Coming Home

Conrad Pegues

With October comes National Coming Out Day, a day set aside for closeted lesbians and gays to "come out" by making a public statement about their sexuality. In addition, it is a day to disseminate information to the American public about homosexual presence. But the issue of coming out is a complex one, especially if you're nonwhite. Although it is necessary to speak and live the truth of one's life, African American same-gender-loving (sgl) women and men have particular issues with which they must deal in coming out. It is not simply a matter of public confession to move a person from a stance of silence and acceptance of oppression in their lives. Life for many African American sgls cannot be as elementary as stating our sexual preference to another, publicly or privately, without some kind of personal context to affirm the sense of community after the fact. African American sgls need to know who we're stating our truth to and why: Just who is our audience in the coming-out process? To state who we are in a public context is like a call that needs a response. Call and response is a classic cultural motif of the African American church as a means of establishing a rapport and identity between the individual and the community.

In the African American church, when the minister makes a statement that the congregation agrees with, the congregation may respond with "Amen" or "Say it preacher!" or any other acknowledging words. The preacher's words can carry a common context with which both speaker and listener can identify based upon culture and a common experience in America; the congregation's response is one made on a communal scale to the individual before them. The group can be as small as one other individual or as many as a hall full of thousands. But both caller and respondent are humans who establish meaning for one another through their voice and their flesh-and-blood presence. Bodies and souls become one through the voice to verify and vivify the presence of one another in this space and time and provide familiarity, a sense of home. Call and response comes from an African worldview in which to state who you are necessarily calls for a "village" response that reaffirms one's sense of place in the work whether through drumming, singing, or storytelling. Thus, for African Americans to come out, there is the necessity for a waiting familiar community to validate him or her. No positive response, or no response at all, places African American sgls in a difficult position, with homophobia and heterosexism muffling any response like the hand of a thief in the night, and racism within the white community strengthening the grip of that brutal silence even more. African American sgls are left wondering, *Who am I in relation to the African American community after I come out?* White gays and lesbians have to deal with sexuality with the exception of one issue: race. The issues of race and sexuality make the long road from lack of awareness to self-awareness a perilous one. Race being operative in the construction of America institutionally and socially, many African American sgls have several key issues they must face in daily life in relation to their home communities, which white gay and lesbian America can never provide: a sense of self as an African American and purpose born of it; a sense of belonging to the African American community; and a sense of place within that community.

When whites do have to struggle with establishing a sense of self, place, and purpose, it is without the demoralizing consequences of racism. White gays and lesbians may get ostracized from their communities or family for coming out, but they are still part and parcel of the larger support system that is the white Western paradigm of culture. The paradigm can give them a sense of place that can sometimes be contextualized by a superiority complex because they are white, which is a luxury African American sgls will never have.

When the whole issue of coming out is raised for African Americans in particular, it is not about a lone individual making a public declaration. The whole of his or her meaning in relation to the African American community is put at risk. Self and community are always in a state of dialectical exchange to establish meaning for both. If something happens to the individual, the whole community is impacted and liable to take it personally. The Rodney King beating in Los Angeles, with its resultant civil unrest after the white cops were found not guilty of infringing upon his civil rights, is a prime example of this common sensibility. This intimate language of self and community has an African root that is elicited by Zahan:

> From this point of view the individual does not constitute a closed system in opposition to the outside world in order to better secure his own substance and limitations. On the contrary,

he enters into the surrounding environment, which in turn pen-
etrates him. Between the two realities there exists a constant
communication, a sort of osmotic exchange, owing to which
man finds himself permanently listening, so to speak, to the
pulse of the world (Zahan 1979, 8-9).

African Americans as descendants of Africans have maintained
something of an African mind, which sees the surrounding environment, including other people, as conveyors of information; all things
being like multiple voices, a chorus, weaving together a reality.
Through "talking" with the surroundings, we are constantly trying to
establish a psychological and social order with which to give ourselves
meaning at the present moment. With the presence of white supremacy in American society, our "talk" with our environment and one
another is constantly interrupted and so too are our efforts to define
ourselves on our own terms. To build and maintain a sense of community, African American sgls must have a dialectical relationship with the
African American community about who we are in relation to them.
And the language, somatic and psychological, that must be used is one
that whites cannot speak because it is learned through the experience
of having dark skin in a racist society. African American sgls have to
struggle with the possibility of losing the ability to "speak" on an intimate level with their own community when they come out. The psychic
silence borne of the absence of connection to one's home community is
a form of death behind which the body will follow. The negative context that white supremacy creates around racial identity in America is
forever waging war against the African American psyche regardless of
sexual preference. Few African American sgls can see white America as
a utopia waiting to embrace us if our home community should reject us
after coming out.

Some African American sgls may not be public with their sexuality in the sense of broadcasting it through the white-dominated media,
yet are out in their home communities. There are those African
American sgls who don't necessarily make an issue of their sexuality
unless the situation or community raises the issue. Family, friends,
associates, coworkers, or church members may know about the person's sexuality by their own admission as it comes up in conversation,
but for some it is never an issue of standing before strangers, black or
white, to explain themselves and their sexual preference.

In an interview in *BLK*, the Mayor of Cambridge, Mass., Ken

Reeves, speaks on the issue of race and coming out within a community context:

> The notion that all gay people have to come out in a particular way is a white thing.... I have always felt oppressed by the notion that, in order to be politically "out," you must do it a certain way.... I don't believe I've ever been, in any way, closeted. I literally will not do anything, to speak of, differently, because I wasn't then, and am still not, terribly concerned with other people's definitions" (Hinds 1994, 8).

Reeves, who garnered the attention of *The Advocate,* was asked by a reporter to give the names of ten friends who knew he was gay so that he could check to see if Reeves had lied about not being closeted about his sexuality. Reeves's home community's knowledge of his sexuality was insignificant in the face of the white press working under the definition that "out" is a public confession and/or a press conference in which the white media gets to officialize one's sexuality. The white press often has a hard time believing that the African American community has a system of norms and values of its own apart from white cultural values. Reeves is aware that the whole issue of coming out is different for African Americans. He is not dancing around the issue of sexuality nor is he closeted. He believes that whites are not qualified to define "out" for him and that he has never been overtly concerned about whether blacks or whites knew that he was a man who loved men, but if the issue were raised then he could deal with it straightforwardly and honestly, on the spot. To speak the truth of one's sexuality requires a personal context, relationships between the sgl person and the person or persons asking, not an audience, not white definitions of what it means to live out of one's own truth.

In the African American community, the realm of the personal is important in maintaining the sense of self. How the individual feels about what he or she is doing takes precedence over what an indifferent and hostile mass of strangers might demand (including those gays and lesbians who demand public disclosure of one's sexuality). Reeves borrows from the philosophy of African American sgl dancer-choreographer Bill T. Jones, "Bill says, 'I don't plan a dance, I do what's in my heart.' / Well, what happened was an expression / of what's written in my heart' " (Hinds 1994, 8).

Reeves is making reference to the fact that he did announce that he was homosexual during an acceptance speech at the Greater Boston Lesbian/Gay Political Alliance Awards ceremony. He felt that the "public" announcement was more to keep himself from looking hypocritical as a "friend of the gay and lesbian community" than to simply make a public statement about his homosexuality. Reeves found it necessary to remain true to his sense of self by letting the audience know he was not just an open-minded heterosexual receiving the award. He followed his heart to properly define himself before the audience that brought the award under the auspices of his personal identity and philosophy. In so doing he brought the award back from a purely public sphere to one where it had personal value to him as an individual subverting the whole idea of coming out for the sake of coming out as a public political statement. The public announcement had to have a deeper meaning from him as Ken Reeves and not simply as a gay man going public.

Diffusing coming out as an opportunity for an individual to be delivered from his or her own oppression is overly simplistic in the lives of African American sgls. Feminist and writer/publisher Barbara Smith, who is also an African American woman who loves women, states that there is a definite need for people who are open and honest about their sexuality in the African American community: "We need to have many more people who are willing to be out, in all aspects of their lives, not just in their social and personal love lives....We need people who are willing to be out across the board. It's hard to do that by yourself. The more we do it, the more allies we'll have" (Lane 1990, 22).

Smith recognizes that there is a need for African American sgls to be open about their sexuality whether they are in public or private life. It would be fulfilling this need to make African Americans in general realize that sgls exist in every aspect of the community. Smith also recognizes that being open about one's sexuality is difficult in an air of isolation that implies the need for support of other African Americans in the process of coming to terms with one's sexuality and not hiding it. Coming out is not simply publicly acknowledging one's sexuality. It is a perpetual process that requires support and nurture from others within one's cultural community to provide a sense of cultural identification to counter the attacks and dismissals that come with homophobia, heterosexism, and racism. Survival includes defining the truth of just how diverse African American sexuality is. In addition, redefining our sexuality cuts down on the "black on black" violence against sgls within the community. But Smith further defines her sense of coming out for African American sgls as one revolving around not only the issue of "role models" but also the quality of character set before the public's eye:

> I don't need Malcolm Forbes as a role model—he's a class enemy. And I don't need fascists in the government who are closeted white gay men. What I would like to see, as opposed to the necessity for bringing people out who refuse to identify themselves, is a sufficient level of political sophistication, consciousness, and commitment (Lane 1990, 22).

Smith is not in conflict with Reeves here. Both see coming out as establishing some sense of integrity, so just having sgls who are famous or "leaders" is not sufficient. Openness about their sexuality is not the only issue by which they are judged as positive influences within the community. Other issues, such as their politics and stand on issues of relevance to the larger community, must also be taken into consideration. Sexuality does not a whole person make. As stated earlier, Ken Reeves made his announcement so he would not be misunderstood as being ashamed of his sexuality. Smith advocates the same level of integrity when she states that she wants to see out people who have a commitment to a deeper truth rather than those who simply say, "I'm gay." Smith is not concerned with knowing a person's sexual preference without knowing how they view the world in which they live and how they want to make an impact upon it. Smith, like Reeves, makes the issue of coming out very personal. She needs to know how an individual will respond to her and others based upon a consciousness in relation to women, factors threatening the livelihood of the African American community, and all those "isms" that diminish the quality of life. Both Smith and Reeves are concerned about establishing an identity that gives a wider vision for the African American community's growth beyond its present crisis of self-destructiveness.

Because African Americans as individuals come from a community background that demands a certain degree of accountability to the entire group, there is the necessity to reconcile the personal with the public. To come out in a white cultural context in which the predominantly white media designates a valid coming out as one documented by this culture's tabloid tactics can diminish the African American's personal identity. The matter of coming out leaves African American sgls with the problem of where to establish cultural identity in relation to sexual identity and the question of whether they even should come out.

One of the biggest problems of the race and sexuality issue is played out in the debate of whether one is black/gay or gay/black; an individual must choose which aspect of their identity is primary: black or gay. Depending on which side of the argument one might fall, accusations of hatred or that one has an inordinate affection for whites and their cultural values fly back and forth.

In 1981 Oakland psychologist Julius Johnson surveyed African American sgl men to find out how they identified themselves culturally in relation to their sexuality. His sample was small (60 men) and limited to the San Francisco/Oakland area, but it raised important issues in identifying the conflict African American males have in regard to racial identity as it relates to sexual identity. Moreover, Jordan (1990) argues that the gay/black man was identified as more likely to be out or to come out, interacts more with nonblack gays, probably has a white lover, and is more likely to be concerned with activist issues more aligned with being gay than issues of race. Black/gays could be defined as black men who refuse to identify with their sexual desires, or were most likely closeted to protect career or image, or were out and active, but who distrust white institutions of power. Of course, these definitions are limited, and many people do not fall solely into one category or the other. But in the survey one can see the dilemma of what exactly to do with one's racial identity: Suppress it or utilize it as a tool to define one's place in the homosexual milieu? In his commentary, Jordan does make an important observation when he says, "Who are gay blacks and black gays? Halves of a whole. Brothers" (Jordan 1990, 30).

Black women are absent from the argument and Johnson's survey. Although it might be argued that the survey was a sexist dismissal of their opinion, this writer would put forth another observation. Historically, the issue of racial consciousness for African American women has always been intertwined with a larger sense of protest and uplift that included gender, yet always extended beyond it to include men's issues as well. To women, race and sexual politics have been so intertwined that one inaugurates an awareness of the other.

The black/gay vs. gay/black argument among African American men may be one borne of a burgeoning political awareness. More and more African American men are realizing the need for self-definition of African American male identity and sexual politics. The black/gay or gay/black argument is based upon a false assumption. Who says that being one necessarily negates the presence of the other in one's life? The language and perception that the debate is built upon is itself colonized when people are meant to choose one aspect of themselves over another. Further, the argument is faulty in that it does not take into account that, regardless of sexual preference, one's racial identity is a constant in a racist society and determines the quality of one's life. In addition to race, sexual preference can also be used as a means for the general society to reduce the quality of one's life, as both are considered negatives.

Due to racism, African Americans are always trying to establish where they belong in relation to one another and other racial and ethnic groups in this country. Additional questions of belonging plague African American sgls who must constantly negotiate space with their home community, which is often less than willing to accept sexual difference. One may in actuality be out, but what's the sense of belonging like? If African Americans come from a cultural base that says everyone is a part of the larger whole only to be denied that upon admission of homosexuality, then the ability to love in general is inhibited or wounded; possibly beyond ever being healed if there is no real reconciliation with some aspect of the African American community.

More importantly, commentators often wrestle with the struggle for identity with which sgl African Americans must deal:

> Few men of color will ever be found on the covers of *The Advocate* or *New York Native*. As white gays deny multiculturalism among gays, so too do black communities deny multisexualism among its members. Against this double cremation, we must leave the legacy of our writing and our perspective on gay and straight experiences (Dixon 1993, 203).

The outcasting of African Americans in general by white gays and lesbians utterly "cremates" most attempts for African American sgls to find some peace of mind in this world. As a writer, Dixon wants to see us creating our own image and voicing our perspective. He realizes that it is not a task the white press considers to be its own; nor should it be. To establish a sense of ourselves as belonging to the African American community, we must reveal the various threads of our own contributions to the collective tapestry of our cultural identity. Therefore, we must make the community realize we have always been here and belonged but that now is the time break the bonds of silence that came about due to the community's larger struggle for racial justice, as some blacks needed to prove to whites that we were moral by adhering to a strict code of public heterosexual behavior, regardless of same-sex yearnings.

As if the demands of the African American community reacting to white supremacy were not enough, African American sgls are often put in the position of suspending cultural identification to be a part of the larger, white-identified gay and lesbian community. Or we are constantly trying to define who we are in a sea of white gays and lesbians when there is only one of us on a particular board, or two of us attending a public gay and lesbian function. (This cannot always be blamed on racism since it is sometimes due to internalized homophobia amongst African American lesbian and gays.) Historically, African Americans have struggled to establish their identity and a sense of how to belong in America with the presence of white supremacy. But African American sgls have to establish their identity based upon sexual politics as well, leading to the necessity of a protean state of mind to deal with the multitude of differences inherent in our presence within and without the community. To define ourselves as African American sgls has nothing to do with the hatred of the white gay and lesbian community. Rather, it has everything to do with negotiating space with our own people in a way that does not make us pawns of white racism in totally rejecting our home communities or pawns of a narrow vision in African America as we reject ourselves for the sake of their acceptance.

On the whole, the African American community could not have survived in America if we did not collectively learn how white people perceived themselves and us. Thus, African Americans have always been multicultural. The problem now is that many younger African Americans are questioning the inherited survival tactics that have caused the community to be constantly aware of how white people perceived it. The community's historical reaction to a racist white presence is being exposed in an attempt to define African American presence and the resultant problems that come with living in a racist society. Inevitably, the tradition of survival will be challenged by the necessity of posterity to create its own vision, questioning the fundamental notions of a community mind built in reaction to the presence of white supremacy. With their multisexual perspective, African American sgls will play a role in that redefining process. Lacking the vision to make the necessary changes in how we see ourselves in relation to one another in America at this jaunt in history could be devastating to the whole of the African American community. Lacking a sense of deeper connection with one another as African Americans will doom the whole community to collapse in a maelstrom of unprecedented violence because the reality of various lived truths (which include multisexuality) will be at war with the expectations of known tradition. There must be a vision to reconcile the differences of tradition and necessary changes based upon human need.

Dixon, Smith, and Reeves all establish their vision or purpose as a larger goal of liberation and redefinition of not only the African American community but also the world that impacts and influences it. This expanded consciousness can never be boxed into a lone gay politic of coming out as a matter of sexual preference and sexual preference alone. When African Americans come out, they bring the entire community with them as well as its history of resistance and protest against oppression. Personal consciousness becomes the ground for one's own redemption. The personal seeps into the collective sphere and redeems the African American community of its own homophobia and heterosexism. Ironically, violence is often formulated in the hub of the African American community, the church, which itself was fired out of protest against the injustices inherent in American society.

Ken Reeves (in Hinds, 1990 and Kaplan, 1994) relates quite strongly to the African American choreographer Bill T. Jones in that his instinct for survival as a same–gender-loving man is rooted in the African American community's resistance to racism in America:

My survival instinct and my racial history are inseparable. I inherited from my people a sense of the world being a place of adversity, a valley of sorrow, but the redemption is possible...The black community is the most virulently homophobic, and it bothers me deeply.... I want to be loved by my folks, but I've spent a good part of my adult life being disappointed" (Hinds 1990, 89).

Bill T. Jones sees the African American community as "most virulently homophobic," which I do not totally agree with. The African American community is homophobic, but the reasons behind that homophobia are due in part to racism. Many African Americans believe that the presence of homosexuals in the community reveals to white people that we are lacking in "moral fiber" and satisfies white racist conclusions that we have no control over our libido. Some heterosexual African

American women find homosexual men detestable because of the so-called shortage of male partners for marriage in the community. Rarely do they evaluate the racist system that channels so many African American men into prisons, causes others to commit various forms of suicide at phenomenal rates, and still others to murder one another or turn to drugs. Same-sex desire is not responsible for this tragic state of affairs; white supremacy is the offender, along with African American resistance to redefining the traditional roles of male-female behavior as inherited from a male supremacist system. But Jones's pain and disappointment as it relates to the African American community's homophobia is still valid.

Being a same–gender-loving African American man, Jones knows that the desire to survive and stand up under the harsh scrutiny of homophobia and heterosexism from one's own community can be overwhelming. But Jones's resilience comes through in his art, where he defies homophobia from his own people and racism from the larger society. His art, no doubt, is his vision and his resistance to erasure, as he refuses to turn in on himself destructively as have many other African American males in their response to racism. Jones's art is his coming out as it is an expression of the forces that make him who he is as an African American, a dancer/choreographer, a same–gender-loving man, a person with AIDS—the many facades of his humanity.

Coming out is a perpetual state of growth unto understanding who one is and the possibilities of a life lived in the present. Coming out for African American sgls is then a process of *coming home* and taking responsibility for the issues that sap the vitality from life, ourselves, and our communities. African American community first and then others. Smith says, "Even if white lesbians and gays were committed to dealing with homophobia within the black community, they're not the appropriate people to bring those issues up" (Lane 1990, 22). Reeves says, "We must continue to be ourselves and find our own way of acting up, whether we call people on their homophobic remarks or we insist on connecting civil rights to gay rights, both of which are unfinished struggles" (Hinds 1994, 12). Both Smith and Reeves place the onus of responsibility on African American sgls for defining themselves by their own experiences of race and sexuality as a means of protest within the community. And redefining ourselves in the context of our own communities is our "coming out," which I think is more appropriately called *coming home*.

For me, home is all the experiences and feelings about the place and people I grew up with and which the white gay and lesbian community can never buttress in my life or fully comprehend. My people, my community of black folks, have been like a great black wall of faces and places to surround and nurture me and have kept a lot of the insanity of white supremacy at bay. The monster oak tree at the corner that over the years has shaded both those waiting for the bus to go to work and drug boys alike. The neighbors' houses where I have played, laughed, got mad, and was mischievous. Various friends and cousins' homes where I ate Sunday dinner when my mother cooked chitterlings. The neighbor across the street who often read aloud out of her Bible, reminding me what it is to "act ugly." Learning about life and living after church on the front porch as the sun went down on a cool Spring evening. The attitudes of the haves, have-nots, and the holier-than-thous. My mother and father's 50-year-old arguments about who was right (quite often they both were). Learning about politics and "sold-out" black folks during fiery conversations between neighbors over plates of neck bones and corn bread and buttermilk pound cake. And I have always been in their midst: black and loving men (and deep down they have always known what I was). All of these things are me and vivify my definition of community. And it is what I look forward to when I have been immersed too long in a white world full of strangers whose politics do not include my folks and their pains, their joys and their contradictions.

To return home speaking our sexual truth pushes African American sgls and the larger community to face our own needs and to realize the traumas that leave so many of us open to the self-destructiveness inherent in a white and male supremacist system. So being and living our own truths automatically pushes the whole of the African American community to redefine itself and its own racism, sexism, classism, homophobia, and heterosexist presumption. The media will not come running to see this happen because it does not fit the currently accepted form of "coming out," and most of us are not celebrities behind whom the rumor mills have been turning for years. Many of us are just everyday people trying to make a living and to find some peace and love in this world, which is rarely news worth reporting in the white media. As singer/songwriter Gill Scott-Heron has said, "The revolution won't be televised."

And what actually happens when we come home?

My responsibility to the African American community can be cultivated with the most common tool of human experience in our everyday social lives. As noted earlier (in Zahan, 1979), human interactions lead to the perpetual recreation of our common world, giving it meaning. Because sgls have developed to some degree the consciousness where we do not fear the human potential to touch another same-sex person, we alter the space around us. Sharing our deepest fears and needs with someone of the same sex initiates the realization that emotional bonds are ambiguous and have less to do with gender and more to do with affirming human relationships. Homophobia and heterosexism often interject fear into the sphere of meaning for self and others to destroy relationships, not enhance them.

When the African American community can move beyond the imprisoning walls of homophobia and heterosexism, they are freed to explore a larger definition of what it means to be a man or a woman. When we as same–gender-loving African American men and women speak out and name in all the places that we occupy and interact within the community, then we force our own to deal with the lies they've been taught to believe about us. Like Bill T. Jones's dancing, we must become skillful at improvisation and responding to the moments within our community that present themselves for us to state who we really are. Coming home for us isn't a public announcement to whomever. It's an act of will and speech to say who we are at the calling of the moment, whether in church, at home, among friends, on the basketball court, or while hanging out with heterosexual friends who blame the problems of relationship and community on us and us alone. Coming home is no one-time act of liberation. It's a lifelong process of defining self in relation to the social environment in which one find's oneself at any given moment. It's not looking for the "right" moment to say who we are. Rather, it's letting the moment choose itself for us to say, "I too am your brother, your sister," but in another way that takes nothing away from the power of who we are as African Americans. To redefine self is to redefine the context of community and relations. Roles can no longer be exiguous, based only upon gender as people are pushed to seek deeper meaning for themselves instead of depending on the heterosexist script to establish meaning for them.

The human potential expressed through vision becomes just as important as tradition. Power systems shift. Sex and sexuality are revised as the human body comes to be seen in the light of play and pleasure as well as work that avows its presence as a multidimensional tool for affirmation. A new sexual politic is born. Men can no longer define themselves in the singular context of penetrative sex, but with the whole body as a point of affection and affirmation. The penis does not always have to be the point through which affection is expressed. Women maintain their own greater options in exploring who they are beyond the single role of mother. So many women make the mistake of assuming that womanhood and wife/motherhood are necessarily synonymous. Women are women whether or not they are mothers or wives.

The ability to bond deeply with people of the same sex (which does not necessarily entail sexual activity) collapses the cultural expectations of competition with other males for dominance in their relationships as the quality of emotional needs are given greater focus. Emotional nurture and its resultant bonding is a threat to established heterosexist notions of relationship. The nuclear family transforms into the extended family system, in which members are grafted based upon spiritual, physical, and emotional needs as well as blood ties. The nature of the community is transformed as the truth of our same–gender-loving lives is acknowledged on its many levels.

African American same–gender-loving men and women are not a scourge on the community. We are not pawns sent in by that mythical and anonymous being, "the white man," to destroy our people's sense of family. We bear witness to another truth in redefining what it means to be parents, friends, and partners. When the African American community comes to the expanded consciousness that same–gender-loving African Americans are not the enemy, then our "other sexual" truth may possibly set us all free.

REFERENCES

Dixon, M. (1993). "I'll Be Somewhere Listening for My Name." In *Sojourner: Black Gay Voices in the Age of AIDS,* edited by B. Michael Hunter. New York: Other Countries.

Hinds, S. "Do They Know That The Mayor of Cambridge is Gay?" *BLK.* Jan.1994: 7-8 [continued in the Feb. 1994 issue, p. 12].

Jordan, L. Lloyd. "Black Gay vs. Gay Black." *BLK.* June 1990: 25-30

Kaplan, L. "Bill T. Jones On Top." *POZ.* June/July, 1994: 40-44, 69.

Lane, A. J. "Barbara Smith." *BLK.* June, 1990: 17-23.

Zahan, D. (1979). *The Religion, Spirituality, and Thought of Traditional Africa,* trans. by Kate Ezra Martin and Lawrence M. Martin. Chicago: University of Chicago.

CONTRIBUTORS

Lindon Barrett, an associate professor of English and African American studies at the University California, Irvine, is the author of *Seeing Double: Blackness and Value*, forthcoming from Cambridge University Press. His articles on literature and culture have appeared in various periodicals, including *Culture Critique, Substance, American Literary History*, and *American Literature*. He is an associate editor for *Callaloo*.

Charles Clifton received his B.A. in history from San Francisco State University and an M.A. in liberal studies from Dartmouth College. He is pursing his Ph.D. in African American and gay history at the University of Chicago.

Cheryl L. Cole is an associate professor of kinesiology, women's studies, and sociology. She obtained her Ph.D. from the University of Southern California in 1987 and a second Ph.D. from the University of Iowa in 1992. Her areas of interest are feminist, queer, and cultural studies; body studies; national popular culture; and interpretive and ethnographic methodology. Cole's teaching and research investigates the production of deviant bodies and national identity in post–WWII America. She is the editor of the *Journal of Sport & Social Issues* (SAGE) and the coeditor of the book series *Sport, Culture, & Social Relations* (SUNY Press). She also serves on the Advisory Board of *GLQ* (Duke University Press).

Gregory Conerly is an assistant professor of history at Cleveland State University, where he teaches courses on African American culture and the history of sexuality. His research focuses on representations of homosexuality in the black press and African American lesbigay cultural politics. His work has appeared in *Queer Studies* (NYU Press, 1996) and *The St. James Press Gay and Lesbian Almanac* (St. James Press, 1998).

Kennette Crockett is a 30-year-old writer whose work has appeared in *The Chicago Tribune, Curve, Genre, Girlfriends, Hollywood.Com*, the

Los Angeles Times, and other publications. She has a M.A. in English Literature from DePaul University and a B.A. in English Literature from Mundelein College, both in Chicago.

Henry Louis Gates, Jr. is a leading African American scholar and dapper academic superstar, who has hopped from tenured positions at Yale, Cornell, and Duke to Harvard. When Gates lured to Harvard an illustrious roster of African American intellectuals (including celebrity confrere), he was hailed for having built a brain team that recalled the revered postwar New York intellectuals. Known as "Skip," Gates regularly moves in circles outside the academy, opining on hip-hop, politics, and the arts in, among other publications, *Mother Jones, Entertainment Weekly,* and *The New Yorker*; partying with black media mogul Quincy Jones; and testifying as an expert on metaphor at the 1990 2 Live Crew obscenity trial. Gates, who was trained at Yale as a deconstructionist, originally made his name as a "literary archaeologist" preserving forgotten writings of 19th-century African Americans. A fierce defender of affirmative action, Gates tells about growing up in segregated Piedmont, W.V., in his 1995 memoir, *Colored People.* In 1996, as part of his ongoing efforts to create multicultural expansions of the canon, Gates edited, with Nellie Y. McKay, the first *Norton Anthology of African American Literature.*

Horace Griffin is an assistant professor of pastoral theology at the Seabury-Western Theological Seminary in Evanston., Ill. He obtained a bachelor's degree in religion from Morehouse College in 1983, a master of divinity degree from Boston University School of Theology in 1988, a master of arts degree from Vanderbilt University Graduate School of Religion in 1993, and a doctor of philosophy degree in religion and personality from Vanderbilt University Graduate School of Religion in 1995. His work has appeared in publications and books such as the *Journal of Pastoral Theology* and *Notable Black American Men.*

Philip Brian Harper, an associate professor of English at New York University, is the author of *Framing the Margins: The Social Logic of Post-Modern Culture* and *Are We Not Men? Masculine Anxiety and The Problem of African American Identity.*

bell hooks is a feminist scholar, poet, memoirist, and social critic. A prolific writer, she has published more than a dozen books on feminist theory, racism, education, and popular culture, including *Black Looks, Ain't I a Woman, Feminist Theory From Margin to Center, Killing Rage: Ending Racism, Talking Back: Thinking Feminist, Thinking Black,* and, her latest, *All About Love: New Visions,* an eloquent take on the elusive subject of love. Previously a professor in the English departments at Yale and Oberlin, she is now a Distinguished Professor of English at City College. She lives in New York City.

Earl Ofari Hutchinson is an author, a nationally syndicated columnist, and the director of the National Alliance For Positive Action. He is a welcomed and repeat guest on the *Global Village Network Show.*

Laura Jamison is a freelance journalist in New York City.

Cary Alan Johnson is the program officer for Africa and the Near East at the International Foundation for Election Systems (IFES) and the former executive director of Gay Men of African Descent (GM.A.D), an advocacy, support, and HIV service organization. Johnson has served as regional director for Amnesty International in Washington, D.C., and as AI's country resource coordinator in New York City. He was also the country representative for Africare in Kigali, Rwanda, and worked with the United Nations High Commission in Bukavau, Zaire. Johnson is an accomplished author with work appearing in *Brother to Brother* and *Sojourner.*

E. Patrick Johnson is an assistant professor of performance studies at Northwestern University. Johnson received B.A. and M.A. degrees from the University of North Carolina and his Ph.D. in performance studies from Louisiana State University. A performance artist/poet, he has written and directed a number of theatrical productions as well as performed for national and international audiences including his recent one-man show, *Strange Fruit.* He has also published essays in *Callaloo, Obsidian II,* and *Performance Quarterly.* He is currently at work on a book titled *Appropriating Blackness: Performance and the Politics of Authenticity.*

Jason King is a writer based in the department of performance studies at Tisch School of the Arts. He is also a graduate assistant in the Educational and Cultural Programming office for African American, Latino, and Asian-American Students at New York University.

Contributors

Dwight A. McBride is an assistant professor of English at the University of Pittsburgh. He received his B.A. in English and African American studies at Princeton University and his M.A. and Ph.D. degrees in English at the University of California, Los Angeles. His book *Impossible Witness: Restrictive and Resistive Discourses on Slavery and Abolition* is forthcoming from New York University Press. He is an advisory and contributing editor for Callaloo.

Carmen Mitchell is a graduate student in Afro-American Studies at the University of California, Los Angeles. She researches racialized sexualities and gender as mediated through popular culture. She is originally from Lorain, Ohio, and attended Oberlin College as an undergraduate, where she received her B.A. in African American studies with concentrations in history and media, and a minor in English.

Eugene Patron is a journalist who has written for several academic publications, including the *Harvard Law Review*. He has also traveled extensively across southern Africa. He is currently studying urban issues and cultural geography at City University of New York.

Conrad R. Pegues received his B.A. and M.A. in English from the University of Memphis. He teaches community college writing courses in the Memphis area. His academic work combines disciplines such as African American literature, African ritual systems (especially Yoruba and Bambara), mythology, spirituality, psychology, and history. His works include *Queer Looks, Fighting Words,* and an anthology of African American gay writing.

Townsand Price-Spratlen, born in Bellingham, Wash., and raised in Seattle, has been writing poetry and short stories since he was a teenager. He now lives in Columbus, Ohio, where he is an assistant professor of sociology at Ohio State University. Trained as a demographer, he researches the interaction between location, community, and identity; the effects of social ties and community development on residential mobility and neighborhood change; and the relationship between local area context and individual quality of life.

Vasu Reddy is a lecturer in the Faculty of Human Sciences, University of Natal (Durban), South Africa. He received his B.A. in drama and performance and Afrikaans and Dutch literature from the University of

Natal, and an M.A. in comparative literature from the University of the Witwatersrand, Johannesburg. He is also working toward a Ph.D. in comparative literature with a specialization in the history of sexuality. Reddy is a national executive committee member of the National Coalition for Gay and Lesbian Equality, the organization that successfully lobbied for the inclusion of sexual orientation in the nondiscrimination clause of the South African constitution. He has published on sexuality and literature in South African academic and popular journals.

Craig Allen Seymour is pursuing a Ph.D. in American Studies at the University of Maryland. A staff writer for Lambda Book Report, he also served as editorial assistant on Sharon Harley's book, *The Time Tables of African American History* (Simon and Schuster, 1995). Seymour has also written, reviewed, and presented several papers on popular gay culture on a range of contemporary gay and lesbian themes.

Seth Clark Silberman attended the University of Maryland, College Park, where he received his B.A. in English as well as French language and literature. He obtained his M.A. in comparative literature, focusing on the work of Richard Bruce Nugent. He has also written and presented numerous academic papers and, with Robin Bernstein, coedited *Generation Q: Inheriting Stonewall* (Alyson Publications).

Anthony Thomas has worked as a DJ and at last report was completing law school in Chicago.

Touré is a contributing editor at *Rolling Stone*. His work has been featured in the *New Yorker, The New York Times Magazine, Playboy, Callaloo, The Village Voice,* and *The Best American Essays of 1999.* He studied at Columbia University's Graduate School of Creative Writing and lives in Fort Greene, Brooklyn. He is currently working on a short story collection, *Sugar Lips Shinehot, The Man With the Portable Promised Land, and Other Urban Heroes.* He also plays guerilla tennis.

Margaret Rose Vendryes joined the Amherst College faculty in fall 1999 as a visiting assistant professor of black studies and fine arts. Vendryes received her B.A. in fine arts from Amherst in 1984, her M.A. in art history from Tulane, and her Ph.D. in art history from Princeton. She is an Americanist with particular interests in black American art history and contemporary visual culture and theory. Vendryes wrote her dissertation on the art and life of Richmond Barthé, the late black American figurative sculptor. She was a scholar-in-residence at the Schomburg Center for Research in Black Culture in Harlem under 1998-99 NEH and Aaron Diamond fellowships. Her book on Barthé, which is nearing completion, will include new research on the representation of the black body in modern American art and literature.

Gloria Wekker is a professor of Women's Studies in the Arts at the Institute for Media and Representation at the University of Utrecht in The Netherlands. Born in the South American country of Suriname, Wekker migrated to Amsterdam and has served on many governmental and social advisory boards, including the Ministry of Health, Welfare, and Culture on Ethnic Minorities' Affairs as well as the Ministry of Social Affairs and Employment, Directorate Coordination Emancipation Affairs, both at The Hague. In addition to her government and academic posts, Wekker is the cofounder of Sister Outsider, a Black lesbian women's literary circle in Amsterdam.